Headlines, Deadlines, and Lifelines

George B. Bookman

iUniverse, Inc.
New York   Bloomington

Headlines, Deadlines, and Lifelines

iUniverse books may be ordered through booksellers or by contacting:

iUniverse
1663 Liberty Drive
Bloomington, IN 47403
www.iuniverse.com
1-800-Authors (1-800-288-4677)

ISBN: 978-1-4401-1833-3 (pbk)
ISBN: 978-1-4401-1834-0 (ebk)

Printed in the United States of America

iUniverse rev. date: 4/3/2009

George Bookman, 2007
Photo by Bachrach

PREFACE

What follows is my effort to write the story of my life (to date) and what I know or can remember of my ancestry. I am doing this at the suggestion of my son Charles and daughter Jean who expressed interest in a family chronicle and thought that their children would also like to know about it.

These memoirs are composed of two main parts. First, is the narrative I have written about various parts of my life from birth up to the present, 2008. The second main part of the book consists of a wide variety of texts. I never consistently kept a diary. However, while I was a student spending my Junior college year in Paris, I wrote copious letters home, which my parents saved. Then during World War II when I served in Africa, the Middle East, Italy and Austria, I wrote many letters to Janet both before and after she became my wife, and to my parents, as well as memos to the office, text of broadcasts, etc. Much of this has been saved and appears in the book. Then Janet saved our notes on frequent trips abroad, some of which are in the text section. In addition, there are selected texts of articles I wrote over the years, and notable compliments I received from my journalism or public relations contacts, as well as a few news clippings about me. Also included are texts of my Bar Mitzvah speech and my remarks at my Father's funeral.

I owe a debt of gratitude to my dear, late wife Janet for being so well organized as to save much of the text material. And, of course, as this book shows, I am deeply indebted to her for our six decades of friendship, 57 years of marriage and for our two wonderful children, four grandchildren and - so far - four great-grandchildren.

I began writing these memoirs after moving to New York City from Connecticut in late 2002 to share my life with my dear friend, Ruth Bowman. The act of writing and editing them has been a pleasant occupation for a retired man. Any signs of senescence will be understandable. The book has been written for personal reasons, not to become a New York Times best seller, but if that should happen, I could live with it.

Headlines, Deadlines, and Lifelines

This book could not have been completed without the invaluable and highly skilled help of my friend from Wassaic, N.Y., Sue Metcalfe, who converted my hunt-and-peck typing (on a manual typewriter) to the necessary computerized version. Sue also did the same for the book of letters of my late wife, Janet, titled: "***Dear Ines....Dear Janet***". Sue, thanks for your patience and your expertise.

George Bookman
December 2008

Table of Contents

CHAPTER I

To start at the very beginning, I was born in my parents' apartment at 254 West 82nd Street, New York because – as the old saying goes – I wanted to be near my mother. In those days, birth at home was more customary than in a hospital. The date was December 22, 1914.

My mother was Judith Wertheim Bookman and my father Dr. Arthur Bookman. They had been married about two years earlier and I understand their first baby was stillborn. Two years after I arrived, my sister, Caroline Jane Bookman, was born February 5, 1917.

ANCESTRY

As related by my father, the family goes back to a rabbi, Abraham Loeb Stein, (1755-1851) from Frankfurt am Main, Germany. His daughter married a Mr. Buchman of Burg Brebach, Germany, a printer of Hebrew books. Their son Jacob Buchman, born in 1820, came to New York in 1841. He Americanized his name to Bookman. After doing some selling in the Hartford, CT area, he then went to Alabama, probably as a traveling peddler, and settled in Washington, Alabama, near Selma, Alabama. There he ran a dry goods store and traded in cotton and other materials. (Another branch of the Bookmans settled in Columbus, Georgia where they were successful merchants). From time to time, Jacob made trips north to buy diamonds and other things for the cotton planters. He got to know the family of Simon Meyer, who came to this country from Worms, Germany, also in 1841, first to Hartford and later to New York City. Simon was married to Fanny Ulman. They had three attractive daughters, Caroline, Frances and Rosina. Caroline was the eldest, born in Germany July 20, 1837. In her youth, she taught school in Hartford. In September 1857 Jacob sold his Alabama business for $80,000, married Caroline Meyer, and they settled in New York City where Jacob became a real estate investor and builder. I understand he built a house for one of the Lehman family on East 62nd Street and the building that is headquarters of the Harmonie Club on East 61st, and a house for his own family on 62nd Street

1

between Fifth and Madison Avenue. He also owned some undistinguished properties some of which my father inherited on Broadway and 144th Street and Columbus Avenue and 65th Street. Portraits of the Meyers (hand-colored from photographs) hung in our dining room and also oil portraits of Jacob and Caroline painted around the time of their marriage. My children have those portraits now. (Copies of the portraits are included in this book.)

Jacob and Caroline had 14 children, of which my father, Arthur, was the youngest. Six of their 14 children died in infancy or early childhood. In 1991, Janet and I visited the Bookman family gravesite at Salem Fields Cemetery, 775 Jamaica Avenue, Brooklyn, N.Y., the cemetery of Temple Emanuel.

The plot contains the following headstones: Jacob Bookman b. May 7, 1820, d. October 29, 1902; Caroline Bookman b. July 20, 1837, d. November 27, 1921; Samuel Bookman b. December 11, 1869, d. October 8, 1946; Olga Bookman (Sam's wife) b. September 29, 1881, d. August 13, 1963; Fred Bookman b. March 24, 1874, d. January 26, 1940. At the back of the plot are the six infants' graves. Their other children buried elsewhere or cremated, were Pauline (married Bunzl), Seymour (married Helen Rosenwald), Nellie (single), Bella (married Hoffman) and Abe (married Florrie Newman).

My parents were married February 11, 1912. My mother, Judith, was descended from a Dutch rabbi, Jacob K. Falkenau, who was chief rabbi of Amsterdam at one time. Their daughter Hannah was born in Amsterdam in 1838 and married an Englishman named Louis Schlesinger, who I am told was a spiritualist. They moved to the U.S. but Mr. Schlesinger left to go west and his wife subsequently divorced him. The couple had three daughters Adelaide (married Karelsen), Julia (married Rosenblatt) and the youngest Jeannette, who was born in New York in 1867. She married my grandfather Sol Wertheim in 1887. Their two daughters, my mother Judith (born New York December 15, 1888) – during the great Blizzard – and my Aunt Gladys (born New York 1900) who married Joseph Strauch (later divorced) then Leo Bachrach, who died in 1977, a decade before Gladys who died in 1987, after a long illness.

Sol Wertheim was a son of Baruch Wertheim, born in Kassel, Germany in 1826, who married Yetta Frankenberg. When Baruch came to this country, he also started out in the Hartford, CT. area, but soon moved to New York City where he went into the hide and skin business with offices on Gold Street, in a district of Downtown Manhattan nicknamed "the Swamp". Baruch and Yetta had two sons, Jacob the eldest and Sol, and then five daughters: Bertha (married Schloss); Hattie (married Hiller); Julia (married Rose); Emma (married Byck); and Sophie (married Goldstone).

As the boys grew up, Jacob started a tobacco business, and his brother Sol was a partner. As time went on however, Sol became dissatisfied because Jacob was a high-living gallivanter, rarely in the office and Sol was doing all the work. After a while, Sol quit to join his father in the hide and skin business. Jake had sown his wild oats in California where he sold programs and refreshments at the San Francisco opera, using that next-egg to establish the tobacco business in New York City. Later his business became the General Cigar Company. Jake first married a woman named Hannah, by whom he had three children: Angie (Frink) whom Janet and I knew, Maurice, the very successful banker who established Wertheim & Company and was the father of Barbara Tuchman, the eminent historian, two other daughters Nan Werner and Jodie Pomerance; and a son named Albert. However, Hannah then ran off with a European Baron or Count, which upset Jacob W. so much that he took to his bed for a while. Then he married a safe, solid woman named Emma Stern, who gave him two daughters – Diana (Westa) and Viola Bernard, a well-known New York Psychiatrist.

Records show that Jacob Wertheim was very prominent in Jewish philanthropy, notably what is today UJA-Federation, also the Joint Distribution Committee. At one time, he was on the Board of General Motors Corporation and also served as a Director of Underwood Typewriter Corporation and was a leader in war bond drives and other fund raising during World War I.

When my mother Judith was young, the family lived in Harlem at 16 East 127th Street, until they bought the townhouse I remember at 20 West 77th Street. Baruch was a pillar of reformed Judaism, helped found Temple Israel, then at 125th Street and Fifth Avenue, serving three times as its president. He was highly regarded by business colleagues, as evidenced in the text of a memorial service held in his honor at the Temple February 22, 1901. My mother attended school in Harlem, then went for a year or so to a private school run by a Dr. Sachs, and then to Hunter College, called Normal College in those days.

Sol and Jeanette were members of Temple Emanu-el, NY where they owned seats in a pew. My grandmother had my name inscribed on a World War II service plaque, which was in the front lobby of the Temple and may still be there.

My Mother had a younger sister Gladys (born 1901) with whom she was friendly but not at all close. Soon after World War I, Gladys married a man in the department store business named Joe Strauch. They were divorced and later she married Leo Bachrach who did something in the insurance business. Gladys was an artist, and a good one. For years, I had two of her landscapes in our living room. I still have one and Jean has the other.

I never knew Gladys well until Janet once suggested we get in touch, which we did. After marrying Leo, Gladys bought a country place in Millbrook and we visited there a number of times, also a studio she had for a while on 57th Street and later her apartment on 72nd. The last ten years of her life, Gladys was an invalid, bed-ridden with M.S. I visited her about once a week when I could, and helped somewhat with her affairs. Frankly, I enjoyed Gladys' company – she kept her marbles almost to the end. I helped her write her last will in which she left her estate to me. I asked her – don't you want to leave a share to Caroline? Her answer was: "Why should I? She never comes to see me." Obviously, this led to a rift between Caroline and me which was partially but never fully healed before Carol's Alzheimer's set in.

Sol and Jack Wertheim had a Wertheim mausoleum at the cemetery of Temple Israel, in Hastings on Hudson, N.Y. (Westchester County). Many of the Wertheims and their spouses are buried there, including my mother and father. There may still be shelf space available in the mausoleum for any Wertheim descendents, if it should be needed though Janet and I arranged to be buried in National Memorial Park, Falls Church, Virginia, where Janet now rests. Temple Israel is at 112 East 75th Street, New York City.

On a visit to the Mausoleum in September 2004, I copied from the vault stones the following names of those buried there: (Only in the Sol Wertheim section.)

Dr. Arthur BookmanApril 22, 1877 to August 23, 1973 NYC

Judith W. BookmanDecember 15, 1888 NYC to May 30, 1980 NYC

Yetta WertheimDecember 11, 1832, Vorden, Germany to December 10, 1915 NYC

Baruch WertheimJuly 10, 1827, Wehrda, Germany to February 22, 1901

Jennette Schlesinger WertheimMay 28, 1867 NYC to July 20, 1956 NYC

Solomon WertheimJanuary 30, 1861, NYC to October 27, 1939 NYC

Gladys Wertheim BachrachJune 10, 1901 NYC to October 12, 1987

My father, Arthur, studied medicine at Columbia University, receiving his undergraduate degree in 1897 and from the College of Physicians and Surgeons in 1901. At Janet's suggestion, a few years before Arthur died our friend Dr. Paul Marks, then President of P&S, arranged to have Arthur honored as the oldest living graduate. Arthur established the diabetic clinic at Mt. Sinai, and then left for Montefiore, where for years he was a volunteer physician and President of its Medical Board.

4

When my father died in August of 1973, there was a brief funeral ceremony at the funeral home near the cemetery. Arthur had asked before he died that Kaddish be said for him, and I did this at the funeral as part of my farewell remarks (see Text) even though he did not practice Judaism during his life. My recollection of services for my Mother when she died in May 1980 was that there was virtually no ritual in a brief graveside ceremony, which I believe was what she wanted.

Thanks to a 1976 interview with my mother by my nephew, Michael Kazin, and some dot-connecting by Ruth, I learned just recently (2005) that my mother was introduced to my father by a friend of my mother named Enid Frank. She seated them together at a dinner party because they were both learning Italian – which later became their private "romance language". Ruth recognized that Enid was the mother of John Goldsmith, husband of Ruth's close friend Caroline who died in 2004, and now John and I are close friends.

My Father was never very close to his siblings, except for my Uncle Fred, so we never saw much of them, hence I did not get to know my Bookman cousins as I was growing up. After I married Janet, however, she suggested why not call up Uncle Sam and Aunt Olga Bookman. We did, and we visited them, and hence became quite friendly with my cousin John, his first wife Ruth (who died) his second wife Gloria Ross, and John's sister Edith and John's children. John was an eminent doctor, and a hero of World War II. He was a Navy Officer, captured on Bataan by the Japanese and held prisoner in Japan for 3 12/ years. His story is recounted in the book, "Conduct Under Fire" (Viking) by John A. Glussman, son of another officer who was a POW along with John.

Many years later, I learned a possible reason for my Father's estrangement from his siblings. A lawyer in the Karelsen firm, cleaning out his desk, sent me an old copy of a document about the Jacob Bookman estate. It appeared that Sam Bookman, who was the executor, after several years asked the heirs to approve an increase in his fee for his work as executor. Only Arthur disagreed, so the other heirs each paid his proportionate share of the fee increase.

My sister, Carol, died August 1, 2006. A couple of years before that, her son Michael moved her from her apartment on Beekman Place, New York, to a retirement/rest home in suburban Maryland, near his house. A few months before she died, Carol fell and broke her hip – and never really recovered from that. There was a Memorial Service for her in New York and her ashes are scattered in Cold Spring, N.Y. where she and her last husband, Mario Salvadori, had a country home for many years. Carol was married briefly during World War II to someone I never met (because I was overseas), then to Alfred Kazin, the distinguished writer and father of Michael, and afterwards to Mario Salvadori, a professor of engineering at Columbia University and authority on concrete structures.

Carol's son (with Alfred Kazin) is now a distinguished professor of Political Science at Georgetown University, author of several books on progressive politics in the U.S. married with two children and a wife who is a physician in Washington, D.C.

YOUNGER YEARS

Our family continued to live at 254 West 82nd Street as I grew up, and my Father's office was on West 72nd Street. But as his patients moved to the East side, he moved his practice to 25 East 77th Street, and our home went East also – first to an apartment on East 74th street (when I was in my teens) and then to 3 East 85th Street. They lived there while I was in college and a few years thereafter, but then moved to 33 East 70th Street, where they stayed for the rest of their lives.

I attended a nursery school on the West side and while still very young (maybe 7 or 8) went to a children's camp in Connecticut. I can still recall we were driven to the Sound for swimming where I was stung by jellyfish. When I became 12 or so, I went to a boys after school play group in Central Park, and to a camp the same people ran in Connecticut, called Camp Toltec. My chief memories of Toltec are being eaten up by mosquitoes and swollen with poison ivy. Otherwise, it was fine.

When my sister and I were quite young, we had governesses, first a young German woman (on whom I had a big crush when I was six) and later French women. The last one, Mlle Josse, was very ugly as I recall, and once I slit her raincoat with scissors (when it was in a closet) for which I was soundly spanked by my father. At any rate, I grew up being able to speak German and French, languages that my parents also knew.

When I was 5 or 6 years old, I was given music lessons, starting with the piano and then switching to the violin. I was not particularly good at it, and did not really enjoy it. I recall having to practice the violin in my room in West End, N.J. on beautiful summer days when other kids were playing outside. However, I do have the program of a student's recital in the Steinway Building at 113 West 57th Street on March 25, 1926. Included in the program were a Mozart Minuet (Don Giovanni) played by a quartet including GB on violin, and a Berceuse by Bloch with GB on solo violin accompanied by sister Caroline on the piano. So, by practicing I got across the street from Carnegie Hall.

When I went off to Boarding School I dropped the violin and never really returned to music except as a concertgoer.

My elementary schooling was at Children's University School, on West 72nd Street, run under the Dalton Plan by Miss (Helen?) Parkhurst, who established Dalton. (The school is now named Dalton School on East 89th). When I graduated from there, (Valedictorian, at 8th Grade) I was sent off to be a boarder at the Haverford School, in Haverford, Pa. It no longer has a boarding department but continues as one of the best private prep schools in the Philadelphia area. I graduated from the prep school Cum Laude and went to college across the street at Haverford College (though the two schools had no organizational connection). It was a friend of my parents, Dr. Christian Brinton, an art expert, who recommended Haverford. My years at Prep school were not especially happy at first, feeling as I did that I was a fish out of water, but by my final year, I was quite happy.

Another prep school incident I recall was my experience in Latin class. We had a very fine teacher, a Dr. Newhall, but I was a smart aleck. When called on to translate aloud a passage from Julius Caesar, I hid a small "trot" (translation), inside my Latin book. Dr. Newhall must have known what I was doing, but did not say anything. At the end of the year, I flunked the finals, of course, and had to repeat the year of Latin. The upshot was that I got to enjoy Latin so much that in college I signed up for a year of Latin, which is where I learned to love the poems of Catullus. They inspired my pilgrimage to Sirmio, Catullus' country home, which I describe later in this memoir.

In prep school, I must have been a real problem. I still have a very stern letter from my Father warning me to shape up (See Text). One year the Headmaster, Dr. Wilson, moved me to a room in his house, the better to keep an eye on me. But I must have improved because I graduated Cum Laude. Later I wrote a good letter to Dr. Wilson from Paris, which he appreciated. (See Text) Whatever was bothering me; I must have gotten over it because at Haverford College I graduated Phi Beta Kappa and had no disciplinary problems that I can recall.

At about this time (1930) my parents bought Hill Farm on Sugan Road in Solebury, PA (Bucks County) where I spent my teen summers, mostly working on the farm, chasing girls, learning to drive a car, etc. I loved the farm and that was where Janet and I subsequently spent our wartime honeymoon.

Before Hill Farm, summers had been spent in West End, N.J. and later nearby Elberon, N.J., favorite seaside resorts of New York Jewish families who could afford it. As a young teenager, I became interested in journalism and wrote a weekly social column for the Long Branch Daily Record about the activities of my contemporaries at the various swimming pools and country clubs. (See Text of letter from the Editor). Many memories of summers at the beach, including lots of horseback riding (I became pretty good at it) fireworks, shows on the beach, excursions to the fun palace in Asbury Park, riding the open-air trolley up and down the coast, surf fishing, etc.

In the summer my Father practiced medicine from the house at the seashore, seeing local patients. He took me into his lab on weekends and tried to interest me in medicine but I had little interest in it.

Hill Farm was 120 acres, a good part wooded, but many acres actively farmed by a family who lived on the place, the Bauers. John Bauer, son of the principal farmers, ran the place at the time Janet and I were married and we have warm memories of his friendship. The farm work (haying, etc) helped build me up physically (I was smallish when younger) and must have contributed to my longevity. I fondly recall trips with John into the market in Philadelphia to sell fresh vegetables at dawn.

During my prep school years, my Mother became very friendly with an English woman, Monica McCall, who came to live with us for several years, including years when the family weekended at Hill Farm. Monica was single, and good at outdoor work. So, she and I did a lot of work together at the farm including building stone walls and cutting wood. By profession, Monica was a literary agent with the N.Y. office of a London based firm, Curtis Brown, Ltd. After college, when I wrote the article "Life Begins at Graduation" (see Text), Monica helped me sell it to Ladies Home Journal.

My parents sold Hill Farm in 1950. After that they weekended in Cos Cob, CT., renting a converted stable on the estate of Barbara (Wertheim) Tuchman, a cousin with whom we all became friendly.

CHAPTER II

RELIGION

Haverford School, the prep school I attended, was run by a very straight-laced Presbyterian, Dr. Wilson and the School adhered to the Presbyterian faith. Every weekday morning there was a prayer assembly to start the day and vespers in the evening for the boarding students. On Sundays, I had to go to the Bryn Mawr Presbyterian Church, followed in the evening by the usual vespers.

Naturally, this affected my feelings about religion. As a child growing up in New York, I was not given any religious training that I can recall. My Father was an agnostic, never attended services, and my Mother went along with whatever he wanted. My Wertheim grandparents were members of Temple Emanu-el and attended fairly regularly. A number of years when I was a child we went to Passover at their house on 77th Street. However, no mention was ever made to me of becoming Bar Mitzvah. So, when I spent 5 years at a Presbyterian boarding school it inevitably affected my religious outlook. To this day, I know the Lord's Prayer better than any Jewish prayer. Haverford College was established by Quakers, and that was still the dominant faith when I was at the College. Weekly Friends Meeting was compulsory. For a brief time after college, I toyed with the idea of becoming a Quaker, but did nothing about it.

When our children were young, I signed them up for a Sunday School in Bethesda at a Synagogue, but since there was no follow through from their parents, they didn't like going to Sunday School. They dropped out and I then tried teaching them at home, but the results were laughable…so they grew up with no clear religious orientation.

After marrying Janet, I was exposed to a great deal more Judaism through her siblings. In the early years of our marriage we went to Seders mainly at the house of her sister Minna, then Janet and I started giving family Seders at our homes – first in Scarsdale, then in the country both in Millbrook and, later, in Lakeville. Our most ambitious undertaking was the huge Passover gathering we hosted in Lakeville – March 29-30, 1991. Nearly 50 people attended, with Passover dinner in a large rented tent next to the house. All of Janet's family was there, including nephew Leonard and his wife and children from Brussels, Belgium.

Living in Millbrook and later in Lakeville, we joined the Beth David Synagogue in Amenia, N. Y., where I became quite active, serving for a while as a Vice President and recruiting a friend and fellow member (Frank Roth) to serve as President.

So though I would not say I was a devout Jew, I have been a practicing Jew (off and on) since my late 20's/early 30's.

By the time I was in my late 70's, and we were members of Beth David Synagogue I felt the need for some formal religion in my life, hence studied three years and became Bar Mitzvah. I am glad I did it, even though there hasn't been much follow-through on my part. For more on this see Chapter XXVI.

After getting together with Ruth Bowman in 2002, I joined her synagogue, West End Synagogue, which is Reconstructionist. However, I still do not bond with the ritual and other aspects of organized Judaism.

Even so, there is no doubt in my mind that I am Jewish and want to be buried as a Jew.

CHAPTER III

COLLEGE AND JUNIOR YEAR ABROAD

At Haverford College, my roommate my freshman year was one of the few other Jewish boys in the class, Sam Kind, whose family had a jewelry business in Philadelphia. The next year I roomed with William A. Crawford (Bill) starting a friendship that endured over the years. Bill had grown up as a faculty kid at Lafayette College, Easton, PA, where his father taught Latin and Greek. Tragically, his Dad committed suicide when Bill was a young teen. His mother took Bill and his brother Jack to live in Paris, where Bill attended the American High School, from which he entered Haverford. Bill and I proposed to the Haverford administration that we spend our Junior years in Paris, first time this had been done at Haverford. The College agreed, so off we went for the academic year 1934-35. See my letters in the text section. We lived at 3 Rue de la Grande Chaumière, a short walk from café life on Blvd. Raspail and Blvd. Montparnasse. We also were around the corner from the home of Mrs. Crawford, an extremely charming and handsome woman who, by then, was missing one leg (see Bill's family history for the full story). I attended the Ecole des Sciences Politiques, took courses also at the Collège de France, the Sorbonne and art courses at the Louvre. Winter skiing at Chamonix, summer vacation touring Italy from Naples (and Capri) to Venice. A simply wonderful year that left a lasting impression on my life. Returned to Haverford and graduated in 1936, Phi Beta Kappa.

Two summers while in College I was a paid intern at the New York World Telegram, in the Financial department. Would get up at dawn and rewrite stories from the NY Times for the first edition of the World Telegram, then scurry around Wall Street picking up financial tables and quotes for later editions, with occasional chances to write an article.

My routine and Bill's while studying in Paris was to go to classes or study at home in the morning and early afternoon, then repair to the Dôme café for an aperitif or coffee in late afternoon. I think I once told Tyras that we would discuss the U.S. Constitution at breakfast, which may have been a slight exaggeration, and I'm sure I didn't convince him. He reminded me of it a couple of years later.

One of the pleasures of the year in Paris was the friendship that developed with my Uncle Fred Bookman, who was an expatriate bachelor living on investment income in Paris. About once a month, Fred would take me to a different French restaurant, introducing me to the gourmet life. He also bought me my first (and only) full dress suit from a tailor named MacNab on the Rue St. Lazare. Fred was good company. I saw him a few times when the war forced his return to the States, when he lived in Washington DC for a while. Fred and my father were good friends. Fred let me use his Paris apartment once or twice. Also, I once visited him at his home in St. Raphael, on the Riviera, which he left to my father, who subsequently sold it. I also saw my Aunt Nellie in Paris where she lived in pre-war years.

The Text Section of this memoir contains a large number of letters I wrote home from Paris with great detail about my activities (discreetly), such as operas and concerts attended, speeches made to student groups, even mention of two special girl friends. Scholastically, I did a major research paper on aspects of trade relations between France and the nascent USA, a major paper on the Saar plebiscite, a very explosive issue at the time that, in a way, foreshadowed Hitler's grabs for power that led to World War II. The letters reflect the darkening war clouds of those times and the weakness of the French government, which was also a factor in the rise of Nazi Germany.

Some of my first impressions of Paris, September 19, 1934

Dear People,

It is now Wednesday evening of my first week here in Paris. We have decided to start studying Tuesday. We have found diggings on the premiere étage of a house on the Rue de la Grande Chaumière. I will append the address to this letter before I seal it. It is in the sixième arrondissement. The thing that attracted me the most on entering was the lovely old paneled woodwork. The doors are deeply paneled with some light colored wood and it all looks very antique. The stairs are rather broad but very circular. And well worn. You open one of these doors (on the courtside) and enter a small hallway. Doors directly ahead and to the left lead to two adjoining rooms, which will be occupied by Bill Crawford and me. We haven't yet chosen which room will be infested by which fellow. Then there is a third room, adjoining but approached by another hallway and another entrance which Bill Fry will occupy. All the rooms look out on a jardin and just across the beflowered, betreed and begrassed court is another court of the house on the other side of the block, which belongs to some clubhouse for American girl students. So we are surrounded by beauty on all sides. We have sunlight almost all day long (except in the afternoon, which ends at 4 P.M.). That is to say we sunlight in the morning. Each room has a salamander (little heating stove) and a private washbasin. Also closets and bookshelves and fireplaces. The rent with all meals and service and two baths a week compris is 870 francs per month.

We have seen quite a number of pensions. One was fine, with beautiful rooms and all the baths you wanted and an ample table, etc., etc., but the lady who ran it was a little too motherly. She had 15 other boys and treated them like her sons. It would have been un peu trop bien soigné. She would have let us have pension for 900. We saw all sorts of dumps with all sorts of madams. Young and old, pretty and otherwise. The place we chose is run by a Madame of the safe age of 55 with a son about 30 and a daughter about 25. There is also a French woman who teaches French who eats there but we haven't met her yet.

Tuesday night we went up to the Butte de Montmartre, a very high hill on the top of which is the église of Sacre Coeur. You climb up innumerable dark stone steps and finally reach the top from where you can see all of Paris. It was a clear night and the moon was out and the lights in the valley below twinkled gaily (stupid sentence). It was all very pretty. Next to the church is a square called La Place de Tertre. It is sort of a village green on the summit of this high hill. It is crisscrossed by narrow little alleys, which twist in and about the houses. And as if the houses didn't crowd the streets enough, the people absolutely choke them so that you elbow your way through masses of gay, laughing, dancing, Parisiens and Parisiennes. On the green itself are about a hundred café tables, each one with a shaded oil lamp. As you sit there, all sorts of mendicants and street singers pass by the tables. An old man who screeches something in French about the poor lot of an artist, an enormous woman who trills a French love song at the top of her powerful lungs. The people who sit at the tables are mostly natives, but there are a few tourists. You can always spot them. All the houses around the square are cafes of one sort or another, groaning with people and choking with music (or vice versa). People mill around the doorways or congregate in the streets. Whenever a car attempts to plow its way through the mass of humanity, boys and girls will crawl all over it like so many ants and take a free ride down the street. Then you leave the Place du Tertre and wander along the crooked old streets, going downhill. As soon as you round the corner, into the darkness, it is as if some magician had waved his wand that had changed confusion into order, light into darkness. A block away from the busy square one can't hear a single sound or its wanton gaiety. The old shuttered houses seemed quite bored by the noise. You look up and see the cathedral. It reminds you of the priests you saw who descended the church steps and tried hard not to see a half dozen young men and women who were playing boisterously nearby.

I shall go there again but I am sure it will never be the same. That first impression of a bright patch of noise in the darkness is something to lock tightly in one's memory. An original too unique to be reproduced.

* * * * * *

During the academic year in Paris, much of the time was spent studying, going to theatre or music, fraternizing, sight-seeing, etc. The winter vacation in Chamonix was something else. In addition to learning how to ski, there were nights of carousing until dawn, and then a very ambitious ski expedition up Mt. Blanc through many feet of snow to the edge of glaciers – all in an area where no tourists go in winter. (Described in a letter home of January 4, 1935). Then back to studious normalcy in Paris.

* * * * * *

In the spring of 1935, I took a ten-day break to make my first visit to England, which included an extensive sightseeing swing through the south and west of England, including a number of days in London. My full travel journal for that trip appears in Text Section. Following is a letter home April 12, 1935, briefly summarizing the trip.

Dear Daddy:

I hope that this reaches you in time for your birthday because I want to wish you the happiest of days and all my good wishes and love.

As to what I did. I am rushed for time and this will be a very hurried account.

I arrived in England on a Sunday night, slept on the hardest bed I ever felt, in London at a place Bill had recommended. Left for Oxford by bus arriving at noon. Spent the afternoon and following morning in Oxford looking around which I liked but not so much as things I saw later on. But Magdalen College, by the river, was very beautiful. Then took the bus to Stratford on Avon arriving early in the afternoon. I saw many Shakespeare relics that afternoon and saw the sun set over the beautiful church of the Trinity there. It is right on the river's edge, washed by the lazy waters of the Avon. Framed by green trees, etc. very beautiful. Next day I got up early, looked at Stratford some more, walked in Shakespeare's footsteps to Ann Hathaway's cottage and back (2 miles) then walked to Mary Arden's house (Shakespeare's mother – 4 miles away) along the tow path of a canal so beautiful and so much like New Hope that a lump came to my throat. Then I saw the Arden cottage. All those

"Warwickshire farmhouses" are just like Bucks County houses. Big fireplaces, etc. just like ours. I felt at home. Then back to Stratford by lunchtime. I did almost everything on foot and walked like the wind. You ought to see me now, I look very healthy. In Stratford after lunch I took the bus to Warwick, saw the old part of the town and the castle thoroughly, and took the bus to Kenilworth, the loveliest spot on the whole trip. That red ruin overgrown with ivy, standing on a wind blown hilltop with nothing but the cawing of the rooks to disturb the natural silence. Saw the sunset over Kenilworth in a big orange globe that was very beautiful and very romantic. (I was alone). Then I left there reluctantly and bussed to Leamington Spa. Sauntered up to the station just as a train was pulling out so I ran for it and made it because the conductor yelled to me that it was the last train that day. But it made a complete circuit and would not have reached Gloucester until that night at 12:30. But at Banbury I was told to get out and I took a one-horse train to a changing station in the middle of nowhere, riding with interesting rustic types, and got to Gloucester at 10:30. That was my fullest day. At Gloucester I spent the next morning at the cathedral and there is a funny story about me, the Dean and a church service that you will hear some day. Then on to Bath which I saw for the first time on a rainy afternoon so was not over impressed by the Roman baths. Thought them rather dingy much like the Cave of the Winds at Coney Island. But the next day was beautiful. I went to the bus company and got their bus itinerary for a charabang tour of Bath then I did it all on foot and was through before the bus got started. Saw everything. Bath is as though at the bottom of a teacup surrounded by green cliffs. I climbed the cliffs and got splendid views of the bottom of the teacup. Then I left Bath at noon and went by bus to a tiny hamlet 4 miles from Stonehenge in the center of that great billowing sea of green and brown land that they call the Salisbury Plain. I walked 4 miles to the ancient, mysterious monument, studied it, hitchhiked back. Every moment on my trip and gallery, etc., I studied thoroughly. I did not see as much as some people might but I know a lot about what I did see. Then I went to Salisbury, saw the cathedral and the following day (Sunday) walked to Old Sarum, the "dry town" and famous rotten borough where 10 electors met in Election Field and chose 2 members of Parliament until the Reform Act of 1832. There are Norman remains that were very interesting. I had a regal dinner (aperitif, wine and Curacao – my only drinks except ale the entire trip) and then took the train on a rainy Sunday afternoon for Winchester. We passed through Southampton and I got a glimpse of ships in the harbor. It was raining so hard at Winchester that I didn't get out and stayed on to London. Then in London I saw the usual sights and loved best the galleries. I went to the movies every night – a rare treat for me because I never go in Paris. The National Gallery is marvelous.

I bought a book of photos of the entire Italian school. At Tate's the English school was interesting but not nearly so free and talented as the French school. But of course Constable and Sargent are among the greatest, Turner however did not impress me too much and I thought very little of William Blake. I did like some of Dante Gabriel Rossetti. But the French painting was better. I had dinner twice with the Goldstones who are really awfully sweet people and were as good as gold (not a pun) to me. Then I got your nice letters forwarded by Bill, but unfortunately just the day before I left. I called up Dame Sybil but could not get hold of her. Tried several times so finally wrote her a letter saying I was leaving, so sorry, etc., and hope we would meet at Hill Farm some day. I hope that went over. I am so sorry that I had no time to look up Monica's friends. And especially that I missed meeting her Mother. Thanks loads, Monica. I will write you as soon as I find a moment. (This is a hectic weekend for me. Lots to do before I get down to work). Really, I do regret not meeting more people. But my dashing off, as I did (which I do not regret) mixed up my receipt of mail, etc. so the letters of introduction came too late. I thought London very gay, very rich and in a spending mood. I had lunch at the Cheshire Cheese, took the famous pudding. The place is interesting and if you are willing to pay for the atmosphere it is worth it. But the food is not the best I have eaten, though it is good. Interesting old place. Lots of journalists guzzling beer at the bar. Then one Wednesday I took a rubberneck tour in a bus. It was the only time I did hurried touring but I don't regret it because I would not otherwise have seen the places I saw. The tour went to Stokes Poges where Gray wrote the elegy, to Eaton, Windsor and Hampton Court and passed through many suburbs of London giving me a good idea of the lay of the land as you might say. I will write my impressions of the trip later, as soon as I cool off. Honestly I am terribly rushed by things to do, people to phone, etc.

I liked modern London better than historical London. Of course some of the historical sights were quite interesting but it was London, the big bad, beautiful lively, vibrating city and not London the history book curio that intrigued me. I was just a wee bit tired of sightseeing too. Then I was homesick for Paris, inexplicably. And very homesick for the French language. I even had my hair cut to chat with a French coiffeur, and bought a French newspaper once. When I heard some French people talking in the picture gallery I glowed all over. I came back Friday over a rough channel but it had no effect on me. I am terribly glad to be back but I had a grand, full 12 days of it and liked every minute. Learned an awful lot about art and architecture. Liked the countryside more than London.

* * * * * *

Our deal with Haverford College was that we would take final exams in the regular Haverford curriculum courses after our return home in September 1935. We did, and passed with flying colors.

Another part of this memoir contains the text of my travel diary for the trip I made in the summer of 1935 to the South of France and to Italy after classes were over and before I returned home.

Basically, I traveled alone – except for a few days in Capri when I was joined by an American girl friend whom I had previously been seeing in Paris. I picked up conversational Italian as I went along from the border at Menton, down through Genoa to Rome, and – after Capri – to the Italian hill towns, Florence, and of course Venice. In Venice, I spent a little time with friends of my Mother who wanted me to stay for the Regatta, but I insisted on sticking to my itinerary, perhaps to save money or simply to stick to a schedule. Whatever – it was a wonderful trip, even without the Regatta.

As I review my notes, I see that I had very pronounced opinions on all the glorious architecture and works of art I saw. I did not hesitate to rate them as superb, mediocre or third rate. I wish I was as positive in my views now -- but of course, at age 20 I knew everything.

A highlight of the Italian trip for me was my visit to Sirmio, the peninsula on Lake Garda where the Roman poet Catullus lived. I had studied his poetry at Haverford, and then became enthralled with the Tennyson poem "Ave atque Vale" about Sirmione, which begins: "Row me out from Desenzano to your Sirmione row"…Of course, I hired a boatman at Desenzano to row me out to Sirmio. The heady romance of that poem has never left me. Another highlight of that trip was the glorious walled and turreted town of San Gimignano, which bears some similarity to the remote town of Mestia in the Caucasus (Republic of Georgia) which Janet and I visited about 45 years later.

At the end of the trip, I stopped in Geneva to look at the Students International Union, the summer school in international politics that I attended the following summer on a scholarship.

* * * * * *

My trip to Italy was truly inspiring. Following are letters home from Italy in the summer of 1935. My diary of the trip, with a much fuller account, appears in the Appendix.

George B. Bookman
June 16, 1935

18

Dear People,

At last I have time to write you a letter. (am sitting at a café table on the platform of the RR station of Puggibonsi, a small Tuscan town on the line to Siena).

I'll start way back. At Avignon I arrived on a Saturday evening and ate dinner on the opposite bank of the Rhone, facing the Palais des Pâpes. Sunday I visited the Palais des Pâpes and the old churches of Avignon. It is a walled city and I walked along much of the walk seeing the Pont St. Benezet famed as "Pont d' Avignon" in the old song. The garden on top of the Rocher du Dôme is very lovely. I spent much time just sunning there. Monday was Pentecost Monday and everyone was festive, including me. Bus to the majestic Pont du Gard, which I inspected thoroughly. It spans the Gardon River and commands a fine view of French countryside. Imposing edifice. Vestiges of a past so far, far removed always awe me. Then bus to Nîmes arriving before lunch. Sun was blazing hot. I always eat one picnic meal a day (usually lunch because of the heat at noon). Nîmes has a fine Roman Arena well preserved. The day before I got there they had had bullfights so I was for the time being, disappointed. The Maison Carré is a very graceful Roman relic hardly weathered at all. Fine Corinthian columns, gracefully tapered. There is a park there which is a castle with a view of the rocky countryside and vineyards. The wine is very sweet and very cheap. I always drink it. Then bus to Arles through more of the typical countryside of the Midi, which begins to look like Italy when you get to Valence. At Arles I saw the Roman theatre and a church with beautifully carved doorway and a cloister in Romanesque style. The sun beat down in the cloister yard and dappled the stone floor.

The greatest thrill was seeing a bullfight in the old Roman Arena at Arles. Stone rows of seats packed with marvelous happy people of the Midi. 4 bulls were killed. Toreadors in glistening costume. The hottest and most relentless sun I have ever felt. The bellows of the bull at bay, dust and smell of blood coming from the ring. There was a humorous Spanish man that did clown acts to the great delight of the crowd. After that glorious show I took a bus with a gay crowd of holidaymakers to Tarascon. I nosed around there 2 hours. It is a typical town of the Midi and very picturesque for that reason, though for no other. Interesting associations with "Tartarin," Daudet's sidesplitting novel. Sweeping vista of the Rhône and an old castle in the warlike style of the castles at Avignon and Villeneuve (nearby).

Tuesday I took the train to Marseilles, but it was so hot I didn't get off so stayed on to St. Raphael. St. R. is a very quiet spot, a quaint old port. One of the most intime places on the Riviera. I swam and sunned myself. Wednesday afternoon walked up to Uncle Fred's villa, "Ile Verte". His gardener a very nice man showed me around. It is sumptuous large property, but isn't lived in enough.

From all the windows, especially those on the south, there are majestic views. The sea as blue as blue can be – the stubby fir forest that covers the coastline, a large garden not too well cultivated. Rooms furnished in bad taste. All in all, he is a very lucky man to own the place. I know one person who wouldn't mind having it. Thursday went to Cannes and bathed there. Also visited Nice (No mail from you). Cannes is smaller and nicer for a vacation. It wasn't the season though and the Côte d'Azure was generally lifeless. At the casino de la Jetée at Nice I played with 10 francs, doubled my money and stopped playing. But the Casino is still doing business. Nice is too big and has too many hotels. The Promenade des Anglais isn't as important as I thought it would be. Thursday I drove to Menton via La Grande Corniche. You know how wonderful that is so I won't waste adjectives on it. I get a great satisfaction at viewing miles and miles of land or sea from a high vantagepoint. Menton is the best place on the Cote d'Azure. I will stop there if ever I spend much time on the Riviera. I got a great thrill crossing the frontiers about 2 meters into Italy, buying some Gelati and saying Gracia! Returned via Monte Carlo. I was too young to go into the Casino. (Boo Hoo!) The small port is very lovely and blue. The mountains slope down to form a fine background. Best viewed from courtyard of Prince's Palace. Met a young Swiss chef on the bus and spent the day with him. We ate dinner at Cannes, in a little Breton place where I stuffed myself with Crepes Bretons. Friday train to Genoa, chatted in French with an Italian all the way, learned some Italian. Genoa is very industrial but interesting. Historically only the Palazzo Russo and the P. Bianco interested me. But for atmosphere those tiny alleys near the port can't be surpassed. I walked out along one of the quais and then got a boat (rowboat) back to town after arguing the price down in Italian. From the water I could see how Genoa lies low along the coast, stretching way out. Went to the Villa Dinegri, a park at highest point in the city to get the splendid view. Train in the evening to Pisa. Lots of fun on the train speaking French and Italian with some Italians who were interested in my being a lone American in Italy. At Pisa I spent ½ day (Saturday, June 15) in Piazza del Duomo, wrote you a card there. The town itself, even the Lungarno is dull but the Piazza is magnificent. The Campo Santo was the best.

Then to Poggibonsi with two hour wait at Campali, small agricultural town where I bought cheese, salami, bread and wine for my dinner. Today (Sunday) at San Gimignano. My favorite so far. It was glorious. The Tuscan hills are so very pretty. I walked around the walls of the town after lunch. Sent you a card, which I have not yet mailed. Am now waiting for the train to Siena.

Hope you can read this,

Love,
George

At San Gimignano I saw a Fascist celebration. Very martial spirit.

June 20, Rome
Hotel Hassler & New York

Dearest Family,

I am established in this excellent hotel in Rome, taking the tip of Mother's German friend, Dr. ?? I have a room on the top floor front. All of Rome is at my feet. The hotel is on the top of the Pincio, next door to Santissima Trinita dei Monti. At the top of the stairs rising from Piazza di Spagna. Every night I see gorgeous sunsets from my window – the sunset upon the dome of St. Peter's.

I last wrote you from Poggibonsi. I went from there to Siena where I stayed overnight at the hotel. There I met a young Scottish art student with whom I passed some time. Siena – after San Gimignano - was not quite as wonderful as I had expected it to be. But it was still very, very fine. For art it is the best, of course, as regards the Siennese School. I liked the Duomo very much, especially murals by Pinturrichio. The museum is bulging with art treasures. I couldn't absorb it all. The public square where they have the Palio races I thought one of the finest things in Siena. I may get to Siena again for the races on July 2. It is very feasible. My first evening there I walked around the walls for quite a distance. The moonlight was very wonderful. Took an evening train on Monday to Orvieto and went up in the Funicular to the town, which is perched high upon a volcanic peak. Before going to bed I took a look at the Duomo in the silvery light of the moon. As I walked into the Piazza all I could see was the gigantic outline of the Duomo. The moon and one lone pine tree against the sky.

The next day (Tuesday) I went over the Duomo thoroughly admiring especially the façade and the murals by Signorelli. The entire thing is a gem. The finest Duomo I saw on the trip through the hills. I saw a good bit of Orvieto and the splendid views over the Umbrian Valley but I should have stayed there longer. Rome was calling me, however, and I yielded to the call and left Orvieto Tuesday afternoon.

I have seen many large cities and towns this year. Some are quaint, others pretty, still others are interesting or curious. But Rome is majestic. It surpasses all cities for sheer glamour. And I think the Fascist additions and spirit are perfectly within the tradition of Imperial Rome. My first afternoon I walked over the Pincio to Piazza del Popolo and down to Piazza Venezia. Spent the evening watching life around the Forum. Wednesday I walked along the Tiber, down Corso Vittorio Emanuelle and then to the Capitoline and Mussolini museums. Too many statues there. But I did admire the

Dying Gaul, Capitoline Venus, some portrait busts and a mosaic. The young Hercules amused me. Marble Faun very fine. The afternoon I covered the entire Forum and Palatine hill in great detail. My feet were dead. I met a young Italian fellow with whom I spent the evening. I talked <u>only Italian</u> with him. And what Italian!!

Today, Thursday, it was the Church feast of Corpus Domini. I really walked my feet to a frazzle. Walked to Piazza Venezia, Theater of Marcellus, along Tiber to Protestant cemetery (a lovely spot where I stopped before the graves of Keats and Shelley to recite lines from their poems). Then on to San Pietro fuori Mura where I saw an ecclesiastical procession in full regalia. The church is monumental, ornate and overwhelming. The Catholics must be bled to their last centesimi to pay for such edifices. Then to the baths of Caracalla (by bus). Then on foot to San Giovanni in

Laterano. It did not impress me so much. I don't like Baroque style anyhow. But the Scala Santo (which I certainly did not climb) did give me a very deep impression. Very deep, but I still can't figure out why a Catholic is a Catholic. Then on foot to Santa Maria Maggiore which I thought was very fine because it is simpler than most of the other patriarchal churches. Then to Santa Croce in Jerusalem (Unimportant) and finally to San Lorenzo Fuori Mura. (all this on foot) San Lorenzo is very interesting; it is composed of 2 old churches superimposed. The nearby cemetery, Campo Verano is the loveliest I have ever seen, if you like cemeteries. The marbles are all perfectly kept, the place is a profusion of flowers and it is thick with pine trees. In the distance can be seen the Alban hills.

At lunchtime it is very hot in Rome so I eat very little and do little. During the hot hours I try to be in the shade. I am very sunburned.

I meet many people to chat with. I am having a superb summer, and I am learning Italian. I am so glad to be able to get along in 4 languages. It is an immense advantage.

Tomorrow and the following day (Saturday) I'll go to San Pietro and the Vatican and some galleries if I get time. Sunday I'll go to the Alban hills. Then I may go down to Naples for a few days. After Naples I'll stay in Rome 2 or 3 more days to see some more galleries. Then I'll go on up North. Perhaps to Siena for the Palio race.

The enclosed picture was taken in Cannes.

Lots of love,
George

American Express
Rome, July 3, 1935

Dear Family,

At last I can write you again in proper style. I have been to Capri for 4 days. (I couldn't tear myself away). I really got to know Capri, walked all over it, paddled a canoe to the Blue Grotto and swam in the strange luminous waters of the grotto. Saw the most heavenly sunsets at Capri. July 30 left Capri by boat at dawn and breakfasted on a terrace overlooking the sea at Sorrento. Then tram to Castellamare and train to Pompeii. There I went over the ruins which were exceedingly interesting, but hot as blazes. Pompeii and its environs constitute the last refuge of all the ill tempered mosquitoes and flies in Southern Italy. It is filthy dirty. And the people are a bunch of cutthroat thieves. But I soon learned to be as nasty as the Neopolitans. I speak fair Italian, considering that I never studied it for more than 2 or 3 hours in my life. And I get dramatic, pound on tables, act hard and succeed in getting my way and not getting robbed. But it is very wearing. Only the people around Naples are like that, it seems. Northern Italy is completely different. The afternoon of the same day, June 30 I took a horse and buggy up to the Crater of Vesuvius. What bumps, dust and sun! But the crater was very interesting. With a guide I walked over lava only 4 days old and still red hot underneath. Every once in a while the volcano would roar a bit in a terrifying manner. I returned to Rome July 1 and today (July 3) I am leaving for Assisi. I have learned to know Rome very well and love it better than any other Italian city so far. (Capri excluded). My Italian is really not so bad. I can even converse with some facility. I have a little dictionary. I don't know my plans at all but I do look forward to being with you all again. Only a little over a month now. It is getting very close.

Lots of love,
George

Hotel Pensione Villa Fiorita
Firenze
July 8, 1935
Florence

Dear Mother and Daddy:

Don't mind this paper. I am really at a hotel called "Parlamento" wonderfully situated just behind the Palazzo Vecehio. But they have none of their own stationery.

I have been in Florence 4 days and will stay at least one more. When I leave I will have spent 6 nights here. I really am enchanted by it. The opportunities for views are unsurpassed. I took your wonderful suggestions and walked up Viale dei Colle at sunset also went to Fiesole for the sunset. I have "sunset

23

fever", a sort of habit of being on a high cliff with a beautiful view about 8 o'clock each evening. I took my supper along both times at Fiesole and at Viale dei Colle - wine, cheese, salami and bread. At Fiesole there is the most picturesque Franciscan convent recently restored to its original 13th Century charm after having been disfigured for centuries with baroque activities. It is a little gem of a place with an old cloister, bells, incense, Gregorian chants and a view of the Arno valley and Florence at the foot of the hill.

Enclosed is an article from the "News" which I hope you will save along with this letter.

"Continental Viewpoint" Is Hard To Define But Is Easily Noticed

Individualism, A Sense Of Proportion, And A Feeling Of Despair Are European Characteristics, Bookman Finds

By G. B. Bookman, '36.

Everyone who intends to spend a year abroad keeps a skeleton in his closet; a skeleton described as "The Continental Viewpoint." It is a vague thing, this skeleton, and serves chiefly as an irrefutable reason for going abroad, when all other reasons fail. To this skeleton-keeping rule the three Haverford Juniors now in Paris, W. A. Crawford, W. R. Fry, and G. B. Bookman, were no exceptions.

It is safe to say that no one can define the continental viewpoint, but it is equally safe to assert that after spending several months in a European city, one is quite sure that there exists a viewpoint toward life on the Continent which is quite different from the American viewpoint. Even if one cannot define what one has noticed, the very act of being aware of it is an advantage in itself. We who are here in Paris see the Continent from the Northwest corner, a corner turbulent with individualism. So our conception of the continental viewpoint will naturally differ from the impression received by a student in Italy, Germany, or Austria. Nevertheless some very definite attitudes which are peculiar to the European continent can be mentioned.

One broad current that one finds on the continent (a current that is running underground, to be sure, in certain European states today), is individualism. To be true to all of the Continent, that individualism should be defined in one specific sense, and I would give it the following meaning: on the continent one finds a tendency of men to develop within themselves a part of their personality that is hidden, personal and hardly ever revealed, while on the surface they seem to keep a highly polished social veneer which serves both as disguise and as shield for this secret inner personality. One gets the impression that an American is easier to get to know—really know—than a Continental European. In the European there is a depth which we Westerners cannot approach and perhaps cannot understand. It is a nebulous, invisible thing, this inner personality, but I am sure that it is there.

It manifests itself in the following ways: the continental viewpoint gives great value to self-expression —by art, music, literature or even by conversation. It is realized that if a man does not have an outlet for self-expression he remains a cramped, one-sided and undeveloped personality. Secondly, the continental viewpoint places high value on personalities, men taken for their intrinsic value as men, appreciated one by one for the interest that they can add to society by the mere expression of their own personal characteristics. No one can sip a cafe creme in a Paris cafe at dusk without noticing this, no

Cont. on Page 3, Col. 3

one can listen to the versation all about realizing that these over continental Euro to Paris because they be the city where a give expression to within him. Nor can a day in Paris with above all the doors buildings the wor Equality, Fraternity for a type of indivi dear to the hearts of peans; an individual comes more dear to portion as the onrus ship tend to suppre

Appreciate Beau

One other definit that one gets on the that here they hav proportion. That too i expressions that ca thing and nothing, bt it can be illustrated i the Continent men se aware to Beauty an to Time. True, on th seem almost to live the moment—politics gossip. But undern often finds that they the immortality of E levelling of Time. T paper a photograph donna" of Raphael much more prominen front page than a i Nazi demonstrations A fatalistic prophec met everywhere is classes, and newspa lief that Europe is i old world hegemony, ler called "The D West"—that Americ ored races of the O taking world leader after a series of dy rope will be only a expression."

*   *   *   *   *   *

GENEVA AND NEW YORK

Upon graduating from college, I went to the summer school in international affairs at the Students International Union in Geneva. There were 30 to 40 students, young men, and women, from a number of countries in Europe as well as the U.S. The courses included lectures by visiting experts from Britain and the Continent. The school was funded by a wealthy lady named Mrs. Maude Hadden. After the outbreak of WWII the school moved to Salisbury, CT (of all places) and was renamed the Institute of World Affairs. (It no longer exists.) My best friend there was a young Polish chap. He and I used to bicycle over the border to a French café several times a week for a glass of wine, etc. Also was friendly with a Hungarian girl from Budapest. At summer's end, I drove down to Viareggio, Italy, to meet a good college chum, Johnny Pugliese (later a star Harmonica player using the name John Sebastian). With him and an English chap we drove from Italy over the Alps to Vienna in a beat-up old car to meet up with Bill Crawford. Spent several delightful days absorbing the charm (and beverages) of Alt Wien. At one famous restaurant one night (Drei Hussaren) King Edward VIII and his then girlfriend, Mrs. Wallis Simpson, came in with a retinue and we chatted with the King's entourage. At one point I found myself in the adjoining stall to his in the men's room. A few months later, of course, Edward abdicated to marry Mrs. Simpson, becoming the Duke and Duchess of Windsor.

From Vienna, I took the boat down the Danube to Budapest, a delightful trip, greeted by Hungarians calling "Servus" (hello) as our boat passed under the Danube bridges. Spent several days in Budapest visiting the young lady's family, sightseeing, etc.

While in Budapest, through contacts of the family I visited, I was invited to write an article about the American Presidential election – when Roosevelt was running for his second term. I have the Hungarian translation, but not the original text. However, I recall that a few years later my Mother boasted to a visiting friend from Hungary that I had written for the paper named, I think, "Nemszeti Usjag". Her friend was shocked and said: "don't you know that was a very right-wing newspaper?" What did I know.

Incidentally, while in Budapest I bought myself a handsome red velvet smoking jacket. With the aid of a shoehorn, it still fits me. It hangs in my clothes closet.

After Budapest, I went on to Warsaw to visit my summer school chum whose name I think was Waskowski. Did sightseeing in Cracow as well as Warsaw, then by train across Germany to board a ship home from Hamburg. This was 1936 and I remember feeling quite uncomfortable as the train went through Berlin, where the Nazis were already a threatening force. (A paper I had written in Paris in 1935 discussed the German seizure of the Saarland).

Back in New York by Fall, 1936, I got a job on a community newspaper in Greenwich Village "The Villager" selling ads, writing and editing. In my spare time I got interested in the left-wing youth movement, specifically an organization called The American Youth Congress. Together with two friends, Al Fields and Lennie Engel, we published a newsletter for students called "Youth News Service" – ultra progressive in its point of view. As an outgrowth of that, the three of us started a newspaper feature service containing articles on US politics, foreign affairs, a cooking column, cartoons, advice to the lovelorn, etc. We called it "Press Features" and sent out a sample first issue to small papers nationwide. After a month or so, we ran out of money and closed it up, but when I went to clean out our P. O. box, there were a bunch of checks, which we returned. So much for my venture capitalism.

After about a year on "The Villager" in Greenwich Village, I went to work on a regular, established newspaper syndicate called McClure's Syndicate. My job for them was to make sales trips to territory where no McClure's person had been for years. This took me all over the Eastern and Southeastern U.S. visiting small papers, and actually selling a few features. This was Depression time and at nights in these small towns there was little to do, but each one had a shooting gallery where I'd go and fire off a few clips, becoming quite proficient with a .22 rifle.

Soon after graduation, I wrote a magazine article that was published by the Ladies Home Journal in the June 1937 issue under the title "Life Begins at Graduation". This quite long article purported to speak for my generation of college graduates. It was very liberal, strongly antiwar, strongly favored government social programs, but also spoke up for vigorous personal initiative and enterprise. Clearly I had very strong views and did not shrink from expressing them. (See text section).

CHAPTER IV

TO WASHINGTON

In 1938, Bill Crawford went to Washington from Paris to train for the U.S. Foreign Service. I went to D. C. to visit him and, while there, had an interview with David Lawrence, the columnist and publisher of US News Magazine. He hired me as a cub reporter so I moved to D.C. in the summer of 1938 and lived with Crawford, first in a boarding house on O Street (I think) and then in a rented apartment on 'O' or 'P' Street. I spent about two years on US News-World Report, an excellent experience allowing me to cover practically all the agencies of the U.S. Government, particularly the economic agencies.

In January, 1946, after I had been on World Report magazine a few months, they sent me on a fascinating trip to Turkey and elsewhere in the Near/Middle East. This was when the Soviet Union was making menacing noises about taking over the Dardanelles. President Truman decided to send the Battleship Missouri to show the US flag in the eastern Mediterranean. The excuse was to return the body of a Turkish Ambassador who had died in Washington during the war. The Navy invited a few reporters aboard, including me. We left from Newport News, stopped briefly in Gibraltar and went on to Istanbul. After delivering the Ambassador's body, we were feted in Istanbul and then went on to Ankara where we interviewed the President of Turkey.

From Turkey I flew to Cairo, inquired about going to Saudi Arabia (but could not get a visa because I was Jewish). This was also the time when the Soviets were threatening to grab some Iranian territory that they claimed belonged to Azerbaijan (a Soviet Republic). There was a crisis in the UN Security Council and the Soviets backed down. Had a very crazy flight to Teheran with a green Air Force pilot who was trying to show off and was later cashiered from the service.

In Teheran, the high spot was my interview with the Shah, who was later deposed by the Massadeq revolution. I cannot recall anything he said – this was the young Shah, son of the original Pahlevi.

After Teheran, I flew to Rome. Italy was having important postwar elections and I interviewed Pope Pius XII on that subject. The Vatican newspaper, Osservatore Romano, has a column on the Pope's public activities and I am listed as one of his private audiences, June 2, 1946. His Holiness offered me a rosary, I said I was not a Catholic, but he said I should give it to a friend – so when I got back to New York, I gave it to my parents' Catholic maid – Tessie. God Bless her.

While in Rome, before leaving for home, I got a telegram from David Lawrence, the editor and publisher of World Report Magazine. It said: "All your dispatches have been excellent. Congratulations!"

After about two years on US News-World Report I felt I needed some experience on a daily newspaper and managed to get a job on The Washington Post, then in its old home on E Street (I belong now to a Post alumni group called "the E-Streeters".)

Not long after I started in Washington, war broke out in Europe, then came the "phony war" period, followed by the ruthless German attacks on France and the Low Countries. I recall how Bill and I and our friends avidly followed these somber developments via the press and radio broadcasts. These were chilling events. I recall also covering the press conference where Roosevelt, trying his best to help the British despite strong isolationist sentiment in Congress, announced the "lend-lease" program, explaining it with the simile of lending your garden hose to your neighbor to help him put out a fire in his house. At one of FDR's press conferences, I brought along Bill Crawford, who mentions it in his own memoirs.

My White House assignment for the Washington Post was very exciting and professionally rewarding. I got to write some very major stories. The old clippings I have are too delicate for scanning, but here are some of the story headlines (all with George Bookman bylines):

December 18, 1940
> ROOSEVELT PROPOSES TO LEASE WAR MATERIALS TO ENGLAND:
> GERMAN TROOPS MOVING INTO ITALY, BELIEVED READY TO SAIL FOR LIBYA AND ALBANIA

December 30, 1940
> ROOSEVELT SUMMONS COUNTRY TO BECOME VAST ARSENAL FOR DEFENSE OF DEMOCRACIES
> NAZI BOMBERS LEAVE LONDON IN FLAMES

August 15, 1941
ROOSEVELT, CHURCHILL ADOPT 8 PEACE AIMS: PLEDGE JOINT EFFORT TO END NAZI TYRANNY: BEAVERBROOK HERE TO SPEED TANKS, PLANES

Covering FDR also involved several trips to his home in Hyde Park, N.Y. On one of these trips, June 30, 1941, the Franklin D. Roosevelt Library was dedicated. I covered the ceremony (and saved a copy of the program on which I scribbled my reporters' notes). In 2006, I donated those program notes to the FDR Library. Also, that morning Steve Early, the press secretary, introduced me to FDR whom I had often seen up close but never chatted with personally before.

My days on The Washington Post are best summarized by an article I wrote in 2004 for "Silurian News", the newsletter of the Society of Silurians, a club of old-time New York newspaper codgers.

Robert Phillips/LIFE   Acme

George Bookman (right) with Justice William O. Douglas, on the Chesapeake & Ohio Canal, March, 1954. Douglas challenged editors of the Washington Post to hike the gruelling 185-mile length of the Canal after a Post editorial suggested that it be turned into a highway. Thanks to Justice Douglas, the paper reversed itself and the Canal became the spectacular Chesapeake & Ohio National Historical Park.

George Bookman of the Washington Post, covering British Ambassador Lord Halifax (left) and British economist J.J.Keynes (second from left), after conferring with FDR at the White House on the state of British-American economic affairs, July 7, 1941. Other reporters: Tommy Edmunds (UP?), George Durno (INS) and Doug Cornell (AP).

The Old Days of the Washington Post

By George Bookman

My most substantial newspaper experience came in the 1940s as a reporter for The Washington Post. In 1975, Chalmers Roberts, the veteran and distinguished Washington Post reporter for many decades, was writing a book on the history of the Post and asked me to contribute some reminiscences. My recollections follow:

I left the Washington staff of U.S. News & World Report to join the staff of the Washington Post in the winter or early spring 1940, and left the paper in September, 1941 to join the Coordinator of Information, Wild Bill Donovan, later to become U.S. Office of War Information.

About a month after I joined the staff, Felix Cotton – who has been covering the White House for the Post – resigned (to join U.S. News, of all places), and I was picked for his beat by Frank Dennis. Naturally, I was overjoyed.

Maybe I made an impression on the City Desk with one of my first assign-ments – assigned to cover a chess master's demonstration at the YMCA (or was it checkers?). Anyhow, I wrote a feature-type piece that the desk liked, and they gave me a byline. From there it was only a Queen's pawn move to the White House.

Those nights as a cub on the City Desk were memorable (holidays and weekends, too). Gene Pharo, I think, was Day City Editor, and coolly passed out assignments – a shy, but rather friendly man. And we all remember John Reisling on the night city desk. When things were going hot and heavy, and you had two telephones to your ear and were trying to write a new lead for the final edition, with a few minutes to go, John would say, "Hey, Bookman, while you're resting, would you mind re-writing this wire copy (or hand-out)." John would relax by going out riding the back reaches of Washington in a police car or on a fire truck.

I also remember my brief (but sufficiently long) exposure to the press room at Police Headquarters, one of the most depressing, foul-smelling spots on earth, making the press room in "Front Page" look like Elizabeth Arden's salon.

But enough of that. We all worked cheek by jowl in the city room overlook-ing E Street, and I recall that my desk neighbors for quite a while were, vari-ously, Johnny Oakes, Hedley Donovan, Gerry Gross, Jack Norris. One of the great emoluments of the job was to be asked to do Sunday "brains section" think pieces for its editor Marie Sauer (was that her name?) and after the day's work was done we would hang around (us younger eager-beavers) until 1:00 or 2:00 a.m., writing for the Brains Section.

Casey Jones, the M.E. is chiefly re-membered as a remote, austere figure who could be spied through the glass doors of his office, inevitably rubbing his right eyebrow with his fingertips as he studied the front page of the first edition (and presumably the front pages of com-peting papers).

Of course Casey was famous for his budget-consciousness. After World War II, when I returned from overseas war information duties (after an absence of four years), and asked for my old job back, Casey said I could have it, but at my old salary, so I moved on to U.S. News & World Report and later Time Magazine. The first introduction to Casey, however, when getting hired, was his fa-mous "mountaintop" speech, describing what a great showcase the Washington Post was for a young reporter, a window on the world and the best place to dis-play my journalistic wares, and would a salary of $35 a week be okay? Of course, he was right on all counts.

Eugene Meyer was mostly an unseen presence to me, though I do remember him coming into the City Room occasion-ally after a party at the White House, or wherever, to pass along a news tip. By the way, is the story true that Bob Estabrook got his job as editorial page editor because he happened to ride up in an elevator in the Post building with Eu-gene Meyer, and made such an impres-sion on the way up that Mr. Meyer in-vited him into his office for a chat (and of course was then convinced to hire the bright young man???)

There ought to be mention of Post in-volvement in the Newspaper Guild. I

Continued on Page 6

Reminiscence of the Washington Post

Continued from Page 2

joined the Guild and I think served a term either as Secretary or Treasurer or something. Mrs. Roosevelt would occasionally drop in at the Guild meetings in the District Building. The main issue was the running fight between the leftwing and the rightwing factions. As I recall, Mary Spargo carried the banner for the leftists and Bob Buck (Daily News?) for the right wingers. The politics was hot and heavy, but I don't recall too much about the bread and butter issues.

Covering the White House in those days for the Post was exciting. The Post reporter had a direct line to the Post switchboard from the press-room – one of those table-top telephone models with the receiver on a hook on the stem of the phone. Of course, as the Post man, I always was in the front row around FDR's desk and at Steve Early's briefings.

Those were simpler days, when government was closer to the people – and to the press. The Roosevelts used to throw parties every year for the press. I remember going two or three times, when the entire East wing was opened to the press (at least the main reception rooms),and there was a Conga line in the East Room led by Eleanor R., and ice cream being dished out in the front hall, café tables on the roof of the east wing, and newsmen strolling with their girls in the garden. Never will I forget at about 2:00 A.M. when there were only a few dozen guests still left and my date (who became Janet Bookman) and I were eating ice cream in the front hall, Mrs. R. came up and sweetly but pointedly said: "Isn't it a little late for ice cream?" We took the hint and promptly went home.

The White House regulars used to follow the President to Hyde Park of course on his frequent weekends, and every time I pass the old building in nearby Poughkeepsie that used to be The Nelson House (now some local government offices), I fee a nostalgic twinge.

I don't remember any particular Post goofs of those days, but do recall that the Post did what I thought was an outstanding job in illuminating some of the major problems in the months leading up to Pearl Harbor and the people most responsible, I think, for the top-notch

reporting that was done were primarily Al Friendly (as I recall), probably Frank Dennis for assigning him to the stories, and Casey Jones, for backing him up. It was – and is – a hell of a good newspaper.

Covering the White House for the Post in those years was an exciting job. One of the high points was the secret meeting between FDR and Churchill on the Atlantic when the Atlantic Charter was written. As I recall it, Bert Andrews in the Herald Tribune ran a carefully-written story taking note of the fact that the President was out of town, the British Ambassador, the Chairman of the Joint Chiefs, the Army, State, etc. Rumors sped back and forth across the Atlantic that a big meeting might be in progress somewhere. Then an enterprising reporter for the Daily Mail, I think, named Walter Farr, who never let lack of facts keep him from running a good story, did a story filed (I think) from Norfolk, datelined "Somewhere on the U.S. East Coast," reporting that the President and the Prime Minister were meeting in the North Atlantic. We always believed he hunched the story, perhaps with a few hints from the British Embassy. Anyhow, in a few hours the "White House regulars" were on a train for Swampscott, Mass., where we paused overnight before being summoned to Rockport, Me., to interview a jaunty, triumphant, FDR in the cabin of a destroyer that had just brought him back to the U.S. coast from the nearly-secret meeting.

So tautly staffed was the Post in those days that, while the White House was the highlight of my beat, I covered a lot else besides. Much of the time I also covered Treasury (where Henry Morgenthau held press conferences almost every afternoon), frequently filled in at State, and more or less regularly also covered the Federal agencies such as the SEC, FTC, etc. It was an active life.

I remain an active member of the "E-Streeters," the alumni society of people who worked for the Washington Post when it was located on E Street in Washington, where Eugene Meyer bought it at an auction sale on the steps of that old building.

CHAPTER V

ENTER JANET AND WORLD WAR II

At a party on Halloween of 1940, I met Janet Schrank Madison who immediately got my attention by commenting unfavorably on the necktie I was wearing at the time. That set the tone for a relationship that lasted more than 60 years (57 of them as a married couple) until Janet's death, February 19, 2002. We saw each other frequently after that introduction, taking walks together along the Potomac River and the C & O Canal, and making a wonderful trip together to New Orleans and through the rural Southland. She was then working for the Social Security Administration and, she told me, the women in the office would perk up their ears every afternoon when I phoned from the White House Press Room.

Bill Crawford finally passed his Foreign Service exams and went off on his first foreign assignment, to Cuba. When he left, I got an apartment with two journalist friends: Fred Neal, later a professor of political science in Claremont, California, and Bob Kleiman, later a member of the editorial staff of the NY Times. Janet remembers seeing the three of us from a window facing our apartment when she visited a girl friend in the same building. Janet dated Bob for a while, but I won her away from him. He subsequently married four times, I think, and I've married only once. Both Fred and Bob passed away a few years ago.

In the months before I shipped out to West Africa, Janet and I saw a lot of each other. She had an apartment on Adams Mill Road in Washington and I wasn't far away on 19th Street, if I remember correctly. We went to a lot of parties, including functions of the National Press Club, which I joined, I think, in 1938 (I am now a "Golden Owl", NPC members for 50 years or more, exempt from paying dues). The most memorable party I recall was the annual press party at the White House given by President and Mrs. FDR, in the spring of 1941described above. Janet was my date.

As war approached, Janet quit her job with Social Security and took a job doing research for a war intelligence unit in the Library of Congress. Among the distinguished people she became friendly with there were Ralph Bunche (later of the UN) and Kenneth Landon an expert on Southeast Asia whose wife Margaret later wrote "Anna and the King of Siam".

After war broke out Janet switched to a news-reporting job for United Press (then a major news wire service). Mainly she covered Harold Ickes, Secretary of the Interior, and the War Production Board. She got to know Ickes quite well, became good friends with his assistant, Ellen Downes (and named our daughter Ellen Jean after her). Ellen later married a distinguished Haverford alumnus (Brewster Morris) who became a U.S. diplomat. Janet had many exclusive news stories. She gave up that career when she became pregnant with Jean.

US ENTERS THE WAR

By early fall of 1940, U.S. involvement in the war in Europe seemed inevitable, though we were still officially neutral. In midsummer 1941, I decided to leave the Washington Post to join the staff of an agency then called the Coordinator of Information (subsequently the Office of War Information and eventually the U.S. Information Agency). The staff had offices in a corner of northwest Washington near an old brewery where we churned out pro-allied information for the U.S. and foreign press. The director, at the beginning, was Col. "Wild Bill" Donovan, who later ran the OSS which was predecessor to the CIA.

On Pearl Harbor Day, Bob Kleiman was in a DC hospital to have his appendix out. I remember visiting him around 1 PM and as I left the hospital, Bob's father, who spoke broken English, was coming in, and, when he saw me, said something about "Boil Harbor" – the first news I had of the attack on our fleet.

Soon thereafter, I volunteered for an overseas assignment. I remember being interviewed at the St. Regis Hotel in New York by Col. Donovan before I shipped out for my first wartime post, Brazzaville in the then French Equatorial Africa. In a few minutes, Donovan eloquently described to me the global war situation, how I would fit in, and what was expected of me in Brazzaville. An inspiring sendoff.

Recently, from documents in the National Archives, I learned that Allen Dulles of the Coordinator of Information office, in May, 1942, sent to Col. Donovan a very strong recommendation of me for an overseas post. Dulles said, "Bookman is a man of real ability". Apparently Dulles was proposing me for a job in Secret Intelligence, until he found out I was already assigned to Brazzaville.

CHAPTER VI

OFF TO BRAZZAVILLE

After the attack on Pearl Harbor, I was eager to go overseas. The Washington Post and later the office of the Coordinator of Information had requested my draft board to defer me from military service, but I wanted to get closer to the action. (See texts)

In March of 1942 I was formally appointed to represent the COI (later the OWI) in Brazzaville, French Equatorial Africa, where I was to be in charge of an Information Service for the U.S. Consul General. The reason for having an American information office there was that French Equatorial Africa was the only territory in the Western world that flew the Free French flag – having rallied to DeGaulle when the Germans overran France and set up the Vichy government. Also, a 50 kw radio transmitter was being set up there that could broadcast to French North Africa and the south of France.

To get to my new post, I was to go by ship across the South Atlantic. On a day in April 1942, I boarded a Norwegian freighter, the SS Tamesis, in New York Harbor. But there were German submarines off the coast of Long Island, so our ship was held in port nearly a week. Then one evening in late April we sailed – unescorted. The next morning I woke up hearing voices outside the porthole. I looked out, and we were in the Cape Cod ship canal – a maneuver to avoid the subs. Then we headed out into the Ocean for the South Atlantic. We were at sea several weeks. The tight-lipped Norwegian captain told us one day that we had been followed by a German sub that did not fire a torpedo. Good thing they didn't – later, the captain told us what our cargo was – high-explosive ammo and aviation gasoline. (Possible reason we were not torpedoed – we flew the flag of Norway – which the Germans controlled.)

There were four of us aboard as passengers, all headed for wartime assignments in Africa or the Middle East. One fellow passenger was Elmer Lower, later a top news executive with all three major networks.

36

Our first port was Lobito, in Angola, where we stopped a day or so for refueling. Then on to the mouth of the Congo and up the Congo to the ship's destination, Leopoldville, capital of the Belgian Congo (now Kinshasa) – across the river from Brazzaville.

The details of my work and stay in Brazzaville are best described in a memo that I wrote in November 1944 for the Office of War Information after leaving the area.

* * * * * *

The writer of these notes on Brazzaville opened the Brazzaville outpost May 28, 1942, and remained in charge until his transfer to another post in October 1942. All remarks and comments thus refer only to this early period of the Brazzaville outpost.

The Brazzaville outpost was opened with all the panoply and fanfare that a sleepy Congo town could provide and in a manner most propitious for the influence of the United States. The American acting Consul General, Lawrence Taylor, arrived at Leopoldville toward the end of May, 1942, and prepared to cross the river to open the first American consulate on Free French soil and the first ever to exist in French Equatorial Africa. I joined him and on the morning of May 28, the Consul and I set out across the Congo in a special speedboat provided by Pan American Airways. We were met on the French bank by representatives of the Colonial Administration and Army and escorted to the Palace of Governor Eboué where we were entertained at an official luncheon. In the ensuing days, the Consul and I, working as a team, met all the leading officials and Army officers of the colony. The Consul gave OWI half his office floor space for an office of ample proportions and extended every courtesy and consideration. In other words, OWI started off in the French Congo under the best possible auspices and immediately won a place in the minds of French officials as an agency well accepted by the State Department and sharing equally in the deference accorded to an American Consulate General. It was my policy to do everything possible to continue to keep OWI identified with the Consulate since, in so small a town, and among such a tiny white population, any unnecessary division of functions would have served no useful purpose. We had much prestige to gain from working closely with the State Department, relations were of the best, and there was nothing to lose. Thus OWI letterheads, for example, characterized us as the Information Service of the US Consulate General.

The OWI program in the French Congo was a limited one and its existence even on the small scale of the summer of 1942, was never fully justifiable to me in my own mind. The occasion for opening an OWI outpost in Brazzaville was that the French were building a 50-kilowatt transmitter, which we, presumably, would feed with news and programs. By the time I left after a stay of five months, the transmitter was still not on the air and did not get on until many months after the Allied landing in Morocco and Algeria. Thus, we were confined to providing material for a low power transmitter (about 7 or 8 kWh when functioning properly) and sending out literature to the colonials. I spoke over the radio twice a week, once in French and once in English. The talk in English I am sure was not heard in any English speaking country, but its purpose was to get an entering wedge for the talk in French which was heard certainly in French Africa and perhaps in southern France. In fact, the talks in French must have annoyed some Vichy elements of the population because twice during the series the power feeding the transmitter was cut off during my French broadcasts. As a bit of color, the English talks, which were transmitted at 5 A.M. for short waving to America, were recorded the previous afternoons. Recording was usually done on the front porch of the residence of the French radio engineer and the cries of his children and pet cats often crept onto the wave. The script I usually propped up on a baby's high chair. It made a fine lectern.

We mailed out what, for the population of the territory, were sizable shipments of American literature. I recall a report, which I think was made in late July or early August, that up to that time we had mailed 50,000 pieces of OWI literature. I compiled a mailing list which I think gave complete coverage of the colony, officials, planters, army posts, post offices, schools, hospitals, etc., etc. The reaction to this literature was very favorable and the OWI office received many notes of thanks and appreciation, especially from recipients in remote jungle stations. One heartwarming incident was receipt of a gift of fine native pottery from the head of a mission school in appreciation for a shipment of OWI publications. Colonists from upcountry used to drop into the office frequently and thank for publications and to request more. There was considerable wavering sentiment in the colony at the time, since the landings in French North Africa were still to be made, and our literature may have had some effect in stiffening pro-Allied feeling. We saw to it that our posters were as widely distributed as possible. The matches, of course, were ever popular, and sold like hot cakes on the native black market, despite all efforts to keep them out of commercial channels.

Herbert Black was assigned to Brazza as radio engineer and did a pioneer job in setting up a reception station. Transmission from Brazza of radiophotos was not possible during my term there due to the low power of the station and lack of many necessary materials. However, we arranged for a pioneer transmission from Leopoldville, where the Belgians were most cooperative and better equipped. We will never forget saying hello to New York from the banks of the Congo after the test pictures had gone over the air and, some months later an OWI radio engineer who had been on the receiving end in New York told me that Black, Howard Cooley and I reflected in our voices all the loneliness of that Congo outpost. During the latter months of my service in Brazzaville, we received radio pictures on a regular schedule, posted them in the area, and made them available to the local press. Their use however was very limited, since there were no photo engraving facilities in the Congo except for our own small Davidson apparatus. I have never been able to see the reason for having Davidson, Beatti or radiophoto equipment in the Congo outposts, unless it may have been for the commendable purpose of giving the American technicians valuable experience in doing their job under outpost conditions, perhaps with an eye to results later on in some more populated area. Howard Cooley, the photographer and reproduction man, did a masterful one-man job of setting up our printing and dark room facilities in the garage and bathroom of the house assigned to OWI in Brazza. He made all plans and supervised work by a native labor gang. The location was chosen to provide maximum freedom from conflict with the French Information Service, which had ambitious plans for the use both of their facilities and of ours.

Our relations with the Free French were cordial, but never intimate. The trouble was probably the condition that colored all US-French relations – the fact that our government did not recognize de Gaulle. The Information Service in Brazza was probably more violently pro de Gaulle than any other group of the local white population. All were war refugees; none were old time colonials. They were happy to get news transmission from New York and used a considerable amount of the material, and cooperated in distribution of our literature through the colonial post office. But relations were always on a formal basis.

LEOPOLDVILLE...... From the very first weeks of our mission in Brazzaville it was plain to me that the main OWI office, from any functional standard of judgment, should have been in Leopoldville, Belgian Congo. However, the orders were to open the office in Brazza (presumably because of the awaited French 50 kWh transmitter) and no proper letter of authority to work in Belgian Congo was ever received during my term of office, though it was requested almost every two weeks. I went ahead on my own however in operations in the Belgian Congo and at the time I was transferred I was ready to rent an office on the main street of Leopoldville. I never thought that the US OWI, in the set of conditions that prevailed there, should share office space with the British, a plan, which I understand, was adopted after I left but abandoned after a few months. The Belgians it seemed to me were good objects for propaganda partly because of the importance of their exports to the war effort and their important relations to Europe and also because of the prevalence of a lot of sentiment favoring doing business with Hitler. It had been my plan, as a matter of fact, to put on an ambitious campaign there based on Doug Miller's book "You Can't Do Business With Hitler." Radio facilities were much better, there were newspapers in Leopoldville but none in Brazzaville and there were many more large population centers linked by better communications.

Relations with the US Consul in Leopoldville during my term in the Congo, however, were not good. At my first interview the consul informed me that he had no use for OWI, did not believe it should exist, thought the State Department did not like it, and would give us no more help than he was required to do under Department instructions. I did my best to conciliate him, consulted him from time to time on proposed work, etc., but finally gave it up when I saw it was getting us nowhere. I thought the best plan was just to go ahead quietly on my own, doing my work, and consulting him only on policy questions from time to time. I have sometimes wondered if the attitude of the Consul, which he must have expressed within the hearing of Belgian officials, did not interfere somewhat with our standing and prestige on the Belgian side of the river. This was a very unfortunate case of lack of understanding on the part of one government agency of what another agency was doing. But I believe it is not an isolated instance in the annals of OWI.

No memoir of the early months in Brazzaville would be complete without some mention of relations with the US Army. Before the landing in North Africa, as the Germans and Vichy regime pushed their railroad down toward Dakar, the supply line through Central Africa assumed great importance. The Army made careful surveys of all roads and river routes and began construction of a chain of air bases right smack across Africa's midriff, through the French and Belgian territory in which we were working. Howard Cooley and I flew down to the coast to meet the first American troop transport to land on the West Coast of Africa. We covered the event fully for news and pictures. In addition, I wrote an orientation leaflet for the US troops, including a ghosted letter by their commanding colonel, and notes on the history of the Congo and the Belgian people. The C.O. was delighted to get it and distributed it throughout the unit. We handled the printing at an American mission school. Local papers picked up the leaflet and I think it was probably the most effective propaganda job we did while in the Congo. A few weeks' later contingents of the US Engineer force crossed the river to the French Congo. The US Consul invited all the townsfolk of Brazzaville to witness their arrival and colorful parade. A public invitation was circulated through the town by runners, after the local custom. It was a great event in French-American history. Arrival of the first US troops on French soil in the western world since the last war. The local UP correspondent who incidentally was also head of the French Information Service and also was the censor, filed a story to the United Press. I checked security angles with the American military attaché, wrote a story, and submitted it for approval to the US Consul, acting CG. After he had read it and suggested a few changes, which I made, I filed the story to OWI, NY. A few days later General Richardson, USA, commanding US forces in West Africa, called me across the river to Leopoldville and showed me a telegram signed "Marshall" asking for an explanation of why the story was released, etc., etc., and requesting me to issue no more pictures or news about American forces. Inquiries also came from OWI for an account of the incident. I pointed out that the event was a matter of common knowledge, that the matter of publicity had been taken up with the US military attaché, that the story itself had been okayed by the US consul and that another story had been filed to United Press by its local correspondent without clearing with any other local authority. In my talk with Gen. Fitzgerald, I told him that naturally I would comply with the Army request to issue nothing about US forces but on the general question of future activities, I would refer the matter to OWI headquarters in NY and Washington. I understand some months later Gen. Fitzgerald was court marshaled on charges, naturally, having nothing to do with this incident, and was busted to the rank of colonel and assigned to duty somewhere in the USA.

* * * * * *

One sidelight on the arrival of the troopship in the Congo River. The men had previously been on Ascension Island in the South Atlantic building an airbase there. As we steamed up the Congo, their commander got on the PA system to address the men. One thing he said was : "Men, on Ascension Island you have had a perfect record concerning cases of V.D. No cases at all. Let's try to keep it that way in Africa".

One other sidelight: in Brazzaville I cooperated with my British opposite number, a Col. Bagehot-Gray. He and I agreed that it would be useful to buy a riverboat to share in hauling freight and passengers across the Congo. I left before the deal was consummated, but much later, after the end of the war, I got a letter from the General Accounting Office, questioning the rate of exchange, I had used in calculating my share of the boat. Fortunately, Congress passed a bill canceling all wartime accounting quibbles of that kind.

Part of my job in Brazzaville was to do broadcasts in French aimed by short wave to North Africa and southern France and in English to any English-speaking troops or residents within the listening area. I still have the text of about a dozen of the weekly broadcasts in English. One selection is in the Text section.

CHAPTER VII

TO CAIRO AND BEIRUT

On November 1, 1942, after I got to Beirut, Lebanon, I wrote a letter home with more personalized details of the time in Brazzaville and a description of the fascinating trip from the Congo to Beirut. That letter follows:

* * * * * *

Late in September, I got a message saying that I was to be transferred to Beirut. About the twenty fifth or so of September, my replacement, Jack Iams (Ex of the N.Y. Daily News) arrived in Brazzaville. I spent about two weeks showing him the ropes in Brazzaville before leaving for Cairo and points north.

Now that I am a thousand miles away from Brazzaville, I look back on my experience there with what are called, tritely but aptly, mixed feelings.

Physically, it was unpleasant. It was pretty hot, but never unbearably so. There was always the danger of malaria, there was the daily routine of pills and mosquito nets, and there were the swarms of bugs and the remoteness of the Congo from the epicenters of war activity. Perhaps I was very fortunate but I was never in really bad health in Brazzaville. Howard Cooley and Herb Black (my colleagues) both came down with malaria. Black recovered quite well, but Cooley was left weak by the disease and finally had to be transferred to a kinder climate. Naturally, I am sure that the malarial germs worked their way into my system. From time to time I could feel them playing around in my bloodstream but I never actually had a fever that could be properly called an attack of malaria. Often I felt tired, overcome by a sort of lassitude, but it never interfered with my work. However, it was a relief to step aboard a plane and fly out of that area. You never feel quite comfortable. Subconsciously you are always on your guard against natural enemies, such as bugs and germs. For instance, it becomes a habit to shake out your slippers before putting them on – just in case there may be a poisonous spider or another unfriendly creature hiding there. You also inspected your bedclothes very carefully for the same uninvited guests. You never went out in the daytime without a sun helmet and you had to be careful about wearing sunglasses at noon or on the water. It was a tremendous relief to arrive in a part of the world where you could put your bare foot on the floor without knowing for sure that you would pick up chiggers or other worms, where you could go about bare headed without fear of sunstroke, where you did not have to be constantly in a state of defense, ready to repel attack by bugs and germs.

But Brazzaville had its bright side too. Life was easy, much easier than here. We three fellows had six servants. You never had to worry about getting clothes washed, pressed, or put away properly. That was always done for you silently, automatically, unobtrusively. If you wanted a drink, or a bag carried or a pencil sharpened, you just yelled "boy" and a little brown brother came running to tend to your needs. That isn't so in the Near East. The Arabs are very advanced and high-ranking members of the human race indeed and do not enjoy being yelled at, called boy, or otherwise treated as something less than human. There was more variety of food and more of it. Here in the Lebanon, as in Cairo as well, there are three meatless days a week. White bread is rare. Butter is extremely costly. Next door, in Palestine, people are living under very severe restrictions. They all carry point cards, ration cards, for food and clothing, and the rations are none too generous.

Though the Congo and Brazzaville may seem to you to be lost somewhere in the wilds of Africa away from everything comfortable, life there was much richer as far as food and drink are concerned, than it is here. You didn't feel the war there nearly as much as you feel it here. The blackout for instance. The cities on the Congo of course observed no war blackout. The only blackout they observed was the usual tropical custom of pulling in the sidewalks at 10 P.M. but that was only to be expected.

Cairo is blacked out, Palestine is blacked out, and Beirut is black as pitch on moonless nights. A flashlight is an indispensable piece of personal equipment.

In Brazzaville, we lived like kings. We had a lovely house, as you know, on the banks of the Congo. It did not cost us a cent and living was cheap. Three of us lived together, always providing each other company. It was a small town, a neighborly place where you made friends easily and saw them frequently.

Beirut is expensive as Hell. I am probably going to have to spend my entire salary here, or a large part of it, just to live properly. I am now living at a Hotel, the best in Beirut, called the St. George. But I do not care for hotel life and am looking for an apartment. But apartments are very hard to find, and I will probably have to look a long, long time before I find anything.

I have not met a great many people here, yet, which irks me somewhat, but I think that will be remedied soon. There are a great many British here, a large colony of Americans, connected with the famous American University, and of course the French and the Lebanese.

In addition, there are sprinklings of Greeks, Poles, Czechs, and in fact almost every nationality you could name.

But let me double back on my trail and tell you how I got here. I had expected to leave Brazzaville about October 15 or sometime thereafter. On Sunday, October 11, I think it was, we were entertaining some American fellows at our house, when the British vice consul drove up and told me that I would either leave at dawn the next day, or he could not promise me a seat on the plane for quite a while. I had only about three hours to get ready, but I made it. However, I had to severely shorten or omit altogether a lot of good-byes that I wanted to say. My baggage was way overweight, even though I did cut it down drastically. I left behind your great big brown suitcase with the initials AB. The one that has the expanding sides, and will hold as much as a trunk. I also unloaded some tropical clothes and left behind such things as a camping kit, etc.

At dawn Monday, I left Leopoldville via British flying boat. That aerial trip across Africa was a grand experience. One regret I had at leaving Brazzaville when I did was that I had seen so little of Africa. But the flight across the continent gave me an opportunity to get a quick glimpse of many different kinds of country all the way across Africa. There is no secret about the route traveled by the British flying boats so I guess I can tell you what I saw along the way.

We slept the first night at Stanleyville, far up the Congo River where Henry M. Stanley had a historic fight with native tribes on his pioneering expedition. The flight that day was mainly over the great Congo River or its many tributaries that snake through the Central African jungle. We alighted at midmorning at one Congo River Station, right on the Equator just after a rainstorm. The air was clear and full of the music of tropical birds. Traveling by British airways is traveling in grand style. Each time the plane stops a tender comes out from shore, and the passengers are either taken for a bit of a ride on the river or else are put ashore for a few minutes. It is pleasant too because the plane stops frequently and there are very few times when you are in the air for more than four hours at a stretch.

It took us about two and a half days to span the continent. The second night we slept in Khartoum. The flight that second day was the most impressive of the whole trip. We left Stanleyville somewhat before sunup in a drizzling rain and came out into the sunlight over the fertile hills of Uganda. As the sun climbed up, we came over the Northern end of Lake Albert and then turned down the Albert Nile, headwaters of (I believe) the Blue Nile. The pilot was a good sport and flew us about 200 feet off the ground, over the Albert Nile basin, which is famous as the most heavily populated game region in the world. We were three passengers and we spent our time running back and forth across the plane from window to window as it skirted the treetops, looking at great herds of elephant, hartebeest, wildebeest and packs of hippos wallowing in the sun-warmed mud. We saw no lions or giraffes but a great many other animals, especially large quantities of elephants.

That day we flew through one of the hottest parts of the world and as evening fell, landed on the Nile off Khartoum. Yes, Khartoum was hot. But the dry desert heat was a relief to me. After the wet humidity of Brazzaville, I loved the searing crackling dryness of the desert heat. When we stepped ashore the wind off the desert felt like a suit of long woolen underwear. But it was dry, and to me, invigorating. We stopped at what I think is called the Grand Hotel in Khartoum. The best one in the place. After dinner, I went out with a fellow passenger, The Belgian Minister to Egypt who had just come from a Jap internment camp in Tientsin. We went about the town just enough to find out that Lord Gordon is chiefly remembered there by a night club named after him which features a rather good belly dancer and a fair to middling fandango Artiste.

Later, I learned that the belly dancer had been in Cairo where she had affairs with several British officers until they learned she was a German spy. Instead of executing her, they sent her up the river to Khartoum for the rest of the war.

The next day we flew down the Nile, passed over Luxor a bit too high to see more than just dim outlines of the temples, and landed in Cairo in mid afternoon.

I got a tremendous kick out of the fact that our Cairo office had reserved a room for me at no less a hotel than Shepherd's. Damned expensive but a thrill to stay there, especially on one's first visit to Cairo. I stayed in Cairo about a week.

In Cairo, we landed on the Nile outside of town and I took an airport bus into the city. Leaving the bus in front of the British Airways office, I hailed a horse-drawn carriage, loaded my bags, and told the driver to take me to Shepherd's Hotel. He looked at me, shrugged, turned the carriage around, and pulled up to the Hotel, which was next door. Greenhorn that I was! As I went up the hotel steps, a man came down wearing a British officers' uniform. He looked at me and said: "New in Cairo? This place is a pushover for Gen. Rommel." With which he disappeared into the street crowd. Probably a German secret agent.

The contrast between civilian Egyptian Cairo, which is definitely not at war, and the throngs of allied troops in the streets, hits you in the face. The Egyptians seem to do nothing but try their hardest to make as much money out of the war as possible. That appears to be true in fact of all the Arabic peoples in the parts of the Near East that I have visited. To them the visiting foreign armies, are just a different kind of tourist trade. These tourists in uniform are more numerous and spend more freely than the usual peacetime tourist. Of course, they sometimes get drunk and break a few chairs in a café, or they sometimes attract a little shooting their way from the enemy, but by and large, the peoples along the Mediterranean seem to consider the Allied armies as just one grand opportunity to make money. At the start of the war I am told, Shepherd's Hotel, Mena House and the other big Hotels, closed, thinking that their trade would be ruined but they quickly learned better. Now they are all doing a land office business. It takes diplomatic influence to get a room at one of those hotels and practically takes diplomatic influence to get a waiter.

Another amazing thing to me was to see so many soldiers and officers patronizing the fleshpots of Cairo when Mr. Rommel and his boys were about two or three hours drive by car out of the city. Of course the big British offensive has now started. But when I was in Cairo, it had not quite begun. In fact, it started the day after I left. That may have changed the spirit of the town somewhat, but not much, I'll warrant. Of course a great many of the British Officers and men who are having a good time in Cairo, richly deserve it. They have been out in the desert most of them for months and some for a year or more, without leave in Cairo. They have been living under conditions of pluperfect hell and have earned their right to have a few drinks and dances back in the sinful city on the banks of the Nile. But the most evident officers and most obnoxious are the staff boys from the good families who have the ever so beautifully tailored uniforms, and spend most of their afternoons and evenings on the popular terrace cafes, and at the right night clubs with the not-so-right young ladies. There is a lot of that and it doesn't make a good impression on the casual visitor like myself. It isn't the tough stern kind of living that the other side is probably exposed to. Someone said that Cairo was worth several divisions to Rommel by the very fact of its existence and the influence it has on the morale of the troops who spend their leave there. I think he was right. It turns your stomach to hear some of the conversations at Shepherd's Bar. Gentlemen soldiers who reserve a room by the year at Shepherd's, who gallop out to the desert for a bit of grouse-shooting at the Germans and then come back to exchange hunting stories in polite tones at a chic bar. It doesn't look like war and I doubt if it is.

But there are so many of the other kind of officers and men, chaps who are fighting well and fighting hard, that I guess they make up for the sins of the minority in Cairo who are more in evidence behind the lines, but, I imagine, less important to the winning of the war. In Cairo, I must confess that I too covered the nightclub belt fairly well, which, I guess, weakens the above comments somewhat. I also stole enough time one Sunday to go out to the Pyramids. I went with Elmer Lower, who crossed with me on the boat. He is grand and doing a swell job handling a very fine picture service for our office in Cairo. The other members of our Pyramid party were George Rentz, Elmer's roommate, and Ben Stern from our office whom I knew in Washington. We went to Mena House and had lunch there and then did the Pyramids on camel back. We climbed up inside the big Pyramid but did not scale the outside.

That morning I spent walking through the Mousky, (the native Bazaar section) with Ben Stern. Cairo is certainly filthy. I have now been in a few more Near Eastern cities but I have not seen one yet that is as dirty as Cairo. Nor have I seen anywhere a race of people as filthy looking or generally low down as the Egyptians. They certainly have slipped since Pharaoh's days. A savage black African native is infinitely cleaner, more honest and generally has more self-respect I think, than the best that Egypt has to offer, not excluding probably the royal family. But don't tell the Egyptian minister I said so.

While in Cairo I spent the daytime buying some equipment for our Beirut office. I was all set to come up to Beirut by train with the equipment; in spite of the fact that I heard it was a grueling, dirty ride with no food and no sleeping cars. But at the last minute a young American Army Lt., Karl Quigley, who handles press relations in Cairo for the American Army invited me to ride up to Beirut with him in his Jeep. Naturally, I jumped at the chance. I managed to find another way to forward my baggage and equipment (I hope -----it hasn't arrived yet) and so off I went with Quigley across the Sinai desert by Jeep!

We left very early Wednesday, October 27, drove along the Nile a ways, cut over through Ishmailia and to the Suez Canal, and then struck across the desert. A Jeep is a bit bumpy and doesn't have any upholstered seats, but it is a marvelous way to travel. It goes very fast and can take any kind of bumps or sand at high speed. We whizzed along about 60 miles an hour over the desert through the country where poor old Moses and our ancestors spent 40 years wandering around. They could have cut down their time considerably if they had had a flock of Jeeps.

The desert is glorious. Many colors. Great "Mesas" of sand and rock. Looks very much like pictures of Arizona and New Mexico. By shortly after lunch we had crossed the desert, and then we drove up through Palestine, arriving in Jerusalem in the late afternoon. We came up a beautiful way, hitting Beersheba first and then up through Bethlehem to Jerusalem. Palestine is so beautiful and picturesque it takes your breath away. I can see now how it became the home of so many religions and prophets. It inspires religious feeling. One thing that amazed me was how healthy everyone looked.

Naturally in Brazzaville, all white people look unhealthy. I was yellow when I left and lost about 15 pounds weight. In Egypt, all the Egyppos looked diseased. But in Palestine all the farmers have ruddy cheeks are well tanned, look like stolid, tough people in excellent health.

The deep valleys and rocky ravines I thought even more beautiful, in places, than the Italian hills though of course much more barren.

I hadn't seen so many Jews since I left New York. At Jerusalem, walking through the bazaar section toward the Wailing Wall, I thought for a moment I was back on Fourteenth Street. Sure are a lot of Landsmann in the old country. And they seem to do pretty well for themselves. I didn't get to Tel Aviv this trip, which I am told is practically like an American city. But I did see Haifa and a number of other Jewish communities as we traveled across country and our boys seem to have developed the country pretty well.

We stopped at the King David Hotel in Jerusalem. We had very little time to see the sights. I just got a glimpse of the Wailing Wall and walked quickly through the old town. I plan to go back some weekend and really look around. It looks extremely interesting to wander around in Jerusalem for a couple of days. I did not get out to the Dead Sea either. The mornings in the Palestinian Hills are very cold this time of the year, very invigorating mountain air. In Jerusalem, I fell victim to a very slick Armenian salesman and bought an enormous goatskin Bedouin coat. It is smooth white skin on one side, and shaggy goat hair on the other side. Warm as four or five blankets. But it would look very peculiar in Beirut. Just the right thing for the mountains if I get a chance to travel this winter.

Last Thursday afternoon I arrived in Beirut, after driving up along the Mediterranean, past Tyre and Sidon and a score of other romantic and beautiful places.

Beirut is truly beautiful. That is what everybody says, and in fact, even after living here quite a while. So far, I haven't discovered very much here that I have warmed up to except the absolute beauty of the city and its location. But I suppose I will gradually discover other likable qualities about the place.

We had already had an office established here about six weeks when I arrived. It is in charge of George Britt, a man of about 40 or 45, who used to be an editorial writer on the N. Y. World Telegram for many years and more recently on the N.Y. Post. Of course, an old World Telegram man like me was very welcome. He didn't know me in my W.T. days and I can't say I blame him. He is a very likable man, the type of person who makes you his friend very quickly. He has done an excellent job here of personal salesmanship. He has been here only about 6 weeks and his name is already practically a household word in Beirut. For a newspaperman, he is the best politician I have ever met. The other associate in the office is a delightful chap called Frank Brown, a Professor of Archeology at Yale University.

Later, November 15th

Well the usual thing has happened, this letter to you was interrupted, and I have not had a chance to get back to it until just now, exactly two weeks later. Some work came up the Sunday I was writing to you. And then you know what happened last Sunday…. The American landing in North Africa. When George Britt came up to my room to tell me about it, I couldn't believe it, it sounded too wonderful and thrilling. We quickly got to work on it, and put out lots of pictures and special News Bulletins for the local press, and managed I think, to do a valuable piece of work in helping to cover and make the most out of the news.

Things have changed somewhat since I wrote the first part of this letter… changed for the better for me personally. I have met more people since my first week here, and am feeling quite happy about being in Beirut. I think I am going to like it. I am still living at the hotel, but this morning I saw an apartment a few minutes from the sea, which I think I will hire if I can… all furnished. More Personnel have arrived for our office. Barclay Hudson, a sort of photographer, traveler, and writer is here now handling financial matters, which leaves everyone else free to enjoy life and do some interesting work. We also have a radio operator called Charlie Miller. I am in charge of a daily news service and our picture service and probably am going to take over displays such as public bulletin boards, and such like in a few days. In addition, I am running a weekly English language Radio program, consisting mainly of Jazz Music and directed to the Allied Forces in this area. I announce the program on Radio Levant, which you can't hear from the U.S. so don't bother trying.

I am gradually getting myself a little staff. I have an Arabic translator, and an Arabic Typist, who turn into Arabic the stuff I write in English. And I am getting a secretary in about a week, a young French girl who speaks very good English who will translate my stuff into French because I do not feel that my French is good enough for regular translations of news with the necessary amount of speed and fluency.

My first weekend here George Britt put the car at the disposal of Charlie Miller and myself and we went across the mountains to Damascus. It was a wonderful trip. I could spend pages describing it. (But I won't). I had no idea the Lebanese Mountains were so gorgeous. Driving from Beirut to Damascus you climb up and up to the top of the Lebanese range. The air gets cold and invigorating; the mountains get barren of vegetation and look wilder and wilder as you ascend. Then finally you get to the summit and look down over the other side, and see a great inland valley, fertile and drenched in sunlight. You dip down, cross the valley floor, and then go up again into the dry rocky Lebanon range. More minutes of driving through the desolate uplands and then once more you look down and see the well watered plain of Damascus at your feet, a green garden spot surrounded by desert. It is called the Pearl of the East – and with reason, for the gurgling water whose music you hear everywhere in the city must strike the lonely Bedouin from the arid desert country as something akin to Paradise. I enclose in this letter some pictures that may give you an idea of what it was like. On the way back we stopped at Baalbeck, one of the most interesting sights I have ever seen. Three civilizations can be seen there piled one on top of the other - Phoenician, Roman and then Moslem. The Roman temples, especially one large Temple to Bacchus, are in an excellent state of preservation. You get an excellent idea of the glory that was Rome and what it must have represented to the folk of the Middle East.

* * * * * *

The most important things that happened during my stay in Beirut was that, in the winter or spring of 1943, I proposed marriage to Janet by mail. It was a hand-typed letter that was personally carried back to Washington by an officer friend (don't remember who) and I think hand-delivered to Janet. Unfortunately, the letter cannot be found. But of course, it recalled our friendship and relationship in Washington, contained a declaration of my love, and asked her to wait for me to get home, and then marry me. It appears that she was seeing someone else at the time but in due course, I received a wonderful letter from her in similar terms and saying she would wait for me and indeed would marry me. As explained later in this memoir, she did wait and, after much delay, I managed to get home leave from Italy and we were married in September 1944 in New York. A few weeks later, I had to go back to the war.

As for my activities in Beirut, I spent a very active year until my eventual transfer to Italy, via Cairo in the fall of 1943.

In Beirut, I shared a two-bedroom apartment with an American technician on the OWI staff named Bill Carter. He shared his room with a French-Indonesian woman who had lived in French Indochina. The three of us used to take breakfast together. I also was quite friendly with a Lebanese brother and sister, Emile Lahoud whose sister was quite attractive but whose first name I have forgotten. Last name same as the family name of the President of Lebanon in 2005.

Made a few expeditions in the area: one to see Le Crac des Chevaliers, a castle/fortress from the time of the Crusaders – 12th Century? Another visit to a Moslem or Druse chieftain in the south of Lebanon and go horseback riding over his rolling semi-desert farmland, on a very lively Arab horse. (I used to be a pretty good horseman, trained in Elberon, NJ as a kid at the Montulet stable.)

Also managed a weekend visit to Palestine, then the British mandate, and some years before establishment of the State of Israel. Briefly visited Jerusalem, Bethlehem, Tel Aviv and the Dead Sea, including of course a visit to the Western Wall, among other sights and shrines. Stayed at the King David Hotel in Jerusalem, where I returned with Ruth and her family in the early winter of 2005.

In mid-winter 1943, I came down with a case of yellow jaundice, and had to stay in bed for a week or so. While recovering and before going back to work, (believe it or not) I took a bus trip to Damascus and Baghdad. In Damascus, strolled the soukh (marketplace) also saw a performance of Dervish dancers. Then took the Nairn bus across the desert to Baghdad, then firmly under British occupation. Just did a little unremarkable sightseeing before returning to work in Beirut.

The city of Beirut was a beautiful, seemingly peaceful haven. One time when I had lunch with an Arab businessman from Damascus at the elegant waterfront hotel, the St. George, he showed me that he wore no wristwatch. "I always take off my watch when I come to Beirut", he said.

How helpful our wartime propaganda was in keeping Beirut peaceful, I have no idea. However, let the record show that there were no uprisings or terrorist outbreaks while I was there.

The work in Beirut was primarily dealing with the Lebanese and Syrian press and radio, making sure they received the war news from the perspective of the Allies. One reason for being there and doing this work, of course, was that Lebanon and Syria had been under Nazi and Vichy French occupation until just a short while before we arrived. British forces took over the area, with the French as nominal rulers, in mid-1942. One indication of the attitude of local journalists happened to me when, one day, I offered a local newspaper editor some newly arrived pictures of American landings in the South Pacific. He asked me how much we would pay him to run the pictures. Of course, my answer was: "we don't pay papers to publish news". He ran the pictures anyhow.

CHAPTER VIII

TO BARI, ITALY AND MARRIAGE

Before I went overseas to Brazzaville, I had received draft deferments from Selective Service: once at the request of The Washington Post, when I was covering the White House, and later at the request of the US Office of War Information. By the time I got to Beirut in late 1942, I was getting restless to be closer to the actual theatre of war. I began writing letters to the headquarters of OWI in the late fall of 1942, asking for a transfer closer to France or Italy, and by 1943 I had written letters to Jim Linen, then head of the overseas activities of OWI, requesting a transfer closer to the combat areas.

Finally, in the autumn of 1943 I was told to proceed to Cairo pending transfer to the war zone. I spent a few weeks in Cairo, which, as I recall, included Thanksgiving – as shown in a snapshot of me dancing at a Thanksgiving party in Cairo. Soon thereafter, I was ordered to Bari, Italy, flying there from Cairo.

Just before leaving Cairo for Bari, I wrote a booklet (in English) for translation into German, intended to be dropped over the German lines to influence the attitude of the troops. In German it was called, "Die Nazi Daemmerung" (Twilight of the Nazis), a take-off of course on Wagner's opera.10,000 copies were printed. I doubt it had much effect on the outcome of the war – even though the Germans surrendered less than two years later.

I arrived in Bari in late December, 1943, a very short time after German saboteurs (or bombers) had blown up an American ammunition ship in the harbor and, of course, the place was a mess. I lodged at first with an Italian family in a rented room. I recall the father of the family wore a lapel button with the initials of the Partito Nazionale Fascista – PNF. I asked him what the initials stood for. His war-weary reply: Per Necessita Familiale (For Family Necessity).

In Bari, my job was to supervise the contents of the Italian news agency that fed news to the press and radio stations. It was heavy-duty work with little occasion to travel. I remember one day a U.S. soldier named Lou Madison asked to see me – it was Janet's first husband – just curious, I guess. We chatted pleasantly for a short while.

It was in Bari that I met my friend Roy Block. The Scotswoman he later married (and divorced) Jean McCarraher, whom I first met in Cairo was also in Bari. Then I met John Kobler, the magazine writer, who became my friend until his death in the 1990's. After a while, I left the rooming house to share an apartment with Bill Miller,an OWI official, then a news correspondent who later was an editor at Life Magazine. The British in Bari, of whom there were many, were mostly involved with Intelligence Operations focused on Yugoslavia, just across the Adriatic. I took my meals at a British officers mess in Bari. (See an October 1944 report of mine regarding Bari in the text section.)

Made very few side trips from Bari. One was to the hill town of Matera (years later re-visited with Janet) – an extremely picturesque town on the steep hillsides of a river – with caves used as housing. Of course, there were occasional parties in Bari. The craziest was on the night of Mardi Gras, in a British officers' apartment. After everyone had had a lot to drink, we pulled out service revolvers and shot crockery off the mantelpiece.

In early June 1944, I was transferred from Bari to Naples. On the way over by car, I recall seeing dark smoke clouds in the sky as we approached Naples – an eruption of Mt. Vesuvius.

The work in Naples – and from then on as we advanced up the Italian peninsula was much more intense and seemingly more important than in Bari. As I moved from Naples to other posts in Rome and Florence, I had a number of different titles – a typical one (in Florence) was Deputy Chief of Psychological Warfare for Policy and Propaganda (Forward Area).

Though I didn't save exact travel dates, I was in Naples a couple of months before moving up to Rome – as the Allied forces went northward. In Naples, I had a rented room or apartment near the Bay of Naples – have very fond memories of the fresh octopus in a restaurant in (I think) nearby Posillipo. Am not sure when I moved to Rome, but one letter indicates I was in the Italian capital July 4, 1944. Continued the same kind of work in Rome and then in Florence. One of the most vivid memories of Rome was my visit to the Ardeatine caves where hundreds of Jews and non-Jewish members of the resistance were slaughtered and their bodies dumped there by the Nazis.

While in Rome, I wrote letters to OWI headquarters asking permission for home leave based on the fact that I had already been overseas nearly two and a half years. In late summer 1944, leave was granted and I flew back to New York (via Casablanca in a DC3). I arrived in mid-September and of course went straight to Washington to see Janet. We had been corresponding about getting married and needed to confirm it to each other – which we did immediately.

I must say that at this point, both my Mother and my sister tried to talk me out of marrying Janet, but we were very much in love and I never seriously thought of backing out.

We were married September 22, 1944 in the Rabbi's study at Temple Emanuel in New York. Among those on hand, besides family, were Bill Crawford and Johnny Sebastian (Pugliese), from my Haverford class. The reception afterward at the Beekman, 63rd and Park was, to say the least, somewhat strained because Janet's family and mine had such different backgrounds and really did not know each other. However, the two of us went off on our wartime honeymoon to Hill Farm, my parents' country place in Solebury, Bucks County, Pa. We had an idyllic time for a couple of weeks. Then back to New York and, after putting in a little time at the NY office of the OWI, I flew back to Italy in early November.

Our actual wedding date was September 21, 1944. We had applied for a wedding license in New York City. However, the clerk would not accept Janet's Mexican divorce from her first husband, so we went for help to the Karelsen law firm which arranged a Connecticut marriage September 21, followed the next day by the wedding and the party in New York.

CHAPTER IX

RETURNING TO THE WAR IN ITALY

I spent a few weeks in Rome, and then went up to my new assignment in Florence, arriving shortly before New Years Day, 1945.

In Florence, I was responsible for all the news and propaganda in the forward area of Italy as the Allies advanced and the Germans retreated. While this was mainly deskwork, I did go to the front lines once, at a place somewhat east of Bologna, to observe the news operations closer to the front. However, I must say that I was never exposed to enemy fire during the war.

In Florence, I stayed at first in a hotel near the office but later was able to arrange to share a rented villa across the Arno with several other pysch war types, both American and British.

Our job in Florence, as in areas further South, was to supervise Italian news media in occupied areas, furnish news from the Allied viewpoint as well as regular news, and to do propaganda aimed at Fascists and at German troops beyond the front lines.

One of the moments I remember vividly of course was the day President Roosevelt died and our concentrated work to distribute that news with appropriate comment. I remember that a Washington friend of mine, Arnold Barach, then stationed with us in Italy, wrote the major story on the President's death for our newsletter – and very eloquently, too.

By April 22nd I moved into Bologna, newly liberated by the Allied forces. A report from Psychological Warfare Branch, 15th Army Group, gives a good snapshot of my work at the front. (See Text in Appendix)

By late April and early May 1945, the war in Europe was winding down – certainly going much more favorably for the Allies. As the month of May began, American and Allied forces conquered Milan and on May lst, I flew from Florence to Milan to establish an office for our outfit, the Psychological Warfare Branch (PWB) of AFHQ. On this trip, I also made stops in Turin and Genoa before returning to my base in Florence. May 5 I wrote a letter to

Janet describing highlights of the trip. I also wrote official reports to my boss, Don Minifie, about the trip but I think the letter to my wife tells the story in more interesting fashion.

* * * * * *

May 1945
Darling:

An account of five days I have just spent up where the news was being made.

Left here by plane Monday morning April 30, in a planeload of correspondents flying to Milan, which had just been liberated by the partisans. We took off at 1000 and at 1115, after flying over the recent battlefields landed at an airfield on the eastern edge of Milan. Ours was I think the second Allied plane to sit down there since the Germans left town. The field was completely unbombed and only a small group of people -- members of the airfield staff -- were there to greet us. In a hangar stood Mussolini's private plane which the ill fated Duce had kept standing by waiting for a quick getaway that he was never able to make. There was no transport at the field so we borrowed bicycles from the workmen and rode into town. I strapped my bedding roll, typewriter, and musette bag all on the bicycle and pedaled off for the center of Milan. On the way into town, people turned and stared at me, one of the first Allied soldiers they had seen. The American army had not yet arrived in town, but the Germans were gone – except for small groups holed up in various buildings, such as a group of 200 Gestapo men holding out in the Regina hotel who did not surrender till about 3 p.m. on the afternoon of the day I arrived. I went immediately to partisan headquarters and got in touch both with the partisan military formations and the Committee of Liberation. Had lunch with some Allied special operatives who had been living in Milan for months in plain clothes and had just come out into the open and put on their uniforms. Had to return the bicycle so for the rest of the day was hard put for transport. However, amazingly enough the streetcars were in perfect working order, absolutely unheard of in any Italian city liberated in the earlier days of the Allied offensive in Italy. So, I rode around to see various people all Monday afternoon, using the streetcar and becoming the object of much attention from the populace as I jumped on and off trams. At 4 p.m. that afternoon, the Fifth Army entered the city. I met up with an advance PWB movie truck and fell into line with a parade of tanks and rode along the main streets watching the Army receive the really heartfelt greeting of the population. In northern Italy, I have felt for the first time that the people were genuinely glad to see the Allies and were not pretending. They did not have to put on an act or simulate good will, since it was the people themselves through their Liberation committees and patriot formations who really liberated the northern cities. I arrived too late to see Mussolini's body lying in the public square and later was so busy that I did not get time to go to the morgue to see him in his coffin, but I saw all the pictures and heard all the gory details first hand. Perhaps my failure to see him bespeaks an inactive news sense but I felt no great impulse to see that criminal in his coffin. Our photographer, Nat Knaster, who took pictures of the corpses, said he had to climb over about 200 bodies to get his pix. Stayed in Milan until Wednesday noon, advising on the setting up of our outpost there. Met with the full committee of liberation, who were an impressive group of men. The city is very well administered by the CLN, pending AMG taking over. VCLN has done a beautiful job, for which they deserve great credit. One of the phenomena however is that by their well organized resistance the Northern Italians have preserved the industrial power of N. Italy, which makes that portion of the country comparatively even richer than it used to be as against the badly destroyed southern part of the country. It accentuates the economic gulf between North and South Italy.....which will have great postwar effect!

Milan is a great sophisticated metropolis and all of the public utilities that are the lifeblood of such a city were preserved. When I was there, the word was that patriots had shot about 3000 collaborators in the past few days, and I wouldn't be a bit surprised. The streets were full of them, riding around in the best-commandeered cars, wearing their red Garibaldi kerchiefs, absolutely determined – as one of them said to me – to make a clean break with Italy's past. I don't think they are all Communists – though they look it by their dress – but they have certainly had all they want of Fascism. For the moment, the Liberation Committee and the patriots control the city. The Allies are very popular and very welcome, but have not yet asserted themselves.

Wednesday, after lunch I drove over to Turin via Pavia and Alessandria because on the main direct road the German armies had not yet surrendered. We crossed the Po on a crazy-improvised ferry that can carry one jeep at a time, run by partisans. An unseasonable hailstorm came up and almost froze us to death. Gave a lift into Asti to a miserable looking Italian who said he had been away from home three years. He had been in the Italian army at Trieste on famous September 8, 1943, when the armistice was signed, and the Germans walked in and took him prisoner. He worked as a slave in Germany until he was recently repatriated and was making his way home. Found Turin a beautiful city, perhaps the loveliest I have seen in Italy, with the Alps – still snow-covered -- as a backdrop, and ennobled by stately palaces, leftovers of the days when Turin was Italy's capital and the seat of the House of Piedmont. Arrived just about one day after PWB's shock force and they were very surprised to see me so soon. The streets still rang to the shots of partisans executing Fascists and Fascists sniping at partisans. A dead man was found outside our office the evening I left. The Germans were six miles outside town when I was in Turin and were behaving abominably, gouging out the eyes of local patriots when they caught them…and we got pictures to prove that statement. There was a fantastic scene in the Principa de Piemonte, the leading hotel of Turin, the night I arrived. The town hero, a 23-year-old partisan named Pieret, former employee of a motor works near town, gave a banquet at a tremendous horseshoe table in the grand dining room of the hotel. You met people riding up and down in the elevators with Sten and Tommy guns, just as in peacetime guests rode those same elevators with golf clubs and tennis rackets. Pieret, a brash young man, entertained a motley crew of partisans, American flying officers, a US sailor who dropped in from somewhere, British, Polish and Brazilian officers – at a great feast. Partisans kept running into the dining room all evening bringing food that they had "requisitioned" somewhere in the town. Once during the evening, there was a gunfight in the street outside and a lot of the guests ran out to help settle it. Some Fascist apparently bit the dust. But the band played on. Discovered that PWB had arrived as the first Allied force to stay in the town, and had received the flowers and cheers that ordinarily would have been reserved for combat troops. During Pieret's banquet somebody came in and announced that the war was over in Italy – von Wietinghoff's armies had surrendered. Everybody said "uh huh" and went right on with what they were doing. The news created hardly a ripple. Don't ask me why. I stayed in Turin only overnight. Left there May 3 about lunch time and drove down to Genoa, where I also stayed overnight – also inspecting our outpost there and helping get it going. Genoa has been badly damaged, by bombing, shellfire, and naval guns. PWB got there with advanced armored elements in time to watch and hear the German garrison commander surrender to the US commander. The city reminded me very much of Naples, same poverty and squalor, same – or much the same -- natural beauty. It is not a town I would want to live in. I left there Thursday and drove back here along the coast, out of the way, passing through such famous and beautiful resorts as Rapallo, true beauty spots of the world. Everywhere in Northern Italy, one feels more respect for the Italians than ever before, because they have really done something toward their own salvation, have risked their necks to save their country from total destruction. The Allies are very aware of this and are treating the Liberation committees with considerable deference and respect – which they have certainly earned. One of the interesting phenomena taking place is that the liberation committee, composed entirely of civilians

– politicians – are getting worried about the armed partisan bands and are just as anxious to see them disarmed as are the Allied authorities. There seems to be considerable fear among responsible Italians that armed bands roving the country will provoke a new fascism under another name if not held in check. But for the time being the situation does not yet present that danger. Liquidation of Fascists however is proceeding without too much regard for trial by jury, the direct method being invoked in most cases. Few tears are being shed on that score, even from the Allied side. The ways the patriots settled the Mussolini question, for instance, certainly took a load of responsibility off Allied shoulders and eliminated a lot of legalistic nonsense. He got what he deserved.

It was a thrilling five days; perhaps the most fascinating I have ever spent overseas. I am back now but am scheduled to leave in two days for Switzerland. So, if mail gets a little irregular you will understand why.

So, that is my latest perambulation darling. Got back to find your letter of April 22, which started off saying that there was very little news and went on for seven delightful pages. I was intensely interested, as I always am, in the latest doing of Unit No. 1. Naturally, I have been thinking a lot about names darling and am delighted to hear you agree with Jean Ellen (or Ellen Jean). Personally, I would prefer Jean Ellen. I think we have batted boys names back and forth enough and we should make up our minds so lets pick the very fine, strong, short, friendly name of Tom Schrank Bookman, and let it go at that. It sounds good, rings well to the ear, is a clean strong name, and should serve a young man well. What do you say, darling?

Arnold Barach is here and has been staying with me, in the other bed in my room. He imparts the intelligence that your maid is the daughter of his maid. So, that is another bond between the Barachs and the Bookmans, and I must say we should be indebted to Steffy for her generosity and helpfulness.

The war is over in Italy darling and will be over soon in all of Europe, probably before you get this letter. You are very likely asking yourself when is George coming home, and George is asking himself that too. Here, is as simple a summary as I can write, of the situation.

As I mentioned above, I am leaving in a day or two for that place I prepared for some time ago in New York. PWB very much wants me to go there. Don Minifie will be headman there and he and I are very friendly and I think he is counting heavily on me. I will have an important job to do. I asked him yesterday however whether I could go home in about a month or so. I also phoned Jim Linen about it today and he said if Minifie says okay, then I could go. Minifie says he will try to spare me time to go home and be with you in the last weeks of your pregnancy. So, that is the situation. It is not 100 per cent sure, but I at least have a promise that I can go home, if I can be spared. Incidentally, I received my new draft card today and learn that I have been deferred again for another six months, for occupational reasons.

I have always made it a policy darling to tell you the truth, the whole truth and nothing but the truth, because I knew you could stand it so that is the story. It may turn out as we both dream it will, but neither of us should bank on that wholeheartedly.

Darling, I have been on the road for almost two weeks now, and am dead tired. In between my trips to Bologna and my latest trip to north Italy, I stayed up nights here getting out our forces that went to Venice and Trieste. So you see I have been doing a little work recently.....but I have loved every minute of it.

Under separate cover, I am sending a different sort of account of the last few days.

All my love darling to you and baby.

Today also sent you a big package, which should reach you in about six weeks or so.

I kiss you darling

George

* * * * * *

CHAPTER X

SALZBURG

A few days after my trip to Milan and Turin, I was ordered to go over the Alps to Salzburg, Austria, to establish similar Psy War programs there in the American occupied zone of Austria. This was the unforgettable trip I shared with Roy Block when we stopped our jeep by the side of the road on the Brenner Pass May 8, 1945 to listen to Winston Churchill announcing the end of the war in Europe.

My letter home to Janet of May 11, 1945 tells of that trip and the first few days in Austria.

Austria

May 11, 1945

Darling Wifey:

I hope you have not tired of reading of my travels, because most of my recent letters and probably also many of my future ones will concern travel, bounding around over the map of Europe. As you can see by the dateline of this letter I am in Austria, which I admit is quite a jump from Italy and I am still not quite used to it. But let me tell you about it.

Things have been happening so fast that I find it hard to remember dates, but about a week ago, I returned to Florence from a trip through northern Italy. Within 48 hours I was told to pack and leave for Austria. The first definite news I had that I was to go came late Sunday night and by 2 p.m. Monday afternoon, I was in a jeep and on the road to Austria. So you can see that my parting days in Italy were pretty hectic. I shipped back to NY OWI one duffel bag of luggage, but took all the rest with me.

Monday, May 7 we left Florence in convoy, drove over the Apennines to Bologna and was surprised but very happy to learn when we got there that the Germans had signed unconditional surrender while we had been on the road. There was no particular celebration, but Scotty Forrest, our news editor in Bologna, is in charge of British rations and has special access to supplies of Scotch whiskey so he and I polished off some of his private stock, promising to visit each other after the war. He is a Capetown newspaperman and has been in the army 30 years, active and reserve. Early the next day we set off again northward. Lunched in Verona and at 3 p.m. stopped our jeeps along the roadside to listen in to Churchill announcing the official end of the war. We tuned in on a radio with which one of the jeeps was equipped. Then back in the cars and off for the Brenner Pass. We passed through the territory that had been the hunting ground of American heavy bombers and saw that they had done their work well. Then began a strange experience. The roads were filled with German soldiers and officers, some walking but mostly riding. They had officially surrendered a few days before, but – as you probably read in the papers – were allowed to keep their arms for fear of attack by Italian partisans who don't play the game according to the same rules we go by. The Germans had been permitted by the Allied command to administer themselves, use their own transport and deliver themselves under their own supervision to Allied Prisoner of War cages. So, our tiny convoy made its way northward to the Brenner passing through thousands of armed Germans. It was a very uncomfortable feeling to drive by a German MP standing by the road, holding a loaded rifle. But they kept the terms of the surrender – at least no one took a shot at us. Another strange sight was the large number of freed slaves of Hitler. The most impressive group we saw south of the Brenner were thousands of Czech officers, apparently the staff and students of the Czech officers school who had been sent by the Nazis to work as road laborers in the Brenner Pass, where they would be most exposed to bombing. They had been liberated for a few days now and had put on uniforms that they had not dared to wear since 1939. Columns of these Czechs would swing down the road, singing their national anthem in chorus, singing defiantly as they passed by the Germans. One of the anomalies however was that the Germans, under the surrender terms, temporarily retained their transport and so most of the Germans rode by us in cars and trucks, while the liberated Czechs made their way mostly on foot or on what bicycles or farm horses they were able to find.

The queerest experience was in Bolzano, where we arrived late in the evening to find a place to sleep. We canvassed all the hotels and found they were occupied by Germans. At that time the Germans in town must have outnumbered the Allied troops at least ten to one, probably twenty to one, and they still carried their arms. Finally, we found a hotel that seemed desirable but the manager – a very obvious Nazi – told us that there were no more rooms left. So we had to tell him that either he would find us all rooms or we would throw him and all the Germans into the streets. So then, he found them very quickly. In the dining room, German officers ate at tables near us. One of our boys was in the bathroom and heard a loud knocking on the door. When he was through, he left the bathroom and found an impatient German general waiting for his turn. You probably don't believe this. I know it sounds incredible, but – so help me – it is literally true. I never saw a crazier war than this in its final stages.

The following day Wednesday, May 9 we set off on the final lap to Austria. We climbed up through the Alps, still snowcapped, through some of the most beautiful scenery I have ever seen, and reached the Brenner Pass about lunchtime. We found a standing order out that only Generals were allowed through the pass, but the very able Major who is leading our party did a little fast talking and we got through – over the hump and down into Austria. The scenery on the other side of the boundary, though still of the same character – mountains, water falls, pine trees, etc. – seemed quite different. Austria impressed us as being cleaner, neater, better cared for than regions of Italy just a few miles away. We wound down the Alps to Innsbruck, where we stopped a while. The town, we found was crammed with foreign workers, as are all the towns of Austria that we have seen. The first few days you saw very few Austrians or Germans on the streets, because they were afraid to come out, but the city swarmed with French, Belgians, Italians, Poles, Yugoslavs, Greeks, etc., etc., all wearing their national colors in their button holes in order not to be confused with Germans. The foreign workers, after so long a period as underdogs, were now lording it over their former masters and we saw hundreds of them happily bicycling or driving home in requisitioned vehicles and bicycles. But it is certainly not true that all were slave labor or were treated as such. Many came to Germany to work because they were very well paid and were offered very attractive conditions. Of course, as the war picture grew darker for Germany, things got tougher for the foreign workers. Most were eager now to get home. Almost all have learned a little German. In Innsbruck, we fell in with a company of MP's who used to be stationed in Italy and were so happy to find someone from "home" that they broke out two gallons (sic) of cognac, which we did our best to consume. So, in a very good mood we then struck off for Salzburg. Our first night in Austria we spent in the very quaint village of Kufstein, a quiet small town on a swift-flowing stream, within sight of the snowcapped mountains and not far from the famous skiing resort, Kitzbuhel. Of course, everything was shut up tight because the American army had been in the area only three or four days, so it probably did not resemble peacetime Austria very much except in its physical aspects. One thing should be mentioned in passing: Austria is lucky compared to Germany on the score of destruction by bombing. The places we have seen so far have not been badly hit.

We reached Salzburg on the fourth day and stayed there a while. The famous music festival city is only slightly damaged by bombing. It is crowded with foreign workers and with nervous Germans and Austrians, who do not quite know what to expect from the conquering Americans.

The most thorough enjoyable time I have had was two days ago when two other Americans and I drove out of Salzburg for an afternoon of visiting the surrounding area. Looking at the castle of Heilbrun, formerly the property of the Archbishop of Salzburg, was interesting enough, and it was certainly extremely pleasant to go boating on a glorious mountain lake (the Koenigsee) surrounded by craggy rocky hills still flecked with the winter snow…but the greatest pleasure was our visit to Berchtesgaden and Hitler's house. Berchtesgaden is a very small Bavarian town beautifully situated, nestling into surrounding hills and mountains. It boasts a sumptuous railroad station that bespeaks the fact that this was no ordinary Bavarian way station. From the town down in the valley goes a long winding road, about two miles up the hill to a private estate, that reminded me very much of pictures I have seen of super deluxe dude ranches in the American Far West. Hitler's estate must have been dotted with about twenty buildings of various types. There was a guesthouse, really a fair-sized hotel, with rooms probably for 100 guests. Each guest had his private sitting room, bedroom, and bath. On the upper floor were servant's quarters, hardly less splendid than those for the guests. Next-door was a restaurant and beer room where the Fuehrer's guests could sit, sip, eat, and talk things over. The hillside was dotted with guardhouses, administration houses, etc. The interior of the hill was laced with an intricate system of tunnels, from which elevators led up to the main houses: one to Georing's villa, another to Hitler's, another to Goebbels', etc., etc. Under the hill hollowed out into the rock, was a giant air raid shelter for the population of Hitler's estate. The houses had every modern convenience. Telephones in every room, electric stoves, beautiful tiled baths, etc. In the guesthouse, for instance, was a small newsstand where periodicals and cosmetics were sold. Each bedroom had a panel of four push buttons for summoning the waiter, the maid, the houseboy or the tailor, etc.

But the great pleasure was not to see this elaborate layout of houses, etc., but to see what Allied bombers and Allied Troops had done to it. You may have seen the pictures in the paper. Never have I seen such a beautiful job of bombing. Every single house was utterly smashed into rubble. Roofs blown off, walls knocked down, rooms and floors telescoped one onto the other, entire houses blown into the air…the place was just complete wreckage. And what the bombers did not wreck, the occupying troops finished off. Thousands of soldiers have by now gone through Hitler's house in search of souvenirs. Everything that could possibly serve as a memento of the world's biggest and most dangerous bastard has been carried off. Even the boards from the floor and walls have been stripped away, the plumbing fixtures, pieces of furniture, crockery, etc. I myself took a serving tray, a plate, and a pitcher from Hitler's own kitchen. It was an inexpressible joy to see American soldiers having free run of Hitler's smashed mountain retreat, sacking it, as it certainly deserves to be sacked. I saw French officers going through the house, their faces wreathed in smiles, saying over and over again to themselves, as they thought of poor, torn France: "Cést merveilleux, cést epattant." And so it was. I spent quite a while in Hitler's own house. The framework and most of the walls are still standing. His famous study, with the enormous window, opening out on the Bavarian hills, is still standing, though it has been gutted and stripped of everything, even floorboards and plaster from the walls. The only things of interest still remaining in the room were some bas-reliefs with historic Nazi dates imbedded into cement in the walls of the fireplace. No one had yet tried to remove them.

The study was an enormous hall of a room. The window itself is as big as an enormous house, and gives a clear view of miles of Bavarian and Austrian countryside, mountain peaks, green valleys, and rushing streams. It is a sight that should certainly have had an ennobling influence on the man who used to gaze out of that window, but – to the world's misfortune – he missed the point. Just off this main room is a motion picture projection booth containing the most modern equipment and complete resumes, nicely bound, of every German and foreign picture for the last 5 or 10 years. When the boss wanted to relax, he could just look through the index and pick his entertainment for the evening. It was projected through a wall of his great study onto the opposite wall, where presumably a silver screen once hung. The cellar of his house was filled, when I saw it, with opened and emptied cases of champagne (undoubtedly gone to whet American throats) and dozens of porch chairs where on sunny days Hitler could sit with his pals on the terrace that runs round the front of the house. The great study window was equipped with an electrically operated blackout curtain that covered its entire great expanse like a huge screen. Just outside the Fuehrer's study was a foyer and two bathrooms, one for men and one for women – convenient for trembling quislings issuing from Hitler's study or for right thinking Germans who had to puke shortly after standing in the boss's presence. The kitchens of his house were sumptuous. Electric ranges, peeling machines, ovens, etc., etc. Every device that the most modern hotel kitchen would have. In the basement were the latest washing machines, and so on. The crockery we found unfortunately bore no crest or initials, just plain white ware of a very good quality. We could not go upstairs to see the bedrooms because the bombing had made it unsafe to walk about on the second floor. The house was well camouflaged – but not well enough. Besides being surrounded by guardhouses, its four corners were protected by cement blockhouses where undoubtedly special guards were constantly posted at machine guns when the boss was home. His people loved him so.

A few German children stood at the gate sullenly watching the Americans come out of Hitler's house, their hands full of souvenirs. It is a sight they won't forget for a long time and I hope they learn a good lesson from it.

The other day we went out to the country to interview some personnel we are thinking of hiring. It was a lovely ride toward a suburb called Petting (where they do no petting). Actually, we lunched with a priest who had spent two years in Buchenwald and did not care very much for the Nazis. He was fascinating to talk to, but rather represented a Catholic point of view. Have also talked with leaders of the rather abortive and weak Austrian resistance movement who do not seem to have been very effective. There are plenty of anti Nazis in this country. Austria has no love for the Germans and is happy at being severed from the Reich, but courageous opponents of Nazism are few. Most of them are, I guess, dead by now or so weakened by concentration camp treatment that they are hardly able to live a full life anymore. It should be noted that on the way we stopped at a village brewery and drank some wonderful Bavarian beer. There is hardly any left though. Many of the raw materials for beer making are lacking and the troops drank up everything in sight when they came in, so one has to wait at least two weeks while the new beer is brewed and ages.

There are so many impressions I have of Austria and so much to tell you. I think I have touched only on a few of the high spots in this letter. First impressions are so many and so varied that they take a while to sort themselves out in your mind. The people are afraid of Americans, but do not dislike them. They are somewhat bewildered by what treatment is to be accorded them and are delighted if they are cordially greeted. Children along the road would like to wave to you as you drive by and readily respond to a greeting but are a bit scared to be the first to wave. There is of course immense respect for and fear of anyone in uniform – an old custom in this country, accentuated by the Nazi regime. It is said there is a werewolf organization of underground Nazis but it is apparently not a great factor in this area, though a few incidents have been reported. I think that the Allies will find this part of Austria quite friendly and not hard to govern.

That's about all of my travel notes for now.

Darling: the above part of this letter, rather impersonal, I wrote in duplicate and sent a copy to my parents. Hope you don't mind.

Our little group of PWB people here are somewhat confused as to the future. I can't go into details, but I can say that we did not know we were leaving until a few hours before we got underway and the preparations and plan that had been made for us left a great deal to be desired. So I have no idea how long I will have to stay here, how long it will be before our operation gets really on its feet. Don Minifie is however top policy man here for the Americans and before I left Italy, he named me his coordinator of propaganda policy, so on policy matters I am the Number Two American concerned with propaganda in the American zone of Austria.

I have no idea what our mail address is here so am still using the old one and hope mail will be forwarded. Haven't received any mail from you for a week and don't know when our mail will reach us. That is one of the worst features of this isolation here. I am hungry for news of you and our baby and the apartment and everything. Hope with all my heart that you are feeling well and are happy in spirit and heart, as happy as I am at the thought of our approaching child. How is your tummy? Lots of moving around going on down there? I kiss it darling and think of you…..a beautiful mother whom I love with all my heart.

George

* * * * *

My next letter to Janet from Austria tells of the devastating sight of the Jews and other Nazi victims just released from prison camps.

May 20, 1945
Darling:
Still here in the Austrian vacuum. I note that now under new mail censorship regulations I can tell you where I am. Boy, what a thrill. I am in SALZBURG, AUSTRIA, in the heart of some of Europe's most beautiful scenery. But as far as I am concerned, this is strictly a dead end and like living inside of a gunnysack. No mail comes in here for us at all; we are orphans, babes in the Austrian woods.

It will be fun to tell you about this cockeyed mission of ours when I see you. We have been here about ten days now on a reconnaissance mission and operations have not started. In our Italian theater work, such a state of affairs would be unheard of but that seems to be a matter for no surprise in this area. We are planning to get out a daily paper in N. Germany as soon as proper approval is received and this flabbergasts the people in other German speaking areas who think only in terms of weekly newspapers. We almost fell over when we heard that a city the size of Munich has only a weekly paper. We produce dailies within 24 hours of arriving in such jerkwater towns in

Italy as Bologna. Apparently their conception of things up here and out back in Italy are entirely different. By the way, I see by the papers that Italy has been handed back to the Italian government and so PWB there will probably break up about June 15. So, I had the cream of the excitement there.

Since I last wrote to you, I have been to Linz, which is certainly a good place to have been (past tense). It is all smashed to hell and gone and is overrun by thousands of displaced persons and Allied soldiers. MG there told me there are about 150,000 displaced persons in the Linz area. The Russians are the hardest to handle, seeming to make a specialty of looting German homes, for which I can't say that I blame them after the way the Russian slave workers were treated by the krauts. The Poles are the next most wayward, with the French the best behaved and Italians second best. The Russian DP camps are all elaborately furnished in radios, rugs, curtains, tapestries, etc. taken from German homes. On the way back from Linz we drove through a German PW camp. There must have been about 5000 German prisoners there, all disgustingly healthy looking, sunning themselves in a camp area by the side of a swift flowing stream. We drove slowly through the center of the PW's feeling a bit uncomfortable but no one heaved a rock at us. We were the object of curious and usually, unfriendly stares.

Right after that, we drove down the road to see signs of an entirely different nature. This was Mauthausen, a camp for Jews from Eastern Europe, mostly Polish Jews. There was all of Europe's suffering in its most shocking form. As we stopped our car by the side of a dirty pool of water a few starved skeletons of human beings clad only in rags dragged themselves over to the car. We wondered what they could be. "Jews" they replied. That told the whole story. The spokesman for the group was the best fed and healthiest of the number. He looked fairly well preserved. He said they had – many of them – been through Oswiecim and had survived the cattle car exportations, had seen their entire families executed in gas chamber cars or burned to ashes in cremation bins. Not one of them thought he would live through the war. Their eyes all spoke of suffering deeper than any one of us could possibly imagine. Reading newspaper accounts of the persecution of the Jews in Europe and seeing it written in the face of one of the victims are two different things. They all bore marks of their religion imposed on them by the Nazis: a broad swath shaved, down the crown of their heads and numbers branded on their skins. One said that at the stone quarry where he worked in Poland the German guards were told by their officer to take out 400 Jews to work in the quarry and that if they came back at night with more than 200 they would be shot. So, the guards returned at night with 200. The rest were forced to jump to their death into the stone quarry. Another recounted how mothers entered the gas chambers, knowing full well what was in store for them but taking along soap and a towel so they could lead with them to the peace of death by gas their small children, telling them that they were being taken to a public bath. There was also confirmation of the stories you have read of the great exportations of Jews by the thousands, packed into cattle cars and sealed up for days without food or drink so that half of the car-full died before the doors were opened. Another story was of a band of sick, half starved Jews who were forced to strip in Poland in February and run around a yard in a biting wind, jump into an ice cold pool, run around again, jump into the water, etc. until most of them died from exposure. They were having a hard time getting used to freedom. God only knows how they will fare in this postwar period. Only a few had enough life left in them to be able to enjoy the death of Nazism.

A few days later, I went to Munich on a business trip, and wrote of my impressions of the city – the immense destruction, the famous beer halls, and the attitude of the German people about their defeat

May 23, 1945
Salzburg, Austria
Darling:

It is about two weeks that we have been here, and more than two weeks since we left Florence, and still no mail has been forwarded to us from Italy. You can imagine how rabid is my appetite for one of your letters. One of our officers went back to Italy the other day and he should return here within the next day or two bringing with him a sack full of mail. I am licking my chops at the prospect of sitting down for a wonderful evening of reading letters from you. I'll bet there will be a fistful of them.

It would be hard to describe to you the state of suspended animation and general snafu (confusion) that prevails here among our little band, even if it were diplomatic to write you about it. We have been here two weeks and have not yet issued a paper or a broadcast, which to those of us with experience in Italy where we always put out a paper within 24 hours of reaching an objective is a most peculiar state of affairs. I think operations here will always be complicated by the juxtaposition and overlaying in such a small geographic area of so many different military lines of authority, national occupation zones and conflicts of policy.

Two days ago, I went to Munich for the day to see PWD (Psychological Warfare Division) there. It is not far away: less than three hours over one of those wonderful autobahns, which the Germans copied from American superhighways. The road wound over the crest of the Bavarian Alps. Had it been a sunny day I probably would have been treated to a wonderful view, but it was drizzling and cloudy and beastly cold. We did drive however through some noble endless pine forests, the finest I have ever seen. Along one stretch of the highway, the Germans, in the last desperate days of the war, had created a temporary airstrip. Apparently, every plane the Luftwaffe could muster was flown down to Bavaria and landed on the broad concrete surface of the Autobahn. We drove by scores of them pulled up along side the road into clearings in the forest, camouflaged with pine branches. Almost all had been spotted by Allied planes from the air and had been strafed. There were planes of every type, fighters, bombers, transport planes, observation planes....most of them looking pretty weather beaten and woebegone.

At the outskirts of Munich stands a sign: Munich: Headquarters of the (Nazi) movement. Munich has received its just desserts. The center of the city is completely smashed. We estimated that 70 per cent of the buildings in the city are uninhabitable without major repairs. The suburbs are generally in good condition, but the heart of the city is rubbish. There is not a building that is not either completely destroyed, or has parts of its roof or walls blown away. I understand Munich was one of Germany's loveliest cities. Now it is one of Germany's biggest ash heaps. Many of the side streets are impassable, blocked by rubble. The city is so crowded by foreign workers and bombed-out Germans that any room with walls and roof in good condition is used as a habitation, even if parts of the same building are blown open to the sky. Strangely, two monuments to Nazism have not been badly bombed. One is the Burgerbrauhof, a beer hall where Hitler was almost killed by a bomb a couple of years ago, and the famous Brauhaus beer cellar where Hitler's 1933 putsch started and which became the spiritual shrine of the Nazi party. The latter was open to the public and I looked it over. It is an enormous beer hall, with several great raftered rooms, furnished with bare plank tables and wooden chairs and benches. The largest room of all, where Hitler made his speeches, has been bombed out, but there was another room downstairs that was open and doing a rushing business. Most of the other breweries and beer halls in Munich have been bombed out, so people from all over the city had come to this Brauhaus which was the only one dispensing beer. There were queues of perhaps 1000 people waiting for a gulp of the foamy stuff. I pushed my way up to the bar, where I saw a small group of GI's, who had wandered in. I asked how much it cost for a glass of beer and one of the GI's looked at me as though I were crazy and said: "Hey, bud, where have you been? Don't you know we don't pay for anything in Germany." I said excuse me I'm a foreigner from Italy and am not yet used to the customs of the country. So, I had a glass of beer on the house. A couple of French war prisoners who worked in the brewery as bottle and stein washers and were going home soon, insisted in presenting me with a souvenir mug. I noticed that every GI visitor to the beer hall carried away with him a mug as souvenir of his visit. So did I. All the fancy ones were gone however. The Third Army had picked the place pretty clean.

When you see such destruction as in Munich – and there are many German cities much worse than Munich – you wonder why the Germans resisted as long as they did. Of course, they tell you it was because the SS and Gestapo forced them to resist. But I don't think that tells the whole story. Many of these people lived for months underground in air raid shelters while their hometowns overhead were blown to matchsticks. Why didn't they quit? That is a riddle, which it is fascinating to try to answer. My impression from talking to various Germans is that they knew the war was lost, they knew that further resistance could only mean further destruction of their country, they knew that V1 and V2 could not win the war, they didn't really believe in the secret weapon .. but they kept on fighting. What is their attitude now? In Austria and Bavaria, which are Catholic and were always the least Nazi sections, the people I think would like to be friendly. Of course, there are no more Nazis. No one admits to ever having been one or ever having a friend who was one. It's just like Italy where, if you believed the Italians statements about themselves, there were never any Fascists. The Germans claim to know nothing about the SS concentration camps. Perhaps they are telling the truth on that. At least they seem profoundly shocked when we show them pictures of the horrors of places like Dachau and Buchenwald. I don't think they have a sense of war guilt. They know that the Germans started the war, but they don't feel guilty about it. They are not by any means a broken people. They are determined to rebuild their country as speedily as possible and probably will, provided we let them. Morally, they are very proud and have plenty of fight left. I guess the only reason they quit was that they ran out of weapons. If their bare fists could have helped them, many would probably still be fighting. Though they have seen through some of the Nazi propaganda, yet lots of it they have swallowed. They are all terrified of the Russians. They also believe that Russia and the other Allies cannot remain friends very long. They expect us to be at odds with the Russians quite soon. They expect decent treatment from the Americans but are in mortal fear of the Russians, being sure they will either be killed or enslaved for life if they get into a Russian occupation zone. They wonder whether the Allies will permit Germany to be a unified nation and have any national life, they even would not be surprised if we sent them all to Siberia to work in the salt mines for the rest of their lives. Germany has certainly felt the war this time. There is no mistaking that. Every city is smashed. Everyone has lost a close relative in battle, or has a close kin in a Russian prisoner camp and never expects to see him again. But I get the feeling that these bastards would try it again some day if they ever regain enough power to wage another war.

My own impression so far has been that the Germans are a very well united people and are not ready to blame any particular class of their own people for their defeat, such as the military. Others here believe they will turn on the SS and Gestapo but I see no signs of that yet. There is a great feeling of disappointment with Hitler and his leadership, a feeling that he lied and blundered, but I don't get the impression that feeling is a bitter one and I think his memory still commands considerable respect. Certainly, the German people are not disgusted with Hitler and all he stood for the way the Italian people are thoroughly disgusted with everything that Mussolini stood for. In Italy, practically everyone is violently abusive of Mussolini. You don't hear that from the Germans about Hitler.

It is a fascinating study and I guess I could go on for hours soliloquizing like this.

Love, George

In early June, I wrote of my trip to nearby Linz and then to see the now-liberated Nazi concentration camp at Mauthausen, Austria. Excerpts follow:

June 3, 1945
Austria
Darling light of my life:

Please note at the top my new address, which we have finally obtained. I will repeat it to make doubly sure: Headquarters, Information Services Branch, APO 887, Postmaster, NY NY. As you will note, our name has been changed (once again) but it is the old propaganda mill under different colors. A rose by any other name would not smell any better.

I have received huge amounts of mail from you; all arriving within the last few days overland from Italy by various vehicles that came up over the Alps. It has been a tremendous thrill and pleasure to sit down and read them and learn about your Mother's visit, your Pop's intended visit, my parents visit, your recovery from your first fall, your increasing pregnancy, that you like the names for boy and girl that I suggested, your growing stock of furniture and baby equipment, your news from our various friends around the country, and that you still love me and hope I come home one of these days.

That pile of letters on my desk from you is a bottomless well of joy and comfort to me to which I will repair often for strength and re-inspiration. I enjoy so much hearing all your anecdotes of your life and the things going on around you and inside of you, both physically and mentally. Our baby seems to be making wonderful progress and I know is getting the best care that any mother could provide.

Thank you so much for your very understanding words about my desire to come home in time for the baby's arrival and the slim possibility of that desire being fulfilled. Let me bring you up to date on that question. Don Minifie has now arrived here (thank God) and the situation, not only as regards my personal future but as regards the much-muddled outlook for American information in Austria, is much clearer. As I told you in a letter some time ago, I wrote to Don asking him to try to arrange for me to be returned to the United States. When Don arrived, he told me that he took the matter up with Russell Barnes, Director of PWB AFHQ, and with Jim Linen. Barnes said he did not think he could spare me and Linen said that transportation arrangements could not be made in time anyhow to get me home for the event in July. He said that now, with the redeployment of the army, it would take two months to get me ship passage and air passage was not being granted. Well, that certainly depressed me to hear that, so I wrote immediately again to Linen. I have heard of several other people who wanted to go home and who were able to get passage within a week. So, I said in my letter to Linen that if his refusal was based on grounds of transportation, I wished he would re-examine it in the light of the experience of several others who have recently gone home without difficulty. I further said that if, however, the refusal to let me go was based on grounds of indispensability, I would at least appreciate a letter to that effect. It would look pretty in my scrapbook, if it serves no other purpose. I further suggested the name of another man (Leo Hochstetter as a matter of fact) who I proposed could take over my "indispensable" job. That letter went off to Linen yesterday and I should get the answer in a week or ten days. It will probably be no again, though I did state my case as strongly as I could. I said, as a matter of fact, that I would be prepared to resign from OWI if that is the only way to get home. But resigning from OWI when you are on a Psychological Warfare job like mine is a little like trying to resign from the Army – it is not very easy.

My job here, by the way, has now been confirmed by new orders. I am Coordinator of Propaganda and also Chief of News and Press services. Same double job that I held in Italy, except that I also am in direct charge of press now as well as news, in addition to coordinating all media of propaganda.

To give you a little idea of what I do: Today I went out looking for a new location for our radio operation (studio, etc.) so that we won't have to locate it in a building where it might interfere with the musical life of the city, which is very developed and important to the local economy. Also, I am setting up a display department and spent part of the day breaking in a Sergeant who will prepare posters and photo displays under directives from me. Late in the day, a group of visitors arrived from London PWD to look at our news and press operation and I spent a few hours exchanging notes with them. Then this evening, just as I was getting ready to write to you, in came the man who will be head of our press department and I had to get him filled in on developments to date so that he can go over to Linz to start a daily paper there. That should give you a little picture of how I spend some of my time. Incidentally, I also took a long walk up one of the picturesque hills that overlook Salzburg. At the top, there is a charming old café but it does not serve anything to drink, so I walked my thirsty way down the hill. What makes it all the more disconcerting is that the water here is contaminated so even if I were driven to the desperate measure of wanting to drink water, I could not do so unless I disinfected it first with halazone tablets or something.

I made an interesting trip to Linz the other day. After finishing my business there, I drove about fifteen miles to one of the Nazi concentration camps; a horror spot called Mauthausen. It is one of the least known of their death camps, but is officially listed as one of the dozen or so largest camps. It is situated outside a tiny village, on the top of a hill, well-shielded form the public. As one of the inmates said, if it weren't a concentration camp, it would make a beautiful resort. What surprised me most about the place was the solid permanence of the installations. I had expected to find a group of ramshackle, makeshift wooden structures, in ill repair, supplemented by rough barbed wire enclosures. Instead I found a very elaborate installation comprising main buildings built of granite blocks, garage, terraced approaches, swimming pool for SS guards, athletic field, stone administration buildings, warehouses, etc., well planned driveways, stone gates and fences and about thirty or forty barracks buildings with stone foundations and floors and wooden superstructure. I went over the entire grisly place: gas chamber, crematorium, meat hooks where victims were hung, showers where their naked bodies were wetted down to be more quickly asphyxiated, morgue, dissection room where gold teeth, identification marks etc. were removed, shooting box where victims were sometimes shot in the back of the neck, as a variant to gassing or other forms of death. The place had been cleaned up when I reached there and there were no more corpses lying indiscriminately around. People were still dying in the camp hospital however of undernourishment. The hospital was built within the past fortnight by the Americans. The camp still housed all its former inmates who were awaiting transfer to their homes, and were still trying to get used to the idea that they no longer faced death from the Nazis. The camp was plainly nothing more than a murder factory. I was told that some 200,000 or 250,000 people had passed into the camp in its history. When we captured it, the place contained only about 15,000. Most of the rest had gone up in the smoke of the camp crematorium, which could handle a couple of hundred bodies a day when it was working full blast. Why did the Nazis go to such elaborate pains to hide the camp, to dispose of the victims by cremation, etc.? Probably because they knew, they were breaking the law of God and Man and knew that not even the German people would condone it if they knew. I am no softy where the Germans are concerned but I really do not think the average German knew anything about what went on inside these camps. They knew that conditions in the camps were very tough, but had no idea that they were mass murder centers. Why didn't the Nazi kill their victims faster? In the entire Mauthausen camp, which had perhaps fifty buildings, there was only one death plant with two crematory ovens. Why didn't they kill them faster? The answer to that I think is that not even in Germany could they find enough men so perverted, so devoid of human decency, to man as many of these death factories as they would have liked to operate. It isn't every Mother's son who will earn his living by burning his innocent fellow men to death or gassing them into oblivion.

The inmates of the camp, those still alive when we reached there, were an interesting lot. Largely, they represented an international collection of everything liberal and decent and clean in Europe. There were many Jews, but also many non-Jews. There were several Spanish Loyalists, who had been turned over to the Gestapo by the Vichy French. There were lots of Russians, POW's, and political prisoners. Czechs, Hungarians, Rumanians, etc., etc. I was told at the camp that even some captured American fliers and parachutists were killed at this murder camp, in dark secrecy.

One of the inspiring things at the camp was to see that the American Army had moved an entire hospital unit, complete with US doctors and nurses, into the camp to care for the liberated prisoners. The starving were given special diets and injections of life-giving serums and the sick were being cared for by the latest methods known to American science. The inmates are also now eating American rations. One man told me that they get as much now in one American meal as they used to get in an entire week's rations under the Nazi regime.

My guide, interestingly enough, was not a Jew, not a liberal, or intellectual or other "dangerous character"…he was a plain ordinary common criminal, a poor farmer who about five years ago had shot a game warden rather than be shot himself, an ordinary German farmer who had gotten into a jam. He was shocked deeply by what he had seen in the camp. I asked him what he as a Gentile German who had been through the experience of Mauthausen thought of the Jews. He said that he thought that anti-Semitism had always been present in Germany, but was never taken very seriously until Hitler exploited it. Then it assumed an importance all out of proportion to the true feelings of the people. He thought that Jews were human beings just like anyone else and thought that this attitude represented the feelings of the average German. I asked him what should be done with the SS men. Should we shoot them? Oh no, he said, that would be much too good for them. Let them suffer in a camp like Mauthausen for a few years and then kill them…. but slowly.

Maybe that is enough horror for one letter.

All my love,
George

* * * * * *

Another expedition out of Salzburg that I recall was a trip into the Russian-occupied zone of Czechoslovakia, across the Austrian border. This was strictly unofficial – really a sightseeing tour. An American officer I knew in Salzburg, whose name (I think) was Captain Fred Flott, suggested that he and I take a drive into the Russian zone. He was a language officer and I think spoke Russian. Also, he had a jeep at his disposal.

We set off one morning and drove to the Czech frontier where Flott had no trouble talking our way past the Russian guards and into the nearby city, which I think was Brno. On arrival, we went to the Town Hall, which was the Russian command headquarters for the area, to get overnight accommodations. They assigned us to a midtown hotel. After dropping our bags, we went for a walk in the town park – mid to late afternoon. In the park, we found many Russian soldiers strolling, and we struck up conversations with a group of them. After about a half hour of socializing, we saw a man in plain clothes and trench coat walk up to the Russians, obviously a police or intelligence operative. After he said a few words to them, the soldiers dispersed and that was the end of our chatting in the park.

That evening, we went down to the hotel dining room for dinner. It was filled with Russian officers celebrating the end of the war in Europe. After a while, officers at a nearby table invited us to join them and, in whatever languages available, we talked and became friendly, with many vodka toasts to punctuate the conversation. Around 1 or 2 a.m., I asked one officer who was especially friendly if he would like to ride back to the American zone of Austria the next morning. He said sure, and I told him to be downstairs at 6 a.m. in the morning.

Sure enough, at 6 a.m. he was there in front of the hotel and the three of us took off in the open jeep. It was a chilly morning and after a while, the cold air sobered up our Russian friend. I had thought wouldn't it be great to bring a real, live Russian officer back to our mess in Salzburg, but he had other ideas. As we approached the border, he tapped me on the shoulder and asked to get out of the jeep. Then he flagged a ride back to his unit in Brno. Good, sober thinking on his part and ours.

CHAPTER XI

ELLEN JEAN

All during the spring and early summer of 1945, Janet and I of course were pre-occupied with the expected arrival of our first born, Ellen Jean. I was in Italy and then in Salzburg, Austria and Janet had to cope by herself in wartime Washington. Jean arrived on July 2, 1945 at 8:11 p.m., according to the telegram sent by my parents a couple of hours later that evening (see below). However, due to wartime communications for civilian messages, I did not receive the telegram until July 13 – 11 days later. Meanwhile, on July 5th, I received a message through OWI channels saying: "Tell Bookman its able healthy boy". Then the next day came another message correcting the first one, and saying it was a baby girl. The messages apparently took forever to reach me because my thank you reply to the OWI headquarters in Washington was dated July 7th. So I heard about Jean's arrival through official channels several days after the fact, and finally from my parents more than a week later.

Similarly, communications from me in Austria to Janet in Washington were painfully slow – which must have been extremely upsetting for the new mother.

WESTERN UNION

HQ. INFORMATION SERVICES BRANCH
GEORGE BOOKMAN CIVILIAN
MHE-M115 WASHINGTON
DC 27 3 10H30

Lovely five and half pound Jean Ellen born July Second eight eleven PM both very well Congratulations blessings love.

Arthur Judith Bookman

Received July 13, 1945
　　　　　　Salzburg

051130

　From Clark OEI to ISB

　　Tell Bookman its able healthy boy.

LIAI V LRAR NR 7604
T JJAP
FROM WOIA 051005Q
TO JJAP
QSH GR 30 NY 001

PWB MINIFIE – Advise Bookman correct title is female of the species.
Extremely sorry previous information in our July 3 via another channel was
incorrect.
J.A. Clark
Sent NR 7604 at 2305 WR AR TNX

IBS Unit #1 APO 887
U.S. Army
OWI New York says July third they relayed to me via you important news
item concerning Jean Ellen. Nothing received please investigate and relay
item soonest.

End Msg.

IBS Unit #1 APO 887

FROM Bookman ISB Salzburg   TO OWI New York

Ref. No. SAWAG –057
Nothing on Jean Ellen received please repeat via Rome.

End Msg.

ISB Unit #1 APO 887

Date Receiving time July 5 619P

NR#

To Bookman JJAP Gaynor JJNJ

Prize for years foremost first novel CMA was awarded today to "Jean Ellen", five pound three ounce volume described by one reviewer as "healthy happy novel of childhood destined set new model for such works end it."

CONFIDENTIAL

From: ii corps Signal Officer From Bookman ISBPRECEDENCE: Routine

TO: OWI WashingtonDATE/TIME: 071330

REFERENCE NUMBER SAWAG ZERO SEVEN NINE PD PAREN PASS TO ONAF OWI NEW YORK UNPAREN MANY THANKS JEAN ELLEN ITEM RECEIVED WITH TREMENDOUS INTEREST

> APPROVED BY:George B. Keyzers
> Captain, Infantry,
> S-l Adjutant

On July 4th, less than two days after Jean's birth, Janet managed to handwrite me a note, reproduced on the next page.

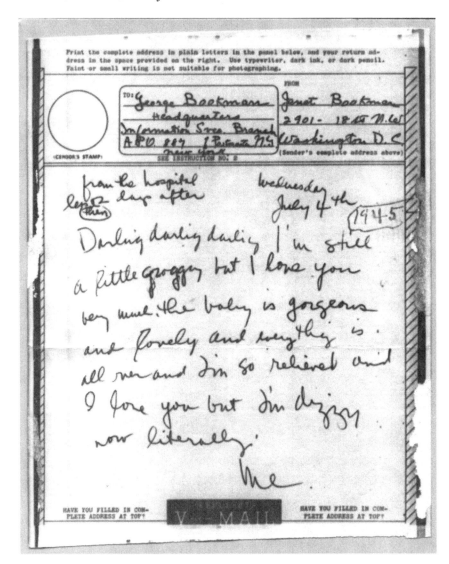

TO: George Bookman   FROM Janet Bookman
HQ Inf. Services Branch   2901-18 St. NW
APO 887   Washington 9 DC
C/o P.M. NY NY

July 5th, 1945 –3 days

Hello sweetheart darling"

I can't sit up so it's very hard for me to write all that I want to -. There's so much I want to share with you. Our baby, I think, is really beautiful - She's trying to learn to nurse and so am I. It's so wonderful to feel her next to me, darling – to feel that a part of you is next to me – it's that wonderful.

I still feel very weak and awfully uncomfortable from stitches. I can't write much because it hurts all over. But the doctor said I'm in fine health. Just received flowers from the Kilpatricks. Haven't heard from you yet, darling. It's so lonely without you . Now they're once more getting ready to wheel the baby in to me so I cant write another word.

Love,
Janet

As shown by the letters following, Janet wrote me repeatedly from the hospital, and after she returned home, but did not receive a telegram or other word from me until more than two weeks later -- though I sent wires and letters about the baby's arrival.

Other war brides were in similar situations, but it was particularly hard on Janet since her family and mine were in New York and she in Washington. Fortunately, however, her mother, Fannie Schrank, was able to come to help.

In fact, Grandma Schrank had a premonition that the baby would arrive ahead of schedule and unexpectedly showed up on Janet's doorstep (coming from her home in Florida) a few days early – which turned out to be absolutely the right time.

Saturday, July 7, 1945
Hello my darling –

I'm still flat on my back and will be so for several weeks more probably and so it is terribly hard for me to write to you. But I'm really beginning to feel very much better though I'm still very uncomfortable. God! Darling how I want to tell you in detail about this terrific experience so that we can share it together! But that will have to just wait until we can be together for good. (Make it soon dear God!) Our baby is wonderful-I think – all that either of us have prayed for - healthy and good and normal and so lovely to look at (but maybe I'm a little biased!) During the past two days I've succeeded in nursing her. I'm trying my very hardest to keep it up because it's best for baby but it's very hard to do and we still don't know if I'll be able to. So far nursing is very painful to me but I don't care because it's good for baby. She's wonderful, darling, and I can't wait until the day when we begin to share her together. Can't write more now – even this one page has been a real effort. Please understand.

Much love,
Janet

P.S. Still haven't heard from you about the birth!!!

Tuesday, July 10th, 1945
Dear darling,

Still no word from you about the baby's arrival and it's beginning to sort of get me down and I wonder whether you've yet received the news. Certainly, I hope so.

Present plans are for my leaving the hospital on Thursday when I'll be allowed out of bed for the first time.

I'm feeling a little glum now, darling, so this letter will probably not be too cheerful. I feel glum because of not hearing from you (which I know is no fault of yours) and also because I no longer am nursing the baby. This is a fact, which I'm finding hard to accept because I wanted so much to nurse the baby because it is so much better for her. But I'm not going to and the explanation will have to wait until we see each other.

The baby seems to be thriving, though and darling George; every time I look at her, I love her more and more. How I hope and wish and pray that soon you'll be able to be with her too so that we can share her together.

Dear Papa – I love you so much and miss you and want you and need you and everything. But I shouldn't talk like this because I know that you're just as unhappy about this lousy separation as I am.

I probably shouldn't have written to you just now because of my mood – but it's visiting hours here at the hospital and I can see and hear all the proud husbands talking with their new mama-wives and I suddenly became green with envy. But I know this mood will pass. This has been a very long letter to write on my back, sweetheart and I'm very tired. Take good care and the baby and I send you all our love.

July 12, 1945 morning
Dear darling, husband, & pappa-

I'm getting ready to leave the hospital now – expect to be out of here by noon today. Am terribly scared – excited – jittery – shaking – wobbly – scared – scared – scared – feel awfully alone without you. My mother and the practical nurse are calling for me in a few hours. My mother will carry the baby; the nurse to tote my valise and I'm still terribly wobbly on my legs. This business is a terrific ordeal and strain without you to lean on darling. I try to be cheerful and everything – but it's so hard – because deep down I want and need and want you desperately – and still no word from you about the baby's arrival. Our daughter is very very healthy, according to the pediatrician - but she is quite small (because she was premature) and as a result needs very careful handling – which only serves to petrify me still more. Today a new life is really beginning for us darling and I hope and pray that we will both make good, wise, and happy parents.

All my love

Janet

TO: Mrs. George Bookman   FROM: George Bookman
2901 Eighteenth Street nw   HQ Information Services Branch
Washington, DC   APO 887 Postmaster NY NY
July 15, 1945
Darling girls:

What a joy! Oh boy, what a joy. (Am I repeating myself? Well, I don't care) I have now received the first direct word about Jean Ellen's coming. It was a telegram from my parents sent July 5 and received July 13 and it says: LOVELY FIVE AND HALF POUND JEAN ELLEN BORN JULY SECOND EIGHT ELEVEN PM BOTH VERY WELL CONGRATULATIONS BLESSINGS LOVE.

So, that makes it official and it was certainly a relief to hear for the first time that you are all right. The telegram took ten days to reach me and that was just about what I had figured it would take. The telegram appears to be sent from Washington. How did my parents get there so fast? I'll bet there is a good story of excitement and frantic train catching attached to that, which will be coming thru in the mails in due course.

I was sure in my own mind that you were all right, but this is nothing like seeing it stated in black and white to give you a sense of relief. I am so anxiously awaiting a letter from you, as soon as you feel strong enough to write, telling me just what you went thru to have our baby, and how she looks, and what you thought, did, and said and everything. I know you will describe to me everything about Jean Ellen just as you kept me completely in the picture during your pregnancy. It is the only way I can even begin to share with you the experience of being parents together. Of course I am very confident that we will be together before too long, but I don't even want to miss anything about these first few months, when we will still be separated. It's funny darling that you should say in your letters that you have a hunch that we may be together for our first anniversary. That is the goal I have been shooting for and will do my damndest to achieve it. I have been thinking along exactly the same lines for weeks, but didn't think I would say anything about it, just in case something goes wrong and I don't make it in time. But that has been my own goal too for several weeks.

I think just as big a thrill as hearing the definite confirmation about Jean Ellen and you being well, was to receive you letter of June 29 written when you received the flowers I sent you. It is such a warm loving letter and I could almost feel you pressing against me as I read the letter. I am so happy the flowers arrived, and apparently, just about three days before Jean Ellen came. I arranged for them to come to you regularly for a few weeks, so that during these most difficult times, I should be a little closer to you than usual, so that whenever you look at the blooms you can remember "that's George" he's right here in the room with me, or at least his love is. What can I do darling to be close to you? Flowers were the best thing I could think of. Through those blossoms, you can communicate with me and I with you. If you wear one in your hair you will be proudly displaying the fact that you have a husband overseas whose heart is just breaking at the seams with love for you and our baby and the only way he can get close to you just now is by writing to you and by sending you a floral offering from time to time.

As I read the letter again, which you wrote while you were still a little weepy with emotion, I can just see you sitting at your typewriter, turning to look at the flowers and then your eyes getting reddish and brimming with tears and your mouth puckering a little as you try not to cry....and I know I love you, everything about you, every inch of your wonderful face and body and every trait in your wonderful cockeyed character.

I have also received some other letters from you. Mail is beginning to come thru again,....in bunches.

At hand are your letters of June 18 and 20, also an old one of May 28 that just came in. In your letters you tell of the possibility of a caesarian birth, your cramps, your weepy moments, and your triumph over the Dide wash man, …Lord, darling, you have had a tough time. You certainly needed someone to gripe to and I am sure you know that you can always gripe to me, to your heart's content. That is what husbands are for (partly). I want to know about your gripes just as I want to know about your happiness. You have had a very tough time, but at least I hope that the days of physical discomfort are almost over now. You have a brand new burden now, but if you can shake off physical discomfort, which is the handmaiden of pregnancy and childbirth, it will be easier to cope with your new tasks, even tho you have to do it mostly alone. I have told you before that I admire you so much the way you have stuck out your chin and handled these various situations as they have arisen. I say it once more – I admire you enormously – because I really really do and know that I will never be able to make it up adequately to you.

I wonder whether you are back from the hospital yet. I guess you must be by now. And you are undergoing the terrific new experience of taking care of your own baby…I guess I can't even imagine what that is like. Visualizing you while you were pregnant was difficult, but not impossible. But visualizing you now as a mother, feeding your baby, washing her, caring for her in every way, is exceedingly hard and I guess I will have to wait until I get home to really know what it is like.

I certainly am getting used tho to the idea that now I am a father and I like it very much – at least, at this distance. I know it is going to mean a world to me when I get home and we start being parents together and meeting all the various problems that will have to face as we bring up our daughter.

I think I told you I had a hunch it was going to be a girl. Someone asked me the other day if I was glad it was a girl. To tell the truth, that is a question I had never asked myself. I had no prejudices on the subject and no particular preference. I just wanted a baby and am delighted that we have Jean Ellen. I must say that I was somewhat disappointed that you did not have twins ….. and after all your boasting about how it runs in the family and the finger of fate pointed to you ….. (just a little kidding, darling) (no pun intended). Seriously, my darling wife, I am overjoyed that you are well and that we have a baby girl and I cant wait to get home to start being a real father to her and a real husband to you.

Just came back from a day in the country at one of the wonderful lakes near here. I drove out last night with four other men: Roy Block, who is a Captain in the Army, is getting married this month to an English girl who isn't up here yet; Jim Williamson, one of our newsmen, a Texas boy, Dave Mayer, a 1st Lt. Delightful guy with a swell sense of humor, very cockeyed and funny; and Lennie Lieberman, a quiet but nice type. Roy Block and Dave Mayer are particularly good friends of mine. We will probably be in Vienna together. I like them both very much and hope you can meet them and their wives after the war. Dave is the boy who has a 15-month-old daughter he has never seen.

We drove out to the lake last night, arriving just in time to sit on the porch of a house and watch the moon go down, while drinking cognac and singing. This morning we lay in the sun (I baked out my cold) and went swimming (which did not seem to hurt my disappearing cold). Slept practically all afternoon and then came back to town to find that our hotel was serving a terrific dinner of roast chicken, soup, apple sauce, and real ice cream. Washed down with a little beer, it was terrific. So, this is Sunday evening and I feel wonderful and am writing to you.

There is a strong possibility I may have to leave for Vienna soon, and God knows what will happen to my mail while I am there and whether I will be able to send letters to you. But if we are cut off from communications, it can't be for very long. I'll let you know before I leave tho.

I was supposed to go to Italy this weekend for the purpose of telephoning you, but Don Minifie made it pretty plain he would appreciate it if I would stick around here, in view of this Vienna deal looming up. I was awfully anxious to phone you, so I more or less badgered him into saying I could go, but then next day my conscience got the better of me (damn my conscience) and I told him I would stick around here, as he had requested. He seemed quite pleased. So, the chances of my being able to phone you from Italy are now very very slim, I'm afraid.

Saturday afternoon one of the battalions of the 42nd Infantry Division was given a Presidential citation. The ceremony took place in the main square of Salzburg, right under the window of my office. It was a stirring military display. Every battalion of the division was represented in the march past the Commanding General to do honor to the group that was being decorated for exceptional bravery in the battle of the Rhine. There was a brass band, the flying colors of the Rainbow (42nd) Div and all the stirring panoply of martial ceremony that makes your blood tingle. I took a lot of pictures and hope they come out.

I guess that's all the news for now. I blow you a kiss, darling and kiss Jeannie too, if she is big enough for that sort of thing.

Love,
George

Monday evening
July 16th – exactly 2 weeks after
Our baby's arrival

Dear darling,

Just got out of bed a little while ago for the first real time since I came home from the hospital on Thursday. But according to the doctor's orders, I have to make bed "my headquarters" for the next three weeks or so. I've been feeling comparatively well, but still find it very hard to write letters – so don't expect the typical "Janetian" letters for quite some time. I just don't feel up to it yet, darling – and that's why I haven't gone into every real detail about the whole terrific experience. It will just have to wait until we can talk about it together.

Our baby, George, is truly wonderful. I know that I'm probably beginning to sound like the typical mother, but I'm not ashamed of it in the least. To me, Ellen Jean looks perfectly beautiful. She is a good little girl, and seems to be adjusting herself very well. I'm still a little worried about her size – she's just such a little thing, darling. But the pediatrician keeps reassuring me that there is nothing to worry about and that she is really in very good health.

The practical nurse I hired is leaving on Wednesday. I asked her to for what probably sounds like a very funny reason – but it really was (and still is) quite serious. The nurse snores all night long, and makes a terrific racket and has kept me awake every night since she's been here. As a result, I'm simply exhausted – which certainly isn't helping to get me on my feet sooner. So I had to ask her to leave when her first week is up, which will be Wednesday.

My mother will take over from there, darling, and I really have the utmost confidence in her ability to handle the baby. She'll teach me all about bathing the baby and all that sort of thing – and I can't wait darling until I start handling her myself – even to her diapering – though maybe that will be your assignment (or one of 'em) when you finally get home.

Darling, you'll love the baby! She has such sensitive and well formed and graceful features – and so many varied facial expressions – and such a plaintive little noise! It just seems futile to try to describe her to you – because no words really can do her justice. I guess I just love her, sweetheart – because she's part of you and our love and all that it stands for.

I still haven't heard a word from you George – for more than 2 weeks now. Something certainly seems to have gone wrong with the mail and communications – and it's most demoralizing, to say the least.

I've lots and lots to tell you, darling husband and pappa – but it's hard for me to write it all out – and I just don't yet feel strong enough to use the typewriter.

Received a note this morning from John Dunning of the New York OWI. He told me about just having received a message from you acknowledging and thanking him for forwarding the news of the baby. I was tickled to receive this note from Dunning because I still didn't know whether or not you'd even heard about it.

The Kleimans visited me at the hospital one evening. Bob looks perfectly wonderful, and he certainly seems to have grown so. He expects to leave for Okinawa and the Pacific area momentarily. (If I had my typewriter before me now I'd be able to tell you much more about him but this will have to do for a while).

This has been a very long letter for me to write, sweetheart – and I've been sitting at the desk here much longer than I really should.

So no more for now, darling. Be happy. God, I just love you so much and want to share our baby with you more than anything else in the world!

Always, always, always,
Janet

July 17, 1945
Darling!

Just received the first letter from you in your own handwriting two days after the baby came, and what a thrill it was. A million thanks for writing to me, even tho your head was probably reeling and you felt very woozy and much unlike holding a pen in your hand and writing a letter. I got a great thrill out of hearing directly from you tho, and having the best possible confirmation that all is well.

At the same time I received long letters from my parents telling all about the baby, and that you were so lucky in having only five hours labor, and that the baby – sez they – is booootiful – etc., etc.

Also, their letters included the fact that the baby's correct name is Ellen Jean. So please excuse me for getting off on the wrong foot. Your letters in which you told me you preferred the name "Ellen" did not arrive until THIS MORNING! After well over a month in the mails. So Ellen it is, a lovely name, and I am crazy about it so please excuse me if my tongue slips sometime and I call her Jeannie....but I completely agree with you as to the name Ellen and am in love with it already. Fact is, I like both names equally well and I think it is a swell idea that her full name includes them both.

Your time schedule before the baby was born takes my breath away. Visit to the Doctor at 1, in the hospital at 3 and a mother by 8:11. Whew. If Ellen goes thru life like that she will probably end up as Presidentess of the

United States, or at least a champion runner. That is what I call getting off to a flying start.

My mother congratulates me on "the swell job as Father that I did! What did I do, that was so terrific? I admit it was very pleasant but it did not seem very difficult, I rather think that a Father at these times is a sort of unnecessary necessity, but it is nice to know that people appreciate your handiwork, even if I had such a fleeting part in making our baby. At least, you can't say that I influenced Ellen prenatally except perhaps by my absence. My mother also tells me that you received a letter from me the morning after the baby came, which of course is wonderful news and is another hurdle you have taken in your stride.

It will be so good to hear from you when you are strong enough to write, but receiving your note and the letters from my folks was wonderful. It was really the first detailed news I had received and went a long way toward appeasing my hunger for some of the details. Their letters however are somewhat sketchy and I know you will sit down and tell me everything in the minute detail. I am so anxious to hear, so the first day you feel strong enough just put Ellen to sleep in her lovely white crib with the lambs prancing on it (hand painted by momma) and sit down to your typewriter and tell hubby all about it.

It certainly was swell of my folks to give Ellen a welcome-to-the-world present, and I will write to add my thanks to yours.

Also got a telegram from my grandmother who, in a burst of enthusiasm, without even seeing Ellen, telegraphed, YOUR DAUGHTER IS BEAUTIFUL LOVE MA. Isn't that typical? But I am sure she is right. Any daughter of yours is bound to be beautiful.

This morning I got a batch of letters from you, forwarded from Italy, all old ones. They were dated June 7, 10, 11 and June 6. They had made the circuit of Europe, apparently and may even have been on a ship that was sunk or something because they were all full of sand, as though they had been lying at the bottom of the ocean a while, or at least at the bottom of a sandy ship's hold.

One of the letters included the small pictures taken when your BIG BELLY picture was also photographed. I must say the one you chose to send me, where you sit on the couch and hold a book, is the silliest of them all. You look as tho you burst out laughing as soon as the man snapped the camera shutter, and are having a devil of a time to keep from giggling. The one with your head thrown back, showing your teeth a la Pepsodent is the prettiest of them all. You don't look at all like an old fatso, in fact I think you kept your figure remarkably well under the circumstances.

While commenting on the pictures, in my facetious manner, I just noticed one stuck inside the envelope that I haven't seen before. It is a chest up view, but this time instead of looking as though you are going to burst out giggling any minute, you are gazing pensively at the ceiling, wearing your most soulful look. Who are you trying to kid? Me? I know you are no angel and am not one bit fooled by these angelic poses. You are a down-to-earth human lovable wonderful girl and the person I love the most in the entire wide world. But an angel? Hell, no. Get out from behind that halo, honey. I know you.

(Incidentally, don't read these letters to Ellen, please, she might get wrong ideas about her momma and pappa.) (And don't leave them lying around the apartment where she can pick them up and peek).

Aren't you sorry you married a loon?

One of your letters (one of the old ones) received today burns my ears off for not writing more often. I have put it in a bucket of water to cool off before handling it with my bare hands. The next letter, however, said, "all is forgiven" so I feel better. Another tells of your really stupendous effort, when you were swollen with Ellen, to scrape and paint the crib. I don't see how you did it and think it is phenomenal. Boy, what a lot of dishwashing I am going to have to do in order to make up for that. Looking over some of the figures you quote on the expenses of this wonderful process of childbirth, I am amazed at how little the layette cost. The medical expenses of course bulk the heaviest, but the layette and furniture, etc., came to much less than I thought they would. You got some excellent bargains and I think the reasons you advance for the various purchases you made, even the slightly extravagant splurges, are all excellent and I am sure I would have agreed with you at the time if I were with you.

Nothing new on the Vienna front. Still waiting. Meanwhile I have written a charter for an American Publication Board for Austria, which will license all Austrian publication; and also have written a directive for our outpost in Vienna, rather a tricky job because you have to bear in mind four occupying nations. That's all for now except lots of love to you and Ellen.

George

* * * * * *

Finally in September, I got permission to go home. I was assigned a jeep and Army driver who drove me from Salzburg to Paris. On the way, I stopped off to see my brother-in-law Joe Schrank, who was an Army captain in charge of Military Government in an area of West Germany around Heppenheim, in the Rhineland. Joe ran a very tight ship. I recall that he required Germans to set up a cemetery for burial of the slave workers from the East who had died while working for the Nazis in the area and had been dumped into a common grave. Some years later, on a trip to Europe in 1963, Janet and I stopped off to see Heppenheim again and paid our respects to the graves of the Nazi prisoners, the graves that Joe had arranged for.

Joe's brother, Norman, was also involved in the war in Germany. As a Sergeant in the U.S. Army he took part in the battle for the Remagen bridgehead across the Rhine and I believe was wounded – losing a finger shot off his hand. The other brother, Mannie (Charles) volunteered for the Merchant Marine (where he had worked before the war). He did the run to Murmansk and one of his ships was torpedoed, but he survived.

After Heppenheim, we proceeded right to Paris but making one stop for a meal in a town in Northern France. We parked the jeep in the town square and went into a GI mess hall. Foolishly, I left in the open jeep a Beretta pistol that Joe had given me and of course, it was stolen while we were eating. I spent a couple of days in Paris before going aboard a troop transport ship for the trip home, where I arrived at the end of September.

This was my first sight of my newborn daughter and of my wife since the birth of our first child. It was a lovely, warm reunion. Of course, I needed a job so I went back to The Washington Post to see Casey Jones, the Managing Editor. As recounted earlier, he said, yes, I could have my old job back (covering the White House) but at my old pre-war salary. So I got myself a job at World Report Magazine, just started then by David Lawrence and later merged with his magazine U.S. News. I wrote a great variety of articles for World Report. When it merged, I left and very quickly landed a job with the Washington Bureau of Time Magazine, due to a friendship Janet and I had with Bob Elson, then the chief of the Time Washington Bureau.

The only opening Bob had at the time was to cover the Latin American embassies, which I did for about a year. This involved attending a lot of carioca parties, also one week in Haiti as a journalism guest of the Haitian government, to cover an International Expo they were having. We were assigned a car, driver, and villa and were able to take a trip from Port-au-Prince to Cape Haitien, and another to the remote town of Jacmel on the south coast. To get to Jacmel required fording a couple of rivers, but once there, it was enchantingly beautiful – so much so that Janet and I even toyed with the idea of opening a tourist hotel in Jacmel. Thank the Lord we gave up that idea, though some years later on a trip to Scotland, we similarly toyed, half-seriously, with the idea of buying a country inn in the Highlands, at a place called the Spittal of Glenshee.

Before starting work at World Report Magazine, Janet and I went on a postwar honeymoon trip to Florida, staying first around St. Augustine and then, for the first time, visiting the Okefenokee Swamp in southern Georgia.

It was totally enchanting and we went back there a couple of times in later years, once with our children.

CHAPTER XII

ENTER CHARLES

The main event of 1948 was, of course, the birth of our son, Charles Arthur, on March 19th. This time I was home before, during and after – thank heavens. We were then living on Nevada Avenue in Chevy Chase, D.C. When it came time for Janet to go to the hospital (Columbia Hospital, I believe), I opened the front door to go out for the car and our Persian cat ran out and climbed a tree. Janet would not leave the house until the Fire Department had come and retrieved the cat for us.

At the hospital, Janet chose the name Charles in lieu of other names she had considered because, as I recall, it was just a short while before Prince Charles was born to Queen Elizabeth who was considering that name – and Janet always admired English royalty. After some years however, our Charles asked us to call him Chip, which we did most of the time until Janet passed away and I thought it was time for me to switch back to his given name.

Momma Schrank helped us considerably after Charles was born, and in a serious illness he had about a year later. Charles contracted a blood ailment and had to have his entire blood supply replaced. Fortunately, he came out of it in fine shape, but we were very worried for a while. He was taken care of, I believe, by our pediatrician, Dr. McLendon, and at Children's Hospital in Washington.

While I was overseas, Janet managed to get us an apartment suitable for Jean's arrival. Janet had been living in a one-room apartment on Adams Mill Road. Larger apartments were very hard to find in wartime. But Janet – taking the problem by the horns – wrote a letter appealing to Morris Cafritz, then a real estate mogul in Washington. Mr. Cafritz came up with an apartment at 2901 Eighteenth Street, a few blocks from Rock Creek Park, where she often aired the baby. A year or so after I came home from the war, we moved to a house on Nevada Avenue, D.C., not far from Chevy Chase Circle. I might mention that during this period our close friends were a newsman,

Sandy Klein (of the UPI) and his wife Hilda. Later, I think they split – Hilda to New York and Sandy to a newspaper in Boise, Idaho.

In 1950, I think it was, we built a new house in the Somerset section of Chevy Chase, Md. The house was built by our brother-in-law, Leon Horowitz, then in the home construction business in Virginia. We were trying to save money, so we told him we did not need a basement. A couple of years later, however, we requested a finished basement, which he built, plus a very attractive sunroom in the rear of the house. The address, if memory serves, was 4921 Cumberland Avenue, a lovely, quiet, sloping street with many trees, etc. We stayed there until we moved to Scarsdale, N.Y. in 1957.

Leon Horowitz and his wife Sylvia, Janet's sister, were good friends and good relatives. For many of our years in Falls Church we were invited to their house for Passover – and many other occasions, also after they moved to Reston, Virginia.

When the children were old enough, we sent them to the Green Acres School, which had a fine country setting out Wisconsin Avenue. It was an elementary school at that time. I served on the Board and we were very active in school affairs. It was there we made some good friends – Muriel and Maury Miller (after Maury's death Muriel married Phil Pear, now deceased); also Edna Lusher and her husband, a Government economist. Edna and Janet were close friends for years.

It was during this same period that we formed our very close friendship with Bob and Mabel Cohen. They were both eminent psychoanalysts, originally from Chicago, and leaders in those circles in the Washington Area. Bob was medical director at one point at Chestnut Lodge, a greatly respected psychiatric hospital in suburban Maryland, and later he was research director of the National Institute of Mental Health.

Janet and Mabel were closest personal friends, played piano duets together and no doubt discussed their own lives together in great frankness. As families, we spent many Thanksgivings together and lived very near each other in Somerset, Maryland. We became good friends with their adopted children, Donald and Marjie, now married to Shelley Beinfeld.

Mabel passed away long before Janet and Bob married a friend from NIH, Alice, with whom we also became friends. As I write this, Bob is 97, somewhat hobbled by walking problems, but lovingly cared for by Alice and still someone with whom I keep in touch.

It was about this time that we met Bernard and Ines Burrows. Bernard was stationed in Washington as Counselor of the British Embassy. Ines and Janet met at the house of Joanna and George Oakes (George was brother of John Oakes, the N.Y. Times editor). Janet and Ines hit it off and we did as a foursome as well. We invited the Burrows to come square dancing with us, and they in turn invited us to join a Scottish country-dance group. We continued that for a couple of years, until the Burrows were transferred elsewhere. While in Washington, they had a daughter, Antonia. Their son, Rupert, was born after their return to England.

Bernard became an expert on American square dancing and learned to be a caller -- which he put to good use making friends with American colleagues later when he became the Queen's envoy to the Persian Gulf, Ambassador to Turkey and then to NATO.

Bernard was knighted by the Queen for his diplomatic services. He also wrote several books – one about his work in the Gulf, another on European Federalism, one on the defense of Western Europe and he contributed to a bestseller on The Third World War. He served as Chairman of the Federal Trust for Education and Research, and in his last years was working on books about humanism and paranormal phenomena.

Janet and Ines began a correspondence in the 1950's that lasted about a half a century. I edited the collection of letters and had it privately published in 2006. It is titled "Dear Ines – Dear Janet – 50 Years of TransAtlantic Letters Between Two Friends". The book is available on Amazon.com and Barnes & Noble.com.

Incidentally, we were very good friends of George and Joanna Oakes who helped get the Burrows friendship started. Tragically, George and Joanna and their son were killed in an auto accident on a New England highway – their daughter, Diana, who was not on that trip, survives.

CHAPTER XIII

US NEWS AND TIME MAGAZINE

During my fairly brief stay at US News-World Report, the highlight was a news trip to Turkey, Iran and Western Europe. This was in 1946, when the Russians were making menacing noises about seizing the Bosporus Straits that connect the Mediterranean with the Black Sea. President Harry Truman decided to show the flag in the eastern Mediterranean by sending the Battleship Missouri (scene of the Japanese surrender the year before) to Istanbul. The excuse was to return the body of a Turkish Ambassador who had died in Washington during the war. A few newsmen were invited along for the ride. We sailed from Newport News I believe, to Istanbul, a trip of 6 or 8 days. We were received royally in Istanbul, with a big Government party in one of the palaces. There also was time for some sightseeing in Istanbul. Then we went by train to Ankara where we were received by the President of Turkey. Also, I remember an elegant luncheon in an Ankara restaurant with some of the most delicious desserts I ever tasted.

From Turkey I flew to Cairo for a few days, tried to get permission to go to Saudi Arabia, but was turned down for being Jewish, then decided to go to Teheran.

The flight to Teheran was on a startup Iranian airline, staffed mainly by former U.S. Air Force pilots. We stopped for refueling in Baghdad and then on toward Teheran. The pilot however was an airman who had not served in WWII combat, while the passengers were almost all combat veterans. So the young pilot decided to show off to his passengers over the Iranian mountains by dipping the wings as we flew through mountain passes. One of the pilot passengers was so angry he drew his revolver and headed for the pilot's cabin, but was restrained by his buddies. The plane detoured to Abadan, where the pilot was taken out and charged with reckless flying, and we went on to Teheran.

In Teheran, it was the time of the Azerbaijan crisis, when the Russians tried to seize the part of Azerbaijan that belonged to Iran. The U.N. Security Council intervened and amazingly, the Russians backed off. It was probably the first success for the U.N.

My main journalism accomplishment in Teheran was to interview the Shah who was later kicked out in the Iranian revolution. If he said anything memorable it may be in the pages of an old issue of World Report magazine, but not in my memory.

From Teheran I went to Rome, where I interviewed Pope Pius VI, who was still in the Vatican. Italian elections were coming up and that was a major topic of the interview. Also, His Holiness gave me a rosary, which I gave to my parents' Catholic house worker when I got back to New York.

Let it be noted here that Harry Truman's decision to show the flag in the Eastern Mediterranean, one of the opening salvos in the Cold War, had some effect because the Russians backed away from their threat to seize the Bosporus.

As I noted earlier, I went to Time, Inc., in late 1948, starting by covering Latino embassies in Washington. After about a year, I became their business and economics reporter in the Washington Bureau. There were a dozen or so correspondents in the Bureau. Bob Elson was in charge when I started. Later, Jim Shepley took over. He later moved to New York to be publisher of Time Magazine. When he left, Jim McConaghy (later killed in a military plane crash) took over. One of my best friends in the Bureau was Anatole Visson, of Russian-Belgian background, who was a diplomatic correspondent. Also Clay Blair who covered the Pentagon, Jack Beal and Frances Levison Low, who married Bob Low. Frances and I once interviewed the notorious Senator Joe McCarthy for an article that, I am glad to say, was quite hostile to McCarthy. The Lows became friends of mine and I am still in touch with them, though they moved to San Francisco.

On the economic front, I did a lot of stories on all aspects. One of my good contacts was Gabriel Hauge, Economic Advisor to President Eisenhower. After Hauge left the White House, he became Chairman of Manufacturers Hanover Bank in New York. He asked me to help him write his memoirs, which I did. Hauge died just before they were finished, so I sent his widow a copy later expecting to have his memoirs published. She didn't get back to me about it for months, and when I asked her she said, "the children don't want the publicity that would involve", so the book was never published. Later, I offered the manuscript to the Eisenhower Memorial Library in Abilene, Kansas and they were delighted to have it.

Another friendly contact in Washington was William McChesney Martin, Jr., Chairman of the Federal Reserve, and the first paid Chairman of the New

York Stock Exchange (before he went to Washington). As I recall, I think I helped him get a child into Green Acres School.

One of the trips I made for Time's Washington Bureau was with the then Secretary of Commerce, Charles Sawyer, to look at offshore oil wells in the Texas Gulf. I spent one night on a drilling platform. This trip also included a night in New Orleans, which was a great experience – long before Hurricane Katrina. There was also a stop in Ft. Worth, Texas where Amon Carter gave me one of his famous Stetsons.

In the economics field, I wrote annual economic reports for Time Magazine, most of my years in the Bureau, also occasional articles for LIFE

I was the main reporting contributor to quite a number of TIME cover stories. Among them were articles on Paul Hoffman, who ran the postwar aid agency called Economic Cooperation Administration, Secretary Sawyer, and Mike DiSalle, who was price controller during the Korean War. I became friendly with DiSalle and he attended a party that Janet and I gave on Cumberland Avenue. Another was the redoubtable Treasury Secretary George Humphrey. One sidelight on that: when I arrived at the U.S. Treasury to interview Humphrey, I was wearing recently purchased blue suede shoes. His P.R. man looked and said, "Are you really going to wear those shoes for the interview?" I changed my shoes. Another subject was an advisor to the President named Joseph Dodge (on budget matters, I think). He resigned the day after the cover article came out, which apparently he had been planning all along, but I did not know. The TIME editors took it in stride.

One of the least remembered Eisenhower cabinet members was the Secretary of the Interior, Douglas McKay. I did the reporting on him for a TIME cover, which gave me a chance for a Western swing. I recall very warmly a day or so in Yellowstone Park, a day at Glacier Park in Montana near the Canadian border, a flight in a small plane over the Snake River Canyon, a trip down the Columbia River, and a little traveling around city areas in Oregon and Washington. I doubt if that issue of TIME sold out, but I enjoyed the trip.

There was a cover story also on Dag Hammarskjold of the U.N. ten years after it was founded in 1945 at San Francisco. I believe I was at the original founding session, probably sent by US News-World Report, my first visit to San Francisco. In later years I was in New York briefly to cover the UN when Soviet President Khrushchev was there and famously pounded his shoe on the table in the General Assembly to protest something or other.

Another article was on Dave Beck, head of the Teamsters Union, who later had to resign due to corruption. After I interviewed him, his secretary, a former nurse, looked at me and said I didn't look very well, and I should call a doctor. I did, and the doctor put me in the hospital to have my appendix removed. There is a picture of Janet transcribing my Dave Beck notes, which I dictated from my hospital bed.

Among other cover stories were Bill Martin of the Federal Reserve, with whom I became friendly, Mayor Wagner of New York (for which I came on a reporting trip to New York), two heads of the U.S. Steel Corporation and a major article on the telephone industry, then dominated by the near-monopoly AT&T.

I also did a cover story on Nelson Rockefeller when he was running for Governor of New York, and followed him around the State. Another article was on C.R.Smith, the formidable head of American Airlines who introduced me to his own private brand of corn whiskey. The U.S. Steel article involved an invitation to that company's annual luncheon for journalists where they gave an award to the one they considered to be the best economics writer. I received the award one year, a handsome Steuben glass owl head, which I still have.

Other cover story subjects: Chief Justice Earl Warren and Sherman Fairchild of Fairchild Industries. A particularly enjoyable assignment was the cover story on Henry Alexander, head of Morgan Guaranty Bank. The only time I could interview him was aboard a cruise ship taking a convention of bankers to Bermuda, so I sailed along and got my interview. The ship's return trip was held up by a storm, so I flew back from Bermuda but not before working in some very pleasant beach time.

I also interviewed Jimmy Hoffa who followed Dave Beck as head of the Teamsters Union. That interview took place very pleasantly at the big hotel in White Sulphur Springs, West Virginia, where the Teamsters were having a meeting. Janet came along and she got on quite well with Hoffa. That was a while before he wound up killed and dumped somewhere in Detroit.

One of the more notable cover stories was March 10, 1952, showing a U.S. Taxpayer being ground up and squeezed into dollar bills -- drawn by the famous Artzybasheff. It involved a lot of reporting on all the economic agencies of the Federal Government.

I have copies of these TIME covers autographed by the cover subjects, with two exceptions: Dave Beck, whose autograph I did not want, and of course the cartoon of the poor taxpayer.

Also, while in Washington I was a panelist a number of times on Meet the Press, and Face the Nation. On the 50th Anniversary of Meet the Press there was a Washington party to which I was invited and attended. I have a couple of tapes of those broadcasts obtained for me by Charles.

Other sideline activities included doing a number of radio economic commentaries for Canadian Broadcasting from D.C., also signing up for a while with a lecture bureau and delivering a few undistinguished lectures at ladies' clubs in places like Pittsburgh.

One of my most enjoyable – and memorable – assignments in Washington was covering the hike on the Chesapeake & Ohio Canal led by Supreme Court Justice William O. Douglas in March 1954. The Washington Post had run an editorial advocating that the Canal be turned into a scenic highway. Douglas wrote to the Post strongly objecting and proposing that the editors come for a hike with him the full length of the Canal, which parallels the Potomac River for 185 miles from Cumberland, Maryland to D.C. When I heard about it, I got TIME to assign me to cover the hike.

As I recall, the hike lasted eight days and I was along for about 4 or 5 days (due to other assignments). We camped out overnight in freezing weather a couple of nights and other nights slept in hunting lodges near the Canal. There were scores of hikers most days, including very prominent conservationists from all over the nation. I wrote stories for two successive weeks, both carried by TIME. The eventual result was that Bob Estabrook, then in charge of the Post's editorial page, who also was on the hike, backed away from the highway idea. Some years later Congress designated the entire Canal path a National Park. In 2004, along with Ruth, I attended the 50th anniversary dinner for the hikers (but without Douglas who died earlier). We were accompanied by Bob Estabrook (now in Lakeville, Connecticut) and his wife Mary Lou, owners of the local paper in Lakeville, Ct.

CHAPTER XIV

TO NEW YORK

Time Magazine tried several times to transfer me from Washington to another news bureau – as a promotion. Once I tried Chicago for a month, which involved an interview with Col. McCormick, who owned the Chicago Tribune. But I decided against moving the family to Chicago, and also had a brief illness that required my going home. I was also offered the Ottawa bureau and, later, the bureau in Rome. That would of course mean uprooting my family, and Claire Luce, the publisher's wife was then U.S. Ambassador in Rome. To me, that was a drawback.

In late 1957, however, TIME asked me to come up to New York, and I accepted. We sold the house in Somerset, Chevy Chase, and bought a very attractive place in Scarsdale, New York. I recall that my brother-in-law Joe urged us to move to Scarsdale, and introduced us to the agent who sold us the house. Anyhow, it was a very fine, large house on the Post Road with 2 or 3 acres of land. The school system there was very competitive and Jeannie was not too comfortable there. So, after a while, she moved to the Barlow School in Amenia, New York and a year or so later Charles also went there. While Jean was at Scarsdale High, I volunteered to coach girls' basketball. They were extremely competitive girls and of course won the area championship without much help from me. As a thank you, the team took me out for ice cream at the end of the season.

We brought our very fine housekeeper, Eva, with us from Washington and her husband came along and lived in a basement apartment. After a year or so they left and we rented the apartment to a friend from LIFE Magazine, Bob and Becky Brigham, New Englanders who, when last heard, moved back to the Coast of Maine – Kennebunkport, I believe. Eva's name lives on in the names of my granddaughter, Alanna Eva and her daughter Eva Jean.

In Scarsdale we became friendly with several neighbors, notably Sidney and Freda Schreiber (he was our doctor), and Frank and Laura Taubes, who lived across the road. However, social life in Scarsdale wasn't really our style. One evening we went to the movies in New York with other friends, Mark and Clara Mae Friedlander. We saw the film "The Apartment" just as they were buying a brownstone at 156 East 71st Street, with an upstairs apartment available. We decided to sell Scarsdale and move to the city. We stayed in the apartment from about 1961 for a few years until the stairs became too much for Janet, when we moved to an elegant apartment at 1085 Park Avenue.

However, it was in Scarsdale that Janet began freelance writing that she continued for some years afterwards. Our neighbor in Scarsdale was Henry Collins, a nature writer who was doing a major book on wildlife. Janet helped him with the editing. Later, when I moved to the

NY Botanical Gardens, Janet did writing and editing for some of the scientists, notably Ian Prance, who later became director of Kew Gardens in England and was Knighted by the Queen. Janet also did editorial work with Joan Marks (wife of Dr. Paul Marks of Memorial Sloan Kettering) who wrote books on women's studies and was on the faculty at Sarah Lawrence College.

Professionally, in New York I had a very busy and satisfying few years. From 1978 to 1960, I was the National Business and Economics Correspondent for TIME based in New York, and then in 1960 moved over to FORTUNE Magazine as a member of its Board of Editors.

In May 1959, a TIME official (Frank Shea) wrote about my work in a memo he sent to TIME ad salesmen, as follows:

May 22, 1959
TO:TIME Salesmen

FROM:Frank Shea

This week's cover story features Dwight Robinson, President of the Massachusetts Investment Trust. Since George Bookman, TIME's national economic correspondent, did much of the basic reporting for the story, this serves as a useful peg to tell you something about George's beat and how he covers it.

Reporter Bookman speaking:
It is now about a year and a half since TIME asked me to come to New York to be its first full time economic correspondent covering the American

business scene, with particular emphasis on the great corporations and financial houses centered in the city.

I have never been so fascinated by any newsgathering assignment. The entire U.S. economy is my oyster, and much of it can be tasted within a taxi or subway ride of the Time-Life Building.

There have been spot stories to cover, major "projects" such as TIME cover stories, and a great deal of editorial "exploration" work, getting to know more about what goes on inside U.S. business, lining up top-level sources for future stories.

So far, this beat has provided a number of major cover stories on which I have done a large share, or all, of the reporting work. These include: Frank Pace of General Dynamics, C.R. Smith of American Airlines, the "Telephone Man" and currently the story on mutual funds. At the depth of the recession in the spring of 1958, I made a tour of U.S. industrial centers, was able to report to the editors that U. S. businessmen were taking the buffeting of the recession with great equanimity, were certain it was only temporary. At the end of 1958 I wrote a memo for TIME's editors, nearly book-length, examining the new forces that make the U.S. economy operate – the shifts in production, the new habits of consumers, the new trends in taste, style, investment, etc. This was the basis for TIME's cover on the Bull Market at the turn of the year in which the workings of the "new economy" that had developed in this country were examined. (Jim Linen also used this Bookman research as a mailing piece – extremely well received. FS).

My beat has included a trip to the St. Lawrence River valley for a full report on the economic implications of the Seaway, a few days in Boston at the height of the Bernard Goldfine uproar digging into that gentleman's labyrinthine business ways. Soon I will be heading for the West Coast for an appraisal of economic story possibilities from the Canadian to the Mexican border, west of the Rockies.

Perhaps the most fascinating assignment has been the chance to penetrate into the inner sanctums of Wall Street for "inside" stories of the financial district. I have sat at the old-fashioned, high-top desks of Morgan partners; interviewed real estate tycoon Robert Dowling on his flower-planted terrace overlooking the Wall Street pinnacles; shouldered my way across the tape-strewn floor of the New York Stock Exchange at the height of the trading day; chatted with Chase Bank President John McCloy in his quiet office; talked privately with steel executive Roger Blough about his upcoming problems with the steelworkers union, secured an exclusive interview with General Motors new chairman Fred Donner (and it is still exclusive, many months later.) I have been to Pittsburgh to talk to leaders of steel union locals in their modest homes within sight of the smokestacks of the steel plants. I have sat in the private offices of investment bankers while they showed me their private calculations on the future of the economy – such figures as Robert Lehman of Lehman Brothers and Sidney Weinberg of Goldman Sachs. And I have listened in great auditoriums where company officials told thousands of stockholders how they were running America's biggest corporations.

One important fact deserves to be mentioned: the name of TIME opens any door in the U.S. business. It has been an invaluable calling card to be a TIME correspondent.

Recently, on the mutual fund story, going to press this week, I talked to leaders of that growing industry in the New York area. This included interviews with Dorsey Richardson, who runs the exciting, new fund One William Street for Lehman's; with a partner of Lazard Freres about their new fund; with Hugh Bullock who runs the highly respected funds founded by his father Calvin Bullock; with Herbert Anderson, who is president of the National Association of Investment Companies and also runs his own mutual fund business, Distributors Group. My work for this story also included talking with salesmen, the men on the firing line who are trying to sell (and with great success) shares in mutual funds to the public. In other words, my reporting ranged from the man with the sample kit to the man with the portfolio.

* * * * * *

In November 1959, I made a major reporting swing through Western Europe for TIME. This involved interviews in London with people like Sir Oliver Franks, Chairman of Lloyds Bank, Sigmund Warburg, of the famous banking family; then Holland to see top officials of Royal Dutch and Phillips; then Brussels where I interviewed top officials of the European Economic Commission; then Paris for talks with a Governor of the Bank of France, General DeGaulle's Economic Advisor, and Jean Monnet, who was instrumental in unifying the Common Market; on to Germany to see such officials as Hermann Abs, president of Deutsche Bank and Ludwig Erhard, then Vice Chancellor; to Zurich for interviews with people like the heads of Union Bank of Switzerland and of Julius Baer & Company; finally to Italy interviewing people like the head of Fiat. (A full list of those interviewed is in the Appendix).

The following letter I sent back to the Business Editor, Joe Purtell, gives a feeling of my reporting and my findings.

14 November 1959
Paris

Dear Joe:

I am now past the halfway mark of my trip through Europe and I thought you might like to have a short interim report on the sorts of things I am finding out that will figure in the research I will write for the Yearend Review.

So far I have spent a week in London, three days in Holland, three in Brussels and am now finishing up five days in Paris. Next, about five days in Germany, two in Switzerland, three or four in Italy, and then I fly back to New York. I expect to return about November 30 and should have my copy written by the end of that week, in other words perhaps by December 6, certainly no later than December 10.

By the time I leave Italy, I will have had about 100 interviews with leading bankers, businessmen, and government officials in the seven countries I am visiting.

I don't want to anticipate research I haven't yet written, however you may be interested in some of the standout impressions I have, which I intend to develop in the research. Among them:

1. Within the past year, there has been a fundamental shift in the world balance of economic power. U.S. policies of aiding recovery in Europe were so fabulously successful that now the tables are turned, the economies of many countries in Europe are actually more dynamic and seem to have greater growth potential than the US economy, at least in the near future.

2. A real economic revolution is taking place in Europe, as fundamental in its effect on the daily lives of the people as the industrial revolution of the 19th century. It is evident everywhere I have been. In France, which had probably the most antiquated economy of all, the change is the most fundamental and startling.

3. Seen from Europe, the U.S. economy has serious problems. The dollar isn't as yet in serious trouble, but the U.S. balance of payments is seriously out of line and U.S. production costs are going up while Europe's have been more or less stabilized. Most thoughtful US businessmen see quite clearly the fundamental importance of the cost-price struggle in the steel industry, now adjourned for 80 days by Taft-Hartley. The issue at least as viewed through European eyes is crucial for the US if it hopes to maintain its economic leadership of the world. Other nations have in the past two or three years faced up to their wage /price problems. We have not yet had our showdown.

4. The economic competition for the US in the next decade or so isn't going to come from Soviet Russia, as Mr. K. likes to say, but rather

from Western Europe. While K. talks of burying us, the French, the British, Germans, Benelux, etc., are breathing down our necks in a production and sales race. If we are going to maintain the conventional gap between our standard of living and theirs, we have a lot of humping to do in the next five-ten years.

5.   The Common Market is an immense political-economic fact in Europe, will be one of the bases of a Golden economic Age for the Continent. Difficulties of gearing the Common Market in with the Outer Seven and avoiding a trade war will be handled without too much difficulty. The vision of one big market for at least 160,000,000 people will be too much for the British and their friends to resist. In addition, the biggest protectionists in the Common Market, i.e. the French, are now learning the lesson that they can get further with a wide trading area with modest tariffs than by hiding behind protectionist walls. Seen from here, the U.S.A. looks potentially more protectionist in the years just ahead than the Common Market area.

6.   US businessmen are very aware of the tremendous potential of this market, are flocking to Europe in great numbers. As one American banker in Paris said: "There are so many American business firms coming over here looking for French partners that my only worry is, will there be enough French firms to go around?"

In the countries I have visited, the old restrictive ideas and economic walls of the nineteenth century, the barriers between economic classes, the cartel-minded business thinking, and many such ghosts of the past are being blown away as people realize that a way of life, like the one in the United States (at least on the economic plane) is within their grasp – and fairly soon. This has myriad facets, results, and consequences, which I hope to spell out for you in research in time for the Yearend Review.

*   *   *   *   *   *

While in New York for TIME I wrote a number of major articles for TIME and LIFE.

For the May 25, 1959, issue of LIFE International, I wrote a major article titled: "*U.S. Invades the Common Market*". This was a very comprehensive article predicting that the Common Market in Europe would become a very important area for U.S. business and reporting how major American corporations were already gearing up to take advantage of it. In a way, the article also foreshadowed the recent phenomenon of "out-sourcing" of jobs, though not to Asia.

Earlier, in a 1954 article for LIFE on the U.S. economy, I had forecast that an incipient recession in the U.S. would turn out to be a small economic decline which, I am glad to report, turned out to be a correct forecast.

The Time Inc. promotion department used me as a speaker at a number of business gatherings. Sample title: "The World Challenge to American Advertising", delivered November 1960, to the International Advertising Association. Also, about that time, I was a panelist for Time, Inc. at a business meeting at the Waldorf Astoria in New York titled "The Great Forces Shaping Our Future". As I recall, at one of these appearances, my Mother showed up in a back row to watch her son perform.

When TIME published its year-end economic review in 1958, my broad-ranging report was issued as a separate booklet, after it had appeared in the magazine.

After I moved to FORTUNE as a member of its Board of Editors in December 1959, there were a number of very interesting assignments. The one I enjoyed the most was an article titled *"The Split-Level Soviet Economy"*, in the October 1961 issue. The magazine, perhaps for cost-control reasons, did not let me go to the USSR but I did extensive interviewing of experts in New York, Washington, and California including the Rand Corporation. I think it was on that trip that I spent a weekend with my nieces Amy and Emily who were studying in California -- an unforgettable time touring the San Francisco Bay area in delightful company.

The gist of the article was that industrial production in the Soviet economy received priority and was expanding very strongly. On the other hand, consumer goods and agriculture were not stressed nearly as much and therefore were lagging. The Soviet consumer received the short end of the stick while industry, especially defense industry, was expanding very strongly. This was Khrushchev's approach and, at the time of the article – October 1961 – it appeared to be working.

Among other articles I wrote for Fortune was a long inquiry titled *"How Good Are Mutual Funds?"* (June 1960). (This may have foreshadowed my working for Dreyfus Corporation about 20 years later). My conclusion in the article was that mutual funds were basically a sound investment and were destined for future growth. I am happy to say this turned out to be the case. The industry grew much more than could have been imagined in 1960.

In 1960, before I switched over from TIME to FORTUNE, I helped cover Jack Kennedy's campaign to win the Democratic Presidential nomination. In this connection, in June 1960 (before the nominating convention) I had a lunch appointment in Boston with Jack's father, Joseph P. Kennedy, the formidable businessman, ex-Ambassador to Britain and ex-Chairman of the SEC. At that luncheon (which Janet also attended), held at the Ritz-Carlton Hotel, Joe Kennedy for the first time disclosed that his eldest daughter, Rosemary suffered from mental problems. I believe Kennedy wanted the story to get out before the nominating convention, so it would not be a distraction later. At the same time, he told us that the family charitable foundation would devote major resources to find cures or treatments for mental illness.

* * * * * *

My life has been enriched by being a member of a number of journalism organizations. When I went to Washington in 1938, I joined the National Press Club and have been a member ever since (now a "Golden Owl" – member over 50 years and exempt from dues). I also joined the Cosmos Club in Washington about 1981, and enjoy its reciprocal memberships in N.Y. clubs. When we moved back to NY in 1958, I joined the Overseas Press Club where I have been a past Board member, a member of the Freedom of Information Committee and, for about a decade, chairman of the Club's Admissions Committee. I also belong to the N.Y. Financial Writers (used to act in their annual show), to the Society of Professional Journalists (SPJ-SDX) and to its NY professional chapter, The Deadline Club (ex-President), and to the Society of Silurians (veteran NY news people).

CHAPTER XV

TRIPS, TRAVELS AND VOYAGES

Janet and I did not wait very long after our children were born to travel together abroad. The greatest attraction was to visit Ines and Bernard Burrows in England, which we did every few years -- and many of our trips abroad were built around those visits. One time we did not visit them ** on our trip to the USSR ** Ines really was very angry with us. Our last trip during Ines' lifetime we did not get to London because we came down with severe colds or flu while staying in Brussels – after our 50th anniversary trip to Venice.

On each of these trips I kept notes of varying length and quality. On the Russian – USSR trip Janet kept very extensive notes – too long to be included in this memoir – but summarized in an article we wrote for <u>Newsday</u> which is reprinted in the Appendix to this book.

Full travel diary notes have been saved among my papers. What follows are brief summaries:

We took the <u>Flandre</u> to Cherbourg sailing July 8, 1955. Spent some time in Paris and environs, including Chartres, then by ferry to England to stay in the apartment of Joanna Oakes' brother Tom Rose and visit with the Oakes and Joanna's parents, the Roses, in the village of Churt. After an antiquing trip to such places as Penshurst, Windsor, Bray, Oxford and Farnham, and an evening at the Glyndbourne music festival, arrived August 1 at Steep Farm (Petersfield) to visit the Burrows. Stayed just two days, then off for the Cotswolds, the Lake Country, then on to Scotland where the highlights included the Kyle of Lochalsh, Applecross and the Spittal of Glenshee. We were so smitten with Glenshee that we even corresponded with the owners of the Dalmunzie Inn about possibly buying it – which, fortunately, we never did. For the excursion to the North, we were armed with advice from Bernard to stop at Jedboro and Melrose Abbey (which we did on the return trip to London), and from Col. Rose who suggested the steep drive to Applecross.

We also attended Highland games in Strathpeffer and of course, spent a couple of days in Edinburgh (though never got to Glasgow).

Back in London (via Fountains Abbey and the Stour Valley) we stayed at Barkston Gardens hotel where we were delighted to find a vase of white campanula dropped off by Ines.

Before sailing home, we bought a Hillman Minx car and shipped it with us – it served as our family car for several years.

* * * * * *

In July-August 1957 we went to Europe again, but did not go to see the Burrows because we did not want to impose on their hospitality. This led to a letter from Ines expressing very hurt feelings that we did not come to see her, even though Bernard had returned to Bahrein. On this trip we sailed to Cherbourg on the SS United States. Our good friends Bob and Mabel Cohen were also aboard – in second class, while we were in third class. We toured Normandy and Brittany in a tiny "Deux Chevaux". This was our first visit to Brittany where we saw a "Pardon", their native religious ceremony. Also stayed in the little town of Locronan where we bought a wooden statue of a saint (Saint Roche, Patron of Travelers) that was in our household until after Janet's death. Crossing the Channel to England, we went to Devon and Cornwall, where we bought the huge brass measure that Charles now has, and also met a Cornish woman who devoutly believed in extra-territorial creatures. In Locronan when the waitress brought around the seafood platter, I thought it was all for me – little did I know I was just supposed to help myself to a portion. Quelle betise!

* * * * * *

In July-August 1963, we took Jean and Charles, then 18 and 15, on their first trip to Europe. We started with a stopover in England to visit the Burrows at Steep where our children spent some time with their children, Antonia and Rupert.

In London, of course, our kids saw Billingsgate, Camden Passage, took a trip on the Thames and saw some plays.

Arriving in Paris (Hotel de Bourgogne et Montana, recommended by my college roommate Bill Crawford), we ran into my very old friend Fred Neal in the Paris Metro, visited the studio of Jane Kleiman (wife of another old friend Bob Kleiman), watched "Son et Lumiere" at the Invalides, went to Versailles and picked up our car, a Hillman Minx. The trip South through France included visits to Autun-Vezelay, the Pont du Gard, Avignon and Arles then to Italy and Pisa and Florence. A highlight in Florence, besides the major Galleries, was visiting the La Certosa monastery where they make a delicious liqueur, and sidetrip to the tiny walled town of Monte Reggione, Siena, and San Gimignano. This part of the trip also included Venice where of course we rode in a gondola and walked to the ghetto, and took a boat tour to Murano, Burano and Torcello. Then heading north for Switzerland, we spent a night on Lago di Garda, of course visiting my beloved Sirmione, the site of Catullus' villa.

After spending a night in the Tyrol at a picturesque town of Spondini we crossed the Alps via the Stelvio Pass, the highest in the Alps at 9080 feet, and with 48 hairpin turns. Then down to the town of Schuls in the Engadine, to spend a few days in an Alpine lodge in the village of Scaarl, one hour by jeep into the mountains where we used a chalet belonging to the family of Hans Geierhass, a Camp Treetops counselor. In that gorgeous area, Charles and I climbed the Scaarl pass to the Italian border – over 9000 feet altitude, and sighted ibex and ptarmigans.

From Scaarl, we drove through Switzerland to Zurich (via Lichtenstein), then into Germany and the Black Forest (where they made up place mats for us while we were having lunch).

In Germany, a main goal was to go to Heppenheim where Uncle Joe Schrank had been military governor at the end of WWII. Saw the cemetery where Joe made the Nazis dig proper graves for the slave workers brought to Germany by the Nazis. Also dinner with relatives of Franz in Karlsruhe in the Rhineland before heading West across France to Brittany. Highlights in Brittany were talking to fishermen in Kerrity, seeing women's beautiful Breton headdresses, watching fish being unloaded in Concarneau, eating fantastic crêpes in Locronan, and walking around the ancient castle of La Roche Jagu in the tiny hamlet called La Roche Derrien. At the end of the Brittany tour we took the ferry from St. Malo (with our car) to Southampton.

From Southampton, we drove through the New Forest to the little port of Salcombe where Charles (Chip) was scheduled to go sailing to France on a sailing vessel, the "Provident" recommended by the famous Captain Alan Villiers. At Salcombe, George took leave to fly back to the U.S. and to work at the Stock Exchange. From that point on Janet did all the driving in England with Jean and briefly with Charles after he sailed back to Salcombe.

Janet and Jean had a very adventurous trip. One place they used as a base was Simonsbath, from where Jean went horseback riding, and they attended sheepdog trials in nearby Porlock. There they met a farming couple with whom Janet became quite friendly, learning much native lore particularly about native foot clogs and weaving. Janet carried on a lively correspondence with this couple, the Davises, for quite a few months. Driving across the moors of southwest England, Janet and Jean also stopped at a "Panier Market" where all goods sold are brought in baskets, also chatted with several of the ruddy-cheeked local women known as "Devonshire dumplings".

Further along, they drove to Glastonbury and Wells to see the cathedrals, passed huge piles of thousands of drying sheepskins and willow thatch also set out to dry. At one point near Glastonbury Janet took a wrong turn and drove to a garbage dump, and in Cirencester was stopped by a cop for cutting in front of his car. Then through the Cotswolds and to Bath where they visited the Pump Room and the Roman Baths.

Returning to Salcombe to pick up Charles from his outing to Brittany, they spent an evening watching a traditional Waiters and Waitresses Dance. From there, they went (with Charles) to Cerne Abbas, a little town where the highlight was meeting the Martins, a family of roof thatchers, whom Janet got to know quite well. Then on to Stonehenge and Salisbury Cathedral from where the three of them drove back to visit the Burrows for one day, before embarking (with car) at Southampton.

* * * * * *

On July 24, 1970 we set off again for Europe, this time by air to London, where we stayed at the English Speaking Union. Much of the week we spent in London was taken up with research on our 18th Century Millbrook home "The Saltbox" at the London Record Office. While we did not find out much new about our property on Woodstock Road, we did unearth a letter at the Royal Geographic Society about a Col. Montresor, the mapmaker for General Cornwallis during the Revolutionary War. Years after the war, he appealed to the General to get him out of a jam with the War Office and the General did so. Montresor based his appeal on the fact that he had helped to fete the General for his return to London from the Colonies, and the General showed his gratitude.

In London, we attended a concert on the Victoria Embankment, saw Laurence Olivier in The Merchant of Venice, "Home" with John Gielgud (Noel Coward in the audience) and went to Kew.

After a week we rented a car and drove to Steep to see the Burrows, mostly visiting with friends of theirs, attending the Chichester Festival (Arms and the Man), a day at the Museum of Rural Life in Reading and spent time with Joanna Oakes' parents (the Roses), and visiting friends of the Burrows who were experts on dowsing and on ESP.

August 7, we left Steep and drove West with stops at Winchester, Salisbury Plain, Cirencester, the Cotswolds, then to Tewkesbury, Hereford, and into Wales. We stayed in a Welsh inn in a stone cottage in a loft bedroom reached by a ladder. The light worked by putting coins in a slot and a beam was so low that I kept bumping my head into it. But it was picturesque.

After a couple of days of exploring Wales, we took the ferry at Fishguard to Rosslane, Ireland, and stayed in Wexford. Then drove across southern Ireland to Killarney, the Ring of Kerry, crossed the Shannon by ferry to the Cliffs of Moher and Galway. From there we took the boat to Inishere in the Aran Islands, were rowed from the ferry to the beach in a carragh. On the beach landladies were lined up for paying guests. We selected Mrs. Kenealy, an excellent choice with a very interesting cottage full of guests including an Irish nun who was there to study Gaelic. We walked all over the rugged island, spent an evening dancing at a cailley (songfest), took a currach trip to nearby Inish-mann island, and another day a boat to Inishmore.

Returned to Galway, went to Loch Carrel for fishing (didn't catch any), then for a couple of days in Dublin, and wound up in Shannon airport for the flight home.

* * * * * *

Our next trip started August 22, 1974 sailing on the SS Leonardo da Vinci to Lisbon. Our itinerary took us across Portugal, northern Spain, over the Pyrenees via a little used pass, then drove Northeast from Pau through part of southwest France to the Dordogne and Les Eyzies area, then the Loire Valley and to Chantilly outside Paris. Then we took the ferry to England, for a delightful week with the Burrows, partly at their newly purchased house in Walham Grove, London, and at Steep. At the end of our visit I put Janet aboard the Russian ship Alexander Pushkin to Montreal and I flew home and back to work.

In Lisbon, one highlight was dropping off some books of Janet's for binding by a Portuguese bookbinder. When we eventually got them back in handsome (and very inexpensive) leather bindings, the lettering on the spines read: The Woks (sic) of Jonathan Swift. After sightseeing in Lisbon area, we took a rented car (Morris Marina), drove East visiting the beautiful university town of Coimbra (older university than Oxford), crossed the Spanish border to a walled city of Ciudad Rodrigo, stayed in an inn built into the Rodrigo castle. Then drove across the plains of old Castile visiting Salamanca, Avila, Segovia (the Alcazar) and to Burgos, where they were having a street fair featuring books that had been banned during the Franco regime, just a few years earlier. Next, we headed north to the Pyrenees, stopping in a very small mountain village called Ochagavia, where they were having a fiesta for the Virgin of the Snows. Janet dancing with drunken Basques in an upstairs café while crowds reveled in the town square. Then to the mountains, crossing the

Pyrenees via a small pass -- Larrau -- so little used that cows were sleeping in the tunnel as we drove -- elevation 8,000 to 10,000 feet, pass open less than 5 years. Then dropping down onto the verdant, much greener French side and on to Pau.

From Pau we drove north and northeast (one stop was the now-industrial town of Bergerac – where Cyrano came from) and along the Dordogne River to Les Eyzies in the heart of the pre-historic Perigord cave country. We stayed at an inn in the nearby town of Tursac where the chief event happened when we complained of bedbugs to Madame who ran the place. In front of a full dining room at breakfast she said, "Oh Monsieur, you don't understand those are "les mouches du vendange" (the grape harvest flies".). The other guests snickered at how she outwitted those dumb Americans.

Of course we visited the Cro-Magnon caves at Les Eyzies, also ancient caves at La Mouthe where an old crone with a kerosene lamp guided us around and we saw remarkable cave drawings of bison, deer, etc. Also visited other nearby caves – the Madaleine caverns where an entire village lived from pre-historic times until the 19th century.

Spent two more days touring sights in this lovely area – St. Cyprian, the castle of Beynac, the medieval art center town of Sarlat including a picnic in a garden spot near Sarlat that looked like the setting for a Renoir painting. Then polychrome cave paintings at Font du Gaume and Rouffignac, known for its 5-mile underground railway to see monochrome wall paintings and mammoths and bison (but mixed with modern graffiti).

Leaving the Dordogne Valley, we then headed for the Loire through beautiful Vienne et Touraine to Amboise, after lunch at Limoge. In this storied chateau area we of course enjoyed "son et lumière" at the chateau of Amboise and then at Chenonceau. Next day saw us at Chambord, then to Paris via secondary roads in the back country, and on to Chantilly where we stayed several nights (in the nearby industrial town of Creil because of no rooms at the inn in Chantilly). It was racing season in Chantilly and we enjoyed that colorful scene, but our main reason for going there was to inquire about our painting by Francois Clouet of King Charles IX. The curator at the museum said our painting was definitely of the period, probably a copy of the original ordered by Charles IX to give to a courtier. The curator was quite sure our painting was of the period because, he said, Charles IX was such a hated king that no one later on would have wanted a copy of his portrait.

Still staying in Creil, we took the train into Paris to attend Synagogue on Rosh Hashonah at the Orthodox Sephardic Great Synagogue. Also spent the next day in Paris sightseeing mainly on the Left Bank and turned in our little rented car after 1800 miles. On September 19th, we took the boat train and then the channel boat to Folkestone and London where we were warmly greeted by our friends the Burrows at their London house, 4 Walham Grove, in the Fulham section.

The next few days we spent with the Burrows at Steep, their country home – visits to Chichester Theatre Festival (Turgenev), to a museum of early farm buildings in the village of Singleton where Bernard was born, walks, Scrabble games and socializing.

Back in London for a big evening party at the Burrows, after a stopover at Wisley Gardens en route. Shopping in London, lunch dates, and an evening at the theatre to see a stupid farce I selected, "No Sex Please, We're British" – an embarrassing choice I made, but the Burrows took it in good spirit. To even the cultural score we also went to the Queen's Gallery in Buckingham Palace to see her pictures, to the Victoria and Albert Museum and to theatre for a play of their choice – Dr. Faustus.

Our next to last full day in London, the Burrows left for Steep and we went antiquing and clothes shopping. The final day we went to the National Gallery, then to Hampstead Heath for a walk and glorious views of London. All the while we stayed in the Burrows' house in Fulham.

Finally, on September 29th, I took Janet and her luggage to the Tilbury Docks where she boarded the Alexander Pushkin, a Russian ship, for a trip home via Montreal – and George headed for the airport to fly back to New York.

A bit of a crisis when Janet landed in Montreal – due to a business meeting, I could not meet the ship, nor could I contact her aboard. Finally, I asked a Montreal film executive (who had done a Stock Exchange film for me) to meet the boat and put her on a bus to New York. He also had to advance her some money because she was out of cash. The end of the story was that George waited for the bus in New York, but it arrived half an hour early – while George was in the coffee shop and it took a while for Janet and I to make connections. Anyhow, the trip to Europe was great.

* * * * * *

We flew to Britain to spend Christmas of 1976 with the Burrows. Supposed to leave the morning of December 23rd but due to mechanical problems we had to sit around the NYC airport all day and switch flights. Finally got to Heathrow December 24th where Bernard picked us up and drove us to Steep. Antonia, Rupert and Elizabeth George were there for the holiday. Christmas Day a traditional holiday dinner, with plum pudding. Next day we took a walk to the Poets Stone commerating Edward Thomas who died 1917 in WWI. Then I helped Bernard build a rose arbour. December 27th a big cocktail party with a dozen people staying on for dinner including John Brinton, a cousin of

Christian Brinton (friend of G's parents), and who formerly lived in Beirut. Overnight guests – the Frasers, she from New Orleans, he a retired diplomat. Next day we went to visit a very artistic couple, he a former architect who makes picture frames, she makes needlework pictures and collages. Then visited the Lubbocks at their handsome country house. They are the dousing couple we had met some years before.

December 29th we went to Brighton with Bernard and Elizabeth George. Dinner at Steep with the Hachards, he a landscape gardener, she a divorcee from Chicago. Thursday the 30th to London to the Royal Geographic Society for a lecture on underwater archeology at sunken cities of the Mediterranean. Later dinner with the lecturer, Nicholas Fleming, who was confined to a wheelchair, and his girlfriend a red haired Polish ex-countess.

On January 1st Bernard took us to visit a Stone Age farm on the Downs. Evening singing and playing piano and guitar around the piano. January 2nd to London to see an exhibit on Pompeii at the Royal Academy then on to Cambridge. Spent the next day in Cambridge, also visited Ely Cathedral, then to Ipswich where G. had business appointment for the N.Y. Botanical Garden. Back to London January 4 in time for elegant dinner at the Brintons in Cadogan Square. Next day to the theatre – Somerset Maugham's "Circle".

Our next to last day in London, January 6, 1977 shopping with Ines in Kensington High Street, then Janet went home to rest and George went off on his own. Bought Janet a bag, walked from Knightsbridge through Mayfair to Bond Street and the Burlington Arcade. Then taxi to the British Museum to see the William Caxton 500th anniversary exhibit, the Rosetta Stone and to re-visit the Elgin Marbles which moved twice in the Museum since I first saw them in 1935. Dinner in Soho with Antonia, then to theatre with Rupert and a girlfriend. Friday the taxi did not show up so Bernard drove us to Heathrow. Fast trip back to JFK, drove back to Millbrook where we found 3 to 4 inches of snow on the ground – being plowed by Jim Alexander, our next door helper.

CHAPTER XVI

RUSSIAN JOURNEY AND BEYOND

Our most ambitious -- and fascinating -- trip was the one we took to the Soviet Union (at Janet's urging) in May-June 1978.

Both Janet and I kept extensive notes on the trip – hers more extensive than mine, and when it was over I wrote an article on the theme of independent travel in the USSR (not with a group) that was published by <u>Newsday</u> (see Text appendix). Our trip included Leningrad, and surrounding areas, Moscow and nearby sights, then the Trans-Siberian Railway to Novosibirsk (capital of Siberia), then by plane to Tashkent, capital of the Republic of Uzbekistan. One of the many highlights there was visiting the ancient Museum city of Khiva, also Samarkand, Urgench and other storied places along the ancient Silk Road. After Uzbekistan, we flew to the Republic of Georgia where the highlight without a doubt was an arduous trek to the Caucasus mountain village of Mestia, which Janet was determined to see after having read about it in an English-language Soviet magazine published in the USA.

After Georgia, we returned to Moscow briefly and then home. The following are my notes written at the time – Janet's much longer notes (40 single-spaced pages) are also available in my files.

1978 Trip

Friday, May 12th: Chip and Betsy met us at the Botanical Garden with young Tyras, and drove us to JFK (where they gave us a knapsack as a going away gift which I still use). Our flight on SAS took off about 6:30 P.M.

Saturday, May 13th: At dawn we were over northern Scotland, then Copenhagen at 6:30 A.M. for one hour; then landed at Stockholm, where we rested in specially-equipped restrooms, until our flight to the Soviet Union left for Leningrad at 10:30 A.M. (NY time); 1:30 P.M. Stockholm time, 3:30 P.M. Leningrad time. Arrived in Leningrad 4:30 P.M. Waited two hours for luggage, due to busy arrivals, then private car to Leningrad Hotel on the Neva River. Dinner in the café bar of the hotel – Borscht and blinis.

Sunday May 14th: Morning excursion tour of Leningrad, brief walk on the Nevsky Prospekt. Taxi to hotel. Rest in the afternoon, then marvelous circus at night and back to hotel by street car.

Monday, May 15th: Morning to Pushkino by private car with beautiful, charming – "My name is Natasha" --. Walked through Catherine's Palace, with special shoe covers. Lunch at the hotel buffet, then to a department store to buy a suitcase, and look at shops. Took a streetcar home to hotel. Evening to the Metropole Restaurant for dinner. Shared a table with a Swedish carpenter and his Russian girlfriend. Meal was fair. Lots of lively dancing. Overpaid dinner – 20 Rubles.

Tuesday, May 16th: Morning excursion by private car to Petrodvorets with guide Nadya, a sweet young thing. Fountains in a park on the Gulf of Finland. Saw industrial suburbs on the way. Lunch in the hotel, then went by ourselves to the Hermitage Museum to see mainly the royal apartments and Russian furnishings. Stranded getting home, but saved by a friendly jazz musician. Snack at the hotel with a Dr. and Mrs. Sawyer from Cincinnati. Then to a ballet program at the Palace of Culture with dancers from the Kirov Company.

Wednesday, May 17th: Repack luggage, check out of room, leave bags in hotel checkroom, then to the Hermitage to see the Flemish paintings, including Rembrandt and the French Impressionists – fabulous rooms of Gauguin, Matisse, Picasso, etc. Then a boatride on the Neva River – warm, sunny afternoon. Then back to Leningrad Hotel to rest and have supper in the buffet with a retired Australian couple. Intourist car takes us to the railroad station where we were met by Intourist and escorted to our seats on the train to Novgorod. Left Leningrad at 7:30 P.M. for Novgorod. On the train I met two men, one was a drunken racing car driver who had a beautiful ring with a flower encased in thick plastic which he gave to Janet. Later on the trip he became very drunk and disgusting. But his friend who had made the ring was very nice and apologetic for his friend's behavior. We were met at Novgorod Station by a girl tourist guide. We stayed at the Intourist Hotel.

Thursday, May 18th: In Novgorod. In the morning, a three-hour guided tour of the old city, the Kremlin and market, war memorial guarded by Young Pioneers, music school and cultural center. Afternoon on our own we went to a monastery. Also visited an excellent museum of wood architecture, log farm houses, church, and other building from the 16th to the 19th centuries. At the monastery a young student named Sergei befriended us, took us to the bus, and followed us on his bike. We went with him and his friend to St. Sophia Church, and walked back to the hotel. Dinner at a restaurant in the Kremlin Fortress, sat with two women, an engineer and an economist. A Latvian man followed us downstairs. We talked in German but some Russians disapproved, and we left hurriedly.

Friday, May 19ᵗʰ: Caught the 7 A.M. train from Novgorod back to Leningrad, and went to the hotel. Tried to phone Moscow, finally succeeded after about six tries and got word of Fred Neal's whereabouts. Taxi to Peter and Paul fortress, visited the Cathedral and prison. Then a private bus driver gave us 'taxi' service to the Winter Palace Square to see a Pioneer parade. ('Pioneers' were like Boy and Girl Scout organizations).

(Vignette on the train): A suitcase was left on the overhead rack. The conductor empties and examines it. Everyone in the train laughed when he picked up a pair of pajamas from the suitcase.

We watched the Pioneers parade for a couple of hours, then stood in line for a taxi. But an Intourist man saw our Intourist shopping bag and got us a free ride to the hotel in a passing Intourist car. Nice dinner in the hotel, and we sat on a park bench until time to go to the train to Moscow.

Saturday, May 20ᵗʰ: Red Arrow train to Moscow, arriving 8:30 A.M. and then to the huge Rossiya Hotel. Brief visit with Fred Neal, then sightseeing through Red Square, the Kremlin, etc. Saw wedding couples at the Tomb of the Unknown Soldier and the Lenin tomb. In the evening, Janet was tired and stayed in bed, while George had dinner in the hotel, talked with a young couple (English and American) who just got off the Trans-Siberian Railroad. Then George went to see the excellent puppet theater and museum.

Sunday, May 21ˢᵗ: Moscow – morning bus tour of the city, including the Sports Complex and Moscow University and the Lenin hills. In the afternoon, Janet rested and I went strolling. One hour visit to the Lenin Museum, then to the National and Intourist Hotels, then to Red Square, and back to our hotel, the Rossiya. Weather glorious, ideal summer weather. In the evening, to the Bolshoi with Fred Neal to hear a Bulgarian Opera. Bolshoi theatre is magnificent. Left early to eat and talk at the Balalaika Room of the Intourist Hotel.

Monday, May 22ⁿᵈ: To the railroad station aboard Car #10 on the Trans-Siberian Railroad to Novosibirsk. We boarded at Yaroslavl station. We are in Car #10, compartment 7, bunks #13 and 14. Met a very nice Dutch couple on their way to Ulan Bator, Mongolia, and China by rail. Lovely little girls about ages 4 and 6 in the next compartment. Very pleasant trip. Early Spring greenery . . . endless hemlock, spruce, birch, larch, etc. To bed at about Kirov after learning how to make up our beds in the car. Restaurant menu in four languages but limited choice – only dessert wine.

Tuesday, May 23ʳᵈ: Woke up to a winter landscape; snow on the ground; endless woods, lots of lumbering, houses mainly wood. We give the little girls stick-on bird-and-flower seals. In return they give us candy. Arrived at Perm, about 10:30 A.M. Crossed the Urals, which seemed like low hills in the early afternoon. Saw a sign marking boundary between Europe and Asia. Reached Sverdlovsk in the late afternoon. Train starts early, and a woman thought her husband was left behind. A beggar on the platform is scolded by the woman conductor. The Dutch couple invited us for champagne and snacks in their cabin – Ruth and Jules Hosman. Then I treated us all to a champagne dinner in the dining car. The waiter laughs when Ruth orders fish, and we tried to figure out why.

Wednesday, May 24th: We wake up as we pull into Omsk. Enormous flat fields stretch to the horizon. Countryside much flatter and more fertile than we had expected. Many freight trains. Tremendous development work. Countryside is like the Great Plains in the USA, with large herds of cattle. Noon at Berabinsk. We buy ice cream in round cake-ring shape. Flat prairie countryside, with birch trees and huge state farms, including horse farms. Villages with mud streets and wooden shacks, each with TV antennae. Looks like the first settlements in American Western frontier country. Said fond farewells to our new friends, Ruth and Jules, also to Ludi, the fat jolly woman conductor (with the gold teeth), and to the male porter. Arrived at Novosibirsk at 9:00 P.M. local time, and drove to the Novosibirsk Hotel. Took a short walk around this large, industrial and commercial city.

Thursday, May 25th: Private tour of the city in the morning. Factories, schools, sports center with huge swimming pool, impressive war memorial – the old wooden houses being torn down and replaced by private garages. Our guide was named Anna. Shopped in local stores. Bought Tyras a pair of red shoes. Rested in the afternoon. In the evening went to the Opera, to see the Barber of Seville, a wonderful performance. Tenor superb, Basso excellent, chorus and acting etc. all top notch, also the orchestra. Amazing to find such outstanding Italian opera in Siberia. Late dinner in the hotel includes cranberries.

Friday, May 26th: Breakfast standing in a bakery across the street from the hotel. Visit in a private car to Academgorodok (Science Town), about 15 miles out. Our guide Olga had limpid brown eyes, especially when reciting figures on non-ferous output. We toured the academic town, which has about 20 or 30 special scientific institutes, all built in the last 20 years. Visited a special school for English – two classes.

In the first class, we sat up front and George talked to them about the solar energy building at the Cary Arboretum. The boys were interested, but the girls were not. Kids asked a few polite questions about books and movies, and we asked them a few similar questions. In the next class, we sat with small groups of kids of junior high school age. One girl showed George a book she was reading (in English) on collie dogs. She has one, a local champion. The boys asked me about radio electronics, short-wave (citizen-band radio), etc. Janet talked to the girls about music. Then back to Novosibirsk, and we took our driver, Olga of the limpid eyes, to lunch. Discussed race questions and religion. Then we went to the airport, and flew to Tashkent in an Ilyushin-52, comfortable and similar to a 727. Tea, etc was served. Fellow passengers were a group of Japanese tourists. The flight lasted from 5:15 PM local time to about 8:15 PM. In Tashkent, we were driven to the Tashkent Hotel, through town, all very modern with masonry architecture in mid-Eastern style. Clear, bright airy, and light. Lovely shaded boulevards, profusion of rose gardens, water trickling in conduits through the streets – "modern Middle East". Before bedtime, walked through the nearby streets.

Saturday, May 27th In Tashkent. A very special day. In the morning, I phoned the Uzbek Friendship Society, and we were invited to an ll:00 AM reception for delegates to a film festival meeting here from Africa, Asia, and Latin America. Walked to Friendship House, a large, old-style building with a large garden. Half-hour of speeches and responses, presided by a large, handsome but tough woman President of the Uzbekistan Friendship Society. Then adjourned to a beautiful Oriental garden for a program of folk dances by what seemed like a top-notch folk dance group. Lovely delicate costumed girls, also men dancers and an Oriental orchestra. Then a buffet tea, with snacks at a long table under the trees, followed by more dancing. Everyone received skullcaps and pins. In the afternoon, we had a private tour of the city led by two lovely young girls, practicing to be guides -- Lena, a Jewish girl, and her friend Bella, married but also about 22. High spot of tour was the central open market. In the evening, we visited a Circus on Ice in a splendid circular new circus theater. High spot was the bears playing ice hockey, which we had seen years ago when the Moscow Circus visited NYC.

Sunday, May 28th: Tashkent: morning by car to visit two kholkuz (collective farms) with our two girl guides Bella and Lena. First to a medium sized farm, 1500 hectares and 100 tractors, then to a very large farm (14,000 people, 3,000 hectares, over 300 tractors) – mainly Korean farmers, a prize farm visited by Brezhnev. Produce is mainly cotton, rice, and some silk. Impressive facilities at the Korean farm – big auditorium, sports stadium, their own hospital, etc. Met with the repair foreman at the first farm and the vice-chairman at the larger farm. Then to a shish-kabob lunch at the outdoor café of the Uzbekistan Hotel with our two lovely girl guides. In the afternoon, we strolled through old native market, looking and buying souvenirs. Janet meets a Jewish man from Kiev. They talked Yiddish and he almost cried with joy. Then to a teahouse for a snack. Five Uzbek girls invited us to join them. One is a medical student, one is a textile engineer. We talked by means of a phrase book. They gave us parting gifts – handkerchiefs. They insist on having a snapshot taken with us. Then to our hotel to pack for Boukhara.

Monday, May 29th: Tashkent to Boukhara. Up early to fly to Boukhara in a twin-engine prop plane like a DC3. Other passengers – English tourists on a Swan tour. Arrived about 10 AM local time after a 1 ½ hour flight. Went to Intourist Hotel on the edge of old Boukhara in a new, rapidly-developing area. We walked to the old town through narrow streets; kids ran up to us to speak in English and French, which they study in special schools. Then we walked through the old shopping area and had lunch in an outdoor café under a 300 year old mulberry tree beside a pool and fountains. At 2 PM we joined the Swan group for a bus tour of the city – the Ark, mosque and a historic tomb maintained by UNESCO with brickwork like basket-weaving. People here speak Tadzik (similar to Persian); also Uzbek and Russian. Fewer Uzbeks and more Persian-looking people. Saw an engagement parade with people blowing big horns. Amazing to find people in the streets who can speak English. Evening we walked to a movie theatre to see a film festival movie, a family soap opera from India with translation in Russian.

Tuesday, May 30th: Boukhara to Samarkand. In the morning walked through the heart of the city, shops and market, visited the Madrassa (Islamic school), now used for brass and copper handicraft, small booths off a central courtyard and people working in the court. Walked all through the bazaar, talked with a Jewish woman selling fruit juice. Bought gifts from native peddlers and shopkeepers. Broiling sun. Went back to the hotel, then in the afternoon drove in a private car to a nature preserve in the desert on an old Silk Road to Samarkand. Our guide, a young Uzbek girl, Mastoura spoke excellent English. Her grandfather was an Afghan. Drove about 25 miles out of town, past very developed collective farms, irrigated land, etc. Then on dusty dirt roads to a small hill crowded with tamarind trees and thorn bushes., a nature preserve for pheasant, jackal, and a couple of camels – none visible when we were there. Most interesting feature – remains of a man-made hill fortress perhaps 150 feet high with a commanding view of a flat valley now only ruins of an ancient moat and walls. Then we flew to Samarkand, 6-7 PM. Bukhara is a very dusty desert town, but Samarkand a lush, green huge oasis, a verdant fabled city.

Wednesday, May 31st: In Samarkand. Morning – private tour of the city with an American couple from Sheboygan, Wisconsin. Guide was named Nicholas, a student of English. Stunning monuments – the Observatory of Uleg Beg discovered in 1908 through a manuscript bought in the bazaar. Cemetery of Shahi Zinda, where Tamurlane's court are buried – fabulous, timeless mortuary row atop steep steps. Saw Uzbeks praying at the tomb of a cousin of Mohammed (in lieu of going to Mecca). Then a badly damaged mosque of Bibi Khanyan being extensively restored. Then the Registan – beautifully tiled huge complex of three madrasses – finally a lovely, peaceful tomb of Tamurlane. In the afternoon, Janet rested and George walked around in the colorful city food market. In the evening, George walked to the Registan to see "Son et Lumiere". The building facades looked absolutely stunning illuminated but the show was mediocre.

Thursday, June 1st: Samarkand to Urgench to Khiva. Up at 4:00 AM for a 6:00 AM plane to Urgench, via Bukhara. Arrive at Urgench 8:30 AM, stayed at the Urgench Hotel, a new two-story motel on the edge of town. Khiva: 76 Madrassas and 94 mosques, and minarets – Islamic center of the 17th to the 19th Centuries. Entered Khiva through the West gate, passed an old madrassa now remodeled into a hotel. Then to the tombs and mosques and madrassas in profusion from the 13th to the 14th Centuries. Also the Avicena Museum of Science, the Museum of local handicrafts, and the jail with a display of the cruelty of life in the old days. Khiva is a real, authentic Williamsburg of Central Asia. Also saw a complete caravanserai now used on Sundays as the bazaar market. Our guide was a lovely young man, Bahram. The three of us ate lunch in the teahouse of a new hotel, sitting at tea benches, Asian style. In the afternoon, rested, then ate dinner on the outdoor terrace of our hotel.

Friday, June 2nd: Urgench and Tashkent. In the morning, hired a car and our guide Bahram to drive to the desert about 20 miles each way from Urgench, west from Khiva. Sand dunes, tamarind trees, lizards, small cacti, thornbush, etc. Right next to the untouched desert was a new state farm being built. New brick buildings, while the sandy dunes were being reclaimed. Interesting contrast. Made a quick stop at the Urgench market where we priced some carpets. Then we flew to Tashkent with a planeload of Uzbeks. Delay at the airport because we had changed to an earlier flight. In Tashkent at the Uzbekistan Hotel we were invited by a reporter for Radio Tashkent English language program to be interviewed on our impressions of Khiva. We have no idea how they knew we were arriving in Tashkent. The reporter's name was Bachtiar Zufarov. Then he interviewed both Janet and George for his program "Salaam Aleicum", a friendship club of Radio Tashkent on the subject of how travel can help international peace and friendship. After the interview, we talked about dangers to peace, the arms race, etc. Dinner at the hotel and early to bed for an early plane to Tblisi, Georgia.

Saturday, June 3rd: Tashkent to Tblisi. Up at 3:45 AM to go to Tashkent Airport. Take off an hour late. Fly over seemingly endless, trackless desert, nothing but black sand. After two hours, reached the Caspian Sea – deep blue. Then soon appeared immense, snow capped mountains – the Caucasus Mountains. Tblisi – a beautiful city along a river, ringed by hills green and verdant from ample rain. Vegetation more like home in June – sycamores lining the streets. At the Hotel Adjara we step off the elevator to a gaggle of tall, black-robed orthodox priests, all staying on our floor, including the Patriarch in a blood-red robe. City tour at 10 AM with a guide Natasha (not like the Leningrad Natasha). A shy, rather plain girl. Up the funicular (George alone) to see a spectacular view, beautiful panorama – lovely city like a more Oriental Beirut. The city is strung out 14 miles along the river, at times through a rocky gorge with towering cliffs. Several beautiful new suburban apartment developments. The entire city looks very solid, clean and prosperous. Private houses are all stone or solid masonry and quite large. We noted many pinups of Joseph Stalin, still a very popular local figure. Trucks have bumper stickers to the effect that "Stalin Lives". Rested in the afternoon; in the evening went to "The Magie Flute" by streetcar at the Opera House. Well done, good orchestra and lead voices, but poorly attended. The orchestra and cast outnumbered the audience. The Opera House was lavish with marble, gold and crystal in Moorish-Oriental style.

Sunday, June 4th: In Tblisi. A fabulous day. Expedition by car 10 AM – 7:30 PM to the High Caucasus via the Military Road. The priests in our hotel said they would have a special Orthodox mass at the Cathedral at Mtskheta, the original capital of Georgia, for the installation of a new Orthodox patriarch. The church, founded in the 4th Century, built in the llth Century. Now filled with incense, priests, worshippers, choral singing. Patriarch dons a golden robe and crown. Exotic, very impressive. The choir was made up of the opera singers we had heard the night before. Then to the high mountains along the Military Highway. We follow the Kiera River, then Aragul River – castles, churches and watch-towers on the mountain peaks. Lunch at an inn at the base of the mountains in Pasanauri. Then we begin to climb on one of the most spectacular and roughest mountain roads anywhere. Well above the snowline, deep drifts still there in early June, raging torrents, washouts. Biggest obstacle – thousands of sheep, moving to summer pasture along this road, blocking traffic. We cross a pass at 7,837 feet – cold, drizzly, low, chilly clouds, then we descend to the Devil's Valley, only rocks, no vegetation, finally to the town of Kazbeki, near Kazbek Mountain (16,650 feet), with glaciers on both flanks. Tea in a deserted Intourist Hotel being renovated. Then back to Tblisi, tired but stimulated.

Monday, June 5th: In Tblisi. Gloomy Monday. Janet feeling that we couldn't go to Upper Svanetia (Mestia). Rainy and cold. George goes to the Botanical Garden alone, climbs up hill and down dale before he found the Director's office. Very cordially received by the Director, Prof. M.A. Gogdishvili, a nice man, a copy of Vol. 1 of Wildflowers of the U.S. on his desk. An English translator and a dendrologist led George through the Gardens. Very densely planted on steep hillside of a rocky gorge, still developing new areas. Lots of medicinal plant research going on, including a cure of baldness and psoriasis. No plans for the afternoon. Wandered in the shopping area; looked at unattractive souvenirs, back to the hotel, no rubles left, made an arrangement to pay for the dinner in dollars. Shared a table with a German couple and early to bed. At dinner, saw a group of men 'living it up' in the dining room who looked like the Georgian Mafia, probably labor union leaders.

Tuesday, June 6th: Left Tblisi and took train to Batumi. Sun is shining and our spirits improved. Early appointment with the Director of Intourist of the entire area re: visiting Mestia. He says the road is being rebuilt, no way to go there, 'not possible'. Janet told him there was air service, but the director said the plane is all booked up. "Come back next year". Then we went to the Georgia State Museum, showing historic development since the days of the cave dwellers. In the afternoon, hired a car, went to the Museum of Native Architecture. Very good German-speaking guide who showed us about a dozen houses from all over Georgia, wooden ones from west Georgia, and stone ones from East Georgia, furnished with implements, clothes, etc. Most unusual was a stone house with a wooden central cupola where everyone lived in one room with a fire in the middle. Authentic peasant houses, reconstructed and brought to the site. Eventual plan is to have 300 houses there. Then went out to the former capital to see, once again, the Cathedral at Mtshketa, which was quiet this afternoon, with a few of the faithful (young and old) lighting candles. Good chance to see the very early architecture, murals, carvings, etc. Then visited a nearby monastery and back to the hotel. Dinner at the hotel, then went to the train for Batumi on the Black Sea. On the highway, a man driving a horse and buggy – probably as a hobby. Natasha sees us off, and tells us a poem: "Always....always, busy. Never loved, never kissed, I'm a girl from Intourist".

Unpleasant surprise at the train to Batumi. We were put in 'soft class' compartment for four people. Janet very upset. Natasha finally gets us transferred to a compartment for two, but in "hard class"; sleep on benches with thin pads, dirty corridors, no service. Train stops every five miles, and the porter pokes his head in all the time because we were using his compartment. Janet doused the whole setup with DDT, but we survived.

Wednesday, June 7th: Arrived in Batumi 9:00 AM, passing tea plantations, palm trees, and holiday resorts on the coast of the Black Sea. Stony beaches, the sea a lovely light blue – oil tankers outside the port. Hotel Intourist on the seafront, faded but very comfortable, across the street from a beautiful seaside park and the sea. Walked through town, somewhat nondescript, Oriental late 19th Century style, lots of vacationers from Russia. In the afternoon, took a tour of the city, including the Botanical Garden and a trained dolphin show at the Aquarium and the beautiful harbor at the foot of the mountain. Very pleasant resort town.

Thursday, June 8th: Batumi and Mestia. Though refused in Tblisi, we got permission in Batumi to drive to Mestia. Up at 5:30 AM for a 6:00 AM departure in a car with our guide Gurami and driver, a war veteran named Gyorgi. Very long trip, 6 hours each way. Total time almost 15 hours. Went by way of Potiania Zugdidi. North along Black Sea resorts and tea plantations, then inland and start climbing into the Caucasus. The first sight was the Ingauri Dam, an incredible structure, partly finished, a key project of the Five-Year Plan. Then we climb along a road cut into the cliff face, just completed, with drops of thousands of feet. We follow the Ingauri River with endless hairpin curves and switchbacks on the 'road' – landslides and washouts at several places. The level section of the day's drive was about 100 miles and the mountain road 110 miles. After three hours of hair-raising drive winding up canyons towards the snow-capped Caucusus peaks, we came to villages with fortified towers and finally to Mestia, which has forty of these stone watchtowers attached to private farmhouses. Lunch in a small restaurant overlooking the Ingauri River, where the waitress spoke English and had worked on the SS Alexander Pushkin. Then we walked through the town, looking at fortified farmhouses. A group of little boys, then a 12 year old little girl greeted us in English. George gave them 'animal stickers'. They ran off in glee. The back streets of Mestia were a warren of houses, farmyards, ancient tools, such as boards for threshing grain, wooden pungs, and woven basketry, and pung bodies to haul stuff. Small but excellent museum in Mestia with ancient artifacts, a herbarium of native plants, and stuffed animals including bear, fox, and wolf. Ancient church displays, beautiful early icons, some of gold and silver from the 11th to the 13th Centuries. The museum director, a Georgian woman, gave us a book in the Georgian language about the museum. Then we headed down the mountain. We stopped for water, and a group of men working on a stone garden wall urged us to stop for drinks. Araki, cheese and bread, were brought out for us. George drank two toasts, and then we left. Down the steep mountain road, hillsides covered with brilliant yellow azaleas. Finally back in Batumi at almost 9:00 PM.

Friday, June 9th: Batumi to Moscow. Strolled through the Batumi shopping district in the morning – ancient workshops, coffee houses, very colorful crowded narrow streets, very Middle Eastern, a few men in white turbans. Left for Moscow by plane at 1:00 PM Moscow time in a four-engine prop Ilyushin. Arrive 4:00 PM, perfect flight. Intourist provided a taxi for the long ride from Damadero Airport, south of the city, through farmland and then enormous suburban apartment developments. To the Rossiya

Hotel, nice rooms. Dinner in the top floor restaurant, sharing a table with "Boris", a Siberian deputy from Krasnoyarsk, who was attending a meeting of Parliament. We conversed with a phrase book and a little German, drank toasts, signed 'short snorters' (dollar bills) and at the end he asked for George's, "Bull and Bear" tie clasp for a souvenir. He was stunned at George's monthly salary.

Saturday, June 10th: In Moscow. Shopping all morning first at the Berioska stores near the Novodivichi Convent, then at the Rossiya Hotel; found good gifts. We vowed to return to the Convent on Sunday. In the afternoon we toured the Armory in the Kremlin with a rather glum girl guide who rushed us through, but the collection was absolutely stunning, breathtaking richness of armor, carriages, jewelry, robes, etc. In the evening we went to the old Moscow Circus in a historic old, round building redolent of animals and sawdust. Stunning high wire, trapeze, acrobats, tumbling, wonderful trained dogs and seals – but no bears.

Sunday, June 11th: In Moscow. In the morning we met the Wisconsin couple from Uzbekistan at breakfast in the hotel. Spent the rest of the morning at Novodivichy Convent and a lovely quiet nearby park. Bought a painting of the convent from an artist working in the garden on a scene of "Smolensk" Cathedral. Orthodox services in the cathedral were filled but there also were young families crossing themselves and burning candles. We sat in the park next to a lagoon; a rainstorm then started so we had lunch in a nearby café and then took the Metro to Marx Prospect, and then to the hotel. In the afternoon Janet rested and George went to the Tretyakov Gallery, seeing mostly 18th and 19th Century realism, portraits, and historical scenes, etc.

Monday, June 12th: Moscow to New York. Up at 5:30 AM for the airport. Bad scene – our luggage was carefully searched and we were fined $220 for excess baggage weight – 20 kilos. Then to the aircraft, a TU 154A, a small jet half empty. One hour 50 minutes to Warsaw. G's first visit to that city in 42 years! Spent one hour at the Warsaw Airport, then on to Amsterdam, where we changed planes for New York, arriving at Kennedy Airport at 4:00 PM and home by 8:00 PM, tired but otherwise fine.

CHAPTER XVII

HOLLAND, ITALY, FRANCE AND ENGLAND (OF COURSE)

The following year, 1979, we traveled to Holland, Belgium and then another very enjoyable stay with the Burrows in England. (Ines had been very disappointed and a bit upset that on our Russian trip the year before we had not made a stop in England).

April 14, 1979, we flew KLM to Amsterdam, arriving Easter Sunday. Of course, we visited the Anne Frank house, then took the train to The Hague to see Jules and Ruth Hosman, the couple with whom we became friends on the Trans-Siberian Railway. Our impression was that they had gone on the Asian rail trek to try to repair their marriage. They traveled by train to Ulan Bator, changed to a Chinese train and went across China, flying back to Europe I suppose. But I guess it didn't work because we heard a year or so later that they divorced (no children).

In Amsterdam, we of course went to the Rijks Museum and other museums. Visited the Portuguese Synagogue and the Jewish Museum where there was a portrait of a Mr. Wertheim, a 19th Century Liberal leader.

Then, with a rented car, we went to Volendam (beach resort), Edam (to buy cheese), Hoorn, then across the Zuider Zee dike, through some very rustic farm towns and to Appledoorn, to see the home and museum of the Dutch royal family. Then a highlight of the trip – to the Kroller-Muller Museum in Otterloo with its stunning art collection set in a large park area. After that we went to Arnhem with its museum display of over 100 farmhouses and other rustic buildings. Then, a ferry ride across the Meuse to the village of America and to Mastricht in Belgium, a center of vast numbers of greenhouses for market gardening.

From Masstricht to Bruges, which we loved (I hadn't been in Bruges since 1935). Did thorough sightseeing including the Groningen Museum. Also saw a street called Biscayen Plats (any relation to Bisgeier?). After Bruges, went by ferry to Rotterdam, then Delft. We were headed for an inn run by relatives of friends of ours in Millbrook. This very elegant place called "Waterland" in the town of Welsen, was the height of luxury – a concert pianist playing Chopin in the drawing room, a bedroom the size of a ballroom with dressing room and huge bath – breakfast in the room served by giggling Javanese girls. Wound up our stay taking sherry with the Countess who owned the place, after walks through the gorgeous gardens of the estate.

April 23rd we took the ferry from Hook of Holland to Harwich and train to London and to the Burrows in Walham Grove. Next day, a concert at St. Martin-in-the-Fields, the National Portrait Gallery, then Christie's where I sold my fine Koran – a souvenir of wartime Cairo – and finally a Tom Stoppard play with Rupert Burrows and Serena, now his wife. Later, a lecture on Turkey, followed by dinner with the Turkish speaker. Also a visit to the Wallace Collection, a dinner with the Brintons (whom we had met before), then a drive after dinner to Steep, the Burrows' country home.

From Steep, we first went to Seven Oaks for overnight with a couple who own a crumbling family mansion with ancient, elaborate gardens; then to Sissinghurst to visit the beautiful Nicholson-Sackville West gardens. Later, on to Leeds Castle in Kent (restored by Kate Whitney's aunt), then to Sheffield – famous for its rhododendron and azalea plants on grounds designed by Capability Brown. After returning to Steep, Janet and I went by ourselves to Oxford. Of course, spent a lot of time in the Ashmolean, a recital at Oriel Chapel, visits to the Bodleian Library and Sheldonian Theatre – and Janet especially enjoyed time at Blackwell's bookstore (where she did considerable mail order business for years).

Back to the Burrows – another dinner party, then walks in Kensington where Janet found the house of Muzio Clemente, and to theatre in the evening. It was election day in Britain and Margaret Thatcher became Prime Minister while we were still in London. Back in Steep, more country walks, dinner parties, a trip to Bournemouth to hear Bernard speak about Europe, and George helping Bernard cut brush and do other outdoor work. Then on May 7, we flew back to the USA – another great trip abroad.

* * * * * *

Our next trip was in September and October, 1981, which covered Rome and southern Italy, then to London staying both with the Burrows, also in an apartment near Covent Garden loaned to us by David Banford (who had bought our house in Millbrook). I left for home October 18, however Janet stayed on in the Banford apartment on Endell Street for another fortnight.

We took an overnight flight on Alitalia to Rome, where we stayed in the small but very enjoyable Hotel Raffaele on the Piazza Navona. Among the sightseeing we did during a week in Rome were The Vatican, Sistine Chapel and St. Peter's; the Villa d'Este in Tivoli, Hadrian's Villa, Santa Maria Maggiore, San Giovanni in Laterano, San Paolo Fuori le Muri and the Catacombs. The most memorable sight though was the Ardeatine Caves where the Nazis killed and buried several hundred resistance fighters and Jews in what was originally a gravel pit. George had seen it at the end of World War II. Now it is an impressive monument to these martyrs. Another day after more Roman sightseeing we walked to the Jewish ghetto for dinner in a kosher restaurant. Our last day in Rome – shopping and strolling in the Borghese Gardents.

Took the Rapido to Naples where we saw the sights (including Posilippo which George remembers fondly from WWII), and a day's excursion to the island of Ischia. Picked up a car in Naples then drove to Pompeii and Herculaneum. Next, a hair-raising drive on the coast road to Amalfi where the narrow curves scared Janet out of her wits – so much so that on the return trip she went back to the mainland by ferry while I drove the car. In Amalfi, George left Janet for the day while he drove to the very beautiful, scenic mountain town of Ravello where Wagner had a home. While George was doing that, Janet staying in Amalfi watched a group of senior citizens doing peasant dances in a town square.

Our next stop was Paestum with its gorgeous, romantic Greek and Roman ruins (re-visited later with the Burrows). After that, a long drive first over tortuous back roads, then the Autostrada to Calabria where we found a small but beautiful hilltop town, Alto Monte, and watched a church procession through the town with a band and worshippers carrying a statue of St. Michael. The next couple of days driving through Calabria and other provinces to the hill town in southeast Italy of Matera, which I had seen briefly during the war. Liked it so much we stayed three days visiting the cliffhouses and the museum with Greek vases and local objects dating back to the Pleistocene. Particularly enjoyed the "Passegiata" when townsfolk stroll the streets in the evening to see the sights and greet friends.

A highlight of our stay in Matera was a side-trip to the town of Venosa in Apulia, where we became friends with a priest, brother Geraldo of the Order of the Holy Trinity. We toured the town with him and then met him later to tour the Holy Trinity Church, built in the 11th Century by the Longobards, on the site of an earlier church. Venosa was a stop on the Appian Way used by the Romans and later by the Crusaders on their way to the Holy Land. There also was a Jewish colony there, as evidenced by Hebrew writing and a Menorah cut into the stone walls.

From Matera, drove back to Naples to turn in the car and take the train back to Rome. At the station, George's wallet was stolen containing passport and airline tickets. Feeling completely stupid, George lined up at the Embassy in Rome next business day to get a new passport, etc., only to find many other experienced American travelers in line for the same reason.

A couple more days of sightseeing, shopping, etc., in Rome that included Yom Kippur. We attended services in the main Synagogue. George asked the man next to him what work he did. In Italian, he said "a miserable profession". When George asked what, the man said he sold postcards in St. Peter's Square. George tried to make him feel better by telling the man he was performing a public service. Later, we found an excellent Jewish restaurant not far from the Synagugue.

October 8 we flew to London, warmly welcomed by the Burrows and driven to Steep for lunch. During our visit, Rupert, Serena and their children Tom and Silva came down. We gave the kids Italian puppets and we all put on a puppet show. Played Scrabble, talked politics, and I worked with Bernard on his wood pile. Then to London where after two more days socializing with the Burrows we moved into the Bamford apartment in Endall Street. Spent several days shopping and museuming at the Queen's Gallery (a Canaletto show), the National Gallery (a show of Spanish Paintings), then dinner with Patrizia Schrank and her kids (Lennie being on a trip to Boston).

The next day, we made a trip to Dulwich to see the outstanding Picture Gallery collection, in the evening a play by Noel Coward, and the next day (October 18) George flew home. Janet stayed in Covent Garden another two weeks, returning November 2.

* * * * * *

Our next excursion started September 16, 1982, when we flew to Paris, later by train to Toulouse, from there through Cathar country and much of the Dordogne, staying partly at a country house owned by my Dreyfus client Howard Stein, then Beaune and Barbizon before flying to London for another visit with the Burrows and on our own in the borrowed Covent Garden apartment. Home October 22nd.

Our hotel this time was Le Ministère, walking distance from the Madaleine, recommended by Bill Crawford. During our Paris stay we saw John Kobler and Rita Stein, also Uncle Joe's ladyfriend (Chris Pizzoli), visited Rue de la Grande Chaumière where George lived as a student and Rue Jules Chaplain where Bill's mother lived. Excursions to St. Denis, to Monet's home in Giverny and to the Pompidou Museum.

Train to Toulouse where we picked up a car, then drove toward the Pyranees to visit Cathar country mainly the mountain town of Montsegue where George climbed to the top up a steep goat track while Janet waited at the bottom. On the way north passed through Tarascon (among other towns), then visited the Grottes de Niaux – also a smaller nearby grotto Grotte de la Vache. Difficult walking through the grottoes, enormous caverns, with a flashlight the only illumination. Driving on, through a little town called Mirlepoix where a wedding was in progress then via Carcassonne to a "Relais de France", the Chateau de Montledier near Mazamet, with a terrific room in a gorgeous restored chateau, with dinner featuring pear soufflé. Toured Carcassone, then Castres, a wool-weaving town with a museum of Goya's war paintings. Our second night in the chateau all lights went out but, even so, they served another fabulous dinner.

Next to Albi, a beautiful cathedral town also with an extraordinary museum of the works of Toulouse-Lautrec. Then to Cordes, a fortified city from the Middle Ages known now as an arts and crafts center. Next goal, the valley of the Lot (St. Cirq la Poupie) and so to St. Ceré where Howard Stein's house was located, and greeted by his manager, an American ex-patriate named Adele Feinstein...house a former presbytery of the church across the road, equipped with nun's beds, prie-dieu catechism desks, etc. From St. Ceré, drove to Castelroux-Bretenoux and the Dordogne Valley, also ancient caverns at Goufre de Paderac, discovered charming village of Carennac with a 12th Century church being restored. Another day went to Conques, another ancient unspoiled town, and later to Montal Castle, built in the 15th Century by a mother for her son who never returned from the wars. Finally, near the town of Autoit found a bubbling hillside stream that made a perfect picnic spot.

After that, we drove to Beaune where we met our friends the Kolkers. Drove 300 miles across Dordogne, Auvergne and to Burgundy, the most interesting sight in town of Roanne where people in Auvergne costumes were forming up for a costume parade. Toured Beaune, then to Autun to see the Ghiselbertus sculptures and a birthday dinner for Janet back in Beaune, about a month ahead of her real birthday.

After Beaune, drove toward Paris by way of Vezelay and spending the night in Barbizon where we bought a print at Millet's home and then to DeGaulle airport to fly to London.

Arrived in London October 5th for a great reunion with the Burrows and drove to Steep the next day. Country walks, outdoor work with Bernard, dinners with the Burrows children, grand-children and guests. Back to London for shopping, more dinner parties, theatre, visit to Lennie and Patrizia Schrank. Trips to the National Gallery and the Tate. Then we moved to the Bamford flat in Endall Street. Trip to see Hampton Court, visit the Courtauld Gallery, evening seeing "Rigoletto" (Jonathan Miller), a trip to Kenwood House and Park, tea with Barbara Miller and son in Covent Garden, evening at an organ recital in Westminster Abbey. Another day toured the Barbican, Tower Bridge and buying shirts nearby. More shopping, high tea at Fortnum & Mason, more theatre. Last day in London visited art dealers and bought Janet a print by Caspar Netcher of a woman making lace – back to the Abbey for Eventide, supper in Covent Garden and finally on October 22nd flew British Airways back to Dulles Airport.

* * * * * *

A memorable trip with Bernard and Ines to share a vacation cottage in the French countryside.

Flew to Paris June 3, 1985, then train to Toulouse to pick up a car and drive to "The Regis" in village of Montflanquin.

Landing in Paris, we went to the Albany, St. James Hotel where we had a reservation, only to be told "no room at the inn" and sent to a commercial hotel PLM St. Jacques in the distant 14th arrondissement, populated mainly by Japanese businessmen. Two days in Paris spent re-visiting my old neighborhood near Blvd. Raspail, strolling around Ile St Louis, Notre Dame, Les Halles, a Chopin recital in the Bois de Boulogne (Orangerie of La Bagatelle). Then June 9th, train to Toulouse to pick up our Citroen. Overnight in Toulouse then drove via Agen and Villeneuve-sur-Lot to our reunion with the Burrows at "The Regis" vacation house outside Montflanquin, getting there about one hour after Bernard and Ines arrived. Spent time together touring "bastides" (fortresses) (Gavaudun, Biron, Montpazier, Villereal,) and winding up at our local Montflanquin bastide, one of the most magnificent. Next day, we set out for Les Eyzies to see the recreated Lascaux cave paintings in Montignac. But, it being Monday, they were closed. So we drove back to Montflanquin but stopping to see a couple of medieval towns on the way.

Next day, went to the "Entre deux Mers" region (between the Garonne and Dordogne rivers) stopping to see ancient abbeys, picnic lunch by a river near a ruin, and other ancient towns on the way home. Another day drove to visit some very interesting scholarly friends of the Burrows. Then a day's excursion to visit some small churches in the Quercy forest. Along the way George found a wild boar farm and enjoyed teasing the boars through a sturdy fence. One day went shopping in larger town of Villeneuve that boasted a French version of a shopping mall, stopping en route to see picturesque medieval town of Pujols. Then a rainy day's drive to Moissac (via Agen) and Montauban mainly to see the Ingres museum showing how many drawing studies preceded his paintings. At the end of the day, back at "Regis" George went for a walk down the country road. A neighbor's dog took a bite out of his jacket (but not his leg). The farmwife with the dog said: "it's alright, Monsieur, we are insured". One day George and Janet by themselves toured to see the Biron castle, an art museum that used to own some important paintings bought by JP Morgan for the Metropolitan Museum.

After several rainy days, a fine sunny day for the four of us to drive to the Dordogne Valley and tour the fortress at Castelnaud – held by the English in the Hundred Years War – across the river from the French-held castle of Baynac. A birthday dinner (and poem) for Bernard in a charming local inn June 19th – then the next day a fabulous expedition to The Lot Valley – Cahors, St. Cirq-la-Poupie. The next day, the Burrows left – after many evenings of Scrabble games and great home-cooked dinners.

We left Montflanquin June 22 for the Poitou area – stopped once again at Lascaux but once again the caves were closed – for lunch. We pushed on, our route including a stop at Chassenau, a Gallo-Roman excavated town with extensive baths, etc. Overnight at a hotel in Montmorillon with one of the finest restaurants ever. After a visit to Poitiers, we detoured to see the chateau at Azay-le-Rideau, then to Loches, Montresor and Vallency, the former home of Prince Talleyrand – noted among other things – for gardens with peacocks and vast parkland. In the area we toured the Chartreuse de Ligon, the pretty medieval town of Loches on the Indre River and the chateau of Montresor, formerly owned by Polish nobility.

From Valency to Bourges passing a huge plantation of poppies which we were told were grown for medicinal uses. After visiting Bourges we continued on to Barbizon (our second visit there), staying at "La Charmettte" an inn where reportedly Elizabeth and Prince Philip spent their honeymoon.

On the last day in France we stopped at Vaux-le-Vicomte, then the palace at Fontainbleau and dinner in the town where we made friends with an artist named Francois Federle – and we wound up buying one of his paintings. The next morning (June 27) left for the airport, but we got stuck in traffic on the Periphérique – and George practically went out of his mind with frustration. But we just made the flight, after turning in the car – last passengers before the doors closed.

* * * * * *

We sailed to Southampton on the QE 2, October 20, 1986 (last trip before conversion to diesel). The ocean was very rough most of the way, and Janet was not well. Pleasant tablemates, a retired policeman from North of England and his wife. Also saw an acquaintance from the Overseas Press Club, Roz

Massow, and had drinks with Ed Newman, the TV newsman. Landed very late October 25th so spent the night at a Southampton hotel and took taxi next day to Rubens West in East Dean (near Chichester) our first visit since the Burrows moved there. Janet spent most of the week in bed, seen by a local doctor who conferred by phone with her doctor at home. George did a lot of yard work with Bernard, and went to visit Petworth once with the Burrows, home of the Seymours and Percys, with paintings by Van Dyck, Lely and Turner, carvings by Grindling Gibbon, gardens by Capability Brown. Janet got up to have dinner with John Irwin, the eccentric scholar, and for lunch when Leonard Schrank family came for a visit. On her birthday, Ines gave Janet a book of English proverbs and George gave her the set of place mats with scenes of East Dean. Rain practically all week. On November 4th, we all went to London, where Janet went to bed and the rest of us went to the theatre one night (Shaw's "Misalliance"), visit with Rupert and his family. Before leaving London, George took his father's fly rods to Pall Mall for repair. On November 8th we returned to the U.S. via Concorde to Washington and then on to NYC on another flight, after Janet had rested in a first aid unit at Dulles Airport. Home the evening of November 6th.

CHAPTER XVIII

NOSTALGIA IN PARIS, CRUISING ITALY, PAPRIKA IN BUDAPEST, CAVES IN THE DORDOGNE

In June 1990, to mark my 75th birthday, I invited Alanna to take a trip with me to Paris. My actual birthday had been the preceding December, marked by a family party. But when it came time for the Paris trip, Janet was not up to it physically so I invited Alanna. We were away June 8 to 17th, 1990.

Flew TWA overnight and stayed in Paris at Hotel Le Ministère, Rue de Serène. Started with a bus tour (after long naps), next day met Sarah Schrank (studying in Paris) and we all went to the Picasso Museum, Pompidou Center, Notre Dame, nearby monument to Jewish deportees, crossed the Seine to St. Julien-le-Pauvre, walk through Latin Quarter, coffee in Rue de la Harpe, crossed Luxembourg Gardens, paid respects to 3 Rue de la Grande Chaumiere (my old pension), dinner at Blvd Raspail, coffee at the Dome. Next day to Tuileries, toured the Louvre (Mona Lisa, Samothrace, Pei Pyramid, etc.), … Alanna shopped near the Pompidou – George managed to lose the package with her dress, so we got another one – later, met Margie Beinfeld on the Left Bank for dinner.

Following day to the d'Orsay Museum – our first look at this wonderful collection – then up the Eiffel Tower (including the office where M. Eiffel met with Thos. Edison), ending the day on the Champs Elysées.

Next, a morning at the Pompidou, then Montmartre and Place du Tertre and Sacre Coeur, later took the Bateau Mouche trip on the Seine – much of the day with Sarah Schrank. Aboard the boat, some Oriental gentlemen offered me a drink from a whiskey bottle so I proposed a toast to Japanese-American friendship. But it turned out they were Koreans – end of a beautiful friendship.

Than a day at Versailles, the palace, Trianon, gardens, Hameau, etc. In evening, dinner at a soufflé place in Paris recommended by the Kolkers.

Next, big shopping at Galeries Lafayette, then to Sainte Chappelle, walked across the Seine to Ile de la Cite, flower market, then Ile St Louis. In P.M. met the Beinfelds for dinner, strolled Ile St Louis, and back to the hotel.

Our last full day in France, took train to Chartres, including climb to top of the bell tower, then to Paris for our final dinner at L'Auberge de France on Rue Mont Tabor. Back to hotel on foot through Tuileries and Place de la Concorde. Flew home Sunday, June 17, dropped Alanna at Alan's in Boston, then was driven back to Lakeville.

* * * * * *

August 16, 1990 we flew to London via TWA where Bernard and Ines took us to Walham Grove. They stayed with us just for coffee, then they had to leave for East Dean where the next day Bernard was Chairman of a flower show. Janet and George stayed two nights at Walham Grove (including dinner with the Rustins), then on to East Dean for just one night. Back in London, Ian Prance (Kew Gardens) came to dinner. Next day the four of us went to Gatwick for the flight to Genoa where we picked up our cruise ship the "Orpheus". The highlights of the two week cruise were Napoleon's villa on Elba, side trip to beautiful Lucca, Pisa, Etruscan ruins near Civitavecchia (at Tarquinia), Naples (including George's side trip to Capri while everyone else went to Pompeii),Herculaneum, Paestum, Palermo, Greek temple at Segesta (near Trapani), Agrigento, long bus ride to Piazza Armerina to see the fabulous Roman mosaics, then Siracusa, Brindisi, Lecce, Ravenna, then finally September 4 our ship docked in Venice after a fabulous early morning ride up the Canal.

Most evenings aboard ship we had lively games of scrabble with Bernard and Ines. Among the most memorable sights were walking around the glorious Greek ruins at Paestum, watching an Italian wedding in the Palatine Chapel, Palermo, the mosaics at Villa Casale (Piazza Armerina), the mosaics at Ravenna, and then the spectacular arrival at Venice. After a day of sightseeing by ourselves, we had a farewell dinner with the Burrows at la Fenice Restaurant, adjoining our hotel. They rejoined the ship for its final leg to Trieste, when they flew to London. We went to Milan the next day where we saw "Swan Lake" at La Scala (choreography by Nureyev), before flying back to the U.S., arriving home September 6th.

* * * * * *

In late March of 1992, I made a trip to Budapest as part of my consulting work on public programs, for the Budapest Stock Exchange, financed by the Hungarian-American Enterprise Fund, an agency set up by Congress. Janet accompanied me on this trip. We spent a week in Budapest during which time we saw Antonia Burrows, went for a day to the horse country east of Budapest, attended a circus, strolled on St Margaret Island and generally enjoyed Budapest. Then by car for several days of intensive sightseeing in Vienna (including a nostalgic dinner at the Drei Hussaren Restaurant where, as a youth, I had seen King Edward VIII). After Vienna, by car to Prague where we did more sightseeing, one day in Carlsbad to see its faded glory, then a very saddening visit to the site of the Nazi showplace concentration camp at Theresienstadt (Terezin).

* * * * * *

In June, 1993, Janet accompanied me on my last trip to Budapest as a Stock Exchange consultant, to attend the dedication of the public information project I had set up for the BSE, along with Bernie Landou. Its official opening was June 2, 1993.

While I don't have contemporary notes on the Budapest trip, we were there for a few days, then flew June 3 to Paris (Malev Airline) for a pre-arranged meeting with Aaron who had come to Paris to spend a month or so using an apartment borrowed from a French teacher at his summer school, Middlebury College, Vermont.

First, a couple of days in Paris. Then the three of us by TGV to Tours where we pick up a rental Fiat. With Aaron doing the driving we then spent 5 days in the Loire Valley, drove through the Dordogne (with a stop at Oradour-sur-Glâne where the Nazis murdered most of the population), to our destination, the lovely Relais de Touron at Carsac/Aillac near Sarlat. We spent 5 days there which included a visit to the Lascaux caves (finally open when we could go). Then drove North stopping at Vichy. (Aaron very interested in the political background) then via Cluny and Beaune for several days at a small town of Arnay-le-Duc, then back to Paris where Aaron moved into his borrowed apartment.

From France we took the catamaran to England, stopped with the Burrows at Walham Grove then down to East Dean which looked tremendously improved since our previous visit three years before. Wound up with a couple more days in London, theatre ("Separate Tables"), etc. Catamaran back to Paris, dinner with Aaron and flew home July 1.

Highlights included visits to Chateau at Blois, then Chenonceau, return to Talleyrand's chateau at Valencay. Aaron and I drove to Chinon where Joan of Arc recruited Charles VII, (while Janet rested). Visited story-book castle of Vese which inspired "Sleeping Beauty", then in the evening to Chambord, dining facing the Chateau (and on the way home seeing a nuclear reactor for the first time).

After reaching the Dordogne, loved our stay at Relais de Touron. Went back to Les Eyzies and to the caves of LaMouthe where our guide was a rumpled man, the son of the old crone who had guided Janet and me there 19 years earlier. Exploring the Dordogne, we went to Domme, a town seized by Protestants from the Catholics in the 16th century – terrific views of the Valley. Another day Aaron and I went to La Roque Gageac, a beautiful fortified town on a cliff overlooking the Dordogne River.

After reaching Burgundy, and staying at Arnay-le-Duc, we went sighseeing in Beaune (especially the Hopital and Notre Dame church – (where a piece of molding fell on Lee Kolker), then to Autun to see the sculpture of Ghisilbertus. Our little town of Arnay-le-Duc had a museum for the beef-raising industry and, not surprisingly, the food at our little inn was of three-star gourmet quality.

Returned to Paris (with a hired driver because Aaron had a bad back). Aaron moved into his flat but he joined us for tea with Patricia and Delphine Schrank, Janet and I for dinner at Mt. Valerian, on a hilltop west of Paris, recommended by our chef-friend from Arnay-le-Duc, "Le Jardin de Camille". Fabulous, including a view of all Paris.

Our brief stay in London was highlighted down in East Dean by watching Bernard judge the local rose show, and strolling around Chichester while Ines and Bernard did "Meals on Wheels". During our visit little Owen Burrows was very sick, but we didn't see him (he subsequently died).

Dinner with Aaron back in Paris at Le Bearn restaurant where we had become buddies with the chef-owner (exchanged postcards later) and then flew home July 1.

CHAPTER XIX

ANNIVERSARY IN VENICE – ADIEU INES HELLO BERNARD AND JULIE

To celebrate our 50th wedding anniversary, Janet and I made a trip to Venice in September 1994. We spent about two weeks in Venice, then visited Leonard and Patrizia Schrank in Brussels and were supposed to go on to London to see the Burrows. But we both came down with bad colds and decided to fly home without the side trip to England. As it turned out, Ines died before we could make another trip to see her.

We flew to Paris September 17, back to Hotel du Ministère. Took a day trip to Chantilly to see the Clouets at the Chateau. Later, visited the Marmiton Museum in Neuilly to see Japanese prints. Janet tired, rested a lot, but I went out walking through old haunts. On September 21st, we flew to Venice (Hotel Fenice). A lot of sightseeing afoot in Venice. One unusual outing – took a gondola to Ca Rezzonico to see a curator to evaluate our Pietro Longhi drawing. Stepping into the gondola, I refused the arm of the boatman and managed to put my leg into the canal, up to the knee. Arriving at the museum with a wet leg, the curator saw us but never invited us to sit down – also he said our drawing was probably not by Longhi but another contemporary artist. Nonetheless later we had a lovely walk for lunch at the Zettere overlooking the Giudecca Canal – and explored the Dorso Duro section of town.

On another day, explored the ghetto, then to the Pieta for an exhibit of Vivaldi musical instruments. Next day, walked to the Arsenale via San Zaccharia, in the evening a concert of Vivaldi music at the Pieta.

Another outing – on foot to the Academia for the wonderful collection of paintings, also explored the Santa Margharita neighborhood where canal boats unload for the vegetable market.

Took a train trip to Bassano del Grappa and a taxi to Asolo, former home of Robert Browning and Eleanor Duse, also source of the little Asolo theatre now in Sarasota, Florida. Also saw the sculpture studio of Canova nearby. The countryside very mountainous (Monte Grappa), scene of battles in WW I between Italy and Austria. Also enjoyed seeing beautiful covered bridge in Bassano designed by Palladio.

One day we took vaporetto to the Rialto, to visit church dei Frari (Titian paintings) and Scuola San Rocco (Tintoretto murals). On the way home, talked our way into visiting the interior of the Fenice theatre, then closed for reconstruction (same theatre that burned down again in 1996).

Later, took a ferry ride to Torcello known for book-binding and carving of gravestones across the water from San Michele cemetery. On the way back by ferry we stopped off at Burano, other islands, the Lido and back to San Marco.

Then an excursion by train to Ferrara and to Ravenna. Enjoyed joining the locals for their evening stroll (the passegiata). Next day to St. Appolinaris, huge church on the edge of town with a mass in progress, fine mosaics at other churches in the town. While Janet recovered from the Ferrara trip, George went to the Correr Museum on Venice history, then crossed the Grand Canal to the Peggy Guggenheim Collection.

Janet quite sick and spent a couple of days in the hotel. While she rested (and was treated for her symptoms) George went out on expeditions. The longest was by canal boat to Padua on the Brenta Canal past many villas designed by Palladio. Highlight: Villa Pisani, 18th Century, rebuilt by Napoleon, and the place where Hitler and Mussolini had their first meeting. Back in Venice, I went to San Marco to see all the mosaics and the Loggia, the Ducal Place, the Bridge of Sighs and the dungeons, later by vaporetto to San Giorgio Maggiore by Palladio. Other sightseeing included San Giovanni E Paolo with its huge equestrian statue out front, also a canal trip to see an exhibit on the "Creches of Paris" with animated scenes and narration by Marcello Mastroanni.

Flew to Brussels October 9th staying with the Schranks. We did manage a car trip to visit Bruges with the Schranks, but we felt lousy, stayed in their house most of the time, cancelled the trip to London. On October 12th, we flew to Paris to connect with our flight home, getting back to Lakeville at 8 PM Connecticut time.

* * * * * *

In early May of 1995, Bernard and Ines came to the U.S. primarily to visit us – and also to see Ines' sister in California who died not long after.

The Burrows were with us 5 or 6 days. While no memo exists with all the details, they spent all the time with us (no interest in going to New York City). We took many walks together in the nearby hills, also had a couple of dinner/luncheon parties for them to meet some of our friends. Bernard examined Janet's garden very carefully and made a number of recommendations for plantings.

To quote a letter of May 17 Ines to Janet:

"We really did love every hour, the walks, the food and entertainment, and most of all the chance to chat and chat and exchange ideas and not only about shrubs and birds but about most aspects of all our lives – an inexhaustible subject."

One trip we made with the Burrows was to visit Olana, the Hudson River Valley home of the great 19th Century artist Frederic William Church. In addition to his landscapes of the Hudson Valley, Church was also well known for paintings he did of the Middle East including Turkey, which were of particular interest to the Burrows.

On the way to Hudson, N.Y. from Lakeville we passed through the little village of Hillsdale, N.Y. After hearing the name, Bernard commented "isn't that a contradiction in terms?" – a witticism I never forgot.

During their visit I took them on a climb up Bird Peak, the highest point on our property, with an overlook of the Hudson Valley. Just as we came over the crest of the hill to Bird Peak, we found a deer standing there – and I didn't plant it at that spot. Bernard was an expert gardening advisor – he staked our roses expertly, gave us a list of plants to improve the garden, advised us to put water lilies in the pond and devised a landscape plan for the driveway.

A beautiful visit.

* * * * * *

About two years later, on April 19, 1997, Ines died in Chichester after a bout of pleurisy. Bernard organized a memorial service for her June 24th, 1997 so we flew to London (via Concorde) June 21st and returned home June 29th, staying at the Westbury on New Bond Street. At the memorial service, George spoke on behalf of Janet and himself. The text of George's memorial remarks follows. While in London, we visited with Ines' son and daughter-in-law, Rupert and Serena, also went down to the Burrows' country home at Rubens West for a gathering of their family and friends. While in London we also went to see the newly reconstructed Globe Theater, and had tea with John Waterfield, an Englishman with a lovely Hungarian-born wife (long a US citizen) to whom Bernard had introduced us because they had a country home near us in Kent, Connecticut. We saw them socially quite a bit until she pre-deceased John. Then the Concorde home again.

* * * * * *

REMEMBERING INES – George's remarks at Memorial for Ines

My wife, Janet, and I met Ines when Bernard served in the British Embassy in Washington about 1950. Janet and Ines quickly formed a bond that led to a long-lasting friendship among the four of us.

Our friendship started with American square dancing. We introduced Bernard and Ines to this very American art form, at which they later became extremely adept. They in turn introduced us to Scottish country dancing. We will always remember the image of Ines, vibrant and thoroughly adaptable, enthusiastically practicing the square dance steps in the suburban basement of a government employee. In between the do-si-do's and the eightsome reels, the friendship between the two women flourished. Once Ines decided you were a friend, the trust was complete. For example, we recall that in those early days when Bernard and Ines had to go to California, Antonia was entrusted to Janet's care for a week or so.

After the Burrows went back to London and then to the Gulf, Turkey and NATO, the friendship was nurtured by an exchange of letters regularly between Ines and Janet – more than 45 years of correspondence, refreshed every two or three years with personal visits, mainly at Steep and later, Rubens West.

Janet and Ines came from entirely different backgrounds, indeed different worlds. Yet over the years they exchanged thoughts about their lives, their children, their political ideas. After Rupert arrived, they had even more in common – each with two children, a boy and a girl of similar ages, and parallel life experiences. As Janet says, Ines had an enormous capacity for friendship. No matter what nabob she was entertaining at the Embassy, or how many jars of vegetables were waiting to be preserved at Rubens West, Ines always had time – usually in the dead of night – to sit at her writing table and share her life and her thoughts with her friend of long-standing across the Atlantic.

And it encompassed more than the grist of daily life such as "how are the children?" or "what are you planting in the garden this year?" Ines wrote eloquently of the latest book she was reading, whether it was Trollope or Max Beerbohm or a Feydeau farce. Or she would comment on Janet's accounts of American dissension during the Viet Nam war years, or on the shortcomings of the modern educational system.

I don't think it would be indiscreet to share with you some of the comments in Ines' letters to Janet on the life she led in the Gulf and Turkey. In her first few weeks in the Gulf, Ines was hostess to a succession of dignitaries that included the C-in-C East Indies, the ruler of Kuwait, 2 or 3 Field Marshals, the First Sea Lord and, to her consternation, a Vice President of the United States named Richard Nixon. Ines' comments was "perhaps I am not truly a lady at heart, but I certainly have to try and pretend, pretty successfully, in this place."

She set high standards for others as well as for herself. Apropos of the square dancing and the Scottish country dancing they led in the gulf, Ines wrote: "I could smack some of the girls for not holding themselves straight…"

And soon after arriving in Ankara she wrote: "Diplomatic life here is, as you can imagine, a good deal grander than Bahrain because of all the other diplomats. One knows at once who is nice and who isn't – at least, I do, being me."

There was no stuffiness to Ines. In one letter she divulges an incident when she and Bernard were on their way to meet the Queen prior to Bernard's assignment in the Gulf. "In the car that we hired to drive us to the Palace", Ines wrote, "I decided that my second petticoat was too long and might show when I curtsied, so I removed it in the middle of Constitution Hill and tucked it behind the seat. I remembered to collect it on the return journey. Bernard pretended not to know me."

Such letters that Ines and Janet exchanged were the threads of which a continuous tapestry of friendship was woven.

Hardly a day went by in our household without some reference to Ines. Perhaps it was to recall the ratatouille she prepared when we shared a vacation house in the Dordogne. Or a hard-fought game of Scrabble the four of us played together, accompanied by Ines' pungent comments.

Ines was a remarkable combination of qualities. She moved in the highest diplomatic circles, and was very much a part of them, yet she was able to stand aside and see herself and her life objectively, and with unfailing humor. She took life seriously, but didn't take herself too seriously. She had so many interests, among them the guitar, and literature. Yet she was totally at home in the kitchens and gardens of Steep and Rubens West, and of course presiding over the dinner tables.

Speaking personally, I found Ines to have unique understanding of the role a husband can play in a marriage. Once we were discussing a projected trip by Janet and me to the Southwest of France. It was Janet's idea to follow the trail of the Cathars in the Pyrenees and then to go to the caves of the Dordogne. My task was to develop an itinerary. With typical insight,

Ines listened and then said: "Oh, I see, Janet says 'let there be a trip to the Southwest of France', and then George does the rest." How can one not love a friend with such perspicacity?

* * * * * *

After the death of Ines, Bernard formed a friendship with Julie Wimbush, widow of a British businessman who had lived many years in Hong Kong. Julie was an advanced amateur artist, hosted an art class in the studio of her home in Petersfield, and was a sophisticated, interesting, and attractive woman. Bernard lived with Julie until his death in May of 2002. Three years before that, in October 1999, Bernard and Julie came to visit Janet and me at our home in Lakeville, Connecticut. The following is an account of their visit that I wrote at the time.

Bernard and Julie (whom we had never met) arrived Tuesday, October 5, 1999 at JFK airport and were met by me and Ray McCarthy driving his sedan. Though she had never seen me, Julie picked me out from the crowd at the arrival gate. We reached our house at 8 PM where Janet greeted them and had dinner ready for the four of us in the kitchen. It was about 2 AM London time and they didn't go to bed until after 3 AM London time.

Wednesday morning Ellen came and strongly urged Janet to go to Sharon Hospital emergency room to get her elbow taken care of, which she had badly cut in a bathroom fall on Monday. It was getting infected, so I took her to Sharon around mid-day, and then the four of us had lunch on the porch.

Our friends rested; then late in the day I took them for a walk to the Overlook. It got rather dark before we came back, but they loved the view from the bench.

Thursday – Kolkers invited to lunch, held on the porch. But first thing in the AM garden room toilet overflowed. Bernard mopped it up and I used the plunger to fix the problem. Wednesday and Thursday before company came Bernard and Julie looked with great interest at the garden, which Janet had beautified with fall flowering plants before their arrival.

At lunch, Lee was in good form and there was animated conversation in which he expressed his strong view about environmentalists, support for Pinochet's regime in Chile, etc. Later in the day, I think our guests walked down to the driveway entrance and strolled around the grounds. Thursday night we had a late dinner at the Cannery in Canaan which was fairly good. At some point Janet and Julie played Scrabble (and again the next evening) and Julie won both times.

Friday, October 8th was a lovely sunny but cool October day. First, Janet had to go to the Doctor in Dover Plains for her elbow. Then we all went to the Fall Festival in Salisbury put on by the churches in the town. Bernard, an avid reader, pored over the bookstalls of secondhand books. He bought one about King Harold and I bought two – one on life in Renaissance France and the other a biography of Disraeli. Then back to the house to rest, and read before a lovely farewell dinner of the four of us at which George toasted the renewal of the old friendship with Bernard and the start of the new one with Julie. Late evening, Janet and Julie played their second Scrabble game.

Saturday, October 9th – Their last day and what a lovely day it was. Rain during the night but clearing by late morning when we set off planning to visit the Saltbox on Woodstock Road in Millbrook. Beautiful drive, fall foliage a bit late due to the midsummer drought and mild weather until this week, but enough red and yellow leaves so they got an idea of the fall colors in this part of the world. We drove down Woodstock Road and stopped in front of our old house, which looked absolutely beautiful and very well taken care of. There was a youngish British couple there visiting the owners who were taking pictures by the pond. We asked if the owners were around – Mrs. Bucheit came out of the house, a stout woman seemingly in her late 40's. Mr. was away for a few hours. It developed that they had been talking about us only the night before in discussing the history of the house and our research. It seems they keep a copy of our Saltbox history article in the guest room for delectation of their visitors. We had been telling B. and J. about the history of the house and Mrs. Bucheit confirmed all we had been saying about our research. With the Burrows watching with great interest, we inspected the old chestnut cellar door that had been chewed by a red squirrel once (later shot by George), then the old barn where Guinea fowl roosted, and then the large new pond where the new owners had put huge grass carp – nearly two feet long.

After leaving the Saltbox, we then drove to Smithfield, and up a steep back road to the Cascade Winery restaurant on top of a hilly ridge that overlooks the Harlem Valley. It was absolutely perfect. We lunched outdoors at a table with a lovely view of nearby fields. Sunshine and temperature were perfect, excellent meal, good wine for Bernard and me. We think they loved it. Then drove down the mountain past the old Barlow School to Route 22 and back to our house. A perfect day.

Then there was just time for a bit of reading, resting, packing, etc., before Bernard and Julie had to leave for the airport.

We were so stimulated by the visit, and so happy about how it went. As I said to Julie before they left, Bernard (and Ines when she was alive) always brought out the best in us, and that happened again this week with Julie and Bernard.

* * * * * *

Bernard died May 7, 2002.

* * * * * *

P.S. - In 2004 (I think) when Ruth and I were in London for a theatre expedition, we went down to see Julie at her home in Petersfield. While we were there, Julie did a sketch of me which I have framed and hanging on my apartment wall.

CHAPTER XX

AMERICAN TRAVELS

When it came to travel, as other chapters show, we were strongly drawn to Britain and Western Europe. However, we did make a number of trips in the United States, especially after Charles and Aaron moved West. After I had my own consulting business, we spent a number of winters in Florida.

Our first trip west of New York was to see Aaron and Wrenna in Madison, Wisconsin about two months after Vivien was born (August 2, 1996) and before her parents married (November 26, 1996).

In March of 1989, we made a trip to the real West, just for our own enjoyment. We took the train via Chicago to Santa Fe. Neither one of us had visited New Mexico before. We had a thoroughly enjoyable time renting a car and touring to Pecos, Taos and the Rio Grande Valley as well as Santa Fe. We returned home after about 10 days.

By 1999 Aaron, Wrenna and Vivien had moved to Oakland, California, which gave us a reason for our most exciting Western trip, in February-March 1999. Janet and I took the train cross-country to Oakland. The most dramatic part was crossing the Rockies above the Donner Pass and getting stuck in a huge snowstorm in sight of where the starving pioneers, in a similar blizzard, were forced to eat each other. Our train was plowed out after 5 or 6 hours and we made it down to California to see Aaron and his family. I had time however to tell Janet she looked good enough to eat – but that never was necessary.

At Oakland, we met up, by appointment, with our niece, Sarah Kramer who drove us on a delightful sightseeing trip down the California coast stopping at such fascinating places as Monterey, Carmel, the Hearst ranch at San Simeon, part of the Central Valley, then Santa Barbara mainly to see the Spanish mission and of course, Los Angeles (including a movie studio tour and a visit to the Getty Museum), then winding up with a week's rest at La Jolla, with a side-trip to San Diego and a couple of hours (quite enough) across the border at Tijuana. Sarah made a film of our trip together which I have in VHS format, including her interviewing Janet and great scenes of sights along the way.

In the 1960's and 1970's we had made several trips to the Okefenokee Swamp, always entering it from the Western side from the town of Fargo, Georgia. We had taken the children there also and we all loved the primitive beauty of the area. Janet and I also had made a swing through the Everglades, which I believe was right after World War II. So we knew Florida somewhat. However, in 1988-89 we joined up with Charles, Betsy, and their boys then in their young teens, for a trip down the Florida Keys. We stayed on Big Pine Key, where we chartered a fishing boat one day and on the other days went down to see the sights on Key West.

Driving north from that visit, Janet and I stopped off at Longboat Key to see our friends Lee and Betty Lee Kolker who were spending part of the winter there. We liked Longboat Key so much that we returned every winter for a number of years. At first we stayed in a motel on the Gulf, then rented an apartment, and in the last few years rented a house on a canal leading to the Gulf on Bird Key, which neighbors Longboat Key. This was all feasible for me because by that time, I had my own consulting business, mainly with Dreyfus Corp., and they were very cooperative with the idea of my doing the work in Florida for a month or two. As I recall, our last Florida sojourn was in the winter of 1997.

We also made one cross-country trip in the spring of 2000 to see Charles and Andrea in their Seattle home. We took the northern transcontinental route. Unfortunately, the most scenic part -- crossing the Rockies -- took place at night. As I recall, we went on by train to Oakland for another visit with Aaron and family.

CHAPTER XXI

THE SALT BOX

In the Spring of 1963, after I had been at the New York Stock Exchange for a while, Janet and I started looking for a country place outside of New York City.

Dutchess County, N.Y. seemed like a logical area, since we already knew it from having our children in boarding school (The Barlow School) in Amenia, N.Y. In May, 1963 the following ad appeared in the New York Times:

Millbrook – Secluded country colonial, 6 rooms, fireplace, bath, no heat, barn, small pond and 29 wooded acres, $15,950. Terms.

We drove up to see it Memorial Day, 1963 shown around by an agent (Mr. Johnson) from Guernsey Brothers Real Estate. As Janet wrote: It was love at first sight despite its sad, dilapidated, abandoned condition. A week later, on Jeannie's graduation from Barlow School (June 8) we paid $1,000. down and bought it for a grand total of $14,000, with just 30 acres at the start. Within a week or so we heard another 30 acres were available and we promptly bought those as well for another $5,000 – bringing that total for house, barn and 60 acres to $19,000.

We then hired a contractor, Alfred Dillinger, to install heat and otherwise make the house really livable – at a cost of about $5900 more. The work took Dillinger about a year and we moved into the house in June, 1964.

In 1971 we bought 8.8 acres down Woodstock Road (not adjoining) for $10,500 and sold it some years later to our neighbor Kate Haddad Whitney (grand-daughter of FDR), who in turn sold it for development after we had moved away.

Our house, named The Salt Box, was a treasure. When first looking at the land, prior to purchase, I went for a walk into the woods and in a few minutes flushed up pheasant and deer. That did it so of course we had to buy the place.

Subsequently we made other significant improvements – enlarged the little pond next to the house, built a second, bigger pond behind the barn, improved the barn and attached a garage to the old barn.

In 1971, we asked a noted architect expert on colonial houses, Daniel Hopping, to draw up a plan for enlarging our little Salt Box. He drew up an excellent plan, adding a large dining-sitting room and enclosed porch on the east side of the house, with a portico and extra bathroom etc., on the ground level. He also made sure to protect the old cistern on the south side of the house that had been there since Colonial days. We went ahead with the construction work according to Mr. Hopping's plan. That was done in the early 1970's but exact dates and costs have not been saved. In 1972 Hopping also drew a plan for a ground floor master bedroom wing, which we also built. Most of the work was done in 1973 and cost around $10,000.

My recreation at the Salt Box was to rebuild the old stone walls and chestnut stone-and-rail fences that lined the dirt road, Woodstock Road. This involved hauling old chestnut rails and some rocks from deep in the woods. Janet's recreation was to take care of the flower gardens. We also tried a vegetable garden but the deer and other critters made that impossible.

In the fields near the house there were many old apple trees. One of our great annual pleasures was to make cider in the Fall with apples we collected from our trees, using an ancient cider press that we had acquired. Our whole family and friends used to gather for this annual event.

The Salt Box started as our country place – weekends and holidays. However, when I resigned from the NY Stock Exchange to work for the NY Botanical Garden, we left our new York apartment (1085 Park Avenue) and moved full time to Woodstock Road which remained our home until we left for Washington, D.C. in 1981, and then in 1983 we moved to Lakeville, CT.

Many important events in our lives took place at the Salt Box.

The biggest event was Jean's marriage to Alan Fincke in June 1969. Jean and Alan had been living together in Cambridge and one day in May 1969 Jean called her mother and said: "Mom, how would you like to become a grandmother and a mother-in-law at the same time?" The wedding was about a month later, in the garden of our Millbrook home, alongside the pond, with the bridal couple barefoot (Alan wearing a Dashiki), a Quaker minister officiating, some 70 friends and relatives attending – including George's aging parents. By the couple's request, a quartet played music on Elizabethan instruments, a vegetarian meal was served.

Other years, we had the Schrank family come several times for Passover services at our house (as we had done previously in Scarsdale and at 1085 Park Avenue).

Many friends came to visit overnight or just for the day. One visit that didn't happen was from our good friends George and Joanna Oakes who were supposed to spend a night in January 1965. We had to cancel due to trouble with a septic tank. On the same trip from Washington to visit prep schools with their son James, the three were all killed on an icy road in New Hampshire. Only their daughter Diana, not on the trip, survived.

Of course we had several visits from other good friends such as Bob and Mabel Cohen, Muriel and Maury Miller (later deceased), from Washington, and Sidney and Freda Schreiber (Scarsdale). My sister Carol and her husband Mario Salvadori also visited one time.

One of our main interests while living at the Salt Box was researching the history of this little, remote country house. With the help of Clifford Buck, a devoted local historian, we researched deeds, wills, land records, family histories, etc., to fill out a picture of the house's history as fully as possible.

The Salt Box appears to have been built around 1792 (same year as the NY Stock Exchange started under a Buttonwood tree). The house was owned for 128 years by the same Quaker family, the Underhills, originally from New England and Long Island. We unearthed a lot of interesting information about the original land grants in the area, the foibles of the first owner, Edward Underhill, and the story of his wife Jerusha who remarried (and moved away) after Edward died at the young age of 41 (after 22 years of marriage and nine children). The place stayed in the Underhill family – varying in total acreage – until the last Woodstock Road Underhill, George T. Underhill, died in 1918 at the age of 90.

We did our research in libraries and records ranging from Dutchess County, NY to historical files in New York City. In 1970 we also did research in London, mainly at the British Record Office. We didn't find anything about the Underhills in London, but it was fun nonetheless.

A detailed account of our research was published in the Yearbook of the Dutchess County Historical Society Volume 52, in 1967.
Janet and I also did quite a bit of historical research regarding the land and buildings occupied by the Cary Arboretum, given by her will to that branch of the New York Botanical Garden by Mary Flagler Cary, grand-daughter of the noted financier Henry Flagler, a founder of the Standard Oil Company. This was published as a booklet by the Arboretum, titled *"Three Centuries on the Canoe Hills."*

CHAPTER XXII

TO WALL STREET

One day in the Fall of 1962 while I was at Fortune Magazine, I got a phone call from Ruddick C. Lawrence, the Vice-President of the New York Stock Exchange for Public Relations. I had known Rud as a Time and Fortune reporter/writer. This time he asked me did I know any one who might like to become Director of Public Information for the New York Stock Exchange. I recommended someone I knew with the Kaiser Corp., but later, as I thought about it, I was interested in the job myself – which may have been Rud's idea all along. Anyhow, he hired me in early November, 1962, as Director of Public Information and Press Relations. (I succeeded Paul Kolton who went on later to become President of the American Stock Exchange.)

Actually, I had in the back of my mind for years the plan that I would one day switch from journalism into public relations. While still in college, I once wrote an essay about myself saying that might well be my career path. No doubt, I was influenced by my family's friendship with Edward L. Bernays who, in the 1930's, 40's and 50's was probably the most prominent P. R. man in this country. Bernays (the nephew of Sigmund Freud) and his wife, Doris Fleischman, who ran their own P. R. firm, were social friends of my parents. I once tried to get a job with him, but that didn't work out, which actually was much better for my future.

At the time the Exchange hired me, they were involved in Congressional hearings on how the Exchange was handling its responsibilities. They wanted me to write "position papers" on various policy matters, which I did. After that, the job became a broad public relations function, covering all aspects of the Exchange's dealing with the media and general public.

One highlight time was the Exchange's 175th Anniversary in 1972, when we staged lectures and other programs at Lincoln Center as well as celebrations in Wall Street.

At the Exchange, I found myself in charge of a department with about 25 employees. We fed market news and comment to the press, also had a section that dealt with magazines, another for radio and TV, another that did internal publications and one that did films including our own documentaries. I also started two house organs, one called "Exchange Report" published for the membership of the NYSE and "At The Market" for the staff. An article about my work from "At The Market" appears in the text section of this book.

President of the Exchange when I started my job there was Keith Funtson, who launched the campaign "Own Your Share of American Business" which, in due time, became fabulously successful. When I came to the Exchange average daily volume was well under 10,000,000 shares a day. Now it runs to around one and a half billion shares per day. Other NYSE Presidents I worked for were Robert Haack and then James Needham.

Without a doubt, the most memorable experience of my time at the Exchange was the day President Kennedy was shot, and the ensuing weekend. I had been at the Exchange about one year, when between 1:30 and 2:00 P.M. on November 22, 1963, the first bulletin came over the wire of the Dallas shooting. Within a few minutes, the Governors of the Exchange stopped trading and of course we were flooded with inquiries from the media as to effects on the Exchange and stock trading. But that wasn't all. That same day, a financial crisis at the Exchange came to a head – the so-called "salad oil scandal". A member firm, Ira Haupt & Company, had extended large amounts of credit to a New Jersey stock trader, taking tanks of salad oil as security for the loans. But it turned out that there wasn't any salad oil in the tanks – owned by a character named DeAngelis. Haupt & Company owed a lot of money to other Wall Street firms, so their bankruptcy could bring down other brokerage houses. The NYSE Board met all weekend to resolve the crisis, which they did by putting together an emergency loan fund to guarantee payment of the member firm debts. I worked all weekend handling the news end of this crisis while the rest of the country mourned JFK. The Exchange remained closed Monday out of respect for the President and when trading resumed Tuesday, the Exchange crisis was resolved – without any public panic.

By Monday afternoon, when Janet and I happened to see some neighbors on the Upper East Side, they wanted to know what I thought of the situation. They were thinking of course of the Kennedy assassination but I thought for a moment they were asking me about the salad oil scandal.

During my period at NYSE the Exchange began to hold Board meetings at major out-of-town cities. I recall impressive and exciting meetings in Washington, D.C., Chicago and San Francisco which were memorable as well as great fun to work on.

It was during that time that I met and became good friends with Myron Kandel, whose varied news career featured, in later years, his investment commentaries for CNN. Another good friend was Dick Rustin of the Wall Street Journal, who retired to Florida. Also at the NYSE one of my assistants was Bernard Landou, who handled radio and TV. Later, when I had moved to the NY Botanical Garden and Bernie left the Exchange, I hired him as my assistant and, when I left the Garden he took over as P.R. Director. We are still good friends. My secretary was Rose Alter, a NYSE career staffer, with whom I am still in touch.

It was an exciting and very absorbing experience to be in charge of public information at the Exchange. My title when I began was Director of Public Information and Press Relations. In June of 1971 – some two year before I left, the title was improved to "Assistant Vice President". Those were the days when corporate titles were not idly handed out.

I enjoyed the atmosphere and friendships at the Exchange. When I turned 50 in December, 1964, the Associated Press sent out a bulletin on its New York wire that said: "Do not contact NYSE News Bureau between 4 P.M. and 6 P.M. They are having a blast for George Bookman in honor of his fiftieth repeat fiftieth birthday. List of casualties will be supplied as soon as available." When I resigned in 1973 to go to the Botanical Garden there was another and bigger blast for me at a financial district restaurant.

While at Fortune, I had written a chapter for Fortune's Guide to Personal Investing. The subject was "An Accent on Foreign Stocks". Later, at the NYSE, I wrote a major chapter on the New York Stock Exchange for a comprehensive book titled "The Stock Market Handbook", edited by Frank Zarb and Gabriel Kerekes (Dow Jones-Irwin). I also contributed to a book on investing by the President of the American Stock Exchange.

In 1973, I decided to leave the Exchange – "for greener pastures", as explained in the next chapter. I always found the Exchange job stimulating, exciting and mostly enjoyable. But once I moved from that job, the next phase of my career was just as rewarding. It included work for The New York Stock Exchange, though not as an employee or official.

CHAPTER XXIII

"GREENER PASTURES"

As mentioned earlier, by the Spring of 1973 I was ready for a change in my working life. The Stock Exchange was still fascinating, but there was now a new administration with Jim Needham as CEO and Gene Miller as Vice President supervising my department (and other departments). A key factor I think was that in 1963 Janet and I bought "The Salt Box" our enchanting country place on Woodstock Road in Millbrook, N.Y. We fell in love with the place and remained in love with it even after we moved away years later.

It so happened that the property we bought adjoined 1800 acres of land once owned by a very rich woman, Mrs. Mary Flagler Cary (daughter of the mogul Henry Flagler), acreage she left to the New York Botanical Garden. I got to know the NYBG officials including the President, Howard Irwin, who had plans to develop the Cary acreage into a foremost botanical research facility.

Dr. Irwin asked me if I would be interested in becoming Director of Public Relations for the Bronx-based Garden and its new facility in Millbrook. It made a lot of sense to me so I accepted the job in July, 1973 – and was promoted to Vice President of the NYBG, in June of 1974.

Not long after moving to the NYBG, we gave up our city apartment at 1085 Park Avenue and moved to full time at The Salt Box. I commuted by car three days a week to the Bronx from Millbrook (in a NYBG car), but always spent Mondays and Fridays working at the Cary Arboretum in Millbrook – just down the road from our house. That made for a regular pattern of four-day weekends in the country.

We also had "pieds-a-terres", sublet apartments of varying quality off Gramercy Park, and in the East 60's and 70's. Later we bought an efficiency studio on East End Avenue, but overpaid and lost some money when we sold it a few years later. But these places were enjoyable conveniences.

After moving to Millbrook, I drove down to the Bronx every Tuesday, Wednesday and Thursday morning and back in the evening in time for dinner. One morning I was speeding down the Taconic Parkway in my company car when a cop stopped me. I explained that I worked for the Botanical Garden, and he saw by my registration certificate that the car belonged to the NYBG. The cop said: "I have never been to the Botanical Garden. Do you think I could visit there sometime?" I assured him we would make him welcome. So then he told me he would write me up for a parking violation instead of speeding – no points on my license. Of course I thanked him warmly. As far as I know, he never called me at the Garden to ask for a visit.

One of the first things I did at the Garden was to arrange a big media event. I invented something called "The Ink-Stained Wretches Fresh-Air Club", had stationery printed, and sent invitations to every newsperson I knew at the daily papers, the financial press, etc. There was an immense turnout for a tour of the Garden and a party. One of those attending was Peter Kihss, one of the star reporters for the NY Times. He wrote a major article, which led to many others by the Times. It got to the point where one of my old P.R. colleagues, Chuck Storer, asked me: "Do you own the front page of the second section of the Times".

The other major event I brought about was a visit to the NYBG by Supreme Court Justice William O. Douglas. In his youth, the Justice had been a student at Columbia and had visited the Garden. And I had come to know Douglas on the famous hike he led on the C. & O. Canal to save it from becoming a highway. So I wrote to Douglas inviting him to come to the Garden, lead a hike through the unique Garden area that was still virgin forest land, and then deliver a lecture on Conservation. He loved the idea and accepted. A crowd of more than 1000 turned out to hear Douglas and, once again, the NY Times gave the story great prominence. (See article in Text section).

Later, when the Garden approached Enid (Annenberg) Haupt asking her to underwrite the restoration of the Garden's beautiful glass Conservatory, she accepted – and one reason she gave was that she was impressed by the excellent publicity the Garden had recently received. (See clipping in Text section).

Fridays through Mondays I spent at the Cary Arboretum in Millbrook doing public relations for that branch of the NYBG. And at one point, for almost a year, when the Arboretum was between Directors, I functioned as its Acting Director – running the place.

Of course, I learned a little about plants, flowers, etc., but certainly never became an expert. Nonetheless, I proposed to radio station WCBS that I do a weekend program on Gardening on that station. The result was "Garden

World", my program on WCBS that ran several times every Saturday and Sunday for nearly two years – until I left the Garden (See sample scripts in Text section). To get material, I interviewed NYBG botanists. Also my then-daughter-in-law, Betsy Cheney, helped me with script-writing.

At the Arboretum, I supervised production of a documentary film about that unique institution – its headquarters was one of the first buildings of such size to be solar heated, and most of the structure was built underground to save energy.

CHAPTER XXIV

BACK TO WALL STREET

In the Spring of 1979 Janet and I made a vacation trip to London and Amsterdam (see Travel chapter). On my return, to the office at the Botanical Garden I found a message to call Bob Bishop at the New York Stock Exchange. Bob was then V.P. in charge of the Member Firms Department, and I had known him well when I worked full time at the NYSE. When I called Bob he asked me if I would be interested in returning to the Exchange to work with him in the Member Firms Department, handling public relations. I told him I would be interested but only as a consultant, not an employee. Bob agreed to that and in the summer of 1979 I resigned from the Botanical Garden and moved back to the Stock Exchange with an office on Water Street where the Member Firms Department was located.

This worked out very well for me. I did a lot of work for the Exchange plus had my own consulting clients. These included continuing work for the Dreyfus Corporation, also writing and consulting for various companies including American Can, ghost-writing columns for Sylvia Porter, etc. I remained at the NYSE about 4 or 5 years, including a final year in the main P. R. office on Wall Street. One of the things I did while consulting for the Exchange was to write a booklet on self-regulation entitled "Just and Equitable Principles of Trade". Dated 1980, a copy is in my files.

In the mid-eighties, Howard Stein, chairman of Dreyfus, called me and said they could use more of my time. Would I consider moving up to their office in the MetLife Building (next to Grand Central) where they would give me an office which I could use for my outside clients as long as I gave priority to Dreyfus. Of course I said yes. When I left the Garden, I arranged that my successor there would be Bernie Landou, formerly on my team at the Stock Exchange.

Being headquartered at Dreyfus worked out very well. I had a thriving P.R. consulting business, with several steady clients. Our home was in

Millbrook (later in Lakeville), and I spent about 3 days a week in New York. My clients also included Time, Inc., the Business Roundtable, the Public Securities Association and the U.S. Department of Energy.

Having vacated our Park Avenue apartment some years before, we rented a succession of studio apartments in New York – on Gramercy Park, then in the East 70's and 80's. For about a year I stayed with my brother-in-law, Joseph Schrank, by then a widower with an apartment on West End Avenue and 86th Street. That is where I was attacked one morning on Broadway by a homeless man as I walked to a coffee shop. He managed to fracture a bone in my ankle. All he really wanted was to be in a city facility, and I watched from the coffee shop window as he lay down in the middle of Broadway until a city ambulance came and carried him away.

Later in my life as a consultant we bought a studio apartment at 88th and East End Avenue which was very pleasant and convenient but sold it in a few years at a loss during a brief slump in the real estate market. After that, and until I stopped working, I stayed during mid week at the Union League Club on 37th and Park Avenue, a short walk from Dreyfus at the MetLife Building. I had access to the Union League via reciprocity from my membership in the Cosmos Club in Washington.

The Union League was very pleasant and convenient. The only excitement came one summer morning when residents were awakened by a fire alarm in the building. We all trooped to the roof on a glorious morning and waited until the minor blaze was put under control by breakfast time, meanwhile enjoying lovely views of New York rooftops.

While on the subject of Dreyfus, I should also mention that the initial contact with Howard Stein, chairman of Dreyfus, was made for me by Dick Rustin, my friend at the Wall Street Journal. Howard offered Dick a job, which Dick declined, but suggested my name. Howard called me, we had lunch at his country home in northern Putnam County, and I started consulting work for Dreyfus in about 1977, while still working at the NY Botanical Garden.

One of the most interesting things I did as a consultant was to advise the Budapest Stock Exchange on its public programs. It came about through a Haverford alumnus I had known, Alexander Tomlinson, who had been a managing partner at Morgan Stanley, and a college buddy of John Whitehead, famed as head of Goldman Sachs, and – after 9/11 – chairman of Lower Manhattan Development Corp. Alec, after retiring from Morgan Stanley, became CEO of a quasi-government agency, the Hungarian-American Enterprise Fund. This was one of several such funds, set up by Congress, to finance the rebuilding of small and mid-sized businesses in eastern Europe all headed by John Whitehead. Alec needed someone to set up public programs

162

for the Budapest Stock Exchange. He went to see the Secretary of the NY Stock Exchange (Jim Buck), who suggested my name. Tomlinson invited me to dinner in New York and asked me if I would be interested. I accepted and in 1991-93 made six trips to Budapest, the last one at the end of May 1993 for the official opening of the Visitor Center at the Budapest Exchange.

To help me in this project, I recruited my old friend and Stock Exchange colleague, Bernie Landou. We created the visitors center with audio-visuals, printed materials and also made a film about investing. Bernie made about 8 trips, while I made 6. We enjoyed it thoroughly and the BSE was pleased. A letter to Bernie and me from Alec Tomlinson appears in the text section.

The Budapest project was done while I was still working for Dreyfus. When I asked Howard Stein if I could go, he readily agreed and told me to enjoy myself. However, one of his vice presidents, when told about it, said: "are we paying you as a consultant while you go to Budapest?" When I said yes, he said "isn't that double-dipping?" But the Dreyfus chairman did not seem to mind.

CHAPTER XXV

KUDOS

Among the benefits of being a correspondent/writer for national publications are the compliments you receive – often in writing – from public figures for the words you write about them.

Over the years, I have received my fair share of these kudos not just about my articles but also about some of my career moves.

When I moved from the Washington Bureau of TIME to become National Economics Correspondent in New York, George Meany, then President of the AFL-CIO sent me a nice sendoff note – I had covered his election as president and many subsequent labor stories.

In New York, one of my early assignments was to cover Nelson Rockefeller's campaign for Governor – and he responded with a personally written note of thanks.

Several notable people sent compliments for the way they were interviewed. For example, Robert Dowling (City Investing) said, in a note written some time after the TIME article about him: "I have thought of this one hundred times and intended when I reached the office to send off to you a telegram. This hardly seems appropriate action at this late time…A great many people have spoken to me – Henry Ford, Mayor Wagner, Governor Harriman, and countless others. All were very pleased, as I most certainly am."

Another was Sherman Fairchild, the aircraft manufacturer, who was very complimentary about an article I did about him. When I moved to FORTUNE he wrote: "I know that Fortune could use you because, in my opinion, they didn't do anywhere as good a job on my story as TIME did."

Also in my file is a personal note dated January 1958 from Thomas E. Dewey (after he failed to beat Truman for the White House), saying (among other things): "For a while I was worried for fear you had left because I made a wise crack suggesting that Time and Fortune should get together when they are thinking of doing pieces on Wall Street law firms…."

For the year end edition of TIME in 1958 I did an in-depth analysis of the outlook for the American economy based on interviews with at least 40 experts around the nation. TIME also published it as a special booklet, after updating, in early 1959. This report drew many favorable comments from notable people. One I especially prized was from Paul Hoffman, who had earlier run the postwar economic recovery program to benefit war-torn nations.

The extensive report I did for TIME in late 1958 on the economic situation in Western Europe also drew many compliments from business leaders. Among them, notes from Henry Alexander, the chairman of Morgan Guaranty Trust, Jean Monnet who really started the movement to unite Europe, Armand Erpf, a banker at Loeb, Rhodes whom I had gotten to know personally, Laurance Rockefeller whom I had also interviewed on US business for TIME, Lucius Clay then at Continental Can (after commanding US forces in postwar Europe), Arthur Burns (ex-chairman of the Federal Reserve Board, and William McChesney Martin, also a Fed chairman.

The biggest rave review of my European report was written by C.D. Jackson, Henry Luce's right hand man at Time, Inc. The first paragraph of his November, 1959 memo says: "You may remember that I was very enthusiastic last year about your U.S. business roundup. I am even more enthusiastic this year over the truly extraordinary job you did on Europe." In his memo he also asked me to give him some ideas on gold and the world currency situation for use in a speech he had agreed to give on the economic outlook.

During my years with TIME, especially those in New York, I was recruited to make several speeches to business organizations. These included: The Sales Executive Club, the American Bar Association (for a conference on continuing education at Arden House, N.Y.), the Public Relations Society of America, and the Export Managers Club. Each led to enthusiastic thank you letters, uniformly complimentary.

Then when I moved from TIME to FORTUNE there was another set of congratulatory letters.

One I particularly enjoyed was from the financial columnist Sylvia Porter. Her hand-written note said: "What wonderful news about your appointment to the Board of Fortune! Boy, has Fortune gained a lot the news service had! My congratulations, George! It couldn't happen to a nicer and more intelligent guy!"

Among others heard from about that move: Roger Blough, the chairman of U.S. Steel; Laurance Rockefeller, Frank Pace of General Dynamics (former Defense Secretary); Sidney Weinberg, the legendary chief of Goldman Sachs, Henry Alexander of Morgan Guaranty, Eugene Black, chairman of the World

Bank. And later, after I did the piece on the Soviet economy for FORTUNE, I received a very enthusiastic fan letter from Harry Schwartz who was then the New York Times expert on the Soviet Union.

CHAPTER XXVI

BACK TO JUDAISM

During these consulting years, I took a step in my own personal development by deciding to become Bar Mitvah – at the ripe old age of 77 rather than the usual age of 13.

As noted earlier, I came from a non-observant and basically a non-religious Jewish family. While always interested in religion, even toying in college with becoming a Quaker, I had no Jewish training. However, after marrying Janet, whose parents were from shtetls in eastern Europe, I was exposed to Jewish observances. Janet and her siblings were not very devout, but they did observe the major holidays, Hanukah, Passover, etc. Janet and I often held family Passovers in our home, celebrated Hanukah with the children, attended some religious services when we lived in Washington and New York.

When we moved to Lakeville, Connecticut we attended the little synagogue in Amenia,

New York, Beth David Synagogue. We liked the group, and were very impressed with the Rabbi, Elliot Stephens and Cantor Jerry Steiner (a NYC psychologist). I became active in the Synagogue, became vice president, and decided around 1990 to study for Bar Mitzvah, taught by the Synagogue's other part-time Rabbi, Harry Rothstein. My whole family was there for the ceremony June 20, 1992 including my two children Jean and Charles, and the four grand-children: Aaron, Alanna, Tyras and Zachary who took part in the ceremony.

My Torah portion was from Numbers Chapter 9, verses 1 to 12 dealing with the first celebration of Passover. My Haftarah reading was Zachariah Chapters 2:14 to 4:7. In my Bar Mitzvah speech I started off by apologizing for being so late to my Bar Mitzvah – about 64 years late. Then I gave what I considered a very frank discussion of my religious background and how I came to this decision. The text of my Bar Mitzvah speech follows.

BAR MITZVAH SPEECH
JUNE 20, 1992
AGE 77
BETH DAVID SYNAGOGUE
AMENIA, NEW YORK

I apologize for being late for this Bar Mitzvah ceremony......about 64 years late, in fact. I never achieved this milestone at the usual age of 13. Even though I did reach manhood, in the conventional non-religious sense, at the usual time, I do not consider that I became truly a Jewish man until today.

That calls for a word of explanation. My parents were both Jewish by birth. However, religion played little part in their lives. And I do not blame them for this in the least. They reflected the times and milieu in which they were brought up, when assimilation was the goal of many Jews in America, particularly German Jews. My father, a doctor by profession, never became Bar Mitzvah or confirmed, as far as I can determine. As a scientist, he did not accept any theory that could not be proven in a test tube or petrie dish. Thus, he rejected any form of Jewish religious practice, and my Mother went along with what he wanted.

I went through the various phases that were common among non-practicing Jews. Denial, shame, avoidance of the subject, and – for a little while – exploring other faiths at the Protestant boarding school and Quaker college that I attended.

I even remember writing a very sophomoric paper at prep school, which I titled in Latin "De Religione", in which I said that religious faith was all right for those who needed it, but (I thought at the time), I could make my way through life without it.

My attitude towards Judaism began changing after I married Janet and met her family, who were somewhat more observant than mine. After our children were born, we had to deal with the question of what religious training they should receive. I'm afraid we were not too successful at that, perhaps because we did not have enough conviction ourselves. My kids will still remember my unsuccessful efforts to conduct a family Sunday school for them, which was more comic than spiritually uplifting.

Other influences on my thinking were the Holocaust, and I suppose also the process of aging. The catalyst, however, for actually doing something about my Judaism was membership in this little Synagogue, Beth David. I was moved from simply worrying about my own ignorance of Judaism to taking action to learn more about Judaism by the warm and inspiring experience of being a member here. Janet and I were deeply moved the first time we attended High Holiday services here, by the spiritual leadership of Rabbi Stevens and by Dr. Jerry Steiner, who acted as both Cantor and lay rabbi of this Synagogue for many years.

Today, I have moved to affirmation of my Judaism. I don't think I am particularly unique in that. To a great extent, I am reflecting the times in which I live, just as my parents reflected their times and the attitudes of their peers. Though it took me a long time, I acknowledge today my religious heritage and affirm it proudly.

And that brings me to today's Torah portion. It comes from the Book of Numbers. The first few verses of "Numbers" deal with the first celebration of Passover. The Lord tells Moses to instruct the people of Israel, to offer a Passover sacrifice at the first new moon of the second year after the Exodus from Egypt.

There is a very special significance to me that this passage discusses Passover. For a Jew coming from the kind of ultra-reformed background that I did, one of the few Jewish traditions that was observed in my family, in particular by my grandparents on my Mother's side, was Passover. After Janet and I were married and had children, there was a bit more Jewish observance in our young family – (or Yiddishkeit, as my late brother-in-law Joe would have said). We lit Hannukah candles. On some years we attended services for Rosh Hashonah and Yom Kippur. But the principal family/religious occasion was Passover. If we were not very observant Jews most of the year, on Passover, at least, we were comparatively good Jews. We ate matzoh slathered with chicken fat, we drank the cups of wine, we ate bitter herbs, we ate in a reclining position, and the youngest among us always asked the Four Questions ... we remembered the bitter labors of our ancestors in Egypt and tasted the freedom that they later found in their desert wanderings and eventually in the Promised Land.

So at least once a year we were good Jews, and we still try to do that, as a minimum, even though the family ranks have thinned and become scattered around the country and overseas.

So Passover has a very special meaning for me. It was the principal remnant of my ancestral Judaism that I preserved over these many years. And now it has become a building block for trying to reconstruct a new expression of my own Jewish religious feeling. I hope that the members of my family who are here today – especially the grandchildren – will regard Passover in that way. Regard it, at the minimum, as your continuing bond with your Jewish heritage, and perhaps – if you are so inclined – use it as the years go by as a nucleus around which you can build your own religious faith, as well as maintain your family ties.

And now, in closing, I would like to thank those who have helped me so much to achieve this happy day.

My wife, Janet, for her patience and emotional support, including her help in coaching me in reading today's service.

Rabbi Rothstein for his dedicated teaching. Rabbi Stevens for officiating today and helping to open my eyes to the part Judaism could play in my life, and Dr. Jerry Steiner for being a good friend as well as a superb Cantor.

My two children and four grandchildren for their deeply appreciated participation in today's services.

And to my relatives and friends who have taken the trouble to make the journey to Amenia today to attend my Bar Mitzvah. To all I say: Shabat Shalom, Gut Shabbas

CHAPTER XXVII

MY DESCENDANTS --- SO FAR

At this point, I should tell something more about my children, grandchildren and great-grandchildren.

As already noted, Jean, my oldest child, was born in Washington on July 2, 1945 – while I was in Salzburg, Austria and I first saw her when I mustered out of the Office of War Information in September. She was named Ellen Jean, the first name honoring Ellen Downes, a very close friend of Janet's when Janet was a reporter covering the US Department of the Interior and Ellen was the assistant to Secretary Harold Ickes. (Ellen later married a distinguished Haverford alumnus and US diplomat, Brewster Morris).

When Jean was a few years old we moved to a house on Nevada Avenue, Chevy Chase, D.C. After a few more years, to Somerset in Chevy Chase, Maryland in the house built for us on Cumberland Avenue by my brother-in-law Leon Horowitz. Jean went to Green Acres School. Then to public schools while we were in the Washington area.

In 1957/58, when Jean was about 12, we moved to Scarsdale, New York and she went to Scarsdale Junior High. However, the atmosphere there was too competitive so we entered Jean in the Barlow School, a co-ed prep school in Amenia, New York. The headmaster there was Francis St John, from the distinguished clan of educators at Choate. Jean was much happier there. While she was still at school in Scarsdale, she went out for girls' basketball and I volunteered to help coach the team – despite my zero knowledge of the game. But the girls on the team were such experts they didn't need my coaching. In fact they won the championship that year and all took me out for an ice cream celebration afterwards.

From prep school, Jean went on to Boston University, where she met her first husband, Alan Fincke, father of her two children. Alan's father was a conservative Presbyterian minister. For a while after college Jean worked in a social service department of the Cambridge city government. When their kids were still quite young, they had had enough of living in Cambridge and nearby area, and moved to Winchendon, Mass. Really out in the country, where they bought an old farmhouse and 80 acres of land. In that area, both kids went to private schools.

Jean had two children with Alan – Aaron born January 12, 1970, and Alanna born May 7, 1973. Jean spent quite a number of years running a gallery in Winchendon for a renowned minimalist artist, Fred Sandback and also worked for the state government for a while. Later in Winchendon, she went back to school, got a Masters degree in education, and for a period of years was the guidance counselor for a junior high school in the area.

While in Winchendon, Jean and Alan were divorced – a friendly parting. Alan went back to the Boston area, Jean stayed in Winchendon and eventually met Dick Hoyt, who is now her second husband. Appropriately, Dick was also in the school system as a language teacher. At present, having sold the Winchendon house, they are retired and live in another old farmhouse with lots of acreage in Lubec, Maine.

Her son, Aaron, graduated from Hampshire College, Massachusetts. On a trip West he met (in Madison, Wisconsin) Wrenna Kolbusz (parents: Dennis and Wendy). They had a baby, Vivien, were married and moved first to Oakland and then to Paradise, California where they have a home on a country road. Aaron has a job as maintenance manager of a factory and Wrenna is studying for a degree in accounting. Vivien was born August 2, 1996 and is now a very bright and talented 12-year old, interested in acting and in writing. Her brother Jasper, also very bright, was born September 11, 2001 – which makes him now 7 years old.

Alanna went to a private high school in Massachusetts then on to Syracuse University where she majored in women's studies and journalism. Right after college she got a series of good magazine editing jobs in New York: Elle Magazine, US Weekly, In Touch and – in early 2006 – to Body and Soul Magazine, owned by Martha Stewart and published in Watertown, Mass, where Alanna is the Editor.

August 23, 2003 Alanna married Jack Muccigrosso, a good friend of hers from Syracuse. They lived first in New York City, then Hoboken, NJ and when she got the magazine editorship they moved to Belmont, Mass near her office. Jack has his own commercial design business working from home and at client's offices.

In September 2004 they had a son, Jonah, who was born in a New York hospital, and now goes to nursery school in the Belmont area. On May 22, 2007, a daughter arrived, named Eva Jean.

* * * * *

Our son Charles was born March 19, 1948. A year or so after birth, Charles (whom we called Chip in his younger years, at his request) had a blood ailment that required a complete transfusion. Fortunately the recovery was complete and he has led a vigorous and healthy life, though one kidney had to be removed a few years ago.

After early years at Green Acres School, a very good primary school in Bethesda, Maryland where Jean also attended, Charles went on to Sidwell School, an excellent private school in Washington. He didn't graduate because we moved to Scarsdale. After a short while in public school in Scarsdale, and after his sister had gone off to the Barlow School, Charles asked if he also could go to Barlow, and we sent him there. A good experience, I think, for he went on from there to Columbia University.

His stay at Columbia coincided with the famous anti-war riots of the sixties, where Charles' main role was to climb up the outside of the President's office to bring food to the student sit-ins. We got a phone call one night from Paul Marks, then Dean of the Medical School and a friend of ours, saying the police had arrested a number of students and taken them to jail – but don't worry Charles is OK. And he was.

At Columbia, Charles met Betsy Cheney whom, after a few years, he married. Betsy was the daughter of a distinguished biology teacher from Hartford, Connecticut (separated very early from her husband). After graduation, Charles got a job with the Lamont-Doherty Geophysics Lab of Columbia, made some exciting trips to the South Pacific and the Mediterranean. He quit to make a big trip with Betsy down to the tip of Tierra del Fuego. Later they moved to Washington, he got a job in oceanographic research and they married.

They had two sons. Tyras, the eldest, born May 16, 1977 and Zachary born May 5, 1980. The family first lived near Annapolis, Maryland where Charles worked for the State environmental agency. Then they moved to Cabin John, Maryland (a D.C. suburb) where, after some time as an environmental consultant, Charles became Director of the Marine Board of the National Academy of Science.

In the meantime, however, Charlie and Betsy's marriage broke up, due in part to some personal problems of Betsy's. Charles began to see a friend, Andrea Jarvela, who was working in Washington. After a while Andrea, who was from Alaska and the Northwest, wanted to move to Seattle. For a year or so, Charlie commuted when he could from D.C. to Seattle. Finally he decided to give up his job at the National Academy and moved to Seattle in early 2000 where he has lived very happily ever since and was married to Andrea in December 2004. He is now an official of the City of Seattle Highway Department, and a step-Grandfather of Andrea's 2 grandchildren.

Ty and Zac both attended and graduated from Sidwell friends. Ty graduated from NYU in New York where he was captain of the wrestling team and a BMOC. He went to work in New York at Bear, Stearns, the investment banking firm, later moved on to another investment firm in Los Angeles. After a few years there, he followed his girlfriend Nicole Giska to San Francisco where Ty is doing very well at a private equity investment firm. They were married in September 29, 2007.

Zachary attended college at the University of Maryland where he was outstanding, and was valedictorian of his class. From there he went on to Yale Law School, and then took a year out from Yale to get a degree in government affairs from the Kennedy School at Harvard. He graduated from Yale Law in the May of 2007. Next he took and passed the Bar exam, then went to Mexico on a Fulbright fellowship. While in college he spent his Junior year at Oxford, and Janet and I visited him there in the spring of 2001. That was the last trip abroad we made together and included a visit to Bernard and Julie at her home in Petersfield, Hampshire – about a year before Bernard died in May, 2002. At present, Zac is law clerk to a judge of the U.S. Court of Appeals in Pasadena, California.

When I celebrated my 90th birthday in New York with a party at the Lotos Club, Charlie and Andrea scheduled their wedding for the same weekend in December. They were married by a justice of the peace in my apartment at 200 East 66th Street (Apt. D1004) on December 4, 2004. Andrea's son, Michael Jarvela and his wife Kerry Keenan live in NYC also with their adopted son, Francis, and daughter, Lucy.

CHAPTER XXVIII

LAKEVILLE – SALISBURY

From our brief second time living in Washington, we moved back to the exurbs north of New York City – this time to a lovely modern Colonial at 199 Belgo Road in Lakeville, Connecticut - a village that is part of the Town of Salisbury, CT.

Our house had about 50 acres of land, mostly wooded with a low-lying swampy section, a pond and a swimming pool. The house was built in 1940 near a hilltop, with woodland rising steeply behind it to a wooded overlook with views of the Harlem River Valley in adjacent New York State. Actually we were only about a half mile from the New York line, and a few minutes drive from the very convenient town of Millerton, New York – with supermarket, movie theatre, restaurants, etc.

Our house, which we later named "Steepwood" in honor of the Burrows' "Steep Farm" in Hampshire, England -- had three bedrooms and three baths upstairs, and downstairs a living room, full dining room, a study and a guest room (with bath) which we used as a TV room. It also had a very large glass-enclosed porch off the living room, an all weather place for informal dining, etc. with radiant floor heating. When the house was sold in 2002, the new owners stupidly tore down the glass enclosure.

We bought the house in July, 1993, and I sold it after Janet's death in 2002. We paid $405,000 as I recall, and sold it for more than triple that amount. The place was bought by an Oklahoma oil man, Aubrey McLendon, the CEO of Chesapeake Energy Corp. (NYSE). He wanted the land, not the house, and eventually sold the house and five acres to Dr. Joel Danisi, who by coincidence had been Janet's doctor when we lived in Connecticut. Danisi subsequently divorced his wife and sold the house, but not before messing up our lovely gardens and abolishing the glassed in porch.

The pond was always a problem. It was supposedly fed from a seasonal stream up in the woods, but we always had to supplement that water supply from a pump in a field below the pond. That worked pretty well and kept the pond in decent shape year-round. The later owners totally neglected the pond and eventually I understand Mr. McLendon filled it in.

We had a good social life in the area seeing friends from Lakeville, Salisbury and our old stomping ground around Millbrook. Also we made frequent trips to New York City usually having a place to stay there, be it an apartment, a sublet or a club.

Among the friends in the area we saw frequently were Edith and Stuart Marks, John and Tilla Waterfield (a colleague of Bernard Burrows married the second time to a Hungarian woman), Bob and Mary Lou Estabrook (ex-Washington Post), Lee and Betty Lee Kolker (Purchase, NY), Bernie Landou and Dick Leonard (NY and Spencertown, NY), Nancy Kahan, Bob and Frances Low (ex-Pawling NY), and friends from our local synagogue, Beth David in Amenia, NY where I celebrated my Bar Mitzvah at age 77 in 1992.

As a steadfast Democrat, I took part in local political activity in the Town of Salisbury. I was a member of the Town Democratic Committee for most of the years I lived there, was appointed a member of the Board of Assessment Appeals where I served several years, and actually ran for public office and was elected – to the Town Board of Zoning Appeals. I served in those posts until I moved away from Connecticut. I established a good relationship with the Trust Department of Salisbury Bank, which continues, even after I moved to New York City.

The Lakeville area is a very civilized, pleasant place to live. We often went on long walks in the nearby hills, swam in the main town Lake Wononscopomac, enjoyed meals at the White Hart Inn and other good local restaurants.

Janet put great time and effort into gardening, sometimes with hired help. She planned and maintained beautiful flower beds in the gardens at the front and back of the house. Day-lilies were among her prized displays. When the Burrows visited us, she got excellent suggestions from Bernard who was an advanced amateur expert, and frequently judged rose show competitions in his home area in England.

The Lakeville-Salisbury area is very popular for older people who want second homes and do not want the glitz of the Hamptons or the seasonal crowds that go to Cape Cod, the Vineyard and Nantucket. Also an important part of its appeal is its easy accessibility to New York –two hours plus by car or by the commuter train from nearby Wassaic, Dutchess County, New York. A good third of the Salisbury population are retired people, another third perhaps people still working in New York or New England but using the area as a second home, and the remainder are the real locals.

Janet and I led very pleasant lives with our base in Lakeville. I kept up my consulting work until about 2000/2001, when I was about 87 years old, making trips into New York for a couple of days a week, often accompanied by Janet for trips to the theatre, concerts, etc. In those later years we often stayed at the Lotos Club on East 66th Street, a bonus of my membership in the Cosmos Club, Washington.

Lakeville-Salisbury was really a very satisfying place to live. Of course, we enjoyed the outdoors, Janet her gardening, I my hiking and unskilled heavy work such as pruning, cutting wood, hauling brush, etc. For me a main pleasure was to have a swimming pool just outside the door. Now that I am gone from Lakeville for about 5 years, what I miss most is the swimming pool.

CHAPTER XXIX

JANET AND OUR SHARED LIVES

There have been many references earlier in this book to Janet, my wife of 57 years, but not as yet a fuller portrait.

In a word, Janet was a remarkable woman. She was born November 2, 1917, in Brooklyn, New York to Louis and Fannie Bisgeier Schrank. Janet was the youngest of their six children (not counting a seventh who died in infancy). Her father came to this country from a shtett in Poland, Radomysl Wielki, when he was about 21. Her mother was brought here as an infant, perhaps one year old.

Janet's mother Fannie Schrank came from a family named Bisgeier. As the name indicates, her ancestors were Jews in the Bay of Biscay area in Spain and emigrated to Galicia in modern-day Poland at the time of the Spanish Inquisition. Janet's grandfather Bisgeier was a distinguished rabbi in New York, after emigrating in 1885.

Janet lived her earliest years in Brooklyn, then the family moved to the Bronx (Hoe Avenue, among other places). Louis worked in the garment trade, had little education (mostly in Poland) and never really learned English – spoke mostly Yiddish. Fannie grew up learning English. While not especially educated beyond early grades, she was much better adjusted to American life than her husband was. Their marriage, I understand, was arranged by her father, and was not a particularly happy one. After the children grew up and left home, the couple separated. Louis lived in a small apartment in Brooklyn, looked after by a couple of his sons. Fannie was more self-supporting in those years as a baby-sitter, and eventually moved to Florida where she appeared to find a satisfying life.

Janet went to school in the Bronx, but did not finish high school, and had some emotional problems in her late teens. However, she became an avid reader as a young girl, a frequent denizen of a public library near her home in the Bronx, the Woodstock branch which foreshadowed her later deep involvement with English literature.

In the late 1930's, Janet (with a little help from political boss Ed Flynn in the Bronx) got herself a job in Washington with a government agency. Also, at that time she married Louis Madison (Matisoff) – a marriage that lasted only a year or two. In the 1940's, as recounted in another chapter, she and George met at a Halloween party in Washington.

Janet was extremely well self-educated. That no doubt led to her very close friendships with women who had extensive educations – Ines Burrows, graduated from a top-drawer British "finishing" school and was the wife of an Ambassador; Mabel Cohen, a noted Washington area psychoanalyst, and Ellen Downes, assistant to Secretary of the Interior, Harold Ickes. Janet's interest in English classic literature, notably the novels of Anthony Trollope, led (partly) to her 50-year trans-Atlantic correspondence with Ines Burrows, which is now published as a separate book. This also equipped Janet to edit books for such friends as the botanist Dr. Ghillean Prance, later director of the Royal Botanic Garden, Kew; and of Joan Marks, a professor at Sarah Lawrence College. She also had a great interest in experiencing other cultures as indicated by our extensive travels in Europe and the Soviet Union. The trip to Russia, Siberia, and Uzbekistan was her idea. She also had a great love of music, played the piano much of her life, and listened to music (mainly classical) a great deal.

Janet held strong political views and did something about them – as evidenced by her reading aloud at the Riverside Church the names of soldiers who gave their lives in Viet Nam.

Unfortunately, much of Janet's later life was plagued by illness. The list is a long one. She suffered from stomach disorder in 1959, back trouble in 1970, castrocondritis in 1972, came down with pneumonia while visiting the Burrows in England in 1981, went to N.Y. Hospital in 1983 with blood pressure and heart problems, broke her fibula in a fall on our driveway in 1985 but also picked up a severe virus that same year, ran a high fever for 10 days the following year. In 1986 on another trip to England, she had symptoms of flu and pneumonia. In the summer of 1987, she suffered a TIA one morning at the breakfast table (while Aaron was visiting). The following year it was heart problems including periocarditis, then in 1988, castroncondritis and Tietz syndrome and that same year an operation for a stomach ulcer was needed. In 1989, her doctor diagnosed Shingles. Two years later she fell in our driveway, hurting her arm and ankle. The next year there was wrist surgery and in 1993 a small stroke. In 1995, Janet needed an operation on her shoulder, and in 1997 suffered from severe bronchitis and emphysema.

Along the way, she had two operations for removal of cataracts and in the fall of 2000, a coronary bypass followed later by removal of a carotid artery.

Nonetheless, despite all these medical problems, Janet remained active, and continued to travel both abroad and in the U.S. However, in her last year, her strength quite understandably began to fail. On the morning of February 19, 2002, she died at our home in Lakeville, CT. At that point, we had been sleeping in adjoining rooms. When Janet did not come downstairs for breakfast, I looked into her room and found her lying face down atop her bed. She had evidently passed away during the night, probably in the early morning. There was a brief funeral service at an undertaker's in Sharon, CT., then a funeral and burial service attended by the family at King David Memorial Park of National Memorial Park, Falls Church, Virginia where we owned burial plots. There is one set aside for me.

Our plots are quite near those of Herbert and Emily Kramer and Janet's sister Sylvia and her husband Leon. Incidentally, we once owned different plots in the same cemetery but when George Oakes, Joanna and their son were killed in an auto accident Joanna's family asked us to let them have our burial sites for that emergency, which we did, and later picked out other sites for ourselves.

As evident in Janet's book of letters to Ines ("Dear Ines.....Dear Janet"), Janet's relationship with her children went through different phases, some of them difficult. In the 1960's and 1970's particularly, Janet and Jean had their problems, no doubt a reflection of the "hippie" times of that period. This of course influenced Janet's reaction to Jean's first husband, Alan Fincke, who fully reflected that period of Timothy Leary, dashikis, Woodstock, etc. as spelled out by Janet in her letters to Ines during those years. Also, there was tension with Jean again regarding Jean's friend Dick Hoyt who became her second husband. To the credit of both women, however, they were more accepting of each other in later years and had a cordial friendship in the 1990's and until Janet's death.

Janet's personal views on the importance of striving, achievement, etc., were also evident in her relationship with Charles, particularly during the period of his wall-climbing protests at Columbia University. However, as he settled into a career and raised two boys along with his wife Betsy, the relationship between Mother and Son evened out and became close, as tradition would have it.

Indeed, in 1981, when Janet and I decided to leave Millbrook, NY we selected the Washington area as our next home, mainly because Chip, Betsy, Ty and Zac were living in nearby Cabin John, Maryland. Two year later, however, partly due to Betsy's emotional problems, and our own feelings of being Johnny-come-latelies in Washington (after a gap of more than 20 years) we moved back north, this time to Connecticut.

Basically, Janet had very warm, deep-seated family feelings. For example, we gave many Passover Seder dinners at our various homes, including the enormous reunion gathering in Lakeville in March 1991. She also made it a point to set up a fund for perpetual care of the grave sites of her father and mother, and spent a day touring cemeteries where Bookmans as well as Schranks were buried, and neighborhoods where the Schranks grew up.

I always enjoyed a warm relationship with Janet's siblings. Her oldest sister Minna (married to Philip Wiltchik) was very friendly to us, and I became quite close to her daughters Elsa and especially Amy (Gorman). Joe Schrank and his wife Edith, a school teacher, were also very cordial and, as mentioned, I shared Joe's N.Y. apartment for a while after Edith died. Unfortunately, their daughter Julie (Cuthbert) died early. Brother Charles Emanuel (Mannie) and his wife Ann were also good friends until Charles died and Ann moved to California where, unfortunately, she came down with Alzheimer-like symptoms. However, I am in touch with their son Bill and wife Bernice who lived a long time in Newfoundland and now in Nova Scotia. At other places in this memoir I have spoken of our friendship with Janet's sister Sylvia and her husband Leon Horowitz, both now deceased. Their daughter Emily Kramer and her husband continue to be among my friends, and Herbert has for years been my family lawyer. Emily's sister Marjorie remains in touch. Over the years, we saw less of Janet's brother Norman and his wife Pearl. In the Thirties, Norman became a functionary of the American Communist Party. After the fall of Stalin he broke with the party and became a right-winger. He was a decorated U.S. soldier in World War II. They had three sons. Tom, a banking official recently obtained the FBI record about Norman. Son Eric lives in Charlottesville, Va. where he is a builder. Son Leonard has run a major world financial agency called SWIFT from headquarters in Brussels Belgium, for many years, where Janet and I visited them a couple of times. My niece Emily Kramer maintains a very complete genealogy of the Schrank family.

The family Seders were memorable. We started our married years, when we lived in Washington, celebrating Passover at the home of Janet's sister and brother-in-law, Sylvia and Leon Horowitz. When we moved to a large house in Scarsdale we gave several family Seders there, but then moved to a walkup apartment in the East Seventies in New York where that was impractical. We also attended several given by Janet's older sister Minna and husband

Phil Wiltchik. Later, when we had our apartment at 1085 Park Avenue, we hosted a couple of elegant Seders. Then after we had our country homes in Millbrook, N.Y. and later Lakeville, CT., we gave Seders for the family who drove up from New York City for the events.

By far the biggest was the 1991 Seder at our home, "Steepwood" on Belgo Road, Lakeville. Brothers and sisters, nephews and nieces and their families came from far and wide: Lennie and Patricia Schrank from Brussels, Bill and Bernice from Newfoundland, Amy (Wiltchik) and George Gorman who were spending the year in Costa Rica, and several mezpucha from California, Maryland, Virginia, Boston and, of course, New York.

The Passover service was held in a large tent adjoining our house, insulated with bales of hay, and warmed by gas heaters. It was a cold, windy weekend and the tent could not be erected until the last hour or so, due to fierce winds earlier. Nevertheless, a good time was had by all – and our religious obligations were very well fulfilled.

Janet's oldest sister Minna was not there, neither was brother Joe. Both they and their spouses had already passed away. However, as I recall brother Norman and his wife attended, as did sister Sylvia, but without husband Leon, already deceased. Janet's youngest brother Charles (Mannie) and his wife Ann were also there and of course, a lot of the next generation for a total of 41 relatives.

Janet's birthdays were important to me – as was Janet. Recently I ran across two birthday poems I wrote to her – one for her 70th and another for her 80th. The poems follow:

TO JANET FOR NOVEMBER 2, 1987

Here's to Janet three score and ten
First in the hearts of her countrymen.
Doting Grandma, Dearest Mom and wife,
She's had a highly successful life.

Born in Brooklyn USA
She stopped in the Bronx on her way.
Lorimer Street, Kelly and all the rest
Helped to make her better best
Poetic school girl, outstanding scout,
She worked herself to go up and out.
Camp Laughing Water was no joke,
She even studied speech to be well spoke.

"Silver Pennies" were her true wealth
And love of music and good health.

In tender years to the Village she went,
To fight war and fascism was her bent.
Then when FDR sounded his appeal
To Washington she went for the New Deal
First WPA then Social Security hired
This young lady who never's been fired.

One Halloween she met a guy named George
From that meeting a bond they did forge.
They walked and they talked by the C&O Canal
Their chats were fascinating, never banal.

They even exchanged letters written in verse
As this sample shows it could have been worse.
"Dr. Madison's poetic pills
Are guaranteed to cure all ills."

When George sailed off for Africa's heart
She wrote great letters though they were apart.
Though the world was torn by war
Each to the other their heart did pour.
Their V-mail romance certainly flowered
Each by the other was overpowered
So George got leave in "Fourty-four
And off to America he happily tore.
On September 23 of that year
At Temple Emanu-El she became his Dear.

Janet got a job with United Press
And became a star reporter, no more, no less
War Production and Ickes were her beats
And she performed many journalistic feats.

But the Allies still fought for victory
So George had to return to Italy.
Months passed and in early July
Ellen Jean let out her first cry.
Janet the war-Mom did it all alone
A fact which her husband will always bemoan.

At last in September of '45
Their marriage truly came alive
Reunited on DC's 18th Street
How great it was, how very sweet.

Not long after they bought their first home
To Nevada Avenue the threesome did roam
Yet one more was needed to make things complete
A guy named Charles was born to our "Giet".

Next they moved to old Somerset
A house built by Leon they did get
Once again Janet did show
How well she makes a hearth and home go.
She raised her kids to be real "menschen"
With a lot of love and not too much tension.

She's made wonderful homes wherever she went,
That show her literary and artistic bent,
The list of houses is almost too long
To recite in this family song.
Seventy-first street on the East side
Then Park Avenue, a street of pride,
Then Millbrook for long happy years
Then Washington that vale of Republican tears,
And now to Lakeville in the Nutmeg State
A home she regards as very first rate.

The Salt Box in Millbrook she loved so true
It was a place whose charm just grew and grew
From the house where Jerusha Underhill trod
To Pan piping over the pond and praising God.

Wherever she went she was surrounded by books
Good friends fill all crannies and nooks.

Other good friends enriched her days
Cohens, Oakes, shed their rays,
Kolkers extended a friendly hand
And in England the Burrows swelled the band.

When loneliness held her in its fetters
She loosened its grip by writing letters. The written work is her touchstone, her pet,
Correspondence to give, correspondence to get.

So there you have a portrait of Janet S.B.
A self-made woman who's rare as can be,
Loved by her husband, her kids and the tots.
Hip hip hooray let's fire some shots,
For today we observe the threescore and ten
Of a lady who's precious to women and men.
Happy Birthday, Janet
Love, George

TO JANET – ON COMPLETING 8 DECADES
On the 80th birthday of Janet née Schrank
I have her very much to thank
For being my friend these 53 years For being matriarch of her tribe of dears:
Two children, four quite grand,
And one great-grandkid has joined the band.
For decades Janet's kept me on my toes
She's guided me through joys and woes,
Janet Bookman's wondrous pills
Are guaranteed to cure all ills.
I wish I'd known her from Day One
Instead just after 27 years were done.
So in front of witnesses this I say,
Long life to my wife – hip, hip hooray!
With much love,
George   November 1, 1997

Anniversaries were also occasions to be celebrated and none more so than our Fiftieth in September, 1994. For that event, we made a trip to Venice staying about two weeks and having a lovely, sentimental time – except at the end when Janet came down with a bad chest infection. Details of the anniversary visit are in the Chapter titled "Anniversary in Venice". (Chapter XIX)

It must be obvious that Janet was not an easy person to live with. Her standards for people around her – friends, acquaintances, children, and husband – were extremely high and not easy to live up to. Certainly, I did not measure up to those standards some of the time. However, it is my belief that basically Janet and I had a good understanding. Certainly, we had lives together that were enjoyable and rewarding most of the time. Despite ups and downs, I stayed with her and she stayed with me – four years of friendship before marriage, almost a year of separation at the start of the marriage due to the war, and a total of 57 years of marriage. Basically, I found the relationship very rewarding and I think Janet must have as well. I know it enriched my life in many ways, broadened me intellectually, led to friendships and outside interests that I might not have otherwise experienced (music, Russian travel, etc.). Though I have now gone on to another emotional relationship, and to other life experiences, I cherish the days and years with Janet and the family we raised together.

CHAPTER XXX

RUTH

Not long after Janet's death, a very old friend, Ruth Bowman, re-entered my life and has been a vital part of it ever since. More than 45 years ago, actually at a party in December of 1961, I met an attractive, interesting woman named Ruth Gurin. The party was at the apartment of Harry and Margery Kahn in New York. Harry is someone I had known since my early twenties, first in New York as young men both working in Wall Street, then when he worked for Paul Hoffman (European Recovery Administration) in Washington, and later in New York again. Once Charles went on a blind date with their daughter, Susan.

As I recall, Janet was not feeling well the night of the Kahn party so I went alone, where I met Ruth. We hit it off very well. She was an art history expert, also a lecturer and broadcaster on art subjects. She had lectured very often at the Barnes Collection outside Philadelphia, and I offered to get her access to whatever files Time, Inc. had on Albert Barnes (actually angry letters to TIME magazine which Barnes signed with his dog's name).

Ruth and I saw each other a number of times, then decided to break it off because she was divorced and I was married.

Actually, Ruth had three husbands and one major long-term relationship. She was first married in 1944 while still a student at Bryn Mawr College (later graduated) to Stanley Finkel, then a naval officer. They had three children: Ann Lee Switzer, now of Victoria, B.C.; Janet Asten of Rancho Mirage, CA., and Mark Finkel, of Englewood, N.J. Her three children have a total of 11 children, who in turn have 10 children. Ann and her husband Gordon are Quakers also very interested in Japanese beliefs (he grew up in Japan where his father worked for General MacArthur). They have no children. Daughter Janet, married to Peter Asten, turned Catholic and has raised her children as Catholics. They have five children including Patrick who has Down Syndrome. Mark became an Orthodox Jew as did his wife, Hava who was originally Catholic. The Finkels have five daughters and one son. Two of their daughters Miriam and Rachel are already married (to Orthodox husbands) and will no doubt add to Ruth's total of great-grandchildren. I have a very warm, friendly relationship with Ruth's family, especially the Finkels who live nearby in New Jersey.

For a period of about 40 years, I never heard from Ruth until about a few weeks after Janet died. Then one day in early March when I went to my mailbox in Lakeville, CT., I found a letter from Ruth, dated March 5. Actually, the return address on the envelope said Ruth Bowman, and I did not know anyone by that name. When I read the letter, I realized that Ruth Bowman was actually the Ruth Gurin I had known 40 years earlier. She had read Janet's obituary in the NY Times and sent me a lovely condolence letter, reproduced here.

March 4, 2002
Dear George:

Upon reading Janet's New York Times obituary, I am moved to send you my deepest condolences.

Although you and I have not spoken in many years, from time to time I have enjoyed hearing news of your life from your friends and family. Either Marjorie Iseman or her sister Gloria told me of your Bar Mitzvah (at 83?) around the time of my own Bat Mitzvah celebration (at which the late Harry Kahn read a poem). Since Wally Bowman's death, I have changed my residence legally back to New York, resuming the art career which, while you had access to Life Magazine files, you certainly helped by letting me read the Barnes Foundation files. I do hope your days ahead are easing.

Warmly,
Ruth

Years earlier, Ruth had divorced her first husband, Stanley Finkel. Then she briefly married Maury Gurin, a public relations man whom I remembered from the Overseas Press Club. What I did not know when I received the letter was that in 1967 she had then married Wally Bowman, a British-born business executive, several years after my brief first relationship with Ruth. Sadly, Wally suffered a serious stroke in 1981 when they were living in Los Angeles where he was a top-level business executive. The stroke lasted about 19 years until Wally died in 2000 in a retirement home in Irvine, California where they lived during his last years. Ruth continued working in the art field in California, but also commuted to New York frequently where she formed a close relationship with Harry Kahn whose wife, by that time, was also seriously ill – incapacitated by an ailment affecting her brain. Ruth and

Harry put together an outstanding collection of self-portraits on paper by modern and contemporary artists, which, after Harry's death in 1999, Ruth inherited and transferred to the National Portrait Gallery in Washington in a donative sale.

After reading Ruth's letter to me, I of course realized she was my old friend from the early sixties whom I had met at Harry Kahn's house, when her last name was Gurin. I phoned her to thank her for the condolence letter, but found she was on a trip out West. When we did get in touch a few days later, I invited her to lunch at the Lotos Club. At lunch, we each felt immediately that this would be an important relationship for us both. The date was March 18, 2002 and we have celebrated it ever since as an important anniversary – actually on the 18th of every month since then and often at the same table for two at the Lotos Club on East 66th Street.

Ruth is a remarkable woman – remarkable in her way as Janet was in a very different way. Ruth is a native of Denver, Colorado. Her father was a communications lawyer who moved the family to Washington, DC when Ruth was still a young girl. He was an author of the basic Federal Communications Act, and then went into a very successful private practice obtaining radio licenses for major newspapers and other broadcasters. Ruth is the eldest of six children. She attended Sidwell Friends School in Washington before going off to Bryn Mawr. Her father, whom I think she idolized, died early and she also had a very warm relationship with her mother.

After our initial lunch in New York, Ruth and I got together soon again when I offered to meet her at the train in Wassaic, N.Y. and drive her to Great Barrington, Massachusetts to see her close friend and Bryn Mawr roommate, "Boots" (Betty Krainis) who, sadly, was quite ill and died not long after.

For a few months, Ruth returned frequently to visit me in Lakeville and usually to spend time with her Great Barrington friend. During this period in the spring of 2002, it was obvious to Ruth and to me that we belonged together. So, in the summer of 2002 I sold the Lakeville house and moved in September to a two-bedroom apartment in Ruth's building in New York, Manhattan House, 200 East 66th Street. At this writing, I am still there, though my occupancy is threatened by new owners of the building who are converting it from rental to condominium at ridiculously high prices.

A few months after our first reunion, Ruth and I went to California to visit family and also to take a look at "Regents Point", the retirement home in Irvine where she and Wally had lived. It was a fine upscale residence for senior citizens, but I did not want to move there for two basic reasons: (1) I was not ready for a retirement home, and (2) I really don't enjoy the Southern California lifestyle which is almost totally dependent on automobile transportation. (I stopped driving a car about two years ago.) Ruth gave up her apartment at Regents Point, sacrificing a substantial non-refundable sum she had paid to move in. She shipped her personal effects from California back to Manhattan House, lending some of her furniture to me to use in my apartment.

Through Ruth, I have met a great many people she has known for years in the art field: artists, museum administrators, curators, collectors, etc.

Ruth can be described as an art historian and museum specialist with more than 40 years experience in public education. She started out working at the Jewish Museum in New York, then was curator of the New York University Art Collection and helped found its successor, the Grey Art Gallery on Washington Square.

The story is that one day, when Ruth was working at NYU, her phone rang and a lady said: "This is Mrs. Grey in St. Paul, Minnesota. I would like to know if I gave $1,000,000 to NYU would they name the art gallery for my late husband". Ruth said she would have someone from the President's Office call her back. A few years and five million dollars later, the Grey Art Gallery at NYU was founded.

While at NYU, Ruth also taught both as a staff lecturer at the Museum of Modern Art and at NYU. Notably, she also taught art on CBS network's Sunrise Semester for 46 weekly lectures.

One of her principal achievements was to discover the murals at the Newark Airport that had been painted by the noted artist Arshile Gorky during the WPA depression days, and then covered up by coats of paint when the Air Force took over Newark airport for World War II. Ruth did detective work, found the murals, had them restored where possible, and arranged for the surviving murals to be hung at the Newark Museum. Recently, Ruth was honored for this with an award and banquet by the Newark Museum.

Ruth also studied art administration at the Harvard Business School, was a Rockefeller Foundation Senior Fellow at the Metropolitan Museum of Art, and was a special assistant to Director Thomas Hoving in an Annenberg-financed project at the Metropolitan.

She has also broadcast and lectured extensively on art subjects, and served as a guide to art collections for many groups both at the Metropolitan and the Barnes Collection near Philadelphia. Ruth holds an M.A. from the Institute of Fine Arts, NYU.

Obviously, this background has led to many social contacts, which I have enjoyed. In addition, Ruth has a rare ability to strike up conversations, and get people to open up – whether at a party, in a museum, or even perfect strangers on a New York City bus. So, life is never dull.

In addition, we have traveled together a number of times particularly to see our children and grandchildren on the West Coast (from British Columbia to Los Angeles) and two trips to London.

As I write this chapter, Ruth and I have been together for more than six years. Needless to say, we are very fond of each other. Also, I have become quite close to her family, including particularly her children and grandchildren and her brothers Paul in Washington and David in London. Also my children and grandchildren seem to be delighted at my relationship with Ruth and have formed their own warm bonds with her.

Ruth and I are connected to each other by a number of very close bonds – shared interests, attitudes toward life, senses of humor and love of family, as well as physical attractions.

We hope to stay together as long as the Good Lord will allow.

CHAPTER XXXI

LIFELINES

As I write these final lines for my memoirs, it is late in the year 2008 and I have reached the age of 94.

At this point in life, I have a great deal to be happy and proud about. I have two children, both of them appearing to be leading well-organized, successful lives and to have found happiness in their married lives. The two children each have two children of their own, each of them also successful, confident adults: Aaron with his devoted wife, Wrenna and two unique children, Vivien and Jasper; Alanna with her usual good judgment happily married to Jack Muccigrosso and parenting delightful son Jonah and newly arrived (May, 2007) Eva. Then there is Charles' brood consisting of Tyras, former N.Y.U. Wrestling Captain, now a hedge fund Asset Manager, who married Nicole Giska, an outstanding young woman, last Fall; and of course the amazing Zachary, valedictorian at University of Maryland, graduate of Yale Law School, Masters in Political Science from the Kennedy School at Harvard, Fulbright fellow in Mexico, Kennedy School fellow, now a member of the Bar and stellar personality, no doubt to be captured one of these years by some discerning and fortunate young woman.

In addition there is now my five year plus relationship with Ruth, one which brings smiles to our faces as well as to those who observe us.

The main sadness in my life is the loss of my wife of 57 years and companion of more than sixty – Janet. Despite the ups and downs of our emotional relationship, there was always a strong bond of mutual respect and shared interests that held us together all those years. I still feel her presence and her approbation (or disapproval) as I go about these later years of my life and have never forgotten the bonds that kept us together.

True, I was born into fortunate circumstances. They did not constitute a silver spoon in my mouth, but I certainly enjoyed a comfortable youth, a circumstance that has continued for most of my life. There was some inherited money in my family (though not a lot), and some of it passed down to me and my sister. However, I can honestly say that I did well during my working life thanks to my own efforts, and to the fact that I always enjoyed working (and still do). I never made a fortune on my own, but always had good and well-paid jobs, first in journalism and later in financial public relations. In 1979, when I left the staff of the New York Botanical Garden, I became self-employed in my own P.R. consulting business which continued until I decided to give it up in 2001, at age 85/86. It was financially the most rewarding period of my life, and completely enjoyable.

Of course, I have been blessed until now with reasonably good health, and long-lived parents, my Father until 96 and Mother to 91. However, I think my attitude on life has been an important factor in my general health and being able to have a useful life this long. I think that most of the time I have had a very positive outlook on life, buoyed by optimism, expecting that good things will happen, which they often do. Also I seem to have a convenient memory, or loss thereof, so that unpleasant events do not stay with me very long. Keeping busy – whether at writing, or going to concerts, theatre, museums, etc., appears to keep my mind at work, and thus, I am sure, helps to maintain physical activity. The love and understanding that exists between Ruth and me has been a vital factor in my life.

I also believe that my attitude about spiritual matters has been helpful. Over the years since my marriage to Janet, I usually have been a member of a Synagogue, even though I have little patience for religious ritual. But virtually all my life since school days, I have had a strong spiritual feeling and belief in God. How much of it is due to true religion, and how much to sentiment, I do not know. But my exposure to Presbyterianism at prep school, to the Quaker faith at College, and then to Judaism after marriage, were important influences. I am sure these sources of spirituality helped carry me through a number of difficult experiences in life.

So I come to the closing lines of these recollections, with a feeling of optimism, with hope and eagerness to live the remaining days of my life. My past 93 years have given me the strength to face the future – With a glad heart and with prayerful thanks for the life I have led up until now.

TEXT SECTION

DETERMINATION

One day I went unto my home,
And there I had a little talk
With Daddy and Mother; and then alone
At night, I resolved to "walk the chalk".

II

Next week when I returned to school,
I plunged into my job with zeal;
And, determined I'd be no laggard fool,
Myself improve, I could almost feel.

III

I slaughtered work all around,
I studied an hour after school,
At seven o'clock out of bed I'd bound
And learn my Latin rule by rule.

IV

Soon, when I went home again,
I saw the fruits of my hard labor.
Oh, my report card was a gem!
Determination is in God's favor.

April 22, 1929   George B. Bookman
Schoolboy Poem

SHORT STORY FROM COLLEGE -

A PENNY A ROSE

BY

GEORGE B. BOOKMAN

On Washington Street, which runs through the heart of New York's waterfront produce market, roses may be had for one cent. All the skill of botanist Luther Burbank, all the scientific culture of hothouse specialists, all the nurture and manicuring of skilled florists combined in one sweet-smelling blossom may be purchased at this metropolitan bargain-haven for a copper.

"Roses, one cent. Ten cents a dozen, roses...." Rasp the leather-lunged vendors.

To Eddie Evers, as he walked from the Subway entrance to the office, a distance of a few blocks along Washington Street, this cry was a familiar one. Every morning for the four years that he had worked for the newspaper some peddler had cried his wares on that thoroughfare, and bargain rate roses were no novelty. But this morning the cry had a special meaning for him. He had met someone who might like roses.

Eddie's friendship or rather acquaintance with Miss Salmon was a case of combustion, but not spontaneous combustion. She was a newcomer to the editorial staff and Eddie had been assigned the task of showing her around the office. After a morning of traipsing around and interrupting hardworking copy men to mumble an introduction, Eddie conducted Miss Salmon to her desk. A smile of thanks for his trouble and Eddie found himself dismissed from the thoughts of Lucille Salmon. And to be dismissed from the thoughts of Miss Salmon meant utter banishment. Business like, of an indeterminate age, which might be 25 or 45, she was attractive in a stern sort of way. Her cheeks were red, but seemed too dull to be naturally so; her hair was of the stringy brown variety, but when concealed by a hat, it gave her an air of chic efficiency. Her outstanding grace was a talent for dressing well. She ran to rather severe suits, but they suited well her type of attractiveness. The more hardened reporters soon set Miss Salmon down as unapproachable. She did not lend herself to long pursuit on the part of the male of the species. Hers was a pleasing but not an enticing beauty.

We left Eddie in banishment. But it did not endure long. He was soon recalled, and quite vociferously. Across the large room a feminine voice rang out,

"Mr. Watcha-call-it. Oh, Mr. Evers, help, I'm on fire." Eddie wheeled round to see Miss Salmon frantically smothering a smoldering cuff. A cigarette stub, left near her desk by a negligent reporter had set fire to the flimsy fringe of her sleeve, and hence the loudly voiced appeal. But by the time Eddie reached her desk, the sparks had been efficiently scrunched out, and Miss Salmon had already begun her work nursing quietly the sorrow of a singed cuff. Hence, when he made his appearance at her side to offer help he again met banishment, more complete, more unsullied than before.

From day to day, Eddie Evers lived in the hope of extracting a smile from the haughtiness of Miss Salmon. He replenished her supply of paper, even put ribbons in her typewriter, but Miss Salmon always managed to be absent at the time and never acknowledged the service. In an attempt to explain her reticence, Eddie concluded that she must be a restrained sort of person, not much given to displaying her emotions. Once, indeed, he thought he had seen the corners of her mouth turn up into the faint semblance of a smile when he had sharpened her pencils, but it might only have been to stifle a yawn.

But hope is excellent mulch in which to propagate the seeds of love, hence Eddie never lost faith. And on the aforementioned morning, when the cry of a rose-hawker penetrated his thoughts with a new significance, that mulch was considerably enriched. The preceding day

Miss Salmon had actually recognized his existence. She had deposited on his desk a sandwich left over from her lunch, with a curt explanatory note bearing only her initials – "L.S." So, as he passed the flower stall, Eddie stopped briefly to fish six cents from his pocket, and receive half a dozen roses.

"Da ladee she lika dees roses," prophesied the vendor. Eddie, annoyed at the divination of his purpose, concluded the transaction hurriedly.

Arriving at the office, Eddie, as inconspicuously as possible, deposited his gift on Miss Salmon's desk, enclosing in the bundle a slip of paper with his initials – "E.E." Making sure that the brilliant colors of the flowers were completely shielded from the gaze of inquisitive reporters and deskmen, he seated himself at his desk on the other side of the room, all aglow with anticipation.

Ten o'clock, the scheduled hour for the arrival of Miss Salmon, rolled around, and she did not arrive. By quarter of eleven, Eddie found difficulty in concentrating at his work, and when at 11:30 she had not yet arrived, his continual craning of the neck forced his boss to ask him if he had slept in a draft all night and was working off a stiff neck.

On his way out of the room at lunchtime, Eddie gave the package, as yet untouched, a mournful glance, and when he returned from lunch to find the bundle still in its virgin state, Eddie's face bore the expression of a doleful cow. At last, at 3:30 he saw her masculine figure brush through the door and make straight for the city editor's desk. In her hand was a fat sheaf of papers and photographs. Miss Salmon had been out on a special assignment, and Eddie's heart submarined as he thought of the wilted flowers.

After a conference with the city editor, Eddie saw the object of his anxiety proceed toward her desk. She had found the package; she opened it, read the initials, and then gazed at the flowers. And then what ecstasy gripped the heart of Edward Evers! As he watched, her face went through preliminary stages of contemplation, dubious pleasure, pity, and appreciation, and then burst into the full glory of a SMILE. Yes, an actual smile. And she glanced over at his desk, but Eddie, overcome by the facial display, lowered his glance.

The remaining hours fled like the north wind. At five-thirty, Eddie straightened up his desk, mustered his courage, and strode over to the desk of Miss Salmon. His arrival was greeted with another smile, as she opened the package of roses for inspection. Inside the rolled newspaper was the sorriest looking collection of devitalized petals that had ever been wilted. The stems were curling into sickly brown coils, and the petals were of a yellow tinge. Roses at a cent a piece – and they were worth just that much!

After thanking him for his gift, Miss Salmon drew Eddie into conversation. He was entranced by her rapid patter, and she took great care to win him to her confidence. They talked of a variety of subjects – newspapers, her latest assignment, his work, the theatre, - and when they looked up it was quite late. They both prepared to leave, and descended in the elevator together. Out on the street, the weather seemed blustery and forbidding. It was dusk and the gray skies were not at all inviting.

"Won't you come to my apartment for a cup of hot tea!" invited Miss Salmon.

Eddie, bashful, hesitated, but she urged him, and they soon found themselves in her small, two-room apartment. She left Eddie in the sitting room and retired to prepare the tea. The windows of the room were screened by heavy drapes over which capered atrocious embroidered dragons. The room was over crowded with furniture – several deep chairs, two tables littered with Chinese art, and a soft, pillowed couch on which Eddie sat. It was hot and stuffy and Eddie's throat became dry. He was quite uncomfortable, sitting here in this woman's apartment. Soon she appeared clad in a loose-fitting dressing gown. It was brown, with the same type of hideous dragons that were on the draperies, the garment was very flowing and she had evidently wrapped it hastily around her, for as she came into the room, it hung part way open. But that was not the worst of it. Something about her face struck Eddie as being queer. Her cheeks were brown, her lips dull – she had removed her makeup. She came and seated herself on the soft couch, uncomfortably close to Eddie, and it became apparent that she had used a liberal portion of perfume, for it hung about her like a heavy, nauseating cloud. To Eddie she was the exact antithesis of youth, of freshness, of vivacity, of prim efficiency – the opposite of everything he had imagined her to be. Instead, she was the embodiment of repressed middle age, a disgusting mass of unsatiated desires, and faded beauty.

She turned off a light, crept closer to Eddie, and sighed.

"Eddie", she said in a horse voice, her mouth close to his face, "Eddie, I want you to call me Lu. We can have so much fun together if you will just be informal with me. I'm really not so unapproachable."

Eddie squirmed inwardly and tried to think of something to say. Finally, he managed to blurt "How about that tea, Miss Sal...Uh, Lu?"

"Oh, yes. We were having such a good little time I almost forgot about the tea," and she raised herself carelessly from the couch, and went into the other room.

When she had gone, Eddie loosened his collar. He felt very uncomfortable and very out of place. There seemed to be just one thing to do. As silently as possible he took his hat from the table and slipped out of the stuffy apartment.

The cold winds, which were whipping the street corners, brought him back to normalcy. A welter of jumbled thoughts ran through his brain: Perfume, faded roses, atrocious dragons, a carelessly draped kimono, stuffiness, roses again, yellow cheeks....

"Roses for a penny" he mused. Yes, even faded roses have their price.

The End

LONG BRANCH DAILY RECORD
MONMOUTH COUNTY PUBLISHING COMPANY
INC.
PRINTERS LITHOGRAPHERS
192 BROADWAY
LONG BRANCH, NEW JERSEY

Summer 1930

TO WHOM IT MAY CONCERN:

George Bookman, bearer of this letter, conducted a juvenile column for me during the summer of 1930 and I am glad to say that I found it to be an attraction to the young folks of this resort.

Yours very truly

Houston Brown

Managing Editor

Dr. Arthur Bookman
25 East 77th Street
New York City

October 30, 1930

George dear,

Your monthly report came this morning with a letter from Mr. Shafer and it has all made me feel a little sad at a time when, on account of the business conditions and the general feeling about New York that things are getting worse, I would welcome some good news of you. After all you know we haven't very much money and we are looking forward to you and Caroline making something of yourselves, and doing well in school is the best preparation that I know of for a success in life. If either of you fail we will feel it is our failure, and that we have been falling down on the job of bringing you up. And you George have so far fallen down badly on your job this year. Your tricks on people are only one evidence that you don't try to get along with them, and you must realize that just getting along with them and earning their good opinion is half of success in life. The other half is doing good work – and that you are falling down on too. Your record of E this month is shameful. You can and must make B.

You're not a little boy any more. Another month like this may end your connection with school. How would you like to have to leave and go to another school with a bad record from Haverford? That is what will face you, and it's mighty hard to live it down.

Now stop acting the fool and trying to make a reputation as a good sport at the price of your reputation for common sense and veracity. I am not deciding that issue between Mr. Shafer and you. Of course I believe in you. But my opinion means nothing at school and Mr. Shafer's does, so I want you to go right to him and do your best to straighten out this matter before you come home. If you can't do anything else you can at least assure him you will behave yourself and get down to work. You should be in college in two years. The way you are working now you will not make it. If you don't, what will you do? Jobs are not easy to get if you have neither college training nor a mechanical trade.

Don't forget your big job just now is convincing Mr. Shafer that you are going to keep out of trouble and do your work. If he is watching you more closely than others, it is your fault. You have known him two years and if you have any sense you know by this time how to conduct yourself so that you will not attract his censure. That is your job. He is your boss and if you want to keep your job you have to satisfy the boss.

George, please stop being a fool, because we love you and you must succeed.

Daddy

New York World Telegram

Friday, August 25, 1933

Dear George,

 I was very glad to have been able to give you the six weeks' experience on the Financial Page, which you have just completed. I think that what you learned this summer should help you a great deal in journalism. Your work handling over-the –counter securities, commodities, foreign exchange, etc. was very satisfactory and you seemed quite eager and industrious. I wish you the best of luck in newspaper work.

Sincerely yours,
Ralph Hendershot
Financial Editor

JUNIOR YEAR ABROAD

PLANS

First draft of letter to Haverford College asking permission to spend my Junior year in Paris.

Dear Sirs:

We, the undersigned, would like permission of the faculty to spend our Junior year studying in Paris, with the understanding that we will be eligible to enter the Senior class in the fall of 1935 and to take our degrees the following spring.

We are all majoring in Government and have very definite plans for study. We believe that a year abroad would be of great benefit to us in the careers we have chosen to follow. Crawford is preparing for the diplomatic service, Pugliese intends to study law and Bookman plans to enter political journalism and eventually public relations.

The central idea of our plan would be to learn a great deal along several lines, which are of outstanding interest to us. We feel that our purpose would be defeated if we had to take the customary number of courses. Our mutual concentration is with Current International Relations and their historical background. Each one of us, in addition, plans to take a cultural course and to do all the voluntary reading time will permit. Our schedules of study are as follows:

CRAWFORD:
International relations (Government 4a)
International law (Government 5b)
Political theory (Government major)
History 3
History of Art (University of Paris)
French 5
Reading in English

BOOKMAN:
International relations (Gov. 4a)
International law (Gov. 5b)
Political theory (Gov. major)
History 2
International exchange (Ec 5b)
History of Art
Reading in English

PUGLIESE:
International relations (Gov. 4a)
International Law (Gov. 5b)
History of Art
Political Theory
History 2
Reading in Italian

Our method of study will be as follows: 1). On the History of Art, at the University of Paris and in Political theory at the Ecole des Sciences Politiques. The rest of the time we will work as guided by reading lists some of which we have already received from the heads of the respective departments here at Haverford. In order to provide a goal for our efforts, we will write papers on those topics from the reading which are of greatest interest to us. We would like permission to turn these papers over to the faculty for their inspection, upon our return from Europe, and to be examined in September 1935 on those courses, which we have starred in the foregoing lists.

We want to take this step for the following reasons: (1) We want to learn a great deal in a specialized field (2) Extra-curricular activities at college inevitably rob much of our time (3) We all feel that the advantage of a year of independent study in Paris will greatly aid us after graduation (4) We are attracted by the prospect of getting the international viewpoint on modern problems.

Respectfully submitted,
George B. Bookman

LETTERS HOME FROM PARIS

1934-1935

Baltimore Mail Line
Saturday, September 8, 1934

Dear Mother and Daddy,

The letter you received from me was mailed at Norfolk. I spent the day in that godforsaken town with two other fellows from the boat: a baron and an ex-Harvard student named Cullison Cady. We hiked to the nearest trolley and rode for a half-hour into the town of Norfolk. It is the most depressing place I have ever seen. Nothing but empty buildings, junkyards, cheap eating places and drab little cigar stores. No beauty whatsoever. We went to the town hall and listened to a trial of a man on a charge of operating a slot machine. He was guilty as hell but the judge had all the evidence stricken out and then told the jury to hand down a verdict of not guilty. It was all a pretty sick-looking picture.

As soon as we left port the purser came up to me and asked us if we would like to have stateroom no. 1. It has a shower and private bath and toilet and two portholes and is fully as large as the other and quieter. It is on the promenade deck. I sit at the purser's table with Bill Fry and Cady and a Mr. Hamilton who is a shrewd businessman and a good fellow. We have a good time together. The beer on this boat is wonderful, being Bavarian beer. Also a keg of Bremen beer which was almost as good.

The crowd is not so very lively. There are only two girls, both married, but their husbands are not on board. One woman is violently blond and does nothing but play cards and she is very lucky. I played once with her and then learned better. But we manage to have a good time. And I think it will get better as the week moves on because I was never the boy to sit back and twiddle my thumbs, so to speak.

There is a German aboard with a monocle who looks like a fairy but he knows a lot about Germany and politics. Everyone here abouts is abed by 1:00 at the latest, most of the old duffers turning in around the scandalous hour of 9:00 p.m. But fear not, I am having a good time. Last night I even inveigled one of the "girls" to dance with me. Hometown boy makes good.

The sea has been like glass up till now but it just started to blow about one hour ago. I have taken sunbaths on the top deck with Cull Cady, and a Russian dancer (female).

It's a funny community and I am drinking it all in. Very amusing.

That is about all the dirt I can think of. So goodbye for the nonce.

Love,

George

LE ROYAL;
HOTEL RESTAURANT
212 BOULVD RASPAIL
PARIS

September 16, 1934

Dear Mother and Daddy

I arrived here in Paris safely and am having a wonderful time learning to know the city. Bill met us at the train and took us in hand splendidly. We put up here at Le Royal and have very nice single rooms on the sixth floor overlooking the Boul Raspail. Just down at the corner of the street is the Dome Café where we have stopped several times to sip a drink (nonalcoholic) and watch the crowds. As soon as we set our bags in the rooms, which was about lunchtime on Saturday, we went out to lunch at a little Russian place where we had a grand lunch with wine compris for 7 Fr. Today we found some places where one can eat for 5 and 5.50. And well too.

Paris is grand. I love it. Saturday (yesterday) we walked around the streets looking at the old buildings etc. Mrs. Crawford was good enough to invite us over for dinner. She is a charming woman and it certainly is a pity that she is handicapped by the loss of a leg. Their home is unique. In front of it there is a garden and since they live on the rez de chaussée they command a wonderful view of the garden and a high lattice overgrown with ivy that screens them from the street. Mrs. C. has very good taste and the house is very simply but effectively decorated. Her younger son, Jacky is terribly alert and keen about everything. He must be about 13 or 14 and knows as much as any American who is just entering college. He speaks French better than English and is always using French words when he can't think of the English equivalent. They are very fine people and I am glad to know them. I sent Mrs. some flowers this evening with a thank you note.

Today Bill called for us and took us around the city. We walked mostly and took our time. We went to see a mass at Saint Clothilde and then walked down past the Chambre to the Seine and then down the Quai d'Orsay past the bookstalls all the way to the bridge which leads to Notre Dame. We were terribly lucky at Notre Dame. For an unusual service was going on. The cathedral was packed to the doors with thousands of young boys, members of la Jeunesse Ouvriere an organization of youths. They were all singing when we entered and the bishop of Paris was there in all his glory. The old walls echoed with the workers' chant from thousands of young throats. It was all very impressive. Some day soon I will go again to see the cathedral empty and notice the details of the construction. Then we went to see the oldest church in Paris St. Jean le Pauvre, which was rebuilt in the 13th century. It is in a very ancient quarter of Paris. The streets are very narrow and the houses hang far over the cobblestones. The streets twist serpentine-fashion around the buildings. The St. Jean is a Greek Catholic church and so the air was heavy with incense.

Sunday is certainly the day to see Paris. We then left Bill and strolled along the boulevards. Near the Sorbonne we found a little restaurant chinois where we had a very good dinner for a matter of 5.50. It was quite amusing, because the garcon spoke bad French and so did we. He was Chinese, of course.

After lunch we visited the Pantheon which was interesting and then sat in the Jardins Luxembourg several hours. We talk French among ourselves all day long. And of course we always speak French to the waiters, and so on. It was grand in the park

today. The sun was out and it was quite mild. Both today and yesterday the weather has been perfect. One of the most remarkable things in the park is that all the French children are so cute. You hardly ever see an ugly one. We watched them playing and riding the carousel. The types of men and women are very amusing also. We had supper at a creamery because we weren't so very hungry. (Special note for Mother: I had Crème Isigny. It was divine.) Then we walked about and talked French. There was a crowd on one of the boulevards arguing about the Salvation Army. They were chattering away at each other and I understood almost everything they said. I am learning to rattle off French, too.

Tomorrow (Monday) I am going to do all my bits like getting the mail, seeing the banker, and perhaps seeing Fay. And looking for an apartment. Mrs. Crawford knows a Mme Wagner who keeps a pension where we can get pension entiere for 1000 Fr a month. She knows the woman and says that she serves very good food and lots of it and that she really looks after her boys. There are several other students living there who study at the Sciences Politiques. We may investigate that. Then Bill has a few others in mind also.

We will try to move as soon as possible because living at a hotel is expensive.

Living is very inexpensive. We haven't paid more than 7 francs for any meal. So far I have spent less than 160 francs which includes checking the trunk and the train ride. (which was very beautiful and interesting). But that doesn't include two nights hotel room rent, which would add 40 more. So I have spent about 13 or 14 dollars.

I am going to bed now. Maybe I'll write some more tomorrow.

Bill just came in and is going to take me out apartment hunting. I think we can get one for 850 Fr. A month. That is tout compris.

Must stop now.

Lots of Love to everyone,

George

AU CENTRE DE MONTPARNASSE
HOTEL
"LES GLYCINES"
15. RUE JULES-CHAPLAIN
PARIS (6e)
CONFORT MODERNE

September 19, 1934

Dear People,

It is now Wednesday evening of my first week here in Paris. We have decided to start studying Tuesday. We have found diggings on the premiere étage of a house on the Rue de la Grande Chaumière. I will append the address to this letter before I seal it. It is in the sixième arrondisement. The thing that attracted me the most on entering was the lovely old paneled woodwork. The doors are deeply paneled with some light colored wood and it all looks very antique. The stairs are rather broad but very circular. And well worn. You open one of these doors (on the courtside) and enter a small hallway. Doors directly ahead and to the left lead to two adjoining rooms, which will be occupied by Bill Crawford and me. We haven't yet chosen which room will be infested by which fellow. Then there is a third room, adjoining but approached by another hallway and another entrance which Bill Fry will occupy. All the rooms look out on a jardin and just across the beflowered, betreed and begrassed court is another court of the house on the other side of the block, which belongs to some clubhouse for American girl students. So we are surrounded by beauty on all sides. We have sunlight almost all day long (except in the afternoon, which ends at 4 P.M.) That is to say we have sunlight in the morning. Each room has a salamandre (little heating stove) and a private washbasin. Also closets and bookshelves and fireplaces. The rent with all meals and service and two baths a week compris is 870 francs per month.

We have seen quite a number of pensions. One was fine, with beautiful rooms and all the baths you wanted and an ample table, etc., etc., but the lady who ran it was a little too motherly. She had 15 other boys and treated them like her sons. It would have been un peu trop bien soigné. She would have let us have pension for 900. We saw all sorts of dumps with all sorts of madames. Young and old, pretty and otherwise. The place we chose is run by a Madame of the safe age of 55 with a son about 30 and a daughter about 25. There is also a French woman who teaches French who eats there but we haven't met her yet.

Bill C. has been grand as a guide. There is still a lot of Paris I haven't seen yet. There are hordes of museums still to be seen. And the Eiffel tower (of course) and the Etoile and the Place de la Concorde (which I only whizzed thru in a taxi).

Monday evening Mrs. Crawford invited Fry and me over to have coffee and we met a great friend of hers, a French count, the great-grandson of Lafayette. He was charming, witty and a brilliant conversationalist. He invited Bill, Fry, Mrs. C. and me to go out to see the Lafayette chateau so we are going on Friday. It is where Lafayette lived. It is in the feudal tradition and quite historic. It will cost us about $2 taxi fare apiece. Well worthwhile, I think.

I have inscribed myself for a course at the Alliance Francaise, which teaches practical French and all sorts of things about Paris to foreigners. For 180 f. a month you get daily classes for 2 hours in Grammar and diction. A conference on some subject like Franco-German intellectual relations in the XIXth Cent or some such baloney but which gives you an opportunity to use high flown phrases in French. And then there are "Conferences-Promenade" in which a trained lecturer takes you to places like the Louvre and the Cluny and Versailles and points out the worthwhile features of the architecture and the paintings and all that. This afternoon I went to the Louvre with the group and saw some XVIII Century things like those of Poussin, Champaigne and Watteau. I wasn't crazy about any of them. The subjects don't appeal to me. The things I do like are little portraits of a man smiling, or someone in a familiar attitude or realistic landscapes and agricultural things like "The Gleaners". I detest symbolism and cherubs. But there is some excellent composition and technical execution connected with that religious school. I can appreciate the excellence of the canvas technically but if it weren't for that I wouldn't look at it twice. Of course I am going to the Louvre again soon. I think students get in for ½ price (one franc).

I walked along the bookstalls with Bill and Fry and bought myself a guide to the Louvre (a sort of miniature course in the history of art) and a novel in French, or rather a memoir called "De Montmartre au Quartier Latin" by

Francis Carco. He reminisces about life along the "Boul' Mich" about 1910. I am reading it carefully looking up the words I don't know.

Tomorrow we are going to see Fäy and fix that all up. And then Friday we go to the Chateau. If there is time tomorrow I will see about my job (?) Then some more sightseeing Sat and Sun. Then move house Monday and then on Tuesday we will start the scholastic year by breaking a bottle of champagne over the first book (figuratively speaking). Et bien, c'est ca.

Please do me a favor. Please save the letters I write home and put them all in one place so that when I get home I may have them as a diary. It is a lot simpler than writing a diary. Although not quite inclusive.

I'll look up Uncle Fred. On the back of this is a map of our rooms.

Lots of Love to you and anyone else who asks for it or deserves it.

George

P.S. I am following French internal politics in the little papers that seem to sprout up everywhere. Stavisky, et al. They are to publish an important document, the rapport Guillaume, tomorrow which may implicate that beggar Cheron and his crew of Radical Socialist bribetakers.
New Address: #3 Rue de la Grande Chaumière
Paris 6e
France
P.S. I didn't copy this from a tourist come-on circular.

#3 Rue de la Grande Chaumiere
Paris, VIe, France
September 28, 1934

Dear Mother, Daddy, and Monica,

It's now Friday. On Monday we moved into our new rooms here at the pension and Tuesday we started work, so I am well along in work now.

Let me tell you what I have been doing and thinking. Friday we all (Bill, W. Fry, Mrs. Crawford, Jacky Crawford and I) went out about 30 kilometers from Paris in a taxi to call on a close friend of Mrs. Crawfords. The close friend is the Count de L'Asturie, a great grandson of LaFayette, and he lives in the Chateau La Grange where Lafayette lived during the latter part of his life. It is a typical example of one of the Old French chateau's and dates from about the 14th century. We drove out of Paris for about an hour or so through beautiful French farmland (they seem to do farming on quite a large scale) and finally arrived at the Chateau. It is approached through an avenue of trees. Around it runs a moat, which is still filled with water, though the original drawbridge has been replaced by a concrete bridge. The count greeted us and showed us all around the chateau. He has collected here thousands of relics of the days of LaFayette: portraits, books, furniture, jewelry, etc. Ordinary visitors pay a small fee to see the chateau but since he and Mrs. Crawford are old friends, we were his guests for the day. At each end of the chateau are two towers and of course there are tower rooms with walls more than nine feet thick. We saw LaFayette's bedroom, the room where Fenimore Cooper lived when he visited LaFayette, and went all over the house. There is some hand painted wallpaper worth thousands of dollars, which was quite beautiful. Then we took a walk in the park around the chateau. Along the paths there are little basins of water for the pheasants to drink out of that were placed there generations ago. (The basins, not the pheasants). When we came in for tea we went to the old chateau dining room which is paneled in marvelous old wood. The beams are uncovered and imbedded in the wall are two paintings of the Count's ancestors. The men in the portraits are dressed in armor so they must date from about the 16th or 17th century. For tea, in case you are still interested, we had tea and cakes and homemade raspberry jam almost as good as Hill Farm jam, and pears and nuts. Some tea. I saved money on my supper that night. After tea we went out to see a historic relic that the count keeps in the barn. It is the first American boat to race with England, that is the ancestor of the Rainbow, which has just won the Cup. The barnyard is just what you would imagine a medieval barnyard to be. With those typical mossy tiled roofs and thatching, and cobblestones, et al. I am very glad that we had the opportunity to go out there. It was very interesting. The count, poor fellow, is practically penniless, but he refuses to sell any of the relics. He lives for them, just about. I don't blame him. They are beautiful things and the chateau is a perfect setting for them.

Saturday, if I remember correctly, Fry and I did some more sightseeing. We went to see the Eiffel Tower (of course) and then to that ugly blot on the French escutcheon, the Trocadero. There are lots of terribly ugly buildings in Paris, I find, but the way they are placed, with broad avenues, parks and lawns leading up to them, make them rather beautiful. It is the most beautifully planned city I have ever seen or heard of. There are so many little conveniences too, that the French seem to have thought of. For instance, handy little signs in the subway to tell you where the darn thing goes to; tickets at crowded autobus stations; big signs in the metro to tell you what station it is; etc.

Everyone takes his time in Paris. They are individualists. We were on the autobus and had just left the Opera. At the Rue de Rivoli, a terribly busy corner as you well know, the conductor dropped a carnet of autobus tickets and they fell out of the bus. He stopped the bus, leisurely climbed down, walked to the middle of the crowded street, looked around to see if any cars were coming, and bent his little fat frame in two to pick up the carnet. Then he strolled slowly back to the bus, climbed on and rang the bell as a signal to go on.

Monday we moved in. Bill and I have rooms connected by a short hall, while Fry has the end room next to mine, but we have closed the partition between the rooms and communicate thru a long, circuitous hallway with about six doors. After lots of diplomacy and intrigue with Mme Vaujany (our landlady) we got all the hangers, tables, lamps etc. that we need. Tuesday we started work. We read and outline a chapter of Government per day. I am outlining the History textbook to get a good knowledge of the background. Which reminds me that we saw Fay. He suggested that I do a piece of research on the devaluation of the dollar in 1778 and its effects on French foreign trade and relations with France. This interests me tremendously because I am eager to learn all I can about foreign exchange. This is the first time the U.S. devaluated its currency and is a very good specimen of devaluation to study. He gave me a long list of books to read as a starter, which I will attack as soon as I finish mastering the textbook. I am making carbon copies of my Government outlines, one copy for the college and one for you, as you requested. Also I am studying French grammar and speak French with Bill and of course at every meal. This is our program, which we follow rigorously: Get up at 7:30, dress, shave, etc. At 8:00 the maid brings in the breakfast (some luxury, eh?) and Bill and I have breakfast together. As we eat I read aloud a few paragraphs each day from the Constitution which we want to know pretty well by the end of the year. Since we are majoring in Government. Then we take a short walk around the neighboring quarter of Paris and at 9 or 8:45 we settle down to work. We work without interruption until 12:30 when lunch is served. Then from 1:00 to about 2:30 or 3:00 we work again. We go out at 3 for exercise. We have been playing tennis in the Luxembourg gardens, which is good fun. All you do is hit the ball once and then chase it for ten minutes. The ground is so rough that no actual tennis is possible. I even had to climb a tree once to get the ball. At 4 we start studying again and study till 5:30. Then we go out to the Dome for a café crème. (That's all the coffee I take, because I drink the marvelous chocolate that the French make for breakfast.) (bad grammar in that sentence.) As you know only too well, the Dome is the hub of Montparnasse, the center of life, and we don't miss a trick.

I have decided that this typing on both sides is very confusing for you so I will continue the letter on page 5.

Supper is at 7:30 and after supper we study. Then we take a walk about 10:00 or 10:30 and so to bed. The meals, I was surprised to find, are excellent. Plenty of everything, and well balanced. There is a son of about 30 who works in a bureau and a daughter who also works and is in love, and rushes in and out of the house like the sea breeze. She is about 26 and rather foreboding looking (I mean forbidding-looking).

Thank you very much for all the letters. I received the letter from Mother about the Citroen people this morning. Sounds very interesting. Thank you so much. And thank Doris Thompson. Or maybe I'll write her when I get the letters of introduction. Which reminds me that I saw Thatcher Grant's friend, Elbert Baldwin, and he was very nice but was sorry that he couldn't use another man even if he worked for nothing. I don't think I have the time for it anyhow (and I am not rationalizing, Mother darling). I had to steal time to write this letter. I have written Kelsey, Comfort and Herndon at Haverford about the progress of work.

The draft came and was credited to my account at the Westminster Bank. Thank you. I think I must have been saving money. I have about 550 francs left in the bank from the money that I brought over with me and my rent is paid up till October 24. Not bad? The lists of courses aren't posted yet at the Universities, and since classes don't start until November 8 I will let you know about that later. My room is very pretty today. In fact all of Paris is. It is one of the most beautiful fall days I have ever seen. Last Sunday was wonderful too. Fry and I went rowing in the Bois de Boulogne, and it is an enchanting place. I met a very nice Russian dancer on the boat (feminine) whom I have seen a few times, and I think we are going rowing on Saturday. In the Bois we passed a dairy and I looked in the barn. The cows looked so clean and well kept that I bought a glass of milk – my only milk since the U.S.A. and milk is my favorite delight in life, as a beverage. It was excellent. I am now going out to the Luxembourg for some tennis so I had better stop.

Best of Love,

George

P.S. I hope Monica received a package. At least I posted it.

October 5, 1934

Dear Mother and Daddy

Thank you so much for your very interesting letters. I enjoyed reading the bits about N.Y. politics and was glad to see that you are optimistic about business in the States. I don't feel so optimistic about U.S. conditions. Everyone over here says that England is definitely prosperous. Conditions in France seem to be good financially speaking, but the government is between the devil and the deep blue sea. The men with money have nothing to kick about because they are getting all the gravy they need, but the workers and middle-class people eat blackbread or starve, figuratively speaking. The government is infested by a band of thieves who seem to possess no trace of personal honesty at all. And this devilish party system they have over here makes centralization and leadership impossible. Doumergue is an honest man. We listened to his speech on reform last night. Everyone believes that he is honest – the only honest man left in France, they say. But he is tied hand and foot by the stupid constitution. It doesn't even mention his position as President of the Senate. He has called a meeting of lawmakers at Versailles later in the month to draft a new constitution, which will make him more powerful and provide for separation of powers. The minister of justice, Cheron, is a bribing blackguard and is recognized as such by everyone, even Doumergue. But Doumergue hasn't the power to kick him out. Even in the Palais de Justice there isn't a thimbleful of honesty. Doumergue's speech was largely a violent invective against the communo-socialist Front Commun. Now they are in a rage and are planning a big radical demonstration on the eve of the opening of the chamber of deputies. Things are mighty interesting. The rentrée des classes has brought life back into Paris. The movement in the streets is totally different from what it was 2 weeks ago. Theater, music, politics, schools are all gathering momentum. The season is on, things are moving, but where, no one knows. The government lacks confidence as shown in the drop in the bourse, and the joking that the French assume whenever they mention Papa Doumergue and his Government de Treve.

Since I last wrote you I have been working, mainly. Last Saturday night, however, we all went to see Romeo and Juliet at the Opera. It was quite well done. Juliet was even pretty, although Romeo did tip the scale a trifle the other way. I had never seen it before, and loved the music especially Juliet's gay little song in the first act "Je veux vivre". Saturday (tomorrow) night we are all going to see Faust, so I got a cheap edition of it in French and am reading it. I have read Dr. Faust by Marlowe but that was some time ago and I forget it. The opera is so cheap here that it is well worth while. 12 francs in the peanut gallery.

Sunday I am going to Versailles because they will have the Grands Eaux for the last time this year and I don't want to miss that. I can get out and back for 7 francs compris. I will take a lady friend with me. (Yes, she's a <u>lady</u> in the fullest sense of the word).

Wednesday I got a pneumatique from Uncle Fred who blew into town. He took me out to dinner with Aunt Nellie at the Rond Point. He was certainly very nice to me, as was Nellie. She's taking me to the theater next week and would have done more, but I have to study some time. The New Yorker gets here regularly and is a saving grace.

I enjoyed Mother's exulting letter about Paris. I can't help exulting either when I walk in the Luxembourg and see the Pantheon through the trees, or when I go rowing in the Bois as I did last Sunday. We (the lady and I) went out to the island in the middle of the Lac Superieur and spent the P.M. under the trees. It certainly was marvelous. You go out in a big row boat rowed by one man something on the order of a gondola, but the thing is packed full of humans like a sardine box. We would have gone rowing but the lake was packed with every able-bodied man, woman and child in Paris. And they were all in boats and were bumping all over the lake. But if you lay on your back and looked up through the trees it was like a different world; no rowboats, no nuthin. Just beauty. Stark, naked beauty. This letter is getting to the silly stage so I will make a new start.

We are working hard. As hard this week as last week, strange to say. I am getting a lot out of it too. The questions we are studying are so up to date that it is more of a pleasure to study them than to read a magazine. Saturday I went to the Louvre and took a look at the fine collection of moderns they have. The Camondo collection has some very good Monets and Manets in it. Have you seen them? The one of the cathedral of Rheims, etc.?

It is turning colder. It seems to rain in the morning, and then clear up. Very queer weather. But when it's beautiful it's perfect. Bill has had a cold, but now it is all over and I didn't catch it, fortunately. My study of French grammar is coming right along and of course my conversation gets better every day. I read French very rapidly because I read the newspapers and magazines all the time and books, etc.

So glad Caroline is well and settled and did so well in French. I guess her month abroad did her more good than she was willing to admit. I like this practice of going abroad. You can put me down in favor of it.

Bill and I are going out for a café crème now so I will close.

Lots of Love to you and to Monica,

George

* * * * * *

NOTE: Letter to Dr. Herndon. Don't be surprised at the informal tone – we are on very good terms with Dr. H. Almost a member of the family.

Thank you so much for your very informative letter about Haverford. It was almost as good as a subscription to the <u>Haverford News.</u>

First, to dispose of the subject of "work". We are now on about page 475 in Fenwick and page 500 in Schuman, and of course we have been outlining as we go. When we finish the books, some time in early December, we will mail you the outlines. (At least 150 pages of close typing). This week we attended our first lectures at the Ecole Libre des Sciences Politiques: "Economic Geography" under André Siegfried and "Contemporary Europe and her interests outside of Europe" by René Pinon. We buy, as do all the students, printed copies of the complete course, and before each lecture Bill and I read the ground to be covered. At the lecture we take notes, of course, in French. The courses are both very interesting, especially Siegfried's course since he is such an authority on the subject. Whenever he injects his own personality into the lectures they take on an added interest. At the Sorbonne we are taking a literature course (Molière and Pascal) and we are following a course in the History of Art at the Ecole du Louvre.

We have been saving newspapers since September and now have a complete file of papers of every political color. I have been keeping a complete file of clippings on the Saar question. I intend to write a paper on some aspect of the plebiscite and if things seem quiet enough I will top it off by spending a week in Saarbrucken before, after and during the plebiscite (January 13).

I recently finished reading "International Government of the Saar" by Frank M. Russle, which presents a great many useful facts but is terribly biased against the French. Also read (in German) "Die Volkerrechtliche Stellung des Saargebiets" by Edward Bissel which is biased in Germany's favor but is typically German in that it is written with tremendous scientific exhaustiveness. Also read "Finance and Politics" by Paul Einzig. He tears right into the French for their policy of building up alliances and destroying enemies by use of the purse. And whenever he mentions England he puts it on a little pedestal and places a halo 'round its head'. But it was very interesting for opening up a new channel of thought on International Politics. I read it along with the chapter in Schuman on Empire building.

We have had an interesting lesson in Government these days watching the petty politicians of the Radical-Socialist party throw out Doumergue in order to save their own skins. The present Flandin government is just a continuation of the rickety old coalition. It often reminds me of that poem

"The One Horse Shay". It will hold together until it goes over a big bump – and then, crash! France may have another "Sixth of February" on her hands.

I am always eager to hear more gossip of Haverford. Bill sends his best regards.

Sincerely,

October 13, 1934

Dear Mother and Daddy,

Thanks so much for your letters.

These have been exciting days. We were all at tea at the Dome with Mrs. Crawford when we heard the news of the assassination. We immediately bought a paper and read the details. Then we went to the Crawford's; turned on the radio and heard that Barthou had been assassinated also. (Early reports said he was only slightly wounded.) I went out in the street and mixed with the crowds. The kiosks were being besieged by hordes of people, all eager to get a newspaper, and there were none left. Bewildered and stunned by the news, the crowd stood around the kiosks, waiting for the arrival of more papers, and passing the time by arguing among themselves. I listened to the arguments and joined in some of them. Most of the people blame the police for the incident, and it is obviously their fault. France is in Deuil National, and Barthou will be buried today. We are going down to the Espladade des Invalides to watch the funeral procession. All talk of Prince and Stavisky has dropped away. The "attentat" is the sole topic of conversation. Here, at the pension, we talk about it at every meal. There is talk of war in the air. Reports of the new book by Johannes Steele interest me tremendously. He is the chap who scooped the world for the N.Y. Post on the German "blood purge" of June 30. I think he knows what he is talking about. But despite all that, I don't personally expect a war for a long while. But probably the wish is father to the thought. I am sending Monica a little account of some impressions of the assassination – what it has done to French psychology. Maybe she can use it. If not stow it away for me in a dark corner. I would like to save it. But it is "hot news".

Saturday we saw Faust at the Opera. I liked the music very much especially the Soldiers Chorus. But the plot didn't hold water so well. However, I am reading Goethe's Faust in French now and Goethe's version of it is really

221

great stuff, I think. I like the philosophy he works into it. It is long and weighty but very good food for thought. Tonight we three fellows are going to see Lohengrin at the Opera National. I am looking forward to a very nice evening.

Today we gave each other a test in international law and international politics, covering all the ground we have gone over so far. That means that it included 175 pages of Schuman "International Politics" and 175 pages of Fenwick "International Law". We each made out a test and then graded the other's paper. Bill got a 70 and I got a 95. But Bill complained about the type of test I gave him. It was very progressive. The first question counted sixty points and read "Choosing either Italy or Germany as your example, show how the forces of international law and international politics played a part in the country's history". It required a broad knowledge of principles and then a good knowledge of facts about history, treaties and laws, etc. He had a little difficulty with it. I still like that kind of a question, although he thinks it is too hard. The test he gave me was factual and I had little trouble with it. Did I tell you that I went out to Versailles on Sunday? I took a friend along and we started out at 10:30 and got back at 7 in the evening. We took our lunch along, which my Madame kindly made for us. We went all through the Grand Chateau and the Trianons and the beautiful little Hameau of Marie Antoinette and then we saw the Grands Eaux. It is the most beautiful sight imaginable to stand in the terrace in front of the Chateau and look down toward the Basin d'Appollon and into the distant meadows and to see fountains playing on every side. When we first arrived (by train) the park was almost empty. By lunchtime we had finished looking at the Chateau. (We saw all the paintings, which were very interesting from the point of view of history. I was quite comforted to see the little cozy, private rooms of the King and Queen because all those other square, cold rooms looked so very impersonal.) Then we took lunch sitting on a fallen tree in a meadow a few hundred yards outside of the Chateau grounds. An old man who was puttering around the meadow came up and gave us some mushrooms he had gathered. We thanked him very much and I gave them to my friend. She cooked them at home for supper and said they were quite good. Everywhere you look in the park there is something to please the eye. A view up a path isn't just a path; it is usually set off by a fountain at the end of the path, or a grove of trees, or a pleasing curve of the terrain. Everything is so well groomed. We saw the beautiful Temple d'Amour, and sat for a time at the far end of the lake watching the Hameau. About three o'clock the park started to fill with droves of people. Earlier in the day almost everyone around spoke English or German, but then all the French people came to see the Grands Eaux. They played from 4 to 4:30. The park is a very pleasing to the eye, very beautiful, but after a while all the regularity and precision about it gets tiring. I still like the roughness of Hill Farm. The entire outing for two people came only to a little over two dollars, about 30-odd francs. *Paris is filled with Germans – mostly forced or voluntary exiles.

We are continuing to read the textbooks. It will take us to Christmas vacation to finish them both and properly digest the material. Once we know them cold, all the rest of the books will be snaps because there is so much in the textbooks that will be touched on in the other books. We will be able to skip quickly over the other books, reading only the chapters that seem new to us or important.

I am of course still studying French grammar and am reading a history of France. Just finished a book on the Saar territory. The most useful reference book we have is that little book of maps, which Monica gave me before I sailed. Thanks Monica, very sweet of you. We still read the U.S. Constitution every morning at breakfast.

Monday night Aunt Nellie took me out to dinner at the swanky Brasserie Weber where they give each lady a tiger lily gratis. She had a very good-looking and intelligent girl there for me to meet une Autrichienne, Mlle Gaby Deghy. Quite rich, I understand. I saw Nellie off on the Washington Thursday. It was nice to hear all the American voices, or rather it was amusing. But I didn't feel the slightest urge to stay on the train as it pulled out of the station. Not the slightest. Fred is taking me to dinner Monday night. It's very nice to have such attentive relatives. Nellie said she wouldn't be surprised at all if you (Mother) should suddenly trot over here in April or May. Nor would I. By the way, how is that aviation stock doing?

Got a letter from one of the fellows at the World-Telegram (I sent him a postcard.) Things seem to be going along as ever down there. I am going to write Hendershot a letter. Heard from Sibyl but she didn't even mention the accident case. I wonder how it came out.

We can still play tennis in the Luxembourg, although it is getting darker and colder. There were two very cute little English girls in the park yesterday playing ball. They were about 8 and spoke perfect French and had a swell English accent. It was very amusing to listen to them. I am almost ready to start working on my History paper. Very soon we will register at the Sorbonne and the Science Politiques. I hear the Science Pol is a swanky place to go to. Everybody dresses up like a prince who goes there. The Science Pol Ball in the winter is the chicest ball of the season.

I still have 1, 978 francs in the bank. So I have saved a good bit so far. By the way if there are any snapshots of Mother, Monica, Daddy or Caroline lying round, I would like some. I have a big picture of Daddy already and a snapshot of Caroline, but nothing of Mother or Monica. Just so's I don't get you mixed up with some other people when I land next summer, I had better keep a photo handy. Mistaken identities can be quite bothersome.

We read Othello to each other aloud the other night. It is not by any means Shakespeare's best play, in my opinion.

That's all I can think of just now so goodbye and lots of love,

George

3 Rue de la Grande Chaumiere
Paris Vie

October 21, 1934

Dear Mother and Daddy,

I certainly enjoyed your letters. The clipping was very amusing (the one about not raising hogs). I am terribly sorry to hear that Baba is having some trouble. I am writing him today.

Since I last wrote you there has been a lot going on here. A week ago yesterday, Saturday, I went to Barthou's funeral. The procession came up the Esplanade des Invalides to the Invalides. I got a place in the crowd right near the line of march and saw everything. But the press was terrific. It almost squeezed my breath out. The people were at least 30 deep and everyone was pressing hard and leaning toward the front. The funeral was quite colorful. All sorts of dignitaries, Lebrun, Doumergue, the members of the faculty in robes, the members of the Court in their robes, all the cabinet members, the Guarde Republicaine in their bright helmets and with red and black plumes. The students of St. Cyr with bright uniforms and white plumes. The Anciens Combattants all carrying banners of their regiments, 2000 African Spahis in blue pants and long flowing robes all mounted on white horses, several regiments of infantry some in blue and others in khaki. We saw Marshal Petain and General Weygand, and corrupt old Cheron and Laval and every other famous man. The sky was overcast and somber and the crowd seemed a bit scared by all the international developments. The front of the Invalides was draped in black crepe. Doumergue made a short and very impressive speech and then the services were broadcast to the crowd by Haut-Parleurs stationed here and there around the square. Toward the end, as the soldiers filed by I got a place on a stone wall from which I could see over the crowd.

It was a veritable sea of faces – there must have been at least 500,000 people on the square alone.

Yesterday I went to Poincaré's funeral. (Lot of funerals these days). The spirit there was different. The crowd seemed to have recovered a bit from the assassination. When Cheron passed a week ago there were hisses and mutterings. But when he walked by this time people laughed aloud at him. (He has resigned the portfolio of Minister of Justice under public pressure). The day was equally cloudy yesterday, even more so. The funeral took place from the Pantheon, which was draped, in black and deep purple. It looked very beautiful up against the cloudy sky, half hidden by mist. There were more honors paid to Poincaré than to Barthou. More dignitaries and more soldiers. But it was a bit depressing to go to all these funerals.

Monday night I went out with Uncle Fred to the Auberge de Père Louis, a restaurant. I had snails for the first time and liked them immensely. I didn't even think about the snaily side of them. They tasted very, very good, with that green sauce. Then we went to the Actualités and saw some newsreels. It was the night Poincaré died and the minute the poor man gave up the ghost they had resumes of his life on the screen. It was certainly an example of American efficiency applied in France. (Pathe runs the Actualités in France). They had some shots of the assassination. They showed the debarkation from the Jugoslavian cruiser and then the start of the ride up to the Bourse of Marseilles. Just as they got to the Bourse the picture was cut and the next scene was "after the assassination" and showed mob panic in Marseilles. Everyone in the theater hissed at the censorship applied by Sarraut, Minister of the Interior. It did him lots more harm than good. There were only two men on horseback near the car and they were in front of it.

The night of Barthou's funeral we had tickets for Lohengrin but it was called off because of the deuil national. We also had tickets for Rigoletto last night but that was postponed until tonight so we are going to see it tonight. We have been going only to the Opera National, the state-financed one, on the Place de l'Opera. But since Carmen is being given at the Opera Comique next Saturday, I think we will go there to see that.

I received a letter from Comfort thanking me for the one I sent him and one from Dr. Herndon with lots of news about Haverford. I was shocked to hear that Dr. Kelsey is very ill and probably won't live very long.

This morning (Sunday) Bill Fry and I took the Subway all the way out to the Porte de Clignancourt and went to see the Marchée des Puces (Flea Market). Have you ever been there? They have everything under the sun: suits, stoves, food, paintings, radios, hardware, junk, guns, shoes, blankets, rugs, and of course, fleas. Anything you can name can be bought there. I saw some lovely copper kettles and cauldrons that would go well at the farm. Also some beautiful guns and pistols with chased barrels and metalwork. One old poignard of about the 17th century lavishly carved and with an antique mechanism. The district around there is certainly "the other side of the railroad tracks". Thousands of little wooden shanties, each with a garden or mudhole in front, and winding muddy street, with a cobblestone every few feet. I didn't buy anything, though I could have spent a fortune there if I had had the inclination. There were some Americans there, you can see them a mile away. There was a very nice copy of the Mona Lisa there, which for all I know might be one of the famous stolen copies. It was really quite "frappant".

Studies are going along quite well. I have finished studying my history textbook. Monday Bill and I will matriculate at the Science Pol and the Sorbonne. Courses start Nov. 3. I am reading lots of books about the Saar. There isn't a one that isn't prejudiced. But it looks to me as though the only proper thing is for the Saar to go to Germany. If France gets it, it would lead to a war, and would be a very bad settlement of the situation. And of course the status quo is out of the question. That would be almost as bad as if France won the plebiscite. However, no matter who wins the plebiscite, the League of Nations has the final say in the matter. We have been reading the League Covenant to each other at breakfast as a rest from the U.S. Constitution. It's rather interesting but I am becoming a confirmed Positivist or realist in International Affairs. I can't take much stock in brotherly love. It would be wonderful if it existed, but it just ain't. (in international affairs)

Saturday (yesterday) I went to a tea dance at the American Church. There was quite a gay young crowd there and I had a very nice time. They were about 2/3 Americans and 1/3 French. Bought a Baedeker guide to Paris on the Seine for 12 francs which is a very good guide because it gives the history of everything under the sun in and near Paris. We may go out to Chartres next Sunday to see the cathedral. Tonight I may go over and take a look at Notre Dame because I hear it is illuminated every Sunday night and is very beautiful. Am going out with Uncle Fred Monday night. (He invited me to meet him every Monday night and he is going to make me into quite a connaisseur of restaurants). (He doesn't think he will go to the states; hasn't decided yet.) So far I have read and outlined almost 300 pages in each of the very meaty textbooks we are studying, have outlined the history book and done lots of reading for pleasure. Also have read some French classics. I make a practice of going to the Louvre every Thursday afternoon (it's free for students at that time). I have a guidebook and am studying a different school every time. Starting with the Italian primitives and going up. Some of those primitives are very amusing, as well as being quite beautiful paintings.

There is one of some poor little saint being beheaded that is very bloody but so bloody that it is funny.

The Russian dancer's name, in case it is of any interest, is Virginia Balke. She is Russian once removed. I will ask her if she knows Albert Ballin. I don't know about the professor Andre Sigfried, but will look into it.

The weather until today has been quite midwinter Parisian. Bitter cold for two days and then just a warm drizzly fog. The cafes are very cozy in the cold weather. They close them up with glass partitions and have Brassiers sprinkled all around to keep you warm. If you sit near one it is quite comfortable. There is an entirely different atmosphere between a café in the summer and a café in the winter and I have been able to notice it because of the sudden temperature changes. Today, on the other hand it is very nice out and there are some blue patches in the sky. Funds are holding out well but I will be able to use the draft when it comes because I have to pay my immatriculation fees and my rent this week.

The pension is still as good as ever. Food is excellent and varied. But there is one constant and that is – grapes. This is the grape season and since there is a "crise" in grapes this year we have them all the time for dessert. But they are very good. The family is very congenial and my French is getting very polished. I met an Algerian girl at the dance the other day and we got along splendidly. I don't even think she knew I wasn't French.

I bought some prints for 50 centimes, and put them in my room. One is a copy of a Rembrandt (self-portrait) and the other is quite gaudy, bawdy and colorful. Four typically French young ladies. Serves to lighten up the room a bit, but I keep it hidden behind a door and keep the Rembrandt in the open. I thought that since I am in Paris it wouldn't be at all proper not to have some undressed ladies somewhere in the room so I got some for 50 centimes and there you are.

I am glad you are so optimistic about financial conditions. I read a very interesting article the other day in the "Journal des Debats" which spoke about the real estate situation here in Paris. All the new buildings since the war are tenantless or are renting at as much as 50% reductions from the normal rent, but people who have houses built before 1914 have no trouble in renting them. That is because of the great rise in all costs since the war, I imagine. And also that some people contracted long-term leases before the war at a figure, which today is abnormally low. Hence they can easily sublet their apartments.

Did I tell you that last Saturday night I went to the Grand Guignol Theater to see what it was like? Bill suggested it. What a suggestion! They specialize in gory mystery plays and murder plays. The program was "L'Accident de Studio 16" in which a girl's throat was slit on stage "Jack L'Eventreur" all about Jack the Ripper and in which a girl is knifed on stage and a man hung by his neck. They finished off with a comedy "Le Roi des Cocus" which was very raucous and a welcome relief from the blood and thunder.

Living in Montparnasse is a valuable experience. I don't think I will ever be able to be shocked again. You see every sort of flouting of every convention that ever existed. The first time you see incidents of that kind you're shocked, the third or fourth time it is amusing and from then on it is quite natural and you hardly even raise your eyes to look. I am now in that stage.

I was glad to hear about all the livestock at Hill Farm. It must have been grand there as the leaves were turning. That is one thing we don't get here. The leaves turn brown and then drop off. I have been playing tennis and getting exercise that way. There is a student's club that just opened which has a swimming pool and we are going there to use it when it gets going.

This has been a long letter so I had better sign off. Lots of Love to Monica and Caroline and a bouquet to "The Distaff Side".

Love,
George

Monday, October 29, 1934

Dear Mother and Daddy,

This week might be called "national trotting-around week" because that is what I have been doing most of. This was the eventful week when I got my card of identity and registered at the Sorbonne and the Sciences Politiques.

And thereby hangs a tale. It took all of 2 ½ days of good, hard work to get the carte d'identité. You have to have a certificate of domicile, then the local prefecture in your arondissement puts an O.K. on it. After getting that O.K. we went down to the head Prefecture of Paris on the Seine near Notre Dame and there we had the thing countersigned and approved. By that time the other offices were closed. The next day, bright and early, we went to the Sciences Po and got a card saying we were "auditeurs" of the school. We thought that would entitle us to a reduction on the carte. But no. We had to be full "élèves" of the school. So then we went to the Sorbonne and registered there. You register at the main building of the Sorbonne on the Boul Mich but to pay the registration fee you have to walk way down to the Seine to a dingy little office, and then all the way back to have your picture pasted on the card. I enclose one of the pictures. Aren't they beautiful? That's what I look like after getting that carte d'identité. After getting the Sorbonne card, since it was about 1130 we rushed down to the Prefecture hoping to get our cards, but no. The grim-looking woman official looked at the clock, and since there were <u>only</u> 20 minutes left before her lunch hour she wouldn't let us be interviewed for the cards. So we went all the way home and then all the way back and finally I got my carte d'identité for the student's rate of 20 francs. Or rather, I got the provisional card. They don't give you the real card until 3 months later, so they have time to look into your history and see if you have been a good boy or not. At the Sciences Politiques we are trying to be admitted into André Siegfried's course on Economic geography, which is the best course in the school.

I joined up with the American Church.. They give dances and teas twice a week – Wednesdays and Saturdays – I play basketball there. I did it for the first time Wed. night and had a swell time. Grand exercise. Then after the practice 15 of us all went to a restaurant nearby and had a big stag dinner. (That doesn't mean that we ate stag-meat).

Uncle Fred, whom I had dinner with Monday night last at the Escargot, is planning a trip down around Africa and then to South America and up to New York. It would leave France in January and take 3 months. But he has no final plans made yet. Isn't sure what he'll do. I'm going out with him tonight too.

Saturday Bill Fry and I went to Chartres. We left at 10 and got back at 6, took our lunch along. Going down on the train we met two elderly ladies from San Francisco. I saw it coming so moved my seat to another carriage where I talked French with some French girls, but when they left I went and talked with these Americans. One of them spoke German so I spoke German with her.

Chartres was grand. The town impressed me as much as the cathedral. As to the cathedral, Bill C. had loaned me a list of the meanings of each vitrail so we went around the cathedral and in front of each vitrail I would give a little lecture to the old ladies. (One was called Miss Cook). I didn't like the outside of the cathedral nearly as much as the inside. It is so simple inside. The main points of architecture such as arches, ceiling, wall, columns, etc are very simple and beautiful. But when the ornate, gothic style appears, I cease to be crazy about it. I went all over the cathedral. Up to the tower and then I met a graduate of Smith and we went down to the crypt together. A very eerie place. We were piloted by an old crone who showed us the remains of the Roman temple that was built there and lasted until the 9th century. And we saw a 30-meter pit with 3 meters of water at the bottom of it where they throw the sinners, or where they used to, if there were any sinners in those days. The most impressive part was a long, narrow chapel, extending the entire length of the transept, underground. At intervals along the walls are tiny candles in red glass shades and at the far end is the altar, a patch of light in the subterranean darkness. You can understand the pagan charm that the Catholic religion exercises over its members when you stand in that gloom, your eyes fixed on a mellow, flickering candle far, far away in the darkness.

The most interesting part of the town, as you no doubt remember, is down the hill behind the cathedral. We walked down there, toward the Porte Guillaume. There is an old tower from the 12th century "La Tour de la Reine Blanche" You can see the wooden beams set in the mortar, the style of the period.

The old gateway spans a river, and at the edge of the river we saw women washing linen on stones that have been worn smooth by being rubbed, century after century, with rough peasant linen. On the way back I spied what looked like a ruined church, behind a wooden wall. We entered the courtyard behind the wall into what seemed to be a junkyard, and there was L'Eglise de Saint André, dating from the 12th Century, and now a ruin. It is used like a barn to store city property. The arches are just beginning to get pointed, very early Gothic. The pillars and stonework are all very massive. it looks as though it had been swept by fire at some time. Not many people seem to know about it.

Back at the cathedral, we visited the chapel, built more recently, and not as impressive. There is one small window which is my favorite because of its colors(by the cathedral proper). It sheds a sort of a royal purple color, being composed of red and blue stains. The two towers of Chartres, the one early Gothic and the other late Gothic seemed to clash, and I didn't especially like the effect. But when considered singly they are excellent examples of architecture. An old verger in the chapel tried to sell me a monograph he had published on the cathedral. He had been there 30 years and taken pictures of every statue and statuette around the cathedral. It was all very interesting, but I had no money (so I said). But I chatted with him and he told me that he had never had a University training but that he read a lot about cathedrals, etc. He sleeps in a sort of a closet just behind the altar of the cathedral.

We went out third class on the chemin-de-fer and it cost 30 francs apiece, approximately. A very valuable and interesting day. Saturday night I had one of the grandest experiences I have ever had. I saw Carmen at the Opera Comique. Never have I seen any production of anything so beautifully, lavishly, authentically and expertly done. When they swung into the Toreador song I could have jumped up and screamed for joy. As it was, I did yell bravo several times, as did almost everyone else. It was a superb production. Mlle Poccidalo did Carmen and Veriere did Don Jose. After it was over I went around back and waited for the artiste to come out. There were about 30 of us out there, and when she came we all applauded and shouted bravo and she signed autographs for people and kissed all the women and made a little thank you speech.

Sunday we all took Mrs. Crawford over to the Colisée on the Champs Elysees. It was a beautiful day and there were just crowds and hordes and regiments of people walking past our table. Everyone seemed very gay and prosperous. It is hard to put much trust in talk of war when you see thousands of Parisians having a grand time on Sunday, all "en dimanches" and laughing and joking.

The other night I went to a boite chansonier with Bill, "Les Deux Anes". It is one of those tiny little theaters they have in Montmartre. They made cracks about all the politicians and have a revue and jokes and songs, mostly about politics. They talk French faster than anyone on the street talks it and I had to key my hearing up about 100 percent to catch it all. But I understood it so well that I got the jokes before anyone else in the theater and four or five times my loud, booming guffaw almost brought the house down. Once they told a joke I had heard before in English about a rival Catholic and a member of the chosen race. I almost split with laughter and everyone turned around and looked at me (I was in the 1st row balcony). They make cracks about anyone who comes in late and stop the show to ask them questions. One man wouldn't give his coat to the vestiaire so the actor took time out and told him to give it to the vestiaire; the man wouldn't so the actor remarked, "Ah, oui. C'est la crise".

I received notification of your instruction to the Central Hanover to pay me 125 dollars and have instructed them to convert it to francs and credit to my franc account. Thank you very much. I think your suggestion of 175 Dec 1 and then 100 dollars January and February is very good. It suits me perfectly if it suits you.

Thank you for confirming the dress suit. I am going to see about getting one some time this week. Bill says that there are two pretty fine English tailors, notably the West End Tailors. I'll go down and see what they can quote me. Thanks a lot for letting me pay for my own neckties and collars. I am more than anxious to. I am quite excited about the dress suit and top hat. It ought to knock 'em dead, as we say in French.

The radical Socialists are having a Congress over here and getting all stewed up about nothing at all. The crux of the matter is that they all want to appear to be helping Doumergue, yet none wants to sacrifice one franc of graft or one bit of power. They aren't sure yet whether they even will go to Versailles to redraw the constitution. The poor old Senators are scared of losing their power. As one paper remarked, if they grant Doumergue the power to dissolve the chamber he'll dissolve it, and if they don't grant him that power, he'll dissolve it anyhow.

I heard that someone at the American Church wanted a Latin tutor so offered my name. Haven't heard yet what became of it.

You have probably heard from Mrs. Crawford (This item is for Monica mainly) If you haven't, here's the crux of the matter. During her experience with her leg, etc. she wrote a sonnet sequence and would like to see them published. She gave them to a French agent who put them in the hands of an American associate where they have been gathering dust. I told her Monica might be able to do something, or might not. But that it wouldn't do any harm to have them sent to you. She is addressing them to Mrs. Bookman because the N.Y. agent may have heard of Miss McCall and may get suspicious. She is willing to sell them singly to magazines, or any other way. She has a friend, a Mrs. Coyle (Kathleen or Catherine Coyle, I believe) who writes very impressionistic novels at high speed and doesn't have a red cent. Not even a stick of furniture in her room. Claims the publishers have victimized her. Personally I don't think much of the stuff she writes on general principles, but then I am no famous agent. "Flock of Birds" is one of her opuses. I suggested that you might be able to handle her stuff, since her agents are so rotten. By the way, bonus legislation is coming into the fore again, and I think that you may find a market for that old dusty manuscript of mine. The American Legion Conv. voted recently to fight for a bonus in the next Congress. So we may have a chance.

Please give Baba my best and all my wishes and also Ma.

Haven't heard from Caroline in a dog's age. Is she still in the family? Or did she get a divorce?

Finished reading two books, one in German, on the Saargebiet. By the way, I saw the Sainte Chapelle, the other day. It is rich in color isn't it? Warm, glowing. Very beautiful.

That's all I can think of. The enclosed is the program of a deadly concert I went to Sunday night. The pianist was awfully mechanical and the violinist was very scrappy. But she had a good original treatment, which compensated somewhat. Do you know them?

> Lots of love from me, and regards from Bill.
>
> George

PS Went to the Louvre Thursday PM as usual and studied XVth Century Italians and XVI Century. Lauritz Melchior is here singing the Wagnerian operas. I am going to hear him.

P.S. Saw Riggoletto. Wasn't so crazy about it, though I like Verdi's music far better than Gounod's.

November 4 (Sunday)
3 Rue de la Gde Chaumiere, 6e

Dear Mother and Daddy,

I certainly was interested in your letters with the valuable suggestions about the article I wrote, etc. Monica's letter hasn't arrived yet. Tomorrow, Monday, I am going downtown to see Heinzen of the United Press, and a few other people whom I have in mind.

Tomorrow also, the universities open. I have my first class on Tuesday at 11 with Michaut, professor of French Literature at the Sorbonne. The first half year the course studies Pascal's "Pensées I and II". The last half they study Molierès "Don Juan". Or maybe it is vice versa. Then Wednesday at 3:15 I have a class with André Siegfried at the Ecole Libre des Sciences Politiques which I will call the "Science Po" from now on when I mention it. (That's what all the students call it). On Thursday at 11:15 I have a lecture on "Modern Europe and the interests of European countries outside Europe" with Prof. René Pinon at the Sciences Po. I haven't yet decided about the Art course. I could take a course at the Ecole de Louvre for 120 francs because at the Sorbonne there is no complete course in Art. They just take up special periods in different courses and I want a general view of the subject. Mais nous verrons.

I did quite a lot of work this week, reading a very interesting part of the International Politics text on "Imperialism". We are up in the 400's in both books now. Considerably more than ½ way through. I also finished a book on the Saar, and read "Finance and Politics" by Paul Einzig. It blames the entire depression on France's ruthless financial policy, and makes England (very nice place, Monica) out to be just one notch lower than the Angel Gabriel. His writing is very emotional and he gets all in a froth at France, and then runs back and whitewashes England. But it was good food for thought.

Last night (Saturday) I saw Rosalinde given by the Atelier. (As You Like It). They called it Rosalinde to avoid confusion with another production playing at the same time. I had never seen a mise-en scene of any Shakespeare production, which was as good. And for a comedy of the type of "As You Like It", I really thought that French sounded better than English. There is much more gaiety in the French language, and the speeches which would sound forced and overacted in English sound perfectly natural in French. Jacques Coppeau was in the cast, and he has a very big reputation.

I spent some time seeing tailors recently, and will see some more tomorrow. I think I can get an excellent job done on coat, pants and vest for a little over 1000 francs. The hat will cost 150 francs. Is that all right? I can probably get a few shirts made for about 50 or 60 apiece, and may even get them ready-made if they conform to the vest well enough. I could use the draft soon to pay for them. If there is any balance either way you can add it to or subtract it from the next month's check. As to the form in which to send the money over, unless Roosevelt cuts up right after the elections and does some devaluation, I think francs would be the best form, at the present. The government looks pretty weak here. Old Papa Doumergue made a speech last night threatening to go home to his little garden cottage at Tournefeuille if the politicos and grafters didn't stop blocking his reforms. He is the only disinterested, honest man in the Government, and if he goes it will be too bad for France. There isn't a man left with an ounce of integrity or impartial leadership. And France can't stand any more partisan, grafting government. The German propaganda in the Saar is raising howls from the French press just as much as the French military maneuvers near the Saar are irritating the German papers. Personally, I don't expect to see anything very serious come out of the Saar plebiscite. It looks like a foregone conclusion that Germany will get it and that France and the League will be glad to get rid of it. But there are almost as many indications to the contrary.

Upton Sinclair seems to be providing lots of entertainment in the States. I am anxious to see what will happen at the elections.

Uncle Fred took me on Saturday to hear a French Marshall speak on "Mon Ami le Roi Alexandre de Yougoslavie" It was at the Ambassadeurs, chicest theater in Paris (Champs Elysées). The speech was very dull because the old marshall couldn't be heard past the third row and what he said wasn't very startling, but the crowd there was very interesting. Very rich, aristocratic people. And the lobby was filled with Republican Guards in helmets and flowing plumes. It was quite a nice milieu to be in.

Went to a Halloween party at the American Church, which was good fun. Bill had his face blackened with charcoal in one of the "stunts" but he took it in good spirits. They had dancing and there was quite a nice crowd. I may go to MacNab for my dress suit, or MacDougall. Uncle Fred has been very nice about running around and getting me samples prices, etc. Because I have to study.

Took a walk around the Ile de Saint-Louis, Place des Vosges, and the very old quarter around there behind Notre Dame and behind the Hotel de Ville. It was very interesting. The streets were dark already when we (a graduate of Smith and I) started out; it was already darkish and the darkness blotted out all the 20th Century innovations. You could very well have imagined yourself back in the 17th Century Paris, the time when that particular quarter flourished.

All Saints' Day was a holiday here (Nov. 1) and everyone was out on the streets in their Sunday clothes. I took some time off to see what it was like. That's the nice part about a Catholic country, you get a holiday from the office, much more often than in the States. But the clerks etc. work much longer, later and harder than clerks do in New York, for instance. They start in at 8:30 or 9 and finish at 6. But then, I forgot the fact that they get 2 hours off for lunch, which isn't so bad.

The New Yorker came today, radiating joy and happiness and cosmopolitan atmosphere all over the place. It is certainly a very welcome addition to our family life over here. By the way, the pension is still very satisfactory, even more so. I am a great pal of Monsieur now because I admired his perfectly awful paintings. My French is coming along like a houseafire. Partly due to French at the table, partly to French opera, plays, etc., partly to French girl friends, and partly just due to France in general, I am making progress through the grammar book.

Wrote a letter to Hendershot the other day and will write the Managing Editor there soon. Also intend to write Bernays.

I was very glad to hear that Baba is better. Please give him my very best. I am writing him, soon.

There are a lot of good operas playing this coming week. Bill is in here as I type trying to decide what to see. We have seen so little and there is so much to see. The theater here is having a good season. There must be about 30 houses lighted, and there are some quite good things, according to comment. Amphitryon 38, a modern version of the old story, is quite well thought of. Then Sacha Guitry is in something or other. I wish I had the resources to see some of them. But I am getting a lot out of the Opera.

> Can't think of any more bits so Bon Soir
> and lots of love,
> George

PS The Pipe Caroline gave me is getting very good use. I like it very much.

November 11, 1934
3 Rue de la Grande Chaumiere
Paris, VIe, France

Dear Mother and Daddy,

Thanks for your letters. You can imagine that I was quite saddened to hear of the death of Dr. Kelsey. I had expected it though. He was the youngest member of the faculty, in spirit.

This week I have done a great many things. First of all, I had an interview with Ralph Heinzen, European director of the United Press. He was a grand fellow, and didn't have all the shee-shee about him that most editors seem to have. He came down the hall to greet me, helped me off with my coat, and treated me like his own brother. I told him what I had done and he said that if there are any riots in the streets as there were last year or any other really BIG news he will use me as a reporter. Also he may ask me to help out on some of the night shifts in the office. And he is going to get me a police card that will admit me to anything I want to be admitted to – such as the Chamber of Deputies. We had a little chat about int affairs, etc. and then he helped me on with my coat and accompanied me to the elevator. I never met an editor who was so cordial. They usually growl in their beards and get rid of you in about 2 minutes flat.

Caroline's poison-ivy experience must have been painful. Very negligent of the Botany professor. I sympathize with Caroline, to the bottom of my heart.

I attended my first lectures this week. The lectures at the Sciences Po are in a wonderful, modernistic building furnished in up-to-the-minute style. Everyone claps the professor before and after the lecture. Bill and I bought together printed copies of the entire course, and we read each lecture before it is delivered. And then in class we take notes. Taking notes improves my French tremendously, because I take notes in French. Since the classes meet only once a week, the professor packs a lot of meat into each lecture. And the courses are very interesting. I am taking, as you know, "Economic Geography" with André Siegfried, "Contemporary Europe and her interests outside of Europe" with René Pinon. At the Sorbonne I am taking a course studying "Moliere's Don Juan intensively this semester. I read the play the other day and it is a queer thing. Half farce – half supernatural. The second semester the course takes up Pascal's "Pensées". At the Ecôle du Louvre we are going to take a History of Art for another 75 francs.

I received a letter from Kunkle, editor in chief of the Haverford News, telling me lots of pleasant things. My resignation, which I offered to the News Board due to my enforced absence of one year, was not accepted and they gave me some new title on the masthead like Foreign Editor, or something like that. So I immediately sat down to the typewriter and tossed off my impressions of studying in Paris. By the time I finished typing, the article was really quite good (if I must say so myself). I don't know how it took form, but when I read it over everything was as though I had outlined it before starting to write. I said the two greatest differences between studying here and studying at Haverford are (1) We are not isolated from the rest of the world here. (2) We are completely independent. I will have to send them more articles in order to live up to the editorship they gave me.

About those reports. Of course you understood, didn't you, that the reports will be in the form of outlines of the reading I have done? And I am sending you the outlines of both of those enormous textbooks at one time. I will have them finished some time in early December. Everything that I wrote to Haverford I have written to you also.

Last night I saw <u>Siegfried</u> at the Opera National. I had never seen one of the Ring Operas before and was tremendously impressed. To me Wagner now seems so far above all other composers of Opera that there is no comparison. People like Verdi and Gounod are incapable of treating a theme as lofty as the Niebelungenlied. It takes a supreme master to put into music the romance and lore of an entire nation, and especially of the German nation, and I think that Wagner has done it to perfection. It also occurred to me how far Germany under Hitler has fallen from the noble traditions of its folklore. Bill C. was terribly depressed by the music. I will never take him to hear Wagner again. He moped around all evening and is still in a mopey mood. He was already depressed when he went to the Opera and it put him in a blue funk. He is reading Barry to snap out of it. I have Shaw's St. Joan on my table and a book on Italian poetry since Dante, which I mean to read soon.

We three play basketball once a week with the American Church team. It is grand exercise. Last Wed night I played steadily for an hour and a half. After that they give you a very nice supper.

I ordered my dress suit at MacNab's, a Scotch tailor on the Rue de Rome. I am getting a soft black material, not glossy at all. And a diamond-pique vest with three buttons. Silk lining in the coat, and all the pockets I want. The whole to cost 1010 francs. (coat, vest and pants). It will be ready in ten days. I am having the first fitting on Tuesday and I think Uncle Fred is coming along as an impartial observer. I haven't ordered any shirts yet, but will soon. The entire outfit will come to about 1500 francs, or $100. I hope I receive the draft soon so I can pay for the stuff and have it in my wardrobe. I am very excited about seeing how it will look on me. I will have to pick an A#1 girl to take out the first time I wear it.

Today is Armistice Day and there have been some very gay parades up near the Etoile. At Salle Pleyel (now called Salle Rameau) Gigli is singing soon. Bill Fry has an abonnement there and goes to a concert every Sunday afternoon (Paris Symphony Orchestra). They give various programs. Last Sunday he didn't like it because they gave a lot of Stravinsky. Toscanini is conducting two concerts at the Theatre des Champs Elysées.

I may go to some of these concerts. But at present the Opera is sufficing.

This week the government fell, as you know. They kicked out the last honest man, Doumergue, and put in a cabinet that can't last more than a few weeks or months. It is only a coalition and a postponement of the eventual disaster. There may be a coup d'etat here by the Croix de Feu or by a man called de Villis(?) an old army man and now an editor of a paper. I took a swing around Paris the night Doumergue resigned to see what effect it had on the people. It had been expected for some days, so no one was terribly excited. There was a feeling of tension however. People seemed to be terribly tired of all the rotten politics that has been going on. Some day, soon, they will become really angry and then things will begin to pop. The greatest interest now is Germany's rapid rearmament and the war-scares that Lord Rothermere's <u>Daily Mail</u> is throwing out.

Enclosed is a carbon copy of a letter to Haverford.

Love to all,
George

My best to Ma and <u>Baba</u>.

George B. Bookman

November 19, 1934
3 Rue de la Grande Chaumiere
Paris, VIe, France

Dear Mother and Daddy,

Your newsy letters were very interesting. So glad that Baba is himself again.

Work is coming along well. There are less than 75 pages to finish up in one of the books about 250 in the other. (That other one is endless) It has 800 pages. What we have read in these two textbooks will cover most of the ground that is covered by a lot of the other books on our list. And of course we are not going to do paragraph-by-paragraph outlines of <u>every</u> book we read. It has been pretty grueling – outlining each darn paragraph of these two fat books, but we got it done and (or will in a week or so) and there you are. You can have the outlines for a Christmas present.

Let's not send any packages across the water, by the way, this Christmas. It always costs twice as much in francs as it does in dollars, to start with, and then French postal rates are very high anyhow and transatlantic shipping rates are almost prohibitive. A 20-franc present would probably have to bear postage amounting to 50 francs. And that isn't exaggeration. But if you want to send any, I won't kick. I have been keeping a weather eye out for nice things to bring back in my trunk. Saw a beautiful old oak chair the other day and on it, in delicate carving were the letters "AMB" It amused me and I am sure it would have intrigued you, but it would be pretty hard to bring home a chair. So I just look at it every time I pass it, but don't buy it.

I have been going to lectures and enjoying them very much. Siegfried's lecture the other day on the character of the English people was really a gem. Very humorous and very shrewd observations. He was said by somebody or other to be the foreigner who best understood the English people. And that's going some, isn't it, Monica?

Courses at the Ecole du Louvre start this week. Fridays and Saturdays at 5 P.M. Friday they treat ancient art and Saturdays, they treat modern and XIXth Century Art. They have a different professor for each school and period. So you really hear the experts on each field. The classes take place right in the Louvre, in the soussol and you feel as though you were in the correct milieu for such a course. You are.

Uncle Fred took me to a wonderful restaurant last night. It looks like a dump when you come in. You expect to see a lot of truck drivers sitting around but instead the people at the tables are very well to do and all look as

239

though they knew good food. They come up to the chef and ask him how the wife and kiddies are getting along and chat a bit and then place their orders personally. What food! I had a coq au vin that is making the mouth of the typewriter water as I write the words. He has decided on his winter plans: he will take a cruise on a British boat that goes down the West Coast of Africa to the Cape, a week in Africa, then up the East coast a bit and across the Indian Ocean to Bali (week in Bali) Java, Singapore, Malaya, then back to Aden and the Suez Canal and back to Southampton which is the point of departure also. It stops at about 15 ports or more and takes 2 ½ months. He has a big double cabin to himself. Sails January 26 from Southampton, and is quite enthusiastic about seeing some more of the world. He sends you his regards.

I haven't yet decided on my plans for the Christmas vacation but probably will before the week is over. My dress suit is coming along very quickly. Will have it almost finished by next Friday, except for the lining and other last minute things like that.

It looks very snappy and will be a great success. I am sure.

I have tickets for Lohengrin next Saturday. Gigli is singing here as the duke in Rigoletto. I would go to hear him but I don't care so much for the Opera that he is singing in. So I suppose I won't go, unless I change my mind at the last minute. Toscanini conducted 2 concerts here and the place was sold out weeks in advance. He will conduct two more later on and there isn't a seat left under 80 francs, so I imagine that I won't go. Rather, I know very well I won't go.

This week I read some Bernard Shaw and some Petrarch. I am sorry this letter is so short, but I have to go to a class at the Science Po and if I don't finish it, it won't catch the boat. There will be lots more in the next letter, to make up for it.

Lots of love,
George

Love to Monica

November 29, 1934
3 Grande Chaumiere
Paris, VIe

Dear Mother and Daddy,

240

I was so proud to read that Daddy has been made President of Montefiore Medical Board. I wish he had been here this week, I could have used another doctor. The reason I haven't written for a little while is that although I am now all cured, completely and unequivocally restored to my former good health, I was in bed for 5 days with a bad intestinal infection. It came from something I ate. I had Dr. Kresser whom you recommended and he was very good. Saturday the twenty fourth I felt awfully tired and feverish and hadn't felt right for several days. Also had loose bws. So I went to this Dr. Kresser and he saw I had 103 temperature and ordered me to bed and kept me on a regime. From day to day the temperature gradually went down and today I am out of bed, dressed and at work once more and eating like a normal human being. Of course he doesn't' want me to eat everything under the sun yet but I can eat most things. And I feel perfectly fine. I was well taken care of. Mme was very nice to me and put up no kick about all the extra trouble and treats me like a baby that has to be watched. For several days I had bad headaches and tired eyes and so I couldn't do any work but I am now working hard to make up for that. Fred came to see me once and several young friends dropped in frequently. It wasn't so bad but I am dead sick of beds and I never want to see one again, (until tonight). Anyhow, it is all over now and I thought it would be better to let you know when it was all over, since you couldn't do anything about it any way except worry. And now you needn't even worry. He hasn't sent any bill yet or mentioned it. That will all come in good time, I imagine. I tried to tell him as gently as possible that my father is a doctor and say it in an insinuating tone of voice. I don't know whether it registered or not.

Sorry to have missed Aunt Bella's birthday party which must have been a lot of fun. She certainly is a gay belle, at her age.

I am eager to hear more about the work with the Music School. Sounds like just the sort of thing you like to do and can do very well. What's their new idea? As soon as I may go out – probably tomorrow – I will go to the tailor's for the final fitting of my dress suit and then I will be completely outfitted but for the shirts. I may get them ready-made since I am so easy to fit.

I have arranged from now on to pay my landlady every 2nd of the month so if the draft gets here about the thirtieth or 29th that will give me plenty of time. So far I have saved about 1000 francs.

I have not seen a newspaper much during the past few days. But most French opinion believed that Flandin is only a temporary stopgap and that he has stayed in office this long only because there has as yet been no crisis to challenge his security. The talk of war gets more and more imminent. But I think Germany means business and the others are bluffing. Germany will seize the Saar and the others will have to like it or suffer in silence. Just the same way Germany assassinated Dolfuss. No one raised a finger against her. (At least not for long). Hope I'm right

As you can well imagine I haven't received many new impressions these last few days that you would care to hear about. New impressions of the wallpaper (which is a virulent-reddish combination of cherries) – but that is all.

I did read Shaw's "Arms and the Man" which kept me in stitches all the way through. And the New Yorker has just come with some good things in it, but that is about all. But I will soon be in circulation again.

I received a very nice card from the Spiesses this morning wishing me a Happy Thanksgiving. It was quite touching and very welcome. Bill Crawford and Bill Fry are going off tonight to a big turkey dinner at the American club which I cannot eat so I am staying home. But I have a lot to be thankful for, anyhow.

The lectures at the Ecole du Louvre are very good and are given with many, many slides of actual works of art, etc., which makes it ever so much more interesting. I went to one and missed the second, but will attend all the rest, I expect.

Well, that is all for now.

Lots of love,
George

Here's to you, Monica, …..!

George B. Bookman

December 6, 1934

Mother dear,

All my thoughts, experiences, memories and all of Paris from Montmartre to the Quartier Latin wish you a very, very happy birthday. And lots of happiness and all my love, and a thousand kisses and I hope everything comes out all right.

I also thank you a million times for the check. And I have been thinking of ideal ways to spend it. Unhappily, the series of Toscanini concerts is over and I didn't get to hear one. When I phoned for seats all they had left were 100-franc seats. But last Sunday I went to a concert at Salle Gaveau. Heard a program of Brahms 1st Symphony, Liszt, Rimsky-Korsakoff and Beethoven.

With the very welcome $5 you sent me I could go to about five concerts, or I could buy some reproductions of some of my favorite old masters in the Louvre. Or I could get some interesting old prints of Paris, or a lot of books, or a set of Molière or some other author. Or some snappy shirts and neckties (very improbably). Or a bottle of champagne (most improbable). But I am going to spend the money in a way that I would spend it if I were with you, in the way that you would probably spend it if you were in Paris. And what's more, I'll spend it on December 15. I think I will use it to go to the Opera Comique. I don't yet know what they will be playing that night, but whatever it is, it will be good, I know. And I will get myself a good seat, a libretto (and perhaps take a friend) and have a grand time and come home and think of you and hope that you have had as happy a December Fifteenth as I, and so to bed.

There has been a sort of struggle going on in my mind. Whether to enter into American activities here in Paris, or whether to keep away from the Americans and stick to French friends, French amusements. It is so easy to slide into the ways of going from one American Club to another, speaking and thinking English. But I have virtually made up my mind to let the American activities go to h—l, and to get all out of the French side of Paris that I can. After all, I can get all the Americans I want at home, and I didn't come here to polish up my slang, or to improve my wisecracking. There have been lots of things influencing my decision, not the least being the departure for America of a very sweet girl with whom I spent most of my time during the first months in Paris. I have come to the decision that there is a great compensation in steeping yourself in your work and that there is no better recreation to be had than a twilight stroll around the Quartier Ste. Genevieve behind the Pantheon, or an afternoon spent in the Louvre or the Cluny. My French is really (boasting again) quite good both conversationally and otherwise. I take all my notes in French at lectures, and write some letters in French. Also do a little composition from time to time. I read the stuff almost as well as English and am getting so that I can run my eye down a column of newspaper print and get the same sense almost as easily as though it were the New York World-Telegram I had before me.

Work is going splendidly and I am getting a bigger kick out of it than ever. Today I was reading all about the theories of Kant, Fichte, Hegel and Nietzsche, et al on government. I have finished one of those big textbooks and in one week I will have finished the other. I will send you the outlines as a Christmas present, or possibly as a New Year's present. The work I am doing now is really interesting – reading about political philosophy, staking down the gist of the books as I read them and then writing a critique of each book. It puts lots of ideas into my head about philosophy and all sorts of things like that. On the side I am reading a book called "Apollo" which is a History of Art and an excellent one. It is full of pictures and illustrations. The best book of its kind that has ever been published, I believe. I have it in French, but it has been translated into almost all languages. The courses at the Ecole du Louvre are very interesting. They are accompanied by slick slides showing all the great art treasures and explaining every little point. I am making progress also in reading the gems of French literature. Have read some of the earlier things like the Chanson de Roland and other crude beginnings of Literature. Then I read some Villon, which I liked very much. Have read "Le Cid" of Corneille and "Discours de la Méthode" of Descartes. And I have on my table copies of lots of other things, which I am going to read. For what is equivalent to a nickel, or sometimes 3 cents or 4 cents you can get cheap, paper-bound editions of all the greatest classics of the language. At the end of the year if any one author has fascinated me a great deal I think I will blow myself to a set of his works.

The most popular piece of music we have here (we have a phonograph) is Beethoven's Sonata in A. It has a great sentimental value for me since I always played it when a certain good friend came to visit me. We play it incessantly, as a reveille in the morning, a bugle call at noon and as taps at night. It is our theme song.

Read Bronwing's "Pippa Passes" the other night. It was a queer thing. Interesting little narrative and some spots of brilliant poetry. But typically Browning all the way through – right down to the last pentameter. Your comments on music were very instructive: I mean when you told me not to try to compare French, Italian and German music. I had no conception of the different ways the three types of composers went about their work and what you said about them helps me to place them better in my own mind. I think I'll be able to appreciate them much better now.

I am coming to think less and less of the modern French Theater – I mean the avant garde. Uncle Fred took me to see a play called "Le gout du Risque" and I took myself to see Max Dearly (excellent actor) in "Azais". They are both typical French farces of the neo-bedroom type that make you laugh but which really aren't very funny when you come to think of it. At one point in "Le Gout du Risque" I laughed out loud when I shouldn't have because the fake whiskers on the butler were so obviously stagy. But it is all very amusing and good for the French. (I mean for my knowledge of the French language). But there are some good things in town, I understand, although I haven't had the chance to see them yet.

Today I saw Gitta.* It was grand seeing her, but I arrived at her hotel at a quarter to twelve and at one o'clock her train left for Budapest. You can imagine what a nice long chat we had. There were about 16 other artists and managers in the room all chattering away at top speed, making cracks about the Judson management (I can remember artists making cracks about Judson ever since I was old enough to spell the man's name) and they were all making dirty cracks at every other living pianist except Gitta (Victor Witgenstein in particular). And Gitta was running from one end of the room to the other in an old blue shirt, tearing her hair out by the roots, worrying about tickets, about being met at the station, the fact that she would have to spend one day in Budapest because there was no train on Sunday; the room was liberally strewn with open valises, clothes were hanging everywhere, mostly from the floor, newspaper criticism covered every square inch of space that wasn't occupied by a suitcase or an artist. And amid all the hullabaloo she had time to show me a picture of her baby, Rachel Judith. Very pretty child. The criticisms in London and Holland and Warsaw were wonderful and she is having a grand tour. She is not giving any concerts in Paris so I won't be able to hear her. After Budapest she goes to Monte Carlo, then 2 weeks in Italy and finally home late in December. She looked very tired – probably practices much too hard when she should be resting for her concerts. But it was all typically musical, typically Gitta to see her running around in a little blue blouse, tearing her hair, making funny faces, sly wisecracks and dramatic gestures of despair. It was the most hectic scene I ever witnessed but it was very amusing and as stimulating as a Pernod. She sends you her very best love.

*Gitta Gradova - A pianist and close friend of my Mother

As my plans are working out now, I will be here in Paris on the 22 but either late that day or late on the 23 I will board the train for Chamonix. I bought a swell pair of skiing shoes for 110 francs and all the rest of the equipment is going to be lent to me by some young Vaujany (the son of the family that runs this pension). So I will save a lot of money. I would have had his shoes too, but they didn't fit me. Were about a foot too short for my big clodhoppers. I will stay in Chamonix from the 23 until about the 2nd. It will be a bit expensive, but my exchequer can stand the strain. I intend to spend about 800-900 francs during the vacation. We are all chipping in to buy Madame a little present for Christmas – probably a set of coffee cups, which she needs badly. And I think I'll send Mrs. Crawford a plant or something innocuous like that. Bill will stay here all during the vacation and Bill Fry is going on a bicycle trip with some Americans to the Midi and the Côte d'Azur. I will probably take the same trip this summer if I still have any money left (I'm sure I will).

The stomach trouble is practically all cleared up now. It was a pretty serious attack while it lasted – 103 fever and all that – and I have no idea what caused it. But it is all over now so that's that. I haven't eaten anything "queer" and haven't the slightest idea how it happened. But I am 100% now so it is a thing of the past and we won't talk about that any more. I had an after effect of it called spasms of the colon (yes, I've had my spasms in my day) which was very painful, but that is also all cleared up.

This afternoon I had intended to go to that old barn, the Trocadero, to see them give "Le Cid". But just as I was about to leave who should walk in the door but a fellow who graduated from Haverford last year, Dick Pleasants by name, captain of the football team in his Senior year and lots of other important things. He majored in French and is now over here on an exchange fellowship teaching English in a French lycée at Chartres. It seems to be a very lonely life and he looked a bit depressed. Doesn't seem to be getting all out of it that one could. Chacun a son gôut.

The letter to Citroen never came, by the way. It may be just as well because the other day Citroen told his creditors he would commit suicide if they didn't lend him some more money. So they did. He is in a very bad way.

But the international horizon tonight is really quite pink. Laval has just told the League that he won't use French troops in the Saar and Britain has just said that she and Czechoslovakia, Russia and Italy are prepared to send in an impartial international police force. Everyone here is breathing easier and can sit back and start to enjoy life once more. I had a feeling all along that the Saar question wasn't worth a war. It seems to be justified. The psychological factors weren't ready for a war on either side of the Rhine. The Saar would be a wonderful pretext for a war – practically perfect – but no one wants the war – yet. A little stir was caused by an article published by "Le Journal" said to be a confession of Karl Ernst that he had been ordered by Hitler and Goering to put fire to the Reichstag. Everyone believes Hitler burned the Reichstag and this seems to be absolute proof. But it could also be just a good way to sell newspapers and to stir up nationalistic feelings. There are lots of over-clever journalists in Europe. Sauerwein's articles are very interesting and exceedingly well written. He had an interview with Mussolini and wrote a corking article about him. In home politics it is the ex-police-inspector Bonny who is giving all the fun. He has been arrested for fraud in office and now he is telling tales on all his ex-accomplices. Just a grafter who couldn't keep his mouth shut. The others are just as corrupt but they know when to retire from the public eye. This fellow was foolish enough to sue a political review "Gringoire" for some nasty but perfectly true things they said about him in their columns. Of course every paper in town made him the laughing stock of Paris and the journalists who testified in court added to his misery. It was a holiday for the humorists and mudslingers on all the Paris papers. A busman's holiday. And of course M. Bonny got the drubbing of a lifetime in court and his fate was screamed in black headlines by every paper. Anyone is a fool to ruffle the feathers of the French press.

I went to the Luxembourg Museum the other day to look at some of the moderns who are represented there. I came away with rather a low opinion of modern painting and a much greater esteem for the old masters. But then I may be falling into the same fallacy of comparing 2 different things – of trying to reduce to a common denominator 2 kinds of art that are striving in absolutely different directions. Be that as it may, I saw some canvasses which I liked a great deal, but most of them had no appeal for me, in fact a lot of them disgusted me. Much of the modern canvasses seem to be a lazy man's type of painting. A stab at something that is left raw and unfinished. Or a hurried attempt to slap something down on canvas that should be carefully worked out and that should be done with great pains. I still think there is nothing that can beat the Flemish school, Surrealism to the contrary notwithstanding.

This has been a very long letter, but in it I have tried to give you some of my ideas on Paris. Some of my reactions and thoughts, memories and experiences. It is the best sort of birthday present I can think of to give you. Sort of like opening the window of my soul for a few minutes (I hope I have a soul) and letting you peek in to see what Paris has done to me.

Goodnight and lots and lots of love and kisses, and I hope you have a wonderful birthday. I will think of you at the Opera Comique.
George
Love to Daddy, Caroline and Monica and everyone else.

George B. Bookman

December 11, 1934

Dear Mother, Daddy, Caroline and Monica:
Hello and Merry Christmas and a Happy New Year.
You'll probably get this about a week before Christmas but you could put it in alcohol and preserve it until Christmas and then read it again and it would have the desired effect.

I am starting on a "great adventure" the 22n of December. I signed up with a sort of organized group trip to Chamonix. You pay 660 francs and get 12 days in Chamonix, all expenses such as board and room, railroad, etc. paid.

Free entrance to the Casino, free skiing lessons. The house that is running the trip is a reputable one, "France Tourisme", so it is likely that I won't be forced to eat nails or sleep on a shelf. But you never can tell. Anyhow, I am going. If the accommodations are good, so much the better, if they are otherwise I'll have to work out a solution. The skis I am borrowing from Jean Vaujany, son of the Madame who keeps this pension. He is also lending me all the other trappings that go with the skis as well as a pair of skiing pants.

The dress suit is all finished and I wore it Saturday night. It fits perfectly and really looks very, very swell. The occasion was a ball given by the nurses of the American Hospital. It was certainly a very medical crowd. Everywhere you turned there was a doctor, an intern or a nurse. Doctors as a class seem to get more fun out of life than almost any other class of men. There was champagne galore, all contributed by the doctors, and cakes and sandwiches, etc. Someone had sent us tickets for it and we certainly enjoyed ourselves. The party got a little boisterous when they had a medical Paul Jones. But doctors will be doctors, as you no doubt know. Thank you very, very much for the dress suit. It is the most useful thing I could imagine (except a monkey-wrench) and it is very good for my morale to wear it. Not that my morale is in such a very sickly condition.

Are you going to be at the farm or in the city for the vacation? I'll think of you as celebrating the Weinachsten feast at Solebury until I hear to the contrary. Joyeux Noel.

Saturday night (December 15, Mother), I am going to the Opera Comique where the Russian Ballet of Paris is giving a dance recital. They are doing a lot of very grand things, including the Russian dance (I can't spell its real name) from Prince Igor.

Sunday I spent in the Cluny museum. Really, I have never been so interested in that sort of museum before. I can't explain it, but I was fascinated by the old shoes and tapestries and porcelains and especially the painted tiles from Limoges that they have there. I never thought very much of that sort of thing before, but I am beginning to see what it is all about and to appreciate it. The best way I have found to get myself to appreciate it is to say to myself "Suppose you tried to do that". I immediately have a profound respect for the work of art in question, which isn't hard to understand when you consider the little tours de force executed on the back of these Christmas cards. I bought a little pamphlet on the styles of French furniture, fully illustrated with pictures of different tables, chairs, etc., so now I may be able to tell a Louis XIV from a Louis XV. Or vice versa. Heard a very interesting lecture on the artists of Egypt the other day by the curator of the national museum at Brussels who was called by one paper "not only an expert in art, but an apostle of art." He has a great love for the Egyptian relics and knows them through and through.

He described the methods used in an Egyptian atelier, and showed slides of some newly excavated finds that haven't been made public yet.

If it weren't for the fact that the postage is so terribly high to America on packages, I would send all you beautiful ladies several Chanel dresses apiece, with a fistful of neckties for the masculine side of the family, but as the French say, "La Crise" is upon us, so I hope this will take the place of the original Chanel models and silk neckties. (Rather a vain hope).

Lots of love and Merry Christmas
George

December 15, 1934

Dear Daddy

Here they are: the outlines of the most important books we've read so far in Government.

You're not supposed to read the big piles of paper – not a letter has been changed since it was first typed. There are dozens of typographical errors on every line. They aren't supposed to be read – they're just mute witnesses to what we've been doing

Merry Christmas to the whole Family.

Lots of love,
George

I was forced by the post office people to send the outlines under separate cover.

December 15, 1934

Dear Family,

To celebrate your birthday, Mother, I am sending off these outlines. I would drape them with flags if the postal regulations allowed it.

Thank you very much for all your letters. I got six letters last night and everyone else at the table got green-eyed with jealousy. Aunt Belle wrote me a very interesting letter, enclosing 60 francs and a clipping on the bridges of Paris. Very interesting, especially the 60 francs.

Tonight I am going to the Operá Comique to see the Ballet Russe perform. It is supposed to be very good. A week from tonight I board the train for Chamonix. Got the letter from Mr. Kauffman with the names of some people he knows here. It was all a bit vague. I haven't done anything about it yet.

I am more pleased than ever every time I go to a lecture of André Siegfried. He is really a privilege to listen to. He is a great man. All the papers are talking of him; he makes addresses on current questions all the time, writes for the reviews. An article he wrote called "The crisis of Europe" attracted a lot of attention. He believes that Europe as a world center is passing out of the picture. He brings that out in his course too. I sent an editorial about that article to my professor at Haverford, Old Doc Herndon.

The Haverford News sent me a copy of a recent issue. To my surprise I was listed as "Paris Correspondent" so I have been getting busy and have sent them a few articles.

Financial note: I could use the monthly check at about the usual time this coming month (January) because I pay my rent on the first day of the month and it makes things difficult if there's no wherewithal to pay it. I'll be back in Paris on the 2nd or 3rd. Have made no decisions yet about a trip to the Saar. I'll decide that when the time comes.

I hope the cocktail party is a howling success. I am sure it will be. Drink a couple for me. The invitations are certainly original. I can't think of a much better place for a dance than your new apartment – nor of a much better gal to give it than C.B.

Did you see the crack about Pitts Sanborn in the New Yorker, issue of November 24? I'll enclose it in this letter.

I am really getting pretty interested in the study of art. However, yesterday I set out with the intention of walking down to the Louvre to see some Greek sculpture. I walked down by way of the Rue Saints Perès, which is just lousy with art-shops, if I may use the crude expression. I looked in every window, and lingered at every shop, and when I got down to the Quais I just loafed along, looking at all the prints and books. By the time I got to the Louvre it was so dark you would have had to use a flashlight to see any Greek sculpture. (It gets dark at about 4:30 now).

There is going to be a lecture on Venice at the Ecôle du Louvre on Tuesday to which I think I will go. Later on there will be lectures on Florence and on Rome, also.

Everybody is patting the League of Nations on the back for its great work in clearing up the troubled international situation last week. It looks as though the nations have decided to postpone hostilities at least a year or so. It might be the beginning of that warless world we have heard so much about. But, much as I would like to believe it, I don't. Young Flandin has stuck at his post longer than most people gave him credit for. It looks as though he might get some constructive legislation through the Chamber on wine and wheat without running into a political monsoon. He hasn't struck any bad bumps yet and there aren't signs of any in the immediate future. But the scandal situation – Bonny, Staviski, Prince, et al – is just as bad as ever, if not worse. They let Bonny go scot free after arresting him because (it is rumored) he promised the department of justice that he wouldn't tell what he knows about the corruption in the government. So now he is out on provisional parole and has plenty of spare time to arrange watertight alibis with his friends before he is called to the stand again.

> Plenty of Christmas cheer and mistletoe
> and lots of love,
> George

January 4, 1935
3 Rue de la Gde Chaumiere

Dear Mother and Daddy,

This has all the earmarks of a long letter, so I had better do things systematically. First, I want to thank you ever and ever so much for the very welcome checks and present of books and nice letters. They all came just on my birthday, when I got up for breakfast.

The books I chose (as soon as I got back from vacation) were, you will be surprised to hear Priestley's "English Journey", and (of all things) Lord Chesterfield's Letters to His Son which I find great reading. Will tell you more about my impressions when I read more of them.

My vacation was really grand. The trip I took to Chamonix really didn't turn out to be so bad (I mean the organized excursion). I left the evening of the 22nd and on the train met two French fellows and we planned together to take some skiing trips when we should get to Chamonix. The ride was tiring. At every station we'd pop out and buy beer or a sandwich or some coffee. There was singing almost all night long until finally the singers were just too tired to vocalize any more and dropped off to sleep. I will never forget the first view of the Alps that we had from the train window. We threaded our way along the valley and in the distance rose the peaks of the French Alps. There was not much snow to be seen from where we were, but the bare rock was certainly a majestic sight. Here and there were torrents, which seemed to crash down hundreds of meters onto the rocks below without following any channel at all. They just seemed to leap from the top of a cliff and arrive at the bottom, smoking frothy mass. Everyone in the train was on the lookout for snow and there were cries of joy when some was finally spied. We changed trains at St. Gervais-Le Fayet and were hauled up the mountainside by a little narrow-gauge cog railway. The higher we rose the more snow we saw until finally at Chamonix we found about 30-40 cm of snow. The change to the Hotel was quickly made and I spent the time until lunch sleeping off the effects of the train ride.

I never battled so much in my life as I did my first afternoon on skis. Every little mound or gentle wave of the ground seemed a Mt. Blanc. It was as though someone was deliberately pulling me down hill all the time. I just couldn't get up hill. When finally I did arrive at the summit of a hill, after many groans and puffs and tumbles in the snow, the descent was very easy – but so short.

But the first hundred falls were the hardest. Bit by bit I caught on to the idea of skiing and in two or three days I was doing all sorts of things like Chrstiana stops and Stemmbogens (all very technical terms which I got out of a book on skiing which I bought for myself.) During the days at Chamonix I spoke nothing but French. I went around all the time with two French chaps from Paris who were great fun and we had grand times together. We skied all day and in the evening we painted the town a violent scarlet. Part of the time I spent with a group of younger people (ages 12 to 17) and their parents who were very nice bourgeois French people and very nice to know. I was the only American in Chamonix, or so it seemed because with one or two short exceptions, I didn't meet anyone who spoke English the entire time (and didn't especially care to). One of the fellows I went around with had spent some time in Wales and spoke a very lopsided, broken English. The vacation was utterly different from anything I had ever done before, and certainly utterly different from what I had been doing in Paris. For ten days, I threw my inhibitions to the winds and led a loud and lusty life of good, hard sport in the day time and good, hard laughing all night. I now realize that after all I am at heart a very conservative and well-bred person, and it was quite a novelty for me to bang around the town at night making lots of noise and singing in cafes and dancing on tables, etc., etc., etc. The life we lead here in Paris is usually of the most staid, dignified and placid sort. There are some exceptions, but the general tone is quite serious. So the ten days at Chamonix were a "vacation" not only from studies, but also, I believe, a vacation from myself. Now that I am once again in the old, pleasant rut of books and studies and chatting with Bill etc. Those ten days all seemed rather forced – forced laughter running all through it. But it was a grand feeling at the time. Like the man who all his life has wanted to kick his boss in the face and finally does it. It is much more easily said in French. Pendant dix jours, j'ai vraiment bien rigollé. Let me confess some of my undying sins, in my frank straight-from-the-shoulder way. The Reveillon of Christmas Eve and of New Year's eve were the most fun. Christmas Eve we started out, if I can still remember, at a café where we had oysters and cold meats, etc. and four carafes of wine and a bottle of vin de marque (a Burgundy I think). We were four fellows and had a grand time and being generally boisterous. Then after wandering into another café for a sip of something and a game of pool we went to a hotel where there was a dance. It was all very en famille there but we sat down and ordered a bottle of Champagne. By the time the Champagne came we realized that it was just a little bit too en famille for four young bloods to bear (they even got up and marched around the Christmas tree like one great, big happy family). So we stopped the waiter as he was in the very act of uncorking the Champagne. With a few detours, we arrived at a nightclub (the only one Chamonix boasts) then we ordered drinks to pass the time away until midnight. But for some reason or other everybody in the nightclub seemed to be somebody with his Aunt Mary. In other words, it was quite dead. So we countermanded the four covers for dinner and made a rather noisy and not too graceful exit. Then the next stop was the "Casino" – a big, overdone, barn of a place, which has seen better days. By the time we got there we were quite gay. So we cheerily ordered another bottle of Champagne and then wandered backstage where we found a troupe of six English chorus girls. Which, of course, was just milk and honey to us. They were really very lady-like chorus girls, in the last analysis, if you want to analyze that far. They were dancing at the Casino for an engagement of several days and while their engagement lasted we were steady customers (at the Casino). Anyhow, they added to the gayety of the Reveillon. (The French idea of a Christmas Eve is midnight mass and then sitting up all night in a café drinking, dancing and laughing). (The same goes for New Year's eve, but they leave out the midnight mass). Well, at the Casino, you might have said of us "they know not what they do". But when we returned to our table and found that the waiter had walked off with the half-full bottle of Champagne, we certainly had full command of our properties. We walked out without paying. Then we went to the hotel (it being 4 A.M.) and got into our skiing clothes. Then with our skis on our shoulders we came back to the Casino, like good little boys, and paid for the Champagne. Then we turned our faces toward the beckoning mountains and with our heads full of the fumes of the flowing bowl we started to climb one of the high peaks near Chamonix – the Brevent. Snow was falling, and it was bitter cold, but we climbed for two and a half or three hours. The path, with no exaggerations, was no wider than the top of your piano and a good deal narrower in many, many spots. On the downhill side was a sheer drop of some hundred meters with a nice gentle landing among pine trees and boulders at the bottom. So we made up our minds to stick to the path. As dawn broke (a beautiful sight) we turned around and started the descent. In the semi darkness it was no funny matter to go down that steep, twisting path. If you didn't turn when the trail turned you went shooting off into space, only to hit earth a few hundred meters below. The best brake was to fall down, so I fell down at almost every step. But I improved as we neared the bottom and at the end of it was falling every 3 meters instead of every meter. About 8 in the morning we reached the hotel, had breakfast and crawled into bed. A nice, old-fashioned Christmas Eve.

For three days we put behind us the pasteboard glamour of Chamonix nightlife and hit the trail for the mountains. In other words, we took a three-day skiing trip. The destination was Mt. Envers, of which more later. The patron at the hotel wanted us to take a guide and used every ruse to make us. But one of the fellows with us had spent five summers and winters in Chamonix, knew the trails like the inside of his pocket and is a good skier and very prudent. So we thought we didn't need a guide, besides we didn't want to part with the nice fat sum that the guide gets for his services. To get revenge on us the man at the hotel didn't put enough food in our rucksacks (I used Daddy's old and very serviceable sack). But when we set out we weren't aware of how much food he had given us. For five hours we climbed, through a heavy snowstorm, with occasional stops at little shacks along the trail. All the way up we followed a railroad track, which is used in summertime by the PLM but in wintertime is impassable for a train. The track at one point ran through a tunnel and we had to get out a candle and for twenty minutes marched in the darkness, with only the faint light of the candle guiding us. There were five avalanches covering the trail at different points, and they were the only dangers but they were rather dangerous. The snow at those points was 3 or 4 meters deep and as you crawled across the face of the avalanche you risked the very great possibility of sliding into eternity a 1000 meters below, but we were <u>extremely careful.</u> After five hours of climbing we arrived at the Summit of Mt. Envers, 2500 meters above sea level and 1500 above Chamonix. (One hour of the five was spent in eating lunch). We turned a corner of a mountain and at our feet, 500 meters below was La Mer de Glace, which is a wide glacier cut by many crevasses and looking for all the world like a sea that has frozen in its tracks. The refuge where we spent the night was perched on top of a hill. Right next to it was a hotel, closed of course during the winter, and with ominous signs at each window "Beware of the wolf traps". The refuge is very historic. It was built in 1779 and on the four walls are tablets engraved with the names of famous people who have stopped there. For example: Shelley, Byron, Napoleon III and Empress Eugenie, Pasteur, Ruskin, George Sande and Liszt (they were together) and a long list of other famous people. The hallowed walls that housed all these people at different times were quite simple. One room with a dirt floor, about as large as the entrance hall at 3 East 85th Street. A fireplace, a door and two windows. Walls about a yard thick, mats made of interwoven rope. These were indescribably dirty, dusty and moldy. At night we used them as covers – they were all we had. A fire was imperative. One of us had to be awake to put wood on the fire. I gave him the title of La Vièrge Vestale. The fire guardian looked more like an Indian guide. He'd sit crouched before the flames, staring at the castles in Spain that were forming themselves in the yellow light. And behind him on the cold floor, shrouded in many thicknesses of dirty rope mats lay two snoring forms. We went to bed at 7, got up as soon as it was light. Slept very little because it was too cold to sleep. One lifesaver we had brought with us was a bottle of rum. Jacques, one of my comrades, had the presence of mind to take an enormous swallow of it the first night, so from then on we lacked the warmth-giving firewater. The daytime we skied around Mt. Envers, making ascents and descents and practicing turns, stops, etc. There was no one there but ourselves on that windy waste. Ourselves and the snow and perhaps the ghost of Georges Sande who could be heard fluttering around the refuge from time to time, if one looked long enough into the flames.

The third day we returned to civilization more because of the lack of food than because we were tired of the mountain life. It was grand to cook your own food, burn your socks in the fire and freeze your nose off; smoke a pipe for the warmth it gave your hands, tumble in the virgin snow and have a whole mountain to yourself. If we wanted water to drink we opened the window and filled a bucket with the snow that was piled as high as the windowsill. If we wanted soup, we did the same. We cooked in the flames, and over a small alcohol stove that we had brought along. The stove really was a wonder of efficiency.

The descent took 50 minutes. We found our traces across the avalanches and walked in the old tracks, which made things a lot easier over those dangerous passes. And on the open trail we whizzed along at 30 miles an hour or so, between a cliff on one side and a precipice on the other. In fifty minutes of fast skiing we were back in the bosom of Chamonix life.

There was skating the last few days at Chamonix and I did some of that, but had a better time on skis. Did no sledding at all. The night before New Year's Eve we went skijoering behind a big autobus. There were some forty of us. Mostly people from Paris who were in Chamonix on a three-day excursion organized by the big newspaper "L'Intransigeant". Some Chamoniards, and we three fellows. Some of the people stayed on the bus, half rode on sleds (luges) and a number of hardy souls (we three included) went on skis. The object was to hold onto a rope and be towed along. The road was very slippery and several people fell, but no one was hurt. I managed to stay on my skis. The destination was a little bôite de nuit about 5 miles away. Very tastefully furnished and very "sympathique" and in time. We forty had come together, were the only clients that night, and so a merry time was had by all. Dancing, wine, games such as "coup d'oeil a l 'Américaine" and la danse du mouchoir. In all, quite boisterous and rousing good fun. Then the return under a starry sky (this was all at night, of course) through the snow and back to Chamonix.

One night at Chamonix we were out latish and met up with three Chamoniards who were completely potted. So to have some fun we stood them a bottle of wine (they call it un "cannon" de rouge in argot). One chap had a feather in his hat and his battles with that feather, his attempts to comb his hair and to light a match were really screams.

New Year's Eve we also had a reveillon. It started out being "mortelle". We went to a café and just couldn't get gay. Then to the bôite de nuit where we had a very strong punch and that had no effect on our spirits. Then to the Casino where we had a big fight about getting a table (the place was packed to the doors.) Finally we sat down at a table with two women of sixty. They were a little surprised to see us invade their camp, but not too displeased. We danced, (not with the beldames) opened some Champagne, ate some oysters, but were still feeling blue. At 2 we left. Then we returned to the bôite de nuit, had another punch. Danced a little. Things seemed to go better. All of a sudden the door opened and in blew harsh, unfamiliar sounds. English was being spoken. A half dozen American and Englishmen came in with two Canadian girls. One was dressed in a costume (for a costume ball) that was quite abbreviated. The girls acted as though they hadn't seen a white man for months when they heard I spoke English and danced good, old American style. (I will never learn the valse tournante). The three-piece orchestra took on a sort of inspired second wind when they noticed that there were people in the bôite who really wanted to dance their feet off. And for two hours we made the rafters ring with the pounding of our dancing feet. Then at 4 A.M. they left (the Canadiennes). We issued forth into the street where snow had started to fall and found four Chamoniards, drunk. They invited us to a little "bar louche" where we sat up till 7 singing folk songs and drinking innocuous vin rouge. At 7 we went to the hotel for breakfast, bought a patisserie, and dragged our whirling heads onto the pillow. The next day I returned to Paris.

I had a grand time, and am a little ashamed of it. It is something I don't do here in Paris. I learned lots of argot and French slang, drank a bit, exercised like mad, danced a lot and laughed all day. Spoke nothing but French. To return to Bill with his sedateness and politeness and reserve, and the quite cloistered life here full of learning was a shock. The life we lead here is infinitely more "mouvementé" than life at Haverford, and life at Chamonix was infinitely more of a giddy whirl than life in Paris. I think the Paris pace is my natural pace and I am glad of it.

But I enjoyed myself. By cracky, I did.

So much for that. You have probably read with pain, as did I, the enclosed note from Dr. Kresser. What shall I do about it? Shall I pay it out of my own pocket? It is possible, but would take a big piece out of my funds for the summer vacation. Please advise me. I'll pay it myself if you want me to. It means about fifty dollars.

I paid the months rent out of my Christmas money so you needn't send the check until the end of the month, as you had previously planned. But maybe it is already on the way. I had quite a lucrative Christmas with the presents from you all and the 100 from Ma and Baba (which I was quite surprised to get) and also 5 dollars from Aunt Nellie, 10 from Gladys and 60 francs from Belle. Uncle Fred gave me 200 francs, which was very nice of him. I bought him the New Yorker Album, which pleased him very much. Bill gave me a swell collection of photos of Paris – not of famous monuments but of the little things you see on the street every day. A chair in the Luxembourg Gardens, chimney tops, a man fishing in the Seine. The spirit of the city in photographs. His birthday is the 14th and I think I'll get him a book called "Les Trésors de la Peinture Francaise" which is an excellent collection of reproductions.

I have millions of letters to write. Don't know when I'll finally get them all done. It might interest you to know that you may have tied the knots of fate or something like that when you invited Tris Hearst and Toussia Kremer to the farm. He writes me that he has fallen heavily for her. But don't taunt him with this. I thought you might like to know what the little Russian from across the Brooklyn Bridge does with her spare time.

Last night I went with Bill Fry to see "Le Cid" and "Les Precieuses Ridicules" acted at the Odeon. The acting in the tragedy was terrible and so was the staging but the comedy was well done. Comedies usually are. Especially boisterous ones in which the actors have a good time. I think that the American way of giving classical dramas, by private initiative coupled with a real financial risk by the manager and lots of sweat and worry put into each production is infinitely better than a nationalized theater where the actors perform classics somewhat grudgingly (much preferring new plays) and where there is no effort made to tempt the public with new ideas. But private initiative in classical drama is not very often met with. The Odeon, anyhow, is a bit run down.

The pictures you sent me are very amusing. Sometimes I think they resemble you and sometimes I don't. Looking at them as I type, I have decided what they look like. They resemble you as you look at the farm (which is as different from you at the city, as black from white). All of which was meant to apply to Monica as well as you, mother 'o mine.

By the way I hope you are still stowing my letters away in a dark corner for me as I asked you to do, early in October. I really would like to keep them as records. Fry and I gave the Crawfords a bottle of champagne for Christmas, which they liked very much. In fact it made them quite gay, Mrs. Crawford said. She is a very fine sort of woman but has one or two amusing faults (as have we all). She reads papers omnivorously and is continuously making mountains out of molehills. Prophesying catastrophes that never happen and attributing untold importance to minor details in the news. She will single out a street fight at the bottom of the inside page and say that that is a sign of the approaching civil war in France, a discovery, the first faint sign of the impending doom. Just at present I can't get terribly worked up over the impending doom. One week I can and the next week I can't. This week I'm off impending dooms. She also believes greatly in astrology but despite those bad traits (you're meant to laugh at that) she is a splendid person. Tomorrow I will start working again, haven't yet decided what book to dig into. Possibly I'll read some French literature. Or maybe take a dig at American History. (once again)

Got a letter from Tom Brown full of gossip of the campus, and a letter from that redheaded------Priscilla Comfort. It made me laugh. Told me what she was doing. Exactly the same things she was doing at this time last year, with no variation. The same dances, the same boys at college, the same sodas in Ardmore. It all seems so far away. We were talking about readjusting to campus life again next year among us three here. Bill C. has made the adjustment before, but still he was younger then and I think he has become pretty set in his continental habits. But we decided that the best thing to do anywhere you are is to live as the people around you are living and keep stored away in the back of your head your ideals and pleasant memories. That is what he did at Haverford, and that is what I will probably do. I know that is what you would tell me to do. I think you used to write me letters to that effect when I was at school. By the way somewhere, I don't know where, just know, I have a packet of clippings from your letters with your words of wisdom preserved for eternity. Maybe there was some good subconscious reason after all why I should go into a store and pick out of several hundred books "Lord Chesterfield's Letters to His Son".

That is all the bits I can think of just now. Maybe before I seal the envelope I'll think of something else. Paris is gray – as gray as ever during the winter months. But it gives signs of lifting and cool, clear, crisp days are promised us. I look forward to spring and the Bois de Boulogne, and canoeing with Japanese lanterns, etc., etc., etc. I'd better stop or I'll go on like this all afternoon and then dash off to a concert or something equally flighty, when I should be here at my desk pounding out letters. This has been quite long, hasn't it? So I'd better sign off before I think of anything else to say.

Lots of love and thanks for everything. I really had a Merry Christmas, a Happy Birthday and it looks as though I am going to have a really happy New Year.

George

P.S. I never saw anything as majestic as the sunset over Mt. Blanc. With the tips of all the mountain peaks stained pink by the disappearing rays. Like a lady's fingernails with bright red polish. A very stern, haughty lady. The mountains were almost too big. Something like Wagner's music – it's too big to be comfortable.

Thanks for your 2 cables. They were grand to get. Made you seem very close.

January 13, 1935

Dear Family,

I haven't written as early as I should, partly because I have been working too hard and partly because the boats didn't sail when my letter was ready. But here I am.

I am glad to hear that you didn't read those fat outlines. That would have been very useless, boring and foolish. I have been ticking off books at the rate of about one a week. Finished a 670 page book by Felix Morley on the

League of Nations this week and outlined it. Bill Crawford and I are taking two courses under Fäy at the Collège de France. One course is on Lafayette and is a public course with about fifty or so attending the lectures. The other course, which meets the morning following the public lecture, is a sort of supplementary course. We are about ten in a small classroom and sit around a table with Fäy as around a dining room table. The private course takes up each lecture topic in detail and studies the documents and texts, which bear on the topic. Fäy is having some rare documents on Free Masonry photographed and we are going to read them together in class doing an "explication de texte" a French method of study, which Fay warmly approves of. It is a rare privilege to study under him – one that I will profit by and never forget. In his first talk to the small class he gave his opinions on modern literature. As you may have heard, he is a worshipper at the shrine of Gertrude Stein. And this spring he will give a course on Franco-American poetical relations and probably will take that chance to extol Gertrude to the stars. The difference between studying under men like Fäy and Siegfried, and studying under the mediocre professors that one finds at home is astonishingly great. There is so much of value that I get from listening to Fäy and Siegfried that has no relation at all to the course, just bits of philosophy injected here and there. Along that same line is Rufus Jones, professor of Philosophy at Haverford and perhaps the greatest living Quaker and among the leaders in social and religious thought. He is touring Europe, visiting Quakers and doing research and he is in Paris today. We heard him speak twice at different meetings and have renewed a contact established with him at Haverford. He is a "grand old man" of 70 with a mind as keen, in fact hundreds of times keener, than ours. I am writing back to the NEWS about his activities, a task that falls in with my duties as "Paris Correspondent".

I may have told you that I joined the "English Debating Society" at the Sciences Po. They are sending a team to London Jan. 30 to debate in English with the London School of Economics. The team will be composed of 3 French fellows because the topic is Resolved that under the present circumstances rearmament is the one way to avoid war, and they will be expected to voice the views of the French government. I suggested the topic and Wednesday night I am speaking on the Negative side, so as to give the team practice in rebuttal. The London debaters will probably be supporting the disarmament views of the British government. They have asked me to come along on the trip to London. They will be there about 4 or 5 days. From a Wednesday (30 I think) to a Sunday. It would cost me 500 francs. I haven't decided yet. I would like to go, can afford it and will probably do it.

You asked me when Fred sails. He sails Jan. 26 on the Angora Star (Blue Star Line) from Southampton. He and I are having dinner together tomorrow night, as we do every Monday, and going to theater.

Last night I saw "La Bohéme" at the Opèra Comique. It is a beautiful thing, isn't it. The picture of student life in the Latin Quarter was interesting and very, very real. I paid 5 francs and stood up for most of the performance in the very top of the house. That all helped to make the Bohemian atmosphere register more deeply. I think this after noon I will go to hear a concert at Salle Gaveau. They are playing Beethoven's 7th and a number of other things I want to hear. Mischa Elman gave a recital here recently but I didn't attend.

The other day I went to the Rodin Museum. For some reason or other I wasn't tremendously impressed. But I will go again. I must have been in an off-mood. Because there certainly is something there if I can only bring myself around to seeing it.

The fate of the Saar is being decided as I write. I think it has been decided for the last 1000 years that the Saar is German and that this is just a sort of endorsement. But if it turns out the other way you can mark down one bad guess for me.

I never had such a palate-tickling sensation as the other day when I went to the tearoom run by the Turkish mosque here in Paris. I ate some Baklouwa and Turkish paste (now I know Mother is jealous) and had their thick, black coffee. You could cut the coffee with a knife. When I finished it there was a half-inch of thick, black slime in the bottom of the cup. But the piece de resistance was a papery, honey-sweet cake called Baklouwa. I liked it so much I bought six pieces to take home.

Tomorrow morning I will start on my research for my History paper. That should be interesting. Research itself, especially in a French library, is quite an experience. I have been reading myself to sleep at night with Priestley's "English Journey". He writes in a remarkable facile style and really beautifully in spots. But I don't feel he did enough with the material he had. Once in a while I read a letter of Chesterfield. Remarkable sound common sense. It is getting to be one of my favorite books.

I went to the Musée Carnavalet, which houses relics of Parisian history. Not being Parisian myself, I missed some of the thrill that a Frenchman gets when he sees the relics of the Revolution. I still think that the Louvre and the Cluny are the two best in Paris. I spent Thursday afternoon learning about Greek and Roman sculpture at the Louvre. Went to dinner today to the home of the pastor of the American Church with Bill C. and Bill Fry. The pastor has a copy of the Mona Lisa which was declared to be the finest existing copy, and declared to be such by the man who expertized the Mona Lisa when it was recovered. It is astounding to see such a perfect thing in a private home. He also has an equally good copy of LeBrun's picture of Mme Lebrun and her daughter, and one of Rembrandt's self-portraits. All of them look like originals.

There isn't much other news.

Lots of love,
George

PS No news from you in ages.

January 18, 1935

Dear People:

Your bright-eyed boy almost caused a cabinet crisis and a second world war today. This is how it happened. At the Sciences Po there is an English Debating Society to which I belong. They were going to debate the London School of Economics Feb. 1 on a topic, which I proposed: Resolved, that in the present circumstances rearmament is the one way to prevent war. That is the French view and the negative is exactly the British view. We are to sail from Calais for London (by Dover) Jan 30. It happens that M. Pierre-Etienne Flandin, Prime Minister of France, is honorary president of our debating club and he sails for important diplomatic conferences in London Jan 31. The London School of Economics accepted the subject and everyone was quite enthusiastic about it. I was all ready to give a speech in the negative here in Paris to give our team of French fellows practice in rebuttal. Then the administrator got hold of the news (I mean the school administrator). They looked at the subject and said it was much too good – too controversial. Finally, the argument got so bitter between the Pres. of our club and the Administrateur de l'ecole that they decided to refer it to honorary president and Prime Minister Flandin. So to the sanctum of the Prime Minister they went with my topic for the debate in hand, and he vetoed it. He hasn't given out any opinions yet on disarmament and if the debaters who are sort of under his aegis said rash things, the London papers might pounce on it and botch the diplomatic conference. So that' s my little good deed for the week. Instead of the rearmament subject, they are going to debate on this insipid topic: Resolved that national security needs international organization. It doesn't mean a thing, that is why they chose it.

However, I am going to London with the team. It will cost less than 500 francs. We leave the 30th, a Wednesday, and get back Sat or Sunday the 2 or 3d. There will be about 12 of us and we'll be banqueted all over the place and also have time to see London. I will make it a point to stop in on Monica's parents. I wouldn't want to leave London without paying my respects. What is the address, please?

Apropos of the debate, I telephoned the above story immediately to Heineken, chief of the United Press. He liked it and sounded as though he was going to send it over the wires. Did it ever come out in American papers? He said he would phone me soon and ask me to help out in my spare time in the office. He mislaid my card otherwise I could have spent the Christmas vacation working for the United Press. I wish I had known that.

By the way, don't get the idea that my Xmas vacation was spent in a smoky barroom and in bed. It wasn't. Ten hours a day (almost) I was out in the snow skiing hard and skating hard; and that 3-day ski trip was three days of glorious outdoor life. So there, you and you and you.

I have really been working like a Trojan this week. No week has ever passed so quickly. I have much too much to do and I like it. I am always in a grand humor, when I have too much to do and find that I am actually doing it all. I have been working all day on my Fäy history paper. I have been through 2 libraries so far, read everything they contain on my subject. I wish I could cite the books I have read that have nothing on my subject, but had to be read anyhow. They would form an impressive list. The work is about 1/10 done, or so it seems. There are no books on the subject, you have to cull items from here and there and everywhere: original sources, etc. Of course, I have been attending all classes, debating in English and in German, if you please. On February 11 I am making a 45-minute speech before the Foyer de la Paix, a youth organization, on "Laissez-Faire: Politique de la Jeunesse Americaine". The speech will be in French. So I have plenty to keeps me busy. In addition to that I try to read books for amusement, almost impossible. Read my government. Am reading "The Economic Consequences of the Peace" by J. M. Keynes. Probably the best book out of the millions that have been written on that hackneyed subject. And written in 1920 when the clouds of war had not yet cleared, at that. Going to operas (am seeing Madame Butterfly Saturday night for 5 francs again at the Opéra Comique). Saw a classic at the Odéon last night, or rather a semi-classic "Madame Sans-Gêne" about a bourgoise woman at the court of Napoleon I and the dust she stirs up with her outspoken mannerisms. Very amusing but the acting was mediocre.

I also do a little writing. Wrote my ideas on religion, of all things, the other night. I am beginning to think that it would be a good idea to take one day out sometime next spring, for a real, old-fashioned rest. I have not experienced for weeks the feeling "Now what in the devil can I do to pass the times?" There are always so many thousands of things clamoring for attention that I spend my spare time deciding what to do. (Don't take that literally).

My old friend, Marian Halpert gets here about the third or fourth. That will be one more pleasant distraction.

Bill Fry may go skiing. Bill Crawford seems to be slacking on his work. I don't know whether it is that, or whether he just goes slower than I. I have found out that I am only supremely happy when I am much better than anybody else around me. If I can excel everyone I feel fine. Of course that only applies to fields in which it is possible for me to excel. I don't feel downcast because I can't run a hundred yards in ten seconds or paint a picture like Rembrandt. But in the work I am interested in and believe I am good at, I am very happy when I excel and sad when somebody beats me. So far I have had plenty of cause for happiness. That quality will probably always keep me out of the gutter and keep me with a sound suit and a clean shirt on my back (at least).

I must write other letters and I must go to an art class (history thereof).

So goodbye and lots of love,

George

* * * * * *

What a shock to hear you bobbed your hair! (I liked it **long**). But you must look about 35.

January 27, 1935
3 Rue de la Gde Chaumiere
Paris, VIe, France

Dear Mother and Daddy,

Please congratulate Caroline for me if you see her or phone her on the 5th. I am writing to her, of course.

I am sending you copies of reports to Herndon and Comfort about my work so far. There is a lot of news in those letters that I won't bother to repeat here. You can fit the three together like a jigsaw puzzle.

I spent 2 weeks working on that History paper and accomplished something. At least I now know where not to look for material. So I have sworn off history for a few weeks and will do Government now for a rest. Sometime in February I will come back to the History. (PS I said goodbye to Fred before he left for the East Indies. He gave me his radio and magazine subscriptions).

Saturday night Bill and I went to see "Ce Soir on Improvise" a translation of Luigi Pirandello's newest play. I was immensely interested by it. He proposed the very original idea that life as lived from day to day is incomplete and that nothing ever works out properly, but on the stage where they have laboratory conditions actors can really live life to the utmost. The theater is true life, whereas our movements from day to day are just cheap imitations of life. And he drives home his point by showing a group of actors acting out a simple little play and he is constantly having them change from stage life to world life and back again with almost electric effects. It was done by the Pitoev Company, the best in Paris, and they used Pirandello's ideas to the best advantage. The scenery, décor, mise-en-scene, acting, lighting, everything was very well done. This afternoon Bill and Mrs. Crawford and I went to the Comédie Francaise to see Racine's Phèdre, and Moliére's "Le Médecin Malgré Lui." I had just finished reading Phèdre. It was acted, in such a violent manner that it almost turned me inside out. The woman who played Phédre screamed her lines like a tigress, but that was marvelous acting. It was a very tragic tragedy and quite tiring on the audience because of the violence of the emotions. Molière's comedy was very funny, a lot of naughty fun poking at doctors. And excellently acted in true Molière fashion. The Comédie Francaise is a very chic sort of place, even boasting an elevator.

I am getting to like public speaking very much and am discovering the knack of it. It is leading me to think about studying law. It does seem a steadier sort of profession than Journalism or Advertising. And I think I might make a good lawyer. I find that I can see through things quite readily and analyze and think on my feet. I might be able to write a good brief. Time will tell.

I have made a record for not spending money this month. Have no idea how much I haven't spent, but it is really an enormous sum. I have not spent almost a thousand dollars this month. Last month I did not spend only 500 dollars. Seriously, though, some unseen influence has been keeping me inside my own bailiwick these days with my ample nose buried in a book.

These outlines which I enclose aren't terribly enthralling but they are more interesting than those two enormous ones I sent you earlier in the year. The Student's Comments on the last page of each one may interest you.

The Saar plebiscite produced no unwonted furor here, after it was all over. But everyone is just as uneasy about Hitler's next move as ever they were before. If the London conferences don't result in some concrete agreement Hitler may do another audacious act. And I am pretty sure he'll get away with it too. France is too scared of him to declare war just now and the "low years" in the army have arrived in which the effects of the war are being felt in decreased military enrollment. So far no new military law has been passed and the militarist papers are screeching for one. Flandin has just passed a mildly inflationary law and the dollar reacted accordingly. I cannot regard this Flandin regime as permanent. Some day soon France is going to demand reform. Flandin is better than average but he won't give them reform any more than the rest of his cronies. They are using a worn out political system that will probably get its much-needed renovation within a few short months.

Lots of love,

George

Give Baba my very best, please. Love to Monica

PS I am not going to England because it conflicts with some appointments I have here that seem more important to me. But I plan to go this summer.

George B. Bookman

3 Rue de la Grande Chaumiere
Paris, VIe, France
February 5, 1935

Dear Mother and Daddy:

Even though the inconsiderate sailings of the boats have made this letter a day late, I hope I am not too late to wish you much, much happiness. Many, many more years of it and all my love.

On Feb. 11 I will be making a speech on American Youth before a French organization called the Foyer de la Paix. You might hold your thumbs for me and hope that I don't fall off the platform. I have been raking together a few ideas on American youth and will try to give the French a picture of what an American youth has to go through before he can become a full-fledged Democrat. There is a difference between American and French psychology as wide as the Atlantic Ocean and that psychology has a great effect on the youth movement, if you can call it that in the U.S. So I will try to explain why the youth movement at home is such a puny thing and then say a few things about what is going on in the U. S. The swing toward the left, Townsend, Huey Long, etc.

Saturday night Bill Fry and I went to a very nice Chinese restaurant behind the Cluny museum. It is the second time I have eaten with chopsticks and I am really very adept at them now. You hold the bowl up to your face and shovel in the rice and meat with the chopsticks. It isn't pretty to watch but it is very practical. The menu has about 40 different dishes you can order. We usually order 2 dishes and since they are so enormous we divide each in half, so we each have a part of the two dishes. Then they give you all the rice and tea you can put away. It is lots of fun.

This last week students were rioting a bit in the streets. The affair started in Montpellier, in the provinces, as a protest against foreign medical students. The French medical students think that foreign med students get easier work and easier exams than they, and are appointed to positions, which Frenchmen deserve. They don't mind the Americans and English , for they study in Paris and then go home to practice, but it is the Central Europeans (Romanians, Hungarians, Serbs especially) who come to Paris, study at the Ecole de Médecine and then set up practice in Paris and take customers away from the French doctors – it is this type of medical student that they manifested against. The students boycotted the lecture halls and paraded around shouting down with foreign medical students. It soon spread to Paris and then the students in the other faculties of the University – the Sorbonne and the law school; etc. took this medical affair as a pretext for political manifestations. So the ultranationalist Action Francaise (royalists) and fascist groups paraded through the streets shouting "La France pour les Francais" and burning foreign students in effigy. But they took it mostly as a big joke. I watched them and even slipped into some of the meetings. It was all half serious. The affair died out of its own accord in 2 days, but it gave the students a good chance to go tearing around the Latin Quarter shouting at the top of their lungs. February 6, anniversary of the Revolution of 1934 in which 20 Paris citizens were shot by government troops, will give more real cause for trouble in the streets.

Marian Halpert landed bringing lots of messages from you. Thank you very much. She went to Switzerland for a month and will be back March 1. Thank you very much for your letters, they were very interesting. I wish you would send the next check in dollars, especially if the dollar rises in value. We are waiting jitteringly for the gold decision. It may mean that we get 25 francs instead 0f 15 for the dollar. In that event I would be very, very disappointed if you didn't send the draft in dollar form. But I have enough money in the bank to last until the end of the month of February.

As I added hastily in a footnote to my last letter, I didn't go to London. The time was too short and I had several debates and other appointments here that had a prior claim. I expect to go this summer. Fry and I have been planing a trip about which I'll write you more later in the year. I wrote a very long and studious sounding letter to the young man who is now in charge of Dr. Kelsey's courses in History. Told him, more or less, what I intended to do in History and my attitude toward the paper. I'm sorry I didn't make a carbon copy of it. It was a very good letter, put in rather strong terms. I intend to work as much as possible at this history paper and if by the end of May I don't have all the work done and haven't investigated the last bit of material available, I will write the paper anyhow pointing out what I have done and what there remains to do and how a future historian should go about doing the rest of the work. Because I will have worked in all the Paris archives by the end of the year and will have a good idea of the field. It may be possible for me to write the paper, and on the other hand it may be a 2-year job. The subject, as I think I wrote you, is "The effects of French Foreign Trade on Inflation of the Dollar During The American Revolution".

I read in "Time" that Eddy Bernays made the "most bizarre suggestion of the week" by asking for a Secretary of Public Relations in the national cabinet. A little bit of personal horn blowing. But I'd like to see him get it, though I don't believe he will. Neither does he, in all likelihood.

I think that in the middle of the month Bill Fry and Bill Crawford are going skiing. So I will have a good chance to get an awful lot of work done. This week I am going to read a few more government books, then I will devote the following weeks to History. In March I will probably read some

French and government again. I have Fred's midget radio here and it is a great thing to have. Listen to the news and classical music. Had Budapest on the radio last night. They announce in German, Hungarian and French and I understood everything except the Hungarian. I am going to try to get time to study a little Italian this spring to help me along in Italy.

I hope Caroline had a good Birthday and Baba also. Give them my best love.

I have received several letters from college and a copy of the News. There seems to be a lot of liberal politics going on there and peace propaganda. I guess I'll have a swell time there my last year, after all. That is, if I make a good showing in September.

But I am not too worried about that.

I have a Fäy course this morning on the other side of the Luxembourg Gardens so goodbye until the next boat.

And all my best love and congratulations,
George

Love to Monica

3 Rue de la Grande Chaumiere
Paris, VIe, France
February 12, 1935

Dear Mother and Daddy,

This week has been public speaking week. I have done a lot of soapboxing. Thursday night I spoke at a Quaker social center on the difference between French and American universities. All three of us had been invited to speak at first, but Bill Fry backed out and Bill Crawford got the grippe. (He is all cured now). So it devolved on me to make three speeches rolled into one. I didn't mind, in fact I lapped up the chance because I like to do it. There was a small group of earnest Quakers or what have you there and I spoke for about 20 to 25 minutes. There was a French girl who had studied and taught in the United States who also spoke. Her speech was a rebuttal of what I had said – she didn't like some things I said about French youth – so we had a very interesting discussion. It was a group of English speaking foreigners who were there mostly to get a chance to speak English. They didn't speak much though. Most of the evening was taken up by a three-cornered discussion between the Young French teacher, the chairman and myself. I learned a lot about American youth and also a lot about French youth that I had never known before. Last night I spoke for about an hour in French before the Foyer de la Paix, a small but vigorous pacifist organization that has been having a series of lectures every Monday by a representative of the youth of all countries. I spoke up for the USA. It startled me a bit to learn that they had asked the American University Union some 6 months ago for a speaker and the staff there hemmed and hawed and said no one spoke French well enough and that it was very, very difficult to find an American who would speak. I thought my countrymen were more vigorous than that. But I was glad that I was the one asked to speak because it was very interesting. There were about 30 or 40 people and after I spoke they all started firing questions. About Roosevelt, about the U.S. and the League of Nations, about American youth and sports, even about American movies. I answered them all and I think I did well by the United States. One Frenchman got up and first criticized everything that I had said about French youth and then asked me a long list of about 6 questions he wanted me to answer. I first rebutted his criticisms of my ideas, with good grace bien entendu but also with force, and then answered his long list of questions. I have never remembered so much about Roosevelt in such a short space of time. Everything I have ever read or heard about the different political questions that were asked came back into my head at just the right time and I could even quote figures to back up my points. I didn't know I had read so much about the questions. But I also found out what I don't know – especially about French youth. But I didn't let the audience know it. You can cover up any lack of knowledge with a bit of verbosity, humor or begging the question. Or else you can listen attentively to someone's question, say yes, yes, and then go on with your speech and completely ignore their question. If gracefully done no one notices it. Bill Crawford and Bill Fry came to hear me, and bought me a glass of beer after it was all over by the way of reward for my efforts. I enclose some handbills that announce the lecture. Next week in the organization's newspaper there will appear a write-up of my speech which they are going to send me. I find that I can think rapidly on my feet. It is necessary, or else you make a very bad showing. But I think I kept the ball in the air for the good old stars and stripes. (ta ra ta!)

Wednesday afternoon, tomorrow, I am speaking in English at a model international conference which is meant to be a model of the one France, England, Germany, etc. will have to discuss the London proposals. I am speaking for Germany. I chose to do it because it gives me the best chance for a scrappy argument, not for any other reason. I have tried to guess exactly what Germany will say and think I have hit it. Which reminds me of one of the questions I was asked the other night. It made me smile to myself, but I answered it with perfect detachment. Someone asked if there is discrimination against the Jews in America. You can picture me answering that, can't you?

Saturday night it was the 21st birthday of a girl friend of ours here so she brought a friend to our suite (?) and with Bill and I providing the male attraction we had a little party for 4. The girls brought some Asti Spumante (white wine) and we provided some bread, Brie (cheese) and fruit. Then we all went Dutch to see "Manon" sitting in the topmost gallery for 5 francs. You get there very early, at 7 o'clock and stand in line till 7:45 and then the bureau for the gallery seats opens. Then you buy your ticket and rush up to the gallery and grab the best seat you can find. It is first come first served. I loved "Manon" as it was sung at the Opéra Comique. Suzanne Fisher, an American girl with a noticeable accent but a beautiful voice sang it. The mise en scène was really perfect. I think I like "Manon" almost as well as any Opera I have seen. It stands second in my list of preferences (with Carmen in first place). The girl that was along on the party for me (whom I had never met before) turned out to be really very, very interesting. She is half-Bulgarian and half-American. Name is Maria Atanasoff. Went to Wellesley and is a fellowship student here. She is brilliant (as to the cerebellum) and not so bad as to looks. Very good company.

I have finished studying about Germans in government reading and it has been very interesting. I read three books: one on Germany before the war, one on the German Republic and one on Nazi Germany. I will now devote the coming weeks to history research and then in the Spring I will read French. (And do some more government). As you know I have Fred's "Commercial and Financial Chronicle" here and it is a grand thing to have. I wish I could always have a subscription to it. My idea of happiness in the periodical line would be the New York Times every morning and the Commercial and Financial Chronicle every week. Doesn't sound like light reading I know, but it is what interests me.

I hope you had a grand day on the 11th. I did and I thought of you a lot. For one week (almost) we had perfect weather, though it was coldish. You could go into the Luxembourg when the mist was on the trees and almost believe that spring had arrived. I have been going around the city in my spare time finding new places to see the sunset from. When I have a complete itinerary I'll take all my girlfriends on the trip. Schemer that I am.

It looks as though Italy will have Abyssinia in short order. I have thought it would be coming quite soon and it seems to have arrived. Flandin, the French Premier, is still holding the fort. He is a Roosevelt without Roosevelt's forceful personality or popularity, or even without his political ability. He has introduced an NRA scheme into the chamber. By the time those deputies are through with it, it will look like an emasculated puppy. Whatever that looks like.

Heard from Baba in a very welcome letter and from some other friends dotted here and there in the US. How is Caroline? Is there still life in her old body? I haven't heard from her for ages.

> My very best love to Monica, and the extra-special variety to you.
>
> George

Enclosed are the notes for my 2 speeches – the one for the Quakers and the one in French. Can you make anything out of them? You might save them for me, along with the letter. Thank you

Letter to Dr. E. M. Wilson
Headmaster, Haverford Prep School

3 Rue de la Grande Chaumiere
Paris, VIe, France
February 15, 1935

My dear Dr. Wilson,

I have been planning for a long while to write you and by postponing it until the middle of the year I can give you a much more concrete picture of what I am doing in Paris than would have been the case earlier in the year.

Last Spring I applied jointly with two other members of the Junior class at Haverford College to be allowed to spend the Junior year studying along specialized lines in Paris. The College administrator considered our petition and granted us the permission. We are to do work in Government, French and American History entirely under our own direction and in September 1935 we will be examined to see if the year "was profitably spent". If the college decides in our favor we will be admitted to the Senior class in full standing.

We sailed from the United States in September (taking a ten-day, hundred-dollar boat) and when we arrived in Paris we devoted the early days of September entirely to getting acclimated, satisfying our curiosity about the city, and settling into an apartment. I have never spent two weeks so full of interest, new impressions and pleasant adjustments. I am now living on the Left Bank with my two classmates in a pension. We have all our meals with a French family, have pleasant rooms with a view of a quiet courtyard, and are conveniently situated in the heart of Montparnasse, just a few minutes from the Luxembourg Gardens and the Latin Quarter.

At the Ecole Libre des Sciences Politiques I am taking two courses. One in Economic Geography under André Siegfried and the other in Contemporary Europe and her Problems outside of Europe under René Pinon. The courses, especially that of Siegfried (author of "America Comes of Age") are excellent. At the College de France I am following two courses by Bernard Fäy on the Revolutionary Spirit of the XVIIIth Century, especially as it affected Lafayette and led to the American Revolution. He is an excellent lecturer, full of new slants on the subject, and almost all of the material he presents in his courses is the result of original research that he has done. In addition I take a course in the General History of Art at the Ecole du Louvre. Naturally, the courses do not take up a great deal of time. The majority of my work consists in reading from a list of books on International Government, Politics and Law. None of my work is supervised, directed or planned except by myself. The only control is that of my own conscience and the thought of the examinations at Haverford in September. I debate about three times a week in English, French and German, and go at least once a week to the art museums and to the opera. In the fall there were opportunities to take unforgettable trips to Versailles and Chartres and I am planning similar springtime excursions. I am also writing a paper on "The effects on French Foreign Trade of Inflation of the Dollar during the American Revolution". It must sound like an awfully abstruse sort of subject, but it interests me a great deal. There are no secondary sources bearing directly on that subject so all my work is the result of original research among the manuscripts in the various collections available here in Paris.

To say that I am enjoying my year would be superfluous. And I feel sure that I am profiting greatly by it. Someone before I left told me that you could learn more about international politics by sitting in a Paris café than by two years of study at home. That is a highly exaggerated statement, but the principle of it is very true, I find. I am sure that my conception of the questions involved in current events would have been much narrower had I not come over here this year. Speaking with students of all nations, taking courses of a type not available in the United States, reading literally a dozen different newspapers of different political complexions has made me alive to a great deal that would have been lost to me otherwise.

We had exciting days here especially at the time of the Barthou assassination and before the Saar plebiscite was arranged for. Things have quieted down considerably, by all exterior signs, but I cannot help but believe that beneath the diplomatic negotiations now going on with Germany there lie immense forces. Big stakes are being played for. At any rate, the atmosphere is highly enervating, highly inspiring to a student of politics.

Life in Paris is a most pleasant experience. In winter there is nothing but continual rain, and a day of sunshine is a real pleasure. But you grow to love the rain, and the gray, misty streets. And furthermore when it is raining you are inclined to study harder.

But Spring vacation will soon be here. I may spend it in England, Holland and Belgium. Or I may take a bicycle trip along the Loire. In the summertime I hope to go to Italy. My plans will probably be decided for me by the extent of my financial resources.

I feel very strongly that a great deal of the value that I am deriving from this year abroad is due to the training I received at Haverford School. I was a very hard animal to train, I admit, but I think that by graduation day in 1932 I was finally trained.

My best to Haverford and kindest personal regards,

George

Please remember me to Mr. Black and Mr. Shafer.

3 Rue de la Grande Chaumiere
Paris VIe, France
February 18, 1935

Dear Mother and Daddy:

Thank you very much for your very welcome letters. You spoke of sending me a "scrap of paper" under separate cover. I have not received it yet. Is it a manuscript? I am anxious to see it. I have been sending letters to the Haverford NEWS regularly and imagine that they have been printed, but I have received no letters from them for several weeks so I don't know what is going on there. The latest one I wrote was about "illusions about French people, which I have lost since coming into contact with them". Just in case you want my private opinion, it was a damn* fine article. *this word slipped in by mistake.

I have been working as usual. The history research has given me some interesting times. The other day I worked long and late in the Bibliotheque Mazarine, affiliated with the Académie Francaise. It is an imposing library. L-shaped with enormous bay windows running the length of the long, narrow and darkish room. In front of each window is the bust of a Roman statesman. It is all very classic looking. I spent much time reading journals and newspapers of the Revolutionary period in America. Found lots of interesting items and some scraps bearing on my subject. It was lots of fun to read those old papers. This morning I set out first for the Ministère des Affaires Etrangères on the Quai d'Orsay where I hoped to consult the archives. You need an introduction to do that, so I went to the nearby American embassy for that. There a man gave me the idea that old banking houses might have papers that would interest me, so I went to Rothschild's, de Neufliz and other old houses. At Rothschild's they have nothing since they were established in Paris only in 1804. But the others may have something on my subject. I am following that lead. Rothschild is a very musty, rich looking place and all the porters and petty functionaries all wear black neckties and morning coats. It's dreadfully formal there.

In the meantime I continue to read government. Letters from Dr. Herndon at Haverford have arrived in which he O.K.'s our reports, etc. and sends us friendly campus gossip. I am immensely interested in the negotiations with Germany. In the weekly debates in English in which I take part I have been upholding Germany's side (merely for the good scrap it gives me) and I made quite a speech on Wednesday last and probably will make another this coming Wednesday. The Germans are too devilish to be beaten by France. But I don't think they were as clever as they might have been in answering to the invitation of France and England about the Air Locarno. They weren't quite polite enough and public opinion here is hostile to them now. They could have arrived at the same result with a little more tact. But that is their affair.

M. Flandin has stayed in office longer than anyone gave him credit for, but I still wouldn't buy any long term French bonds if I had the money, which I haven't.

I heard of a new way of making money hand over fist. The father of a friend of mine has extensive property in Jugoslavia. But he can't transfer it to any other country. So if he wants to luxuriate for a while the entire family returns to Jugoslavia where they live like kings. But back in Paris they must economize. This man buys up Jugoslav govt. bonds in Paris, where they are practically worthless, and sells them in Jugoslavia for almost par value because they pay interest there but not in Paris. Jugoslavia has a credit restriction law. Is that a good idea?

I wrote a letter to Fred Bookman and addressed it to Penang, Straits Settlements, Malay. I hope he gets it for his birthday. That's the first letter I ever wrote to Penang.

I missed seeing La Tosca the other night because I got there too late, but I am going to the premiere of a brand new opera "Gargantua" by a modern composer of whom no one has ever heard. But since it is taken from Rabelais the mise en scene should be interesting even if the music isn't. The premiere took place last night but I haven't read the reviews yet.

I enclose a letter I wrote to Dr. E.M. Wilson at Haverford School. Is it all right? I have sent it already, anyhow.

I spent yesterday at the Bois de Vincennes with a young lady friend. There is a 12th Century chateau there which is very interesting and quite ancient with moats and so on. And a nice chapel with windows of sea green glass as a change from the usual stained glass. It was quite pleasant. It was a perfect spring like day and there were mobs of bourgeois French people there all having a grand time. It seemed that everyone in Paris was trying to climb the tower of the old chateau to see the view at the same time. (There is an unusual view of Paris form the top of the tower.) But the Bois de Vincennes isn't as pretty as Boulogne. But there was a very pretty moon and a nice lake with Greek temples sprinkled here and there on the shoreline and that made up for it. The chef d'oevres of the Museum of Grenoble are here on exhibition and I am going to see them. A friend has loaned me her catalogue. There are many well-known masterpieces in the collection. In the springtime the Italian Government will send a big exposition of Italian art up here for an exhibition. Another cementing of the Franco-Italian friendship.

Fritz Kreisler will play here in March and I will try to hear him. You spoke of getting reports that Paris shopkeepers are grumpy. No doubt these reports include only shopkeepers on the Champs Elysées. I never met a little boulanger or papetier who refused to sell. Probably the denizens of the haute couture find that the patronnes can afford to be snooty. But I even doubt that. Right now France is really getting scared about the decline in tourist traffic and decline in world purchases of Paris "quality manufactures". Public opinion is being regimented by newspaper and radio campaigns and lectures in order to revive the quality goods trade and to make the people more kindly disposed toward foreigners. Because France, nationalistic though she may be, depends for perhaps a third of her prosperity on foreigners.

Financial note of extreme importance: Please send me the next draft as soon as you can, and be good enough to send it in DOLLARS, unless there is a very excellent reason to do otherwise. If you send it in dollars, I may be able to make a little profit on the transaction. It all depends on Roosevelt. I paid the doctor's bill, stiff though it was. But it certainly cramped my budget. Do you think that you could include with the next check about $25, which would be just half the amount mentioned in the doctor's bill? I will take care of the rest. But the payment really did set me back a lot. With $50 I could take a trip to England, Holland and Belgium. I will need the draft very soon to pay for my rent. And if you find it convenient, could you send me the money to cover two months' expenses and also a statement of how much I still have coming to me? I want to start to figure out where I can go this summer, etc. Please don't forget the statement. Thank you.

I saw a sign downtown on the Rue Halévy, just opposite the Opera National that might interest Monica:

F. H. Hodgkinson
Agent for .... And Co.
London – Liverpool – New York

I'm sure it is the same Mr. H. but I didn't get a look at him.

I have been walking a good deal in the very old quarter around the Place des Vosges and also the quarter near the Rue St. Jacques and behind the Panthéon. They drip with antiquity and romance. I found one street (not an alley) which you can almost span with your arms.

There is a full moon tonight, so bon soir and lots of love, which, to be sure, is meant to include Monica.

George

3 Rue de la Grande Chaumiere
Paris , VIe, France
February 25, 1935

Dear Mother and Daddy:

I was very glad to receive your letters and especially the photo. I agree with you that it doesn't look very much like you, Mother. You have a great deal more character and individuality than is shown on the photo. The mouth is very bad. But I am glad to have it nevertheless. I look at it often and try to translate it into what you really do look like.

I have had a very good week. At the present time I am completely alone here since Bill C. and Bill Fry both left for Megève last Saturday. (French Alps, Haute Savoie) They are going to spend about ten days there skiing, much as I did in December at Chamonix. It is good both for them and for me that they are going to be away for a while. Even good friends need a vacation from each other every once in a while.

I have been having busy times. Last Tuesday I saw "Le Bourgeois Gentilhomme" done in toto at the Odéon. It was done with all the trimmings that go with that rousing old piece of Molière: the Turkish ballet, the dancing master's ballet and all other ballets. The music, written especially for the play was an insipid sort of 17th Century thing with no character but the play was well done. It was the best production that I have seen at the Odéon. Thursday I went to the exposition at the Petit Palais of the chefs d'oevres of the Museum of Grenoble, which turns out to be a very rich museum. They had some very fine Italian primitives, the most striking Rubens I have ever seen (St. Gregory, painted entirely by Rubens himself, they say) some excellent Fontaine-Latour (self-portraits and a composition in honor of Berlioz) and then the Spanish school which I liked tremendously: Zurbaran, Morillo and Velasquez. Also some LeBrun. Then one entire wing was devoted to the most inane collection of contemporary painting I have ever seen. There were some Matisses and things by the Cubists and Surrealists and the G. knows whatists. By staring and contemplating Matisse for a while I could see that he had an idea, but with the exception of one or two canvasses (Modigliani's portrait of a long necked, distorted woman) most of the moderns left me flat. It is an art I do not care for because it is so incomplete. Here and there you see a canvass with one strong point - good color, good composition, good design - but there is no one canvass that combines all those elements into an integral unit commonly known as a work of art. I was told a story of a painter who would paint a picture every Sunday and then spend the other six days running around to the picture dealers trying to sell his hasty composition. That is the impression most moderns give me. The exposition was well worth seeing, however. I don't mind seeing contemporary painting - in fact it interests me - but it interests me purely from a clinical point of view. I certainly don't like most of it.

Thursday night I went to the second performance of a new Opera called <u>Gargantua</u>, written by 2 modern composers who aren't well known. The music, as was to be expected, was very bad. Once in a while I could catch a few bars that were really excellent but then it always lapsed back into a spineless mediocrity. The transcription of Rabelais, the mise en scène and direction on the other hand were prodigious. It was all done in a sort of picaresque style. Wherever you looked on the stage something was going on, a little sideshow of a humorous character. The costumes were lavish to an extreme. The sets of Gothic architecture were very well done. The story, crude in spots, was thoroughly amusing. At the end of the first act Gargantua made his appearance to the audience by kicking out the bottom of his cradle and running off the stage with the crib on his back, little tyke that he was. (he had been born ten minutes before). In the second act he was a few months old and was already devouring entire legs of beef and throwing his professors out by the ear. And they brought a marvelous paper-maché horse on the stage with flashing red eyes and real steam coming from its nostrils. The whole was very lavish, very amusing but musically uninteresting.

Wednesday I spoke again for Germany in a continuation of our debates on the London note in re air pact, etc. We prepared the debate with a real diplomatic conference. The preceding week I had addressed a series of some 17 questions to France and England on the 3 pacts involved. Wednesday they answered my questions and I will answer their answer as best I can this coming Wednesday. Last Wednesday I started to refute them, by interposing remarks at the psychological moment, but I will give a full answer on Wednesday.

Yesterday (Sunday) was very interesting. In the morning I upped and went to visit Bernard Fäy. He received me in his beautiful, almost regal apartment. His windows are fully two stories high, draped in one of the rooms by severe but effective white curtains. The whole thing is done in American colonial style, the Washington era. (Since Fäy is a specialist and lover of that period.) We had a short interview in which he suggested various sources that I might consult and gave me some very valuable directions. Then he invited me to come to tea on Tuesday. It was very nice of him, don't you think? I look forward to the occasion. Sunday afternoon I started out by going to Orangerie des Tuileries to see the Nympheas of Claude Monet. Georges Clemenceau, a great friend of Monet, asked him to sum up his entire technique in a series of murals, so near the end of his life Monet executed this group of 8 murals in a little known wing of the Orangerie. They are immense things, four in each of the two, large circular rooms. They represent a shady pool at all hours of the day and under all conditions of light. I was immensely impressed by Monet's technique. At first glance they looked like just so many dabs of paint, but as I looked at them the shadows and impressions began to take shape. Once grasped, the paintings are very beautiful and very soothing, if I may use a word like that. Soothing is the right word, however for there is nothing so restful as to look at his impressions of the chequerboard of sunlight and shadow on a quiet country pond late on a midsummer's afternoon. And then to plunge out again into the windy Place de la Concorde brought Monet's technique into vivid reality. Then I went to the Musée Cognac-Jay (not a liquor museum) a museum donated by the founder of La Samaritaine, a big department store. The museum contains a complete exhibition of 17th and especially 18th Century art. The woodwork, probably transported from some ancient hotel, is very beautifully carved. There are many Fragonards, Guardis, La Tours, a queer Rembrandt (in Rubens' style) and a queer Rubens (in Rembrandt's style). A Tiepolo, portraits by Gainsborough and Groese and many other portraitists of that period. That type of goody-goody portrait-painting and over-technical painting that was so popular in the XVIIIth Century does not appeal to me. All the women had beautiful rosy cheeks and all the men had very smooth features and nice lace frills. The execution, too, is too formal. But it was interesting to see, nevertheless. There are also many examples of Louis XV and Louis XVI furniture which I liked, some horrible French porcelain and some beautiful tapestries. The museum is arranged excellently. Much as one would find it in a private house. There is not too much to look at, and it is all tastefully framed and displayed. Although I don't like most of that XVIIIth Century work, it is very interesting to look at and to revisit.

Bill Fry has a subscription to the Paris Symphony Concerts and since he is skiing he gave me his tickets for yesterday's concert and the concert next Sunday. Yesterday they played the 2nd Symphony of Brahms, a Concerto of Schumann and 2 moderns, one called "Le Parc Monceau" by Ferroud and something by Dukas. George Enesco was the guest pianist. I thought he had a very caressing touch, I could almost imagine that he was stroking the keys instead of striking them. He played very beautifully but the style was not very individual. The Brahms was beautifully played by the orchestra. I liked it very much.

As you know, I am working hard at my history and am greatly interested in it. The more I work at it the less I find on the subject. There seem to be no papers relating directly to it. There are many which nibbled at it in a general manner, and many very interesting papers nearly on the subject, but not quite hitting the nail on the head. It is an excellent experience however and I will be able to write a paper of some interest. Today I did a full 8 hours work in a private collection at the American Embassy. Hugh Wallace, ambassador 1919-1921 at Paris, has left a priceless collection of books on Franco-American relations to the embassy. There I found many documents that are absolutely impossible to find elsewhere, even at the Bibliotheque Nationale. Also there is a beautiful library to work in and I am the only one who uses the entire library. There is a red haired (dyed scarlet) librarian of about 60 years of age who takes a motherly interest in my research and has given me the run of the shelves. There are also many books at the Embassy collection, which one finds elsewhere but it is so much more pleasant to read them there. At the Bib. Nationale one waits fully 45 minutes for books to be delivered, there is lots of red tape, the light is bad, it is too crowded and there are all sorts of queer, illiterate-looking people who shuffle around the place in BEDROOM SLIPPERS. At the embassy there are no interruptions, there are rare documents and there is a beautiful library with ample light and a nice view. Embassy gossip: every one is crazy about Ambassador Strauss. He is very strict but very good. They say that once a ladder was ordered for the library he helped the workmen carry it in with his own ambassadorial hands. He is also very well read, so they say. He knows every book in the Library and is quite the old book lover. I will probably see him before I finish my work there.

I have just returned from a French debate. A young Irishman gave a speech in French, as I did the other day. He read an essay he had written on "Irish Youth Fights the Past". It was rather dry and his delivery was very poor. He didn't know much about it except historical facts culled from a book and he was prejudiced in favor of the Protestant Unionists. But I got a chance to speak some French.

Tomorrow night I believe I will go to hear André Siegfried give a special talk on French Parties and Internal Politics. The talk is especially for American students. Then tomorrow afternoon, of course, I will be going to Fäy's for tea.

Your suggestion, Daddy, that I might continue my history work next year is one that interests me a great deal. It had not occurred to me. It is a subject that I would have to take up with Haverford authorities and one that I would have to decide upon – or rather one that could only be decided upon – after I have done all I can on the topic here. Naturally I will stop at the end of May, since I plan to take my summer vacation at that time. About summer plans, I have none that are definite yet. I still intend to go to Italy via the Cote d'Azur and it looks as though that tour would include a week visiting the Chateaux of the Loire also. But I await your letter with a statement of my account with you to date before I make any definite plans. The same holds good for Spring vacation. I would leave for that about the third week in April, since Easter falls on April 21. I have heard of a cruise down the Dalmatian coast, through the Isthmus of Corinth and to Athens, around Greece and back. It includes several stops and the cost from Paris to Paris is 950 francs. That is all I know about it and I will inquire further on Wednesday. I have asked Cook's to make me an estimate for a trip to London, the Shakespeare country, Belgium, including Bruges, etc. (Ostend to Antwerp), Holland (Amsterdam, Rotterdam, The Hague) then to Brussels, and thence to Paris. I will also ask the American Express for an estimate and then try to make one of my own. I am more interested by the Dalmatian idea though, than by the northward trip.

Financial note: I seem to change my mind on the franc every week but I now believe that devaluation is remote. The government is very strongly against it and will fight to the last inch before it takes a step, which in the eyes of the French bourgeoisie would be a negation of all they value highly.

Before closing up shop this summer I mean to write an essay on the Saar plebiscite. I have a complete file of clippings since the first of October on the question. I will make a nice scrapbook out of them wherewith to impress ye old government professor at Haverford, and I will then write an interpretive essay. By that ambiguous word <u>interpretative</u> I mean that the essay will be more on my ideas than on historical facts. I will probably call it <u>Plebiscite Politics: The Statesman's Newest Gadget.</u> Or something to that effect. But at the present time I am all occupied with History and with government and politics which I sandwich in between trips to the library. (La Tosca is being sung this week and I will make a valiant effort to get there to hear it.)

Your draft is awaited here with bated breath (especially if it is to include an additional sum for ½ of Dr. Kreesser's staggering bill.) ie $25.

So glad you got my telegram of Anniversary wishes. Is Caroline still in the family or has she been excommunicated? I wrote her some letters on or about Feb 5. (long letters too) and have not heard from her. But I still have hopes.

So glad that you are succeeding so brilliantly with your German singer, Mother. Maybe you can help me in my diction some time. If I go to Italy I hear that you can get through marvelously with a knowledge of French, Latin and English and a little book of "Handy Expressions in Italian". How to say it and when to say it, as it were. But if the Spring is beautiful enough in Paris and I find that one of my lady friends has a latent knowledge of Italian I may take some lessons – Italian picnics at the Bois de Boulogne or at Versailles. A good way to learn, don't you think? But as long as this gray, windy weather keeps up I will stick to my research and my dusty tomes. (There is a hurricane sweeping across France as I write. 2/3 of France has been devastated by high winds. Paris is next. But it is nothing serious.

I would like very much to go to bed, so with your permission, I will bid you good night and seal this letter with lots of love and a filial kiss.

George

Ever my bestest and warmest to Monica !!!
I include this 1934 license. It may come in handy if you want to renew my driver's license for me.
Best of love to the farm and kindest regards to the Bauers, if you see them soon.
I think of the farm often. There is a marvelous cheese place on the Rue d'Amsterdam, and sitting before an open fire last Saturday night over a divine cheese sample (au Parmegues) I described Hill Farm to a very good friend (a very intelligent Bulgarian girl, Wellesley graduate, no kidding). Describing Hill Farm gives one a pleasant, warm sensation somewhere near the heart, a nice sensation. All my love,

George

3 Rue de la Grande Chaumiere
Paris, VIe, France
March 2, 1935

Dear people,

I should have sent something by the Bremen yesterday, but I have been very busy. I can't quite figure out why I have been busy, but I have because there are lots of things that I have had to neglect. Writing letters is one of the categories of neglected duties, and since it is noon and a rainy Saturday afternoon is in front of me, I am going to spend the time writing letters.

As I mentioned in my last letter, Bernard Fäy invited me to tea. I went Tuesday afternoon. He has a beautiful home (thanks to a rich aunt who died just in time). The pervading tone is colonial architecture, but one of the studies is done in ultra modernistic style. And that is more or less a key to his nature. Because he is a bit ashamed of being an expert in History. His friends, outside interests and conversation all run to modern art, modern poetry and modernism in general. In the colonial rooms he looks uncomfortable while in the modernistic room he looks perfectly at home. So, in his life, he seems a bit ashamed of being a professor of History (why he is, I am sure I don't know) and all his spare time is devoted to very modern people (in the Bohemian sense of the word). At his tea party there was a German painter named Zerber (I believe)(I am hazy on names), a French painter or art dealer named Gey (I believe, (a short thick heavy-set and jovial man), a Miss Parrott who I believe was the Ursula Parrott of modern novels, and as piece de resistance the parents of Gertrude Stein. They were just what you would expect. Very nice Jewish people of the old school, quite bewildered at their daughter's popularity (as are 9 out of 10 people) and quite unassuming. It seems that Fäy isn't married. He is thick as thieves with Gertrude Stein. They toured America together, giving joint lectures to women's clubs. He is really quite hepped on the woman. I don't know what he really thinks of her writing, deep down inside. What he enjoys most is her personality, and that is understandable. It must have been amusing to see hundreds of Americans making fools of themselves before her trying to read a meaning into stuff that had no meaning at all. He says that they laughed themselves sick over it. She hadn't been back to the US in some 20 years and is still there. Fäy told some professorial anecdotes about his lectures. He finds it very disturbing to lecture at the Collège de France because all his friends come and sit in the front row and he knows just what impression his words are creating in their minds. Gertrude S. used to come to the lectures.

The tea was very amusing. The people were interesting. Fay gave me a few more tips on American history, on the sly. I have been spending lots of time at the Embassy and am now engaged in reading a manuscript in 18th Century French and very, very difficult to decipher. The handwriting is even worse than mine. It takes an hour to decipher a page or two and is quite laborious, but full of information on my topic. Very romantic business, reading original manuscripts.

**I have been permitted to use the archives at the Quai D'orsay and at National Archives, a special privilege.

When I haven't been at the Embassy I have been going to courses or reading. (Except for a few dates, which don't count). I heard André Siegfried give a lecture on French politics Tuesday night. It was excellent, in fact marvelous. That word is not too strong for his lectures. He said in France there is a parliamentary Opposition only because of the fact that there is a Right. The Left exists only as a means of fighting the Right. And they believe that the best way to beat an extreme Right ticket is to vote extreme Left. He drew the differences between Paris and the provinces, and added something very interesting. He said that the kernel of French politics is the opposition between those who favor the principles of the French Revolution and those who oppose these principles. The provinces, it seems, are very strongly attached to the Republic and wouldn't stand for a dictatorship. He also mentioned the very grave split between Parliament and the People, a thing which I have mentioned to you before in my letters. That is the reason, I believe France is in for a change in government.

Wednesday I spoke, as usual, at the Debating Club and carried on my German argument. They seem to find my speeches interesting, which make me feel very good.

I received a letter from Sam Kind this morning thanking me ever so much for my Bi-monthly letters to the news (once every two weeks equals Bi-monthly.) He told me about the technical changes in the paper and changes in the editorial staff. They are starting a vigorous, modern policy now. Quite in opposition to traditional policies and a thing I urged them to do for some time. I am still Paris Correspondent and may be a sort of special feature writer next year. Maybe. If I had stayed on I would have been a managing editor possibly, but that is all over now.

Thursday night I went to Mrs. Crawford's for dinner with her and her son Jacky. Had a very pleasant evening, chatting with her. She has gone through an awful lot in one lifetime, more than 2 or 3 people have gone through. And she has come out wonderfully and has very admirable courage and gaiety. She is now quite happy. Believes in astrology and is always predicting quite horrendous political happenings, but outside of that she is quite fine. Also she looks about ½ her age.

Last night (Friday) Marian Halpert pulled in from Switzerland alone. I saw to it that she was properly lodged and taken care of. I will give up writing anything in longhand from now on. You say my handwriting is bad, but I thought you were just indulging in a mother's privilege of exaggeration. But Marian confirms the impression about my handwriting, so I'll give it up as a bad job. Too late now to do anything about it, except learn to type better. I would like to learn shorthand some time, before I start working, or while I am working (night school perhaps). Or a summer before Law School, if I should go to Law school. Seems remote though (Law School seems remote).

I have learned a lot about the diplomatic service, from the inside, by chatting with the librarian at the Embassy. She doesn't know that I have learned though. A general happy-go-lucky air combined with a dependable inside seems to be the formula for success, according to her. But that needn't be a rule to go by.

This afternoon at 5 I am going to hear Das Rheingold given at the Chatelet in a special performance with special artists chosen from the Opéra and the Opéra Comique. It will probably be above average, and might well be excellent.

I have received big folders and estimates of costs of trips to Spain and to England. Spain would be very beautiful and not so expensive, but the English pound is dropping like fury and I might go there. They say there is going to be a big drop in gold currencies, what with the English pound going on the toboggan. I hope so. I'll go to England before the prices rise. I just got another idea. I believe that the best plan for Easter would be to go to London and stay there for ten days. Really learn something about the city. Take a trip or two to the environs and then come back, having spent a good deal less than I would on a voyage circulaire. I wouldn't see Belgium and Holland, but that wouldn't break my heart. Then I would have more money for the summer. Yes, I think I will do that. But plans can always be changed.

*Key to my character below.

It isn't very amusing for you to read this letter and have to follow the meandering course of my mind. Because all I do is sit down to the typewriter and start thinking with my fingers on the keys. The result is what you are reading. I hope you like it.

Bill C. and Bill Fry get back early Monday morning. I will be quite glad to see them. I think Fäy's course starts this week; i.e. the course on relations between French and American literature (an excuse for Gertrude Stein).

**Important Please!

I haven't yet received the draft but am awaiting it. I also want you especially to send me a statement of my account with you, please, Daddy. I must know how much I have before I make vacation plans. Please be good enough to send it to me soon. And oblige, your son. Thank you.

Mardi Gras comes this week (March 5) and there will be some gaiety, no doubt. And no doubt, in fact it is a certainty, I will join in it.

I have been talking over plans to study Italian with Marian. We may buy an Italian grammar book and study it together. When we have mastered some fundamentals we can get hold of an Italian and exchange English lessons for Italian lessons. History repeats itself, one might say. Which was meant to be a cryptic remark.

Spring is making a desperate effort to come in, but the persistent rain and cloudy grayness have had the edge so far. But the days are getting longer and the blue patches in the sky more frequent. We have hopes. The Luxembourg Gardens looked springy this morning despite the rain. I will now sign off for a day or so but will no doubt continue this letter later on and send it off to you in three days.

PS By all means, Daddy, why not take the trip to the gardens of the Old South. I can't imagine anything much more beautiful. You would have a grand rest.

PPS Idea for Santa Claus. I need a new typewriter (but this one will last till next X-mas),

Continued Monday, March 4, 1935

Both the Bills blew in this morning from the Alps looking very red-cheeked and healthy and winter-sportsy. They had a grand time in Megève. Went to bed early every night and had the usual exercise. They were very good boys, by all accounts. Fry is already back in his routine of study and I imagine that Bill Crawford will follow suit tomorrow.

Saturday, as I predicted, I went with a friend to hear Das Rhinegold. It was done without acting or stage setting. Just a full-sized orchestra and the singers in ordinary concert clothes. But I have never heard anything so impressive. I am fully convinced that Wagner is truly great now. If an entire house full of people can listen attentively for

2 ½ hours without a break to nothing but music – nothing to look at or otherwise distract you – the composer must be great. Everyone in the audience was on the edge of his chair for the entire time (no intermissions during the entire 4 acts). I loved it. He builds up climaxes in a way that I have never heard equaled. And the first, long notes in the overture were wonderful to hear. They say that Wagner expresses the spirit of the German people in his music. Nothing is more true. But one might even add and say that the German people express the spirit of Wagner in their lives.

Sunday I spent walking around Paris until dark with Marian, who needs to be introduced to the nicest parts of Paris. At 5 we went to a concert at the Salle Rameau (ex-Pleyel) where they played all the fugues of Bach. The first few were interesting, but they played 15 - no more, no less - of the fugues and it was quite boring by the time the concert neared conclusion. The same theme repeated for 2 hours just didn't stand up under the treatment it was given. A little Brahms would have been all right, but 2 hours of the same theme was too much. An interesting item was a duet on clavichords, for which Bach wrote some special fugues.

Today I spent at the Embassy library deciphering my manuscript and I actually finished it. So now I have read every line that bears on my subject at the Wallace Collection of the Embassy. I was granted permission to use the national archives and archives of foreign affairs and will go there next (after a day or so at the Biblioteque Nationale). The work is still very interesting. By the way, I rode up in the elevator with Ambassador Strauss this morning and he said good morning to me and I to him. He looks very intelligent and capable. Also quite friendly. They make quite a fuss over him here. Almost strew lilies in his path, but not quite.

Wednesday I go to hear a lecture on "The French Newspapers". It is in the evening and they serve free buffet after it - so why not go? Besides, the lecture (as a pure after-thought) will be interesting. Tomorrow, on the other hand, is Mardi Gras. So I have made my little plans and am to go dancing in the evening. (Work while there is yet daylight, of course.)

Received a card from Uncle Fred sent from the faraway island of S. Helena – where a famous XIXth Century citizen of Corsica died. Guy called Napoleon.

I bought a little Italian grammar with handy phrases in the back of it and have been looking through it. Donna immobile. Isn't that good Italian? And good horse sense? PS I like my Italian accent. I am sure I inherited it. (from my very talented parents) (That means you).

I would like to mail this so will close soon (when I have nothing left to say.) I happened to go to the American University Union and in chatting with the secretary down there I heard that this pension where I am living – chez Vaujany – is the best one for the money in all of Paris. I had started to grumble but now I am more enthusiastic than ever. (All grumbling was to myself of course, apropos of lack of variety in food and table conversation). But I really don't see now how she gives us the good service and good food she does for the money. We almost bathe in butter at each meal. I like the pension despite the one or two faults that it has. I am only glad that it hasn't more faults than it has. And Mme has turned out to be a very sweet person. Tries hard to please. Did I tell you that for Christmas we bought her a set of after dinner coffee cups.

Well good night and have a rousing old Mardi Gras.

Lots of love,

George

Love to Monica, of whom I think <u>very often.</u>

3 Rue de la Grande Chaumiere

Paris, VIe, France

March 11, 1935

Dear Mother and Daddy,

I was so glad to get your letters and especially the statement of my financial position with you. I had no idea that I was so rich. At present my bank balance is 3800 francs or thereabouts which is about $250 figured very roughly but conservatively. With the 505 that you say I still have to my credit with you that makes $775 dollars, a very tidy sum. Now will you believe that I can live within my income? I intend still to go to London for the Easter vacation. I received a very nice letter from my good old Aunt Sophie Goldstone, of all people, who lives in London and told me to be sure to call on her. I will, with the greatest of pleasure. It was a very nice letter.

You might be good enough to write me some addresses of London people whom I could say hello to. I have lost the ones you sent last time. I really don't think it is a false alarm this time. I am going (I believe), I would leave about the 19th of April and return on the 28th. I could easily shorten my stay if so inclined.

I have been doing a lot of history work these past weeks and have done all the work I intend to do in the Bibliotheque Nationale. Starting today I will spend the time in the Archives of Foreign Affairs at the Quai d'Orsay. They keep very diplomatic hours there. The Library is open from 2 to 6 five days a week, so I will have to make the best of it, in the time allowed. In the mornings I will continue to read government and to write a paper on the Saar plebiscite. I am pasting up my newspaper clippings about the plebiscite, a long job. My paper will not require too much research because it will contain my own ideas more than anything else.

Recently wrote a bit for the Haverford NEWS on "the continental viewpoint". I said that no one could define it, but by living in Paris for several months you were aware that it did exist. Then I went on to tell about some aspects of it that occurred to me. I will show you all these articles this summer. They sent me several issues of the NEWS with my articles in them. The papers were good to see, and it was interesting to read about the college activities going on as usual. Debating has taken a new lease on life there.

The Greek civil war is interesting the papers now. Everyone expects some international complications. I don't know enough about it to guess. Hitler's diplomatic cold is now cured and he has invited Sir John Simon to Berlin. That cold was one of the most stupid things Hitler could have done. Someone ought to give him a course in how to be oily, or how to keep up pretenses. But he is the kind of a boy who gets to the head of the class, stupid or not.

Sunday I went to the Russian church, a sight that everyone should see. The music is so very beautiful that you can't believe that human voices produce it. The deepest base imaginable (reminded me of dark, polished woodwork for some reason) sustained by a wonderful chorus of feminine voices. It seemed a very paternal religion, inviting the sinning children all to come and be cleansed of their sins. Possibly that impression was due to the liberal use of gray-bearded men, well-paunched. Not a few had hair arranged a la Rapsutin. The music I thought was very sad, suffering sort of music. Tragic. Nothing gay about it at all, no elation at all. We left the church and stepped out into what I would call a typical Russian scene – the city was blanketed with snow. Friday, Saturday and Sunday were snow days here in Paris and a white carpet covered most of the city. The wind was bitter chill and Bill Fry succumbed to a cold which he's getting over. The spring sun, so long awaited, has just broken through now (noon, Monday) and I believe that winds and snows have gone for good. At least I hope so. Paris weather is so capricious that it is well worthwhile to hold your tongue in your cheek when making weather predictions. Had a nice Italian dish of spaghetti on Sunday at a restaurant I know of. Then in the evening (after a very pleasing afternoon) I went to a dance given by the pension where a girl I know lives. The girls were largely in costume but not the men. It was quite gay and lots of fun. Lots to eat and some Vouvray to wash it down. I must now go to the Quai d'Orsay. More later.

Later. I have spent the afternoon thumbing through hundreds of letters signed by Franklin, Vergennes, Genet and their contemporaries. It is a strange feeling to read the letters written by their own hand. Practically, however, it is a wearisome process because the useful information bearing on my paper is thinly scattered in those letters.

The week holds in store opportunities for lots more work and then a date or two at the end for relaxation. This evening I will probably read and go to bed early (a luxury that I am always glad to indulge in).

I am writing to Ma and Baba at their Florida address, hoping they will still be there.

Love,
George

3 Rue de la Grande Chaumiere
Paris, VIe, France
March 17, 1935

Dear Mother and Daddy

Naturally, I was quite pleased to get your letter with the item about Dr. Wilson's letter. Then just the next day I got a letter from Wilson himself with a carbon copy of his note to you enclosed. He said:

"Dear George: Two days ago I read your article in the Haverford News and then wrote to your father the letter of which the enclosed is the copy. I am more than grateful to you for the trouble you have taken to write me so fully. I am sure all your former teachers will be glad to read the letter, so I am circulating it among them. I think it is true that you learned something about English style when you were at Haverford School. It is plain from the article in the News and from your letter that you are making a fine use of your year abroad. You have discovered the true method of education. If you make your public spirit, your devotion to your Church and your religious life match your intellectual spread, you will be a citizen of whom any country may be proud. No man may neglect the deeper issues of his life and hope to weigh heavily in the affairs of his day. That is my best and most affectionate word of greeting to you. Faithfully yours, E.M. Wilson."

A very headmasterly note, isn't it? It probably reminds Monica of Sundays in England. It brings me back 3 years to Sundays at Haverford. But I am very pleased to learn that I have a staunch supporter in such a man as Dr. Wilson.

I am writing numerous letters today, Sunday. Will write to some friends on the World-Telegram and to Hendershot, and to Bernays if I get the time. It can't hurt to keep those contacts alive. I am getting more and more awake to the value of contacts. It seems to be the sad, but inescapable truth that the way to get to the top is to know the right people. Perhaps that explains my letter-writing activity.

The article to which Dr. Wilson refers may have been the one on war and peace. If it is, and you read it, please bear in mind that the editor of the News cut the article exactly in half. The second half told about the reasons and arguments for Peace in Europe. And in the conclusion I said that Europe will have another war. Some references in the first part of the article seem superfluous when the second half is left out. But the Haverford News is cramped for space. I may send you some of the articles. I may include them in this letter. If I do, be sure to save them for me because I value them and want to put them in my scrapbook.

I have worked this week along the usual schedule. Every afternoon from Monday to Friday, I spent 4 hours at the archives in the Ministry of Foreign Affairs, which is open only afternoons 5 days a week. I have been making some progress in the research. It is still interesting and the paper may amount to something. I have been working on my paper on plebiscite politics. To please the people at Haverford, I will fill up the first chapter with historical references, the result of some research. If the historical part could be cut down, the paper might be something worth submitting to magazines. It will be much better written than the bonus thing, Monica. On rereading the bonus paper I found that it had much too much slang in it and was a trifle "cheap". This plebiscite paper will be better written. But to be salable it would have to be revised. Because for a Government thesis at Haverford, and a magazine article 2 different standards of knowledge and treatment prevail.

Dr. Herndon (Gov. professor) wrote me sending a list of readings in Political Philosophy that we will be responsible for on our Major exam in the spring of 1936. It includes Plato, Aristotle, Hobbes, Bentham, Machiavelli, Locke, Rousseau, Dante, Duguit and others. I will try to get some of it done this spring. My program for the rest of this year is as follows: continue to do History and Government until April 19th, and try to do some work on the Plebiscite paper in spare time. April 19th sail for England. Come back about the 30th and spend the first three weeks in May reading political philosophy and French. Then spend the last two weeks of May reviewing the work of the year. June 1 or thereabouts take a bicycle trip to the Chateau country, come back to Paris and leave immediately for Italy. A month or 1 ½ months there and then back to Paris and sail for home and you (which I will be more than eager to do).

All this is subject to change. But the studying must be done. By hook or crook.

Marian Halpert, who had been here for a week or so, had to return to Lausanne to stay with her mother who had, quite typically, worried herself sick about her daughter. I saw her to the train. Last night I went in style (full dress) to the Opera Comique with a Bulgarian-American friend to see "Sapho" by Massenet from Daudet's novel of the same name. I didn't know what to expect but was quite agreeably surprised when it turned out to be a very good opera. It was done in modern dress, which seemed a bit strange, but the music was quite lovely although it contained but one aria that might make a bid for immortality. The dramatic qualities were unexpectedly well developed, especially the third act which works up to a beautiful climax when the trusting young student is disillusioned, and rather cruelly disillusioned, about the woman he has idolized. Some of the scenes were so true to Paris that they made you squirm in your seat. The staging was excellent, and the singing (some voices) was the best. After the Opera we went dancing at the fastest and chicest spot in Paris, Le Boeuf sur le Toit. It was my one and only and last fling of "aristocracy" or "plutocracy" in Paris. There is nothing I like better than to act the grand seigneur. We had a marvelous time. But one cannot do that more than once a year on a student's income.

So this afternoon I am going to hear some Wagner at the Chatelet, a concert hall. And I will sit in the 3-franc seats. The top gallery at that theater is an enormous barn of a place: dark, rangy, and almost windy. There are nothing but worn wooden benches (without backs) to sit on, and the entire gallery is illuminated by only two tiny blue lights. They give an eerie light, just sufficient to make out the form of the benches and stairs. But the music is wonderful. I will tell you all about it later.

Friday afternoon, the 22nd, Bill and I are going to Fäy's for tea to meet, as he said, his two "golf-playing nieces and an American girl". He is unmarried and takes quite a pride in his nieces; they say he is a very good uncle.

I think I will acknowledge Dr. Wilson's letter. I don't know what I'll say to him, but I will write anyhow. As to the articles included in this letter, they represent about half of what the NEWS has received from me. I think most of what I sent has been printed, but they haven't been very regular about sending me the issues. The other articles, of which I have only the original manuscripts, were better than the enclosed. They were about my general impressions of Paris. I am thinking of writing one on the lack of blue blood in Paris, if I can find enough to say about that or another on "Spring Comes to Paris".

The farm must be grand this time of the year. I often long to spend just one weekend there with you, and then hop back here before Monday morning. But I will be with you there in about 4 months.

My dearest sister, Caroline, has owed me a letter since her birthday. Pretty soon I will be tempted to break down and write to her. What is eating the dear girl!

I may write some more after the concert.

LATER:

Well, I am back from the Wagner concert and it was just grand. They played the overture from the enchanted vessel, Prelude to Lohengrin, Venusberg scene from Tannhauser, forest murmurs from Siegfried, Voyage to the Rhine from Gotterdammerung, Prelude and death from Tristan and Isolde, Holy Friday music from Parsifal, and as dessert they played the best selections from Die Meistersinger. What else could one ask, for a perfect afternoon? I went with my Bulgarian friend, the Wellesley graduate.

I have just been reading Hitler's statement to the world accompanying his proclamation of military service for the Reich. Of course, it is just the recognition of a fait accompli, but its diplomatic effect will be enormous. It changes Germany's position completely from that of humble beggar to that of proud dictator to the rest of Europe. However, by what I hear and read I cannot believe that the war will come soon. It will come, sans doute, but not for a year or so. 10 months possibly, but not before that time. One good reason to believe that the war isn't a risk that must be dealt with in a few weeks is that the Flandin government is too steady to suit Hitler. Of course, Flandin is just balancing as on the top of a rail fence, but Hitler wouldn't get nasty without taking pains to create a weaker internal situation in France. Or if he lacks the means to do that, he would wait until France is weak of its own accord - and he won't have to wait too long either.

Not a very cheerful way to end a letter, but it is the way I size up the situation. Sorry to be such a cold realist.

But the above sentences have not the slightest cooling effect on the warm and devoted love that I enclose with this letter.

George

A great big kiss for Monica. (an enormous one, in fact.)

3 Rue de la Grande Chaumiere

Paris, VIe, France

March 22, 1935

Dear Mother and Daddy:

The "Bremen" sails tomorrow and I feel that it ought to be carrying you a letter so here goes.

Remember the cable I got from the Haverford News? Well, I "scouted" the streets, as they asked and whipped up an article, which I sent them the very morning the cable came. It took about two hours, from scouting to mailing. But I think the article is of some value. Perhaps they or I will send you a clipping of it. The sum total of it was that there is no war scare in Paris and that Hitler's armament move has made the French people not only distrust Hitler more than ever (nothing new) but it has also made them distrust their own government more than ever (nothing new either, for that matter). I wish there was a way of cashing in on the articles, but that seems to be out of the question while I am still in my journalistic diapers.

Tuesday night I went to hear "La Boheme" at the Opera Comique, sung by Giuseppe Luge and Mlle. Marengo from La Scala de Milan. Their voices were just grand. There were some Italians in the gallery with us (at 4 francs) who just went wild with joy. The Lugo and Marengo, being both Italian, sang all their scenes in the mother tongue while the others sang in French, but the combination was not at all bizarre, and was on the other hand very pleasant. One particularly good spot was the solo of the philosopher when he is about to sell his old coat to buy some medicine for Mimi who is dying. He sang it in a deep, throaty but rich voice, in Italian enunciated with much feeling and passion. They raised the curtain with Cavaleria Rusticana, sung in French. I like it very much, but one could feel all along that it should have been sung in Italian, and in fact would not really fit any other language. It is the most traditionally constructed opera that I have ever heard. At every step along the stage the singers burst into some wonderful aria. Every nod of the head is the happy excuse for an immortal song. But enough of that.

Spring happens to be here, and it couldn't have arrived under much better conditions. On the first day of Spring, and in fact every day this week, the sky has been a clear Mediterranean blue, the sun has been warm and caressing, and every trip to the gardens reveals another tree is in bud. Wednesday Bill and I went to the Bois de Boulogne in the afternoon with the intention of doing some rowing. There was a long line of students with their lady friends waiting for boats, so we just went on to one of the wide stretches of lawn, leaned up against a tree and let the sun work on us. The place was full of children who were very amusing to watch. But don't think that is a daily occupation of the three Haverford students in Paris. Not at all.

I have now completely exhausted the resources of the Ministère des Affaires Etrangères as regards to my history essay. I may do some more work at the Archives Nationales and then write the essay. I am collecting material for my paper on plebiscites.

The German insolence has everyone here interested. Some are excited and nervous about it, others, like your son, are inclined to take it in their stride and wait to see what happens. I don't expect a war, as I said before and will say again, for at least ten months. Papers here are coming out with analyses of Germany's economic capacity to wage war. It is almost nil. But that is an argument neither for nor against. The true reason, I believe, why Germany will have to wait a while, is that she has not made alliances that are strong enough and an iron band of pacifist countries is quickly forming around her. As soon as she makes sure of Japan, Poland and Hungary, (and there is a very, very slight, almost negligible chance of keeping England neutral) she will be ready to fire the first shot.

Incidentally, I firmly believe that another war would be a most horrible disaster for the entire world, but what I believe or what several hundred thousand people like me believe does not change the facts. There will be another war and the world will take the consequences – and probably come through it somehow.

I read of Negro riots in Harlem. I hope they are not as serious as they sound, because they sound mighty serious. Not only for New York, but for several continents. But that is a big question.

By the way, I have decided that I am a rank capitalist, opportunist and a lot of other dirty names. But I like it.

Thank you for sending me my license with the enclosure. I will sign and send it today.

This afternoon Bill and I go to Fäy's for tea. I may tell you about that when I return.

Paris takes on an entirely different aspect in the springtime, as you may already know. The cafes by the simple expedient of taking down their little glass enclosing walls transform themselves from dovecotes for the shivering doves that inhabit Montparnasse to the gathering places of the international hautemonde that one reads about. The old pastime of watching the queer human parade walk by your table comes once more into vogue, the cafes lost their cozy, inn aspect and become rejuvenated into their well known "sidewalk" and "cosmopolitan" aspect. (bad grammar).

On the first day of spring I took tea with Mrs. Crawford, a rare pleasure. But with the longer and warmer days she will probably be going out more frequently and such opportunities will become less rare. She is an alarmist but a charming woman. Many alarmists are. (Charming women). And so are many charming women. (Alarmists).

If Sunday is as beautiful as I am hoping it will be I will be going to Fontainebleau, taking my lunch along with me. Received a letter from a London Hotel, in Russell Square, which promises bed and breakfast for 5 shillings. You can't do much better than that.

Later. Well, I am sorry to report that the Fäy tea was rather dull. We were intended as bread and butter for his young nieces who play golf. The rest goes without saying.

In the evening Bill and I intended to see a French propaganda movie called "Germany Under William II and Under Hitler". But there was such an enormous line of French patriots in front of the theater that we could not get in. So we just strolled along the Champs Elysées and came home to bed early. Today I will study and then, it being Saturday, take a few hours off. Sunday I hope to picnic at Fontainebleau.

Lots of love,

George

Love and a very happy Spring vacation to Caroline if she is home for that yet. And I hope that she'll answer my letters.I just received your 2 letters of March 14th and March 13th. Thank you.

3 Rue de la Grande Chaumiere

Paris, VIe, France

March 26, 1935

Dear Mother and Daddy:

Just a short note between trips to the Library to let you know that I am alive and happy.

I went to Fontainebleau on Sunday with a friend and picnicked. It was drizzly when we set out but we persevered and were rewarded for our pains by a brilliant sunny day from noon on. Went through the Chateau, which is a sterling example of the decorative arts in France. All furnishings are of the very best crystal of Roche, all carpets from Aubusson, all plates and vases from Sevres, etc. Nothing but the best. The oldest part dates from as far away as Louis IX, and the latest parts were done by Louis Phillippe. There are wonderful carved ceilings, meters thick, done by Francis I and the floors of the rooms reproduce in many kinds of wood the design of the ceilings.

The park is very large, that is to say the forest. The trees are immensely tall and have no branches on the lower trunk. They are all far apart and the forest floor is clean as a whistle. It isn't as cozy a forest as yours at Hill Farm. But then at one end is an enormous pit on the style of the Grand Canyon called the Caverne des Brigands. It is formed of glacial rock in all sorts of shapes and sizes and gives a wasty, desert appearance. The day turned out to be very warm so we curled up next to a warm rock and read poetry, studied some Italian and had a generally nice time. Returned to Paris late in the afternoon, about 7 P.M. It was the first time I had left Paris since January. The longest I had been in one city without a break for some 7 years. I was very glad to get out for a while. It seems that many young French people camp in the woods over the weekend because we saw many of them on the train going back with us who had enormous Alpine sacks with provisions for 2 days.

My plans for a trip to England are taking shape rapidly. I would leave here April 15th by the Dieppe-Newhaven route. Then go immediately to the country by Oxford, Stratford-on-Avon, Gloucester, Bristol, Salisbury, Winchester and then back to London arriving the night before Easter. Then I could spend all the time I wanted in London and environs and return to Paris when good and ready.

You will no doubt note that I am in a hell of a hurry and am dashing this letter off. More details in the next letter. Went to a speech on New Turkey last night that was very interesting. It was given by a young Turk who is all enthused about Mustapha Kemal. It seems that Kemal is the answer to what Turkey had been waiting for for 50 years. They all love him a great deal.

The Hitler Juggernaut rolls on and seems to be crushing all resistance under it. (This is prophecy, not pro-Nazism).

I will write a less hurried letter soon.

> Lots of love to yourselves and a hug to
> Monica,
> George

The same to Caroline if she is vacationing with you.

3 Rue de la Grande Chaumiere
Paris, VIe, France
March 29, 1935

Dear Mother and Daddy

This year has been flying on toward its end much too quickly. I have no idea when I am going to do all the things I would still like to do, most of them will probably have to be left undone. The spring days are getting warmer and warmer but there is still enough of a chill in the air to remind one that winter has not been left far behind. Last Sunday, I went to Fontainebleau, this Sunday I will probably go to St. Cloud, which they say, is a very nice park. It is not at all far from Paris, being almost within the city limits. Yesterday (Thursday) was Micarême, the middle of Lent, which is a holiday in France, due to the prevalence of Catholics. The schools and universities and many shops were closed, and in the afternoon I decided to put away the books and go out for the rest of the day.

I went with Bill Fry out to Auteuil where they have horse racing. For five francs we entered the turf, or whatever they call the cheapest standing room. There was an enormous crowd of very nondescript French people and at the time we got there it was between races and everyone was betting. We watched and tried to figure out what it was all about. There are hundreds of little betting booths and enormous signboards, visible for half a mile, with the horse's names, numbers and the odds. We watched one race and then ventured five francs in another, just to see how the things worked. Naturally, our horse, the favorite, didn't win, so we spent the rest of the time watching the races and left the betting to the experts. Between races all the sharpers, bookies, vendors of "hot tips" and lists of "sure wins" got in their work. They collected a little knot of about twenty people and then started to harangue them until someone broke down and bought their "hot tips". The horses didn't seem to run very quickly. Perhaps it was because the course was a steeplechase and not a flat race. But it was very interesting to watch, and especially to watch the people. Judging by what I saw around me, no one gets very rich by betting on horse races. It was a beautiful day and a good one to spend outdoors. After the seventh race we took the metro home (Don't worry, I'll not become a follower of the ponies).

Last night Mrs. Crawford invited us out to dinner so we bought her a big bunch of bright yellow jonquils and went over to dinner. She has a marvelous

French cook and we dined royally. Then we all climbed into a taxi and went over to the Champs Elysées where they have some very good newsreels. They showed a picture "Germany Under William II and Under Hitler" which was a series of shots of Germans marching in perfect order and with very happy faces. It was meant to show the French audiences that the Germans are not forced to parade and march as much as they do, but that they do it because they like to do it. It was a good attempt to explain the workings of the "ame Allemande". But there was one thing that absolutely brought down the house. They showed a short shot of Mussolini making a speech to thousands of young Italian blackshirts. He stood on a balcony, thrust out that formidable chin of his, gesticulated belligerently and shouted at the top of his lungs: "Our contribution to the peace of the world is supported by millions of hard steel bayonets." Then he just thrust out his chin as far as it would go and let the Italians massed in the street below go wild with joy. The French people in the theater clapped and cried very strong enthusiasm for him. They would probably like someone with a personality like that. They have lacked any sort of personality for such a long time.

In one day or so I will have done all my research for History and then I will write the paper. I have to go to the Ministry of the Colonies to get special permission to use some documents they have charge of. I have not come to any startling conclusions by means of my research. The sum total seems to be that, just as anywhere and any time, the smart Frenchmen profited by U.S. inflation and the dumb Frenchmen were caught short and had their ears clipped. I have already started to write my plebiscite paper, and I have all my clippings neatly pasted into three volumes. But I am not terribly pleased with the prose that I have set down so far. Perhaps my pencil will work better this morning.

This afternoon I am going downtown to make arrangements for going to England. Could you send me a check for the balance of my account with you? Or if you don't like to send that much at one time, could you send part of it? I will need about a hundred dollars when I go to England April 15th. If you send me a check for it then I can get pounds for it right away without having to change it into francs first. I would like any further money you send me in the form of a check, if that is convenient to you.

I have received no recent letters from you, but the boats get in tonight and I imagine there will be something then. You spoke about hay fever injections. I suppose it would be a good idea to take them, only it is difficult and messy to do it myself. I haven't received the box yet.

I took a walk the other day in the most populous section of Paris and one of the oldest too. It is around the Gobelins factory, the Rue Mouffetard to be exact. The streets wind and curve downhill and there are very tiny alleys with old, quaint names. Not so quaint to see, but giving quite an old-world atmosphere, was a big fat rat running down the street chased by two cats. I didn't especially relish that, but I suppose it is all part of old Paris.

We have had more debates on the German question, which is certainly coming quickly to a head. They have been manifesting about the death sentences in Lithuania against four Nazis. The Germans are being fed Memel propaganda and when they are ripe and the time is advantageous Memel will probably become German again. I don't know just how Hitler is going to try to do it, but he probably has it all figured out. Chances for peace in Europe look very thin unless France, Britain and Italy take a very firm attitude. If they would all do what Mussolini is doing - just quietly increase their army and air forces - Hitler would probably think twice. As it is, the damn fool doesn't even think once. Latest rumors are that Hitler told John Simon everything he wanted: Memel, Austria, Polish Corridor, etc. and Sir John found it a bitter pill to swallow. As I had guessed, Hitler will go back to the League if it is completely reorganized along Nazi lines. The French people are being lathered up into a good hearty hate of Germany once more. One paper calls him an "enfant terrible" who demands more and more attention all the time. The more you give him, the more he asks.

I am pretty sure that I can see what the final result of it all will be but I don't quite know what to do about it. I suppose the best thing is to have a good time in spite of the gathering clouds, which is the policy I am following. One very true thing was said in a newspaper editorial yesterday. One writer stated that there is still a powerful force of <u>inertia</u> that keeps us out of war. And until something happens to sweep away that inertia there will be no war. I still hold to my ten-month guess, but may have to revise it within a week. July seems to be the traditional month for dangerous international situations, and 1935 may be no exception to that rule. But at present there is certainly no war atmosphere. There is hate and fear of the Germans, but no desire to fight about it.

I have to go off to a lecture by Siegfried on the political economy of Canada now, which will probably take my mind off Germany for a while.

Goodbye and lots of love,
George

Happy April Fool's Day
Your loving son (nobody's fool)

BONNINGTON HOTEL
SOUTHAMPTON ROW
LONDON, W.C.1

Dear Mother and Daddy

No doubt you are very surprised to see this letter coming from London. So am I. Today is Monday, April 1$^{st.}$ On Saturday I was sitting around in Paris, talking to Bill. It suddenly occurred to me that there was nothing to prevent me from taking my vacation then and there and that is just what I did. I was not getting enough work done and was getting stale at it, so I just packed my bag, went down and bought a ticket and pulled up stakes early on Monday morning (this morning).

For 202 francs I got a round trip ticket London – Paris and vice versa. At 10:15 this morning I left the Gare St. Lazare and went to Dieppe. The channel steamer – called the S. S. Worthing, in case you care to know, took 3 hours (usual time) to make the trip from Dieppe to Newhaven. It was bitter cold on the Channel but not rough at all. There was a bright sun in the late afternoon, which made the Channel look bright blue – very pretty. Many English people on board. We landed at Newhaven at 4 P.M. and I climbed on the train and had my first English tea in England. The chalk cliffs were very beautiful such a striking, bleak whiteness. One can tell while still miles off shore that the island you are coming to is not France at all. It has such a very different spirit from France.

We got to London – Victoria Station – and instead of taking a taxi to a hotel I summoned all my courage and took a bus and, by George, I got there.

My hotel is not the one shown on this letterhead, even though I do use their nice stationery. I am at the Berkshire House Hotel – 33 Guilford Street, off Russell Square London W. C. But I am leaving tomorrow morning for Oxford, Warwick, Kennilworth, Stratford on Avon, Bristol, Bath, Salisbury, Winchester and intermediate points. I will get back to London about April 7th. But don't write to me here – write to my usual address and Bill Crawford will forward the letter to me. I might change hotels.

You ought to hear my English accent. It would split you. I find it hard to accustom my ear to the accent. I always think the clerks, conductors, people in the street, etc. are going to talk French and I listen in French. So when they talk English I often miss some words. But that will soon wear off.

What I have seen of London so far looks grand. All I have seen has been from a train window or a bus window.

It was an exciting and inspiring feeling just to pack up and leave at 48 hours notice. I am looking forward to a grand 2 weeks here in England and then to 6 weeks of concentrated work in Paris before the summer vacation. Now I want to trot out and take a look at London. So   Cheerio

Love,
George

BONNINGTON HOTEL
SOUTHAMPTON ROW
LONDON, W.C.I.
April 1, 1935

Monica dear,

This is a grand island you have here – what I've seen of it. The people are all so dreadfully clean cut and well turned out. It's been said many a time, but I really do think that they all look just as though they had stepped out of a bath.

My hotel is a dingy little place but cheap - /5 – for bed and breakfast. No running water. But everything else in the place runs, especially the bugs. (No, it's not as bad as all that).

I was a bit confused at first over the money what with crowns and guineas and florins, shillings and whatnot but I had it all explained to me and am straightened out now.

The channel wasn't nasty at all. Choppy, but not rough.

Later letters and postcards will contain some impressions of England. Up to the present time I have seen very little. (I have been on British soil 3 hours).

Congratulations on your new office. And lots of affection -
George

DIARY - TRIP TO ENGLAND – SPRING 1935

In the Spring of 1935, having slaved away (?) at my studies in Paris for about seven months, I decided I needed a break. So I took a 12-day vacation touring part of England. My travel diary follows.

Trip to England April, 1935

Monday, April 1 -, London, England. Berkshire House, 33 Guilford Street (off Russell Square)

Saturday after noon I began to notice that my taste for work was going decidedly stale on me. So I determined to take my Easter vacation here and now instead of waiting 2 weeks. Accordingly, I bought my ticket (200 francs round trip) that afternoon and drowned my troubles in good red Bordeaux. A gay afternoon, an unimportant evening comprising Helene Vaujany and a nude dancer, an unforgettable and exquisite Sunday with Mary – art galleries, the puppet show, café viennois and Monday morning found me steaming toward Dieppe. A crowd of dreadfully clean – looking English people aboard. Lunch of 2 sandwiches and a banana. The one funneled channel steamer. The fog and the wintry blast. The rocking of the boat and the grand feeling when I realized I wasn't going to get a bit seasick. The sun about 3 P.M. The beautiful English girl on the other side of the deck who smiled in her sleep when the sun caressed her face. The white cliffs rising up sheer out of the marble blue sea. England gives out an aura even miles off shore that marks it unmistakably as England. We landed at about 4 P.M. – very little customs chichi and then entrained for London. Good, hot English tea and toast with a newspaper aboard the train. Frightfully cozy way to catch the English countryside fly by. It isn't as trim or as economically exploited as French land, but looks more personal, more homey. A flock of sheep nestled close one against another. A real English cottage peeking out from beneath its thatched roof. The feeling that if there isn't primrose around the door there should

303

be. Then London started – Croydon, North Croydon, East Croydon and finally Victoria Station. I became suddenly unbelievably brave and took a bus straight away to Russell Square. Found this cheap hotel without trouble. It's dreadfully bare and has a shilling-in-the-slot gas meter just like in "Angel Pavement" by Priestley. Wrote letters at a hotel on the square, bought a bus guide, ate a dreadful English supper at an ABC restaurant – really poisonous – just like my only full meal in Canada in 1933.

After supper I wandered around Rosebury Avenue and that district and then took the bus to Piccadily Circus. Saw Charles Laughton do an outstanding piece of acting in "Ruggles of Red Gap" – at Plaza Theatre, a cinema palace with a rug that you can wade in.

In England I feel distinctly like a foreigner. Much more so than in Paris (which is like home to me). I use an English accent – grand sport – but find it difficult to understand people because I still listen in French and am dreadfully surprised to hear English coming out of their mouths. But London is by far more cheerful than Paris. People can actually dress here. Top hats even to a picture show. Lighted shops late at night, no shutters, many smiles; light, gay intonations. The King's Jubilee has everyone on the patriotic go. They played "God Save the King" after the movie and everyone stood up in the most reverent silence. A patriotic nation – deeply, religiously, traditionally patriotic through love. Quite different from French patriotism. And so to bed. I like London.

Tuesday, April 2 - Boarding house 16 St. John's St., Oxford.

I had the honor last night of sleeping on the hardest bed that ever abused a man's tired limbs and robbed him of his well-earned rest. But nevertheless I was up at 8 in time to eat an English breakfast of bacon and eggs and to take the 10:30 bus to Oxford. The trip (about 60 miles) started – and a long start it was – in the middle of London. Then suburb after suburb flicked by – Chelsea, Hammersmith, etc. until finally London tapered off and we were out in the country. The edges of London are documentary proof of the post war industrial revolution that has taken place in England. The city is fringed by brand new, spick and span factories catering to the newborn consumption goods trade. Makers of gloves, typewriters, autos, tires, garden tools, etc. The limits of London have expanded mushroomwise since the war to give room to these new, clean factories.

The countryside we traversed was exceedingly pretty after leaving London. We went by way of Slough, Henley, etc. The scenery in Buckinghamshire reminded me very much of Bucks County, Pennsylvania. But the houses bear no resemblance to America. Most of them are made of real brick with red, weather-beaten tile roofs or equally weather-beaten gray thatched roofing.

Tall poplars silhouetted against the sky, a cottage perched high on a wooded hill so that it seemed to be put there for effect, not built there for permanent use. A herd of sheep with their leggy white lambs. Two horses looking out into the warm sun from their clean stable and then we climbed a hill, rounded a turn and the spires of "Oxentown" lay at our feet. I found this S/D boarding house, had lunch at Lyons' and set out to see Oxford. Map and guidebook in hand, I toured the various colleges. I dressed English fashion – gray pants, black coat and vest, no overcoat, but just gloves and a hat. The cold wind, which the April sun did nothing to ameliòrate made me regret my determination to play the English gentleman.

The colleges are very sentimental looking. Easy it is to see how old grads can moisten at the eyes when coming back to Oxford to look up their old diggings. Today I kept on the hill; tomorrow I will visit the colleges along the Thames. The quadrangles, planted at this season with jonquils, give a very bright appearance and set off well the tan- colored stone of the buildings. The chapels are not very beautiful but are full of tradition. I liked immensely the garden of Trinity College, the cloistered quad of New College, and the stained glass windows of New College chapel. At All Souls' a student picked me out as an American and showed me the Hall. It contains a fine Lawrence and a Reynolds. The students eat on Saturdays and Sundays in the Hall, otherwise in the commons. The colleges are very much alike in architecture etc. and general spirit. Many battlemented turrets, spires and cloistered walks, flagstone courts. The rooms look dingy, but it is all soaked in tradition. I visited the Bodleian library, which contains many more books than I ever imagined (1 ½ million) and has an underground bookstore. There are many very old and interesting manuscripts on view. "Pope's Essay on Criticism", a letter written by George V when a boy. Addison, Tennyson and others. Shelley relics including his copy of Sophocles that was clutched in his hand when he was drowned. Then the Radcliffe camera – dome-shaped reading room of the library. A fairly good view of the city from the tower of the camera.

There are very few students in evidence anywhere. All studying is individual (tutorial) which explains the long and frequent vacations. Otherwise as one student told me "they wouldn't be able to stick it".

The English don't have the peasant spirit. They have the gardener's spirit. The large farms are just overgrown gardens and everyone, even the lowest class, tries to be a gentleman in some sense of the word. Everyone dresses alike – tab collars, gray pants and brown chequered coat.

The colleges are very peaceful and quietly graceful, cloistered and aged, but very much alike.

I wrote 12 postcards, had dinner with ale and Gorgonzola cheese, went to the "Red Lion" for ale and then home to bed for a bath and a smoke before going to sleep. My landlady here has a clubfoot but outside of that she is quite regular. I feel much more like a foreigner in England than in France, strange to say.

Oxford is indeed the city of spires and the city of bells. But the spires are a bit stuffy and too numerous and similar. The bells however are clear, silvery and beautiful. Goodnight diary.

Wednesday, April 3 - "Old Red Sun" Bridge Street, Stratford-on-Avon.

Up at 7:30, a gigantic breakfast and then the entire morning devoted to seeing more of Oxford. I saw Magdalen College and made the lovely "Addison's Walk" which tours a vernal meadow and follows the banks of the Cherwell River. The cloistered quadrangle and especially the noble Norman tower are the best in Oxford. Wharton College has a choir window in the chapel quite beautiful from the outside but disappointing from the interior. The immense quad with its rounded, Romanesque arches at Christ Church is very impressive but is pale in comparison with the "Hall" and especially the Cathedral Church of Christ. It dates from God knows when, has a fine tracery – web-work vault in the choir, some excellent windows and generally pleasing proportions. The hall is the largest and most imposing in all of Oxford, contains some excellent portraits and perhaps 1 Holbein of Cardinal Wolsey. At Magdalen the Hall is done in beautiful paneling, quite unusual. Christ's Church Meadow is very pretty, green and shady. Very English. A walk in the meadow gives a good view of the Norman spires.

I caught the Stratford bus by the skin of my teeth (made it 20 minutes late) and arrived here in time for lunch. The country-side passed through on the way was very rolling; all farmland with many stately poplars framed against a windy sky, the usual but picturesque shops and several quaint red brick towns.

I love Stratford-on-Avon as I have never loved any other European town. It is so very much warmer, more personal, intimate and individualistic than Oxford. The boarded Queen Ann cottages, the Shakespearean relics, the quiet flowing River Arden which washes the feet of Trinity Church, the church spire rising from a grove of trees and the soft greenness of the river banks. I lingered long over the relics of Shakespeare. There is certainly no reason to believe that Shakespeare was obscure in his day. There are no less than some 66 references to him in contemporary writings and he is always spoken of as "Gentle Shakespeare" or a great bard. The guides at the birthplace were eager to talk and I drew them out on their favorite subject – Shakespeare. They worship the man – in fact the whole town does. As one man said, "What would Stratford be without Shakespeare? Not much." It would still have the beautiful lazy, Avon, but the distinctive character of the town, which sets it apart from the rest of England, would be lacking. Beautiful oak beams, fireplaces, but not as good as at "Hill Farm". Several signatures of the poet, the folio editions. The first folio is the same as at The Bodleian Library, Oxford. The attic rooms are tiny romantic little pigeonholes. The garden is very English and contains every plant that is mentioned by Shakespeare. They are all native, indigenous plants proving that William S. knew and loved them all. Saw house of Judith S. (daughter). New House (site of Shakespeare's house in which he died) was built in 1492. (Very hard to believe) It contains very interesting Roman and Anglo-Saxon remains dug up while making a golf course, of all things. The garden is again, a model of English gift for careful and loving gardening.

I had time to walk to Trinity Church and inspect the exterior and the lovely riverbank. The Church is on the river's edge and is the most beautifully situated church I have ever seen. It's like a diamond in a red velvet case to see this gem of a church in its vernal setting. I walked along the river, past the Memorial Theater (an enormous and unimportant site) strolled over the bridges to watch the sun set over the valley of the Arden.

A big tea with Devonshire cream, a light supper (at Judith's). How to spend the evening in these English towns is a great problem. I spent mine in walking through the cool night air, nosing around town and drinking ale. The poet's birthplace looked very real, very peaceful at night.

The shrine is not over-commercialized. It is treated with just the right mixture of common sense and religious devotion that make for good taste. Good night! (I have a bed warmer in my bed) I wrote some postcards, mostly to women.

Thursday, April 4 – On the train between Kingham and Gloucester.

This has been a grand day, varied full to overflowing and not yet over. Some idea of the things I have done is given by my itinerary. Stratford on Avon, Shatlery, Windsor, Wilmcote, Stratford on Avon, Wilmeate, Kenilworth, Leamington Spa, Banbury and now I have changed trains at Kingston and am railing toward Gloucester (alone in the carriage).

Arose at 7:30 and by 8:30 I was standing, hat in hand, before the immortal doggerel in Trinity Church, Stratford on Avon, that marks the grave of William Shakespeare. The church itself is interesting, being one of the 5 existing churches whose nave tends to "represent Our Saviour on the Cross" as the verger told me. The entire Shakespeare clan is buried in the chancel, with their feet facing the altar.

Leaving the church and its rapturous riverside setting I stopped in at the Guild Chapel and the five Century old school, but found them closed to visitors during the term.

It was now raining but that made the country even so much greener so in the steps of the poet, the rain beating in my face, much as it must have in his, I walked those measured yard to the farm house of Ann Hathaway. In a brisk walk, William could have done it in 15 minutes. The path itself is a bit disillusioning as it crosses the back of a group of rather tawdry workmen's gardens. But the house of Ann, inexactly termed a cottage, is a gem. The easy flowing Shattery Brook runs past its door. The old beamed rooms, the settle, the bed, are all there. The garden and orchard, in strict Elizabethan style, make a good frame for the house. It is a charming place. I walked quickly back to Stratford, found the way to the canal, and then set out along the old towpath for Wilmcote, site of the house of Mary Arden, Shakespeare's mother. The canal cuts through the most beautiful Warwickshire land. Green fields fringed by shady groves, sheep, a swan or two floating gracefully along the quiet canal, a rustic farmer to lift his cap and reply to my "Good Morning". And then, with the rain still beating in my face, my 4 mile walk was up after 40 minutes of most pleasant striding along the mossy path, and I found myself in the tiny hamlet of Wilmcote. The large farm house with its dovecote and L-shaped group of buildings reminded me more than strongly of my home at Hill Farm, Solebury, Pa.. The dovecote is unusual, containing perhaps 500 separate holes for doves. In an adjoining shed are some modern pigeons, quite alive and nesting in fact, but they refuse to go into the spacious dovecote which has housed dozens of generations of their ilk. The barn is a museum of old Warwickshire farm implements. They are not so very crude, and some are even ingenious. There is everything from a one-man hand plow (pushed by the chest) to a machine for cutting off young horses' tails and a wash wringer. (immense) The house is in the Queen Anne Style, with a beautiful beam over the fireplace and a second floor containing a rush mattress and a lady's silk- covered saddle, among other things. Some of the flooring is 500 years old and slopes like a drunken sailor. Pretty English garden.

Back into the rain again, train to Stratford-on-Avon, a quick lunch and then the 12:30 bus to Warwick. A ride through beautiful rolling country, drained by the lazy Avon River, passing through a number of red brick and wood and plaster towns that haven't stirred since Shakespeare's days. At Warwick went immediately to the Castle. The entrance drive is imposing and as you turn a corner the mighty towers rise immediately before you in surprising majesty. I toured the castle through the beautiful cedar room, red lacquer room, Great Hall, gunroom, chapel, etc. There are several excellent

Van Dykes and Rubens and Romneys, all painters of the period and in their best style. The windows give a majestic, expansive view of the entire valley, up and down the River Arden which flows quickly past the battlements of Warwick. The old growth of trees has been cut down within a circumference of 3 miles and there is a sparse growth of new trees within that radius. (New - 400 years old). The castle is still used by the young Earl. The Italian garden and its conservatory command another sweeping view of the verdurous valley. If it had been warm and I had had time to linger, I would have stretched out on the grass and feasted my eyes on that typically English thrilling medieval vista.

The rest of the town is very, very old – a good example of a medieval town. It has a gate at both ends, in good state of preservation. The tower of the church is reached by a road. I climbed way up to the top and got a good view of the country. It was still raining. I visited and climbed the South gate; nestled close to it in authentic medieval fashion are the guild houses, dating from the early 1500's. It is in the wood and plaster style, with shields of the various guilds on the beams and fine mullioned windows.

Bus to Kenilworth, where I was set down in front of the castle walls a little after

4 o'clock. A bit of snow did flurry for a while but as soon as I started to visit Kenilworth a strong sun came out, the sky turned brilliant blue and the air was fresh and moist. Kenilworth is entirely in red stone, while Warwick is gray. Kenilworth is in the very ruins that Cromwell's men left it in when they demolished it to keep the King's men from fortifying it during the Civil War. Its red stone is half hidden by glistening ivy, thickly matted and centuries old. Rooks fly and caw about the crumbling pile. The lake, once 2 miles wide is now a grassy meadow. The old banquet hall is indicated only by the framework of its windows in the beautiful perpendicular style used by the Normans, and by a few stumps of columns. It is a spot that beckons with romance; I have never seen a sunset more of a lover's sunset than when the big orange disk disappeared tonight behind the town of Kenilworth. The Norman's keep dates from 1120 and there is a GateHouse, built in the 13th Century, which I visited. It is lived in by a private person today and is chock full of stuffy collection of bric-a-brac, but its walls, its paneling and alabaster chimney taken from the Leicester building and Great Hall of Kenilworth Castle when Cromwell's men demolished it, are very interesting. The paneling is carved with the design of Leicester's emblem, a gnarled oak staff. When Darby owned the castle, Elizabeth, Queen of England, came to visit him. He spent 5 years preparing for that visit and a good 10,000 pounds into the bargain. She stayed 19 days. That was the heyday of Kenilworth. It is now a romantic red and green pile, swept by the winds of Warwickshire, baked by a midlands

sun, washed by English rains, covered with ivy and inhabited by nothing but the swooping, circling rooks. It is just the thing to bring sentimental tears to the eyes of a romantic lad far, far from his home.

I left Kenilworth, suitcase in hand, took a bus to Leamington Spa. As I walked leisurely to the railroad station I heard the puff of a train. I was just able to jump on the train, which was bound for Gloucester by the roundabout way of Oxford and Swindon. But I got off at Banbury, ate a sandwich and took a tiny local train to Kingham. In the car were country types, the conductor was rudely but heartily joking a country girl who was to be married soon. I joined in the laughter at his "newlywed" stories. At Kingston I got a train for Cheltenham and here I am in a 3rd class carriage at Cheltenham waiting for the train to leave for Gloucester.

Warwickshire must be the most beautiful part of England. I have really loved every minute of the time, every inch of the way. And this hectic day of riding, walking, and shuttling in rain, snow and sunshine has been one of the most enjoyable days I have ever spent.

I am going to sleep at the Wessex Hotel near the RR station, Gloucester, after tucking eggs and chips and a cup of coffee under my belt. Cheerio!

Friday, April 5 – Firge's Hotel, Eastgate Street, Bath

This morning I was up latish and out in the street in Gloucester before 9 A.M. Went immediately to the Cathedral. It is really a church within a church – the shell dates from the 11th Century and is in Norman style (like Romanesque) and the tracery and later additions superimposed are XIVth Century perpendicular work (like Gothic). While I was looking around the verger told me there was to be a service at 10:00, I thought I'd watch so he ushered me to a pew in the choir. In walked the dean and his retainers bearing staffs, etc. and I found I was one of 2 devouts, boxed in between the dean and the assistant preacher (?). I did not have the remotest idea of the routine of the service so took hints by copying my fellow worshipper, evidently an old hand at the game. I also acted as though I were under great emotional stress (sort of a Resurrection) in order to cover up my infidel character. I thoroughly enjoyed the service – both as student and as Jew. It gave me a better idea of the meaning of Christianity. That's all, I am sorry to say. The cloisters of the cathedral, with nooks where the monks worked built into the walls and the exquisite fan tracery superimposed on Norman walls give an object lesson in English architecture. The Cathedral dominates the town – its spirit and its geographic boundaries. The tower is on the grand scale – the best I have seen in England or France (though Magdalen at Oxford is good). The old streets around Gloucester cathedral are interesting but too modernized to show more than a few traces of this town that has grown from Roman "castra", crossroads, Norman fort and Cromwellian stronghold to modern industrial city and above all the finest cathedral town on the River Severn.

After a quick lunch and a glance at the enormous hogs being auctioned in the cattle market, I wrote some post-cards and made the train (1:55) for Bath. We rode along the valley with the Cotswold escarpment on the left and the Malvern hills on the right. As we neared Bristol the valley narrowed and the lines of hills seemed to intersect.

PS It is surprising what a variety of good and bad accommodations you can get for 5/6 in different towns.

We went through a long tunnel and emerged on the smudgy plain that leads to Bristol.

But the train left me at Maggotsfield and I rolled toward Bath without seeing Bristol. The houses in this county – Somerset - are all built of Bath stone – gray in color and are markedly different from the red brick of Warwickshire, and not so pretty. (Memories of Kennilworth's red ruins!)

Bath was drenched by a pouring rain all afternoon. I found this good and cheap hotel and trudged through the rain to see the town. All at once I found myself in the Roman baths. I had had the idea that Bath was a little hamlet with some mossy ruins to mark the spot where the Romans had once bathed. Not so. I was immeasurably surprised, disillusioned or even disappointed to find that Bath is famous for its hot water geyser that gushed so well that it has been housed in a very modern clubhouse and you pay very stiff prices to dip your finger in its precious waters. I refrained form the dubious pleasure of sipping the sacred liquid in the "Great Pump Room". Some rather shoddy Roman ruins mark the former baths. They reminded me strongly of the cave of the winds at Coney Island or Asbury Park. But perhaps a few hours of sunshine will rectify my bad impression of Bath. I did spend a grand evening, nevertheless. For 6 pence I bought some Essays by Ruskin on architecture, 3 pence of cheddar cheese, 3 pence of crackers, and 2 pence of apples all bought at the town market. Then I stood in the courtyard at the foot of the cathedral munching my bread and cheese in the pouring rain. I could ask for nothing better! My idea of a perfect meal. Then I spent the evening seeing a film taken from Tolstoys "Resurrection". It took all of Anna Sten's miraculous beauty to overcome the grossness of treatment that Hollywood has applied to the story. And so to bed with Anna Sten, Episcopal mass and a prayer for sunshine whistling through my weary head.

P.S. – Walking makes me red-cheeked and healthy looking.

Saturday, April 6 – Goldfish Hotel 14 Catherine Street, Salisbury

This morning I arose bright and early and set out to see Bath completely. I am very happy to be able to record that the sunshine completely changed my first bad impression of Bath. I followed the route, on foot, which an autobus tour takes and really saw everything. Of course I walked a lot – up hill and down dale, but I love it. Bath is a gem of Georgian architecture nestled at the very bottom of a cup of Somerset hills, then through the very middle of town runs the inevitable Arden River. As I walked along the Grand Parade, North Parade Circus, Royal Crescent, I could almost hear the rustle of crinoline, could fancy Sheridan's manservants from "The Rivals" joking together in the narrow streets. The center of town with its superb Georgian architecture (columns, etc.) is a great deal more stuffy and less picturesque than the hills that circle it. Beecher Cliff, Camden Crescent and the other high vantage points all give excellent views of the town, the fine old 14th Century abbey and the opposite hills – notably Sham Castle. It was a beautiful blue-skied day, flecked here and there by large fleecy cloudbanks. At one point I climbed the steep sides of Beecher Cliff, lined all the way up its perpendicular streets by workers houses. How can a laborer feel oppressed when he can step into the street and see all Bath and the Arden Valley at his foot? The abbey has a fine example of the late development of fan tracery. Very classic interpretation of the fan-medium. Almost extremist. I liked Bath, especially the bay windowed shops and the views from the top of the cliffs. But it was XVIIth Century Bath that I liked, not Roman Bath. I didn't drink a drop of the famous water.

Caught another bus and again by the skin of my teeth which took me to a little hamlet on the Great Salisbury Plain called Shrewton. I had a grand lunch there (enormous, juicy fruit tarts) and then set out to walk across the plain to Stonehenge. It is 4 miles one way and I got a lift ¼ of the way going and ½ the way returning. The Salisbury Plain is an enormous green and brown sea that billows across England for miles. Here and there flocks of sheep, like the white caps of the waves, break the rolling monotony. Above there was a clear blue sky, below a rich sea of Wiltshire loam. As I came over the brow of the last hill I saw in the distance the fantastic group of Neolithic boulders that marks the spot where an unknown race gave testimony to their faith in the supernatural. To the East, the West, the North and South of Stonehenge there is nothing but a billowing plain and the huge gray stones, arranged in a semi-circle to correspond with the axis of the summer solstice, loom large against the clear blue horizon. It made me more keen to the vastness of time and space. It made me wonder if we are so much happier in our chromium plated, electrified world than those sun worshippers of the early bronze age. And it made me all the more puzzled as to **why** all men need a faith. As yet the need has not entered significantly into my life. I walked back to the hamlet passing many jackrabbits who have burrows on the plain, and took the bus to Salisbury. Another cathedral town dominated in fact and spirit by its religious pile. All night it has rained hard, but I mixed with the throngs in the ancient public square who are in town for Saturday market night. I could make out through the rain many ancient structures of the 15th Century. I had supper in the Hall of John Hall, a rich 15th Century merchant. After supper I went to see Grace Moore in "One Night of Love". She has a silvery voice and sings "Lámour est enfant de Bohême" from <u>Carmen</u> to perfection.

Trudged home through the rain and so to bed. I write this by candlelight.

I had a glance at the cathedral, but only for a few minutes. It is entirely in Perpendicular style – a perfect example and its crowning glory is its spire of heavenly proportions.

I noticed lettered on the sundial of an old house the following words: "Life is but a walking shadow".

Sunday, April 7 – Ashleigh Hotel, Guilford Street, London

This morning I set out to see some more of Salisbury. Evidently the religious atmosphere of Salisbury needs a long Sunday morning nap because even at 10 o'clock the cathedral was not yet opened. But that didn't bother me. I climbed over the wall and slipped into the cloisters. I looked around a bit but could find no way to break into the inside of the building itself. So I climbed the wall once more and went out of the close, leaving that graceful spire behind me. A beautiful blue sky had turned to gray and the warm sun had disappeared, but I plugged on toward Old Sarum a two-mile walk. I felt tired and rested a bit in the park. Salisbury's official name is New Sarum. When the water supply of Old Sarum gave out and when conflict between the priests and soldiers within the earthworks got obnoxious, the clerics moved their cathedral to New Sarum (now Salisbury) and eventually the whole town followed. Old Sarum is now an interesting, thought-provoking mound rising sheerly out of the plain that bounds Salisbury. It is the famous "rotten boro" where until 1832 less than 10 men would meet in a field and elect 2 members to Parliament. The early monks gave as one reason for leaving the Old Castle-fortress: the rheumatic winds that whistle around the hill. I thoroughly agree with them. I had no overcoat and was thoroughly frozen. To warm up I passed out of the moat and Norman embankment and went across the road to an inn for dinner. I started off with a glass of brandy, sipped near the fire. Then I had a fine dinner and played the lord (I love it) by ordering some wine, and a liqueur (divine Curacao) with my coffee. I played the lord so well that the waiter virtually scraped his nose on the floor for me.

By this time it was raining hard. I took the bus to Salisbury and ran for the 2:25 train to Winchester. It went round by way of Southampton where I got a rainy glimpse of docks, funnels and ships' rigging. When the train got to Winchester, it was raining so disgustingly hard that I didn't get out. I stayed on to London and here I am. Changed hotels (this is superb luxury for the price – 35/ per week) Then I had a Welsh rarebit and stout, bought some aspirin and am now about to doze off hoping that my incipient cold will be cured so that I will enjoy "seeing London".

Monday, April 8 – Ashleigh Hotel, London

My busy week in the counties and my head cold took away a bit of my taste for sightseeing but I did do some. With my guide book, spent the day on Trafalgar Square, Houses of Parliament and Westminister Abbey. The Abbey is not by any means the most beautiful I have seen but it is the most historic. Poet's Corner exceedingly interesting in this connection. But by far the most astounding thing in architecture I have ever seen is the lace-like stone work in the Chapel of Henry VII. The ceiling is like a fine pattern traced in vanilla icing on a royal birthday cake and then all the banners of the Knights of the Bath hang in a blaze of color against the glaring whiteness of the walls and ceiling. I went to the Goldstone's for lunch and they were extremely nice. I spent the afternoon with Aunt Sophie. We covered Green Park, St. James' Park and Palace and then went to the House of Commons. We sat in the gallery and heard a dull debate on India. But the spot is historic and the procedure and attitudes of the ministers is interesting. I had supper with the Goldstones, then took myself--to the movie – Molnar's "The Good Fairy" on the screen. Quite good and very "sweet". I am homesick for Paris and even went so far as to spend 5 pence to buy the Paris – Soir. Goodnight or Bon Soir!

Tuesday, April 9 – Ashleigh Hotel, London

Today I had my failing self-confidence considerably bucked by the receipt of many letters from my family and lady friends. I then went to the British Museum where I spent the morning. It is impossible to see it all – a real maze of exhibition rooms. But I did go rather carefully through the Greco-Roman rooms. I was a trifle disappointed by the Elgin marbles, but I do think them very beautiful. They are earnest of greater beauty that has perished with the passing centuries. Many glorious illuminated manuscripts.

I have never been so amazed by the beauty of art as at the National Gallery. Their collection is incomplete, scanty in many places but each canvas is a priceless gem. I did not see any minor works in the entire collection. In this respect the National Gallery differs from the Louvre. The Italian schools are represented in a blaze of glorious color and design.

It was as though a box of sparkling rubies had been opened before my eyes. I was dazzled by its brilliance. They go very strong on national painting – the British school. I bought myself a book of photos of all the Italian canvasses. I wish I could have bought the entire museum! How I would love to have a good private collection some day!!

I had a haircut and indulged in the great pleasure of speaking French with the barber. I am homesick for Paris – bought "Paris Soir" last night.

I saw the screen version of David Copperfield. It was the best possible treatment of Dickens' great pageant novel but I had the feeling that the actors were weighed down by the burden of the reputation of the book they were dramatizing. Beautifully played, but a bit labored. A very pleasant and even glorious day in the art galleries.

Wednesday, April 10 – Guilford Street

Another day chock full of new experiences. Walked down the Strand in the morning, to the Inns of Court, Lincoln's Inn Fields, etc., a haven of quiet in a busy city. Visited the lower Temple, encrusted with traditions and the glamour of the law. Then down Fleet Street, the river of ink, to St. Paul's supreme achievement of Christopher Wren. The dome is really awe-inspiring. It seems true that Wren has built London. Two out of every 3 churches are in his style and many other monuments are his work. To me London is not a romantic city – historically to me London is a city of the present not of the past. For the romance of the past I go to Paris.

I lunched at ye Old Cheshire Cheese where Dr. Johnson used to enunciate his, "Well, Sirs!" It is heavy laden with that specious quality called "atmosphere". But the bar still has its true characteristics of yore. It is patronized by many an ink-stained pen pusher from nearby Fleet Street. The Famous Pudding, however is worth trying.

The afternoon I took a real "rubberneck" tour with an uninteresting crowd in a bus out of London. We stopped at Stokes Poges where, in the shade of an ancient yew tree, the graveyard immortalized by Gray still harbors in serene peace the rustic fathers. Through the pretty Thames Valley, past "the playing fields of Eaton" to Windsor. It is a mixture of architectural styles and much more impressive from a distance than at close quarters. (Especially after Warwick) But the Park, the long walk leading to Ascot and the views from the parapet are splendid. Then to Hampton Court, which Cardinal Wolsey turned over not too willingly to Henry VIII. The building is much like a French chateau and the exquisite gardens reminded me, with a pang, of Versailles. The same majestic effect obtained by a long piece of water bordered by a lawn and well spaced trees. The park of Hampton Court has more personality and individualism than Versailles, but of course it lacks the grandeur of the Roi Soleil. The tour went through many suburbs of that endless, stretching cobweb that is London. Thus I had an opportunity to fix in my mind the characteristics of several large sections of the city. "Rubbernecking" is banal but instructive.

Had dinner with the Goldstone's, very simple but very warm-hearted people. Then I saw Elizabeth Bergner in "Escape Me Never". Her miraculous acting dominated the entire film. She has a very sensitive technique.

London is very gay and very rich.

Back to bed and gorging myself with stuffed figs while I write this diary and think of Mary and Virginia. Sweet girls!

Thursday, April 11 - Guilford Street

I have decided that this will be the last day of my vacation in England. I will leave (Deus Volens) tomorrow at 9 a.m. (Hope the channel's not rough.)

Today I rose latish, received rather a passionate letter from Marion (whose mushroom romance has quite naturally fizzled out) and wrote some postcards. Also cabled her for a date. Then I went to the Tate Gallery walking along the embankment for a while in a treasured burst of sunlight. I am beginning to learn how to like London – but tomorrow I leave. (Lovestarved). London must be enjoyed as a big, lively city – not as a museum piece.

I had a thrilling time at the Tate Gallery. Some excellent French Moderns and a big collection of the English painters. The English are much less talented, it would seem, than the French. To that statement one must except Constable and John Sargent – the latter truly great. But the others, Turner included, are not at all miraculously good. Turner is interesting, as one of the early impressionists. There were some things of Rossetti in the Pre-Raphaelite vein that had a remarkably vivid and fulsome palette and luscious treatment. Also some good English sculpture.

I had fish and chips for lunch (four pence) in the poor quarter on Vauxhall Bridge Road and then took a nice, clean underground train to the Monument. Climbed it, got a splendid view, descended, bought some shirts and socks, wandered around the Bank – Threadneedle Street, etc. a quarter teeming with men in bowler hats (the future financiers) and men in silk hats (the present financiers). The streets hum like a ticker tape exactly like the Wall Street district of New York but with less democracy.

Then I visited the Tower of London and saw the busy Pool of London (port). I wasn't in a sightseeing mood but was nevertheless dazzled by the overpowering brilliance of the Crown Jewels. All a sparkling array of gold, silver, diamonds, pearls and rubies, etc. I never knew that a simple salt cellar could assume such a glorified form.

Then I returned to Regent Street and found myself in an excellent mood for spending money. So I bought a snappy sports coat in black and white tweed. Bought presents for the folks in Paris and New York and had a nice walk in the late afternoon sun along prosperous Regent Street, to Oxford Circus, heart of the shopping district. London seems in a spending mood, very gay and prosperous on the <u>surface.</u>

Then I had a light supper, wrote to Dame Sibyl Thorndike my regrets, said goodbye to the Goldstones, took a hot bath, packed and am about to get early to bed. Amen.

April 12, - Paris – Back home safe, happy, nervously excited to a maelstrom of women hanging on my neck – and 2 staunch friends.

More Letters From Paris

April 23, 1935

Dear Mother and Daddy:

It has been a longish time since I wrote. The interval has been occupied mostly by work. I had thought that I would write you more details on my trip to England, but I kept a diary of it and will show that to you when I get home instead.

I really was quite homesick for Paris and was overjoyed to get back. The first Gallic syllables, blue shirts and little black mustaches looked awfully good to me. In London I even bought a copy of the Paris-Soir one night to avoid being homesick for this city. In London, as I may have told you, I bought myself a nice tweed coat (sport suit coat) for a guinea and wear it all the time. It is the sort of thing I have always wanted and never had until now. Also some tab shirts and a few socks. Got them all safely through the customs and they are perfect fits and very satisfactory.

Arriving in Paris was a typical arrival. It was raining. Nothing could have made me feel more at home than that steady, beating rain that washes the streets almost daily. But a week or so has passed since that time, buds have opened, trees have bloomed and spring seems to be here.

Yesterday was your birthday, Daddy. I tippled to you in a small glass of Benedictine. I want to thank you both again very much for the very welcome and highly appreciated cash presents. I took myself and a friend together with Bill and a friend of his to see Espoir, a play by Bernstein. It was fair to middling.

I am working on my paper for government and have the writing of it almost finished. Then I will type the blasted thing out. After that I will have to organize my notes for the History paper, write that and type that. Conjunctly I am reading my French classics. Have been highly amused over Voltaire, especially Candide. A rollicking tale with a sprinkling of salty philosophy.

I received your letters and thank you very much for them. I will inquire about the Rabelais but have not yet done so. I certainly would like the Symonds if you think it worth while to send it over.

Easter Sunday (day before yesterday) was coolish but the other days this week have been perfect. You must be having grand fun at the farm. I often wish I could fly over for a weekend to plant some seeds, or watch Monica get energetic. Easter I went to the Louvre and visited several churches. Saw a beautiful service at Notre Dame and had a chance to go up to the gallery around the choir where you get an unusual view of the cathedral. It is certainly one of the finest I know.

My courses are not in session now so I have plenty of free time to stay home and work. I often take my French classic out to the Luxembourg Gardens and sit to read it there. It is by far the loveliest city garden I know. Very satisfying proportions. Soft green and gray hues and the sparkling basin in the center make a very restful effect. I visited Pare Monceau the other day. It is unusual because it has rolling ground. In a very rich part of town, lots of rich looking children playing around. The fake ruins of Roman statues and columns give an effect of antiquity that is not hard to believe. On Easter Sunday I really regretted not being in New York. I would have liked to walk in the Easter parade. That evening I saw a movie called "Central Park" in which typical views of many familiar parts of the park were shown. It was very warming to see. But the nostalgia passed off quickly.

At college the first week in May the Junior class holds a Prom or dance. Since we wont be there Bill and I have decided to hold a little miniature one here ourselves. We may go out in a foursome to a very nice place in the Bois de Boulogne to dance. A place called the Pré Catalan, situated in the midst of the trees and lawns of the Bois, almost on the edge of the lake.

Please be good enough to congratulate Ma and Baba for me on their wedding day. I am writing to them, but you might also give my congratulations by word of mouth for me. And a kiss too.

The Spiesses were good enough to send me an Easter card. We sent some beautiful white flowers to Mrs. Crawford and she was very pleased. That evening we all went out (we three boys and the Crawfords) to a Russian restaurant. It was very enjoyable.

Bill Fry leaves tomorrow by train to take a trip to Italy, Switzerland, Germany and through France. We are giving him a little goodbye supper. He is a good chap and will succeed, but is dreadfully serious about things.

Received several cards from Uncle Fred, mailed from the most out of the way South Sea places. He is now in London. I just missed seeing him by one day.

I beg your pardon for this sleepy letter. There is nothing the matter, I am just sleepy. Yesterday was a jour de fête.

Please give my Love to Caroline and to Monica, and reserve a healthy share for yourselves.

Your sleepy but loving son,

George

George B. Bookman

May 3, 1935

Dear Mother and Daddy:

I couldn't let the <u>Bremen</u> go without a letter to you. After sending off the government thesis I buckled down to work on the history paper, which will be ten times harder to write. I have been organizing my ideas and may start writing today. At the same time I have been reading French classics such as Rousseau, Chateaubriand, Balzac and Stendhal.

At the American Church they are giving a play June 3 and Bill is in it. I didn't want to try out because I have not got much free time these days. But there was a small character part open, which doesn't require much rehearsing, and so I was asked to play it. It won't take much of my time. The play is something called "Icebound". All about a detestable family in Maine. I am a sheriff who has about ten lines to say. But I have a good curtain line in the first act. I am supposed to bring down the curtain by saying "Kinda early for snow. Not but what it won't be a good thing for the winter wheat". Pretty agricultural, eh what?

Bill is growing a beard, but you ought to see what I am growing. Maybe I'll still be wearing it when I get back to the States. It is one week old. It is a long, black shadow lying full across my upper lip. (mustache)

A friend of mine, just back from Italy, has been feeding me full of the wanderlust once more. I have planned my summer, more or less. I think I will leave Paris the 5th or 6th of June and take the train to Avignon. Spend 2 days in that region and then train to Marseille. Bus to Nice via Cannes. Maybe spend 4 or 5 days on the Cote d'Azur and then go to Genoa, Rome, Naples, Capri and the peninsula region; Pompeii, etc., back to Rome; then to Assisi, Perugia and Florence. After Florence to Venice via Padua. After Venice to Verona and then around the Lago di Garda to Desenzano and to Sirmio (a tiny spot on the lake which I want to see for sentimental reasons). Then from Verona to Milan. Milan to Stresa. Stresa to Como (possibly passing through Milan again). Come to Bellagio, Menaggio, Perlezza and finally Lugano. From Lugano I'll take a train across Switzerland to Paris. Naturally I will stay a long time in Rome and Florence, shorter time in the other places. How does that sound? Can you suggest any additions? When I go from Genoa to Rome I will stop a few hours in Pisa. I would probably sail home about July 15th.

I have written to John Pugliese (remember?) who wants to come over here this summer. I suggested that we meet in Naples and go on up to Paris together.

Have received letters from friends in America such as Dave Hart and the redheaded daughter of Pres. Comfort. Dave seems to be having a good year at Princeton. He graduates the year I do. He despises Roosevelt.

Thank you for your letters. I hope Ma and Baba's wedding day was a splendid family function. I am going to make you very jealous, mother. Guess where I went on Tuesday. Bill and I had complementary tickets to the Vernissage of the Salon de Printemps at the Grand Palais. It was a sort of dress rehearsal for the most famous salon of painting in the world. There was an enormous crowd there. Not what I would call a chic crowd, but Paris is not so very chic these days. But a varied crowd. Many artists congratulating each other on their canvasses, many socialites who didn't know a drawing from an etching. Many foreigners, many celebrities. The vastness of the salon is incomprehensible. They have well over 2500 paintings. And the variation in quality is wide. But what surprised me was that the frequency of really bad painting was much lower than I had expected. I was prejudiced before I went and was gratified to see that there were really many canvasses that were worth looking at. But out of all the artists who exhibited, only 8 or 10 have any claim to greatness. There were some excellent portraits by Laurens who died this year. Some Despujols in a very mellow, classic style and a Van Dongen portrait which had some marks of good painting. One enormous mural panel executed by Henri Martin to decorate the Mairie of the Ve Arrondissement was worth the entire exhibition. It was in a very modern style, something like Monet's impressionism. It showed scenes in the Luxembourg, very typical of the spirit of the gardens and of the Ve Arr. The planning and conception was good and the color too. I liked it quite a bit. There were so many, many canvasses for which you couldn't say any word of praise, but which you couldn't condemn either. You know the kind. That impassive, mediocre sort of work that is half way between obscurity and competence. There was lots of sculpture, some of it well done. But nothing that would make me get up in the middle of the night to write home about. They had a tearoom running in conjunction with the exhibition. To see the old waiters that they had rudely dragged from their old age asylums and forced to carry heavy trays was almost as comic as some of the painting on the walls of the gallery.

The exposition of Italian art is the big thing over here. Mussolini is sending hundreds of priceless things up here. The exposition opens May 15.

I bought tickets to hear Lily Pons sing in Lucia di Lamermoor on May 9th. Bellezza is conducting. I think it is "your" Vincenzo Bellezza. I may try to get backstage to see him.

Monday night I am going to stand in line to hear Johann Strauss conduct a program of Viennese music. It is a good month for music here.

I took a book with me yesterday to the Bois de Boulogne and ferried out to the island in the middle of the lake where I installed myself at the foot of a tree. It was a beautiful day; the first real May weather that we have had. I read "Eugenie Grandet", an interesting and well-written novel by Balzac. I bought myself a beautiful map of Europe the other day. Very up to date, even showing all the principal radio stations. People here expect war to come but not just yet. They realize that Germany will get what she wants or burst in the attempt. But they have not yet taken it seriously enough. They are beginning to be seriously concerned about the threat of German armament but not seriously enough. Europe seems to be rubbing the sleep out of its eyes. But she isn't yet fully awake. Hitler's speech on May 15 will probably be very important. Mrs. Crawford has the idea that the war will start in June and she is getting ready to leave the country if it does start. But I don't think it will come as soon as that. It may come in July. If it doesn't come then, it won't come for many months after that. Many, many months.

I think that the war may start this summer, but there are chances pulling the other way, which are just as strong. If it doesn't start this summer, then Germany will probably have a nice little revolution next fall or next winter and peace may be saved for a long time to come. (*original ideas. Not based on any printed information) That is the way I look at it now.

I am going to dash off to a course, so Cheerio and lots of love,

George

P.S. Courses have started again. Heard a magnificent lecture by Siegfried on Japan's place in the modern world.

George B. Bookman
3 Rue de la Grande Chaumiere
Paris, VIe, France

May 1935

Dear Mother and Daddy:

322

Since last I wrote to you spring has really come in with its true warmth and charm. It is glorious to take a book to the Bois de Boulogne, stretch out under an old familiar tree (I always use the same tree) and delve into a French novel. I read Stendhal "Le Rouge et Le Noir" and can say that it is the best-written French novel I have ever read. Grand suspense and psychological analysis. I am now going through some Flaubert.

I have done a good deal of work. Half of it has been reading French and the other has been working on my history paper. The history takes the prize of a furlined bathtub for being the dullest thing I have ever set myself to. I really pity, from the bottom of my heart, the defenseless professor at Haverford who will have to wade through those pages and pages of nonsense about imports of dried codfish, exports of muslin and whatnot. The thing is a snap to write. The only difficulty is mechanical. Finding the time and the grit to keep myself bound to the desk when there is a May sun speckling the courtyard outside, painting the wall of the opposite house. When a warm breeze is rustling the vine outside my window and just two blocks away is a friend who would be delighted to go out to the Bois for the afternoon and help me read my French classics. Ah me!

In case that sentimental pity arouses in your hearts any fears for my seriousness of purpose, I may say that the history is now one third done. Today is Tuesday. I may have the whole thing written out, roughly, by a week from today.

Saturday night Bill and I went up to the American Club on the Boulevard Raspail to hear Louis Bromfield tell how it feels to be a big, bad author. He is a young chap, looks bronzed and healthy from his life on a small farm near Paris, and impresses very well at first sight. But as soon as he opens his mouth one notices that he is a supreme egoist. (As what authors are not?) He told us, not shyly at all, that he was a very popular author, though of course he didn't care whether he became immortal or not. He talked about his subconscious mind and let us see just how it works. Someone asked what he considered his best book. And he answered, "Well, it is hard to tell. There is no 'best'. They are all so good". And all that with an affable smile. But it was an education to listen to him give a bad impression of himself.

I have been rereading some of Lord Chesterfield's letters. They are really excellent things. I might force them down my own son's throat some day. This presupposes, of course that my son, if I have one, will be able to read.

Sunday I went to Chantilly with my friend Mary, the Bulgarian girl whom I like very much. We left early. I took along some gingerbread, Yoghourt and a stick of French bread. And she brought a very aromatic sausage and some fruit. I also had the essays of Ruskin, which we took instead of wine.

His oratory is just as good an accompaniment to a meal as an uncut flagon of Bordeau "red". Even though his ideas often have the strength of one part wine and three parts water. It is the rhetoric that makes them easy to digest. The chateau of Chantilly is not very beautiful architecture, XIXth Century, I believe. But it is in time, small and easy to comprehend. Some of the French chateaus are so enormous they are too much for one mortal to understand. This one has a cozy library with some of the most beautiful bindings I know, an interesting collection of paintings. It has a set of Fouquet miniatures that are quite exquisite and then some ordinary representative canvasses of people like Leonardo, Rafael, Decamps, Watteau, Champaigne, Meissonier, etc. Also some poor work by other well-known painters. It is a nice little chateau. The park is however what one comes to Chantilly for. The parterre, laid out by Le Notre is all done without a speck of color. He used just water and grass arranged very symmetrically, in fact even swans balancing swans. Effective Grecian urns are set off against boxwood backgrounds. Long avenues, lined with turf and formed by well trained plantain trees and poplars, chestnuts, etc. are usually terminated by the brilliant whiteness of an urn visible through the green at a distance of many meters. A quiet canal flows away from the severely planned garden toward a meadow where cows graze in peace and a waterfall goes about its business without too much bustle or noise. We had lunch under a tree in the forest. It was a gorgeous day and the warm sun filtered down through the trees showing through the leaves, which are still a tender green at this time of the year. We read our Ruskin and munched our aromatic Hungarian sausage. Then we visited the chateau and walked as soon as possible to the meadow on the canal. On the grassy bank, shaded by a motherly old Chestnut that spread her lower branches for meters around us, we rested and talked. Returned home before supper on a train packed to overflowing with Parisian bourgeois families who had all been spending the same sort of day of delightful repose in the country.

Monday I worked all day (in spite of the tempting sunlight) and then went with Mary to the Opera Comique in the evening to hear Johann Strauss conduct the well-trained Pasdeloup orchestra in a program of Viennese music. We sat in the gallery and didn't buy a program because they were too expensive. But I recognized a few of the Strauss waltzes. The Viennese music is the gayest sort of balm in the world. No one could be blue, even if he wanted to, while listening to it. I wish you would tell me some stories of Vienna in the 1900's. It must have been a wonderful place. We walked home (there was a bright crescent of the new moon) and had some excellent beer at a café on the left bank where they provide the best brews in Paris.

I am very happy, working and playing in the proper proportions. And enjoying this May weather with all my heart and all my soul. I will write later about my plans for the Italian trip. I haven't yet done any further work on them. But there is time. Manana.

All my love,

George

My warmest and heartiest to Monica and all other members of the family who may be gathered 'round your hearth.
Also a big kiss for Mother on Mother's Day. (and every day as usual)

George B.Bookman
3 Rue de la Grande Chaumiere
Paris, VIe, France

May 10, 1935

Dear Mother and Daddy,

I have not heard from you in some time and hope that everything is all right at home.

Here the weather is too glorious to be true. And I am very pleased with myself because my work is going along at just the rate it should, according to all my plans for myself. I am reading French furiously and hacking out that History paper which, at this writing, is 2/3 done. Last time I wrote it was only 1/3 done. I may have it done completely by Tuesday, as I promised. And then I'll have to type it out, which will be the work of three or four days.

I went to a concert on Wednesday afternoon at the Eglise Saint Sulpice. It was to commemorate the 250th anniversary of the birth of Bach and Haendel. The program included some Bach Symphonies and Concertos by both composers. I didn't think the program was awfully well chosen. The Pasdeloup orchestra played with the finest organist in Paris. But the organist couldn't see the conductor and an intermediate had to relay the signals. So the organ was sometimes a tiny bit out of time with the orchestra. And I could hear the treadles of the organ too distinctly. But outside of that, and a few other things, it was a lovely concert.

Much to my grief, Lily Pons had a cold and so Lucia di Lamermoor was not sung last night and probably I will not be able to hear her at all. Dammit.

I have taken the Symonds book out of the library. The one I have is a one-volume abridged edition which sort of sums up the enormous quantity of material left by Symonds. I am reading the grizzly story of the Popes of Renaissance Italy.

Bill Fry is now in Venice and thoroughly enjoying himself. Bill C outgrew his fit of the "blues" as he always does. He is now very happy. I am extremely happy, for a number of reasons. I have set Cook's office to figuring out the price of the railroad fare for my Italian jaunt.

I have completely closed my bank account and if you send me my balance, as I hope you soon will, I would like it in American Express checks or in a simple check. If that is convenient for you. Please.

Sunday I will probably go to the country again. Just where, I cannot yet tell. They now have cheap 5 and 10 franc round trip Sunday tickets to pretty spots in the vicinity of Paris.

If I want this to catch the Europa I will have to close it now. So goodbye and lots of love, and please write to me soon,

George

Love to Monica.

3 Rue de la Grande Chaumiere
Paris, VIe, France

May 13, 1935

Dear Mother and Daddy:

Thank you for your latest letter with the news of Ma's wedding day, et al.

The days here have been unbelievably beautiful. We have had more than a solid week of azure skies, hot sun, gentle breezes. And of course I have been in the parks as much as possible. Friday afternoon I took a book and a friend out to the Parc Monceau, a little parc du quartier on the south side of the city, near the Cité Universitaire. It is a quartier populaire, full of workmen and badly nourished children, but teeming with interesting faces. It is there that I read some insipid stories by Flaubert. After reading <u>Mme Bovary</u> it didn't seem that the same man could have produced "Trois Contes". There is a lake in the park, just a small one. But enough to harbor some stately swan, some ducks and other birds. And the sun was of that insistently hot quality that starts to turn your brain to wine and sends you dozing off. Then we came back from the park and had tea at La Coupole and did some talking.

Saturday I did some more work and then went in town to get estimates for my trip. It turns out that the voyage I will make will cost me about 800 francs for railroad fare. Cooks tried to sell me a Cooks Tour but I won't take it. I will enjoy all the fuss and trouble of arguing about prices and looking for hotels even if it costs a few dollars more. I am going for the fun, and I consider that half the fun consists in making your own arrangements and taking things as they come, without too many preconceived plans. So I will get a circular railroad ticket for the big towns, but decide on the intermediate stops a volonté.

Sunday I took an all day trip to a part of the countryside, which I have never visited. I went with my friend Mary to the Vallée de Chevreuse, on the southeast side of the city, about an hour's ride on a little used railroad line. Our destination was a little village called Gif-sur-Yvette. The valley is formed by two chains of low, wooded hills and in the bottom runs a tiny little stream, the Yvette. All the houses are heavy with vines of wisteria. The wisteria, and a hundred other flowers, are all in full bloom now and the effect is one of unbelievable beauty. The houses themselves are all new, bald, stucco arrangements of no beauty. But the plain architecture is hidden by vines of the gayest, most fantastic and sweetest-smelling wisteria. We started out under cloudy skies but the minute we left the station at Gif the sun came out, the sky turned blue and we had one of the best days of the year. We climbed a hill and reached the plateau on top of the low chain of hills. The operation necessitated scaling two fences, but we did that with no broken bones, and no broken hard-boiled eggs. There was a sunny grove of trees on the plateau where we spent most of the day. Eating the lunch we had brought, an ingenious strawberry shortcake which she concocted, and being generally lazy. In the afternoon we descended slowly, passing parts of the forest floor that were carpeted with bluebells and other varieties of flowers in white, red and yellow. Grassy banks, young foliage, wild flowers. It was all very unreal. The sort of European forest that one reads about in picture books, but which rarely comes true. But it did come true for me. At Gif-sur-Yvette. Sunday, May 12, 1935. Then we had tea at a crazy little place on the banks of the stream. A garden dotted with little straw-roofed dens just large enough for a table and two chairs. The sort of fantastic place you would expect to find at New Hope (very much like the Mexican place run by the Jewish divorcee at New Hope.) We were home in time for supper.

I have taken some walks along the quais and have picked up some books that I wanted. Will show them all to you when I see you. They have endless stacks of trash along the quais, but there are just enough of the books one wants to own to make one wonder if anyone in the world is lucky enough (or unlucky enough) to have anything he wants.

I received a copy of the Haverford News in which I read that I had been chosen to be a member of the editorial board of the "Record", our class yearbook published at the end of the Senior year. That was very nice to learn.

The History paper is coming along. I may be able to mail it off in a week. Who can tell? I, for one, cannot.

Marshal Pilsudksi has just died, leaving Poland weak at a crucial moment in European history. That is no help whatsoever to peace. But one cannot blame poor Mr. Pilsudski for that. He didn't have much to say about it. Hitler is still regarded as the enfant terrible of Europe. The kind of child you can't do anything with. But I guess you never had experience with children like that, did you? Say no.

The way Mussolini is neatly and decently putting an end to Abyssinia would be a joy to a sadist's heart. The poor Ethiopians are being quietly put out of the way. And they are in a difficult position. Because few people wish to offend Italy at this ticklish time. Italian friendship means a great deal to European diplomats today.

All over France they have been having municipal elections which have done nothing except confirm what we all knew before: that France is in a bad way, a very bad way. Bill is writing a government paper on reform of the French constitution. I am anxious to see what he does with it. By the way, what did you think of the paper I sent to you?

I have not had time to study Italian, worse luck. That will have to wait until I get sur place. There are prior duties here. Lots of things to think about before Italian. And I do regret it deeply.

I bought a roll of film and put into use an ancient vest-pocket camera that I haven't used since I went to South America one Xmas. And I have had the thing for at least 5 years, possibly 7. The cover is peeling off, but it takes good pictures. I took some of the pension on the Rue de la Grande Chaumière and hope they turn out.

If I could get an idea, I would write an article, the last this year, for the NEWS. Maybe if I start writing the idea will come by the time I finish the article. That is in the best journalistic tradition, isn't it?

Goodnight and sleep tight.

Love,

George

George B .Bookman
C/o Central Havnover Bank
20 Place Vendome
Paris, France

Tuesday, May 21, 1935

Dear Mother and Daddy,

Thank you very much for your long and interesting letters. The party for that interesting crowd, including Monica's Mr. Beebee must have been splendid. Just the sort of thing you do well.

I have been very busy. I finished writing my history paper just about half a day after I had planned. That is not so very bad, me thinks. Now I am typing it out, an interminable and very boring job. I will mail you a copy as soon as I finish it. I would like your criticism of my Government paper on the plebiscite question. But don't bother to read the history paper. It is very boring. I warn you.

I have also been reading my French and am very near the end of that reading list. Have enjoyed it very much. I am reading a stupid book by André Gide just now, but I have "Du Coté de Chez Swan" still to do, and others that promise to be more interesting.

I have almost decided what to do in Italy. I will probably leave the morning of June 6 for Avignon. Spend two days in that region visiting Nimes, Arles, the Pont du Gard and Tarascon. Then through Marseilles (about 2 hours or so there will be plenty) and along the coast to Cannes. I'll spend about 2 days there, take some trips such as to Monte Carlo along the Corniche. Then the train to Genoa. One day there, or possibly half a day. Then to Pisa. And the same day to Siena. Stay there about 2 days to see Siena, San Gimigniano, Orvieto and walk in the hills. Then down to Rome. Stay there about 4 days then to Naples where I will spend about 2 or 3 days to see Naples, Capri, Sorrento, Pompeii, etc. Back to Rome for another 3 days and then to Assisi and Perugia, which I may do in one day, maybe two. Then about 3 in Florence, maybe 4. Then Venice via Padua. Two days in Venice then to Verona, Lago di Garda, for one day. Then to Milan for a day and then the Lakes for several days. Then I will go to Lugano and thence to Altdorf on the Vierwaldstettersee or I may go via the St. Gothard. Or better yet, over the little St. Bernard and then to Zurich. From Zurich to Geneva. I am not yet decided on what to do in Switzerland. After a couple of days in Geneva I'll come back to Paris. I am going to try to be here on July 14, and then will sail for home. In the next letter I will send you complete details, with mailing addresses and everything. In the meantime, write to Central Hanover Bank, 20 Place Vendôme. That is the best way to reach me. Of course, I will stay here on Rue de la Grande Chaumière until June 6. I am going down tomorrow to work out my final plans with the railroad people.

Thank you very much for the check, especially the extra thirty dollars which I appreciate very much at this crucial time – the beginning of the summer. It will mean a lot to me in the way of added enjoyments. It is quite possible, however, that I will come home with a few dollars in my pocket. I haven't needed to cash the checks you sent me so I now have $205 dollars as yet untouched, and your check for the balance, which I await, will make it a tidy little sum which I certainly won't spend. I haven't yet received the "Renaissance Italy" which you said you mailed.

Uncle Fred was good enough to send me a royal Jubilee necktie from England, where he is staying. (Ritz Hotel: London). It has crowns and royal seals all over it and makes me feel very monarchist. I'll wear it in Monica's honor one of these days.

Enclosed are some negatives, which you may care to develop to see what my room looks like. On the walls are some prints that I have bought of scenes in Paris. Bill is in one of the interior views, looking very seedy due to a mustache that he started to grow and then, wisely, shaved off. I also shaved mine. One of the pictures shows a garden view from my window. I'll take some more and send them to you.

Last Tuesday (a week ago) I bought several books, among them a volume of Catullus with the Latin and translations in French. I like his stuff a lot. Wednesday I applied for a student identity card which gives you reductions on all museums in Europe and works especially well in Italy. It costs 20 francs and has to be countersigned by the head of the faculty of letters of the University of Paris. That evening I went to a Russian restaurant, K'nam's, in the Latin quarter where they have excellent music. Friday I went to the Zoo at Vincennes in the afternoon. Had a grand afternoon with a friend of mine looking at the animals. They are kept in the modern style that is no bars, no fences. There are ditches and moats around the cages, but the animals have no bars to look through and they are out in the open air, with plenty of space to play around in. That is applying the new psychology to zoos. I thought that the animals seemed to appreciate it. There were 2 splendid peacocks: a white one and a regular, multi-colored bird, who were both showing their plumage to best advantage. They were courting two dowdy-looking female peacocks (peahens) and fluttering their fans to make a big impression. There was a nice, mangy old camel on which I could have taken a ride but didn't. Also some giraffes with impossible necks.

Saturday the weather turned very nasty (it snowed Saturday night, believe it or not!!) and it rained and was as cold as in February until this very morning. The sun has come out today in true spring fashion. But the weekend was forbidding. Saturday night I went to the movies with Bill Fry and saw a good thing all about Ali Baba and the 40 thieves, done in good Arabian style. Fry has come back from his trip to Avignon, Cote D'Azur, Genoa, Milan, Venice, Switzerland and the Rhine. He had a wonderful time; full of many experiences and I am getting names of hotels, etc. from him. He leaves for England in a few days. After the movies I went to another Russian restaurant I know of and ate a stuffed carp's head. The name appealed to me as much as the fish. It was delicious. An enormous, very intelligent carp with lots of delicious brains. All done in aspic. I enjoyed it very much. Have you ever eaten a stuffed carp's head?

Sunday morning I took the same friend to see the Flea Market at the Porte de Clignancourt. There is a fine choice there of the most atrocious junk one could wish to see. But it is very picturesque. Sunday afternoon I worked until she came in bringing me a strawberry tart, which was very nice of her. Then I went to see "Carmen" in the evening. The singing was mediocre, but since the seat cost me only 4 francs I was not damaged very much. Walked home across the Seine, which looked very inky. Yesterday, Monday, I worked, of course, but went over to the very quaint and very French part of Paris for a few hours, the part around the Canal St. Martin. Walked along the canal and through the quartier St. Paul to the Place des Vosges and then up to the Turkish mosque for tea on the Left Bank.

It sounds as though I do nothing but go out and amuse myself, but I only tell you of the extracurricular activities. Behind all that you must imagine me at my desk, day and night, peering over dusty tomes. The pleasures, which I describe to you, are momentary relaxations. But the major part of the day is occupied, as ever, by work, WORK AND **WORK.**

I wrote to Dr. Comfort giving an account of the year's work.

Last night I listened to the radio as I worked. Lily Pons was singing "Lucia di Lammermoor", Bellezza conducting. I told you that I missed the performance because she had a cold the night I had tickets for. But over the radio last night her singing was exquisite, wonderful, miraculous, etc. It really was startling. She got a tremendous ovation at the Opera. People went mad with enthusiasm.

I must type out some more of my paper. Please give Aunt Bella my sincerest wishes for her health when next you see her, Daddy.

Love,

George

George B.Bookman

May 31, 1935

Dear Mother and Daddy,

This is the most exciting day in France for several months. For many days now gold has been leaking out of France, confidence has been gradually undermined and the do-nothing Flandin ministry has been subjected to attacks and criticism. Flandin, his arm broken in an automobile accident, tottered up to the rostrum of the Chamber of Deputies yesterday, leaning heavily on his brother and doctor, and asked in a weak, despairing voice for plenary powers. What he would do with the powers once he had them he did not indicate. Before he finished his speech he announced that the Minister of Finance had resigned. That was a shock to everyone and did not help Flandin at all. Then he turned over the session to the 20-odd orators who were inscribed and crawled home to bed. As he slept the deputies pronounced his death sentence. At 1 o'clock in the morning they voted by a sizable majority not to give him plenary powers. Flandin's cabinet was history. There is really no one available in France who can be called a great statesman. And only a great statesman can fill the breach today. They are probably going to call Boudsson, chairman of the Chamber of Deputies, a fairly honest man who is respected. But he is just mediocre and mediocrity is too weak to meet the present crisis. The people on the street are downright disgusted with the Third Republic. I went to the Quai d'Orsay last night at 10:30. The bourgeois and their wives were walking up and down in front of the Chamber of Deputies, chatting, looking anxious. Across the bridge, the Place de la Concorde was a blaze of light because yesterday was a public holiday, Ascension Day. But on the South side the Chamber of Deputies loomed up large and dark. No one was allowed to get near the fence, which surrounds it. A cordon of gendarmes guarded all approaches and on the quai, almost out of sight, 200 blue jacketed men waited – for emergencies. They don't want another "Sixth of February". No one is sorry to see Flandin go because he was just a puppet put in by the radical-socialists so that they would not be interfered with in their game of robbing the taxpayers. Now that the situation is serious, and now that any foolish slip might bring a financial panic, the Chamber will have to act in lightning speed and with unusual sagacity to restore confidence. I don't think they will do it. There probably won't be any great conflagration, but the political system, already rotten to the core, will disintegrate and finally dissolve in dust. A fascist, nationalistic movement will probably get control in a few months.

I have my plans for my trip worked out. All are subject to change, especially as to length of stay in various places.

I will take one suitcase, a large one and won't buy the railroad ticket till the last minute. Nothing else will be reserved. I am having nothing done by Cook's. Doing it all through the CIT, Italian railroad bureau.

I might come home on the Normandie, which sails July 24 and takes only 4 days, but on the other hand there is the Arnold Bernstein Line, dirt cheap, well recommended by former passengers. It takes ten days. The drawback is that it docks at Weehawken, N.J. That is almost the end of the world, isn't it? If I do take that line, I certainly would not want you to troop over to Weehawken to meet me. I love you too much to impose that on you. It sails July 30 and arrives August 10.

As I told you in a previous letter, the Italian Art Exposition here is the most marvelous and talked of thing that has happened in art history since Michaelangelo was born. I went to it Tuesday afternoon and it is astounding. It takes your breath away. Every wonderful painting is there. Michaelangelo's "Holy Family", "Flora" and four other things in his best style, "Chaste Suzanne" by Tiepolo, Botticelli's "Venus", lots of Fra Angelico and Piero della Francesca, exquisite portraits of Messine, the best work of Mantegna, in fact every Italian painter of importance who ever wielded a brush, and the most important canvasses of each man. (canvas is inexact, but figurative). There is wonderful sculpture by Michaelangelo, Donatello, Verrochio, etc. and drawings by all the artists and bronzework, etc. It is an amazing experience. I must visit it at least twice more to get anything out of it. There are enormous crowds that come to see it and people absolutely worship the canvasses. They are too wonderful to be true. The Salle d'Honneur unites the chefs d'oevres and is a glittering array of the jewels of art. I am bringing home an illustrated catalogue, which I will show you. Mussolini did a lot to make it all possible. By the way, Il Duce is very popular here due to his personality.

I have been book hunting again and have several wonderful bargains. The play I am acting in is coming along haltingly. I have been reading political philosophy: Machiavelli, which I liked immensely. He has the right idea, the correct approach to politics. It should be looked at factually because it is a very hard, practical business. I don't care for idealistic approaches to it. Rousseau's Social Contract sickened me. But I am now reading Plato, who is of course terribly idealistic. I don't favor his approach to the subject, but I have discovered that Plato is not as dull as I had always imagined. His dialogues are often spangled with very amusing sarcasm. I am reading the Republic. It is good reading.

Went to a typical foire du quartier the other night. Shooting gallery, electric cars to bump each other in, medicine shows, barkers, snake charmers, roulette wheels, etc. I won a bar of chocolate. There were many of the old style shows with the barker, a girl dancing, and a trained monkey to catch the crowd. Avancez, messieurs-dames. Un franc seulement, cent sous. It was very amusing.

Yesterday was a public holiday and, while the Chamber of Deputies debated, I strolled through Paris. Along the quais and over to Notre Dame. I climbed the tower once more to look at the view and those cynical gargoyles who sneer at the Latin Quarter. There I met an American family from Missouri (Yowsah). They were typically American, in the good sense. (You see an awful lot here who are typical in the worst sense). They came on the Bernstein line with their car ($85) and are going to drive through Europe. Notre Dame is one of the loveliest spots I know. It was choked with school children, there on pilgrimage, when I visited it yesterday.

The summer vacation is almost here but I have noticed that I don't feel as anxious to throw off the yoke as in other years. I like the life here very much. There are no set rules and no set goal toward which I point. At college you know that at such and such an hour and a certain day in June the studies will be at an end. Here I do not have that feeling and rather enjoy the life, not grinding very hard, but still doing a full day's work. But I do look forward to Italy and Capri and will be glad to get down to the Midi. Fred has sent me a letter to his caretaker so that I can stop in at Ile Verte, his estate, and see what it is like.

After a bad week the weather has turned in the proper direction and is Mayish again. Or almost Juneish. But it is not warm when the sun is down. Not at all summer weather.

I cashed one of the checks at the Central Hanover where they were very nice and treated me like the Lord of something or other. I will buy American Express checks before I leave. I leave a week from tomorrow.

Thank you for the bulletin about the International Union at Geneva. I may go there when I get to Geneva and may see about taking part in the discussions for a few days. If the money holds out, I might stay some length of time. But I really should get back to the States before the middle of August. I have studying to do before college opens, lots of it. The exams are week of September 16. And I am ever more eager to be with you again.

I must go out now and see what they have done to replace Flandin. As I wrote you when he took office, he was only a makeshift stopgap, weak and temporary measure on the part of his political backers. France has just started to solve her troubles, or to realize them. The fall of this cabinet is the first scene of Act I.

Lots of Love from your dutiful son,

George

And lots of love to Monica from her dutiful friend and admirer.

Enclosed is an article from the "News" which I hope you will save along with this letter.

"Continental Viewpoint" Is Hard To Define But Is Easily Noticed

Individualism, A Sense Of Proportion, And A Feeling Of Despair Are European Characteristics, Bookman Finds

By G. B. Bookman, '36.

Everyone who intends to spend a year abroad keeps a skeleton in his closet; a skeleton described as "The Continental Viewpoint." It is a vague thing, this skeleton, and serves chiefly as an irrefutable reason for going abroad, when all other reasons fail. To this skeleton-keeping rule the three Haverford Juniors now in Paris, W. A. Crawford, W. R. Fry, and G. B. Bookman, were no exceptions.

It is safe to say that no one can define the continental viewpoint, but it is equally safe to assert that after spending several months in a European city, one is quite sure that there exists a viewpoint toward life on the Continent which is quite different from the American viewpoint. Even if one cannot define what one has noticed, the very act of being aware of it is an advantage in itself. We who are here in Paris see the Continent from the Northwest corner, a corner turbulent with individualism. So our conception of the continental viewpoint will naturally differ from the impression received by a student in Italy, Germany, or Austria. Nevertheless some very definite attitudes which are peculiar to the European continent can be mentioned.

One broad current that one finds on the continent (a current that is running underground, to be sure, in certain European states today) is individualism. To be true to all of the Continent, that individualism should be defined in one specific sense, and I would give it the following meaning: on the continent one finds a tendency of men to develop within themselves a part of their personality that is hidden, personal and hardly ever revealed, while on the surface they seem to keep a highly polished social veneer which serves both as disguise and as shield for this secret inner personality. One gets the impression that an American is easier to get to know—really know—than a Continental European—and that in the European there is a depth which we Westerners cannot approach and perhaps cannot understand. It is a nebulous, invisible thing, this inner personality, but I am sure that it is there.

It manifests itself in the following ways: the continental viewpoint gives great value to self-expression —by art, music, literature or even by conversation. It is realized that if a man does not have an outlet for self-expression he remains a cramped, one-sided and undeveloped personality. Secondly, the continental viewpoint places high value on personalities, men taken for their intrinsic value as men, appreciated one by one for the interest that they can add to society by the mere expression of their own personal characteristics. No one can sip a cafe creme in a Paris cafe at dusk without noticing this, no

one can listen to the hum of conversation all about him without realizing that these men from all over continental Europe have come to Paris because they believe it to be the city where a man can best give expression to the qualities within him. Nor can anyone spend a day in Paris without noticing above all the doors of all public buildings the words "Liberty, Equality, Fraternity" which stand for a type of individualism very dear to the hearts of many Europeans; an individualism that becomes more dear to them in proportion as the onrush of dictatorship tend to suppress it.

Appreciate Beauty, Time

One other definite impression that one gets on the Continent is that here they have a sense of proportion. That too is one of those expressions that can mean anything and everything, but I think that it can be illustrated as follows: on the Continent men seem to be more aware to Beauty and more aware to Time. True, on the surface they seem almost to live for things of the moment—politics, nationalism, gossip. But underneath it all one often finds that they are aware to the immortality of Beauty and the leveling of Time. In last night's paper a photograph of the "Madonna" of Raphael was given a much more prominent place on the front page than a picture of the Nazi demonstrations in the Saar. A fatalistic prophecy that I have met everywhere in discussions, classes, and newspapers is the belief that Europe is losing her age-old world hegemony. What Spengler called "The Decline of the West"—that America and the colored races of the Orient are fast taking world leadership and that after a series of dying gasps Europe will be only a "geographical expression."

Cont. on Page 3, Col. 3

DIARIES FOR SUMMER 1935 AND 1936

TRIP TO SOUTHERN FRANCE AND ITALY, SUMMER 1935

These are diaries that I kept for summer vacation trips in 1935 and 1936.

In 1934/35 I was studying in Paris at the Sorbonne and Ecole des Sciences Politiques. When school was over I traveled to the south of France, a pretty comprehensive tour of Italy, then for a week at the Students International Union in Geneva, then back to Paris and home to the USA.

In 1936, I had spent the summer studying at the International Students Union, Geneva, and then went off on a trip. I headed first for Florence, Italy, to join up with my college friend John Pugliese (Sebastian), and we went for a few days to the Italian Coast at La Spezia. I kept the diary through the stay at La Spezia, but unfortunately discontinued it then. The best part of the trip came afterwards, when John and I and an Englishman drove a car over the Alps to Vienna for a few days; then I went on my own to visit a young woman friend from the Students Union at her family home in Budapest, and from there to visit a male chum who lived in Warsaw. From there I took a train to Hamburg, then caught a boat to NYC. Unfortunately my impressions of the central European part of the trip were not chronicled in the diary.

Voyage to Côte D'Azure, Italy, etc., Summer 1935 AET SUAE 20
Saturday, June 8 – Avignon, Hotel Lance (Rue de la Republique.)
Left my well loved red walled pension and closed the door behind me, perhaps for the last time. Bill was indulging in the charms of a red head and so was not up to see me off. A long and hot train ride from Gare de Lyon 8:05 A.M. to Avignon (6:00). Passed through the flat and fertile French

farmland along the Seine and Yonne rivers. The fields were splotched red with poppies. Groups of trees along the rivers and canals much as in a Corot. The same quality green. After Dijon, grape vines became noticeable and the "allure du Midi" made itself felt. It was a beautiful cloudless day. A hot and copper sun beat down on our train as it sped along the valley of the Rhone after Lyon.

I didn't know what to expect at Avignon and was immensely surprised and pleased at what I found. I had time to sit in a café and then walk around the walls of the Palais des Pâpes, up the Rocher du Dom and see the view. As soon as I realized that I would get a soul filling view of the entire valley from the top of those rocks I was glad. The Rhone, a silver ribbon which, through millenniums of flowing has cut a deep path for itself through the heart of Provence, winds round the base of the Castle. From the cliff one sees the town with its countless roofs of fawn colored tile, then the wide river in the green, leafy plain, and on the opposite hill another old fortress of the XIIth Century. I descended the Rocher du Dom, walked along the river's edge to get a view of the perfect city ramparts and then contemplated for a while that romantic old ruin, the 4 remaining arches of the Pont d'Avignon. I crossed the river then had an excellent dinner on a terrace with a view of the imposing Palais painted by the rays of the setting sun. Returned by the narrowed and most infamous old streets of Avignon. Bill Fry said he discovered 2 brothels when he toured the town. I saw at least 10. (But entered none). Avignon is a lovely town and a lazy town. But then, I imagine all the Midi is lazy. The pace of life is langorous and easy. They must make love slowly too, but passionately. The town is harmonious with its historical relics. Et la vie est doux.

Extremely tired, I crawl between the sheets.

Sunday, June 4 – Avignon.

Rose latish, visited the old Eglise St. Pierre for Pentecost service and likewise the main church – St. Marie du Dom, on the hilltop. They are both early gothic with 1 central nave, no transepts. Visited the Palais des Pâpes under the guidance of a guide who was a typical homme du Midi. Full of human song ----and exaggeration. The palace is massive, with excellent architecural work especially in the arches and vaulting. The day was hot and I could do little else but sit in the sun and vegetate. I ate a picnic lunch on a bench in the beautiful hilltop park that overlooks the Rhone. Paté de fois gras, bread and cherries. Then after a long rest in the shade I crossed the River and visited the Tour Philippe le Bel, which used to command the approach of the pilgrims to the old Port St. Bénézet. It has a splendid view from the top of the turret across the valley to the Palais des Pâpes and the rooves of Avignon clustered at its feet. Then a little farther on, past Villeneuve, a sunbaked hamlet, lies the massive Fort St. André. The sun was oppressively hot. People didn't walk, they crawled. You had hardly enough energy to cross to the shady side of the street, yet you always did. The old Fort has a magnificent double towered gateway but inside it is overgrown with weeds. Nothing to compare with Kennilworth for Romance. (I think of Mary often) Took a bus back to Avignon and collapsed into a café chair. But soon I lost the lassitude and, with renewed energy, I walked along the outside of the city walls. Watched the gens du Midi playing their local game, Boulles. It absorbs them and its pace is slow. All life here is slow. Had dinner opposite the magnificent turreted city walls, saw a movie (that amusing film, "It Happened One Nite") and returned home at midnite to bed.

Pentecost Monday, June 10 – same Hotel, Avignon

I really had luck today, and splendid fun. Since it was Pentecost Monday everyone was in an especially good humor. The buses were filled with excursionists, many prices were reduced. I set off at 8 A.M. with a crowd of picnickers to the Pont du Gard, a majestic Roman aqueduct that spans the valley of the Gardon, a small river. Its construction is an excellent example of the Roman arch. Three tiers of arches one above the other, no mortar or cement used at all. Between arches 2 and 3 runs the conduit through which the water used to flow down to Nimes for the use of the emperor or local governor. They must have been a thirsty crowd, those Romans. Nimes is an excellent introduction to Roman antiquities in Italy. I visited the large and well preserved Roman arena with its 4 galleries, its "vomitories" through which the people ascended to the seats. It is used for bullfights today but I missed seeing the show because it took place yesterday. Then to the Maison Carré, graceful in spite of its mass. Much airier and lighter than the Eglise de la Madeleine at Paris. Friezes not so good as the Parthenon (Elgin Marbles) by a long shot, but same motifs. Interesting collection of Roman bottles, coins and pottery. Those Roman girls must have thrown their bracelets away after wearing them once. One sees many Roman jewelry bracelets, etc. picked up in public places. Then along a canal to the public Jardin de la Fontaine, former Roman baths. In one corner is the ruined Temple de Diane, a curious structure that has 3 naves. Fine Roman arches. Only a few traces of what was once a Porch of Corinthian columns just like the perfectly preserved Maison Carré. I then climbed to the highest point of the city, the Tour Morgue, where you get a fine panorama of the great plain, broken here and there by long ranges of low hills. The vegetation is scrubby and there are many hard rocky formations, mostly chalky-white. Many cedars which, when silhouetted against the sky, make a sharp, severe, and almost Italian outline. Had an ambulatory lunch, mostly fruit and ice cream. Then bus to Arles. Arles is full of Roman remains. I first visited the old Eglise St. Trophime. It has a very finely carved Romanesque doorway with friezes, statues of saints and arches (vaulted) all well preserved. The interior of the church seems Romanesque. It is not very interesting. But the piece de resistance is the lovely cloister. Reminded me of the cloister at Gloucester or Westminster Abbey. Two sides are Romanesque (with rounded arches, unadorned vaulting) and two are gothic with slightly pointed arches and a vaulted ceiling in very simple, early style. The sun was very hot and the grass plot enclosed by the cloister broiled with the heat. Some of the sun seemed to flow in through the arches of the cloister and dapple the stone floor with a golden yellow light.

Then I visited the Théâtre Antique, which is in very bad repair but gives an idea of the majestic size of the stage and amphitheater. Two lone columns are all that is left of the stage proper. The Romans, it seems knew how to live. Bread and circuses.

But Arles, on this Pentecostal Monday, provided its own bread and circuses, proving to my complete satisfaction that the gens du Midi also know how to live. There was a bullfight in the Roman Arena (not as good an arena as at Arles, but pretty fine none the less). A BULL FIGHT! Wouldn't Mary have loved it. Four bulls were mis a' mort in this Course aux Taureaux by 2 toreadors and their assistants. All in the traditional Spanish costume, scintillating and sparkling in the hot sun. They threw kisses at the ladies, tossed their hats, waved their cloaks; the band played Toreador music from "Carmen". The arena was packed with these amusing Provencals who laugh, drink wine and dance in the sunlight. Some of the bulls were ferocious and tossed the toreadors on their horns. Some needed to be stabbed 3 and 4 times with swords and then with a dagger (in the head) before they would crumple up and die. Then 2 stout drag horses would come prancing out and drag the dead bull around the dusty ring and away to the music of the local band. Then a man with a sack of sawdust sponged up the pools of blood in the ring. The toreadors seemed pretty scared or maybe only careful of the bulls. I enjoyed it immensely and was not very worried by the carnage. The people who packed the old arena were lots of fun. There was a humorous Spanish band and at the end of the show a bull was turned loose in the ring for the practice and delight of about 50 local blades who showed off their prowess (?) in the ring. The bulls are first maddened by the toreador's helpers and are stuck with darts in their back, and then the toreador comes, hiding his sword under a bright red cloth. He maddens and tires the bull, poises his blade and then plunges it home in the bull's back. The crowd goes quite wild. A splendid setting for a picturesque show.

Bus to Tarascon (standing up all the way because it was so crowded with holiday makers). At Tarascon I had time to look at the Rhone, the magnificent Chateau du Roi René and then to sit at a café on the main street of Tarascon and drink in some more of the atmosphere of the Midi. The accent is almost like Italian or Spanish and very hard to understand when spoken by old peasants. But it is contagious. The people are all so happy and smile so readily. Quite a new view of life that one gets in this sunny, smiling country where the wine is sweet and the songs are gay. I was happy and smiling too. Why not? This is a splendid vacation. Bus to Avignon where I dined too expensively (30 fr) at the Hotel Crillon. But I was very hungry. Mailed postcards and so to bed. A ¼ moon tonight. Oh me!

Tuesday, June 11, 1935 St. Raphael (Var) Hotel de Genève at Azur.

Left Avignon at 8:00 and had a very hot and uncomfortable train ride. It was so disagreeable that at Marseilles I didn't care to get down so I missed seeing Marseilles. Tant pis. But as soon as I got to St. Raphael and felt the ocean breeze I was refreshed. Put on my white linen suit, ate an ambulatory lunch and then went to the beach. I hired a cabine (2 francs .50) and stretched out in the sun. Read Victor Hugo's poems. It is Tuesday after Pentecost and the town is deserted. Not much life. I took short swim about 3 o'clock but mostly just laid on the beach. There are palm trees growing along the boardwalk. The palms don't seem as natural here as in the Caribbean. But the opalescent blue water and general allure reminds me a lot of the Caribbean Sea. The water is so blue that any white caps seem to be an unusually hard, brilliant white against the dark blue background. The water was coldish. About 5 P.M. I walked up a wooded hill out of St. Raphael on the Route du Valescure to Fred Bookman's estate, "Ile Verte". A sexy girl showed me the gate. The gardener and his wife, very nice and hardworking people, showed me all around. A beautifully situated house, very spacious but furnished in bad taste. The view from the balconies of the Mediterranean Sea, the Estival range of mountains, the Alpes Maritimes behind Cannes are magnifico. At the foot of the hill lie St. Raphael and a neighboring town. At a nearby airport hydroplanes zoom over the water, cutting white paths in the clean blue water as they land. Fred should live there more than he does. It is a shame to neglect a beauty spot like that. He ought to turn it over to his nephew for good keeping. The place needs tasteful fixing up. What couldn't Mary and I do there! Fred had some crazy ideas for things to do there, the gardener told me. There is a basin of water, which he wanted to change into a canal with basins at each end. Also he wanted to have a pool of crocodiles, of all things. Are all bachelors like that?

Walked back to town and had dinner after an aperitif (St. Raphael, sec).

In the Midi the laborers start at 4, work till 12 then knock off till 4 again then work till sundown. It is impossible to work, so they say, in the hot hours.

There was a moon tonight, which shimmered over the blue waters. The palm trees were silhouetted against a dark sky. Too romantic for me – traveling all alone. I sat at a café in the old port and watched the moon shine through the trees and on the water, painting with silver light the masts of the boats lying in the harbor.

A high wind came up around 10 o'clock so I strolled a bit more and then turned in. But the moon shines on as romantically as ever.

Hugo's poetry is so good – technically – that it is boring. And it bores chiefly because none of his ideas are original. He just takes tried and true saws and recasts them in noble phrasing. But the noble phrasing is worth its reputation.

G'nite.

Wednesday, June 12, 1935 Modern Hotel, Rue des Serbes (16) Cannes

Left St. Raphael, a lovely and intime coin, early in the morning and put up at this inexpensive and comfortable hotel in Cannes. Another room with a view of palms, a blue sky and a blue sea. Then I took the funiculaire up to Super-Cannes. There is an observatory (payante) which I climbed and got a splendid view of the entire littoral. All of Cannes was at my feet and behind me were the Alpes Maritimes and the snow capped Italian Alps. The Estoral were on one side and Nice on the other. Altitude about 800 metres. Very worthwhile and an inspiring sight. Wrote a card to Mary on the top of the mountain and then descended by funiculaire. Had an ambulatory lunch at the city market which was very good and then I went to the beach. I got a very red sunburn and I now look like a cooked lobster and I feel hot and burned. But it is quite bearable. Took a pirogue, a tiny boat like a kayak, out into the sea. It was rough however so I turned back in. The proprietor persuaded me to fill out the hour I had paid for with a canoe. But it was too big for 1 man to have much fun with. I am not such a good sailor (as far as the stomach is concerned). Did a kip and full turn on a horizontal bar with the greatest of ease. After some sun basking and studying a little Italian I took the bus to Nice. It stopped right on the famous Promenade des Anglais. Got a sweet letter from Virginia, which I immediately answered. Also bought some Italian lire. Then I went to the casino and played Boule. By sticking mainly to #7 my 10 francs grew to 25 so I walked out with my winnings and started for the Roulette room. But you need a card for that so I couldn't get in. Returned to the Boule but my lucky streak was over and I lost my winnings plus my original stake. Tant pis. Then walked around Cannes, had an aperitif at the best café on the Promenade, (right in front of Jay Gould's Casino (closed)). Wrote many postcards to everybody and then had a good Italian dinner (and low priced) at a Crèmerie. The proprietor gave me a card to his brother-in-law, an innkeeper at Salsamagiore. Nice is much larger than Cannes, much more international. Many more foreigners and oodles of hotels. It isn't as sympathique as Cannes. But the Cote d'Azur in general would be more fun if I weren't alone. But I like it. Perhaps V?

Returned to Cannes in my white suit, changed into something warmer and less conspicuous. Walked along the Croissette and looked at the moon on the blue sea. Bought ice cream from an Italian and said, "Gracia". He answered "Prego". Looked at the large number of motley and not-so-motley boats in the port, had a café at the best café in Cannes (like the Colysée only cheaper) and then had some distraction. And so we say nighty, nite, Virg. The Cornice tomorrow. I had my picture taken today but haven't yet seen the prints.

Thursday, June 13, 1935 Cannes –

Today I took the Grande Corniche drive. Starting from Cannes at 8:15 in a snappy autobus we went through Nice and then climbed high until we could look back and see the city at our feet. Then a drive along the dizzy heights of the Corniche. The form of the coastline, traced out in the thick blueness of the sea was readily visible. The day was magnificent and all the towns, red-rooved, stood out magnificently against the sea. I really believe there is nothing more satisfying than to see the world spread out at your feet like that. We humans look so small in the midst of all that space. We stopped at a halfway house where the strong French fortifications were clearly visible and the Italian frontier was only 14 klm away. The forts date from those post war days when France and Italy were on very bad terms. Then we descended past Villefranche and its large harbor and above Monte Carlo. Arrived at Menton, which seems much more picturesque and lovelier than Cannes, plus "intime", and the beach is rocky like at Nice. I had an enormous thrill when I walked 2 meters over the Italian frontier and bought some ice cream. "Gracias" "Prego". Tomorrow I'll roll right across the frontier with the greatest of ease. (Knock on wood). Menton is laden with bright flowers. More tropical than Cannes. Lemons and bananas grow there in profusion. Lunch (expensive) at a tea roomy sort of place done in the style of an English Inn. I was very sleepy, perhaps the result of the wine. I made a fast friend of a young German Swiss, a restaurant cook on his vacation. He was in the bus with me and we became comrades. At Monte Carlo we tried to go to the Casino. I was too young, damn it. He won 50 francs. I sat on a bench and contemplated the Englishmen who hang around the Casino gardens.

Everything is de luxe – even the people. If they aren't de luxe today, they used to be and are now broken down but still de luxe in spirit. Gambling makes them jittery. The gardens at Monaco just below the Prince's Palace are lovely and the Prince has a splendid view of the symmetrical port, blue sea and high mountains from the courtyard of the Palace. There is a surly guard d'honneur in snappy white uniforms to guard the Palace. Monaco is like a toy. In fact the entire Cote d'Azur gives me a papier maché feeling – as tho it were all fake, hollow stage setting – its beauty is too perfect, the colors too heavenly. It isn't dirty enough to be real. Monaco is the most toy-like of the entire coast. Pleasant but hot ride back to Cannes. We had the bus photographed in the morning and picked up the photos on the way home. I came out very well. Also the photos of me in Cannes came out fairly well. I spoke French all day. Letter from Ma and Baba. Back at Cannes at sundown. I went swimming (undressed on the beach) with the Swiss fellow. It was cold but invigorating.

Had a good and cheap supper at a little Crèmerie run by some Bretons. Gorged myself on some delicious crepes Bretonnes, the specialité de la Maison. Said goodbye to my Swiss friend. Came back to the hotel, repacked my bag entirely and early to bed. Domane Italia! The Corniche was really grand. (Tho I was sleepy).

Friday, June 14, 1935 – Hotel Washington, Pisa
Left Cannes early, chatted about youth with a café proprietor. On the train, which went along the seashore, I met an Italian who spoke French. We chatted all the way to Genoa. At Ventimiglia changed trains, had a customs inspection, etc. No trouble. Saw my first Italian Carabinieri in their snappy uniforms of olive green of which they are very, very proud. You feel the regimented spirit here. They venerate ll Duce as a great hero and a strong man. They obey rules and are orderly because of ll Duce's power which can be felt everywhere. Going to Genoa we saw some lovely Italian scenery, cities with wash hanging from every window. Genoa is very industrial and we passed many factories. At Genoa I checked my bag at the station. Walked down Via Balbi, which contains the University with an interesting court and staircase. Then Via Garibaldi and the Palazzo Rosso. It is sumptuous but in good XVIIth Century taste. Some fine marble work. Excellent Van Dyke portraits of the family. A Titian and Strazzi, whose earthy work I like. Gorgeous ceilings painted by local artist, Ferrari after whom the Piazza de Ferrari is named (Main Square of Genoa). Through wonderful narrow streets (you can reach out and span them). Crammed with people, lined with shops. Bought a pastry. The streets all go steeply down hill from the main thoroughlanes, they twist and turn. Walked along the waterfront and out to the lighthouse

through great shipping wharves, Genoa's big industry. Got a boatman to row me back to town after arguing about the price. Splendid view of Genova from the water. It spreads out long and low along the waterfront and it is very compact. Walked along the waterfront and up via San Lorenzo to the Cathedral which is stunning and curious with its black and white marble and the cloister nearby with slightly pointed arches is made more lovely by the old, time-worn well in the center of the cloister garden. Nearby is a small church, too gaudily decorated but a square lined with houses formerly belonging to the aristocracy. They are very interesting with their black and white and black and yellow marble. Walked through the main streets, Piazza di Ferrari, via Quattro Septembre lined with fine stores. Then to the parks of _Aquasola and Villa Dinegro. From the top of the grotto in Villa Dinegro a splendid view of all Genoa. It was a splendid day, very blue sky and sea. Lots of activity in the harbor. Returned to town, had a cheap but adequate meal (spaghetti included) and then train for Pisa. Lots of fun on the train with 5 Italian men 2 of whom spoke French. They were very jolly and we had a good time. One was a Sicilian soldier quite a nitwit. Got this bare but cheap hotel at Pisa at 11:30 P.M.

Saturday, June 15 - Albergo (?) opposite Station at Poggibonsi
   Slept very late this morning in Pisa, had lunch at the hotel and then went to the Piazza di Duomo (on foot, of course) over the Ponte di Solferino. The Arno looked rather plain and uninteresting as it flowed through Pisa. The Piazza di Duomo is magnificent. There is the Campanile (famous leaning tower), the Duomo, the Baptisterio and Campo Santo all in white marble. The Duomo is encircled by white marble steps. Green, closely clipped grass is the only other element except for the clear blue sky, which outlines the domes of the Cathedral and Baptistery and the superimposed colonnades of the Campanile. I first entered the Duomo. A simple cross plan – set in bold relief by the black and white marble. A Cimabue mosaic in a half dome, very Byzantine. Some Andrea del Sarto which was hard to get a look at. But the cathedral, the best I have so far seen in Italy (my 2nd Duomo) is fine. Very noble columns (trophies of war). The galleries around the top, especially on the altar are very curious. Typical Italian style. The glorious façade kept me occupied for many minutes. I sat and looked at its rows of white marble columns from the steps of the Battisteria which is opposite. The Baptistery is absolutely round, all in marble. The Font is beautifully carved, fine inlaid work. A perfect echo due to the bell-shaped dome. The pulpit by Giovanni Pisano is very delicately done. Amusing, sensitive faces of priests. It is octagonal and each side represents a biblical scene. I like painting better than sculpture. It is warmer and I understand it better. Then I climbed the

345

tower (Torra). The leaning of it makes you think you are drunk. I went to the very top and saw the view of the Italian hills, the town of Pisa and the Arno stretching away, flat and dull toward the sea. The sun was brilliant and blazed on the white marble. On a platform just 1 colonnade below the top I lay on my back and gazed up through the marble circle to the blue sky. Glorious. Down and bought some very fine postcards. Then to the Museo (Opera del Duomo) which has just been opened. I admired some sculpture of Giovanni Pisano (very religious and soft) tiles of Luca Della Robia and other things brought mainly from the Campo Santo. Some unimportant sculpture by Guardi and a curious Arabian idol (sort of a winged dragon in bronze). What I liked best at Pisa was the Campo Santo. It is a glorious cloister with Romanesque windows enriched with Gothic tracery. Majestic dimensions. A happily ornamented grass plot in the middle, a hot Italian sun filtering through the tracery onto the stone cloister floor. The walls are covered with frescoes. Those on the left as you come in are the best – they are by Oreagna (?). Depict scenes from religious (monks) life. Very humorous. Very lively faces. Well preserved. But the technique is too evident. Quite primitive. Those by Renezzo Gozzoli on the right–hand wall are also good (pictures of the Medici family at the tower of Babel). The others are less interesting. The Campo Santo was very interesting. Walked back to the station via main streets of Pisa and the Lungarno Reggio, which is rather bare. Train at 4:20 intending to go to Siena. Had to change at Empoli and waste 2 hours there. So I walked around the town which is a very plain little agricultural town with no interest. The Arno runs through its outskirts. Bought my dinner there, which I ate on the train later. Salami, cheese, bread, red wine and 2 peaches. I can make myself understood pretty well in Italian and thoroughly enjoy the process. Certainly glad that I am making all my arrangements myself. On the train toward Siena I chatted in my broken Italian with some fellows who took a great interest in the fact that I was an American all alone in Italy. They told me to get off at Poggibonsi to see San Gimignano so off I got and here I am. It is a quaint mill town. The moon is shining over the hilltop and on the roofs. There are many people in the streets – Saturday nite I went to the movies and saw Enrico VIII ("The Wives of Henry VIII" to you). Buona Notte.

Sunday, June 16, 1935 – Pensione Senese Via di Camollia, Siena

A superb day in every way. Set out by bus about 8:30 across the lovely Tuscan hills. They are green – an ashen, graying green. Green in all its forms – ranging from yellow to blue – is the only color. Around a bend in the road and the strange square towers of San Gimignano stood up against the sky. Entered the town by the Porta San Giovanni above it on the inside is a curious frescoe badly preserved. All the town is old and authentic. Dripping with XIVth Century atmosphere. Very much like Bruges. The buildings are all in Siena-colored brick, a sort of burnt brown. Via San Giovanni is only large street. From it crazy steps and inclined alleys lead to the side streets. Via San Giovanni debouches in the Piazza della Cisterna. In center is an old well (cisterna) and the houses, some topped by the ruins of the old towers, are all old. Some with the Tuscan double-arched windows. Every store harmonizes with every other. Comparison with Bruges is irresistible. Adjoining this piazza is Piazza del Duomo. I used my French guidebook, very good. The Piazza has on one side the dull façade of The Duomo with a broad flight of stairs. Opposite side a curious arcade closed at one end, used as a municipal market, which was in full swing. At left the Palazzo Publico and a portico with a frescoe. At right private houses. It was a festive day for Fascism, the last day of school and there was a big demonstration of Giovanezzi (youths) which I watched. Marching in perfect order and in different uniforms. Figli della Lupa, Avanguardisti, Fascisti. Tiny Italians with tiny guns. Fiery patriotism. Youth is keynote of Italy. The oldsters feel out of it, but they admire it.

Visited the Duomo Frescoes of Gozzoli and fine work of Berna who died too young to be famous. Chapel of Santo Fina with 2 frescoes of Ghirlandaio and the oratorio (little side door) with Annunciation. Ghirlandaios are the finest things in the Collegiata. They impressed me very much. There was a church service for the Fascisti who marched like Crusaders with banners waving into the cathedral in military order. Saw Palazzo Publico fine XIIIth Century courtyard embellished by frescoed family seals. A noble staircase heading to Municipal council rooms, Now a Museo Civico. Salone di Dante (he was ambassador) and Pinacotheca Municipale with Byzantine crucifix paintings, some fine Filippino Lippi and some Mainardi who, with Gozzoli, seems to be the local hero. Glassware and faience in best Tuscan style. The new Museo della Basilica is worthwhile. A Byzantine Christ in wood. A fair Perugino like the one at Paris exposition. Clerical robes of which the custodian was very proud but over which I could not get enthused. Then I visited the church of Santo Agostino at the end of the town. It is a bare, poor barn of a place but the choir has a glorious array of Benezzo Gozzoli better than his work at Pisa. (If Gozzoli be glorious) Fine portrait heads. An excellent dinner on a terrace which had an unblemished view of the most heavenly Tuscan hills. I will never see its likes again. Unbroken vista of the accented hills crowding one upon another. Olive trees, waving wheat, blue sky and classic white clouds. And a ½ liter of wonderful Chianti wine which made me slightly dizzy. After lunch I walked all the way around the city walls (about 1 hour) pausing often to drink in the Tuscan scenery. The town is circled by a wall with round, crenelated fat towers. Inside are the square towers, probably from earlier fortifications. Passed the Fonti, series of arcades in Romanesque and Gothic style which shelter a fountain where women still do their washing. I loved San Gimignano and splurged on postcards. Bus back to Poggibonsi and a last glimpse of those square towers as the bus rolled over the hills. Two hours wait at Poggibonsi during which I wrote a letter home. Train to Siena, passed many ruined castles. At Siena, with my heavy bag on my shoulder I climbed the hill to the town and put up at this ritzy pension in an old house with impressive ceilings, enormously high. I took full pension and am not so glad. Won't do it again. Walked around La Lizza, public park built on the old city walls. Got my first view of the 3 hills of Siena and the towers. Very lovely skyline.

At supper I met a Scotch art student. (The rest of the pension are old maids, all English, who are waiting in Siena for death). We walked at sunset around the walls of the town from Porto Camillia to Fonte Ovile, an old fountain sheltered, like at Gimignano by an imposing Romanesque portico. A glorious, fat, yellow moon. Back up steep streets to the center of town for coffee. We talked politics, women (of course) and art. I was surprised to see how much I knew about art. At the pension we showed each other postcards of things in Italy. I got a great pleasure in showing my postcards. He is a very decent Scotch lad, knows a lot about art technically. We exchanged tips on tourism.

I read Italian newspapers with a fair facility, using Latin and French to piece words together. Speak very badly but make myself understood. I know no syntax. Buona Notte.

Monday, June 17, 1935 – Albergo Cornelio, Orvieto
Up early this morning to walk my feet to a frazzle all day seeing Siena. I liked Siena less than San Gimignano. Perhaps its size, 3 times that of San G. – had something to do with that impression. But it is nevertheless a treasure house and a lovely hill town. I first walked along the main street past many old private Palazzi, mostly in Renaissance style with very graceful windows. Gothic also. It was a fine lesson in that kind of domestic architecture. Then the Campo, the enormous public square where the 3 hills of Siena (I tramped up and down all three) converge. On one side is the crenelated Palazzo Civico with a tall tower – a poem of grace. I did not climb it. The tower is tall and slender and the most graceful I have seen for that kind of architecture. It is square. A fountain by Jacopo della Quercia on the opposite side of the enormous campo site of the Palio Races July 2. Then to the Duomo. Its façade, rich with statues and gothic design is excellent. What impressed me most were the ruins of the immense cathedral planned by the Siennese builders of which the existing Duomo was to be only the core. One can see from the

ruined nave that they started that the projected structure would have been the most imposing in all Christendom. As it is, it juts out over another church, San Giovanni and its black and white marble shining from the highest spot in Siena are imposing enough. The chief attractions of the inside are the unique floor, all done in polychrome marble inlaid with extreme artistry, and the library. The marble floors, partly covered today for protection, are as well designed (human bodies, faces, etc.) as the paintings of the period. The medium must be very difficult. A chapel (San Giovanni) with some very good heads by Pinturrichio and a John the Baptist by Donatello, which was hard to see. It looked less interesting than the one I saw at Paris. The church nave with black and white zebra-like stripes is very curious but impressive and not at all grotesque. The Pinturrichio murals are a glorious symphony of color. Remarkably preserved. But the movement is very stiff. The heads have no very direct muscular and anatomical relation to the bodies. Still primitive in that respect. Good composition, but quite mechanical. Colors, however, are glorious. The Museo Opera del Duomo is dull except for some works of Duccio and then a small door, which leads out onto the end wall of the old, ruined nave of the unfinished cathedral. Splendid panorama of the city giving me a chance to fix its geography well in my head. The Tuscan hills surround Siena in a riot of green. Then I visited the Battistera San Giovanni, once an independent church and now nestled up under the choir of the Duomo. Its bronze font is article of chief interest. Panels by Ghibuti, Donatello, etc. but I don't know enough about bronze work. In the Duomo was a splendid pulpit by the Pisano family. The panel of the Last Judgment especially fine. I used 2 guide books – Baedecker and The Guide Joanne. The latter is much more detailed and better for art and history. Then visited some more private palazzos. Tried to get a student card at the University (modern building). Then went to church San Francesco at the edge of town where there are 2 cloisters both influenced by modern buildings. I walked very self consciously, through the monk's seminary. Nearby is San Bernadino, a small Oratorio of 2 floors containing highly overrated frescoes by Sodoma. Nuts. Good lunch at pension. (My Scotch friend had a toothache.) Then I went to the Pinacotheca. A splendid modern museum in an old Palazzo. Wonderful for studying Siennese school. Scores of paintings by all the masters of Siena. Siena in the primitive years took the lead but it seems to me that Siena never developed like Florence. Siena remained static but Florence learned from Siena and then stole the laurels by developing and improving the Siena technique. The XVth Century and early XVIth Century stuff from Siena is still primitive.

I was very much touched by a statue of La Madelina in baked, glazed, painted clay by Cozzarelli (1450-1516). She is all alone in a sort of chapel.

Only the torso and head are extant. Tears, real tears stream down her face and the afternoon light played softly over her delicate features. I half closed my eyes and could imagine that her half parted lips were smiling and moving for me. Even more entrancing than the Mona Lisa. I would return to Siena just to see La Madelina by Cozzarelli.

The school of Siena is too, too sweet. Only about 1450 is there any punch in the canvasses. Usually nothing but very religious sweetness and light. There are a good Cranach and some good Moroni portraits.

Back to the hotel along the endless main street after buying my food for supper. Siena is long from one end to the other, and up hill – down dale. Carried my bag the long distance to the station with perfect ease. Then off to Orvieto via Chiusi (change) at 6:25. Ate excellent supper of cheese, bread, Chianti wine and cherries on the train and read a French and an Italian paper. I read Italian well now. Also met an Italian on the train Chiusi-Orvieto and made a date to meet him in Rome – Palazzo Venezia. I speak damn fine Italian for a guy who is been in the country less than 4 days. (I love me).

At Orvieto I took the funicular up the hillside to the town. It was 10 P.M. and a glorious silver moon shone down on Orvieto. Found this wonderfully cheap hotel (7 lire). It is very arty – there are frescoes on the ceiling of my bedroom of the XVth Century and great wooden beams. Then I took a short walk. Up to the Piazza del Duomo. The Duomo was painted by moonlight. Its rich façade, which seems to be embellished with inlaid mosaic, glistened in the silvery night. As I came into the Piazza all I saw was the great Duomo, a lone pine tree against the sky and the moon. A sight I will never forget. A sight of intoxicating beauty. Walked to the Piazza Publica (it is enormous) past the high Torre del Morro (clock face) and climbed the balcony of the crenelated Piazza Publica. Enchanting view of the roof of the Duomo, the moon and the distant Tuscan hills. And back to bed after a swig from what remains of my Tuscan wine. Tonight's moon at Orvieto, the Chianti and La Madelina at Siena have been today's high spots.

Tuesday, June 18, 1935 - Pension Salus, Piazza del Independenzia, Rome

Up early in my cavernous hotel room and out to see Orvieto. Spent several hours at the wonderful Duomo. The façade is very rich. Central portal is Romanesque and the earliest of the structure. Then came the other lower parts. The upper part, especially the spires, are in the highest Gothic. Entire thing is Gothic. Gothic roof. Strange circular absidal chapels which form rounded buttresses when viewed from outside. Sculpture on base of columns outside are among the best I know. As good as Pisano's pulpit. The large rose window is the most delicate I have ever seen from the outside. The inside of the Duomo is very impressive, black and white marble. And very simple.

The Signorelli murals in chapel on the right are piece de resistance. Same self-assured treatment of bodies as achieved later by Michaelangelo (who studied Signorelli). But Signorelli's bodies, for all their strength and realism, seem sordidly human, while Michelangelo's are supremely divine. The murals are very striking and tho not beautiful, they are excellent painting. Saw Etruscan tombs and other paintings in the Opera del Duomo. Then I walked along the city walls getting glorious views of the Umbrian hills especially from the old Fortezza. Orvieto must have been an impregnable fortress, perched on its rocky height. Then I went to the Pazzo, the old XVth Century well that goes deep, deep (200 feet) into the bedrock. I descended the stairs, led by a boy with a candle. It was very cool and dark at the bottom. Ascended by another staircase. There are 2, which wind around the well. Very curious thing.

Then an early lunch (11:00) and down the funicular to the train. I left Orvieto too soon. Should have stayed longer. But Rome was calling.

Very hot train ride to Rome. Trouble with hotel arrangements and cab. Got this bare room too near RR station. Then walked to American Express. Letters from home with name of a good hotel. Got money changed. The hotel suggested was in the Piazza Santissima Trinita dei Monti. I went to see it, up the Spanish steps from Piazza di Spagna. It is very snappy and chic but I got a special rate. The room I'll have tomorrow is on the top floor, front with a glorious view of the city of Rome from the Pincio. I see across Rome to St. Peter's etc. Wonderful. Then I walked along the Pincio hill, with wonderful views that got me all excited about Rome, down to Piazza del Popolo then along Corso Umberto I to Piazza Venezia. Passed many baroque churches and homes. Nuts to baroque! Saw lovely Fonte di Trevi. The fountains of Rome! The Piazza Venezia is overwhelmingly impressive. The huge monument in dazzling white marble is worthy of the eternal city. Grim Palazzo Venezia with Mussolini's little balcony distinctly visible. Sat at a chic café and contemplated it all. Then climbed the monument with fine views of all of Rome. I constantly studied the map. Seeing the Forum, Colosseum, etc., got me all in a lather of enthusiasm for Rome. There are so many ages side by side here. But the most impressive monuments are products of Imperialistic ages. Mussolini is in that fine old Roman tradition. Supper at a Trattoria just off the Piazza then a sunset walk around the Forum. My feet almost killed me. Then bus home to read the New Yorker and doze off to bed. Rome is a grand city and I love it. The others were interesting, pretty or quaint, but Rome is Majestically Grand!

Wednesday, June 19, 1935 - Hotel Hassler, Piazza Santissima Trinita dei Monti, Rome

Slept till about 8:30 this morning at Pensione Salus and then went down to check out and pay the bill. A big argument with the desk clerk who wanted to charge me seidici lira (16 lire) when I had made the padrone agree to tredici (13). I thumped the table with my fist, yelled "Basta", lost my temper and felt like poking the dirty, greasy clerk. I finally won the argument. Took a carriage to this splendid hotel and installed myself in my front room with view of the entire city, especially San Pietro. They are very nice here. German I think. Lots of service.

My first full day in Rome and I have almost walked my feet to the bone. They are absolutely frazzled. Set out, about 10 A.M. and walked to the Tiber (muddy and sluggish) along its banks past the Castel St. Angelo with San Pietro in the distance. Then down Corso Vittorio Emmanuele past many baroque churches, some of which I visited. Stopped in at the GUF and was told to return later for my museum card. The heat is pretty bad during noon hours. Entered the Gesu, fine example of baroque, if you like baroque. Then walked around the quarter to the South of the Piazza Venezia. Turning a corner, I saw a very familiar face and recognized it immediately as Mrs. Keyser. I called out her name and she turned round and recognized me. We exchanged a few words and I promised to phone her. Had lunch for less than 2 lire consisting of a big cheese sandwich and almost a quart of MILK! Milk, my first love – my cherished drink. The first real dose of milk since America and it was good milk too. Spent the hot hours in the Capitoline and Mussolini museums. I was tired by the countless rooms of statuary. Remember best the Dying Gaul, Infant Hercules, (humorously pudgy) and The Capitoline Venus (very appealing). Also a beautiful Roman woman with a fan shaped coiffure worse than Helene Vaujany's. Then I sat just outside the Senatorial museum and had a lot of fun bargaining with a postcard vendor. I made him pare his prices to the bone and finally bought some views of Rome – dirt-cheap. Then, in the blazing sun I visited carefully the entire Forum Romanum, Palatine Hill and Colosseum. At each step my feet got heavier but my interest held up pretty well. The grand manner in which it is all done impressed me. I liked the House of Livia on the Palatine with its well-preserved frescoes of Roman origin. The entire Forum, Palatine and Colosseum are a very exciting and inspiring array of dead glory. Some splendid views of Rome from the Palatine. Then to the GUF office by cab to find about 30 priests fighting it out for their cards in a very unpriestly manner. I return Friday for mine. Walked home in time to see a wonderful streaky sunset from my verandah. A cold bath refreshed me a lot. I got all dressed up and had dinner at La Rosetta, excellent restaurant near the Pantheon recommended by a friend of Mother. Had a fine spaghetti dish, chicken liver and fruit, etc. But it was expensive. Spent the evening until quite late with the Italian I met on the train to Orvieto. He is pretty soft and I don't know whether to trust him or not. Agreed to go to a dance place (Citta Giardino) with him tomorrow night. Bon soir. I am glad to speak so many languages. (self-praise) I spoke Italian all evening.

June 20 to July 2, 1935

No daily entries for my diary in the period June 20 to July 2 because I was otherwise occupied with a visiting girl friend from Paris, Virginia Balke, whom I had originally met on the ship from the US to France the previous year.

Just before she arrived I had spent a day tramping around Rome, seeing famous sights – Santa Maria in Cosmedine, the Protestant Cemetery, San Paolo, Caracolla baths, San Giovanni in Laterano, Santa Maria Maggiore, Santa Croce in Jerusalemo, San Lorenzo fuori Mura and The Campo Verano – all in one day.

We spent four days together in Rome, which included a trip to Ostia on the coast. Another day to Rocca di Papa by train and funicular, also walked to Genzano on Lago di Nemi. Later in the week I went on my own to St. Peters, the Vatican and the Passegiata Margherita and the entire Janiculum Hill.

On June 25 we went to Naples – frightfully dirty but very colorful. Then to the Isle of Capri for four delightful days. This included swimming in the Blue Grotto, spending time in Anacapri, the Villa of Tiberius and the Faglione Rocks. From Capri took the boat just after dawn for breakfast in Sorento, then by train to Castellamare and from there to Pompeii. Got a horse and driver to take us up to the crater of Vesuvius – an ancient nag. Walked all around the crater, saw lava only four days old. Red hot and still moving. The Italians we saw in the South all seemed like consummate thieves, eager to rip you off if they possibly could. I actually got to enjoy arguing with them over prices, etc. It was good, clean sport. Will never forget one old guy we met in a flyspecked café, who was probably a racketeer deported back to Italy from Chicago. His motto, he told us, was "Don't Trust Nobody". Good advice for Italy.

We returned to Rome and after a day or so Virginia went back to Paris – a wonderful experience for me as a young man, and I am glad to say, we parted as friends.

The next day I resumed my bachelor travels.

Wednesday, July 3, 1935 – Piazza Santa Chiara, Assisi

My first bachelor day in a fortnight. I enjoyed my solitude but thought somewhat about Virginia. I get more out of traveling – more vivid impressions – when I am alone. Did errands and shopping all morning in Rome and then took 12:37 train for Assisi via Foligno. Sat next to a healthy mother who nursed her baby at the breast all the way from Rome (4 hours). She seemed to typify the new Fascist policy of increasing the population.

At Assisi I took the bus up to the town. It is situated half way up a hill in the middle of Umbria. Returning to the hill towns gave me a thrill. I do love these Italian hills. Above the town, crowning the hill, are the ruins of a XIVth Century castle. At sundown I walked up there and sat down to contemplate a glorious view that takes in an entire fertile valley bounded by olive planted hills. Nearby sheep bells were tinkling and in the valley the carillons were ringing vespers. The sun sank lower and got more orange as the shadows lengthened. Assisi's churches and brown stone roofs and towers were painted with warm rays. I climbed down the hill just as the sun dipped over the horizon.

Dined on a balcony overlooking the largest public square, had some coffee and gelatin and returned to the hotel and to bed early and alone.

Thursday, July 4, 1935 – Albergo Parlamente, Via di Leone, Firenze

Today I spoke many languages. For considerable lengths of time I carried on in English, French, German and Italian.

Up at 8 and out of my bare little hotel to see the frescoes at San Francesco of Assisi. It is an enormous fortress-like monastery with a 2 storied basilica attached to it. A noble courtyard and portico to the lower church. Then the interior – dark, mystic, fervently religious. The frescoes of Giotto, Taddeo Gaddi and the other pupils were quite beautiful and historically interesting and their religious fervor was in direct harmony with the "dim religious light" of the lower basilica. Beautiful woodcarvings in the sacristy. And a 2 storied cloister of an interesting, rambling shape that looked very timeworn and romantic. Views of the hills from holes in the cloister walls. The upper church is abandoned, for no good reason at all. It houses beautiful Giotto frescoes of the life of St. Francis and there is a Cimabue Madonna overhead. The upper church echoes – I recited the Lord's prayer to find out. I liked Assisi better at sunset than in the morning. They do commercialize St. Francis a bit too much.

I bought some presents and an ashtray with the wonderful motto which I know and love so well: L'amore fa passare il tempo, il tempo fa passare l'amore.

At noon I took train to Perugia. It is also on a hill above the station. I walked up, leaving my bag at the Deposito. Had a good lunch at a fine little back-room restaurant near Piazza Garibaldi.

Then I walked to the main square and looked at the noble old town hall and lovely fountains. Then up to the chapel of San Severo when I saw

Raphael's first independent work, a lovely creation but still not free of Umbrian influences. Altercation about postcards with the guide in which I came out on top. Then visited Perugino murals in the wonderful old Cambio - old exchange room. Chatted with the guardian – a hearty old duck – in about 3 languages. Then the Museo Vanucili where some Perugino and especially a triptych of Fra Angelico inspired me most. This museum does the same for the Umbrian school as Sienna does for the Siennese school. Down the hill to the oratory of San Bernadino whose polychrome façade is richly sculptured. Met some very nice Americans, man and wife. I didn't like Perugia as much as Assisi, but I did like it. Should have stayed longer. Perhaps I should have enrolled as a student in the Royal University. I may do that some day maybe.

Then train to Florence arriving at 9:30. The first thing I saw was the Dome of Brunelleschi. Cab to this excellent hotel which is just behind the Palazzo Vecchio and Piazza della Signoria. Dirt cheap and fine hotel (12 lira). Had ice cream on the Piazza and contemplated the wonderful architecture of the Palazzo. Walked along the Lungarno, past the Uffizi and over the Ponte Vecchio. The goldsmith's shops were all sleeping. Back to bed, quite tired.

Friday, July 5, 1935 - Albergo Parlamento, Firenze

Today was one of the fullest and most interesting days I have spent since I've been in Italy. Up rather late after a good sleep and to the Palazzo Vecchio. Inspected the apartments and admired especially the chapel with murals of Bronzino in his striking, humanistic style and vivid coloring.

Climbed to the very top of the battlement tower and got the splendid view of Florence. The town sits in a pocket formed by the Arno running down thru the Tuscan hills. Excellent view of the Duomo from the tower of the Palazzo. Some fine examples of Italian furniture in rich old wood in the old rooms. Then I looked at Loggia di Lanzi with its statues. The streets nearby and the Piazza della Signoria itself are used today by the business men of Florence as a trading market and everywhere one hears quotations, figures being argued over. A good lunch with white wine near the Piazza then I wrote some postcards and inspected Piazza del Duomo. Looked at the wonderful bronze doors of the Baptistry. Especially main doors by Ghiberti. The expression and beauty worked into those bronze relics by the artist is almost miraculous. Looked at exterior of Duomo and its splendid Campanile. They were both closed at the time. The dome is very pleasing architecturally but it falls far short of the simple majesty of San Pietro of Rome. Its shape is very curious.

I spent all afternoon (3 hours) in the Uffizi Gallery. I covered everything in the gallery but the last hour I was pretty groggy. But for 2 hours I absorbed splendidly. Bought some reproductions. Admired especially Donatello, a Perugino portrait, Filippo Lippi, portrait of Andrea del Sarto by himself, Leonardo's portrait of a woman in brown and of himself. The Raphaels, Madonna of the Goldfinch and La Belle Jardinière were, of course, perfect. But too perfect to move me deeply. I noticed a tondo of the Holy Family by Signorelli which must have been the inspiration to Michaelangelo for his masterpiece because it is almost exactly the same composition. Titian's Duke of Urbino and his wife was fine and there were some good portraits by Tintoretto. Many excellent foreign schools – Flemish portraits which I like so much, excellent Holbein, superb Cranach studies of Adam and Eve, Rubens – 2 large canvasses overrated, but some good portraits. Claude Lorrain and an exquisite Mme Vigée Lebrun portrait of herself. Some Rembrandt but I have seen better canvasses of his. It was a glorious experience – The Uffizi Gallery.

I then bought myself 2 rolls, some cheese, tomatoes and a banana, tucked a copy of French XIXth Century Poetry under my arm and set out for the Viale dei Calle walk. Across the Ponte Vecchio with its many shops all displaying tempting leather goods and jewelry and down the Via Roma past grim but perfect Palazzo Pitti. Many art shops. Out Porta Romana and to the left up a shady, winding road passing San Miniata and coming after ½ hour walk to the Piazza Michelangelo. I arrived just at sunset and the Arno was a river of gold. Golden lights glinted through the arches of the Ponte Vecchio. The Duomo and the tower of Palazzo Vecchio rose up against the reddening sky. In the distance Fiesole was easily visible. I ate my simple supper on the steps of the Piazza and watched the evening sun go down. Then went to a café on the Piazza, had ice cream and then a glass of good Curacao while I watched the lights go on in the valley, contemplated the copy of Michelangelo's David and read poetry of Victor Hugo. That is the way I like to live. Walked home along the Lungarno. There is a crescent of a waxing moon. A splendid day in every way.

Saturday, July 6, 1935, Firenze

Today I saw a great many valuable monuments. But too many. I did not absorb some as well as I should have.

I take my breakfast at a nearby Paneficio (bakery) where they have good coffee. First went to the Baptistery and admired the mosaics of the interior and the effect of its dome. Also looked at the superb "Gates of Paradise" once more. Then the inside of the Duomo, which I did not like. Very bare and ugly, Renaissance architecture needs beautiful materials – polychrome, marble, etc. If it is just done in plaster and left bare, the architecture is not sufficient to create a general impression of beauty. Then to the Opera del Duomo containing 2 singing pulpits of a marvelous beauty. The angels singing by Luca della Robia and on the other pulpit by Donatello are very famous. Justly so. I contemplated them a long while. Then up via Cavour caravan to Palazzo Medici which has some sumptuous rooms and a fine garden. I did not pay to get in though I should have. Then to nearby San Lorenzo. It has an unfinished, raw brick façade. The interior, with a wall by Michelangelo, was very disappointing. Some Donatello statues of interest. Around in back one reaches the New Sacristy and the Capella dei Principi. The latter is a striking creation in polychrome marble and rich jewels. It is octagon, has a noble dome and the general effect is one of blazing grandeur. The bare chapel of the Medici contains two monuments by Michelangelo, both of supreme artistic importance. For perfection, harmony of sculpture and architecture, force, anatomy, power and volcanic strength, the tomb of Lorenzo Magnifico cannot be surpassed by anything in Christendom.

Then I went to San Marco. The church is disgustingly baroque. The chief interest center around the two cloisters and the monks' cells, etc., decorated with frescoes of Fra Angelico. In the Ospizio are the chefs d'oevres of his "chevallet" works. I admired especially a little flight into Egypt and some triptychs.

Not being a catholic, or not even being religious in the formal sense, there must be a lot in painting of this kind that escapes me. (Unless my lack of faith is an advantage, instead of a detriment.) But it takes no religious sweat to marvel at the colors of Beato Angelico's palette. And the tasteful, the primitive way he expresses motion. The quaint street scenes, lacking a third dimension. I like his work. His large crucifixion in the chapter house impressed me a great deal, especially the roguish face of the thief on the left of Christ who insulted him. (On my right). The annunciation at the head of the stairs going up to the monk's cells is also a first rank piece and it did really hold me a long while. The cells are curious and interesting. The frescoes they contain are of varying value. Fine portraits of Savanarola in his old cell. A wonderful fir tree in the center of the first cloister.

Had a very milky lunch in a dairy. Then home to rest. In Florence, I rest every day from 1 till 3 because nothing is open at that time anyhow and it is very hot. Today was a Sabatto Fascista and everything was closed in the afternoon except the churches. So, I went first to Santissima Annunziata where I admired Andrea del Sarto's frescoes. But I should see them again because I wasn't sufficiently alert to get the best out of them. The Spedali degli Innocenti has fine Luca della Robia plaques of infants in swaddling clothes. I got into the Pinacotheca free (it is payante) and saw the Adoration of the Magi by Ghirlandaijo.. He is one of my favorite painters and this is one of his finest canvasses. There are a great many figures represented but the composition is such that the canvas is not at all crowded and each fine, rude face stands out sharply. The Pinacotheca has a nice little "cocotte" collection of paintings and statues of many schools. Then after sitting in a park for a while I went to Santa Croce, a large Gothic church with a bad modern polychrome façade. The Gothic interior pleased me immediately even though it is unadorned. The open work of the wooden ceiling is fine. The church is a basilica of the Franciscan order and the place is crawling with Franciscan monks. There are some excellent Giotto and Taddeo Gaddi murals, which are very important. Then I walked home, washed up and then to Piazza Vittorio Emmanuela for a cappuccino (café crème). Then walked down the fashionable Via Tornabuoni past the fine, grim stronghold Palazzo Strozzi with well-wrought iron fixtures, and also past Santa Trinita a gothic edifice which I will have to visit when the light is better. As the sun was beginning to sink, I walked up the Lungarno Corsine and Amerigo Vespucci. An art shop caught my eye and before I knew it, I had yielded to temptation and purchased a little cast of The Venus de Medici for 25 liras. The shop was filled with copies of many paintings in the Uffizi, any of which I would have liked to have bought. The proprietor painted them. He used to do portrait paintings in Alabama, USA and urged me to buy some of his paintings, which I politely avoided. The Venus de Medici is the first objet d'art in my collection. I hope to buy many more and less humble ones. With Venus under my arm I walked along the Arno and to the Cascine Promenade. It is a lovely park in the Italian style. I sat on the river bank and watched the setting sun paint great crimson sweeps in the sky, dye the windows on the Ponte Vecchio a gay crimson and inundate all of the valley in the evening glow. In the distance was Viale dei Colle and San Miniato surmounted by "Italian clouds" of a classic whiteness. Then walked back to town, had a good dinner just off Via Tornabuoni and some ice cream on the Piazza V – Em., which was crowded with people it being Saturday night. Bought "Gringoire". It looks as though another French Revolution were not far off.

Buying postcards will send me to the poor house. I spend more on cards than for my rent and meals combined!

Sunday, July 7, 1935, Firenze

Another splendid day full of new thrills. Went in the morning directly to the Pitti gallery and was first to enter after the official guards. There are some of the most precious jewels of plastic art in the Pitti but unfortunately along side of them are many inferior paintings. I admired especially the Raphaels – portraits of Angelo Doni and his wife and the Madonna del Granduca. The latter is a heavenly creation. Play of light on the mouth and nose is quite wonderful. I don't especially care for the fat cheeked baby in her arms. I liked some portraits by Sustermans who seems to be a very good painter. Another "concert" of Georgione in same spirit as "Concert Champetre" in the Louvre. What I enjoyed – really enjoyed – the most were some Rubens. A large painting called the Consequences of War and especially "The 4 Philosophers", a group portrait of himself, brother, and 2 contemporaries. In the background is a bust of Socrates (?). There is too much weak stuff of the decadence in the Pitti gallery. No primitives at all. I saw the royal chambers and especially a wonderful bathroom used by Napoleon's Marie Louise when Nap was at Elba. It was sumptuous and the furniture was all there – untouched since the turn of the last century. Beautiful views of the Boboli garden from some of the windows.

Then I walked through the passage over the Arno from the Pitti to the Uffizi. It was Sunday and crowded with people (entrance free). But the people in the passage were far outnumbered by the paintings on the walls. The corridor is hung with portraits of everyone who ever was anybody since the beginning of time. Mostly inferior painting. But very interesting collection. Statesmen, artists, courtesans and, no doubt, some rogues. Then I walked through the Uffizi having a most wonderful visit with the canvasses that I had already seen once before. I followed a guide who talked in English, French, and German and got a great secret pleasure out of horning in on all three languages. Ran across the nice couple that I met in Perugia. Slept long after lunch and then took a tram up to Fiesole. The best views are on the right so that is where I sat. The entire valley of the Arno gradually revealed itself as the tram rose. Up on the hill was Fiesole, in a crotch between two summits. I visited the old 11th Century Cathedral which is quite wonderful for architecture. An unusual raised choir. No transepts. Gorgeous Etruscan-Romanesque arches. There was an impressive service with music going on. Then I went down to the Etruscan and Roman ruins. A small museum, the stones of an arena and a theater and large Cyclopean walls built by the Etruscans. On a fir-grown hillock, beside the mossy stones of the old Roman Theater, with a view of Tuscan hills and valleys toward the north, I sat with my back against a fir tree and read some Victor Hugo.

Then I descended and climbed up to the Franciscan convent church. I have never seen a more perfect little relic of medieval Italy. The church is of the XIVth Century in prime Florentine ogival style, recently restored after being massacred with baroque. It is warm, religious, and very beautiful. The air was heavy with incense; a Franciscan service was being intoned by the monks. I sat on the church steps and contemplated the little churchyard bounded on one side by an old cloistered passage. In one corner a bell, in the center a crucifix in a lovely little shrine, and beyond it an unbroken view of the valley of the Arno and Florence down below. I went down to see the views. Chatted with a well-traveled American tourist. Ate my supper on the church steps, steeping myself in the tranquil beauty of the scene. I drank too much white wine with my dinner. Slightly dizzy I went down for another look at the view, walked around the town square a while and then took the tram down to Florence. On the way down it was dark and the lights of Florence twinkled in the valley. I was reminded of the views of Paris from Sacré Coeur. Down into the valley of light and to my bed very early. Sleepy with wine.

Monday, July 8, 1935 – Firenze

Had a very restless night. Got up at 3 A.M. and read over diary letters, looked at postcards etc. until 4 A.M. when I fell into a fretful sleep again. Didn't wake up until the scandalous hour of 11:30 A.M. So I rushed out and up to the Academia to see the David of Michelangelo. I have rarely been so impressed by a piece of sculpture. In fact, never. I share Mary's enthusiasm for it. The conception, anatomy, and modeling are masterly. Of course, it is exceptionally well shown. The Academia has also some rather unimportant primitives. But I will never forget the strength and power in that head and the hands of David. It is the work of a genius – a super man. I bought for Mary as a birthday present a large reproduction of the statue (10 lira) and for myself some postcards of it. (1 lira 50 centesimi). Then a good lunch and home to write postcards to friends. After that, I went to the Bargello. The palazzo itself is splendid. A wonderful piece of architecture and all dripping with medieval atmosphere. The collection is much like in the Cluny museum and hence interested me a lot. Some armor, some Limoges, glassware of Venice, porcelains, faience, brass work, wonderful ivory carvings. Then some statues of Michelangelo notably Drunken Bacchus, and a winged mercury of Giovanni Bologna. Very tender, whimsical John the Baptist of Donatello. His St. George did not impress me so much. I liked the Bargello. The setting is splendid. Met a very nice American chap, Junior at Harvard, and a government major with whom I toured the Bargello. We became good friends and went to San Lorenzo together. Then to take a look at the Hospital of the Innocents. He had taken a corking good art course at Harvard and knew a lot about architecture. He gave me some tips on it. We climbed the Campanile from where one gets a fine view of Florence and excellent point of view to admire Brunelleschi's dome. Then across the Ponte Vecchio and to the Pitti which we looked at from the outside. Back to town for a good dinner and then we went to a café in Piazza Vittorio – Emmanuele and argued and talked about politics and social trends. Said good night and I went to get some ice cream and then returned to the hotel. Wrote a letter home and will go to bed shortly. Wrote letters to Tris, T.D. and Puggles.

Tuesday, July 9, 1935 – Firenze

I had intended to top off my stay in Florence by going to Vallombrosa today but I woke up too late to catch the bus so I had to change my plan. But in spite of that, I had a grand day. I was out by 8 A.M. and walked 4 miles out to the Certosa Galluzo, an old fortress-like convent built in 1341 on a hillock covered with fir and olive trees. The convent, aside from its situation and some of the cloisters, is not very interesting. But the monks are great characters. They manufacture Certisimo – a chartreuse liqueur there. I visited the Farmacia and distillery, but didn't buy any liqueur. However, I tasted some chocolate and liqueur filled candies that were very good. In the Distillery I saw a sign asking the brothers "per l'amor di Dio" to please wash the bottles well.

On the flank of the wooded hill below the convent, I found a shady spot to install myself. There I took some snapshots, read Victor Hugo and thought about Mary. She is coming back into my thoughts much more frequently now and I remember delicious details of our wonderful days together in Paris.

I got a taste of nature in the woods below the convent. I had walked out by the flat Via Nuance so I returned by the Via Vecchia which climbs some hills and has some good views of the surrounding country. Had a dairy lunch near Pitti Palace, took it very easy after lunch. I had been carrying with me all morning the David I bought for Mary so I mailed it. Also wrote Bill Fry. Sat in a café, read the paper, then in the middle of the P.M. I walked out to the Cascine and finished my Victor Hugo on a park bench. "La Rose de L'Infante" impressed me a great deal. As the shadows lengthened, I crossed the river and climbed a very steep road up Monte Oliveto (I love the names). The best view is of the fertile plain to the West, but there are also some good views of the wooded hills studded with villas to the East, above San Miniato. Then I descended and climbed again, higher, to Bellosguardo a superb point of view for all of Florence and the valley of the Arno. You almost hang over the city and the big attraction is that from Bellosguardo you see the Palazzo Vecchio, The Duomo and Campanile, the Pitti and other monuments from the façade. The setting sun was behind my back as I looked at Florence and the shadows and play of the evening light was the best I have ever seen it. I think the view from Bellosguardo is better than from Fiesole, but of course, you don't see the river or Ponte Vecchio. Crowning the hill is the Villa Umbrellina, one of the most beautiful in Florence. I slipped in for a few minutes to admire the garden but slipped out again when the caretaker came around selling tickets. Superb situation for a villa. It used to belong to a Russian nobleman.

The view was so wonderful that I wished I could draw it. I tried sketching on a scrap of paper and had a lot of fun making a terribly childish primitive drawing.

Went down to town for a big dinner after which I sat through part of a useless movie for no good reason at all.

I eat lots of ice cream. It's grand here. I am packing for tomorrow I leave Florence.

Wednesday, July 10, 1935, Hotel Roma, Bologna

After a last look at The Palazzo Vecchio I took a horse cab to the Florence station. At the station, I bought "La Franc-Maconnerie et la Revolution Intellectuelle du XVIII e Siecle" by Bernard Fay. It is more or less a collection of his lectures, which I attended this year. I read it intermittently all day, marking it carefully. It is of great interest. He has struck on something entirely <u>new</u>. A rare achievement.

A pleasant train ride through the glorious Appenines, but there were a lot of tunnels that spoiled the view a bit. Arrived in Bologna at 11:00 and put up at this good hotel, well-situated three steps from Piazza V-E.

Bologna is a city of arcades and colonnades. Every city street of any size is flanked by a colonnade. The public squares are very charming with their fountains and Gothic palaces. Bologna is full of very interesting old Palazzos, mostly in Gothic style, and largely done in brick. Historically and architecturally, it is an interesting town. But it is a cold sort of interest for it lacks any warmth of spirit and tradition. I didn't feel that Bologna had a pleasant spirit about it. Decided that half day of sightseeing was plenty for Bologna.

First I admired the old Palazzo Communale. Inside it has five staircases in a very early style. I liked best the Palazzo di Re Enzio. In the courtyard is a lovely, graceful fountain. A staircase like at The Bargello and superb Gothic architecture in brickwork. Fine windows.

Then I visited the church of San Petronio. The façade is decorated only on its lower portion. It is an example of the highest form of Gothic in Italy. A very lovely interior, long nave, high gothic vaulting. Some beautifully colored stained glass windows, but too few in number to dim the light enough. A curious meridian line area which I watched the sun creep over at noon. I liked San Petronio perhaps because it was so definitely gothic. It was left unfinished and has no transept. I had lunch that cost me too much and then went to see the leaning towers. They are interesting, I suppose, but I wasn't enthusiastic about them. Sat in a café and read, bought a ticket for La Forza del Destino, an opera of Verdi to be presented in the evening. Then I went to the Pinacotheca, which is excellent for the art of Bologna, Ravenna and Ferrara. The primitives have a little more life in their expression than the Tuscan and Siennese schools, but the expressions are so inane that the compositions lose value. Francia's work as shown is the Pinacotheca looked insipid. Raphael's St. Cecilia, the gem of the collection, is a very charming work. But I didn't like the figure of St. Cecilia herself. So dowdy, pudgy and different from Raphael's usual women. The woman on the right and the man in thought on the left are excellent. It seems to show a very, very strong influence of Michelangelo. A good Perugino if you like Perugino.

The Carracci paintings were so-so. Ludovino was the best of the brothers. Some excellent Guido Reni, especially the portraits. I began to see a bit more in Guercino. He isn't so bad as I thought. Reni's pastel "Ecce Homo" is one of the finest things I have seen. An interesting collection of modern paintings also. Some Bernardo Strozzi, but much as I like his work I can't say much for these examples of it. A very fine, astoundingly fine group of drawings by Albert Durer.

I left the Pinacotheca and walked past the University to San Giacomo Maggiore. Chiefly interesting for frescoes by Francia and Lorenzo da Costa (Francia's teacher). And a chapel in the ambulatory contains Francia's masterpiece, a Madonna with angels, musicians and four saints. It is a fine, soft painting, much like an early Raphael and raised my opinion of Francia a lot. The oratorio with frescoes of Francia and Costa all remarkably well preserved and lighted is as fine a document for those painters as the Library of the Duomo at Sienna is for Pintorrichio.

Then to the unusual church of Santa Stefano, composed of eight different buildings. It is the finest thing in Bologna. Four churches, a cloister and a courtyard all in the finest Romanesque style and constructed in warm red brick. The earliest church on the extreme left is of 800. The octagonal one is very fine, must have been a baptistery. Crypt under the main church very fine. The old cloister is of the greatest interest. A rare gem of Romanesque work. Santo Stefano is perhaps the best thing in Bologna.

I then thought I'd walk out to Madonna di San Luca, to get the famous view from the Adriatic to the Tyrenean Sea. A 2-mile colonnade leads to it. I trudged along it. It was terribly tiring. When I got to the bottom of the hill on which is the church I was too tired to go up. So I sat and ate my supper (yoghourt, bread and fruit) in the colonnade. It wasn't a nice day and the views would have been over clouded anyhow (rationalization). Took train to town. There are loads of food shops in Bologna. I bought some of those thin, crisp bread sticks and then went to the opera. Got a choice seat in the second row center of balcony and ate my bread sticks.

The opera was so-so. An amusingly fat heroine with a good voice. Lots of scenes with Franciscan monks that made a good effect in their brown cowls. A good baritone. No music that will stay with me very long. I was terribly sleepy, but I enjoyed seeing an Italian opera. The acting and staging was pretty Hamish. To bed at 1:30 A.M. The opera house roof was opened to the sky, making it very cool and pleasant.

Thursday, July 11, 1935 – Albergo, Montecarlo Calle Specchiere, Venezia

Slept late in Bologna and took a train at 11:30 for Padua. A long ride through flat agricultural country during which I read some Fay. Checked my bag at Padua station and walked into town about 2 P.M. First went to the chapel Madonna del Arena with frescoes of the life of Christ by Giotto. They are wonderful things, and very easy to admire, well lighted. I like them fully as well as those of Assisi. The Pieta is a marvel. Hardly looks like a primitive. Then in the Eremitani Church I saw some murals by Mantegna. These were very well done. He is a very athletic painter. The figures were strong and vigorous motion was well shown and they did not have any of that heavy grossness that one often finds in Mantegna. Excellent perspective.

Then down through the central squares of town: Piazza Cavour, Garibaldi, Frutti, etc. Saw the old university court and some fine old municipal buildings. Then to see Donatello's interesting equestrian statue and the church Santo Antonio. With its many domes, it looks rather oriental and Venetian. I liked its interior a lot. A long, Gothic nave surmounted by Domes. The chapels of the transept are wonderfully wrought. Many devouts were there. They touch the tombstone of the saint and pray. Saw women kissing relics and bibles, etc. It all disgusted me a bit. I don't fathom it at all. Saw some unimportant Titian murals in the Scuola del Santo, went to the lovely park-like Piazza V-E II and then walked to the station. Ate lots of ice cream. Cassato is delicious. In Venice, I took the public boat to San Marco and installed in this hotel. Good dinner and then to the Piazza. The patriarch of Venice had just died and the whole population was fighting to get into the cathedral to see his corpse. I managed to push my way in. The sight was impressive but it was treated like a public festival by the people. The priests sang mass continually. My first impressions of Venice are quite thrilling. I could write for hours about it. Suffice it to say that there was a moon over the Piazza San Marco making it look exactly as Napoleon described it. An enormous ballroom with the sky for a ceiling. To bed latish.

Friday, July 12, 1935, Albergo Montecarlo, Venezia

Up in the middle of the morning and sat on the Piazza to watch the funeral of the patriarch. There were many soldiers and still more priests, monks and church dignitaries. Even an archbishop. The funeral wasn't so impressive. I've seen better in Paris. After a pick up lunch and a look around the St. Mark's - quarter walked to Palazzo Pesaro to see the Mostra de Titian. There are too many of his things there, thus one sees the mediocre canvasses as well as the good ones. Of course, he didn't always turn out masterpieces and many of his religious pieces fall far below that classification. I was most impressed by the male portraits, the Ascension of Verona museum, and the portrait of a lovely girl called "La Bella" who this time isn't in his over-fleshy vein. Also the excellent canvas Madonna of the House of Pesaro from Frari church and the very seductive piece Danae from museum of Naples. The things sent by the Louvre are excellent examples of his finest work. Note superb composition of Venere del Pardo. The entrance price was very steep (10 L.)

Boat to San Marco and then down Riva del Schiavoni to see some churches. San Giorgio in Schiavoni is very interesting. Carpaccio murals downstairs show remarkable treatment of action and drapery for primitives. Some look much further advanced than primitive school. Upstairs Palma Vecchio decorated the Chapter House. Fine Renaissance façade. Looked at the old Arsenal nearby (port of Venice) and then returned to San Marco. Then I walked east to see more churches then you could shake a stick at. Saw San Salvatore, etc., across wonderful old Ponte di Rialto , saw the oldest church in Venice. Then after lots of walking, I saw the Frari - very fine and full of interesting monuments and Titian paintings. Returned by boat to San Marco.

On my previous ride from Palazzo Pesaro to San Marco I noted carefully, with Baedeker's help, all the old Palazzos on the Grand Canal. Excellent way to see Venetian domestic architecture of all the ages.

I forgot to say that at midday I visited San Marco. I like it immensely. It has such a rich, oriental atmosphere. It is warm and looks well loved.

Took a ½ hour gondola ride (5 lire) through small canals of Venice. The traditional beautiful Venetian courtesans at every window, of course. The gondolier sings out "cave" as he turns corners and with what dexterity they maneuver those boats! Such a restful, gliding sensation. Dangerous and romantic mode of transportation. Glided under Ponte dei Sospiri.

Had a good dinner and then coffee at a café on the Piazza. Saw nearly the most beautiful girl I've ever seen. She was Marian's type but much more beautiful, full, happy, American features. The most expressive face and gestures and an entrancing smile. Very dramatic, flowing type of brunette beauty. A lot of good it did me!

After some more ice cream (gelato) I came home to bed.

Saturday, July 13, 1935, Venezia

I committed the delicious sin once more of sleeping until noon. I can't help it. Sightseeing and eating ice cream tires me. After a snack lunch, I walked to the Academy, eager to visit it. (Had haircut) But found it closed due to the pestiferous Sabbato Fascisto. So instead, I went out to the Lido. Out and back on the snappy 'diretta' steamer, train to the beach and cabin all for 5 lira. Had the thrill of bathing in the warm, salty Adriatic and the self-satisfaction of doing a lot of gymnastics on the horizontal bars and rings on the beach. I still am a pretty good gymnast. The Lido beach is fine soft sand. Venice is full of Germans. Everywhere you turn, you see their Bavarian costumes and hear their guttural tones.

At 6 I went to 113 Ponte della Salute to meet Mrs. O'Toole. A charming Italian woman very sensitive and keen minded. A nice house and a friendly dog. We went to Harry's Bar where we had aperitifs with Mr. & Mrs. Taylor (Gladys Axman) I don't know how she got him. He's a nice chap and seemed to be completely normal – mentally quite rich. Mrs. O'Toole was exceedingly interesting. We got along very well. She recommended me to dine at "A L'Angelo", near Ponte del Angelo. A lovely terrace on the canal with a view of gondolas gliding by in the dark. Coffee on the Piazza with newspapers and so to bed.

Sunday July 14, 1935, Venezia(really written in Verona)

I slept very badly due to the pesky Venetian mosquitoes. At 4 A.M. I rose and dressed and since the hotel door was locked I stayed in my room and read Fay's book. At 6:30 A.M. I managed to get out into the street. Venice was waking up.

The thrill of being on the streets of Venice walking along the canals while the sun was yet low, watching the city's pace accelerate into the activity of a summer Sunday morning is one I will never forget. I watched the night end officially when an Italian youth came down the Calle leaning heavily on the shoulder of two of his comrades who seemed to have imbibed less. Then dawn broke. The city looked so different at that hour. Everything was clean and fresh (except human faces). The light was clear, the bread was warm, the fruit on the streets was still fresh. The people in the street were of a different sort than any other hour of the day. At first the "gens du quartier", climbing sleepily out of bed to do matutinal chores. Then I went down near the harbor. There were sailors, country people disembarking, gondoliers brushing up their gondolas. The port was the center of activity. I was impressed with the feeling that Venice – its true character – is an Oriental seaport. It still has a bit of the atmosphere of the days of the Doges but you must look for it at dawn or after dusk – not when the XXth century innovations flourish in the midday sun.

I looked around Piazza San Marco until 9 enjoying immensely the human spectacle. It was a holiday crowd and hawkers and petty thieves did a brisk traffic. I attended an early mass in wonderful old San Marco. At that time people were sleepily religious – but very religious. I don't understand it, but it's at times beautiful, at other times disgusting slavery.

At 9 I went through the Palazzo Ducale. Was impressed chiefly by the grandeur that <u>must</u> have flourished there in the old days. Tintoretto's "Paradiso" didn't bowl me over but I did appreciate the accuracy with which it was planned and the way the details stand out plainly in that enormous creation. I liked Tintoretto's work as shown in the Palazzo – easy to trace his heritage from Michaelangelo. The old prisons were forbodingly interesting. The Ponte dei Sospiri was closed so I couldn't cross it.

Then I went out to the Academia. Tho I was rather sleepy I remember well the five portraits by Titian, Carpaccio's Scuola Orola. Longhi's genre painting was amusing, as usual. I didn't appreciate the primitives as much as I should have - Lorenzetti, Bellini, etc.

I then went home (about 11:30) and closed my eyes and didn't open them until 4:30 P.M.

After dressing and shaving I went to the square. Feeling rather spiffy, I had my picture taken against a background of the Palazzo Ducale. As the sun sank I climbed the Campanile di San Marco and enjoyed the splendid panorama of Venice. An excellent way to appreciate the colors of the Venetian water and sky and to understand the position of Venice in relation to the mainland. Why a town ever grew up on those mud islands is more than I can say.

At 6:30 or so I crossed to Mrs. O'Toole's and everyone was there. Excellent cocktails on her lovely terrace. Had a grand time. Heard a slick story about <u>Pitts Sanborn's trill.</u> The crowd she had is very easy to get along with. After supper we met again on the square for the Tombola - a sort of lottery. Everyone in Venice was in the square, shouting and hoping to win money. There was a moon. Mrs. O'Toole brought her mother, a peppy old girl of 80 odd years. Mrs. O and I got along famously. I even got to put brandied sugar in her mouth. I really regret not being able to stay for the Reddentore next week. After seeing her mother home she and I took a walk along the moonlit port on the Punte della Salute. We talked over a glass of a beer. I saw her gallantly home. Not bad stuff. To bed at 12:30.

Monday, July 15, 1935 – Hotal Royal Mayer, Desenzano

Up very early in Venice. Down the grand canal on the little Vaporetto. A last look at the Palazzi, Ponte di Rialto and the incomparable Piazza. Then the train for Verona, passing through olive country. The silver trees stretched far away and in the background the mountains could be seen. But the spirit of the country was still of hilly Italian farm land.

I liked Verona, though I didn't stay very long. The Scaliger family seems to have built the place. Without the Scaligeri, Verona would be only a Roman ruin. I checked my bag at the station and took a train to Piazza Erbe. A narrow oval, filled mostly with vegetables, fruits and nick-nack stands as far as I could see. But there were some historic columns and a nice fountain. The square is bordered by Gothic and Renaissance palaces and dominated by 2 towers. Adjacent is Piazza dei Signori - one of the finest in Italy to demonstrate municipal architecture. On three sides are splendid Gothic and Romanesque palaces. On the fourth side is the gem – a symphony in stone – the Loggia del Consiglio. It is built in Renaissance style – the work of the brothers Sanmicheli. A more perfect and tasteful example of Renaissance decoration I have never seen.

Then nearby, just off the square, is Santa Maria Antica. It is Romanesque, religiously Romanesque. Splendid pillars and stern, simple yet warm vaulting. A small church, yet it flows with the simple warmth of Romanesque style. The very ultra-Gothic tombs of the Scaligeri are not so bad – but the Gothic decoration is too ruthlessly carried out. They spared none of the details.

I then had lunch and wrote my diary for previous day (late, I'm sorry). Walked across the river by the Ponte Navi and got a view of the rushing Adige and above it the green hills, dotted with castle turrets.

The sun was very hot but I went to see the Arena. Italians seem to consider the Arena of Verona its finest – at least its most typical landmark. I disagree. It's a nice Roman arena and the ruined top flight of seats is picturesque. But Verona has better things. Romanesque architecture and the Loggia are the attractions of Verona to me. (and the Museum).

Then I crossed the large Piazza Bra' and walked to the river to pay my respects at the tomb of Romeo and Juliet. A snappy little guide showed me the way across a military stable yard to the Old Shrine. It is a quiet, green little corner. A cloister, a tomb, a jet of water, a statue, and a tear. Thousands of visiting cards have been placed in the tank in the hope that their owners will be lucky in love. I had no cash in my pocket but compromised by signing my name on one of the dusty cards already in the tomb. It is a pleasant, shady shrine.

Then I walked too damn far to Porta Nuova and past Porta Palio to the church of San Zeno. Perhaps the most perfect Romanesque church and campanile I will ever see. It is done in polychrome marble. The door, ancient as time, is covered with reliefs in metal. The interior is in the lovely, simple Romanesque style. The altar is high and beneath it is the crypt, the roof supported by five columns. I liked this church of San Zeno.

Then to Castel Vecchio. I liked this the best of everything in Verona. It is a romantic old castle of the XIV built by those industrious Scaligeri. It is perfectly restored. Almost too perfectly. The restorator has injected a bit too much of his own personality and made the stern old castle a trifle on the pretty-pretty side. The banqueting hall is now a music room. But the rooms are filled with relics and some paintings that I didn't care for. There are no restrictions and I climbed all over. Little rooms on the top floor, parapets overlooking the castle yard and the authentic XIVth Century bridge over the Adige, a long mess hall for the guards with splendid refectory tables impressed me a lot. It is the kind of a castle that has an endless amount of rooms and cubbyholes. Mary would love it just as I did. I splurged on postcards.

I went to see the Duomo, which is a mixture of all styles, but a pleasing general effect rather on the Romanesque side and a quaint portal.

The Gothic church of St. Anastasia is valuable.

After a last look at the splendid Loggia I left and caught a train for Desenzano.

What a thrill when I first caught sight of the long, thin finger of Sirmione pointing out into Lago di Garda. Carried my bag to the best hotel in town. Felt like acting the seigneur so I did.

Had an over expensive dinner at the hotel, drank coffee and wrote lots of letters (one to Sibyl). Walked around the port and admired the moon over the Lake and so to bed.

Tuesday, July 16, 1935

One of the finest days I have spent since I have been in Italy. I will never forget it. I got up about 8 and set out to find a good way to get to Sirmione. There was a bus and a steamboat, both cheap. But Tennyson's poetry kept drumming in my head. I had to row out from Desenzano to Sirmione. So I made a price with a man who hoisted a funny little sail, (quite useless except as a sun shade) placed his oars and we set out. The water of Lago di Garda in the morning is ruffled by a cool breeze from the mountains, but it is still a rich azure-blue. To the south was the peninsula of Sirmione. To the north rose the blue Brecian Alps. A bright blue sky and hard white clouds to wreath the mountain crests. I have never seen a more beautiful lake. Not even Nemi approaches it. We rowed and chatted in Italian. The old chap at the oars was an amusing peasant and we got on well. The scenery was intoxicating. And the pleasure of "rowing out from Desenzano" went right to my head. As I said in a letter to Dr. Lockwood, I feel tonight as though I had been hitting sentimental nails on the head all day with very sentimental hammers. The water grew calm and greenish as we neared shore.

I treated the oarsman to some of the sweet vino di Lugano (bianco), tipped and paid him, bought myself some Lugano for lunch and then went off to see Sirmione.

First to the castle built by the Scaligeri in exactly, the same style as the one at Verona. A nice old castle right on the port with drawbridge, etc.

Then I walked up to the end of the island. Sirmione reminds me irresistibly of Capri. If you cut the long peninsula arm that comes from the shore, the extremity is just the shape of Capri; a small and a large hill with a town in the middle, and a castle (the grotto) on the left hand hill. The silvery olive trees against the azure water are also like Capri scenery. The grotto di Catullo is an old ivy covered ruin of romantic interest. It crawls with lizards who basked their little bodies in the hot sun. They say the

Grotto is the ruins of a villa of Catullus' time, and of Roman baths.

For 2 lira, I spent all day swimming and rented a suit into the bargain. I swam out into the shallow lake, sunbathed on the rocks, looked at the mountains in the bluish distance – and read Catullus. Ate lunch – bread, deliciously piquante, ripe Gorgonzola cheese and vino di Lugano. After 4:30, completely saturated with the beauty of Sirmio and with Catullan iambs, I climbed down and went to the town. Had coffee and wrote lots of letters (home and to Dr. Lockwood, my Latin Professor).

Had a fine and inexpensive dinner on a terrace with glorious view of the sunset over the Alps. Then the boat back to Desenzano. A bright yellow moon rising fat and jolly over the hills. Chatted in German with a nice German priest on the boat.

And so here I am in Desenzano, ready to go to bed and officially close one of the most radiantly sentimental days of my life.

Tennyson, Catullus, Italia, Sirmione, Desenzano. Those words stand for some of the most invaluable treasures in the world.

Wednesday, July 17, 1935 – Albergo Lusanna 11 Via Vittor Pisani Milano

Through some strange combination of happiness and expectation, I didn't sleep for a long time last night. My mind was very keen, clear and active. I felt supremely self-confident. Plans kept running through my head: plans for a journalistic career as foreign correspondent, plans to organize political discussion forums at Haverford, to write up my trip under the title "Travels without a donkey", to write a book on the dictatorships in Europe today, to revolutionize the American book business by publishing cheap $1 paper bound editions of new books as on the Continent as "Continental Editions" Inc., etc., etc.

This morning I got up early in Desenzano, had a last look at the blue lake and peninsula of Sirmione and took an 8:30 train for Milano. All morning I spent reading letters at the American Express. What a glorious batch of letters. Mary wrote me a note embodying all her sweet understanding and mature intelligence in 3 superbly written pages. I probably love her. I hope so. Bill wrote bubbling with love and excitement over some new girl. Pilster appears to be ccarrying on the glorious traditions and will spend the year in Europe. I hope he falls in love while he's here. It helps. Dave Hart is spending a very usual existence but his mind is well occupied as ever. Poor Virginia is homeward bound on a freighter, stony broke, no job. I hope she doesn't drift into a shameful, horrible obscurity through lack of money. Mother and Daddy are smeared with jam and are watching the farm wax fruit with the seasons. Ma and Baba are in England, as comfortable and unworldly as ever. And Mary. Where is she? Her spirit and laugh is with me at this moment.

Changed money and bought my ticket to Stresa, Geneva and Paris (214 lira). Around the Lakes would have cost a damn sight more. I'm sorry to miss it but I don't want to hit Paris stony broke. Must have enough for cafe-crème. I don't have nostalgia for Paris because Italy is so perfect. But I'll be glad to get back. I wrote lots of letters – dashed them off to everybody; Uncle Fred, family, Virginia, Palister.

During the lunch hour, I visited the Duomo. The description of it as a fountain turned to stone is exact. The effect is breathtaking. The interior is finer even than the exterior because of its simplicity. Splendid vitrailles glow with a medieval warmth and spangle the pavement with soft gules of light. Out of the darkness rise masssive Gothic pillars crowned by well wrought capitals in German style. But for some reason, I like Chartres better. The ambulatory of Chartres is unmatched. And then the Vitrailles are of the stuff that the hand of man will never equal. Also the crazy spire of Chartres and especially its romantic position thrill me more than the Duomo of Milano.

I climbed the campanile where one sees the forest of buttresses and spires, a wonderful way to appreciate how medieval masons did their work.

A view of all Milan. It is a city of the fascist regime. That is its only atmosphere. A new, spick and span, thriving, throbbing metropolis. It is more American than anything in Italy. But it is hot! God, it's hot.

I went to S. Maria delle Grazie and saw the Cenacolo Vinciana. It is on the end wall of a bare, uninspiring monk's refectory, one used as a stable by Napoleon. The paint is slowly peeling and may not last long, but enough was to show the warmth, artistry, mastery of line and perspective and color that went into it. I like the faces. Each one is a character study of the apostle whom it represents. All types of men are represented at that table. Leonardo must have understood human nature, a very hard thing to do.

Then I had my broken watch chain repaired and just sat in a coffee house reading all letters, etc. At 6 I went to a movie. The perfect beauty and scintillating sex appeal of Anna Sten in Nana. In Italian, which was good for what ails my Italian. A good fish and tongue dinner at a little place near the Duomo and then home to bed quite tired.

Thursday, July 18, 1935 – Albergo Reale, near the station, Stresa-Borromeo
Well, little diary, you have gone places and seen things. You've been to Domodossola all by yourself and back again to Stresa to me. I left you for a while, quite unintentionally and was overjoyed to retrieve you.

Up early this morning in Milano and took a train through the rather dull Lombard plain to Lago Maggiore. The wooded shores of the lake were quite beautiful and also quite un-Italian. Italy stopped when Lago Maggiore began. It is on a grander scale than Italy. But the Borromeo islands are still Italy in spirit. At Stresa I walked to the Lido where I swam in the lake, dove, read Fay and climbed up a rope. Also ate a very little lunch. The sky clouded over, the water became choppy, and it started to rain. The first rain since I left Paris except for a bit at Genzano. When it stopped raining, I walked home and then I set out for a walk in the hills. Went up for about an hour to Alpino, way above Stresa from where you discover a majestic panorama of the Lake, the Alps and the islands. But the sky was overcast and the water looked gray and forbidding. When it drizzled, I ate bread and cheese under a railway bridge. Then I went up further, left the road, and plunged off into forest paths and across fields. Came upon a stony brook just like at Hill Farm. Trudged up through the wet, fragrant forest until rain came again. I took refuge in an abandoned hay shed where I sat on sheaves of oat and straw while literally sheets of water came down out of the skies and ran down the straw roof of my shelter. I let my mind wander over a thousand things. (999 were Mary) (How she would have loved it. It was like our Sunday at Gyf sur Yvette, Vallée de Chevreuse) I tried to count up the nice girls I have been interested in in my life. Got to 20 and lost track. Felt happy, healthy, and strong. What a wonderful summer. The woods were very American. When the rain stopped a bit, I climbed down from my perch, pulled my pants above my knees, and tramped barelegged through the wet woods. Then down to Stresa with a bright blue flower behind my ear.

Good dinner at the hotel where I am taking pension for the 2 days I expect to be here. It's a good hotel and cheap.

A few cakes, coffee and wine in the town of Stresa where I wrote to Bill, Sally Kunkel and Dave Hart and back to bed. A nice view of lights across the lake from the Promenade. Good night, you miscreant little diary.

Friday, July 19, 1935 – Albergo Reale, Stresa
A splendid day devoted entirely to what might be called physical culture. Slept like a brick, got up early and read papers on the lakeshore. The water was blue but not azure. A dark, thick blue. Stresa looked more Italian under the sunshine than yesterday in the rain. About 9 I rowed out to Isola Bella. Visited the sumptuous chateau and beautiful, well-manicured Italian gardens. Saw original draft of the agreement of Stresa signed by Mussolini, Ramsay Mac Donald, etc. Also, the table at which they all sat. Then I rowed to Isola Madre, a long pull. The garden is more informal and in the English style. More sympathique. Many subtropical plants. White peacocks just as Mary and I saw at Vincennes that day. That "camel and picture" day. Then round back to Stresa, another long pull. The whole business took 3 hours. I was at the oars about ½ the time.

The view of the bluish Alps and the towns nestled on the lakefront was magnificent. But Garda is less exploited and pleases me more as a lake. Though of course it has no wooded hills, and they are worth a lot.

I ate my bread and cheese for lunch on a shaded rock in the middle of a stream a few minutes up the mountainside from the stream. Then I broke into a nearby pasture and lay on my back gazing at a splendid panorama of lakes, island, and mountains. Then I descended and went swimming, dressing in the bushes. Finished Fay's book on the beach. He was in too much of a hurry to finish his book. The end disappointed me. I put down my book and struck out for a little island between Isola Bella and Isola Pescatori; about 1 ½ km off shore. At least that far. After swimming about 20 minutes to ½ hour, I got pretty damn tired but plugged on. Then I got a cramp in the right leg. I hailed a nearby boat and they rowed me to shore – for a price, to be sure. It never entered my foolish head what would have happened if there had been no boat nearby. I was only a few score metres from shore when the cramp came. There must be some hidden power of love that is watching me constantly and saving me from the consequences of the foolish things I sometimes do.

On shore, I chatted with some Italian boys. Tried to explain the game of American football in my broken Italian. Before supper, I walked about ½ hour up a path in the woods and watched the sunset over the mountains and lake. Ate like a horse at dinner. Had coffee and ice cream in town. And now I'll go very gladly to bed. I got butter and jam with my breakfast at this hotel. An unheard of luxury.

Saturday, July 20, 1935 – Hotel Nouvelle Gare, Rue des Alpes, Geneva, Switzerland

I left Italy this morning but perhaps to dull the blow, nature had drenched Lago Maggiore in rain and enshrouded her in gray clouds. So I shed no tears as I sped across the border. Left at 10:30, rushed through the Simplon tunnel, pulled by a clean electric train. Then as soon as we left the tunnel in Switzerland we were in the majestic, overpowering Alps. Snow on many of them. Mountain torrents, etc. Strange that the scenery is so "big" and the people so "small". I rather enjoyed the official luggage and passport business. They were very nice about it. Spoke all languages and read papers in all languages except English on the train. Then around Lac Léman with a glimpse of stern, gray Chillon. The weather was bad and rainy. Arrived Geneva about 4. Went to American Express. Few important letters and one from Bernstein Line about my cabin. Bought French francs. Put up in this plain hotel. Walked around Geneva and looked at the unimpressing League of Nations buildings. Was very tired. Had dinner at a wonderful cheap place 7 Rue du Cité. Walked around the old part of the town which is very up and downsy and picturesque. Went to see Charles Boyer in "La Bataille" wonderful war picture illustrating Japanese psychology, damn good.

It seems to be a pretty quarter my hotel is in. The street corner on which I live was occupied by 3 "poules" last night. The surest sign that I am no longer in Italy. Bon soir. It seems strange to hear French again on the streets. I rather miss Italy, now I'm out of it. I was happy there.

Sunday, July 21, 1935 – Geneva

Slept very late and got up very refreshed before noon and walked to Chemin Rigot. Presented myself at the Union Internationale des Etudiants and was immediately taken in hand by Mrs. Tulles, the directrice. Lunched then with a group of very sympathique young people, played ping pong, talked. Talked to Prof Mitrany who is conducting a seminar there. I am trying to be admitted to the course for 1 week. I said I knew a lot about propaganda in international politics. Went swimming in the icy waters of the lake from somebody's private beach. Rode there with some girl on a bicycle. Had tea at the union and talked French. A very pleasant "international" afternoon. Went to look at the new Palais des Nations. I could write a good article about it calling it the white elephant of international brotherly love. The baby on the doorstep of the community of nations. From its terrace, one has a splendid view of Geneva, Lac Léman, the mountains, Mt. Blanc, etc. Had a cheap supper at my little "Rat qui rit" coffee and papers at a café and so to bed early and quite content for tomorrow at 9 I am to try to make a big impression on Mrs. Hadden who runs the Students Union.

Monday, July 22, 1935 – Geneva

I spent the day at the very pleasant process of making my adjustments at the Students Union. Up early and bought Paris and Milan papers which I read under the trees in the League park. Then to the Union for a Seminar on "peaceful change" all morning. I did a lot to liven up their rather idealistic and vague arguments. An interesting morning though nothing much was done in the way of decisions. Ate lunch there. The community spirit is quite wonderful and old Prof. Mitrany keeps very youthful with all those striplings. Two chaps from English Debating Society of Sciences Po were there as well as Joan Limburg, late of Dalton School. Several interesting men, less interesting women.

In the P.M. I did bits at Amerexco about my ticket home. Then met some of the students (1 French fellow, 3 girls) and we tried to go sailing but it was too late. We beered instead. Talked lots of French. Dinner at the Union was a gay birthday party for one of the fellows with lots of fun and parlor games. I left when dancing started – not to run the danger of stealing anybody's girl and to get home early. Walked home under the stars. Wonderful view of Mt. Blanc today clear and white in the dazzling sunlight. I eat lots of the good Swiss chocolate. My 4 languages are an immense advantage.

Tuesday, July 23, 1935 – Geneva

Today has been so full of new avenues of experience and new triumphs if I may say so. Up early and read the papers walking to the Union in the glorious morning sun. The seminar was dreadfully elementary but I did my bit to liven it up. Afterwards I volunteered in the League of Nations Committee to rewrite Art XIX. Some job! Had a financial talk with Mrs. Hadden and made a big impression on her by flattering her Union. She knows Caroline at Geneva. She's a toothy, officious woman, the kind that "means well". Her husband is a very fine, though browbeaten gentleman.

I shelled out 10 francs ($5) with a promise to send five more dollars later from America.

After lunch went to town with a Pole, speaking French and we had been with a French chap – we three. Back to the Union to hear Pittman Potter, arbitrator for Abyssinia, talk on Italo-Abyssinian conflict. He knew very little about it and didn't impress me. I popped lots of questions at him.

The big event today was Tamara. She is Polish, 26 years old, carries herself beautifully like a dancer. Blonde hair and very Polish mannerisms, mixed with Russian. We walked and talked before supper, getting home latish. I presented her with a peacock's feather. She knows a lot about people and life. Has lived and loved a lot.

After supper, I went to a party given by Helen Hiett, an American on the top floor of a house near the Lake. A balcony. There was Tamara, the hostess and her American sister, a Yugoslav, 2 Germans, an Englishman, a Dane and I, whatever I am. (Everyone thinks I'm Italian). After drinking and singing together until midnight, we went beering. Then I walked Tamara home to the Union, the process taking 1 ½ hours. I had time to whisper many sweet nothings in her ear, put a flower in her hair, fail to kiss her, discuss all sorts of human values and fall for her name and her bright Polish scarf. At the end she rested her head on my shoulder and decided that I was just a très gentil garcon. That seems to be my fate, despite my little occasional successes. A nice boy – but NO John Gilbert. Bon Soir. A very happy day, full of new and promising contacts.

P.S. The next morning, looking at Tamara in the morning light I realize the reason I like her is that she combines very neatly the maturity and savoir faire of Virginia with the vivacity and intelligence and Slavic allure of Mary. But she doesn't combine them perfectly. She piques me. Not too much more.

Wednesday, July 24, 1935 – Geneva

Up and out to The Union only to find no course – professor sick. So, I read my papers under a tree in the League Park and also rewrote Art XIV in the Union library. Then I went sailing on the Lake with Thierry (French fellow from Sciences Po) and Dick Cutler, an American girl qui n'est pas mal and some other girl called Gertrude (elle est môche). The sailing was grand sport. Thierry and Dick did the navigating because they knew how. The sun and wind, etc. were grand. We lunched on cheese, bread, plums, and chocolate. Then I slept for 2 hours in the afternoon and then put on my white suit and went up to The Union. A testimonial dinner to Prof. Mitrany (swell grub) after which he made a good tho idealistic talk on the press and international relations. He's been on the "Manchester Guardian" and knows good people. Clear but not novel ideas on propaganda.

Went out with Thierry but did nothing much - coming home I met up with a Pole from the Union. We had a beer and a Kirsch together and talked and at 12:30, I came home to bed. An unimportant day. Not enough Tamara. I was too quick.

Thursday, July 25, 1935 – Geneva

Up and to the Union with my papers. But breakfast first in a patisserie where I met two "goils" from the Bronx and gave them tips on Italy. The seminar was good. A good argument for optimism about the League showing what a changed morality it has already introduced. Then a hot discussion on revision started, led by Tamara for Poland but the Prof. cut it off when it got interesting. Ate lunch there then came in town. Money troubles at Amerexco. No news about my check yet. Rested then sat on a bench on the Quai just watching people go by for two hours. It rained so I sat in a café. Then ate supper of bread, Gorgonzola, and grapes under a tree in a public square. Went to a dance with the Union crowd at a hotel behind the new S.O.N. Spent most time with Dick Cutler and a fine girl. Rather nice evening. Walked home with Joan Limburg (of all people) and a Persian diplomat, "Ali Baba". It rained. Money worries me a bit.

Friday, July 26, 1935 – Geneva

My last full day, I believe, at Geneva this trip. And what a day! The League of Nations committee read its stupid report at the seminar, which I attacked vigorously. Advanced theory that Covenant is quite a strong document. Only the volonté of the nations is weak.

Ate lunch there. Tamara was friendly. Went to town and had an enormous load taken from my heart when the letter from Paris honoring my check arrived. I took the money largely in $.

Then I went to get my wash at a little blanchisserie. They charged me twice what it was worth, I refused to pay. We argued and I called a gendarme. The whole affair was most protracted but rather amusing and good for my French. They thought I was French. In the end, I had to pay the scandalous price she asked, of course. Then to the Union to hear a lecture by a German on Nazi foreign policy. His explanations were exactly, word for word what I had said all winter long at the Sciences Po English Debating Society. He knew his stuff and it was most interesting to see his German mind at work.

Took leave of the Union and paid the stiff sum they ask.

Had an enormous but cheap dinner in town.

Then to a dance, informal, on Rue Peschier, given by Posnansky, editor of Journal des Nations. The Union crowd, a select few at least, were there. Hietts were there. But most important was Tamara. I had just enough Vodka to get into fine fettle. She read Polish poetry to me and I described sunsets over Assisi to her. We strolled homeward together getting more enchanted with each other every minute. Along the lakefront we sat and read Lamartine's "Le Lac", which, in many ways, was beautifully appropriate. I made her. At the crucial moment, I pulled from my pocket the coral necklace from Capri and attached it on her neck. She melted into my arms and stayed melted. She likes me – even loves me – very much. It has been a sweet and unexpected romance for her. We walked slowly home, stopping frequently. She came out to the bottom of the garden in her negligee to kiss me goodbye – Au revoir -vraiment <u>au revoir</u>. I have a trinket – her hair band – to remember her by. She is 26 and coming to NY and will write me. A sweet breeze from the Polish fields, half-Bohemian, half aristocrat, half-Mary, half-Virginia. Marvelous understanding of people. And the most intoxicating Slavic allure – Tamara.

Saturday, July 27, 1935 – "Les Glycines, Rue de Jules Chaplain Paris VI

A splendid day of mental hopscotch. Up at 6 A.M. to go sailing with some Union students, but since there was no wind they didn't show up and I returned to bed and slept until high morning. Then lunch at the Rat qui Rie and aboard the 13:20 train for Paris.

All the way, I just slept and thought about my life and women and read some of Leconte de Lisle's workman-like verses.

I thought about Tamara. She was a sweet and perfect experience. Nothing to detract from its beauty. A walk at sunset together, a peacock feather, a glance or two, a few words in a garden, a glass of vodka, some lines of Polish poetry, "Le Lac" by Lamartine, a coral necklace from Capri, an embrace, a last kiss in the early morning at the bottom of the garden sparkling with the dew. Of such stuff was our friendship made. She is much my senior but I felt that she did look up to me. Il parait que je plais aux femmes.

Helen Hiett said last night I have a lot of poise. If it is true, it is because I have forced poise on myself. I am really inside of me, as awkward as a country bumpkin and twice as self-conscious. But I act outwardly as though I were cool as a cucumber. Thus, they think I have poise. I thought of Mary as Paris approached. A Pole on the train translated for me the words that Tamara wrote in Polish for me. They mean "Nostalgie – après toi" but in Polish it means much more and is much sweeter than that. A sad, delicious melancholy after a loved one has gone. "Tu es comme un doux soufflé de vent des champs Polonais" I told her as we parted. What will happen if we meet in N.Y.? Also thought of plans to return for a year's study in Geneva. The atmosphere there is one I like.

Paris – je t'adore. I'm back again. This time my feet and heart just took up again where it had been broken off last June. By habit, I strolled from this excellent little hotel, where they know me, to the Dome. By sweet and unforgettable habit, I sipped my "bock"! Then took a sentimental tour of the quartier, stopped at the door of 214 Bld. Raspail, the door of 3 Rue de la Grande Chaumierè and the door of 4 bis Rue de Jules Chaplain then home to bed.

The crowd at the Dome is more tourist and international than when I left and a larger crowd. The French faces lack virility and strength compared with Italians. Mais Paris, Je t'aime toujours.

Sunday, July 28, 1935, Les Glycines Paris

A very enjoyable day with the Crawfords. I got up around 9 and wrote letters to Ma and Baba, Fred, Mrs. Tullis, etc., then I took a walk to the Luxembourg. Went into the galleries and admired again La Pensée de Despoujols. Saw a little painting of "Concert Colonne" which reminded me of happy days with Mary. Then lunch sitting on a chair in the Luxembourg Garden - bread, paté and a tomato. Then I came home and found that the Crawfords expected me for lunch so I went with them to the Lotus. Bill is fine and has been working hard (?) and having lots of women. Then we went to the Champs – Elysée for café (Florian's). Then we came home. Bill came to my hotel where we looked at my souvenirs de voyage and bulled about women. Out to the Dome for a beer and some more talk. Before we knew it it was 7:30. We all ate together (Bill, Mrs. C and I) at Dominique's - excellent Russian cooking. Then we went to the Dome (just Bill and I) and who should come along but Jean Vaujany, slightly drunk. He kept us until 12:30 telling about all the American women he had slept with. But it was a very pleasant day. Seeing Bill again and Paris and the Luxembourg and talking over the wonderful year we have both had.

Monday, July 29, 1935, Les Glycines, Paris

Rather a Haverford day. Rushing downtown to get my steamer ticket, I saw Sandy Wood and Sid Hollander at the Surcouf. I jumped off the bus and we had breakfast together. They are going back to USA today. Then I went to the bank. Lots of letters from home. Caroline's summer is working out all right. Virginia has worries, mostly maternal or obstetrical. Then right over to Bernstein Line where with no trouble at all I got my ticket. I am sailing tomorrow. I really don't realize it and probably won't realize the real sadness of leaving Paris until the boat starts to pull away from Le Havre. The rest of the morning spent getting my trunks ready, chatting with Bill. Lunch with "sole frite" at the Surcouf. Then after lunch downtown with Bill. I cabled family and Ma and Baba. To the American Embassy where we called on good old, ever youthful Molly (Mrs.) Murray.

Then we had tea with Mrs. Crawford's Count de l'Asturie at her home and Bill and I adjourned to the Luxembourg. By some unspoken understanding between us we both wanted to be photographed together. So we did. God! How well we know each other! Through and through. We sat and talked in that exquisite dream garden. We were to meet Bob Lewis and Glessner for supper but they didn't show up so we dined together at Krimsky's. Glorious Russian meal improved by a sexy brunette across the aisle who flirted with us.

After supper, at the Dome, we ran into Glessner and Lewis with 2 smooth American babes. We all went dancing at Casio and then to Les Oubliettes where I enjoyed very much the lusty, old French songs and the interesting décor. The babes, especially one tall brunette, were smooth. Too bad Glessner stuck so close. Getting that whiff of America before sailing was just what I needed. A nice way to spend my last night in Paris, linking up the old life with the new.

Bon soir, bonne nuit, ma chère Paris je te quitte pour peu de temps, j'espère.

From July 30 to August 9, 1935 at sea on S.S. Ilsenstein, Arnold Bernstein Line

Written August 8, 1935

The trip has been interminably long, but has changed considerably since it started. The first few days aboard I was bored stiff so took to going around with a hard drinking loose talking crowd. They are very quick-witted but only artificial and smutty. Sort of a racetrack crowd. I have as roommate a Robert Brain, Franco- British advertising man. Interesting chap. A violinist – astronomer, tubby and cheerful, dispenses cigars and stories. There are many others. A newlywed couple – beautiful, worldly-wise wife and baby-faced husband. My table is very dull. Hardly any conversation.

The nicest person on the boat is Mme. Georgette Mauquin, Franco-American wife of a physicist and none too happily married. She is very sweet, intelligent, and demure. I want to see her on shore.

The latter part of the trip has been better. I got over a vague blueish feeling at leaving France – attended German beer parties, dances, etc., with great pleasure. Acted as a cockney waiter, Italian waiter, and a lover in 4 languages on amateur night.

But tomorrow, the 9th, we land. I have read "One More River" by Galsworthy, ""Cranquebille" and others by Anatole France and "Juan Discovers America" by Eric Linklater. It is a bubbling, enthusiastic impression of the American scene by a clever, imaginative Scotchman. A silly but amusing thread of plot to tie together impressions of this romantic land of opportunity that I will see again tomorrow. The book has whetted my appetite considerably to plunge once more into the thick of the American scene. I hope that acclimation will not be difficult. I must not live on the memories of my perfect year abroad – of adolescent freedom. I must create new interests in America and center my life about them, giving only a proportional space to European memories. While I am in America, America must be my life, not Europe.

Tomorrow we land and I will have the strange thrill of seeing once more the faces of people who really love me. The Bernstein Line is very, very satisfactory considering its cost. They do a lot for you.

I am not completely "chez moi" on a ship. I am a land animal. There is always something in the background against which my mind must fight and I am not at ease, although I may be brimming with health. There is little to do but smoke and drink, two very poor pastimes, for all the times I have indulged in them. I did accomplish one thing. I learned to smoke cigars.

Article from Haverford College Magazine - 1935

Below Avignon

By GEORGE B. BOOKMAN

A
T ANY time of the day, the Gare de Lyons always seems to be full of people rushing off from Paris to distant parts of France. On this particular morning in early June the platform was crowded with travelers trying to pass the time until the starting whistle. French people have always impressed me as a race that hates to catch trains at the last minute. You always see them arriving well in advance of traintime. They waste no politeness in claiming the best possible seat and then set, very carefully, about the business of installing themselves for the trip. For the duration of the train ride each French voyager creates for himself, in his corner of the compartment, a comfortable, middle-class home in miniature. That bit of wooden bench takes on the character of its occupant for a few hours. The individuality of American train-travelers seems blotted out by the plush stuffiness of the railroad cars. Frenchmen, on the contrary, create a bit of their own personality when they take a seat for a train ride, and the character of the compartment is altogether subordinated.

I had arrived early to watch the spectacle and had chosen an empty compartment. Before we started a young man came in and sat down on the bench opposite me. He was wearing the English national costume, brown coat and well-worn grey flannel trousers, so I asked him a question in English. We chatted on the way down from Paris. He was bilingual, a French-man who had always lived with English people in Geneva, doing secretarial work for the League of Nations. The country we were passing through became greener, more agricultural. For a time we followed a lazy, shady canal and passed snug-looking barges. The landscape was the sort of thing that Corot would have painted very beautifully—many shades of green, trees that looked all leaf, patches of cool water. Our talk palled a bit so the internationalist busied himself with "Foreign Affairs" and I leafed through some poetry of Victor Hugo.

I was headed for Avignon. It seemed a good way to start a summer trip which, I hoped, would eventually take me along the Riviera and then through Italy. I knew, rather vaguely, that the Popes had once lived in Avignon. I thought of it as a barren sort of place, probably dominated completely by the papal palace. But I had little curiosity about Avignon, be-

17

382

THE HAVERFORDIAN

cause all my hoping, planning and dreaming for this vacation junket had been centered on Italy.

Five hundred years ago Avignon was entirely dominated in fact and in spirit by the palace of the Popes, who had taken flight from hostile Rome and built themselves a stronghold on the banks of the Rhone. Today Avignon is still very Catholic, still clerical, but the empty papal palace does not set the tone of the town. Today Avignon is the seat of an army corps and the spirit of the town is typified better by the hundreds of soldiers, both black and white, who overrun the streets, the cinema theatres, and the sidewalk cafés. The word "Pope" no longer sums up the spirit of the place, even though the sand-colored mass of the palace still stands out against the sun and a battlemented wall still circles the town.

My first Sunday morning in the South of France I climbed the Dome Rock on which the Pope built his fortress and looked at the valley beyond. With the passing of centuries, the Rhone has cut a broad, silvery path through the heart of the wine-country of Provence. Just over the edge of the cliff I could see the fawn-colored roofs of Avignon, clustered close together inside the turreted walls, and far below, the ruins of the old Pont d'Avignon, on which these happy people are said to have danced together, jutted out into the swift-flowing waters. On the opposite bank of the river remains of a castle and a fortified tower built to command the bridge, reminded me of the feudal history of the town. But I turned my back on the river and looked at those tiled roofs and Avignon became once more a centre of the wine industry, a pillar of middle-class, home-loving France, and a soldier's town.

* * *

I never did find out what Whitmonday means to the Catholics. To me it meant seeing the Pont du Gard, Nimes, Arles, Tarascon and a bullfight. It meant laughing and drinking wine and singing in the sun with the people of Provence, holidaying under Mediterranean skies.

In the case of most of the cities I visited I had some slight shred of knowledge on which to pin all my later impressions. The beauty of the women of Arles was the hook on which I expected to hang my memories and experiences in that town. But when I finally trundled down the shady main street in a crowded bus on Whitmonday, I saw that the reputation of the ladies of Arles was chiefly legendary. I went to a bullfight instead.

Arles has a romantic old pile of a church, Romanesque door, sundappled courtyard and all; it has the broken remains of an antique theatre.

18

BELOW AVIGNON

But what I shall always remember about Arles is its bullring. The legions of Caesar brought to Arles the strength to erect an enormous amphitheatre, towering three arches high, steeply banked by stone seats. Today just enough of it has crumbled down to make it a medium between the glory of Rome and the bourgeois enthusiasm of southern France. The arena, in its French decadence, softens the Roman qualities in these Frenchmen; and with the grandeur of its proportions it ennobles their Gallicism. These people are the better for their arena: Panem et circenses.

Together with a thousand or so French families I pushed my way into the enclosure and climbed the great stone steps to one of the upper rows. It was my first bullfight and I sat on the very edge of the stone bench. Several enthusiasts near me were examining "form sheets," picking the bulls and the toreadors who looked promising. A large section of the stand was occupied by a brass band, evidently home-grown, that coughed and wheezed with just enough cadence and tempo to produce something sounding vaguely like the Toreador song from "Carmen." Entire families had turned out in troop formation to watch the bullfights. Those who had come bareheaded shaded themselves from the sun with sheets of newspaper. Women waved handker-chiefs, children climbed over each other, men laughed and slapped their knees. Some sang, others sat staring in tense anticipation at the ring.

Far below, at the bottom of the stone wall formed by the tiers of stone galleries, a dirt enclosure had been carefully raked and swept for the fights. At the far end, opposite the spot where I was sitting, a heavy wooden gate swung open and the band of Spanish toreadors and matadors marched proudly into the dirt ring. They waved their tri-cornered hats and bowed low to acknowledge the applause of the crowd. They were dressed in the bright silk costume that I had always associated with Spanish bullfighters. With supreme self-confidence they took up their posts around the ring and waited for the bull.

At a given signal from a toreador gates on the side of the ring just below me were opened and a heavy bull rushed out into the ring. It was a fine specimen, with long, dangerous-looking horns. For a minute the bull seemed bewildered but then it caught sight of one of the toreadors, lowered its head, pawed the ground and charged. The man slipped behind one of the wooden screens that are placed at convenient intervals around the wall of the ring, and the bull crashed ponderously into the wall. Most of the men in the audience rose to their feet and yelled for action. The six toreadors cautiously approached the bull on foot, holding darts poised to throw. The

19

THE HAVERFORDIAN

animal was at bay and knew it. It breathed heavily through its nostrils and snorted at the attackers. When the toreadors were about five feet away the bull charged; they sidestepped and as it lumbered by they threw their darts and stuck them in its flank. The bull then tried to shake the darts from its back; it jumped in the air, landing heavily on all fours, it lowered its head and bucked, sunfished, and kicked. But the darts stuck. Then the matador chosen to deliver the final stab, climbed over the low wooden wall and approached the bull. Hidden behind his scarlet cape was a thin steel sword. The matador bowed to the ladies in the stands, motioned to his assistants to retire and then set about the business of killing the bull. For a moment or two he waltzed around the animal, angering it by flourishing the crimson cape under its nose. The bull tried to catch the matador in its horns, but the matador always stepped agilely aside. The men in the crowd were on their feet again, watching for the blood to flow. The bull came to rest, pondering the next move and trying to catch its breath. The matador stood just in front of the animal's head, bared the steel blade, rose up on his toes, and then with lightning speed plunged the sword deep into the bull's shoulder. For ten seconds the bull swayed and then pitched heavily to earth. A pool of thick blood formed where its head touched the ground.

The crowd shouted hoarse approval of the matador, men threw their hats into the ring, the band struck up "Toreador." The heavy gates at the far end of the ring opened, two stout truck horses came out, a harness was hitched to the dead bull and its body was dragged in triumph three times around the ring, to the accompaniment of martial music and lusty cheering.

20

SUMMER, 1936: GENEVA, ITALY, AUSTRIA, HUNGARY, POLAND AND HOME

Back home from France, I returned to College at Haverford to finish my Senior year. Bill and I both took exams covering the work done abroad and did very well. I resumed my major in Political Science with Prof. John Herndon and took other courses. Graduated in the Spring Phi Beta Kappa. In my final year, worked on the Haverford News, saw a lot of a girl called Eleanor Brodsky (who later married a guy in St. Louis), went to the Senior Prom (I think) with Toussia Kramer, daughter of my mother's Russian friend, Isa Kramer. Toussia later married a doctor named Kermit Pines who, as it turns out, had a brother who once seriously dated Ruth Bowman.

After graduation, I had a scholarship to return to the International Students Union (Union Internationle des Etudiants), in Geneva, thanks to the good impression I made the previous summer on Mrs. Maude Hadden, the American millionaire lady who supported it. So I spent most of July and August 1936 studying and absorbing international impressions in Geneva. One particular friend was a Hungarian girl whose family I later visited in Budapest, and a young Polish chap named Wladimir Wachkowski, whose family invited me to Warsaw. So on my way home I made a swing, first to Italy to meet up with Johnny Pugliese (Sebastian), then Vienna to meet Bill Crawford, then to Budapest for the Hungarian girl (name escapes), next Krakow and Warsaw, then home via boat from Bremen (passing very uncomfortably through Hitler-dominated Germany).

Very briefly, kept a diary for just the first few days, starting with the bus and train trip Geneva to Florence:

Sunday, August 30, 1936 – Hotel Coronna, Milano
A hurried departure from Pension Villa Mon Plaisir and Marie-Louise. Left Geneva 7:15 by train along the lake and past Chillon, etc., to Martigny.

Then a beautiful bus ride up to the St. Bernard pass which took about 1 ½ hours. Passed through little historic villages along the road. One where Napoleon had lunch, and, as the sign said, "breakfast". Got the impression as our open postal bus twisted up and around the narrow Alpine road, that these mountain formations are just boils or abscesses on the earth's skin, thrown up in some prehistoric time. It is a hard feeling to describe, but I got the feeling that these mountains are not an integral part of the earth's surface, just an accident on its crust. A summation I never had before because in the distance great mountains look so unreal. Had lunch at the Pass in hotel opposite the hospice. Only pilgrims coming on foot get free meals at the hospice. The building is rather bare, with some 100 (?) beds for travelers and a baroque chapel. The great dogs are to be seen playing behind the hospice. There was snow quite nearby, which I fooled with. Slept on a rocky crag overlooking the road. Then at 3:30, down to Italy in a rattling bus chatting with a French hairdresser. No difficulty at customs. The ride going down was more impressive than the ascent, perhaps because you can get a more comprehensive view of the valley, etc. on the way down. At Aosta I spent 2 hours, had coffee-latte and went to an exhibition of local art. One building had religious objects. The best were XIVth and XVth century woodcarvings. There was a very lovely buckle with filigree work in gold lace. Another building housed contemporary examples of local woodcarving, which showed that the native skill of that region in this form of art is not at all dead. Many farm implements, bowls, etc., smoothly chiseled.

Café- latte in a soldier's café. Then a happy train ride from Aosta to Milano (changing at Chivasso) chatting with two Italian girls and a boy. To bed tired as a dog in a strange hotel in Milano.

Monday, August 31, 1936 Villa of Mrs. Roatta, San Gervasio (on road between Florence and Fiesole)

Took 8:00 train Milano to Firenze. I was very glad to see the Tuscan hills once more. Landed in Florence at 1:30 when Puggles met me. He looks fine, well rested, and healthy. In love with his new impressions, a bit awed by his experience of being abroad – just as I was in Paris. We had a grand afternoon just sitting in café's, walking through the beautiful streets of Florence, talking. In the evening, we went by train to the villa of Mrs. Roatta, partly English wife of an Italian doctor. The villa is a gem – XII century tower and XIVth century wings remodeled into a very livable place. Fine circular staircases leading up to our 3rd floor rooms where an unbelievably modern bathroom greeted us. A courtyard dripping with old world atmosphere, lovely cisterns. Dinner at a refectory table with a group of poet- philosophers and medical students. Also dinner guests were Frances, John's beautiful blond sweet-as-honey friend, and an Auvergnate French girl, not good looking, but pleasant enough. We sat in the Italian garden, drank liqueurs, and listened to one of the men recite poetry in French and Italian. Then danced and so to bed. A charming evening.

Tuesday, September 1, 1936 Pensione Marchesini, Forte dei Marmi, Italy

Johnny and I took the early morning train with the girls, Frances and Renee to Viareggio where Kenneth Smith, John's typically English Cambridge student friend, met us in his smooth car. Day on beach with the girls. I hope to see Frances again in N.Y.C. She is quite clever. A very good day. Early to bed at this nice pension.

Wednesday, September 2, 1936, Pensione Marchesini

A superb loaf on the beach all day, bit of rowing out to sea in the P.M., swimming far off shore in the blue green waters, laughing and diving in the hot Italian sun. The meals here are good. Cappuccino in the evening, chatting about American vs. English college life. Then after a while on the beach looking at moon and water, we went to bed.

The next morning, Wednesday September 3rd (probably), Smith and Puggles and I set off in Smith's car for Vienna. We drove day and night, stopping only for meals, sleeping (I think) in the car. I recall once at 2 A.M. getting into an Austrian Alpine village with a flat tire and rousing a repairman who fixed it. In Vienna, we met up with Bill Crawford (by appointment) and all stayed in some small mid-city hotel. Did a lot of sightseeing but especially recall dinner at an elegant restaurant "Die Drei Hussaren" (still there and still elegant). After we started dinner, the then King Edward VIII came in with Wallis Warfield Simpson with retinue (just back from a Mediterranean cruise). They sat at an adjoining table and when Bill went to the pissoir he found himself standing next to the King. A few months later the King abdicated and married Mrs. Simpson.

After Vienna, the others dispersed and I went by myself to Budapest by boat down the Danube (of course not knowing that nearly 60 years later I would be in Budapest doing public relations for the Budapest Stock Exchange). I went to visit the family of a very nice Hungarian girl I had been friends with in Geneva. While there, through her family's contacts, I was asked to write an article on the upcoming 1936 Presidential election in the U.S. It was published in a Hungarian newspaper (and I was paid a modest fee). Years later I learned the paper was right wing. While in Budapest, in addition to the usual sightseeing, I bought a red velvet smoking jacket, which – amazingly -- I still have (even though I don't smoke any more).

After Budapest, I went to visit my summer school pal Waskowski in Poland. First stop, Krakow where, in addition to the city sights, also went to the fabulous ancient salt mines underground outside of town, also to the Czestochova Monastery. Then to Warsaw for a week of sightseeing, spending time with my Polish friend and his family, consuming vodka, etc. Then train through Berlin (uncomfortable under Nazi control) to catch a ship home from Bremen.

Haverford News

(college newspaper)

Tuesday, February 26, 1935

IS PEACE POSSIBLE?

Editors Note: The following is a
student's analysis of the possibilities
of war in Europe.

By G. B. Bookman, '36

Any intelligent man would say
that it is an utter waste of time
to write an article on the topic
"Is War Coming in Europe?" One
third of the people who read the
newspapers believe that another
war is just as inevitable as another hurricane; another third
believe that the machinery of
peace has made another war impossible;; and the final, more cau-
tious, third consider any attempt
at political forecasting just as futile as trying to tell the color of
a cat on a dark, moonless night.
So perhaps the least useless contribution to the ever-growing literature on Our Next War would be
a simple listing of the chances for
and the chances against another
world conflict.

The ideal way to go about the
task would be to draw a line down
the middle of the page and list on
the left side all the signs pointing
toward war, and on the right side
all the signs pointing in the other
direction. For the present, an
imaginary line will suffice.

The first argument on the left
side of our line—the "war" side—
is the armaments race now going
on between the nations. There are
some people — attaches of the
French Foreign Office especially—
who try to maintain the fiction
that increasing armaments ensure peace. But when it is considered that every major war in
Europe has been preceded by an
armaments race between the two
contestants, and that every armaments race between two unfriendly
European nations has been followed by a war, that argument is difficult to believe.

"War argument" No. 2 is international distrust. The semi-
official Paris paper "Journal des
Debats" commented as follows on
a speech made by Hitler's assistant, Rudolphe Hess, in which he
pleaded for peace: "This speech
agrees entirely (as do all the political moves made by Mr. Hitler
since he came to power) with the
Machiavellian designs announced
with impudence and affrontery in
"Mein Kampf: to bulldoze French
vigilance until the moment when
the German army and German nation believe they are ready to attack and to conquer us. The visit
and the soothing words of Mr.
Rudolphe Hess have, without doubt,
still another purpose; to find in our
country the "life-blood of war,"
the money which Germany needs
to fight us." This quotation is not
unique, on the contrary it is typical of French comment on any re-
approachment with Germany. A
short time ago Hitler declared to a
representative of the French war
veterans that his only interest was
the peace of Europe. There isnt'
one French paper that believes a
word Hitler said, and when French
papers are unanimous on any question, it is a safe bet that the
French people themselves feel the
same way. The chief reason why
Hitler's pacifistic words are not
believed is that he has firmly and
plainly stated in "Mein Kampf"
that he intaends to enlarge Germany's boundaries to pre-war dimensions, and he considers war
one of the best means of carrying
out this plan.

Hitler's Book Widely Read

And so "War argument" No. 3
must be the bible of national-
socialism, "Mein Kampf." In this

Cont. on Page 5, Col. 3

HAVERFORD NEWS

IS PEACE POSSIBLE?

Cont. from Page 2, Col. 4

longish and rather badly written treatise on Nazi philosophy Hitler recorded the purposes of his politics. And it is plainly written, in black and white, that his plan includes reestablishing those 1914 boundaries, by war, if necessary. The book is as popular in Germany as "yo-yos" or miniature golf were in America at the height of their popularity. It is read in every school, discussed and explained as carefully as a passage of Caesar in a high shool Latin class, and even given to young bridal couples as a wedding present. France believes that Hitler's true purposes are revealed in "Mein Kampf" and that anything he says to the contrary is mere sham.

The fourth sign of war, on the left side of the ledger, is historical precedent and the violent tempermental differences between a Frenchman and a German, two war-causes which go hand in hand. Ever since the days of feudal campaigns, romanesque art, and craft guilds France and Germany have been on the opposide sides of the fence. French soldiers have always fought against German soldiers, never have they combined against a common enemy. If France and Germany had been separated since the Creation by a wide sea, or even if the French and the English had changed places, making the English the next-door neighbors of the Germans, chances for war in Europe today might have been as remote as the chances of a war between the state of Pennsylvania and the state of New York. It is the fundamental difference between the spirit of the French people and the spirit of the German people that has been the cause of so many European wars. The man who is at heart an artist, an artisan, a romantic individualist cannot live at peace with the man next door who is at heart a blustionalist, an ardent collectivist, tering patriot, a pugnacious na-

Cannon Merchants to be Feared

As sign of war No. 5 we might write down on the left side of the page the activities of cannon merchants. That does smack very much of the table-thumping school of political oratory, but recent revelations make it impossible to deny that the trade in arms has something to do with the frequent occurence of wars. Congressional investigations, best-selling books, and sensational articles may have exaggerated the facts, but all this smoke of indignation against the cannon merchants makes it impossible to deny that somewhere there must be some fire. It manufacturers of cosmetics can sponsor beauty

of fascism is militant nationalism. Benito Mussolini explained the tenets of the fascist credo, which is common to many European countries today, when he said "with regard to the future development of humanity and aside from expediency and political considerations, Fascism does not believe either in the possibility or usefulness of perpetual peace and rejects pacifism as cowardice and denunciation of struggle. Only war carries human energy to the highest tension and prints the seal of nobility on the people which have the virtues to confront it. All other proofs of quality are substitutes which never make a man actually confront himself with the alternatives of life and death. Doctrine, therefore, which is prejudiced in favor of peace is foreign to Fascism."

Germany's determination not to cooperate with the League of Nations is a seventh factor making the future of peace very uncertain. And, of course, another reason to expect a war in Europe is the eternal opposition between Germany and her friends who want to reverse the treaties of 1919 at all costs, as against France and her allies who will give their last ounce of fighting strength to keep those treaties intact.

THE POST-GRADUATE

COMING OF AGE FOR '36

BY

GEORGE B. BOOKMAN

I turned twenty-one this year, election year. There are half a million young men in America like me, all coming of age in 1936, the 4th year of the reign of Roosevelt II.

In choosing this momentous year to become full-fledged adults we have stubbed our virgin toes on a real problem, the biggest problem of our lives as political animals. It has been said many times, in many different tones of voice, that America is "at the crossroads". Well, this time it is American youth that is at the crossroads. The signs point in at least four directions and all the roads look equally treacherous. The signs at the crossroads are confusing.

-"Tired? Hungry? 40 years to Dr. Townsend's Comfy Rest for Old Folk. Pay as You Go."

-"Thirsty? Just Whistle 'Every Man a King'".

-"Stop and Relax! This is Frank's Place. Free Tables for Basket Parties. Bring your own Lunch."

-"Two Miles to Father Coughlin's. We Fix Flats".

During our minority we read the papers, we argued about politics with our fellows at school, college, factory and office. We began forming opinions of our own. We were weaned on Harding's prosperity and woke up crying in the dark of night of 1932 for more of the same kind of milk. We didn't get it.

Now that we are twenty-one, now that we are going to work, leaving college, looking for jobs, the politics of our fathers becomes a more serious business for us. We must make a decision. What formerly were idle arguments about candidates and party platforms now take on fresh meaning as we scratch our heads, trying to decide what to do with that all-important vote that we may now use.

There is a legend flying around somewhere that American youth doesn't care a hoot about politics. That has been true in the past but, fortunately, it is no longer a fact. The young people of this country since the start of the Depression have become more and more interested in their political welfare. They want to do something about it. Observers may see them joining left-wing parties as active members, signing and circulating petitions to representatives, holding model Senate meetings and discussion groups of all flavors. True, we haven't descended into the streets yet to fling bricks through windows, rush madly about with placards or chirp angrily outside government offices. But beginnings of this kind of activity can be seen in the students' nationwide Strike for Peace and opposition to the R.O.T.C.

The fanciful idea that American men and women who are coming of age are young Babbitts who accept the status quo without a murmur is an obvious falsehood as the events of the past year have shown.

So we are interested in doing something about the political future of this country. What is the nature of the choice, which faces us?

We who are coming out of the cocoon in time to go to the polls want to do the right thing with our ballot. We don't want to see it go down a political sewer to be washed out to sea with thousands of other ineffectual votes. Our ballot must be used for our benefit, to give American youth a chance for a safe future.

Exercising youth's eternal prerogative to ask questions, we ask what the present political parties have to offer to brand-new voters. We walk past the showcases looking at the displays set out to catch young, keen appetites.

Will it profit a young man of 21 to give his first vote to a conservative, property-owning party? These parties of the right have been in power alternately, guiding the country through the swiftest period of industrial growth that any nation has seen. Members of the two great parties built the factories and mills in the hometowns of our earliest days, they organized the offices and the nationwide services that we know as an inseparable part of America. Theirs was the energy, the dynamic organizing ability and the knack for turning a penny – honest and otherwise – that now forms this country's national wealth. But these same men pledged to the two great national parties, own the wealth, sit at the big, important desks and give the jobs. They are the "ins" and we are the "outs". And since the start of the depression the chances of getting "in" on this industrial picture are getting slimmer and slimmer for us. Their parties represent vested interests; we have no vested interests but a spiritual birthright. They are in the seats of the mighty and we haven't yet earned enough for a hard bench in the peanut gallery.

That is one version of the story. But there is another version that gives the brand-new voters, turning twenty-one this year, even more of a right to ask their elders very embarrassing questions about the two biggest nationwide parties.

While the two great, capitalist parties should get the credit for their bulls-eyes they cannot escape blame for the times they have missed the target. True, they set the country going on the road of mechanization, put up factories, produced a thousand shoes where one stood before, put a thousand automobiles on the road where one rickety horse grew before and today these men are the nation's leaders. But they have gone too quickly and have barged into a hopeless economic tangle. Youth does not blink at cold facts, and the young men who will vote for the first time in 1936 realize that America is in the most complicated industrial and social situation that a great modern country has ever faced. Young men know that jobs are few, that fathers and brothers have come home from the factory with empty pay-envelopes. Unemployment has struck into the homes of most of the brand-new voters. The one-industry towns, in which many of them live, have sunk into a financial morass. The federal government is spending money to help young men and women, realizing that in some measure the country is responsible for their future happiness. The government is trying to give these young people a financial boost on borrowed money. It is discouraging for a young man, just twenty-one, to be a ward of charity before he has held his first job. It is the start of a practice that may sap the vital energy of American youth, and smacks too much of the condition of young people in post-war Germany, pensioners of the government, faced by a jobless future.

The two great parties of our fathers are responsible for allowing industry to get so far ahead of social science that 12,000,000 people in the country can find no work. It was their idea to cut the value of the American dollar and divorce us from gold. Economists of their generation think it possible for America to flood the world with the products of her farms and factories, feed foreign countries with unlimited loans and then raise high tariff walls to make imports and repayment impossible. They got us into the World War, they lynch Negroes, and they employ peon labor. Our elders voted for the two parties that let commerce get so far out of hand that we spent money we haven't yet earned to try to bring it back. There is a heavy score against the two traditional nationwide parties. Young voters have sufficient cause to be dissatisfied with their explanations and wary of their promises.

The only other place to put the newly acquired suffrage to work is far to the left. A party of radical liberal coloring makes a strong appeal to young men who are entering a bewildering political scene. These parties that beckon from the twilight zone of revolutionary thought have the advantage of demanding a marked change from the status quo. Their appeal is full of dynamic emotion; their promises have never been tried in practice so they fall with a seductive sound upon young ears. Prophets and planners for all schemes of social leveling and economic planning make a tremendous appeal to young minds by offering them the predominant place in the industrial life of the future. Gray heads will go into retirement and the country will be run by its youngest adults, if the mirages that pinko orators describe become realities. These radical parties want to junk everything that we have tried and failed with so far, and make a fresh start. And that is full of romantic attraction to a class of young men who won't have anything to lose if our present institutions are scrapped.

If the political temper of our youngest voters were the same as in hot-blooded Latin American republics, they would have rushed into the streets of the capital city long ago, with a wild-eyed revolutionary leader at their head to demand industrial equality and social justice and the triumph of individual economic liberties. But the hitch is that Americans – young Americans who will be able to vote for the first time in 1936 – are not built that way. Their blood does not boil over political squabbles. It simmers. They don't run mad-dog fashion after the first political panacea that comes along. They are generally careful, intelligent and cold-blooded. They can wish for a new order without going out to knock a lot of industrialists over the head. Young Americans are too dispassionate, calculating and logical in their thinking to be easily swept away. They have enough Yankee shrewdness to look twice at the left-wing platforms. America distrusts a radical who calls himself that, as Norman Thomas discovered in 1932. If he is a radical at heart, but calls himself by another, less disquieting name, America may vote for him. So young Americans are not ready to follow the Pied Pipers of Socialist and Communist parties without a lot of serious thinking. If the changes can be made within the present political system, they will want it done that way.

We who are going to mark the ballot for the first time in the fall of 1936 don't want to repeat the mistakes our elders have made. We feel the pressure of social change and want to yield to it to some degree. We realize that it would be eminently clever for us to throw in our lot with a party that stands for a slow but steady shift to more liberal ideas. Thus to forestall the trend of fate would be an act of prophetic vision. We know that if today's problems are ever to be solved, if we are to enter industry and commerce with an even chance for success, capitalism must be opened to liberal influence. Provision must be made for security in old age, the crazy lurches of the industrial cycle must be evened out and the workers must be protected against the hardships of periodic unemployment that arrives through no fault of their own. Proper housing and food must be provided for those at the bottom of the scale and place must be made in modern life for the skill and manpower that now lies idle. We have seen the evils caused during our youth due to the lack of sufficient social wisdom of this kind, and we are prepared to meet these legitimate demands. A liberal social philosophy is the only sensible course for a generation that lived its adolescent years after 1929.

The verdict that will be delivered at the polls by young men who have come of age since the darkest days of the Depression should be interesting to those whose business it is to take the temperature of public opinion. Politicians will be interested in what the newest class of voters have to say about the activities of the past four years. We who will vote for the first time this fall will be seeking a man and a party of intellectual honesty. We will want promises, but will expect them to be kept. We will not be in the mood to listen to excuses for the mistakes of the past. We will demand concrete plans for the future, for we are too young to have a past. With the reasons for the greatness as well as for the failure of the two national parties in mind, we who are coming of age will go to the polls prepared to revamp the economic system if that be necessary. We will prefer to let the familiar parties do the job, but will not be afraid to entrust it to some radical, untested group if the older parties fail us.

Twenty-one-year-olds will use the ballot this fall to vote for a safer future in a more liberal America.

* * * * *

Note: No records if this was published.

From: Tel. BOgardus 4-1729

ARGUS PRESSCLIPPING BUREAU
OTTO SPENGLER, DIRECTOR
352 THIRD AVE., NEW YORK

TERMS: Payable in advance
$40—for 1000 clippings $12—for 250 clippings
$22—for 500 clippings $6—for 100 clippings
No time limit
WE FILE NEW YORK DAILIES FOR 12 MONTHS
ASK US ABOUT "THE BOOKSHELF SCRAP BOOKS."
Sizes: 6 x 9¼, 9 x 12, 11 x 14 and 18½ x 23½.

NEW YORK SUN

JUN 26 1936

STUDENTS FOR GENEVA

Six Sail Tomorrow for
International Seminar.

Six students will sail from New
York tomorrow for the twelfth mid-
summer seminar of the Students
International Union in Geneva.
Headed by George R. Brockman of
3 East Eighty-fifth street they will
leave aboard the liner Columbus.
Two others have already departed.
   During the session they will study
International economics and political
as well as world problems. The
speakers will include such men as
D. C. Tait of the International La-
bor Office, Sir Norman Angell and
Prof. Pitman B. Potter of the Grad-
uate Institute of International Stud-
ies.
   Those sailing tomorrow besides
Mr. Brockman are James E. Mar-
shall of Indianapolis, Reuben Mary
Nielsen of West Palm Beach, Char-
lotte D. Sharp of New Philadelphia,
Ohio; Frances M. Armstrong of
Silver Spring, N. J. and Harry F.
Stimpson Jr. of Chestnut Hill, Mass.
Rita Abrons of 117 Overlook Circle,
New Rochelle, and Robert Cum-
mings of Brookline, Mass., were the
who have already sailed.

1935 – 36, ~~1978 Trip~~

397

Bylined article published in Ladies Home Journal, June, 1937

Each June finds a quarter of a million of our young people graduating from college. What does America hold for them—what do they hold for America? A member of the class of 1936 says

Life Begins at Graduation

BY GEORGE BOOKMAN

June/1937

IN JUNE each year about 250,000 young men and women graduate from colleges in this country. As one of that quarter million, I have heard many strange statements about "youth." So many of them have been wrong, so many have been silly that I wanted to write down my impressions of this business of stepping out into the world.

When I left the college gates behind me last year and entered the world as an ordinary young citizen, there were two adjectives in my mind that I had always heard applied to the world. The world was described as "big" and "bad." My first taste of ordinary citizenship came as I hunted for a job. And during the entire length of this job hunt I found that the world was neither big nor bad. Its bigness turned out to be no more frightening than the size of the crowd at the state fair, and its badness no more wicked than the Old Lady Who Lived in a Shoe and Had So Many Children She Didn't Know What to Do.

Of course, I was terrified before my first interview with a big businessman. But that first interview, and the interviews after that, soon taught me that the man behind the smooth-topped desk can be just as human and affable as any other two-legged creature. I found that if I was persistent, if I didn't tire of phoning, calling and waiting, I could eventually come face to face with any employment officer. When I actually shook hands with these tycoons of business it became apparent that graduating into the world, even at its worst, was no more disagreeable than getting into a cold bath.

BORN during the World War, suckled on Harding prosperity and grown to manhood during the dark night that followed 1929, my generation has a strange inheritance. We were inevitably stamped at birth with the marks of the conflagration in Europe. As the century wore on, its turbulent disturbances changed our lives, in many cases wrecked our homes. At college I knew boys who had tasted bitterness, poverty and grief while their chins were still beardless. David, who was my best friend, taught music, waited on tables and

did odd jobs which not only paid his entire college expenses but also helped support his father, who was out of a job. Leon, who expects to be a writer, dropped out of college in his freshman year after the tragic suicide of his father and worked in a canning factory to support his mother and two small sisters. When he came back to college to finish the education that had been so rudely interrupted he was certainly not a "typical college boy"—Hollywood style. He and many others like him were sobered by the depression.

TO APPRECIATE what is being experienced by young people graduating from college it is essential to bear in mind our political and economic heritage. If we are to believe the philosophers of the Sunday illustrated-magazine sections, the youngsters before the depression were permanently drunk, always traveling at high speed in a bright red roadster, and living on dad's dividends. If that is true, then we who graduated in the wake of the depression have a good explanation for some of the discomforting headaches of the early thirties. We are products of the hangover era.

For the bathtub-gin generation, life was a gay and easy vacation, clipping coupons was drudgery and their most serious problem was whether the ice would hold out till Joe could phone down to the drugstore for fresh supplies.

The men I graduated with will put up a howl if the ice runs out, but they take that question in their stride. For their adolescent years were spent in a world that came tumbling down about their ears. Because the years of our teens were hard ones for America, we have a deeper understanding of hardship. We are better prepared to fight because we have seen what fighting means. Poverty and unemployment won't terrify us, because we have been poor already and unemployment has come close to us.

Leonard, who used to talk about music with me over an occasional glass of beer at college, won't lose his nerve if he doesn't find a job teaching piano for several months after he leaves college. His two older brothers, both architects, lost their jobs in 1931. To kill time, they used to think up parlor games. One rainy day they invented one with commercial possibilities. Leonard spent his afternoons getting orders for the game, and the two architects filled them at a workshop set up in their boardinghouse room. In this way Leonard earned a big slice of his college expenses and his brothers were able to tide themselves over the depression period. So my friend Leonard has seen unemployment; he has no reason to be afraid of it. Many others of my classmates have had similar experiences.

Such words as "technological unemployment," "relief" and "social security" became as much a part of our everyday vocabulary as "Volstead," "speakeasy" and "boyish bob" had been to the graduates of the twenties. When enforced idleness was at its worst in our college town, the college opened its doors to the unemployed. For one winter we sat in classes with earnest, eager men who were victims of the depression; we wrestled with them over the same French irregular verbs. The strike for peace, volunteer work in soup kitchens, jail sentences for illegal picketing were unforgettable parts of our heritage.

One interesting effect of this new attitude of young people toward the world they are entering is seen in the professions and trades they choose. The college yearbooks four years ago, listing the intended occupations of the graduates, named "respectable" professions in a large majority of cases. It was considered the thing to do to choose law or medicine, engineering or the ministry.

OFFICIALS of the bar associations in many states have announced that the legal profession is overcrowded; cities have too many aspiring young doctors; and architects have suffered most as a group from the effects of the depression. As a result, young people are going into work that is intensely practical. Two classmates of mine enrolled in a nursing school after graduation. They want to become male nurses. Three men in my class are prepared to go into the hotel business, and are taking postgraduate work in hotel administration to fit themselves for bottom-of-the-ladder jobs as night desk clerks. My friend Larry had always

intended to become a lawyer and perhaps drift into local politics. The years at college changed his mind. He is now working as an estimator with an air-conditioning firm and expects to make air conditioning his lifework. Recognizing the shift away from the professions, the universities and colleges are introducing courses to meet the demand. Catalogues list such subjects as "dude ranching," "co-operative management" and "public relations," which students are seriously picking out for permanent careers.

THERE are many new experiences for me and my classmates. When I first went to look for a job I had the strange, new sensation that I was a commodity with a market value. In college no such idea ever existed. If I did good work I got a good "grade"; bad work merited a bad grade. But, good or bad, the professor had to read my themes, had to accept me as a member of his class. On the other hand, when I ask an employer for a job he appraises me from a dollars-and-cents standpoint. He asks himself, "Is it worth fifteen dollars a week to me to let this fellow potter around my office?" I found that it's a hard job to sell twenty-one years of raw young college man to a prospective employer.

Another new sensation is the knowledge that for the first time I have complete power over my own life. I hold in my own two hands the power to make myself into a respected citizen or a failure. No teacher, parent or professor is responsible for my actions. At the age of twenty-two, not one year out of college, I sit with my destiny in my lap and can toss it any way I wish. Another discovery: I found that the business life of the nation had been arranged in very precise patterns long before I made my appearance. It must be quite different from the day when my grandfather went to work sweeping out the back room of a grocery store and from there rose to success in the brokerage business. The paths to success in this world that we inherited have been laid out already and we must follow them. Forty years ago the uncle of my closest college chum was an ambitious cub reporter on a Western newspaper. His reason momentarily impaired by one of those periodic brainstorms that afflict newspapermen, he *(Continued on Page 416*

Life Begins at Graduation

(Continued from Page 27)

packed up his toothbrush and typewriter and moved to New York. With an irreverence that still makes many hardened reporters shudder, he marched into the city room of the old New York World and walked up to the editor's desk.

"Well?" snapped the city editor, hardly glancing up from a sheaf of copy.

"I'm from the West. I want a job as reporter on the World," said the typewriter Lochinvar.

The editor wavered for a moment between anger and surprise, then swiveled back in his chair and asked, "What can you do?"

"I can write," was the young man's answer.

He got the job.

According to the success stories of leading businessmen, many of them started in a similar way.

Today, as college graduates are finding out, it is done quite differently. To slide down the well-marked groove and find your way to your first job today, you must comply with set rules. If you get a job it is often because you have a "contact," your record on an application form reads well, and luck has favored you.

QUICK success is just as easy today as it was when an immigrant boy landed in New York and built a huge fortune with the materials he found in an expanding, rising America, but the first chance comes harder. A young man has a longer fight on his hands to make a start than the young Westerner who broke into his first job on the New York World just by asking for it.

But once we get past the employment office, we are on the same footing as the young Woolworth, the young Edward Bok or even the young Mae West. If we have what it takes, we can play to packed houses.

A set formula of orderly procedure marks one aspect of the world as we found it when we graduated from college. The other aspect is chaotic, a crazy quilt of divergent tendencies that challenge attempts to understand their meaning. We entered a world that is trying to spend its way to prosperity; we found nations signing peace pacts that were the seeds of future wars; we found present wars being waged as a preparation for future peace. We were graduated into life at the time when half the world is pitted against the other half in a titanic struggle of ideologies, each claiming, as did the ex-Kaiser, that God is on its side.

WE FOUND bargain-rate divorces that are supposed to enable men and women to find happier married lives; at the same time we were taught that marriage is for keeps and its object is the lifetime union of two people who want children to inherit their name. We graduated with instincts and eagerness for an early marriage and found that income is just as important as love in making a happy match. We met face to face for the first time with the unruliness of the world and had to decide whether to be shocked by its novelty or to accept it as a matter of course. We continually stubbed our toes on things that wiser men have learned to avoid, and due to our inexperience we often made the mistake of thinking that a straight line is the shortest distance between two points.

We start this thrilling experience of life after college with very definite expectations. Our list is as long as a child's letter to Santa Claus. We all hope for comfortable incomes, satisfying jobs, beautiful wives, intelligent children and active, useful lives. But we want to do something more. A young law student whom I know was asked by an older man what he wanted to do with his life.

"I'd like to make this world a better place to live in," he answered.

What are the specific things that we want to win from the life we are now starting? They fall under the classifications of work, marriage, security, world peace and personal leisure.

THE prime expectation of young people is to work at a job that will be more than just a job. To be fully satisfying, it must give a young man a chance to infuse something of his own personality into his work.

Every young man has a mental picture of the perfect job. He may see himself as publisher of a news magazine, he may imagine himself as conductor of a great orchestra, or as star salesman for a brush concern. But no matter what it is, that perfect job must always give us an opportunity to do creative work. An innovation in presenting news, a new interpretation of a Beethoven symphony or a sure-fire sales method may give that satisfaction.

If it doesn't come from the daily job, we will get it at home in a hobby. Many of us may be tied to unexciting, mechanical work in filing rooms, shipping rooms or at clerks' desks that offers nothing more satisfying than the monotony of a dull routine. To balance this, we will take up spare-time activities that do give us a chance to add the color of our personalities to work distinctively our own. Many of my friends are getting a great deal of enjoyment out of amateur photography, and the reason is easy to find. It gives a creative outlet that our jobs do not often supply.

YOUNG people have pulled in their horns a long way where salaries are concerned. Some years ago, when the happy vision of two chickens in every pot stalked in the land, it was the general opinion of college graduates that a fast roadster, membership in the country club and perhaps even a seat on the stock exchange were prerequisites to the full life. Their bread had to be buttered with caviar—and beluga at that. Those dreams are as dead as the false prosperity that inspired them. The New Deal, bringing with it a broader horizon of living for the average man, has made him willing to give up the second helping of dessert in exchange for a free ticket to the municipal art show. "The finer things in life" are being prized more than a new couch for the sitting room, and sundry other luxuries that used to worry us before the Roosevelt culture campaign.

NOW THAT SPRING IS HERE

BY GRACE NOLL CROWELL

Now that spring is here, the old
   fields wear
Their beautiful new garments that
   are spun
From dew and moonlight, wind and
   rain and sun.
So shall I step from my dark frock of
   care,
And put on gladness as the fields have
   done.

So shall I slip my cloak of weariness
From off my shoulders, and be glad
   today;
New hope within my heart, and my
   new dress,
Threaded with faith and courage,
   shall be gay
As the shimmering flower-dotted
   fields today.

Young people, being most impressionable, have been the most eager and willing to readjust their economic requirements to the new way of American living. In New York City two young people I know, the man not yet twenty-one and the girl still in her teens, have been happily married for two years and living the full life in a walk-up cold-water flat on an office boy's salary and hopes. Their case is typical of the new mode of living that young Americans, barely out of college, have adopted. Realizing that the lines of advancement in the new giant-sized organizations that typify American industry move slowly, they have reduced their salary expectations and turn to leisure-time activities in the home and society for added compensation. Europeans have been living that way for centuries. Perhaps America is becoming mature. Instead of grumbling, wistfully dreaming of a far-off swivel chair and a push-button board that may sometime be theirs, young people face life with an interest more in present pleasures and a willingness to get along on less. Rising interest in music, painting, sports contests and low-priced vacations in the country is a sign of the trend of this country—and its young people—toward more emphasis on leisure-time activities. Shortening working hours, mechanization of industry are the causes. Longer play time and shorter work time are the effects. Live on less and enjoy it more is the formula to which young college graduates are adjusting.

AFTER the college graduates have solved the problem of a satisfying job, the problem of marriage usually comes next. The day is long past when a diploma was a one-way ticket to a job and an option on the boss' daughter. The diploma today is worth only its weight in paper unless you have experience to back it up, and the boss' daughter is probably window-shopping in Reno for her third husband. Initiative can earn good jobs and better salaries for a young man if he waits long enough. Luck and a certain amount of foresight can bring him a satisfying position in the working life of the country, where he can have the pleasure that comes to a creative artist. But nothing can bring marriage and the cash to pay the rent to most college graduates as soon as their normal instincts make marriage desirable. For many of us, supporting a wife is out of the question. Marriages are being delayed, and as a consequence families are getting smaller.

THERE are two very pretty sisters on our block, both engaged to fellows who went to high school with me. The girls realize that their men won't be able to get married for several years, so they are both working in a department store now. They are mature and ripe for marriage and should be having children. There are many young people all over the country in the same situation.

This has brought about a real revolution in the marriage habits of the young people who are not in the high-income classes. The old-fashioned idea of the husband as breadwinner and the wife as the keeper of the home fires has been crippled by the lower salary expectations that young people have been forced to accept. An equal division of labor supporting the household is the rule in many of the new marriages. Of course, such an arrangement is possible soon after graduation.

But children are just as important today to a permanent and happy marriage as they have always been. And with starting salaries in most lines as low as they are today, and the price of bread, butter, rent and permanent waves mounting steadily, the homes of the young newlyweds aren't going to ring with the happy laughter of little kiddies for a long time. Babies cost money. No money; no babies. When the men that graduated with me get married they will think of it more as a partnership than as a means to propagate their kind. Many of them will go into this sort of relation, but still more will prefer a long term of enforced bachelorhood. Then, as they are nearing thirty and the girls on the block are getting really desperate, these young men will be ready to get married and raise children in the normal, happy way. It means a tough break for all those unborn children whose pleading voices will probably haunt us in the dark hours of the night, but the present economic system is at fault. It is the best birth-control device that's been invented.

THE Government is being paternal to a large section of the population. I graduated from college with the firm conviction that I didn't want any Federal hand to rock my cradle, stir my soup or keep the wolf from my door. I was as anxious to be independent and as confident of my ability to get along on my own as the first frontiersman who drove into the West with rifle and ax. But even at college I grew very familiar with the paternal activities of the Government. The National Youth Administration gave employment and aid to a portion of the student body. At the age when their fathers were dreaming of worlds to conquer, many of the men who graduated when I did were wards of the Government.

Take Lou as an example. Lou was captain of the football team, a husky, outspoken Irishman with a big heart but a small income. At a time in life when the strength of his arms and the force of his mind should have been the only social security he needed, Lou had a vested interest in Government aid. He grew from adolescence to manhood behind the financial skirts of the NYA. His sociology professors taught that he has a right to a happy and restful old age, a right to health insurance, a right to support when he is jobless. I suspect that when Lou reached out his hand to meet the world his palm itched expectantly. He has been taught that modern civilization takes care of its own; he has seen this principle carried out by agents of his national Government when they gave him a part-time job, bought his textbooks for him and set his father to work writing captions on pictures for the WPA guidebook to America.

IT is not Lou's fault if he starts business life with the conviction that the Government owes him something. Thousands of young men graduate from college today with this new concept of social stability. They accept it as a necessary piece of furniture in the national household as readily as they accepted the radio in their own home.

Older generations will say that modern youth has been softened by social security. A little starving made a man of you in the old days, they will say. But we have been educated to believe in a higher standard of happiness for Americans; we have been taught that scientific advancement should bring equal progress in human comforts; the copybook virtues that we learned came from Franklin Roosevelt's speeches instead of McGuffey's reader. Social security will not soften us. On the contrary, it will require strength, determination and courage to preserve these gains against future attacks. The old guard were toughened by scrapping for the right to live; we'll win our spurs in the fight to keep that right.

IN NO field are young Americans so completely agreed as in their views on war. Almost without exception we see no excuse or valid reason why America should ever enter a foreign war. But that opinion is new to young people. The boys I knew at high school were easily fired with enthusiasm to fight the Japanese. At the time when newspapers were selling the "yellow peril" to the public we'd joke about the prospect of meeting some geisha girls on an overseas expedition; we were thrilled with the picture of defending our country from a supposed foreign menace. Recent years have changed all that. Mark this: there is nothing temporary, nothing flighty about our opposition to war. It is a deep-seated hatred born of intelligent study, backed by militant action and reinforced by a penetrating knowledge of the actual facts of war. We are not going to give up what may be a fruitful career, a chance for a successful marriage and a useful life just to hang on a barbed-wire fence fighting someone else's battles. Our parents didn't invest money in our college education merely to have us walk out of a dugout and get a few ounces of shrapnel in the stomach. Social security and postdepression philosophy weren't devised to preserve human happiness just long enough to clap all able-bodied men into uniforms and send them out to sink in a sty of blood and mud. Legislation to civilize trade practices, raise wages and shorten hours was not enacted so that the War Department could fatten a herd of robots to be fed to foreign cannon. The steely determination of young college graduates to keep their country out of war is one of the most powerful forces in American life today. It equals the faith of a twelfth-century crusader and packs a hard punch.

THE men who are graduating into active life in this country are not the type who are asking for any favors. True, we expect a lot from life. But we expect nothing that we are not willing to fight for, just as past generations fought to clear the frontiers of the West, to hammer out an economic empire across the seas and to build a smooth-running structure of mechanized industry. Two distinct methods of realizing these hopes lie before us. One is organized political activity; the other is independent initiative. One implies a "youth movement" with all the stuffed dolls, crackpot speeches, mistaken eagerness and juvenile lobbying that plague sincere programs of that type. The other means slower progress, wasted effort, personal disappointments and lack of leadership that always handicap a fight based on unorganized personal initiative. Both the youth movement and individual effort will have a part in securing to men and women of my generation the benefits which we expect. Both influences are already at work.

The American youth movement is still in its swaddling clothes, but is proving to be a very noisy child. It became vocal in 1934, when the first American Youth Congress was (Continued on Page 420)

(Continued from Page 118)
called. Since that time membership has grown to 1305 organizations, which are said to represent 1,650,000 people between the ages of sixteen and twenty-five. An additional three and a half million of our people are represented as co-operating with the American Youth Congress.

That's a good section of young America; school, college, farm and factory have a voice in the organization. It is sponsoring a bill in Congress at Washington to provide jobs and vocational training for young people, going farther than the present National Youth Administration. The bill, known as the American Youth Act, is being pushed by buttonholing, political pressure, campaign songs, pilgrimages, demonstrations, fireworks and petitions all engineered by a steering committee of young people in New York and Washington.

A HEARING on the bill in 1936 at Washington brought leading statesmen into contact with the problem, and since that time Washington has had an increasing respect for the intelligent seriousness of purpose of the young men and women sponsoring the bill. Whether it passes or not in the form proposed is immaterial. What is important is the fact that there exists an active and articulate group among young people who know how to pull political strings, formerly reserved for pork-barrel parties, and know how to get what they want. That is one method used by my generation to realize its ambitions.

The other method is painstaking personal initiative. This will move best through the vote that all these young people possess. Already they have Roosevelt, a President who represents their majority opinion, and future elections will shape the course of American progress still more to suit their preconceived expectations from life. But the vote will not be their only tool. Each day of their private lives, every resource of their trained minds, every grain of grit in their character will be devoted to hewing out a life in America along the liberal lines that they have been led to expect.

I GRADUATE into life and find a world that is neither big nor bad, a world where I can be happy and successful if I can show the same fighting colors as men of my father's generation. My first impressions are hazy; it is difficult to reconcile the chaotic state of politics and national finance with the rigid formality of the business world. I am beginning life at a time when vast social changes are taking place in this country, and as a result my expectations are tuned to the new pace of American progress. I will be happier with less, but will want to do creative work in a warless world in which government takes an ever-larger part in the daily affairs of the average man. To achieve these hopes and to make the world a better place to live in, men and women of my generation are prepared to wage a tenacious fight. And we pitch eagerly into life with the hope of being pioneers in a free and more liberal America.

Private Enterprise - An effort 1937-38

WORLD WAR II

March 16, 1942

To: Dorsey Newson
        Administrator, U.S. Coordinator of Information

From: George Bookman

I would like to represent the Coordinator of Information in Brazzaville, French Equatorial Africa.

Last October when American entry into war seemed many months away yet certain at some distant date, I decided that my services belonged to the government then and for the duration. Therefore, I left a position as White House and State Department reporter for the Washington Post to work for the C.O.I.

My draft board voluntarily decided that I should be deferred (2b) from military service to work for the C.O.I. Now that the United States is at war I am unwilling to retain this deferment unless I can work for the C.O.I. in a job that entails more hardship and sacrifice than being "city editor" of the news room in Washington.

Unless I am selected for the C.O.I. Foreign Service in a spot such as Brazzaville – where my newspaper training can be used and where I can take a larger share of hardship – I intend to resign from the C.O.I. to enter one of the armed services. (Shortly after December 7 I applied to the Marine Corps but was told I was too old to qualify for a commission after a year's service in the ranks. I therefore decided to continue working for the C.O.I. until either I was selected for foreign service or was told I would not be selected.)

My superiors think I am qualified – by training, experience, knowledge of languages, etc. -- to represent the C.O.I. in Brazzaville.

I think there is a tremendous job that can be done for the United States in the way of propaganda, using Brazzaville as a base and I would like to be the man to do it.

Finally, since I am deferred for service in C.O.I., I would like to justify that deferment by taking on a tough job like the one in Brazzaville -- or else I intend to resign for military service.

G.B.B.

March 16, 1942

MEMORANDUM

To: Mr. H. Dorsey Newson
From: Irving Pflaum, News Director
        U.S. Coordinator of Information

Subject:George Bookman and Brazzaville

George Bookman became City Editor of our Washington News Room soon after it was organized. He came to us from the Washington Post on the strong and personal recommendation of Steve Early, at the White House, and others.

Mr. Bookman had covered the State Department and the White House for the Post for some time and was well liked at both places for his dependability, accuracy and good judgment.

In supervising the City Room of this office, he has shown loyalty, judgement and an excellent sense of news and of human values. Under novel and trying circumstances he managed to keep the City News Room organized and functioning smoothly at all times. He has had to handle people of difficult temperament, under stress and he has always succeeded in handling them very well.

Bookman is unmarried and in good physical condition. Soon after the attack on Pearl Harbor, he volunteered his services with the U.S. Marine Corps, but we convinced him to remain with us temporarily to see if he could be given a post somewhere near the firing line. He informs me that unless he receives such a post, he will resign from this office and join the armed forces.

Because of his character, experience and his knowledge of French and people, I feel that Bookman would make an able representative of this office in Brazzaville, and I recommend him for that post.

IP:mt

English Language Short Wave Broadcast from Brazzaville – July 1942

For July 11
Bookman broadcast

We take pleasure now in presenting Mr. George Bookman, the
representative in Brazzaville of the Office of War Information.
We have invited Mr. Bookman to gi tell his impressions of Free
French Africa each week at this time. This is his third broadcast
from Brazzaville.

...

Hello, America. This is a festive weekend in Free French Africa.
The traditional gayety of Bastille Day, the fourteenth of July,
has now been intensified by the announcement from Washington inm
Thursday
xxxxxxxx that the United States will give full military recognition
to the Free French.

This piece of news -- that Admiral Stark and General Bolte
have been designated as military representatives to the French National
Committee in London -- is still spreading to the distant corners
of this colony.

Even major news like this spreads slowly in Central Africa.
xxxxxxxx llxxxxxxxxxxxxxxxxxxxxxxxx
The first stage is to tap it out in morse code over the shortwave
radio, or read it over the air in the night news bulletin addressed
to the isolated posts deep in the jungle and desert of Free French
Africa.

The Free French about a year ago had the foresight to distribute scores of shortwave receiving sets to their remote outposts in
French Equatorial Africa. So news like the announcement in Washington
is taken down far in the jungle by French administrators who sit
with a pencil in hand and their ears glued to their radio.

~~The unknown white man who was not very familiar with the network tom-tom drums~~
From then on news has to travel by methods that are not ve
~~unknown~~
familiar to Americans, methods adapted to the primitive conditio
of darkest Africa.

The whiteman who heard ~~Friday night~~ Thursday night at his
jungle outpost that Free France had won military recognition
probably posted the bulletin on the door of his office. The next
morning at market time when the natives came into to town to sel
their chickens or their manioc or their papayas he may have read
the bulletin to a native chief. The chief in turn would tell the
to his tribe, for the natives here are greatly interested in the
progress of the war, especially when it concerns France. From th
point on the news would travel into the uncharted interior by
of tom-tom
native runner and by the century-old ~~network~~network ~~that is~~
drums that is still the quickest way to spread news in Africa.

The tom-toms are such an efficient news service that a
short while ago they amazed an American military mission that ar
on the West Coast of Africa. The American military men arrived
far up the coast in British West Africa. Their arrival was a dee
military secret. They took every precaution to screen their
destination andlet no news leak out about where they were going.
At the British port the American officers boarded a plane and
flew almost a thoudand miles south to a landing field on French
African soil. When they stepped out of the plane they were extre
ly surprised to find an official delegation waiting to greet them
in spite of all the secrecy of their arrival. The news had travel
south by tom-tom faster than the plane. So that is how the news
of America's military recognition of General de Gaulle reached t
most distant corners of Free Frenchb Africa.

page 3 for July 11

The reaction in Free French Africa to the American action
is best represented perhaps by a headline I saw in one of the local
papers last night. It read : THE UNITED STATES ACCORDS FULL
MILITARY RECOGNITION TO THE FREE FRENCH. And then the next line
said : THIS TIME THE STEP IS DEFINITE.

In other words, the Free French are extremely pleased at the
action taken by Washington. But at the same time they have been
expecting a move like that for a long time and consider that they
have earned recognition by their deeds on the field of battle.

The Free French in this African capital have followed with
great interest the events of Free French week in New York City.
Form their point of view, Free French week was a demonstration of
the natural sympathies of Americans for that section of Frenchmen
wh are still fighting for the liberation of the homeland. So they
considered it only fitting and proper that the non-official
statements of Free French week, such as the speech by Wendell Willk
the other night, should be followed up by an official act of the
Government.

There is a ceryain amount of wondering here as to just what
the practical results will be of military conferences between the
Free French military leaders and Admiral Stark and General Bolte.
~~Ixxthnxxxxxx~~ Those Free French who consider the United States action
to be more than just a gesture of friendship think that it may have
very practical results in the outcome of the war.

~~Mxinxlnskxxxinxxxxxhhim~~
One Government official told me: "It looks as though the
United States is getting ready in earnest to open a second front or
the continent of Europe."

His view was that the Free French are going to be called in
as major participants in any allied attack on the German positions
along the continental coast. He believes that the big allied push
toward Berlin, when it comes, will be a joint undertaking of the
Americans the British and the Free French. His viewpoint is that
Free French participation xxxx in the second front is absolutely
necessary to ensure the wholehearted cooperation of the Frenchmen
still living in France who will have to undergo a great deal of
suffering when the second dront opens up. This government official
believes that if the British and the Americans invite General de
Gaulle to help lead the allied invasion of the continent the move
will be better understood by the French people in France whose
hxxxxxxxxxxxxxxxxxx cities and towns, whose farms and pastures will
unfortunately have to be a battlefield once again before France can
be set free.

So that is one interpretation of the announcement in Washington. It is the interpretation of an official of the Free French
government here who admits that he has no inside sources of informati
about this phase of United Nations policy, but bases his theory
on what he calls plain common sense.

But wuite apart from the opening of a second front the
Free French in this wild anduntamed country think that they and
their Free French comrades in other war areas can make a large
contribution to the war effort in return for military recognition
by the United States.

They point to a long list of military accomplishments
that have already been achieved in many areas from Africa to the far
Pacific.

xgxnmxjormxilxkxryxxxnxxffxxtxxfxxthxmxxxxxxxxxxxxxxxxxxxxxx

Their army is of course the outstanding military contributi
the Free French can offer outside the continent of Europe. At
present their army is doing a variety of tasks for the United Nat

A very importst part of the army is holding Syria, a keyst
of the Middle ᴱastern defenses of the Suez Canal and the oil fiel
xixxxxxthxxxM of the Mediterranean ᵁasin. As you remember, it was
Free French and British troops who captured Syria from Vichy troo
that were encouraged to resist by the Nazis. And now large contin
of the Free Fᵣench are encamped in Syria and are making it a str
hold for the Allies. They are doing a big job there getting read;
to give a hot reception to any germans who try to pay them a visit
fromᵒ Crete or Greece and at the same time guarding the flank of
rich oil fields of Iraq and Iran.

Another impirtant section of the Free Fᵣench Army has
been playing a large role in the defense of Egypt. The Free Frenc
resistance at the desert outpost of Bir Hakeim some weeks ago won
them thxx laurels from the British ᵁrime Minister and from the
American ᵂar ᵁepartment. And now the soldiers who wear the cross c
Lᵣraine are participating in the British counterattack against
the ᵁermans who are trying to forcexx theirway to Alexandria. If
the ᵁermans are thrown out of Egypt, as seems possible, the Free
French will deserve an important share of the credit. They had to
retire from Bit Hakeim when their position became untenable but t
are digging their toes into the sands of Egypt and their battlecry
there is "They shall not Pass."

One of the toughest French fighting forces in existence is
small but well-knit army that is holding the northern desert, that
the southern border of Libya where its hot sands border the top of

page 6 for July 11

French Equatorial Africa.

That's the country of trackless desert, now water, no
vegetables, no meat but an occasional lean sheep and no men
except an occasional Bedouin and small detachments of sun-parched
French soldiers resolved to hold the desert bastion of Africa or
die in the attempt.

And so far these determined soldiers of Free France have been
very successful in that task. Not only have they hold their
furnace-hot border, but they have pushed deep into the Italian
desert and now hold outposts in Libya that some months ago flew the
flag of Mussolini. In an offensive last Spring the penetrated
so far north into Libya that they siezed Italian strongholds that
are only a few days automobile ride across the sands from the
Mediterranean. These French soldiers are sure they can make
in a vital military contribution to the United Nations by preven'
the Axis from breaking 'hrough that desert frontier and startin'
a march down through the center of Africa.

The Free French Navy also points to t'
military effort it ismaking in return for American mili'
recognition. It is patrolling the sealanes in conjunction '
British fleet. The Free French airfoce too, though small '
is playing a role of its own in the nighlt y allied bomb'
Europe from bases in Great Britain.

Another miliyary effort of which the Free F'
proud is their role as guardians of the supply line '
Important lnd and air communications run through Fre'
territory in Africa. It is the job of the Gaullist'
communications, to defend them and to see that th'
used to carry supplies eastward to the warfronts

413

page 7 for July 11

all the way form Libya to China. This too is a miliyary effort.
There isn't as much glory in pulling a truck out of a sandhill or
a mudhole, but it is a job the French are doing and of which they
are proud.

The Free French have more items they add to theirlist of
military accomplishments, the list that they point to as the reason
why they have been given milijary recognition by the United States.
For instance they point to the bases they have turned over to the
United States in the island of New Caledonia. They speak of
the rob they are playing on the security of Madagascar and of
the ialdns of St. Pierre and Miquelon.

To sum up, the Free French are immensely pleased
that they have been given full military recognition by the United
States. But they think they have earned it.

And This is George Bookman saying goodbye till next week.

end

1943

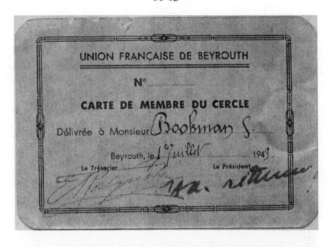

Psychological Warfare memo from Bari

Authority: NND 735006
By MS NARA Date 7/21/06

RG20B EGG
HISTORIANS RECORD OF
PSY WARFARE BRANCH
ITALY PWB POLNA
BOX 4
2 pages

P.W.B. Italy
BARI

Memorandum to: John A. Pollard   27 October 1944

From: George Bookman

William J. Miller and George B. Bookman arrived in Bari on December 28, 1943, to assist the British in opening the Bari news operation for press and especially for Balkan radio purposes. On arriving we found John F. Trow, Jr. (subsequently killed in an accidental fall) in charge of the Bari news division and aided by Gunner John Cox, British Army, and Captain O.C. Anderson, AUS. The news division was quartered on the top floor of former Fascist party offices. The Italian Government news & information department was on the first floor of the same building, in the same rooms where the Fascist propaganda office used to be quartered. The monitoring station where we intercepted news was about three miles out of town, in charge of Leonard Lieberman of FCC. The radio station, where news was broadcast, was more than a mile away, in the opposite direction.

No teletypes were available at the start, and all news hauls to and from the monitoring station had to be done by car. Henry Fischback was made chief of the Italian translation section. In short order the Morse monitoring division, under Fred Annunziata, was transferred from the distant villa to a room adjoining the news room, thus eliminating the overland haul of monitoring material. Study was made of moving the news division down to the radio station, but this was never approved because of insufficient space at the proposed location for the various country experts and for intelligence desks needed to advise the Balkan news editors.

On the death of John Trow on February 2, 1944, William Miller became chief of the news section, and George Bookman was named deputy. Also in Bari, responsible to PWE, was an English news editor named Gerald Sharpe, who in early January 1944 began acquiring a staff of Balkan language experts.

From the very start a major problem in Bari was the matter of relations between the American news editors, who were producing a basic news file in the manner of other PWB outposts, and the Balkan radio editor, who was never satisfied to base his broadcasts exclusively on the basic news file. Even the formation of a Balkan PWB and the departure to Cairo of Mr. Sharpe did not solve this problem. Basic news output was needed for the Bari press and for the Bari radio Italian-language programs, as well as for the information of English-speaking officials in Bari. Adaptation of this output to the needs of the Bari radio desks was a problem that was not satisfactorily resolved until perhaps June 1944, and it was always a source of tension between British and American members of PWB, Bari.

The Bari operation thus fell into two distinct fields: a small basic news office mainly for the benefit of the Italian press and radio;

George B. Bookman

- 2 -

and a constantly enlarging Balkan radio department. To a large extent both fed from the same news trough, but not without friction. Bari Basic News received various additions of Allied personnel -- Miss Marguerite Wilmott, an English subject, and Lieut. Darryl M. Price, AUS. Balkan News Desk was augmented by personnel from Cairo, all British and all employes of PWE. The fusion of effort between the British and the Americans in Bari never worked out as well as it did in Rome, Naples, and other places in Italy.

As time went on, preparation of news for Italian consumption took up a decreasing part of the time of Bari Basic News. Mr. Fischback left to organize the Naples translation section, and Miller and Bookman took over his work in addition to carrying their other duties. Teletype connection with Naples was installed, on an Air Force circuit. Sufficient time to receive a full daily file of news in Italian was not available on this circuit until three or four months after its installation, but I understand it is now operating very well and has saved much time and personnel in Bari. Connections are also available with Rome, for filing news direct to the news headquarters for Italy, in Rome.

Bari, by its location in one of the poorest sections of Italy and far from the main bases of Allied operations, was poor in mechanical resources for a news operation. The building where we were located had no central heating. The only available heat came from wood stoves installed by PWE (British) in rooms occupied by PWE employes. PWB provided no budget for fuel, so rooms occupied by PWB employes were unheated, except in instances where PWB people could "scrounge" from PWE. Mimeograph machines broke down every day. We used old Italian models. No electric or American machines were available for at least the first six months. Our production room used to handle eighty stencils a day, many of them calling for 500 copies, and produced them on one or two old Italian hand-model machines.

The Morse monitoring division under Annunziata operated on a 24-hour basis with Italian operators exclusively, aided by one American enlisted man. With this staff, Reuters and OWI circuits were covered 24 hours a day. In addition, there was a regular coverage of PWB circuit from Rome, and of Tass and PWB from Algiers (JDJD).

The news typing staff, doing English news in English, was exclusively Italian. Most of them did not understand a word of English. The quality of their work, however, became surprisingly high with practice.

About June 1, when Bookman was transferred to Naples and thence to Rome, and when Miller resigned to reenter newspaper work, Maurice Rice took over as news director in Bari. After establishment of the main PWB news office in Rome, the Italian-language operation in Bari was considerably cut, enabling Bari news room, now manned mainly by PWE personnel from Cairo, to concentrate almost exclusively on Balkan radio work, which became increasingly important.

The writer's firsthand knowledge of conditions in Bari ends June 1, 1944, the date of his transfer to Naples.

Report regarding occupied Bologna, April, 1945

April, 1945

RG 209 E6
Rec of OWI
Rec of Historian
Area File
1943-45
Box 2
2 page

PWB,15th Army Group, Weekly Activ
to 28 April. '45 - # 45/18

Area I: Italy

Summary: 4/22. PWB "S" force entered Bologna & had paper, Corriere dell'Emilia
on the streets in half hour after arrival, also sound trucks
4/23: Pamphlets: 3 power warning re prisoner treatment: "Russians
are in Berlin – urge listening to 5th & 8th Army Radios,time, band
4/26: AFHQ approves Press Plan for Northern Italy & issues it.

Summary: Italia Combatte rec'd & broadcast military instructions and messages
daily & hourly with feverish activity. Patriots urged to cooperate, esp
with CLN. warned vs German routes. Emergency instructions regarding
emergency civilian administration carried by NBC and all Italian stations
Monitored first broadcasts of patriot liberated stations. Radio Free
Milan relayed our instructions & used our news file. Proclamation of
Gen.Clark (App. J) to citizens of seized cities, summarising what they
were to do, avoid, etc. Special Death or Surrender leaflets nickled 9
special targets. "Russians in Berlin" delivered few hours after Moscow
announcement: Been prepared in advance
    Permission sought to send "S" forces into cities liberated by patriots
ahead of troops. Weather prevented.
    Bologna Outpost existing a week. All sections working except radio
which getting started by moving mobile transmitter from Lucca. Newspaper
within ½ hour. Sound trucks also used for news. Gen. Erskine Hume
made his speech to Patriots from PWB sound truck. Propaganda display
opened & documentary films shown to public at specially reduced rates.

Reactions: Only from 8th Army front – POWs had seen leaflets up to 90%
Whole series of reactions: POW liked Frontpost and most of them believed
the news in it. Tho forbidden to keep leaflets, most did in case. Some
few thought leaflets & papers exaggerated some news.
    Radio: Deserting Paratrooper regularly listened to Altantiksender-Sol-
datensender West on leave in Chemnitz. Recognized Rosenburg's humor.
He also heard voice of 8th Army. Another said that listening to Sol
datensender was more because "forbidden fruit" than from interest.

Leaflet Rocket container for use of 4-5" rocket been improved & 10 containers
being prepared for field trials

Propag.to N.Italy: exhortations, commentaries, features replaced by material to
"inform, instruct or encourage" population
    Italia Combatte: Special instructions bdct daily & hourly, activity reported
in communiques. Relayed by Free Milan. 4/23 call for Appennines rising;
4/24:call to Patriots north of PO; 4/25-6:call to Piedmont, Lombardy,&
Liguria. Clark's special messages to Patriots

Bologna (G.Bookman) Emergency over & now continuing operations. Arrived 4/22, paper
already printed. 50,000 copies prepared in Florence been distributed. Also
stories written for Rome. Corriere Alleato printed in Bolgna. Got generator
going for press. Talked with Gen. Hume & Rt.Hon.MacMillan re Press Plan fo
1 CLN daily & PWB daily. They approved. Told Committee that if they got
own power could print 40,000 daily, while PWB print 90,000. Increase their
latter. 4/23 a bollettino published & posted. Radio Engineering seized its
target but transmitters destroyed. 5th Army mobile radio summoned to city
& antenna errected on towers in city center. 4/24 conferred with Hume for
program of propaganda to assist disarming patriots on 25th. Corriere Alleato published again with full page on item, also wall papers. 4/25: engineering staff go full PWB Italian news file; monitoring got NBC. planned
produce Corriere dell'Emilia in Bologna for first time. "S"Force that
produced "Corriere Alleato" moved out. Same day Hume used PWB soundtruck
for Surrender Patriot arms. CLN paper Rinascita. only 1 issue, no generato

to 28 April,45 -PWB,15th Army # 45/18.

Bologna "B" Force: left to enter Bologna on 21st but only part of force permitted into city that day. Rest on 22nd. Corriere Dell'Emilia been printed in Florence at 2 A.M. & 50,000 distributed. Not til 26th was printed in Bologna. But 2 # of Corriere Alleato printed in Bolog. Arranged with CLN and other groups do setup a coop printing establishment, to arrange for 1 CLN paper and PWB paper. Radio taken over by PWB. Germans destroyed greater part of studio control panel but some can be salvaged. Antenna left intact & work with 1 kw which PWB will install. plan to use Mobile transmitter on 4/30 & other be ready in 2 weeks. On 4/23 set up Bologna news desk for outgoing news. 1st Eng.News Bulletin on 4/26. 7 panel portable exhibitions, for 250 square feet of space opened in Bologna, 4 mobile sound trucks of 5th Army coop with PWB on news broadcasts, AMG directives and orders & to scotch rumor that war ended with Milan's fall. 4/29th opened 2 movie houses with OWI & MOI shorts, newsreels

Letter to Janet - From Bari

VMAIL
TO: Miss Janet Madison
2630 Adams Hill Road, NW
Washington, D.C.
April 23, 1944
Darling

Hello Hobart 8321, you lovable dazzling light of my life. I am sitting on the balcony of my room writing this letter. That may sound picturesque, but it isn't. The balcony is just about big enough to hold a chair, a small table, my typewriter and me. Over my head, low enough so that I can touch them, are a maze of trolley, telephone and electric light wires. The street is narrow and is unfortunately a main throughfare for military convoys that rumble by exuding carbon monoxide. Across the street is a Special Service theater and long lines of troops queue up there to try to get into the theater to see Marlene Dietrich who is in town. They are very disappointed they hear she is ill, but feel better when they are told she will be on the stage tomorrow. Inside the room my landlady, a pertly chubby woman in her late forties with a voice like a banshee and a figure like a full grown bull is washing the floors and every once in a while she sticks her head out on the balcony to ask what I am doing. She thinks I am working and says since it is Sunday I should not be working. The great thing here on this balcony is the sun – and the fact that I am writing to you, and every feature of your darling face and figure and personality is in my mind, taking shape in the glint of the sunlight on the keys of this little machine. (A truck just went by ... rumble .. rumble.) Some Ities are looking at me in a puzzled way from the balcony across the street. The hell with them. I'd better get on with this letter because I just looked up and saw that the sun is disappearing behind the building across the street and in a little while this porch may get chilly.

Great comings and goings here. Morris Gilbert has been here from London and filled me in on the big intramural squabble that led to several big time resignations in our outfit several months ago. The whole outline and shape of the program I was sent here to work on is still rather vague but there are some high powered memos floating around the Mediterranean that are supposed to put everything right – if memos could win the war we would be in Berlin by this time.

The brightest thing of the week was the arrival from Cairo of a friend of mine bearing gifts – a gift, to be exact – those beeeeeeooootiful sumptuous handkerchiefs that you gave to Jim Clarke to bring to me. Jim is still somewhere near the pyramids but the handkerchiefs are here, and I thank you very very much for them darling. It was a sweet thing to do and once again to get something that came from your own hands was a great pleasure for me. Jim Clarke himself is supposed to come up here sooner or later. He wrote me a nice note saying he hopes it will be sooner, but there are so many things going on now in the way of hi-powered planning, etc., that no one really knows where he will be tomorrow morning. Wasn't this outfit always that way? Le plus ca change, le plus c'est la même chose – toujours confusion . ah me.

The clipping of Bob Lewis and the fine ship that has been named after him was a sad thing to read, yes, but also an inspiring thing as well. If he had to die, what a fine way to be remembered. Thanks for sending it. Yesterday marked the second year since I left American shores. April 22, 1942. I stepped aboard a ship in Brooklyn, NY, and then waited in the outer harbor almost a week before setting sail for Africa. Two years darling. That is an awfully long time. I am so hungry to get home to see you. It is a consuming desire, and there is nothing that can be done about it just now. Such great events are impending in the next few months that our little lives and wants seem awfully piffling compared to them. So many lives are going to be ended and maimed, and so many lives are going to be freed from Nazi slavery, that our little personal problems are dwarfed. But to me our little personal problems, as I stupidly call them, are God damn important! And I still want to come home, Armageddon, or no Armageddon. But you know the situation. The end of this second year is a time for stocktaking. Some things I would have done differently. I would have been more assiduous about cultivating certain people. I would not have cultivated some others. I would have traveled more in Central Africa before leaving it. I would not have stayed on so long in Brazzaville without being much more frankly critical of the whole idea of having a Brazzaville office. Some little things like that I might have changed if I could have seen the plan of the two years spread out before me when I started. But by and large it has been a glorious experience. And I consider myself fortunate in many respects that here I am in Italy, much closer to the front and to exciting events, than many of my friends whom I knew back home or with whom I have worked since coming overseas. I have seen and learned so much, have changed so much in some superficial but useful ways, have such a solid background of unusual experience now in politics and human relations. It has been an experience in which I think, by and large, I can take pride. But one element has been lacking all the while, the element that could have made it completely happy, and that element of course is you … but that is almost too much to have asked of the Gods of war. Maybe we will find when we meet again that this long separation has been all to the good, maybe God wanted it that way, and it should be that way, and we will reap benefits from it. I hope that will turn out to be the case.

During the last few days I have seen a few attractions that I want to share with you. The other day I saw the film "The Song of Bernadette." Now, you know I'm no Catholic, but that film impressed me more I think than anything I have ever seen on the screen. It was beautifully done – technically --, one might critique a few details, but generally the film was done in excellent taste and the acting was superb throughout. A person of any faith could not fail to be impressed by the religiousness of the picture; the bare faith and devotion of Bernadette to her vision quite divorced form the attitude of the established church. It was so carefully done that a churchman could not find fault with the film, yet a non-churchman could see the faults of the church and at the same time feel the intensity of the religious passion of the young girl. If you want to make me happy for the Fourth of July, send me Franz Werfel's book "The Song of Bernadette."

Last night I went to see the opera La Boheme. It is my favorite opera and I recaptured some of the sentimental love for it I had in those long ago and faraway days when I used to go to see it in Paris. I hope you will not reproach me my love of Paris as she used to be before the war, and that opera forms a large part of the picture I have of life in Paris. But there again I could see plainly that at almost 30 I am not the stripling I was at almost 20. The opera and its recollections of Bohemian life in a Parisian garret still makes my heart sing, but not in the old way. I have newer, fresher memories now that do the same things to me – like when you envision our meeting at Manteo, NC, or when I think of horseback riding with you in the hills of Virginia….. those Parisian memories have receded into their logical places as one of many thing that went to make up the peculiar combination of emotions, habits and inhibitions who sits now at this typewriter and bemuses himself with writing to darling, darling Janet…..so understand me if once a year I come home at dusk, pin a bouquet of violets to your dress and take you off in a hansom cab to see La Boheme.

The Merry Widow, which I saw last week, was an amazing thing to see in wartime Italy. A cast of 150 English people in dazzling costumes doing a production whose lavishness would do credit to London or New York. But though the music is delightful I wasn't too impressed by the opera as a whole. Last week also I went out to spend the evening with some Yugoslav Partisans. They gave a performance at a nearby town to commemorate an Anniversary – six months of Allied shipping to their struggling movement. The performance was choral singing by a military choir, a mixed choir and other voices, mostly of partisan and some old Yugoslav songs. The most touching moment of all though was when a chorus of five little children came out on the stage. The oldest was about 9, the youngest perhaps 5. Two of them were missing a hand. One was missing a leg. A fourth was blind. The M.C. said you are now looking at the victims of Nazi aggression. With which the children sang a song about Marshal Tito. Then a little blond girl stepped up and made a speech from her heart about war and the fight against fascism. Then they all stepped into line and sang – in English – "It's a Long Way to Tipperary." There wasn't a dry eye in the house. We can't teach these partisans anything about propaganda. They wrote the book. After the show there was raki smuggled away from enemy held territory, and dancing. I made a point of dancing with the most rugged looking partisan girl I could see on the floor. She was about six feet tall and just as broad, and looked as though she ought to have a couple of hand grenades in her belt – probably she just took them off for the dance. The partisans are a terrific bunch. I could write reams about them but probably shouldn't. But as some very sage observers say, a revolution of worldwide significance is taking place now in Yugoslavia and we here get the backwash from it. That will have to be another chapter in my book "Brooklyn to Berlin Behind a Typewriter" or a Psychological Commando Tells All.

Probably the most disturbing news item of the week to the deep social thinker was a dispatch from Cairo reporting that in a poor section of that Egyptian capital a woman gave birth to a monkey. The creature died a few hours later, but doctors said it had every feature of a normal monkey.

Now I ask you, class, to think that one over. Darwin, as we all know, was right. But here is the human race doing Darwin one better. Darwin only went so far as to say that man is descended from the apes. What he did not envision was that the life cycle might progress to a given point and then turn around and go BACKWARDS. That story from Egypt may just impress you as the pipe dream of a correspondent who had to file something so he dreamed up a good one. Maybe, but … maybe not. Perhaps we have now passed the peak of our development as human beings and are returning slowly, gradually to the ape. Perhaps that strange birth in Cairo was the first stroke of the clapper of doom against the bell of eternity. (Lousy sentence). (My landlady has just stuck her fat peasant head out here again….she is just the type who might give birth to an ape. I must speak to her about it tomorrow). But enough of these digressions…..You know something of the Mendelian theory of heredity. The genes that go to make up each human being are a combination of millions of influences and microbial matter. Could it be that once in a billion births the ape characteristics that lie dormant in each one of us have combined in this instance to produce a monkey, and the human characteristics that usually predominate have receded. Maybe. But also it could be that this event in Cairo is a warning to the human race……..Or maybe the explanation is much more simple than that….maybe the lady in Cairo lived near the zoo and every time she walked by a monkey winked at her until finally she gave him her telephone number……….anyhow it is an interesting subject for speculation ---- and I hope I haven't bored you.

The movie across the street has just let out; there are great crowds of soldiers moving down the streets and trucks beginning to rumble away again. The sun has finally dipped down behind that building and in a little while I ought to put in an appearance at the office to let them know I am alive…so darling I kiss you goodbye and send you a very very warm hug….

All my love,

George

xxxxxxxxxxxxxxxxxxxxxxxxxxxxxxxxxxxxxxxxxxxxxx which means lots and lots of L-O-V-E and K-I-S-S-E-S

Report from Northern Italy, 1945

From Milan

May 1, 1945
Milan
To: James Minifie
From: George Bookman

Arrived Milan airport about 11:15 April 30 to find it completely unbombed and Mussolini's private plane standing in one of the hangars, ready for a getaway which he was never able to make.

Rode into town with all my baggage on the only available means of transport – a bicycle. Allied forces had not yet arrived and citizens stared in amazement at the small posse of Allied correspondents pedaling their way into town.

Had a good lunch at Albergo Milano with some of your OSS colleagues who were probably wearing their uniforms for the first time in months, after a long period of underground activity. Transport was the paramount difficulty and made it impossible for me to get my story off on the plane for Rome that left the airport (several miles from town) at 1730 hours. About 1630 I met Gnudi, who had just arrived in town. His team was waiting on the edge of the city. I advised him to go right back and lead them in, which he did, leading his convoy into town ahead of the spearhead of the 34th Division and thus drawing cheers from the dense crowds along the route that were repeated even more lustily later for the fighting troops. Tanks drew the greatest acclaim.

Contacted by CLN and Gen. Cadorna, the patriot command immediately, but by the time I had transport organized for myself, Gnudi, Mike Noble and Astley were in town so I decided it would be better to let them get cracking at their own jobs than to undertake the press and radio liaison myself.

We apparently stand in well with IV Corps and through Major Nobel's suave persuasion and the friendliness of Colonel Walker PWB has collared the best hotel in town, The Plaza, just near the Duomo. Mess is in a restaurant across the street. Today through the CLN we have obtained sumptuous offices at Via Cesare Cantu No. 3, five minutes from the hotel, with space enough for 15ᵗʰ Army Group – and then some. Completely furnished, including typewriters. As you no doubt know, everything is in perfect working order here: light, water, trams, telephones, etc.

The CLN has the situation well in hand. Everything is beautifully organized by them. They even have a billeting and real estate office that assigns facilities to Allied units. Their various sections (Economic, Financial, etc.) have complete dossiers of statistics on every phase of life in north Italy, and they have very obviously collared all available cars, in which Garibaldi-kerchiefed young men, armed to the teeth, ride around all day.

I sent to Rome via courier plane leaving early Tuesday morning a news story summing up the first impressions of the city, and the entry of Allied troops which was effected about 4 p.m. Monday. My impression was that the patriots, by dint of their excellent organization, had pretty well completed the major epuration tasks by the time the Allies entered, and what remained to be done was finished off yesterday, as was made plain by the rattle of gunfire in the side streets after dark last night. But all is done in a calm, cool and suave manner --- they don't tell the Allies about it, perhaps because they don't want to bother us when we are so busy with other things.

The bloodstains were all washed away by the time we entered and the only sign that revolution had passed over the city was the number of patriot police, guns at the ready, riding and walking through the streets. Even Mussolini's body had been removed from Piazza Loreto -- at Poletti's insistence I heard -- and transferred to a morgue whence it was buried yesterday next to Pettacci in the German corner of a sort of Potters Field. A military chaplain spoke a few words. The burial ceremony lasted five minutes. Nat Knaster, PWB photographer, has unique pictures of the bloody, battered bodies of Mussolini, Pettaci and Starace in their plain pine coffins just before the lids were nailed on. Knaster said he had to climb over the bodies of about 200 giustiziated Fascists to get these exclusive pictures. They have been airpouched to Rome.

Herewith some sectional details:

Press: Corriere Alleato was printed in advance in Mantua and trucked in, but when we saw the issue, done on a rustic press, badly inked, etc., we decided not to distribute it. No great loss, because only 15000 copies were printed. Further, we decided not to issue Corriere Alleato the first night, because with so few hours remaining it would have been impossible to put out a paper worthy of PWB in this city where five daily party newspapers are being published complete with pictures, careful articles and competent news services. We thought it would be better to make haste slowly. The next

day (today) being May Day, and all workers being on holiday, we decided
not to publish today either. So the first issue of the PWE paper will be
out about noon tomorrow (Wednesday). I took the risk of changing the
press plan and telling Noble not to call the paper Corriere Alleato or even
Corriere di Lombardia. The reason: I am sure the public would confuse it
with Corriere della Sera and would jump to the conclusion that the Allies
have taken over Corriere della Sera. They are discussing an appropriate
title now, but I think it will be called Giornale di Lombardia or Giornale
Lombardo. Gnudi, Noble and I met today with entire CLN and discussed
the press plan with which they were already familiar. Longhni, by the way,
is no longer president. He is head of Finance Commission of CLN now
but still very influential and seems to boss the others around quite a bit.
New President is due in from Torino tomorrow. Noble told the CLN their
party papers could continue and that PWB would have a paper of its own.
Until paper situation can be ascertained, he asked them to limit circulation
to 150,000 apiece. They were each printing twice that. They agreed. I
told them to use only NNU news, especially due to delicacy of peace rumor
situation, also insisted they not use BBC or Reuter. They agreed. Hope they
stick to it. Then followed a discussion of Corriere della Sera which revealed
Socialists violently opposed to its reappearance but all other parties more or
less in favor, so I'm proposing it reappear as a CLN organ. We told them to
agree on a CLN recommendation and submit it to us. Fourth Corps is very
anxious to have the paper started as soon as possible. Gnudi and I called on
Mr. Hopkinson of British Embassy, who was also most anxious to see the
paper reappear. Incidentally also saw McLean, the US Consul General, but
he had nothing of interest to say. PWB will print in the Corriere della Sera
plant. Avanti and Unita are now printing there and will stay on until further
notice. The plant is immense and in perfect condition. Stars and Stripes
also wants in. PWB has taken over almost entire second floor of the Corriere
building for news and monitoring and communications set-up, including
a wonderful big newsroom. Corriere organization is so well organized that
it is likely we will merely use their machinery, for many purposes, without
creating our own. Other dailies being printed are Italia Libera, La Liberta
and Il Popolo. The first two are being printed in the Popolo d'Italia plant.
There is also Il Popolo Sovrano, of the Republican Party. Corriere Alleato will
use for the time being staff members of Corriere della Sera, but whether to
create a permanent organization is a very big question which you and AFHQ
must decide.

The problem is this: There are now five party dailies. Allied policy
demands that Corriere della Sera start up soon again as the great information
newspaper. Certainly until that happens, Corriere Alleato or some such must

be published. But would there be any need for it after Corriere della Sera resumes publication, especially if the war is over by that time. I seriously doubt it. I would recommend that our paper publish only until Corriere della Sera is on its feet, and then drop out of existence. At that time we should immediately open the door to OWI and MOI and drop out of the press picture. Our control could continue to be exercised through UNN, making that the only authorized news service.

I hope you can find time to think this over so we can discuss it when I see you.

Communications: Jackson Hammons has decided, and wisely, I think, to use the communications setup we found in excellent operation at the Corriere plant. We just take it over. They have far better equipment than we ever had, including hellschreibers, tape recorders, etc.,etc. The radio station also has a communications setup and Hammons is leaving that undisturbed, insisting only that they copy UNN news. We will rig up a teletype (machines on hand) between news room and radio station to feed them monitoring, local news stories, items from news files which we copy but they don't (such as SHAEF file) and also to exchange notes and corrections on the news file as it comes in from Rome.

Radio: Astley looked over the installation May 1 and programs start conforming to PWB directives May 2. The CLN was in control and their commissar for radio for North Italy was being awaited today by the staff, coming from Torino. But he will find Astley on the job. No difficulty is expected, however, as the station was pretty well controlled by OSS and Special Force before we arrived. Astley has arranged that CLN shall do the daily midday commentary and his own men do the long evening commentary. Their physical plant is stupendous. They have a fully developed programming section for musical, prose, chromatic programs, etc., and Astley proposes to let them continue running that, so that PWB will only pay for the news section, but will of course have ultimate policy control for the whole station. The transmitter at Busta Arsizio (Radio del Alto Milanese) is being run by some partisan brigade, but Astley told the engineers to hook it into Radio Milano so they can't originate their own programs. But tomorrow he will see the partisan leader and explain things to him. I suggested that if the partisans at Busta are busting for their own time on the air, that Astley arrange to let them cut in on the linkup once or twice a day for program periods of their own: vetted, of course, by us. Astley says he has the elements of a North Italy radio network. The powerful Milan transmitters, and the possibility of linkups with Venice, Turin and Verona. Turin was blown up, however, after one day of "liberated" broadcasting. (So I am told.)

Another question: Should Astley broadcast Italia Combatte. If that program is to die a natural death in a few days, it seems hardly worth while to put it on Radio Milano now as a new feature. I told him to go through the program each day and pick out whatever material looked essential – such as instructions, special communiqués, etc., and include that in news programs, while awaiting your instructions whether to start Italia Combatte as a regular feature.

Sound trucks: Started work the first day, before S force got in. Soon will not be needed in the city and can work the outlying areas. The city is well served by radio and press. Gnudi and I are to see Gen. Hume tomorrow regarding assistance of sound trucks, and all other media, in disarming the patriots - when he musters up his courage to undertake that ticklish job.

News: Fromer's news room already mentioned above. He is getting together local personnel and will have a good operation here. Attention should be given now to questions of moving AFHQ Rome news operation here, and using the Busta Arsizio transmitter for the purpose. Understand Maj. Ellis is to examine the technical possibilities. Since our news responsibilities are liquidated down south, I think the news operation should move to Milan, if it is technically possible.

General: Gnudi will send you request for priority personnel, second phase, but in general it can be said that this outpost is ready for all its second phase people and is also ready to receive XVth Army Group HQ at any time. By the way, Cohrssen is on the ball and doing a good job. He is remaining in close touch with IC Corps for any special instructions they may have. Also he is broadcasting in German tonight the surrender instructions to Army Group Liguria, on my instructions. These were given out by UNN from Rome so I thought we had better give them maximum publicity in German and Italian. Your other secret special communication was received and the staff here is closely watching Radio Rome for the cue to broadcast it.

Gnudi I think is taking hold very well indeed. He has a good broad conception of the whole operation and is being a good politician, among his own staff as well as outside. He and Noble still are not the best of pals, but I guess that can't be helped. Anyhow, it doesn't interfere with their work.

I am planning to leave with Col. Cust tomorrow morning for Torino and Genoa, and then Florence. Probably will arrive in Florence Thursday night.

George Bookman

Report From Turin

May 5, 1945
To: Mr.J. Minifie, PWO
From: G. Bookman
       Coordinator Propaganda Liberated Italy

Turin

Arrived in Turin 6 P.M. May 2 coming from Milan via Pavia and Alessandria. Left Turin at 1 P.M. May 3 in company of Col. Cust.

PWB offices in Turin were established in the Gazetta del Popolo building, where Lt. Col. MacFarlane has taken over the entire primo piano (first floor). We share the building with the Communist and Socialist papers, Unita and Avanti, on the friendliest of terms. Billets are established in the hotel Svizzera, some distance from the plant. Lt. Col. MacFarelane is living at the Principe di Piemonte, where he stayed on arrival prior to entry of S. Force into the town.

PWB has been received in the most friendly possible manner by the CLN and the population. Actually, PWB's convoy was the first Allied convoy of any size to enter the city after its liberation by partisans. A Nisei recon tank, a Negre recon car and, I think a Brazilian recon party had poked their noses into the city before, turned around and gone back. The population was quite excited by this and was eagerly awaiting the arrival of Allied troops in force. Then, in the late afternoon of May 1, in came the PWB convoy, under leadership of Capt. Hardy and Mr. Albert Harari. They were the object of fervid demonstrations from the population all along their line of march, so much so that upon arrival at their target building – Gazetta del Popolo, Mr. Harari was constrained to make a speech to the populace, which was answered in most cordial terms by representatives of Avanti and Unita. Harari was presented with a blunderbuss, and the PWB operation got under way. Linkup with Lt. Col. MacFarlane was affected that afternoon and by nightfall PWB was installed. The next morning Corriere Alleate was published. Monitoring and Communications set up without difficulty. Some communications equipment was found on hand and is being taken over. Editors have been told to use only JJNJ and have agreed. There is a great shortage of Morse men in Turin and I have asked Genoa to try to supply some. They could use some sent up from 15th AG HQ, if possible.

The main radio transmitter was blown up by the Germans after it had been on the air a day or so as a free station, but several other (I think two) smaller transmitters remain, together with the best studio layout I have seen in Italy. Turin was the main programming station for artistic and entertainment programs. The station has seven staff orchestras and 600 employees. PWB put it on the air under PWB control a few hours after our arrival.

The city is under control of armed partisans. When I visited Turin the Germans were six miles out of town and had not yet surrendered. They were committing fearful atrocities, such as gouging out the eyes of the local partisans whenever they caught them. We have pictures to prove this. AMG had not yet arrived by the time I left town, but the Allied end of things was under control of Number One Special Force, whose operatives had, of course, donned their uniforms and were using their proper names by this time. They were holding the fort pending AMG arrival. They plan to disarm the patriots Sunday at a ceremonial march past - similar to the disarming in Bologna. The patriot control of Turin was exemplified by a scene in the leading hotel, Principe di Piemonte, the night of my arrival. The hero of the moment, a 23-year-old partisan named Pieret, was host at a huge horseshoe table to a dinner party of about 75 people. The guests, mainly partisans, their Sten guns strapped to their backs as they ate, also included three American Air Corps officers who had landed at the Turin strip, an American sailor, a Brazilian officer, a couple of British officers, numerous girls, a Polish officer, etc., etc. Pieret, former workman in a motor factory at Turin, was obviously king for the day. We asked a waiter who was staging the party and, characteristically of Italians, he replied "l'autorita." There was still considerable shooting going on, both by Fascist snipers and patriot execution squads. A dead man was found in front of PWB offices the morning I left. Second phase male personnel were wanted immediately but the situation was not ripe for PWB women to be sent as yet.

In view of expected pressure (rumors of which had already been felt) to restart Gazetta del Popolo and La Stampa as soon as possible, I advised Col. MacFarlane to move his offices to some office building in the center of town, out of the newspaper plant. He was examining the proposal when I left. PWB's target in Turin had been the Gazetta building because of intelligence that La Stampa was bombed out. La Stampa however, had not been bombed out and three party papers are printing there. I was told that at La Stampa there was a much better communications setup than the one we took over at Gazetta. I accordingly advised the OC to look into possibility of moving news communications and monitoring to La Stampa building, but leaving Press section at Gazetta, because of the fact that only two party papers are being published at the latter plant and the addition of ours balances the load on the two plants.

Some sectional notes:

Radio: The CLN appointee as commissario of all radio stations in northern Italy makes his offices in Turin. Lt. Col. MacFarlane asked me especially to look into the radio problem, and I did so with Sgt. Sadun. Sadun was uncertain what line to follow in controlling the radio and what share of the expenses should be shouldered by PWB. I met for a couple of hours with Sadun and the CLN Commissario and, as a result, at Sadun's request, wrote him a letter of instruction which is attached. Briefly, I advised him to follow same policy as Capt. Astley in Milan: i.e., that PWB should take financial responsibility only for news and comment staff, that the RAI organization should be left intact, and that any operation should be done by the Italians themselves. PWB of course to control entire output of the station, but by working through the CLN named director and existing RAI staff. Since RAI seems to have the funds for this purpose, and the CLN Commissairo, ING Carrara, seemed happy about it. I thought this would be the best arrangement. Iver Thomas, with whom I have now consulted, agrees. Major Ellis advises that Turin-Milan program line should be working in about ten days. I accordingly advised Ing Carrara and Sadun to go to Milan for conferences there with Astley and CLN radio manager on exchange of programs, suggesting that Turin be the entertainment headquarters and Milan the news and comment headquarters.

Press: Harari took hold immediately by getting out his newspaper, with the friendly cooperation of the CLN. The CLN papers were allowed to continue, but were to be asked immediately to reduce circulation until paper situation can be studied. Harari planned to ask the papers to cut down to 50,000 circulation. They were printing about double that amount. Also in view of expected resumption soon of La Stampa and Gazetta del Popolo I took liberty of advising Harari to do nothing about putting Corriere on permanent footing as Corriere di Piemonte until talking with Lt. Col. Monroe, with possibility in mind that Corriere Alleate might continue until La Stampa gets on its feet, and then PWB paper drop out. Col. Monroe will take this up.

News: Lt. Darryl Price and Mr. Scazzella and Mr. Irving Richman have made a good start. News distribution well in hand. Communications are the great stumbling block in sending news back. They ask that Radio Turin be monitored from 2330 to 0030 nightly for their news stories until a 299 transmitter can be installed.

Genoa

Genoa outpost, established April 27, had been in existence longer than the other two covered on this trip, and showed it. I arrived in Genoa May 3 at 1300 hours leaving May 4 at 1300 hours, with Col. Cust.

Lt. Col. Harry Klein has sent in several reports, so this survey will not go into detail. Klein has taken hold very strongly and his operation was the most impressive and the most compact of these visited. Political conditions in Genoa are completely different from these in Lombardy and Piedmont. Upon entry, Lt. Col. Klein stopped the party press (five papers) and told them they could not resume until a censor was appointed. They balked at this, but finally gave in. Major Ellis also took the Genoa liberated transmitter off the air, as per his AFHQ instruction, but Klein authorized it to go back on the air after a few hours. The newspaper holiday however lasted until May 3, with an exception made on May Day, when each party was allowed to bring out a special edition. PWB's paper was started day after arrival as Corriere Alleate and thus, while other papers were forbidden to appear, PWB paper got off to a good start and became well known to the population, free from competition. Censor has now arrived and CLN papers are publishing normally. Meanwhile PWB Press Officer, Capt. Stuart, has converted his paper to Corriere Liguro, under private management and PWB control, as per press plan. There is no pressure, says Stuart, to restart Secole XIX, on the contrary entire CLN is against it and no pressure has been felt from Allied Commission or AMG. Apparently in Genoa situation is quite different from that in Milan and Turin, since Secole XIX was not a paper with an international reputation and few people would mourn its passing. Meanwhile, Liberal Party has taken advantage of this situation by issuing a paper called Il Secole Liberale, which sells fairly well, and is printed in the Secole plant. In this plant are also printed the PWB paper and Italia Libera of the Action party. The next few days will show the competitive strength of PWB's paper.

PWB, arriving with advance elements of S Force in time to witness the surrender of the German garrison commander, received a jubilant welcome from the population. As indicated above, Klein has taken a very strong line that others might not have attempted – but he has gotten away with it. AMG seems to be taking the same tone. Press plan originally provided for only one CLN paper in Genoa, not six, and the CLN demanded to know whether

PWB objected to six papers on grounds of politics or paper shortage. PWB had to base its case on paper supply, so compromise was reached by which all six parties have a combined circulation equal to that contemplated for the single CLN paper: 60,000 copies daily. PWB paper has circulation of 100,00, including provincial distribution, which is now being effected by sound trucks and will be supplemented by civilian trucks very shortly.

Radio operation is very primitive, since Genoa was always a relay station. What studios there were have been blown up, so PWB has set up a crude studio in an office building. They asked my advice on construction of studios and I said the most that would be permissible would be remodeling in the radio location, soundproofing of one or two rooms, provided total cost did not go above $200 or $300. An alternative plan that would have cost $7000 was turned down. As soon as program line from Genoa to Turin is repaired, Genoa should take most of its programs from the north Italy net, perhaps with brief local news periods.

News section is very well set up under Capt. Holmes. JJNJ is being mimeographed and distributed 24 hours daily. Radio newsroom is being moved into main newsroom, from whence completed scripts will be rushed to microphone. Basic News will be issued as soon as communications needs are filled, meanwhile BBC being distributed. Italian outgoing news well in hand, but communications is the difficulty. However Holmes has found a signals channel to get copy to Rome in 20 hours. They could use a 299 transmitter.

INTERVIEWS FOR TIME IN EUROPE

1959

December 2, 1959
To: Johnston
From: George Bookman (New York)
Yearend Review (Biz) – X
PRINCIPAL PERSONS INTERVIEWED ON EUROPEAN TRIP:
OCTOBER 26 – NOVEMBER 30, 1959

LONDON

Douglas Saunders, Manager, J. Walter Thompson, 40 Berkeley Square
Sir Oliver Franks, Chairman, Lloyds Bank, 71 Lombard Street
Sir Jeremy Raisman, Vice Chairman, Lloyds Bank, 71 Lombard Street
Julian Salmon, Director, J. Lyons & Co., Ltd., Cadby Hall
John Evans, Deputy Economic Counselor, U.S. Embassy, Grosvenor Square
Brewster Morris, Counselor of Embassy, U.S. Embassy, Grosvenor Square
Economic officials of British Iron and Steel Federation, Steel House, Tothill St. S.W. 1.
Robert Beam, U.S. Treasury representative, U.S. Embassy, Grosvenor Square
Donald Tyerman, editor, The Economist, 22 Ryder Street, St. James, London S.W. 1
Brian Rootes, managing Director, Rootes Motors, Devonshire House, Piccadilly
John Treasure, Director, British Market Research Bureau, 47 Upper Grosvenor St.
Sir Edgar Cohen, Second Secretary, Board of Trade, Horseguards Avenue
Sir Thomas Williamson, General Secretary, Union of General and Municipal Workers, Thorne House, 4 Ensleigh Gardens, W.C. 1
Mark Abrams, London Press Exchange, 110 St. Martins Lane

Anthony Barber, M.P. Economic Secretary of the Treasury, Great George Street

James Rose, Director, International Press Institute, Chancery Lane

Harold Wincott, Editor, Investors Chronicle, 110 Queen Victoria St.

A.Talbet Peterson, Manager, Morgan Guaranty Trust Co., 33 Lombard Street

Ian McIntyre, Producer, British Broadcasting Co., Broadcast House

Graham Hutton, Economist, 9 Curzen Place, W. 1

Mr. Winn-Williams, Bank of England, Threadneedle Street

Sir Simon Marks, Marks & Spencer, 82 Baker Street

Sigmund Warburg, S. Warburg & Co., bankers, 9 King William Street

HOLLAND

Prof. Sardus Posthuma, Managing Director, Nederlandsche Bank, 33 Noordeinde, The Hague

Anton Dirk vas Nunes, Regional Coordinator, Royal Dutch, Bataafsche Petroleummaatschappij,N.V., 700 Van Alkemadelaan, The Hague

W. A. de Jenge, Phillips, N.V. Eindhoven

E.van Lennep, Treasurer General, Ministry of Finance, 20 Kneuterdijk, The Hague

Sidney James van den Bergh, Vice President, Unilever NV., Museumpark 1, Rotterdam

Johannes Meynen, Vice President, AKU, Arnhem

BRUSSELS, BELGIUM

P. Colin, President, Kredietbank, 7 Rue d'Arenberg (also Mr. Wauters, Vice-President)

Mr. Lamfalussy, Economic Adviser, Banque de Bruzelles, 2 Rue de la Regence

Ambassador Forthonne, Ministry of Foreign Trade, 8 Rue de la Loi

M. Jean Frere, Director, European Investment Bank, 11, Mont des Arts

Count de Liederkerke, European Investment Bank, 11, Mont des Arts

Dr. Walter Hallstein, President, Commission of the European Economic Community, 23, Avenue de la Joyeuse Entrée

Hirigeyen de Courcy, assistant to the Director for Internal Market, EEC

Huge de Grood, Chief, N. American Division, EEC

James R. Huntley, Public Affairs Officer U.S. Mission to European Economic Community

Richard Mayne, Public Affairs Officer, EEC, 23 Avenue die la Joyeuse Entrée

Jakeb van der Lee, director of General Affairs, Overseas Territories Dept. EEC, 58 Rue de Marais

M. Gaudet, legal adviser to EEC, 53 Rue Baillard

M. Deniau, Director External Relations Dept., EEC, 23 Avenue de la Joyeuse Entrée

PARIS

Clarence Hunter, U.S. Treasury Representative, Hotel Telleyrand, Rue St. Florentine

Wilfrid Baumgartner, Governor, Bank of France, 1 Rue la Vrilliere

M. Courtois, Information Director, St. Gobain Co., 91 Rue Faubeurg St. Henere

George Villiers, President, Patronat de l'Industrie Francaise, 31 Ave. Pierre Ier de Serbie

Jacques Rueff, Economic Advisor to General deGaulle, Cite Varenne, 51 Rue de Varenne

M. Groupiron, Information Director, Renault Co., 10 Ave Emile Zola, Boulogne-Bilancourt

Guy de Carmey, Director, Eurinvest, 15 Blvd de Lessert

M. Burnard de Margerie, Banque de Paris et des Pays-Bas, 3 Rue d'Antin

Daniel Petit, Sect. Gen., Compagne des Agents de Change de la Bourse, 4 Place de la Bourse

M. de Murard, Rothschild & Co., 21 Rue Lafitte

Pierre Uri, partner, Lehman Bros., 55 Rue de Cherche Midi

M. Gildas Le Nean, economist, Pechiney, 23 Rue Balzac

M. Caillen, Information Director, Machines Bull, 94 Ave. Gambetta

George Hereil, President, Sud-Aviation and Panteries de la Chappelle, 104 Ave Champs Elysees

M. Cahan, Deputy Secretary General, OEEC, Chateau de Muette

Pierre Meynial, V.P., Gen. Mgr., Morgan Guaranty Trust Co.

Jean Monnet, President, Action Committee for U.S. of Europe, 83 Ave. Feche

GERMANY

Dr. Walter Behrens, Economist, Opel Plant, Russelsheim

Dr. Opel, Economist, German Metalworkers Union, Frankfurt

Mr. Joseph Neckermann, President, Neckermann Co., Frankfurt

Dr. Jessen, Assistant to the President, Daimler-Benz, Stuttgart
Dr. Emminger, Economist, Bundesbank, Frankfurt
Dr. Hermann Abs, President, Deutsche Bank, Frankfurt
Jurgen Eick, Economic Editor, Frankfurter Allgemeine Zeitung
Dr. Harkert, Foreign Trade Director, Ministry of Foreign Affairs, Bonn
Henry Tasca, U.S. Economics Minister, and U.S. Treasury Representative, Embassy, Bonn
Prof. Ludwig Erhard, Minister of Economis, Vice Chancellor, Bonn
Dr. Franz Etzel, Minister of Finance, Bon

ZURICH, SWITZERLAND

Alfred Schaefer, General Manager, Union Bank of Switzerland, 45 Bohnhofstrasso
Dr. E. F. Aschinger, Economics Editor, Neue Zuricher Zeiting, Bellvueplatz
Dr. F. W. Schulthess, Swiss Credit Corp., Paradsplatz
Richard Krenstein, Arbitrium Bank, 9 Alpenstrasse, Zug
Walter Kull, Director, Swiss National Bank, Bersenstrasse, 19
Hans Baer, Julius Baer & Co., Bahnhofstraat 36
Mr. Tiemster, International Press Institute, Munstergasse 9
Gottlieb Duttweiler, Director, Migres, Limattstrasse
J. van der Muhle, Privatbank und Verwaltungsgesellschafft (Brown Beveri), Barengasse 29

ITALY

Prof. Vitterie Valletta, President, Fiat Co., Turin
Dr. Guido Cesura, Assistant Administrator, Pirelli Co., Milan
Dr. Elio Genella, Economist, Mediabanca, via Falodrammatici 10, Milan
Prof. Piero Sacerdoti, President, Riunone Adriatica di Sicurita, via Manzeni 38, Milan
Dr. Livio Magnani, Economist, Financial Correspondent, Rome
Giuseppe Ciarrapico, Economist, 9 Via Tagliamonto, Rome
Vincent Barnett, Chief of Economic Division, U.S. Embassy, Via Veneto, Rome
Ettore Lolli, Director, Banca di Lavoro, Via Veneto
Guide Carli, Ufficio Scambi, 123 Via Quattro Fontani

NEW YORK

David Karr, President, Fairbanks Whitney Corp., 745 Fifth Avenue

Fred Steiner, Banker, 110 East 57 Street
Ben Moore, Economist, Twentieth Century Fund, 41 East 70

KUDOS AND P. R.

NEW YORK STOCK EXCHANGE

ELEVEN WALL STREET

NEW YORK 5, N.Y.

G. KEITH FUNSTON
PRESIDENT

January 3, 1961

Mr. George B. Bookman
Fortune Magazine
Time & Life Building
Sixth Avenue at 50th St.
New York 19, New York

Dear George:

  I can't think of a more pleasant way of beginning the new year than extending my congratulations to you on what sounds like a challenging and significant new position with Fortune Magazine.

  Since I didn't see you at our press luncheon on Wednesday, as I had hoped to, I want to take this opportunity to wish you very well as a member of the Board of Editors. And I hope that it won't be long before we can get together.

  It was good to hear from you and I'm delighted to learn this good news.

      Sincerely,

      Keith

BOARD OF GOVERNORS
OF THE
FEDERAL RESERVE SYSTEM
WASHINGTON

OFFICE OF THE CHAIRMAN

January 5, 1961.

Dear George,

On my return to the office after
a short time away during the holidays, I find
your nice letter of December 19 and am delighted
to learn of your new association with Fortune
Magazine. Congratulations!

I will look forward to seeing you
and want to wish you the best in your new job.

Cordially yours,

Bill

Wm. McC. Martin, Jr.

Mr. George B. Bookman,
Fortune Magazine,
Time and Life Building,
New York 20, New York.

George Bookman

In NYSE Post

George Bookman, a member of Fortune magazine's board of editors for the last two years, has been named director of public information and press relations for the New York Stock Exchange. Prior to joining Fortune, Mr. Bookman was national economic correspondent for Time. He succeeds Paul Kolton, now executive vice-president of the American Stock Exchange.

George B. Bookman

November 7, 1962 — AMERICAN BANKER

Bankers Federal S&L, NY, Appoints Two as Directors

NEW YORK.—William H. McConnell and Louis F. Meola have been elected to the board of Bankers Federal Savings and Loan Association here.

Mr. McConnell, a vice president of American Export Lines, has been with that company since 1950. Prior to joining American Export, he had been with Cunard Steamship Lines.

Mr. Meola is a certified public accountant who has been active in the savings and loan industry. For a time he was with the Savings and Loan Bank of the State of New York.

He is secretary-treasurer of Halkey-Roberts Corp.

GEORGE BOOKMAN

Who has been appointed director of public information and press relations for the New York Stock Exchange. He succeeds Paul Kolton, who has resigned to become executive vice president of the American Stock Exchange.

POLICY QUESTIONS: George Bookman (left), Director of Public Information-Press Relations and Philip Keuper, Assistant Director, look over latest edition of **Exchange Report**, a new membership publication dealing with policy issues and high-level planning.

VOICE OF THE BIG BOARD

News and Views of the Exchange — Via PI-PR

What do you say when a phone caller asks you for tomorrow's volume, averages and issues traded? Or when, in the middle of the Penn Central crisis, a youthful voice pipes into your ear, "What is the plural of money?"

Fielding questions like these is just one job of the Exchange's Public Information-Press Relations Department, headed by George B. Bookman, a former editor of *U.S. News and World Report*, correspondent for the *Washington Post* and *Time*, and editor of *Fortune*.

"The most frequent callers," says Bookman, "are newsmen who are under tremendous pressure to get their stories completed before a deadline. They may need statistical information, data on rules and procedures, or information on a decision just reached at a Board of Governors' meeting."

Bookman, who joined the Exchange eight years ago, has guided the department to its present mix of news and policy reportage, external and internal communications, media and membership contact. "The change in character of the department," says Bookman, "has been in the greatly increased attention to interpreting policy issues, providing public relations services for other Exchange departments, and working on a tremendously enlarged program of communications with the membership."

The number of newspapers in New York may have declined by three since Bookman came to the Exchange, but the department's contact with the media has grown geometrically: Local newspaper coverage has become more intensive, many New York news bureaus for out-of-town papers were opened, and an upsurge in specialized finance magazines and close coverage by the TV networks have kept the department on its toes, on the phone and at the typewriter.

The News Bureau, a six-man team within the department, provides the huge volume of information needed by newsmen on a daily basis. "Besides being specialists in the various news media—newspapers, magazines, broadcasting—each person in the News Bureau handles a specialized beat within the Exchange, such as the Stock List or Member Firms Department," says Assistant Director Philip J. Keuper, formerly an editor at *Business Week* and Associated Press financial writer.

Coordinating the high-volume flow of information in and out of the Exchange is News Bureau Manager Jim Hill, another alumnus of the A.P.'s financial department. Says Hill, "The challenge is in providing accurate information—fast." Hill arrives before the Exchange's official 9 a.m. starting time and is ready for action when the opening bell sounds on the Floor at 10 o'clock.

The start of trading signals the beginning of the busiest part of the News Bureau's day, since events on the Floor take precedence over any other job. Any delay in the ticker, a halt in trading in any individual stock, hourly volume and the NYSE indexes are all recorded and reported.

Dick Callanan, whose more than 40 years' experience with the Exchange have earned him the dubious advantage of being able to answer just about any question (Secretary Aileen Lyons, at the NYSE 18 years, runs a close second), monitors the pulse of trading on the Floor and keeps the news services posted on developments as soon as they happen. Tie-lines direct to the two foremost financial wire services—Dow Jones and Reuters—make instant communication easy.

Keeping people posted, however, was a frenetic experience, Callanan recalls, in November of 1963 when questions out-ran facts. Rumors had reached the Floor that President Kennedy had been shot *but nothing further was known*. Almost immediately Callanan was buried by phone calls as to how the market was reacting and what the Exchange was going to do. The telephone lines were so jammed that The Associated Press, *Journal-American* and *Newsweek* sent their reporters to Callanan's office. The record shows that the Exchange stopped trading at 2:07 p.m.,

3

but Dick Callanan didn't leave his office until 9:30 that night. The last newsman to leave was Phil Keuper, then a reporter for A.P.

George Bookman never really broke away at all that weekend. It was also the weekend that final arrangements were being made, after intensive efforts, so that customers of bankrupt Ira Haupt wouldn't suffer. "It was terribly important for the Stock Exchange to open trading Tuesday morning with the Ira Haupt problem resolved—important for public confidence in the stability of the economy at a time when political stability had been shaken," says Bookman. "With public confidence on the line, we took a calculated risk in order to meet news deadlines. We called the press and TV newsmen to the Exchange in the evening and summarized the Haupt rescue plan even though it hadn't been totally and absolutely confirmed. We had to make it possible for the news to break the next morning. Our risk was in trusting the newsmen not to break the crucial story until they had our final okay. They all lived up to that trust and the news was published and broadcast early Tuesday

morning, with a helpful effect on investor confidence."

To satisfy the astounding demand for information, the News Bureau whips out an average 7,500 words per month in news releases on a wide range of subjects—rules changes, record-breaking volumes, new listings, important speeches, CCS developments. This information reaches thousands of newsmen, members, industry leaders, heads of universities.

Magazine, book and newspaper feature writers also look to PI-PR for facts, figures and background material about industry developments and don't hesitate to dip into the Exchange's history or any other subject that piques their interest. Charles Storer, a former A.P. newsman and Assistant Manager of the News Bureau, handles all queries of this kind. Questions have run the gamut from *Time* magazine's: "Did Franklin Roosevelt say the presidency of the Exchange was the second toughest job in the world?" to a request for information from an author writing a book about member firm branch offices which operated aboard ocean liners in the '20s (so you could use a leisure

hour in mid-ocean to buy or sell stock). "We were able," smiles Storer, "to locate a former broker who had been assigned to one of these shipboard brokerage offices."

In addition to working with feature writers, Storer researches and writes *Perspectives on Operations*, a nuts and bolts newsletter on developments in the operations area of the securities industry. Distributed to more than 4,000 members and allied members, it offers guidance such as what industry trends to consider in switching from a manual to a computer operation, how Exchange Automation Services will work, the status of CCS expansion.

The listed companies section of the News Bureau focuses on a different area. It provides a clearing house of ideas for improving corporate communications of NYSE-listed companies with their employees, shareowners, the financial community and the general public. "This is done through employee publications, reports to shareowners, news releases and advertising," says Charles Parnow, a former U.P.I. newsman and head of the section. Parnow and William DeMeo,

NEWS RELEASE: Kathleen Considine (right). Secretary to Eugene Miller, and secretaries Rose Alter (left) and Christine Anico review final changes.

WIRE SERVICE LIAISON: Richard Callanan and Aileen Lyons phone important news to wire services.

ANNUAL REPORT: Lee Ehrenreich (rear, left) checks out final copy for the Annual Report with Secretary Selma Johns, Terence McCarthy (left) and John LaBarbera, of the Advertising Department.

NEW LISTING: At listing of Electronic Data Systems Charles Parnow (right) talks with **New York Times** photographer. William DeMeo (center) arranges for press photos with Bernard J. Lasker.

EMPLOYEE COMMUNICATIONS: Susan Klein talks with Eugene Miller, E change Vice President for Public Relations and Investor Services, to gath material for profile in this issue.

Public Relations Coordinator, work closely with the Exchange's Stock List Department to keep the companies abreast of Exchange policies on timely disclosure of corporate information and provide editorial and photographic services to companies being listed.

In September of 1969, Parnow and DeMeo helped Dayton-Hudson plan and execute its flower show on the steps of Federal Hall in connection with its listing on the Exchange. Sales of flowers earned more than $4,000 which was donated to the Seaman's Church Institute. It was, all in all, a dramatic, fragrant and profitable celebration for all concerned.

"We even gave blood," recalls DeMeo, "when Technicon was listed"—blood donated by Phil West, Vice President in charge of Stock List, for analysis by Technicon which sells equipment for such ests.

The Radio, Television and Film Services division of the News Bureau is managed by Bernard Landou who has had ong broadcasting and film experience. Landou's office houses stacks of film, a projector, viewing screen and one of the hree broadcast booths from which 250 stock price broadcasts are sent out weekly o thousands of radio stations across the country. Broadcast represents the widest audience for market information. TV networks get in touch with Landou for deails, clarification and guidance when an important news story breaks. And Landou alerts them to news of interest. Seventyive million people found out about the Exchange's first 100-million-share week in he short space of one-half hour by watching the network newscasts at 7 p.m. Friday, January 29.

It has become commonplace to have TV crews filming the Floor of the Exhange particularly in the last few years

when Landou has escorted crews from Mexico, Japan, England, France, Germany, Switzerland, Italy, and Canada and provided technical assistance and other guidance in their shooting of trading activity.

Landou, the Exchange's film coordinator for "Market In Motion"—our most recent film which throbs to the electronic beat of the Moog—is now working on another one, an educational film to be done in full animation.

Backing up the News operation are Mike Janssen and Bob Koster who keep an extensive clip file of news coverage of the Exchange and see to it that news releases and other material reach newspapers and the other media throughout the city as quickly as possible.

Editorial Planning and Special Projects, perhaps better described as "important-miscellaneous" is managed by Lee Ehrenreich who prepares written documents interpreting the Exchange's views on economic developments, changes in public law or policy, and securities industry operations of particular interest to the investing public.

Ehrenreich has measured out his nine-year employ at the Exchange in putting out eight annual reports and twenty-five quarterly reports for the Exchange. Other highlights have been editing reports developed by the Research Department, congressional testimony and speeches, and preparing policy statements on other Exchange-related activities.

"We probably have done miscellaneous assignments for every department of the Exchange," Ehrenreich claims. Another product of Editorial Planning and Special Projects is AT THE MARKET, edited by Susan Klein, which reaches 4,000 employees, retirees and newsmen.

The PI-PR Department also publishes

Exchange Report, written by Keuper. This newsletter for management of NYSE member organizations with a circulation of 9,000 focuses on policy issues and high-level planning—the latest capital rules changes and their impact; advantages of incorporation for member firms; how to save operating costs.

"The best issue so far," says Keuper, who keeps in close touch with block traders, management, analysts, and registered reps, "was the Q and A on the new SIPC legislation. There was really nothing at the time that put the legislation in easy-to-read form and which answered almost all of the questions that would be asked. *Exchange Report*," he points out, "can probably be read in about six minutes"—especially since it eclipses unnecessary pronouns and articles and comes across in staccato, hot-off-the-press style. Keuper sees the newsletter as one of the landmarks in "a whole new function for the department in concentrating on the Exchange's other public, which is its own membership." And along with this expansion of the department's activity and greater involvement in policy as it is being made, Keuper says, "the capabilities of the people in the department have been growing as well."

As a unit, the PI-PR Department acts as a consultant to other departments in the Exchange on public relations and communications problems. In this function, PI-PR people have prepared and edited internal booklets, prepared speeches for technical and professional groups, provided suggestions on recruiting, and assisted in the preparation of executive correspondence. And everyone in the department has already enlisted the aid of new executive Assistant Terence McCarthy whose duties at the Exchange include a wide range of special writing and editorial functions.

The department has just held a day-long news conference for local and out-of-town newsmen at which top Exchange officials Robert W. Haack, Richard Howland, John Alexander, William Freund, Fred Stock and Stan West spoke about paperwork, Floor automation, the pros and cons of institutional membership, techniques for member firm surveillance, and the composition of recent volume. After this event, the members of the department might agree with this reporter's surmise that sometimes it's a welcome relief to be asked the plural of money. ∎

BROADCASTING: Bernard Landou goes over the hourly stock report with Donna Ippolito in broadcasting booth while Jean Monroe (at phone) checks out market information recorded on tape. Fran Grilletto (in foreground) reads latest volume figures om inquiry station.

NEWS SEMINAR PLANS: Jim Hill (left) and Charles Storer work out details for day-long seminar for news media.

5

The New York Time:

JUN 2 3 1971

SENIOR POSTS FILLED AT STOCK EXCHANGE

Robert W. Haack, president of the New York Stock Exchange, announced yesterday that John J. Alexander Jr., Lee D. Arning, Samuel A. Gay and Eugene Miller had been named senior vice presidents of the exchange.

Mr. Alexander is in charge of the exchange's Electronic Systems Center, Mr. Arning is in charge of operations, Mr. Gay handles administration and finance and Mr. Miller is responsible for public relations and investor services.

All had previously been vice presidents and all will continue to report to Richard B. Howland, executive vice president.

At the same time George B. Bookman, Joseph A. Hays, George M. Hunter, Jeremiah J. O'Donohue and Stan West were named assistant vice presidents. All are department directors.

447

THE NEW YORK BOTANICAL GARDEN
BRONX, NEW YORK 10458

FOR RELEASE: AMs Friday, July 27, 1973

The New York Botanical Garden announced today that George B. Bookman, Assistant Vice President of the New York Stock Exchange for Public Relations, has been named Director of Public Relations for the Garden.

The announcement was made on behalf of the Garden's Board of Managers by

Dr. Howard S. Irwin, President.

Mr. Bookman, who has directed the Exchange's public information and press relations activities since 1962, will direct informational programs for the Garden both at its Bronx headquarters and at the Cary Arboretum, an 1800-acre center of plant science that the Garden is developing in Millbrook, New York. He plans to start his new duties in the early Fall.

The Botanical Garden, established in 1891, ranks among the leading botanical and horticultural institutions of the world. It has been known particularly for the collection of living plants at its 230-acre Bronx campus, its Herbarium containing some four million-plant specimens, and for botanical research at the Garden headquarters and through expeditions to remote parts of the world.

With the recent acquisition of the Cary Arboretum property, the Garden has been moving more actively into environmental projects, community-action programs, and education.

The Garden's future plans include working with major corporation and governmental units on environmental problems, expanding the Garden's communications with the general public, constructing a Plants and Man exhibit building in the Bronx, developing new scientific and educational facilities at the Millbrook site, and possibly establishing a Botanical Garden facility in Manhattan.

In announcing Mr. Bookman's appointment, Dr. Irwin said:

"The New York Botanical Garden intends to move ahead rapidly as a more effective force in our home communities of New York and Millbrook, and also nationally and internationally. In accomplishing this goal, we are fortunate to obtain the services of George Bookman to help us become better known to the public. His broad experience in journalism and public relations will add an important new dimension to the Garden's activities."

Mr. Bookman, who is a resident of Millbrook and New York City, was a journalist for more than twenty years; serving as White House correspondent of the Washington Post, associate editor of U.S. News and World Report Magazine, national economic correspondent for Time Magazine in Washington and New York, and a member of the Board of Editors of Fortune Magazine. He left that post in 1962 to join the staff of the New York Stock Exchange.

Mr. Bookman has been active in journalism organizations, and recently served as president of the Deadline Club, the New York professional chapter of the national journalism society, Sigma Delta Chi. He has also been active in conservation matters in the Millbrook, N.Y. area, and is currently a member of the Thompson Pond Committee of the Nature Conservancy, in Pine Plains, N.Y. Mr. Bookman and his wife, Janet, have had a home in Millbrook since 1963.

GEORGE BOOKMAN

George Bookman Elected Vice President Of New York Botanical Garden

George B. Bookman, Director of Public Affairs for the New York Botanical Garden, has been elected Vice President of the Garden. In his new post Mr. Bookman will be responsible for development activities as well as public affairs.

Mr. Bookman, formerly an assistant vice president of the New York Stock Exchange, joined the Botanical Garden staff last September. His career has been spent in journalism with such publications as Time and Fortune Magazines and the Washington Post, and in public relations.

In addition to his work at the Botanical Garden in the Bronx, Mr. Bookman is also responsible for public affairs and development at the Cary Arboretum in Millbrook, New York, an 1800-acre property where the Botanical Garden is developing a collection of trees and woody plants and a center for applied environmental science.

Mr. Bookman is a resident of Millbrook. He is active in journalism and public relations societies, and was recently president of the New York Professional Chapter of Sigma Delta Chi, the national society of professional journalism.

George Bookman Named Vice President Of Botanical Garden

George B. Bookman, director of public affairs for the New York Botanicla Garden, has been elected vice presidnet of the garden. In his new post, Bookman will be responsible for development activities as well as public affairs.

Bookman, formerly an assistant vice president of the New York Stock Exchange, joined the Botanical Garden staff last September. His career has been spent in journalism with such publications a Time and Fortune magazines and the Washington Post, and in public relations.

In addition to his work at the Botanical Garden in the Bronx, Bookman is also responsible for public affairs and development at the Cary Arboretum in Millbrook, an 1800-acre property where the Botanical Garden is developing a collection of trees and woody plants and a center for applied environmental science.

Bookman is a resident of Millbrook. He is active in journalism and public relations societies, and was recently president of the New York Professional Chapter of Sigma Delta Chi, the national society of professional journalism.

FRIDAY, MAY 10, 1974

The New York Times/Edward Hausner

Justice William O. Douglas touring New York Botanical Garden in the Bronx yesterday with Robert Abrams, right, Borough President, and Dr. Theodore Kazimiroff, a historian of the borough.

Justice Douglas, in Bronx Park, Gives Brief for Nature

By PAUL L. MONTGOMERY

Supreme Court Justice William O. Douglas halted in a wooded glen at the New York Botanical Garden in the Bronx, watching a pair of mallard ducks nesting at the edge of a pond. Around him the dogwood and rhododendron were in flowers and the wind whispered in the high leaves of shagbark hickory, hemlock and tulip trees.

"What are your predators?" the 75-year-old outdoorsman asked. "Foxes?"

"We have very few," said Larry Pardue, a plant specialist at the garden. "Mostly it's the people."

Justice Douglas spent the afternoon yesterday at the botanical garden, touring its woods and plantings, warning of incursions on the nation's wilderness, giving a speech about his love of botany and presiding at the reopening of the park's nature exhibitions.

The ceremony was for the refurbished Exhibit Hall in the garden's museum building, reopened after two years or renovation. The displays range from a study of pollution in the Bronx River to a demonstration of the garden's new scanning electron microscope as applied to botanical problems.

The events also marked the beginning of Bronx Week, the borough's annual celebration of itself and its cultural and community resources. Through May 18 there will be a wide variety of fairs, concerts, art exhibitions and tours scattered through the borough.

Historian Acts as Guide

Justice Douglas, delayed by a dentist's appointment, spent an hour in the botanical garden's Hemlock Forest, one of the last uncut woods in the city. Mostly he loped along at a woodsman's pace and listened to his guides—Dr. Howard Irwin, president of the park, Mr. Pardue and Dr. Theodore Kazimiroff, an indefatigable historian of the borough.

Wildlife Ennumerated

Dr. Kazimiroff rattled off the variety of wildlife found in the forest—red fox, raccoon, possum, rabbits, muskrat, quail, pheasant, barred and great horned owls, redshouldered hawks. Skipping agilely about, he showed Justice Douglas an Indian rock shelter, tenderly pointed out a two-year-old hemlock seedling an inch high, marveled over a patch of northern white violets (which the photographers promptly trampled), and presented the Associate Justice with a 1,000-year-old quartz arrowhead of the Algonkin period he had found in the park.

They paused at a 15,000-year-old glacial cup formed by the advent of the last ice age. The gouged rocks were covered with scrawled names like "Ducky" and "Nick."

"The graffiti is modern," Dr. Kazimiroff said.

"It's everywhere," said Justice Douglas.

In his walk, he was sometimes reminded of his own experiences in woods as remote as Oregon and Siberia. When an oak shattered by lightning was pointed out, he had seen long ago in the West.

"I was standing on a ridge, watching the lightning play on a ridge across the valley. I saw lightning hit three trees in a row, in the space of 100 yards. Each one went up like a struck match. It was a beautiful thing to see."

Depredations Are Noted

The outdoorsman also spoke of depredations in parks. He said one of the more pernicious trends was the National Park Service's policy of building roads through parks instead of around the perimeter.

"The thing that is most destructive of the West is motor vehicles," he said. "There's a thing called a dune buggy that is raising hell with the Mojave Desert."

Justice Douglas spoke with Bronx Borough President Robert Abrams, who walked with him, and again in his speech, of the closeness to nature taught him by the naturalist John Muir.

"Flowers, plants, trees are like one's neighbors," he said. "They have names, habits and temperaments. Get to know them; come on speaking terms with them; introduce them as friends to the children. The more one sees and appreciates the beauty of the earth, the less destructive he will be."

Justice Douglas, in Bronx Park, Gives Brief for Nature

By PAUL L. MONTGOMERY

Supreme Court Justice William O. Douglas halted in a wooded glen at the New York Botanical Garden in the Bronx, watching a pair of mallard ducks nesting at the edge of a pond. Around him the dogwood and rhododendron were in flowers and the wind whispered in the high leaves of shagbark hickory, hemlock and tulip trees.

"What are your predators?" the 75-year-old outdoorsman asked. "Foxes?"

"We have very few," said Larry Pardue, a plant specialist at the garden. "Mostly it's the people."

Justice Douglas spent the afternoon yesterday at the botanical garden, touring its woods and plantings, warning of incursions on the nation's wilderness, giving a speech about his love of botany and presiding at the reopening of the park's nature exhibitions.

The ceremony was for the refurbished Exhibit Hall in the garden's museum building, reopened after two years or renovation. The displays range from a study of pollution in the Bronx River to a demonstration of the garden's new scanning electron microscope as applied to botanical problems.

The events also marked the beginning of Bronx Week, the borough's annual celebration of itself and its cultural and community resources. Through May 18 there will be a wide variety of fairs, concerts, art exhibitions and tours scattered through the borough.

Historian Acts as Guide

Justice Douglas, delayed by a dentist's appointment, spent an hour in the botanical garden's Hemlock Forest, one of the last uncut woods in the city. Mostly he loped along at a woodsman's pace and listened to his guides—Dr. Howard Irwin, president of the park, Mr. Pardue and Dr. Theodore Kazimiroff, an indefatigable historian of the borough.

Wildlife Enumerated

Dr. Kazimiroff rattled off the variety of wildlife found in the forest—red fox, raccoon, possum, rabbits, muskrat, quail, pheasant, barred and great horned owls, red-shouldered hawks. Skipping agilely about, he showed Justice Douglas an Indian rock shelter, tenderly pointed out a two-year-old hemlock seedling an inch high, marveled over a patch of northern white violets (which the photographers promptly trampled), and presented the Associate Justice with a 1,000-year-old quartz arrowhead of the Algonkin period he had found in the park.

They paused at a 15,000-year-old glacial cup formed by the advent of the last ice age. The gouged rocks were covered with scrawled names like "Ducky" and "Nick."

"The graffiti is modern," Dr. Kazimiroff said.

"It's everywhere," said Justice Douglas.

In his walk, he was sometimes reminded of his own experiences in woods as remote as Oregon and Siberia. When an oak shattered by lightning was pointed out, he remembered something he had seen long ago in the West.

"I was standing on a ridge, watching the lightning play on a ridge across the valley. I saw lightning hit three trees in a row, in the space of 100 yards. Each one went up like a struck match. It was a beautiful thing to see."

Depredations Are Noted

The outdoorsman also spoke of depredations in parks. He said one of the more pernicious trends was the National Park Service's policy of building roads through parks instead of around the perimeter.

"The thing that is most destructive of the West is motor vehicles," he said. "There's a thing called a dune buggy that is raising hell with the Mojave Desert."

Justice Douglas spoke with Bronx Borough President Robert Abrams, who walked with him, and again in his speech, of the closeness to nature taught him by the naturalist John Muir.

"Flowers, plants, trees are like one's neighbors," he said. "They have names, habits and temperaments. Get to know them; come on speaking terms with them; introduce them as friends to the children. The more one sees and appreciates the beauty of the earth, the less destructive he will be."

VOL. CXXVII....No. 43,864   Copyright © 1978 The New York Times   NEW YORK, MONDA

$5 Million Gift Restores Conservatory

Garden Under Glass in Bronx Scheduled to Open March 18

By LESLEY OELSNER

In a shimmering glass house shaped like a cross, a hippopotamus will be standing, as delicately as he can, in a bed of white pansies. Nearby will be a giraffe.

In a second glass pavilion the earth will have turned to desert, hot and dry and cactus-studded. There will be an underground tunnel at the end of the desert, leading out.

Inside the tunnel, someone will be growing mushrooms.

This is the Conservatory of the New York Botanical Garden in the Bronx—the new version, innovative, varied and sparked by such delights as animal-shaped topiary trees.

Garden Will Reopen March 18

Officials of the Botanical Garden announced yesterday that the turn-of-the-century Conservatory will reopen on March 18, after being closed two years for extensive restoration.

The officials also announced a gift of about $5 million, to pay for the restoration, from Enid A. Haupt, the philanthropist and former publisher of *Seventeen* magazine. The gift includes a previously announced donation by Mrs. Haupt of $850,000 in 1976.

The Italian Renaissance-style structure, dubbed by some the "Crystal Palace," will be renamed the "Enid A. Haupt Conservatory of the New York Botanical Garden."

The original Botanical Conservatory was completed in 1901. It was hailed as one of the truly elegant structures of the world—an ornate, sometimes soaring work, made up of 11 glass-enclosed greenhouse spaces running one after another in an arcade vaguely shaped like the letter C. The spaces add up to nearly an acre of land under glass; for the centerpiece, in the middle of the C, there is a 90-foot-high double dome.

Building Deteriorated

But after a while, the lovely building began to fall apart. Glass broke. Metal rusted. An ornate doorway true to style was replaced by an improbable Bauhaus-style entry. The heating system collapsed.

It was decided to demolish the building. Then the structure was declared a city landmark, and it was decided to renovate it, with the city picking up a hefty part of the bill. Then the financial crisis came, and the city had to renege.

Finally, it was decided to go ahead with the renovation, using private funds. The Garden didn't have enough money for what it expected the project to cost (at that point, the estimate was about $3.5 million.) It went ahead anyway on

The New York Times/Edward Hausner

A view of the domed Conservatory of the New York Botanical Garden in the Bronx, on which a $5 million restoration is nearly completed.

Welders working on steel girders under the dome in the New York Botanical Garden's renovated Conservatory

$5 Million Gift Restores Conservatory in Garden

Continued From Page A1

faith; one official noted, hoping the donations would come in.

The restoration is not quite complete—wood still covers some gaps in the glass; scaffolding is still up, at a doorway to the central dome; one greenhouse space had not a single plant, even last Friday. A troupe of workmen were hurrying about, hammering, carrying plants, patching up.

But Howard S. Irwin, the Botanical Garden's president, and Carlton B. Lees,

The Conservatory will be open from 10 A.M. to 4 P.M., Tuesday through Sunday beginning March 18. The admission charge will be $1.50 for adults, 75 cents for children and the elderly. On opening day, admission will be free.

senior vice president of the Garden and the supervisor of the restoration, insist that the Conservatory will be ready for opening day nevertheless, appearances notwithstanding—"It's like a dramatic production," Mr. Irwin said Friday—all coming together at the end.

The plants, in any event, are on hand. Most, in fact, are home-grown, at the Botanical Garden.

The underlying concepts are well established; they are taking form rapidly, in the landscaping and flower beds of the various greenhouse spaces.

Each airy space has a theme—and often, a unique climate. There's an American desert, and also an "old world" desert; there's a fern forest with a waterfall; a place for subtropical plants, and a space for children. The new tunnel—which connects the two ends of the C—

will have moss and aquarium plants as well as mushrooms, and also house plants that grow under artificial light.

In the children's greenhouse, called "Greenmuse," there will be for opening day a special theme: grocery story botany. Cans of tomato soup and other grocery goods will be on simulated store shelves. Nearby, tomato and other plants will grow. The idea is to get the child to connect the plant and the finished product.

The Conservatory will have another space for children too, downstairs, to be used, among other things, for classes by the garden's four teachers, working in conjunction with several public schools. Materials for the children's sections were bought with funds donated by other contributors.

Most are on Exotic Side

The huge central dome will be devoted to palms. At the moment, there are some particularly big palm trees there. They are "opening day palms," Mr. Lees said. They are the focus of attention now, not because they are particularly special—on the contrary, they are fairly common—but because some of the garden's finest specimens are still "just seedlings," and won't be ready for 20 years or so.

Mostly, though, things on display, and planned for display, seem exotic. In one garden space, devoted to landscape elements, there will be a bay tree encircled by a seat made of turf. It's the kind of seat used in medieval castle gardens, Mr. Lees said, for the ladies of the castle.

Nearby, there will be a type of landscape element called parterre, with low boxwood plants laid out in scrolls and swirls. These types of plantings, according to Mr. Lees, are "mostly things to

be looked at from palace windows."

"How many people in the Bronx have seen parterre?" he asked.

Throughout the Conservatory collections, pathways wander in and out around trees and plants. There are no long straight aisles, and no "don't touch" signs either.

"We've got too much of that in our lives," Mr. Lees explained. "I want them to meander."

Mrs. Haupt, an ardent horticulturist, and a member of the Botanical Garden's board of managers, said in a statement:

"Restoration of this beautiful complex has been a marvelous experience. Growing flowers and living with nature enhances life enormously. It gives me great satisfaction to share this philosophy with the public."

A member of the Annenberg publishing family, Mrs. Haupt pledged the remainder of her $5 million gift last fall, and since then has paid most of it, as bills for the restoration have come in, according to a vice president of the garden, George B. Bookman.

The precise amount of Mrs. Haupt's donation will depend on the final bills. With the exception of some relatively small expenditures already covered by other funds, such as a $75,000 Federal grant, the Haupt gift will cover the full cost of the physical restoration, ranging from replacement of glass to construction of the tunnel, to revision of the heating system.

Some other donors had previously given contributions for the Conservatory's repair. For the most part, these gifts have now been "shifted over," with the donors' consent, for other Botanical Garden uses, Mr. Bookman said.

George B. Bookman

Sample "Garden World" broadcast weekly on WCBS

WCBS-Radio

April 9
(Clausen)

Daffodils, Narcissus and Jonquils

You've been around and you know all about the bees and
the flowers. But can you tell the difference between a daffodil,
a narcissus and a jonquil? Let's try to straighten that out.
This is George Bookman with Garden World.

Daffodils are the flowers of Spring and many poets have
extolled their beauty since the time of the ancient Greeks. The
Egyptians and Romans were botn familiar with them as cultivated
plants and later Shakespeare mentioned them time and again.

Botanically speaking, Daffodils, Narcissus and Jonquils
are all part of the same genus Narcissus, although one usually
thinks of daffodils as the flowers with large trumpets and a
single flower on each stem. The name Jonquil, on the other
hand, usually refers to stems with several very fragrant blossoms
on them.

There has been a great deal of breeding work done on
Narcissus, particularly over the last 100 years. As a result
the group became so large that it was decided to divide the
family according to the size, shape and color of the flowers.
Catalogs specializing in bulbs list daffodils in groups such
as Trumpets, Large-cup, Small-cup and Doubles.

There are Narcissi suitable for all positions in the garden.
The miniature species such as the Petticoat Narcissus, native
to the Mediterranean, are suitable for rock gardens, while

the larger Trumpet and Large-cup types are perfect for bedding, cutting or forcing. Many of the groups are ideal when planted in drifts and naturalized in an informal part of the garden.

Since the flowers are already present inside the bulb before it is planted, culture is simple and almost foolproof. Heavy or light soils in sun or shade will produce a good show of flowers, but for this to repeat the following year, it is well to make the soil conditions well-drained and friable. After the bulbs have flowered, a light dressing of bonemeal or some other slow-release fertilizer will help to build up the bulbs for next year. Since the flowers bloom so early in the Spring before the trees are in full leaf, the shade of a tree that sheds its leaves is quite acceptable as a planting location. When the trees come into leaf, the bulbs will benefit from some shade while the foliage is dying down.

So enjoy the host of different kinds while they are in bloom. Perhaps you will agree with the poet Shelley who described the narcissus as "the fairest flower among them all."

From the New York Botanical Garden, this is George Bookman with Garden World.

George B. Bookman

The Millbrook Round Table, Millbrook, N.Y., Wednesday, August 22, 1979

Bookman retiring from Cary to peace of Wall Street

by TRINK GUARINO

The man is no gardener, but every weekend George Bookman can be heard on CBS Radio offering expert gardening advice on his "Garden World" spot.

Yet when he began his show, Bookman knew very little, if anything about gardening.

How does he do it? He is the consummate public relations professional, the reporter who has honed his skills to such a fine edge that he can disseminate any kind of information to any audience making it imaginative and interesting at the same time.

Whether it's a corporate conglomerate or the New York Botanical Gardens, whether it's the New York Stock Exchange or the Cary Arboretum, George Bookman, director of public affairs at the Cary Arboretum knows how to nose out the news. He has an unerring instinct for zeroing in on what makes his client most interesting.

Will retire

Bookman will be 65 at the end of this month and he plans to retire from his position as director of public affairs for the Cary Arboretum. But he does not plan to put whatever gardening know-how he has gleaned to use in his backyard.

Instead Bookman will take on new challenges at the New York Stock Exchange where he hopes to help that institution deflect impending government intervention.

Despite the fact that Bookman has spent the last six years shuttling between New York City's Botanical Gardens and the Cary Arboretum, his grueling schedule has not tired him. He is nowhere near ready to retire.

Since Bookman took over public relations for Cary and the Botanical Gardens, he has put both institutions on the map.

Focus attention

The radio program "Garden World" was itself designed to focus public attention on his clients. "Here I was surrounded by plant experts who needed the support of the public. CBS was looking for a garden program and I volunteered to do it," Bookman relates. What better way to bring plant scientists to the public eye.

In addition to the radio program, Bookman has written countless press releases, published newsletters and annual reports, and gotten information about the Cary educational programs into the media.

He organized Friends of the Cary Arboretum, an organization that now boasts 650 dues-paying members who provide substantial financial support to the institution.

Cary Friends also work in the greenhouses, conduct guided tours, assist in laboratories, manage the educational building's gift shop and help run concerts, receptions and lectures all designed to bring community support to the Cary Arboretum.

Organized publicity

When the innovative, solar-heated plant and science building was constructed, Bookman organized press conferences in New York and Millbrook bringing the building to public attention in the New York Times, on CBS and on the wire services.

Groundbreaking ceremonies in 1975 were attended by 1,000 people including the Commissioner of the Department of Environmental Conservation. The entire affair, it's atmosphere in an open meadow and the attendance was coordinated by Bookman.

In addition, Bookman has produced two films about the Cary Arboretum. "A Gift of Land" which is a general documentary and "A Building in the Sun," about the plant and Science Building.

For two years, while the Cary Arboretum was between administrators, Bookman took over the job, becoming administrator as well as public relations director.

Through it all, Bookman upheld the other half of his job with the New York Botanical Gardens of which the Cary is a branch.

Just as he organized and effected a major public relations campaign for Cary, Bookman also brought the Gardens into focus in the public eye.

Even Bookman, known for his modesty and the understatement of his own achievements admits he "had a lot to do with" changing the Gardens from a "rather quiet, backwater institution to a well-known, well-respected Botanical garden."

Since Bookman began his public relations campaign, the Botanical Gardens, once visited by mostly hard-core botanists, is now regularly used as a backdrop by television crews, film makers and advertising agencies. The gift shop has also noticed a tremendous increase in business.

While Bookman is unwilling to toot his own horn, he agrees that he didn't achieve place-

457

Bookman ready to retire
to peaceful life on Wall St.

ment on the front page of the New York Times science section just by taking a few reporters out to lunch.

"I had to think up innovative ways of presenting the Gardens so that the news media would recognize a good story," Bookman explains.

Some of the "good stories" he suggested to science reporters included scientific discoveries by Dr. David Karnosky, use of a Cary botanist in the New York Times' regular series on scientists at work, and the reopening of the Garden's Conservatory.

The wire services recently ran a national feature story on Dr. Patricia Holmgren, head of Cary's herbarium. "I just thought that she made a good story since she is a woman and the head of a very important scientific facility," Bookman comments modestly.

Bookman began his innovative public relations campaign almost the minute he set foot in the Botanical Gardens. He called all the journalists he knew, which after 25 years in journalism included a rather large group.

Formed club

He wrote a catchy letter inviting each of them to an afternoon of fresh air that they'd never forget and subsequent membership in the Inkstain Wretches (a tongue-in-cheek term for journalists) Fresh Air Club.

"Over 150 active journalists arrived for a late afternoon tour, dinner and drinks on a pay-as-you-go basis," according to Bookman. "They loved it. I did it twice and I still get asked when we're going to have another," Bookman chuckles.

Bookman's ability to pinpoint the most appealing qualities in his clients, how best to win friends and influence people, grew out of basic reporting skills rooted in his early days as a reporter.

He started as a cub reporter for the now-defunct New York World Telegram, working summers and vacations until 1936 when he went to work for U.S. News and World Report.

"I had a chance to cover every story in Washington. It was incredibly good experience," Bookman comments.

From the newsmagazine, Bookman went to work as a general assignment reporter for the Washington Post.

"I thought I should get some experience with the basics like covering fires," he laughs.

But, Bookman covered very few fires at the Post in his two months as a city news reporter. After two months, the Post's White House correspondent quit, and Bookman was offered his job.

For two years Bookman covered the White House under Franklin D. Roosevelt's presidency. "It was all very exciting," Bookman comments "In those days reporters were invited to many White House social events. It's quite an experience dancing the Conga Line in the East Room with Eleanor Roosevelt.

Went overseas

Bookman left his White House beat in December 1941, just before Pearl Harbor was bombed. He joined the United States Office of War Information, a government agency whose job it was to bring news of the Allies overseas.

He was sent to the Belgian Congo, now known as Zaire. There he operated a shortwave radio using his fluent knowledge of the French language to broadcast news of the Allies to occupied France.

From the Congo, Bookman was sent to the Mideast, including Beirut and Cairo. "It was my job to keep the natives friendly," Bookman laughs.

Following his service in the Mideast, Bookman worked for news services in Italy and Austria until the end of the war.

War over

When the war was over, Bookman returned to Washington, going back to U.S. News and World Report where he specialized in reporting business and economics.

Two years later, Bookman moved to Time magazine where he remained for 14 years as national correspondent for economics.

In 1960, he joined the staff of Fortune Magazine to write business articles, by this time developing extensive experience in the fields of business and economics.

Two years later, he left reporting for news media altogether and began his current career, putting his reporting skills to use promoting a client.

Stock exchange

His first public relations client was the New York Stock Exchange. In 1962, he became Public Information and Press Relations Director. He later became a vice president of the New York Stock Exchange.

"It was a very high pressure job," Bookman declares. "They were very difficult years with the Security and Exchange Commission (SEC) constantly breathing down our necks," he says.

In addition to smoothing relations with the SEC, Bookman was responsible for helping the Exchange's member businesses cope with the morass of paperwork required by the SEC. He also tried explaining to the general public the problems faced at the Stock Exchange during the steadily declining economy.

Walked tightrope

Somehow he managed to walk the tightrope between reporters, Stock Exchange management and government officials. He was elected president of the Deadline Club, a group of professional journalists. He served on the board of the Overseas Press Club. He was a member of the Financial Writers Association and he served on several committees for the National Press Club in Washington.

But after 11 years, Bookman was ready for a break. He purchased his home on Woodstock Road in Millbrook intending to use it as a weekend retreat.

"I really needed an escape valve from city life," he comments.

After a few months, Bookman and his wife Janet became

George Bookman

interested in the history of the rural area and of their own home which was built in the 18th century.

The Bookmans began a series of articles for the Dutchess County Historical Society.

Dr. Thomas Elias, then administrator of the Cary Arboretum, saw the articles and asked if the Bookmans would be interested in doing a similar series for Cary, which had just acquired the land adjoining the Bookman's property.

"Three Centuries on the Canoe Hills" was the result, originally published in the Dutchess County Yearbook and then re-printed in a separate booklet.

Took charge

Howard Irwin, president of the New York Botanical Gardens saw the booklet and asked Bookman to take charge of public relations for both Cary and the Gardens.

"It seemed like a wonderful way to relax in the country," Bookman muses despite the fact that his dual job required that he work three days in the city and two days in Millbrook each week.

Even with his hectic schedul

Bookman managed to find tim for several other corporatior for which he still serves a public relations consultant.

With his "retirement" fror Cary imminent, Bookman plan to make consulting a full tim job. His new position at the Nev York Stock Exchange is o ficially that of consultant.

Avoid intervention

There, he hopes to develor public relations campai designed to convince Securities and Excha Commission that the S Exchange is doing a goo regulating itself without tervention from the SEC.

"I really don't want to be public relations departi anymore," Bookman (ments. "I'm delighted to somebody else do the adm tration leaving me the fu creative work," he says.

Still, Bookman is sorr leave Cary. "It has be wonderful experience, bu time to look ahead to challenges," he says.

The Bookmans plan to r in residence in Millbrook Bookman commutes to tl "I'll still stay a Friend of and I'll still be able to 1 friends," Bookman says.

THE WALL STREET JOURNAL, Wednesday, September 5, 1979

George Bookman Rejoins Big Board as Consultant

By a WALL STREET JOURNAL Staff Reporter

NEW YORK—That hardy public relations perennial, George B. Bookman, has rejoined the New York Stock Exchange after six years as vice president, public affairs, for the New York Botanical Garden, where he also has conducted its "Garden World" radio program.

Mr. Bookman, who headed the Big Board's public and press relations program from 1962 to 1973, a period that included some of the exchange's lushest and most fallow years, has been retained for two years as consultant to its regulation and surveillance department. His main task will be to improve communications between the exchange and its member firms on regulatory matters.

As the voice of the Big Board for 11 years, Mr. Bookman, currently 64 years old, gained the respect of many in the financial community for straight talking during Wall Street's turbulence in the late 1960s and early 1970s, when the member-firm community was under severe operational and financial pressure. Earlier, he played a key role in the Big Board's program to popularize share ownership among the public.

As the voice of the Botanical Garden, Mr. Bookman gained local popularity via his radio show, which has been carried in New York by WCBS for the past two years. Although Mr. Bookman rejoined the exchange yesterday, two previously recorded shows, dealing with Jerusalem artichokes and indoor palms, will be aired this weekend. The show then will be taken over by Bernard Landou, a former Big Board aide who joined the Botanical Garden staff earlier this year.

George B. Bookman

ALLIED POWERS EUROPE
SUPREME COMMANDER

October 25, 1955

Dear Mr. Bookman:

It was most kind of you to send me a copy of the <u>Town Journal</u> containing the article you wrote as a result of your visit to SHAPE. I am intrigued by your pen-name, and will be on the lookout in the future for articles by "Jim Snyder."

I deeply appreciate your having given SHAPE and NATO this much-needed publicity. If this alliance is to continue to do its job, it will be because of the efforts of men like yourself. You are now listed on our books as a staff member, job-description: "SHAPE Booster," so don't think you can get away with only one article!

I enjoyed your visit last July, and hope you can visit us again soon.

With warm regard,

Sincerely,

ALFRED M. GRUENTHER
General, United St ates Army

Mr. George Bookman
4821 Cumberland Avenue
Chevy Chase 15, Md.

461

HUNGARIAN-AMERICAN ENTERPRISE FUND
1620 EYE STREET, N.W.
WASHINGTON, D.C. 20006

ALEXANDER C. TOMLINSON
PRESIDENT
AND CHIEF EXECUTIVE OFFICER

July 19, 1993

Mr. George Bookman
Mr. Bernard Landou

Dear George and Bernie:

This is to acknowledge and congratulate the two of you on the completion and formal opening of the Visitors Centre at the Budapest Stock Exchange (BSE). This important project, carried out from start to finish under your supervision and following your designs, reflects great credit on you and on the BSE. Indirectly, of course, it is a credit also to the Hungarian-American Enterprise Fund, whose selection of the two of you to carry out the project at our expense was well justified by the resulting success.

There was little to work with when the Fund first asked you to consider this project. Even the assigned space was ill-defined and appeared inadequate. The vision you brought to it and your close attention to every detail were of tremendous assistance to the BSE personnel. Your obviously professional approach gave them great confidence in undertaking something for which they had no previous experience or background. I may add that your detailed progress reports made it easy for us at the Fund to follow the project from conception to completion with the same confidence. It was particularly satisfying that you were able to adhere so closely to the budget agreed upon.

You have indicated your interest in providing similar assistance to other new stock exchanges in Central and Eastern Europe and Russia. I have no hesitation in recommending your services based on our experience, and I am sure that the BSE officials would say the same thing.

We very much appreciate what you have done and are pleased with the results.

Sincerely,

Alexander C. Tomlinson

PHONE (202) 467-5444 • FAX (202) 467-5469

Farewell to My Father

July 24, 1973

Dear Dad:

I am planning to make an important change in my professional work and thought I would write you a letter about it, so that you can read all the facts.

For some time I have wanted to figure out a way of spending more time at our home in Millbrook, now that we are enlarging it. I had thought that in a few years I might retire there, and start some sort of consulting business, which would bring me into New York several times a week, or else occupy myself with free-lance writing.

However, quite recently something much more attractive came along. As you may know, the New York Botanical Garden has acquired an 1800-acre tract that adjoins our Millbrook property. I have become friendly with the Garden officials who are developing a very large Arboretum on that site. Our conversations have led to their offering me the job of Director of Public Relations for the NY Botanical Garden, dividing my time between their headquarters in the Bronx and their project in Millbrook, which is growing very rapidly. While the salary will not be as high as I receive at the Stock Exchange, my expenses will be reduced by giving up the New York apartment. I will still be in the city several days a week.

The job attracts me for a number of reasons. I will be in sole charge of public relations. I will also be deeply involved with general management of the Garden, which is in a very expansionist phase of its development. The job can be structured to suit my interests as I grow older, and I will probably be able to gradually spend more time in the country and less in New York, if I so desire.

Naturally, I have regrets at leaving the Stock Exchange. They offered to make me a full Vice President in charge of public relations here, replacing my boss who recently resigned. However, I have chosen to try something new – a third career, if you will.

The enclosed news release, to be issued Friday, gives more details.

I look forward to seeing you later this week.

Love,

George

Remarks by George Bookman

At Cremation Service for Arthur Bookman
August 24, 1973

Ferncliff, New York

Mother has asked me to say a few words as we gather here for Daddy. I plan to express a few of my thoughts about Daddy, and then to read a traditional prayer, which both Mother and Daddy, before he passed on, requested.

In keeping with Daddy's philosophy of life, this is a very simple ceremony. He would not have wanted any eulogy, and it is not my intention to recite his professional accomplishments. The whole world knows what they are.

I do however want to talk about some personal aspects of his life. First of all, I want to speak of him as mother's husband of more than sixty years. The strong and lasting bond that existed between them, his feelings of love and devotion as a husband, are symbolized by the dozen yellow roses that now stand beside his coffin. As you know, yellow roses were a symbol between them, of their love, and he presented them on important occasions in their lives, anniversaries and so on, as reminders of his love for her.

Just yesterday, Mother told me a story I had not heard before that tells something of their relationship. On one of their last walks together at Cos Cob, before they left there, he said to Mother: "I never expected to be so happy." And Mother, quite typically of her, promptly replied: "And never did I".

As the story indicates, Daddy was capable of very deep emotion, though he did not often show it on the surface. He was not demonstrative. But to his marriage, he made a very deep commitment that lasted all his life thereafter.

Now I want to speak of him as a father, to Caroline and me, and also as a grandfather of Chip, Jeannie, and Michael, and as a great-grandfather.

He was a true father. He was not a pal, but rather a true father in the sense that he set an example, he encouraged his children, and his grandchildren,

464

he believed in them. He lived by his own principles and was true to them. In that way, he set an example for his children, but he did not try to impose his ways on them. His standards were strict and strong, and he offered wise judgment and understanding. Yet he didn't insist that everyone must follow his path.

Daddy was a true liberal, in the older classical meaning of that word. I mean by that he deeply believed in laissez-faire in personal behavior. Set high standards for yourself, but let others do things their own way, recognizing however that they must pay the price for their behavior. He was not censorious of the conduct of others, but rather believed in letting each person follow his own path, provided he was aware of what he was doing.

Another word that comes to mind about Daddy is, he was a true democrat, with a small d. He believed in the democracy of the mind, the democracy of individual achievement. He believed that all of us are equal at birth, and again at death, and in between we make what we can of the talents we have been given. That also explains why he wanted the simplicity of this type of funeral.

In another aspect, he was a true intellectual. Janet and Mario in particular are familiar with this aspect of him. He believed in the power of the mind, of the intellect, and the importance of ideas. For example, those books lining the wall of the living room at home were not there as decoration. He knew them intimately. They were old friends, familiar to him for many years. His mind abounded with curiosity about a tremendous variety of things. He was, of course, a scientist. He had a questioning mind. This influenced his attitude toward religion. In these matters, Daddy was an agnostic. His philosophic position was "I do not know" the answers. Yet as a scientist, he never tired of continuing to seek answers.

In that same vein, he was a realist. He was objective about himself, and about life. He knew who he was, and what he was. He was never confused in that way. And one of the things he knew he was, was a Jew. Though Daddy was not observant, did not take part in organized religion, he knew he was Jewish. And before he passed away he asked that the Kaddish, the traditional prayer for the Dead, be said for him, and Mother agreed.

It is the duty of the son, indeed the privilege of the son, to read the Kaddish for his departed father. I will read a portion of the Kaddish, the part that seems to me most in keeping with Daddy's views about religion, first in Hebrew, and then the English translation.

Yisborah, vyishtabah, vyishpo-ar, vyis-romam, vyisnasay, vyishadar, vyisaleh, vyishalai shmay d'kudsho brih-hu; l'ay-lo ul-lay-lo min kol, br-rhoso vsheeroso, tush-bhoso v'ne-heh-mo-so, daa-mee-ron b'o-l'mo, vi-mru; Amen.

Y'hay shlo-mo ra-bo min shmayo v'hayeem olaynu val kol yisro-ayl vi-mru, Amen.
Ose sholom bimromov hu yaase sholom olaynu val kol yisroayl vimru, Amen.

The translation of that portion of the Kaddish:

The departed whom we now remember has entered into the peace of life eternal. He still lives on earth in the acts of goodness he performed and in the hearts of those who cherish his memory. May the beauty of his life abide among us as a loving benediction.
Amen.
May the Father of peace send peace to all who mourn and comfort the bereaved among us.
Amen.

Now let us have a final moment of silence to think our own thoughts before we leave.

Trip to the U.S.S.R.

50 CENTS
DEC. 10, 1978

THE LONG ISLAND NEWSPAPER • NASSAU EDITION

Travel

TO RUSSIA, ALONE—Group and package tours of Russia are available in great numbers, but if you want to travel alone, it offers many rewards. Page 1

Penny-Wise 3

TV Book.

Leisure Sports
Lap swimmers face the toughest opponents: themselves and the clock. But they enjoy it. Inside Travel, after Page 5

Travel
While most visitors tour Russia in groups, independent travel is possible—but for the 1980 Olympics. Inside Part II, after Page 75.

Travel
Sunday, December 10, 1978

The Russian Connection

For the Go-It-Aloner, Rewards Aplenty

By George and Janet Bookman

Group and package tours are all the rage these days, and this kind of travel-by-the-busload has come into its own in the Soviet Union.

Group travel not only suits the requirements of the official Soviet travel agency, Intourist, but it also suits many Americans who feel more secure in an alien land by traveling in groups. There's financial security, too, in knowing the precise cost of a trip halfway around the world (winter packages start as low as $613 for a week).

On a recent four-week tour of the USSR, we saw many other tourists, and virtually all were being shepherded through the country in well-organized bus groups. But if you are an individualist, you can "do your own thing" as a tourist in Russia. Unlikely as it may seem in this collectivist land, we found it simple, usually pleasant and comparatively inexpensive to travel alone.

We didn't encounter many other "non-group" travelers during our approximately 9,000 miles in the Soviet Union, but the few we met enjoyed their trips immensely, as did we. To be sure, we had to submit an itinerary in advance to Intourist. The trip we planned included several days in Leningrad, with a visit to the historic city of Novgorod, a weekend in Moscow; a three-day ride on the Trans-Siberian Railway; two nights in Novosibirsk, capital of Siberia; a flight south to Tashkent, capital of Uzbekistan, with visits to the fabled cities of Samarkand, Bukhara and Khiva; a flight to the Republic of Georgia, with visits to Tbilisi and Batumi; and finally two more days in Moscow before flying back to New York.

As is customary, we were required to make all hotel and travel reservations in advance by buying vouchers, and we booked several side trips in advance, too. But except for these arrangements, our time was not committed in advance, and we were free to make our own plans each day as we wished—whether it was simply to stroll through a vegetable market or department store, to visit museums on our own, or to hire a car to visit a collective farm. In every city, we came and went as we pleased, including the

—Continued on Page 8

For the Olympics, Packages Only

By Judy Loveless

The time: July of 1980. The place: Moscow. The event: Summer Olympics.

Forget every Olympic event you've ever watched on the tube or on location. These will be different. Forget every stereotype you've ever had of the Russian citizen—guzzling vodka, trekking across the tundra with a fur-lined hat, and dancing trepak. You've been misled. Ignore any tours you've ever taken, any tickets you've ever purchased. Moscow's Olympics will be special.

There's only one catch. You'll have a difficult time getting there—even if you act now, even if you're prepared to spend the small fortune required, even if you can accept the rigid package limitations projected for the event.

First and foremost, tickets for Americans are extremely limited. In order to go at all, you must be on one of the teams, an official or very fortunate. A spokesman for the Russian Travel Bureau, which is handling all Olympic travel and ticket arrangements in the United States, says

—Continued on Page 9

For the Go-It-Aloner, Rewards Aplenty

—Continued from Page 1

frequent use of subways, street cars and buses.

We signed up for "first class" travel, roughly equivalent to American economy class. This entitled us to a modest twin-bedded hotel room with a private bath wherever we spent the night, and "soft class" private sleeping compartment on the Leningrad-Moscow train and on the Trans-Siberian. Our flights within the huge country were on the classless Aeroflot planes—in seats that were comfortable but a bit smaller than on U.S. domestic airlines.

In each city, we were entitled to a two- or three-hour sight-seeing tour in a private car with an English-speaking guide—but were under no obligation to take it. On arrival and departure at each airport or railway station, we were entitled to a private chauffeured car to or from the hotel, and free baggage transfer. That was one of the delights of this form of independent travel. During our four-week stay, we had absolutely no hassle with our six pieces of luggage, and so were able to avoid the usual frantic activity going to or from airports.

Intourist, that all-pervasive and seemingly all-powerful tourist agency, kept its end of the bargain meticulously. All the services we had paid for (with one interesting exception) were delivered, though sometimes Intourist's concept of "first class" services—plumbing, for example—left something to be desired. We swiftly grew accustomed to having a deferential driver and guide meet us at airports and railway stations, and we took it for granted that our luggage would be in our hotel rooms a few minutes after we checked in. It always was.

Indeed, so meticulous was Intourist that three times during our trip, various Intourist representatives recalculated the fares we had paid in advance in New York, and gave us substantial refunds.

One refund we wish we hadn't received was on the fare for the overnight train from Tbilisi to Batumi, in Soviet Georgia. We were puzzled when we were given the refund before the trip. At the station, the reason became painfully clear. Though we had paid for a private compartment, we were ushered into a cubicle with four beds, and not at all private. Two strangers already were in their allotted beds.

When we protested, the train commandant was hurriedly summoned and found us a two-bed compartment—the only one on the train. It was in "hard class," two leatherette-covered boards stretched over wooden benches. During the night, when the stubble-bearded porter kept opening our compartment door as we fitfully tried to sleep, we realized how the official had solved our problem: He had given us the night porter's own compartment.

For food, we were entirely on our own throughout the four weeks. We must confess that there were days when we envied members of tour groups who never had to study a menu or talk to a waiter in Russian or Uzbek, and had no worries except to get to their group table before the dining room closed.

But our adventures made it worthwhile. We ate in native restaurants in marketplaces, where the custom is to go up to the kitchen counter and point to the dish you want. This usually eliminated the language problem except for occasional confusion involved in paying. The public markets offered surprises, too. We had expected them to be as fly-specked as those in Syria, Baghdad and Iran, but we found the Soviet versions spotless—whether we stopped at mealtimes or just for snacks or juice.

Our food adventures included taking lunch with the bazaar merchants in the center of Bukhara, beside the cool waters of an ancient reflecting pool. We also shared bread and stew with five young, black-braided Uzbek girls in the public market of

George Bookman, a former Time correspondent, is vice president of the New York Botanical Gardens; Janet Bookman is a freelance editor.

Tashkent, and ordered an excellent Sunday dinner at a neighborhood restaurant in Moscow by pointing to dishes on nearby tables.

For more formal dining, we enjoyed the Soviet custom of seating strangers together at tables. This is how we met a Swedish carpenter and his Russian girl friend in Leningrad, and learned about his contract to help build a hotel for the 1980 Olympics; listened to imprudently candid complaints about Soviet life from a Latvian radio engineer who was a regular listener to the Voice of America; and exchanged ballpoint pens and short-snorter bills in Moscow's huge Rossiya Hotel with a Soviet deputy from the Siberian city of Krasnoyarsk.

Even eating on the Trans-Siberian Railway was a pleasant adventure. Several times a day, the dining car porter came down the aisle selling borscht, stews and occasionally tomatoes or fruit. To break the monotony, we sometimes clambered through the long, bumpy train to the dining car for full meals; other times we stuffed ourselves with snacks bought from platform vendors during stops.

Our sidetrips, which we arranged easily through Intourist and without notice, were among the most rewarding parts of our holiday. For each sidetrip, we rented a car, driver and English-speaking guide at a total cost of about $10 an hour.

One of the most interesting of these tours was to Akademgorodok ("Science City"), about 15 miles outside Novosibirsk in Siberia, where we were invited to visit two English-language classes at an elementary school. We had a chance to tour the town, which is entirely devoted to research; to see the comfortable homes for high-ranking professors and research scientists; and to talk with the children, in English, about career goals and hobbies.

Another day, in Uzbekistan, we arranged tours to two collective farms, including one staffed by Korean farmers whose forebears had settled in the USSR generations ago. We also hired cars, on the spur of the moment, to visit a nature preserve in the Kyzyl-Kum desert outside Bukhara, and to see the stark, sandy wastes—now being irrigated—in the serpent-infested Kara Kum desert west of Urgench.

Our most extensive sidetrip was to the ancient Caucasus town of Mestia in Upper Svanetia. The farmhouses were built of stone in the Middle Ages,

A tour group heads for the Kremlin.

and each farmhouse has a stone defense turret five or six stories high—not for use against foreign invaders, but against neighboring families with whom the occupants carried on "Hatfield-McCoy" blood feuds for many centuries. We had read about the town in a Soviet magazine, and asked permission to visit it before leaving home.

But in New York, they told us to ask in Moscow; in Moscow, they said ask in Uzbekistan; and there they said ask in Georgia. In Tbilisi, the capital of Georgia, most people we asked had never heard of the place, and the Georgia tourism director told us that it was impossible to visit. Bureaucracy being what it is, we decided to make one more attempt at Batumi, where our Intourist guide also had never heard of the place, but he dutifully checked with his supervisor. Within an hour, he returned with the good news: Yes, we could leave for Mestia by car the following morning, and he would accompany us. The trip was costlier than our other sidetrips—$220 for a 14-hour round trip of about 350 miles—but, as it turned out, well worth it.

Mestia was as picturesque and dramatic as we had expected. The rugged, narrow road, curling up into the High Caucasus, was surrounded by snow-capped peaks and roaring waterfalls. Our knuckles were white with tension through most of the drive. The roadbed had been carved out of sheer rock cliffs, and was periodically obliterated by landslides. It was the most beautiful, thrilling and frightening auto trip of our lives, but we were amply rewarded by spending a few hours walking the ancient cobblestones and muddy lanes of a town that has existed since the Stone Age. Children ran out from the ancient stone battlements to greet us in English or French, and farmers proffered glasses of fiery raki liquor when we stopped to rest.

Language was a problem on the trip, and yet it wasn't. We traveled with a phrase book and pocket dictionary. And a few hours spent studying the Cyrillic alphabet paid dividends, at least enabling us to tell the difference between "His" and "Hers" and to read street signs. German is the foreign language that older Russians seem to know best, and English is the one studied by most younger Russians. Sign language, however, is of the utmost utility, and one quickly finds that the experience of a misspent youth playing charades at parties suddenly becomes a prized attribute.

As far as overall costs are concerned, travel in the Soviet Union must be one of the last remaining bargains. (Getting there isn't that bad, either, through April 30, a 14-45-day advance-purchase excursion fare—book 30 days ahead—runs as low as $473 round trip.) Our 5,000 miles of plane travel in the Soviet Union cost about $400 each, or about eight cents per mile, and 3,000 miles of train fares including sleeping compartments ran under $150 each, or less than five cents per mile. About 1,000 miles of local excursions by private car, with driver and English-speaking guide, cost somewhat more—closer to 50 cents a mile.

Hotels in Moscow and Leningrad were $60 a night, but elsewhere it was $30 a night. Buffet breakfasts in Moscow and Leningrad also were great bargains—all you could eat for a ruble, or $1.50 at the official exchange rate. We usually went into a local snack bar or meat restaurant for lunch, where the typical cost was about $2 or $3 apiece. Dinner could range from $3 or $4 each to several times that at a popular "name" restaurant in Moscow—but still not expensive by New York standards.

All this is not to say that independent travel in the USSR isn't hard work. You have to check your own travel arrangements and order your own meals while coping with an alien language. But if you have an independent nature, and don't like being herded around on a tour bus, it's a fascinating way to win your spurs as a seasoned traveler. ■

43RD STREET ● NEW YORK, N.Y. 10017 ● (212) 687-2430 ● V

'NO NEWS ALL THE TIME...' or, 4 weeks away from it all in Russia this summer

(Editor's Note: George Bookman, associate member of the OPC Board of Governors, wrote the following exclusive eyewitness report for the Bulletin's readers.)

Never, since I bought my first trench-coat 40 years ago, have I been so starved for news as I was earlier this summer on a four-week sightseeing trip to the Soviet Union. My month-long starvation diet served as a reminder of how well-fed we are in the United States with media information.

My wife and I managed to learn some tourist Russian (with the help of pocket phrase books), but not adequate for reading the Russian press, or understanding Soviet radio or TV, which might at least have given us a Kremlin's-eye view of world news.

Our itinerary first took us to Leningrad and Moscow; then after three days and two nights on the Trans-Siberian Railway, to Novosibirsk, the capital of Siberia. From there we flew to Tashkent and other cities in Uzbekistan in Soviet Central Asia; then on to Tblisi and Batumi in the Republic of Georgia and finally back to Moscow and Warsaw, Amsterdam and home to New York..

The first symptoms of news hunger set in when we were in Leningrad. A tantalizing few copies of the International *Herald-Tribune* and a few London papers were available at the newsstand of the Leningrad Hotel, I was told, but they were always gone by the time I appeared to make a purchase.

One day, after I hadn't seen a "western" paper for about five days, I spotted a three-day old copy of *The Washington Post*, which some recently-arrived traveller had left lying on a chair. As I settled down in the lobby to read every word, several other news-starved tourists, including three Americans and one English-speaking Dutchman, watched me enviously and hovered in the background, ready to grab the paper as soon as I had done with it.

By the time we reached Moscow, I was hungrily stalking the newsstands, snatching up newspapers in any language that I could read. Soviet newsstands often carry an array of Communist newspapers from Western countries, and wherever I went in the USSR, from Moscow on, I bought copies of either *L'Humanite* from Paris, or the Communist papers from East Germany, Italy, or London. Several times I also happened upon copies of the New York-based Communist newspaper, the

Daily World, successor to the *Daily Worker.*

Some of the most readable material available in English or other Western languages in the USSR were undated feature articles in a weekly magazine called "Moscow News" that the Soviets published in several languages and distribute to all tourist offices. While I was in the Soviet Union, the main news pages of this handout were filled with articles about the success of Comrade Brezhnev's visits to West Germany and Czechoslovakia, but the back pages contained interesting features lifted from American publications and news services. Thanks to these features, I was able to keep posted on such news as the latest doings of "Big Foot", sightings of Unidentified Flying Objects in the American southwest, and new theories concerning the lost continent of Atlantis.

One time in Uzbekistan, we had a fleeting brush with news when a reporter for Radio Tashkent sought us out to interview us on our impressions of his country, for use in an English-language short-wave broadcast. After the interview, we talked briefly about "detente," disarmament and President Carter's speech to a NATO meeting in Washington. It was an interesting discussion, but I felt considerably handicapped because the Soviet reporter had the latest news, at least as supplied by Tass, and I had no independent source of information.

Coming home we flew via Aeroflot, the Soviet airline, to Amsterdam with a brief stop in Warsaw. Passengers were literally locked in the transit lounge and not allowed to visit any shops in the airport concourse. The pangs of news-hunger by this time were very keen, and I remember trying to induce an airport official to act as my agent and buy me a newspaper — without avail. But it was only three more hours to Amsterdam's Schipol airport, where I had a veritable feast of newspapers and magazines from New York, London, Paris — every capital in the Western world! Home bound across the Atlantic I didn't sleep a wink, so busy was I gorging myself on real news for the first time in a month. As they say, it's good to be back.

470

Bookman Bar Mitzvahed

PHOTO BY NANCY LEWIS

George Bookman of Lakeville was bar mitzvahed last Saturday in Amenia's Beth David Synagogue. He is shown here in front of portraits of his paternal grandparents.

BOOKMAN BAR MITZVAH:
Journal Lakeville, CT June 25/92

Better Late Than Never

By NANCY LEWIS
Staff Reporter

When George Bookman, 77, was bar mitzvahed last week at Amenia's Beth David Synagogue, he felt the need to apologize for his tardiness. He was late, he said, by 64 years; though he had reached manhood in the conventional sense, he only truly became a Jewish man at Saturday's ceremony.

The Lakeville resident had studied the Torah for three years in preparation for his bar mitzvah. Jewish boys and men must read from the Torah — the first five books of the Old Testament — in its original Hebrew; they must also study the history of the Jewish religion before being bar mitzvahed, a ceremony which is analogous with Christian confirmation, and which is usually done when a Jewish boy turns 13.

Mr. Bookman said that he is not unique in affirming his Judaism as an older man. The recent increase in mature men opting to be bar mitzvahed is

likely a reflection of the times, he said, just as his parents' rejection of Jewish religious practice resulted from their times.

Though Jewish by birth, religion played little part in Bookman's childhood. He received no religious instruction since his father, a doctor, "did not accept any theory that could not be proven in a test tube or petrie dish" with what her husband wanted. George Bookman's mother went along

This attitude was a reflection of the milieu in which his parents were raised, Bookman said, when assimilation was the goal of many Jews in America, particularly German Jews.

Bookman said that as a young man he went through all of the phases that characterized non-practicing Jews of the time: denial, shame, avoidance of the subject and exploration of other faiths.

While in high school, he wrote a religious paper in which he wrote that religious faith was fine for those who

needed it, but he could make his way through life without it. At age 74, that changed.

Though his attitude toward Judaism began to change after he married his wife Janet whose family was more observant of Jewish tradition than his had been, religious observance was still perfunctory at best during the couple's years of raising their two children.

Bookman worked in the fields of journalism and public relations, serving as an editor of Fortune and Time magazines, the Washington Post, and U.S. News and World Report. He was also director of public information for the New York Stock Exchange, a vice president of the stock exchange and vice president of the New York Botanical Garden, which had a branch in Millbrook. Still, pursuit of his Jewish heritage took a back seat.

Then the Bookmans moved to Lakeville and, influenced by the Holocaust and the process of aging, Bookman decided to join Beth David Syna-

gogue in Amenia. This was the catalyst for actually doing something about his Judaism. Instead of simply worrying about his ignorance of Judaism, Bookman was moved to learn more about his heritage by the "warm and inspiring experience of being a member" of Beth David Congregation.

Rabbi Elliot Stevens tutored Bookman in Hebrew and the Torah, a task which Bookman found "very difficult" though he speaks French, German and Italian. Hebrew means learning a whole new alphabet, he explained.

Bookman's paternal grandfather immigrated to the United States from Germany in 1842. For a time, he peddled housewares from a wagon through the South, finally setting up business in a small town near Selma, AL. There he dealt in cotton and general merchandise. Later, he moved north and married Caroline Meyer of Hartford. The couple lived in New York City where Mr. Bookman was involved in real estate and house construction.

When George Bookman read from the Book of Numbers at his bar mitzvah last week, it held a very special significance for him. The passage deals with the first celebration of Passover and that was the one Jewish holiday he did observe as a child and an adult. Passover, the "principal remnant of my ancestral Judaism that I preserved over these many years . . . has become a building block for trying to reconstruct a new expression of my own Jewish religious feeling," he told the relatives and friends gathered for his bar mitzvah ceremony. He urged them to also use Passover as a nucleus around which to build religious faith and maintain family ties.

Bookman was recently elected vice president of Beth David's board of directors.

Photo Section

Simon Meyer

Great Grandfather

Fannie Meyer

Great Grandmother

Jacob Bookman

Grandfather

Caroline Meyer Bookman

Grandmother

Judith W Bookman
by Ambrose McEvoy, 1912,
her wedding year

Sol and Jeannette Wertheim
Grandparents

Baruch Wertheim
Great Grandfather with sons Sol and
Jacob at office, Gold Street, New York City

Aunt Gladys Bachrach

Grandpa Sol Wertheim,
Sister Caroline, and George
West End, NJ, June 1920

George – age 3 or 4

Graduation – Haverford
Prep School - 1932

Graduation photo, Haverford College, 1936
Photo: Haverford College Library, Haverford, PA: College Archives

George at Hill Farm 1936   Janet, 1936

In Wet Suits enroute to West Africa
S.S. Tamesis, April 1942

At Pyramids, Cairo, 1943
(with Bob Lewis, Haverford classmate)

Janet and George Wedding
New York, September 22, 1944

Honeymoon at Hill Farm
September, 1944

George, Janet, Jean, and Charles
at first house, Nevada Avenue, Washington, D.C. 1949

Family in Scarsdale about 1960

90th birthday party for my mother, December 15th, 1978
l to r: Mario Salvadori, Carol, Judith Bookman, George,
Jean, Charles, Betsy, and Tyras (age 1 ½)

Janet's parents, Louis and Fannie Schrank

Schrank Siblings (Around 1946): l to r Bottom: Sylvia, Minna, Janet
l to r Top: Charles, Joe, Norman

Schrank in-laws: (Around 1946): l to r Bottom: Pearl, Leon, Ann
l to r Top: Phil, Edith, George

The Family – Janet's 70th birthday, 1987

With Bill Crawford, college friend and Paris housemate,
At 40th Haverford Class Reunion, 1976

In Baalbek, Lebanon – 1942   At the Brenner Pass, May 9th, 1945

Beirut – 1943   Aboard USS Missouri en route to
Turkey with Adm. Hillenkoetter,
March 1946

Covering visit of Lord Halifax and Economist J. M. Keynes on the White House Porch, July 1941 with reporters (l to r) Edmonds, UP, G. B. B., Washington Post, Durno, I.N.S., and Cornell, AP. Credit: AP photo

With Justice Douglas, C. & O. Canal hike, 1954

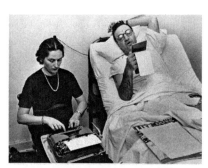

Dictating notes to Janet after appendectomy, 1957

Floor of NYSE, 1971, with Chairman Denunzio and President Robert W. Haack

My parents
Arthur and Judith Bookman
Cos Cob, Ct. 1966

With Alanna in Paris June 1990
for my 75th Birthday which
occurred December 1989

The "Saltbox" in Millbrook, NY,
1974

"Steepwood", our house in Lakeville,
CT, 2002

At my desk
NY Stock Exchange, 1970's

At the NY Botanical Garden,
1975

With Charles, Ty, and Zac,
Long Boat Key, FL, February, 1991

George's Bar Mitzvah, June 1992 in Amenia, NY
Left to right: Cantor Jerry Steiner, George Bookman, and Rabbi Elliott
Stevens

Jean Bookman Fincke

Dick Hoyt

Aaron, Wrenna, Vivien, and Jasper
At 90th birthday, New York

Aaron and GPa
2003

Wrenna, 2003

Zac

Vivien and Jasper Finche

Dancing with Vivien at
Alanna's wedding

Alanna and Jack Muccigrosso

At Zac's Yale graduation, May 2007
L to R: Ty, Charles, Zac, Betsy, George

Zac Graduates from University of Maryland, 2002
l to r: Ruth, George, Charles, Zac, Ty, Betsy, Andrea

Nicole and Ty
2007

George and Aaron
2004

Vivien, 2004

Jasper, 2004

Grandpa Alan Fincke with Eva and Jonah,
Fall 2007

Alanna and Jack with Eva,
Summer 2007

Jonah and Eva, Fall 2007

Members of the Bookman/Schrank family at the wedding of Tyras
and Nicole in California
September 29, 2007

Ruth at son's wedding, March 1977

Ruth and George at George's 90th birthday

Ruth and George in Israel. 2004

Ruth and George, 2006

Printed in the United States
215231BV00002B/1/P